D0145889

CONSUMER BEHAVIOR

SOUTH-WESTERN MARKETING ADVISORY BOARD

JAGDISH N. SHETH, CONSULTING EDITOR
Robert E. Brooker Distinguished Professor
of Marketing and Research
University of Southern California

Roger Blackwell
Professor of Marketing
Ohio State University

S. Tamer Cavusgil
Professor of Marketing and International
   Business
Michigan State University

Elizabeth Hirschman
Professor of Marketing
Rutgers University

Vijay Mahajan
Herman W. Lay Chair of Marketing
Southern Methodist University

Robert Peterson
John T. Stuart III Centennial Chair
   in Business
The University of Texas at Austin

Kenneth J. Roering
The Pillsbury Company—Paul S. Gerot
   Chair in Marketing
University of Minnesota

David Stewart
Associate Professor of Marketing
University of Southern California

Seymour Sudman
Walter H. Stellner Distinguished Professor
   of Marketing
University of Illinois at Urbana-Champaign

M. Venkatesan
Chairman, Marketing Department
University of Rhode Island

CONSUMER BEHAVIOR

A Decision-Making Approach

C. GLENN WALTERS, Ph.D.

Dean, College of Business and
Distinguished Professor of Marketing
Nicholls State University

BLAISE J. BERGIEL, Ph.D.

Associate Professor of Marketing
Department of Management and Marketing
Nicholls State University

ST60AA
PUBLISHED BY
SOUTH-WESTERN PUBLISHING CO.
CINCINNATI   WEST CHICAGO, IL   CARROLLTON, TX   LIVERMORE, CA

Copyright © 1989

by South-Western Publishing Co.
Cincinnati, Ohio

All Rights Reserved

The text of this publication, or any part thereof, may not be reproduced
or transmitted in any form or by any means, electronic or mechanical,
including photocopying, recording, storage in an information retrieval
system, or otherwise without the prior written permission of the
publisher.

ISBN: 0–538–80200–6

1 2 3 4 5 6 7 8 9 Ki 6 5 4 3 2 1 0 9 8

Printed in the United States of America

Market-driven philosophy is probably the hottest concept today in business practice. And it is not limited to business organizations: many public service organizations, including the post office, health care, public welfare, and even the tax collecting agencies such as the Internal Revenue Service, are interested in being market- or customer-driven organizations.

A number of forces are responsible for this changing focus from technology or operations to market or customers. First, most sectors of the economy in all advanced countries tend to be mature and, therefore, buyers' markets with excess capacities, intense competition, and oligopolistic structures. More importantly, in many industries, customers are both economically powerful and technically sophisticated to make the products or services on their own rather than buy in the market place. In short, customers are capable of becoming competitors. This is especially true in service industries including insurance, telecommunications, and training and education.

Second, in recent years many industries have achieved excellent scale efficiency in their manufacturing and operations, especially following the great successes by the Japanese companies. Quality Circle (QC), Just In Time (JIT), zero defect, and flexible manufacturing concepts have contributed significantly in manufacturing excellence.

The next frontier for both efficiency and effectiveness is marketing. Top management seems to be more and more convinced that a company's competitive advantage or vulnerability lies in the marketing area. Indeed, the marketing productivity challenge may be the next wave of corporate commitment. Obviously, this is creating more interest in a market-driven philosophy.

Finally, with the emergence of a global economy and significant offshore competition in virtually all sectors of an economy, markets are becoming more complex. Domestic market understanding seems to be less useful as companies enter offshore markets. The excellent domestic marketing practices are not doing so well in international markets. Therefore, marketing managers are relying more on understanding customers and are willing to adjust their marketing programs, where necessary, to succeed in foreign markets.

In short, the modern marketing concept suggested by such eminent scholars as Peter Drucker, Theodore Levitt, and Philip Kotler is finally implemented in marketing practice. Peter Drucker was the first one to suggest that the purpose of business is to create and retain customers. Theodore Levitt talked about the marketing myopia inherent in a technology-driven philosophy; Philip Kotler suggested how the modern marketing concept focuses on customers and their needs, and not on products or sales.

The role of understanding the customer in a market-driven philosophy is obvious. A market is composed of customers and especially the end-user consumers. Knowing why and how they make buying decisions becomes the foundation for the market-driven philosophy. This knowledge base becomes a key competitive advantage for a company.

In this respect, *Consumer Behavior: A Decision-Making Approach* is a very timely textbook. Furthermore, Professors C. Glenn Walters and Blaise Bergiel have written a textbook which has at least three distinctive and unique features as compared to other textbooks in the area.

The first, and probably the most important, unique feature of their textbook is its managerial orientation. Indeed, this may probably be the only textbook in consumer behavior which explicitly addresses the role of product, promotion, price distribution, and service in consumer's decision-making process. In other words, it discusses how the consumer uses information provided by the marketing practice as she or he makes purchase decisions.

Second, I was very pleased to note that the textbook addresses the area of postpurchase behavior, and especially what happens when the consumer is dissatisfied with her or his purchase decision. Customer satisfaction is an extremely important concept for improving marketing efficiency and effectiveness. The textbook discusses such issues as business ethics, consumerism, and complaint behavior as mechanisms for abating consumer dissatisfaction.

Finally, the textbook provides an integrative conceptual framework which is both rich and simple. It focuses on four areas of consumer decision making: problem recognition, search for market related information, evaluation and decision, and post-purchase assessment. These four areas of consumer decision making are then examined in the context of basic determinants (such as needs, perceptions, past experiences, and personality) and environmental influences (such as marketing, family, society, and culture).

I am very pleased that Professors Walters and Bergiel agreed to publish this textbook as part of the marketing series at South-Western Publishing Co.

Jagdish N. Sheth
University of Southern California

It is time for a change in studying consumer behavior. No change is needed in the content of the subject; that has become established since the mid-1960s. We now have a grip on the important variables of consumer behavior, and we are beginning to develop some confidence in the relationships. Consumer behavior has probably come further faster than any previous subject in marketing. Consumer behavior is rapidly maturing as an integral part of the marketing curriculum.

A change is needed, but it is a change in the manner of presenting and teaching consumer behavior. In the past most of our presentation was spent simply describing the internal and environmental variables of consumer behavior. Very little attention was given to the decision process that consumers engage in when acting in the marketplace. It is this decision process that lies at the heart of consumer behavior, and that is where the emphasis has been placed in this new approach to the subject. The book is organized around the steps in the consumer's decision process: problem recognition, search for information, evaluation and decision, and postpurchase assessment. The emphasis is always on the decision process. The basic and environmental determinants of consumer behavior are integrated into this decision process. However, none of these determinants have been slighted in the presentation. This decision-oriented approach to consumer behavior is more logical. It provides an easy flow of material for the instructor without changing the essential components that must be taught. The instructor should feel comfortable with the specific topics presented. This approach solves a major problem for students who had difficulty understanding the relationship between a decision process and the variables of consumer behavior when they were presented as essentially separate subjects. Previous texts spent two or three chapters discussing the decision process and devoted the remainder of the text to a description of the basic and environmental determinants. The decision approach is also inherently more interesting for the teacher and the student. It should aid understanding.

The authors have not neglected the effect that consumer decision making has on business management. Each chapter presents examples relating its subject to business management. Furthermore, each step in the consumer decision process has two chapters dealing with business policy related to that step. All aspects of business management are included. Market segmentation is covered, as well as are the four P's (product, place, promotion, and price). There are also chapters on international marketing decisions, consumer research, and management's adjustment to change.

This book is written for advanced undergraduate students. A basic knowledge of marketing and the social sciences is assumed, but since we do not expect that the student remembers every detail included in previous courses, some repetition is necessary. The concepts included in the book were selected for their relevance and importance for explaining the consumer decision process. They may sometimes be difficult, but the attempt was made to relate to students rather than to impress scholars or talk down to students. References are used for three purposes in the text. Some refer to specific research findings quoted in the text, some provide in-depth knowledge of the subject under discussion, and some demonstrate positions contrary to those taken in the text.

So many persons have contributed to this book, directly or indirectly, that we cannot publicly thank all of them. However, several persons must be mentioned. We want to thank our Consulting Editor, Jagdish N. Sheth from the University of Southern California, as well as all members of our Marketing Advisory Board. In addition, we thank the reviewers of the text: Gordon C. Bruner II of Southern Illinois University of Carbondale, Stephen W. McDaniel of Texas A & M University, Donna Tillman of California State Polytechnic University, and M. Venkatesan of the University of Rhode Island. Their contributions materially improved the final product.

We thank our secretaries, Debbie Portier, Sherry Schrivner, Jerry Fremin, Hazel Folse, Mona Zeringue, and Margie Guillory, whose help with the typing and technical aspects of the book were invaluable. We thank Dr. Donald Ayo, president of Nicholls State University, Dr. O. E. Lovell, vice-president of Academic Affairs, whose support was important to the development of this book. We also thank Dr. Bill Roe and Rose Edwards.

C. Glenn Walters
Blaise J. Bergiel

PART I
OVERVIEW OF CONSUMER DECISION MAKING

1   The Nature of Consumer Decision Making   1

PART II
CONSUMER PROBLEM RECOGNITION

     Section A. Consumer Problems and Results   32

2   Introduction to Consumer Problem Recognition   33

3   Consumer Problems Founded in Needs   57

4   Problem Recognition Leads to Motivation   79

     Section B. Business Response to Consumer Problems   100

5   Target Identification Based on Problem Recognition   101

6   Product Development to Solve Problems   129

PART III
CONSUMER SEARCH FOR INFORMATION

     Section A. Patterns of Consumer Search   158

7   Introduction to Consumer Search   159

8   Internal Consumer Search   181

9   Family Information Sources   203

10   Social Groups as Information Sources   229

11   Cultural Values Guide Consumer Search   251

     Section B. Business Policy Affecting Search   278

12   Distribution Strategy Reflects Consumer Search   279

13   Promotion Influences Consumer Search   305

PART IV
CONSUMER EVALUATION AND DECISION

Section A. Elements of the Consumer Decision   326
14   Introduction to Consumer Decision   327
15   Consumer Evaluation of Alternatives   349
16   Consumer Purchase Decision   371
17   Consumer Decisions Consistent with Personality   397

Section B. Business Policy Influences Consumer Choices   416
18   Price and Service Affect Consumer Decisions   417
19   Response to International Consumer Decisions   441

PART V
CONSUMER ASSESSMENT OF PURCHASE

Section A. Consumer's Check on Purchase Results   470
20   Introduction to Postpurchase Assessment   471
21   Favorable Assessment Results in Consumer Loyalty   493
22   Consumer Actions When Dissatisfied   515

Section B. Business Adjusts to Consumer Change   540
23   Business Use of Consumer Research   541
24   Management Adjusts to Market Changes   565
      Index   601

CONTENTS

PART I
OVERVIEW OF CONSUMER DECISION MAKING

1   The Nature of Consumer Decision Making   **1**

Chapter Objectives 2 / Why Study Consumer Behavior 2 / Who Is the Consumer 4 / Consumer Behavior 8 / Marketing Strategy Depends on Consumer Knowledge 13 / Consumer Decision Process 19 / Plan of the Book 27 / Questions 27 / Notes 28

PART II
CONSUMER PROBLEM RECOGNITION

Section A. Consumer Problems and Results

2   Introduction to Consumer Problem Recognition   **33**

Chapter Objectives 34 / Nature of Consumer Problem Recognition 34 / Sequence of Problems 37 / Who Identifies Consumer Problems 37 / Consumer Problems Reside in Product Assortment 43 / Problems Identified by Inventory 48 / Degree to Which Problems Specified 54 / Questions 55 / Notes 55

3   Consumer Problems Founded in Needs   **57**

Chapter Objectives 58 / Consumer Needs 58 / Consumer Problem Is to Satisfy Needs 60 / Needs That Require Satisfaction 62 / Other Perspectives of Needs 69 / Problem Varies with Importance of Need 69 / Consumer Problem of Unsatisfied Needs 75 / Questions 77 / Notes 77

4   Problem Recognition Leads to Motivation   **79**

Chapter Objectives 80 / Consumer Motives 80 / Consumer Decisions Are Motivated 80 / Types of Consumer Motives 85 / Consumer Motivation Differs 89 / Consumer Actions When Motivated 95 / Concluding Note 97 / Questions 98 / Notes 98

Section B. Business Response to Consumer Problems

5   Target Identification Based on Problem Recognition   **101**

Chapter Objectives 102 / Marketing Target: Relationship to Consumers 102 / Decide Firm's Abilities: Consumer Implications 103 / Groups Making up the Marketing Target 106 / Can the Target Be Reached? 117 / Develop Strategy for Each Target 120 / Consumers Are Basic to Marketing Strategy 124 / Questions 124 / Notes 125

6   Product Development to Solve Problems   **129**

Chapter Objectives 130 / Identification of the Product 130 / Problem Recognition during New Product Development 133 / Problem Recognition over the Product Life Cycle 140 / Problem Recognition and Product Deletion 144 / Problem Recognition over the Adoption and Diffusion Processes 145 / Problem Recognition Related to Product Attribute 148 / Questions 153 / Notes 154

PART III
CONSUMER SEARCH FOR INFORMATION

Section A. Patterns of Consumer Search

7   Introduction to Consumer Search   **159**

Chapter Objectives 160 / The Nature of Consumer Search 160 / The Importance of Consumer Search 161 / Consumer Search Requires Communication 161 / Internal and External Consumer Sources 168 / Determinants of Source Selection 169 / The Amount of Consumer Search 171 / Patterns of Consumer Search 172 / Questions 177 / Notes 178

8   Internal Consumer Search   **181**

Chapter Objectives 182 / Internal Consumer Search Involves Attitudes 182 / Functions of Attitudes in Internal Search 183 / Internal Search Depends on Learned Attitudes 185 / What Internal Search Reveals about Attitudes 192 / Consumer Attitude Stability 194 / Consumer Attitude Change 196 / Questions 199 / Notes 200

9   Family Information Sources   **203**

Chapter Objectives 204 / Family and Household 204 / Family Organization Affects Information Sharing 207 / Importance of Orientation of Information 209 / Information Flow Parallels Family Roles 212

/ *Information Sharing Changes with Life Cycle 218* / *Life-Style Under-lies Information Sharing 222* / *Questions 226* / *Notes 227*

10   Social Groups as Information Sources   229

Chapter Objectives 230 / *Reference Group Sources 230* / *Information by Type of Reference Group 231* / *Factors of Reference Group Information 234* / *Social Class Sources 240* / *Information Varies by Social Class 242* / *Importance of Social Influence 248* / *Questions 248* / *Notes 249*

11   Cultural Values Guide Consumer Search   251

Chapter Objectives 252 / *Cultural Identification 252* / *Culture Underlies All Consumer Search 255* / *Attributes of Culture That Affect Search 258* / *Cultural Characteristics Affecting Search 260* / *Racial and Ethnic Subcultures 262* / *Religious Subcultures 267* / *Subcultures Bases on Age and Marriage 267* / *Questions 274* / *Notes 275*

Section B. Business Policy Affecting Search

12   Distribution Strategy Reflects Consumer Search   279

Chapter Objectives 280 / *Distribution Methods: General Observations 280* / *Product Line Influences Consumer Search 284* / *Single or Multi-Unit Stores Affect Search 288* / *Non-Store Option Affects Consumer Search 290* / *Store Locations Affect Consumer Search 293* / *Exterior Store Design Affects Consumer Search 295* / *Interior Store Design Influences Consumer Search 296* / *Questions 303* / *Notes 303*

13   Promotion Influences Consumer Search   305

Chapter Objectives 306 / *Promotion: Definition and Overview 306* / *Promotion Affects Internal Search 311* / *Promotion Affects External Search 313* / *Promotion Gains Consumer Attention 313* / *Promotion Educates Consumers 314* / *Promotion Motivates Consumers 317* / *Promotion Moves Consumers to Action 321* / *Questions 322* / *Notes 322*

PART IV
CONSUMER EVALUATION AND DECISION

Section A. Elements of the Consumer Decision

14   Introduction to Consumer Decision   327

Chapter Objectives 328 / *The Consumer Decision 328* / *Types of Consumer Decision Theories 331* / *Perception Underlies All Consumer Decisions 333* / *Manner of Perception's Effect on Decisions 335* / *Perceptual Characteristics Affecting Decisions 337* / *Perceptual Factors Affecting Decisions 340* / *Consumer Perceptions Change 345* / *Questions 346* / *Notes 346*

15   Consumer Evaluation of Alternatives   349

Chapter Objectives 350 / Alternative Evaluation and Preference Ranking 350 / Identify Available Consumer Alternatives 351 / Organize Information for Evaluation 355 / Select Criteria for Alternative Preference Evaluation 356 / Comparison of Consumer Preference Alternatives 358 / Rules for Preference Evaluation 361 / Consumer Decision Ready State 365 / Questions 367 / Notes 368

16   Consumer Purchase Decision   371

Chapter Objectives 372 / Consumer Decision 372 / Decision Making by Individual Consumers 374 / Factors Affecting Individual's Decision 376 / Decision Making Within Families 381 / Factors Affecting Family Decision 383 / Misconceptions about Consumer Decisions 387 / Questions 393 / Notes 393

17   Consumer Decisions Consistent with Personality   397

Chapter Objectives 398 / Concept of Personality 398 / Consumer Decisions Controlled by Personality 401 / Psychoanalytic Contribution to Consumer Decisions 402 / Trait Contribution to Consumer Decisions 405 / Type Contribution to Consumer Decisions 408 / Gestalt Contributions to Consumer Decisions 411 / Personality and Consumer Decisions: An Evaluation 412 / Questions 413 / Notes 414

Section B. Business Policy Influences Consumer Choices

18   Price and Service Affect Consumer Decisions   417

Chapter Objectives 418 / Price and Service Adjust Physical Product 418 / Consumer Prices 419 / Price Policies That Influence Consumers 421 / Service to Customers 429 / Services That Influence Consumers 431 / Service after the Sale 437 / Questions 437 / Notes 438

19   Response to International Consumer Decisions   441

Chapter Objectives 442 / Multinational Consumers 442 / Management Must Be Available in the Market 444 / Management Must Be Culture-Conscious 447 / Income Limits Purchasing Power 457 / Management Must Respond to Attitudes 460 / Tips for International Managers 466 / Questions 467 / Notes 467

PART V
CONSUMER ASSESSMENT OF PURCHASE

Section A. Consumer's Check on Purchase Results

20   Introduction to Postpurchase Assessment   471

Chapter Objectives 472 / Consumer Assessment Defined 472 / Nature of Consumer Assessment 473 / Consumer Equilibrium: The Desired

State 477 / Assessment Results from Dissonance 478 / Consumer Re-Establishes Equilibrium 483 / Results of Prepurchase Assessment 486 / Results of Postpurchase Assessment 486 / Questions 489 / Notes 490

21   Favorable Assessment Results in Consumer Loyalty   493

Chapter Objectives 494 / Consumer Behavior When Satisfied or Resigned 494 / Satisfied Consumers Are Loyal 496 / Advantages of Loyal Customers to Sellers 502 / Reasons Why Consumers Are Loyal 504 / Factors That Cause Consumer Switching 506 / Create a Climate for Loyalty 510 / Questions 512 / Notes 512

22   Consumer Actions When Dissatisfied   515

Chapter Objectives 516 / Individual Responses to Dissatisfaction 516 / Group Approach to Dissatisfaction: Consumerism 518 / Development of Consumer Cooperation to Solve Problems 519 / Consumerism Today 522 / Current Sources of Consumer Dissatisfaction 524 / What Consumerism Has Accomplished 528 / Future of Consumerism 535 / Questions 536 / Notes 536

Section B. Business Adjusts to Consumer Change

23   Business Use of Consumer Research   541

Chapter Objectives 542 / Nature of Consumer Research 542 / Sources of Consumer Data 546 / Demographic Consumer Research 550 / Cognitive Unstructured-Undisguised Research 551 / Cognitive Unstructured-Disguised Research 554 / Cognitive Structured-Disguised Research 558 / Cognitive Structured-Undisguised Research 559 / Consumer Research Ethics 561 / Questions 562 / Notes 563

24   Management Adjusts to Market Changes   565

Chapter Objectives 566 / Management Must Respond to Market Dynamics 566 / Total U.S. Market Increases—But Slowly 566 / Markets Based on Household Characteristics 567 / Income Conditions Household Markets 574 / Expenditure Patterns of Consumers 579 / Geographic Market Changes 590 / Questions 598 / Notes 600

Index   601

PART 1

OVERVIEW OF CONSUMER
DECISION MAKING

The Nature of Consumer Decision Making

CHAPTER OUTLINE

I. **WHY STUDY CONSUMER BEHAVIOR**

II. **WHO IS THE CONSUMER**
- A. Consumers Versus Influencers
- B. Potential and Realized Consumers
- C. Final Consumers and Industrial Buyers

III. **CONSUMER BEHAVIOR**
- A. Purchase Decision: Goal of Consumer Behavior
- B. Basic Determinants
- C. Environmental Influences
- D. Communication

IV. **MARKETING STRATEGY DEPENDS ON CONSUMER KNOWLEDGE**
- A. Marketing and Marketing Strategy
- B. Market Segmentation
- C. Product Policy
- D. Distribution Policy
- E. Promotion and Price

V. **CONSUMER DECISION PROCESS**
- A. Problem Recognition
- B. Search for Market-Related Information
- C. Evaluation and Decision
- D. Post-Purchase Assessment

VI. **PLAN OF THE BOOK**

CHAPTER OBJECTIVES

After completing your study of Chapter 1, you should be able to:

1. Discuss why we should study consumer behavior.
2. Identify and define who is the consumer.
3. Identify and discuss the key elements of the purchase decision.
4. Describe how marketing strategy depends on consumer knowledge.
5. Identify and explain the key elements of the consumer decision process.

The consumer buying process is so familiar that we tend to accept it as a casual, uncomplicated act requiring little thought. Seldom do we consider the complex business decisions that make products and services available when, where, and how we want to purchase them. Even less attention is devoted to the consumer. What types of inner and external forces are at work that cause the individual to want certain products, why are specific brands and stores preferred over others, and what decision processes led to the final choices? In spite of the experience of every individual as a consumer, these and similar questions are not fully understood. Such questions go to the very roots of human behavior and must be answered before the marketing executive can develop effective marketing strategies to satisfy consumer needs.

This book is about consumers, and how a better understanding of people, in the process of consuming, can lead to more efficient marketing operations.[1] The book is a marketing text because consumers are a basic ingredient in marketing. The emphasis is on the interrelationships between consumers and marketing managers, but the perspective is from the consumer's side of the market. This book is a practical book. It deals with generally accepted concepts that can serve both to specify types of consumer information useful to marketers and to provide insights for interpreting these facts.

WHY STUDY CONSUMER BEHAVIOR

Consumer behavior has two sides. On one side is the consumer, on the other the marketing manager. We are all consumers, but the art of consuming is an inexact activity. Some of us may become marketing managers, and consumer orientation is essential to marketing strategy.

The direct benefit from a clear understanding of consumer behavior is that it can make us all better and more prudent consumers. The improvement can result from:

1. A greater appreciation of the complexity of decisions facing consumers.
2. A better understanding of our own motives and decision processes as consumers.
3. A sounder choice of products, services, brands, and stores.

All individuals should be interested in consumer behavior, because at some point almost everyone becomes involved in buying a product or service. As a buyer an individual makes up one half of the marketing process. In its elemental form,

Photo 1-1
Everyone should be interested in consumer behavior since we are all consumers.

marketing consists of an interaction between a buyer and seller for the purpose of exchanging something of value for something of value to the mutual benefit of both parties to the transaction. One cannot appreciate this marketing process by observing only the seller; a student of marketing has to understand demand as well as supply. Specifically, from a marketing manager's standpoint, knowledge about the consumer provides one of the sounder bases for making marketing decisions. Markets are selected on the basis of consumer wants, as well as their location, numbers, characteristics, and expenditure patterns. The basis for all sales appeal comes from information about the consumer. To ignore the consumer can lead to disaster in a modern economy.[2]

WHO IS THE CONSUMER

Observe a man working in the yard. He is using a lawn mower he purchased, drinking a soft drink his son purchased and brought home, and wearing coveralls his wife picked out at his request. Who is the consumer? Well, obviously there are three different situations. The man bought the lawn mower and is using it. The son bought the drink, but the man is using it. The wife bought the coveralls, but the man determined need and is using them. So, is the consumer the one who determined need? The purchaser? The user? The answer to these questions is not easy because each person had something to do with the outcome. The problem is that we attribute the decision to one person when, in fact, each person is part of a total consumption process. This *consumption process* involves three interrelated activities or decisions:

1. Determine personal or group wants.
2. Seek out and purchase products.
3. Employ products to derive benefits.

As we have pointed out, this process can, and often is, engaged in by several different people simultaneously.

Table 1-1 illustrates how the consumption process is related to different types of individuals.[3] Specific terms have developed that apply in those cases where more than one person engages in consumption.[4] A *demander,* following the lead of economics, is one who has personal wants. An individual deciding on a particular hair style at the hair care shop is a demander. *Purchaser, shopper,* or *customer* are used synonymously to indicate one actively engaged in buying. A grocery shopper purchasing for more than one person fits this description. The

Table 1-1
Consumer Terms and the Consumption Process

Terms for those engaged in consumption		Consumption process
Consumer or buyer	1. Demander	Determines want
	2. Purchaser or shopper	Purchases products
	3. User	Consumes products

Part 1 – Overview of Consumer Decision Making

user is a person who derives satisfaction or benefit from products bought. As you read this book, you are a user.

Consumption may involve any combination of these persons. Two examples can make the point. A person (purchaser) buys chocolate for a friend (user, demander), at the friend's suggestion. An individual (demander) asks his or her roommate (purchaser) to buy a six-pack of beer for his or her friends (users) to drink at a party. A *consumer,* or *buyer,* is:

> *one who determines personal wants, buys products, and uses those products.*

Throughout this book, consumer refers to (1) several persons, each performing a part of the consumption process; or (2) one person who engages in all three activities of consumption. There are places throughout the text where the specialized activities of consumption are pointed out.

Consumers Versus Influencers

Several people may be involved in a particular purchase decision, but we do not designate them all as consumers. Consider a person who has just been promoted and needs a different type of wardrobe for the new job. She needs a new wardrobe consistent with her changed responsibility. That person might consider the dress preferences of new coworkers, ask a friend about a particular retailer's prices, check several newspaper and television advertisements for available styles, and consult with her spouse. What is the status of the coworkers, the friend, the retailer's promotion, and the spouse in this purchase?

Based on our earlier definition, only those persons having the right to purchase or use products are consumers.[5] All other persons who exercise a direct or indirect effect on the consumer are said to have influenced the decision. *Influencers* are persons or things, external to the consumer, that provide advice, information, or pressure to consume in a specific manner.[6] See Illustration 1.1. In the above example, the wife is the consumer. The manager, the friend, and the advertisements are external influences that may or may not affect the consumer's decision.

Even the husband in this instance is an influencer, since he did not perform any activity associated with the consumption process. Rather, he acted as an advisor. The difference between a consumer and an influencer is based on participation in consumption and not on how much the consumer was affected by the information. Thus an individual may share responsibility as a consumer in one instance and be an influencer in another instance.

Potential and Realized Consumers

One important method of classifying consumers is according to whether they are potential or realized.[7] A given person may or may not be in the act of buying a particular product or brand. It is important to marketing managers to recognize which state the consumer is in. We can identify three possibilities: (1) nonconsumers, (2) potential consumers, and (3) realized consumers. A *nonconsumer* is an individual who has no need for a given product and is not likely to have a need

Illustration 1-1
Model of consumer behavior

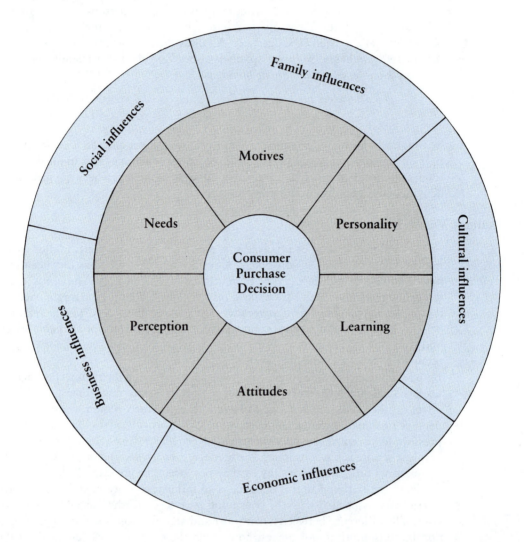

in the foreseeable future. For example, a person living in the tropics who does not travel is a nonconsumer of winter sports equipment. An individual, not currently purchasing, who may be influenced at some future time to buy is referred to as a *potential consumer*. A large enough number of potential consumers makes a potential market which a marketing manager could tap. A person may be a potential consumer for some generic product such as crawfish. The product could be grown and produced almost anywhere, and could be easily within the means of most individuals. If attitudes toward this product could be changed, people could be induced to become potential consumers. A person may be a potential consumer for competing product brands or competing stores. A purchaser of Folger's coffee or a customer of Sears is a potential buyer for all other competitors.

Photo 1-2
These people may influence each other's consumer choices about golf equipment, courses, attire, etc.

Potential consumers are explained by: (1) unawareness of need; (2) low intensity of present need; (3) lack of information concerning available products; (4) purchase from competing firms; or (5) lack of current means to purchase. Potential consumers are important to marketing managers because these individuals represent a means of increasing sales, profits, and extending the company's market share.

Realized consumers generally conform to our earlier definition of purchasers or shoppers, since they are engaged in buying. When a business executive says, "They are one of our regular customers," it means that the designated person is currently negotiating for the firm's products, or that they purchase regularly from the store. The manager means the same thing when instructing a salesperson, "Go wait on that customer." The major task of the business, where current customers are concerned, is keeping them satisfied in order for the business to meet its objectives (i.e., profit, sales, market share).

Final Consumers and Industrial Buyers

Any person engaged in the consumption process is a consumer, but these buyers can be identified by the type of market to which they belong. The two major types of markets are final consumers and industrial buyers. The *final consumer* market consists of individuals who buy for personal consumption or to meet the collective needs of the family or household unit. The final consumer removes products from the channel of distribution because there is no further sale by marketing organizations. The final consumer buys for the sole purpose of using up the product in order to obtain satisfaction.

Industrial markets and *industrial buyers* consist of organizations that purchase products to meet organizational objectives, i.e., resale to make a profit. The product bought by industrial buyers is resold as is; it becomes a part of some finished product that is sold; it is consumed in the production of finished products; or it is used to facilitate the selling of other products or services. Industrial buyers include: business firms (manufacturers, wholesalers, retailers, and agents); governments (federal, state, and local); and not-for-profit organizations (universities, hospitals, churches, etc.). It is common to use the term "consumer" when referring to household or final consumers and "buyer" when referring to industrial consumers. Since this book is concerned only with the final consumer, the term "consumer" or "buyer" refers to final consumers unless otherwise specified.

CONSUMER BEHAVIOR

Consumer behavior is a subdivision of human behavior. To understand the one we must clarify the other.[8] Every thought, feeling or action experienced by individuals is a part of human behavior. Our motives for getting out of bed in the morning, our frame of mind toward others upon rising, the sensations we obtain while eating breakfast, and the activities we undertake that guide us through the day are all human behavior.

Consumer behavior is more narrowly conceived. It concerns specific types of human behavior that are market-related.[9] The definition can be derived from our earlier understanding of a consumer. In this book, *consumer behavior* is used to mean:

> *those decisions and related activities of persons involved specifically in buying and using economic goods and services.*

Consumer behavior includes both mental decisions and physical actions that result from these decisions.[10] Although some social scientists limit their definition of "behavior" to observable actions, it is apparent that the reasons and decisions behind the actions involved in both human and consumer behavior are as important to understanding the fields as are the actions themselves.

Purchase Decision: Goal of Consumer Behavior

People enter into activities for many purposes other than consumption, but when acting as a customer, individuals have just one goal in mind. That goal is to obtain goods and services that meet their needs and wants. All consumers face the problems associated with acquiring products to sustain life and to provide for some comforts. Because the solutions to these problems are vital to the existence of most and the economic well-being of all, they are usually not taken lightly. The consumer must make specific types of decisions in order to obtain necessary products or services.

A list of all the considerations involved with consumer purchase decisions would be too complex to set down at this time, but the basic decision areas can be identified. The consumer must decide whether, what, when, where, and how to purchase. The basic decision is whether to purchase or not. This decision can be made before or after entering the marketplace. A consumer may know intuitively that he or she does not want a given product. In this case the decision is simple, and no direct market acitivity is necessary. On the other hand, the decision may be made after entering the marketplace. It may involve a careful or a superficial search and evaluation of the market.

The decision on what to purchase is directly related to product choices. Consumers seek satisfaction or benefits, but satisfaction can only be achieved through possessing goods and services. Furthermore, the accumulation of products allows consumers to store some satisfaction until needed. Thus, it is typically some perceived deficiency of products that is the stimulus causing consumers to enter the marketplace. The individual may have a deficiency in a particular product normally stocked or may want to expand the total number of products presently held.

When to buy is a basic consumer decision. The individual must decide on a convenient hour of the day, day of the week, week of the month, and month of the year in which to act. Of course, timing differs for different products. Some purchases lend themselves to habitual timing, but others do not. For example, a person may always shop for groceries on Thursday morning but may purchase greeting cards only when the need arises. One consumer may buy early in the season, while another may wait for after-season bargains.

Where to purchase can involve much more than the choice of a store. Persons

Photo 1-3
Timing is an important factor in purchase decisions.

Part 1 – Overview of Consumer Decision Making

in a small town may buy locally or travel to nearby larger cities. Within a city, choices must be made between downtown, shopping centers, and malls. Because consumers often make several purchases, they may visit more than one store or trade area. Furthermore, the trade area and store selected condition the availability of specific product brands, prices, and services. Obviously, the choice of a store or trading area is an extremely important consumer decision.

The decision on how to purchase is directly related to the others. It includes decisions about the amount of time and effort to be spent shopping, the number of items to seek, whether to charge or pay cash, the mode of transportation to use, the route and sequence of store visitations, and whether to shop alone or with others. When the buyer has satisfactorily answered all five questions, he or she has made a purchase. How well the consumer answers these questions greatly affects the consumer's standard of living. It is for this reason that the purchase decision is the central issue of consumer behavior.

We can identify two broad types of consumer behavior variables that directly affect how persons make purchase decisions. They are (1) variables that are internal to the individual and (2) variables that are external to the individuals. We shall call the internal variables *basic determinants* and the external variables *environmental determinants* or *influences*. Each type of determinant is explained below.

Basic Determinants

A key element of consumer behavior lies with the individual. The decision to buy or not to buy is an individual decision. One may accept advice or even yield to outside pressure, but the final purchase decision rests with the individual. Marketing managers *cannot* make an individual buy products. What happens is that the individual takes in information from the environment and integrates it into his or her frame of reference. Such external information may then become the deciding influence on a purchase, but the individual still makes the decisions on using the information or not, as well as on how to use it.

There are six basic consumer variables that control all internal thought processes. They are needs, motives, personality, learning, attitudes, and perception. Illustration 1-1 shows these factors arranged around a wheel. Consumer purchase decisions are placed in the center of the wheel because this variable is the focal point of consumer behavior. The object of consumer behavior is to make decisions to satisfy the consumer's needs and wants.

A *need* is defined as any physical or emotional body requirement. A need describes a condition that is necessary for sound mental and physical health. A *motive* is an impulse or feeling that causes one to do something or act in a certain way. Motives make us aware of our needs and give us a reason for acting on these needs. *Personality* is defined as the human characteristics or traits built into a person that make each person different from every other person. Motives cause the individual to act on their needs, but it is personality which makes an indiviudal act in a specific manner. *Perception* is defined as the particular interpretation one gives to objects or ideas observed or otherwise brought to the consumer's attention through the senses. *Learning* means any change in the consumer's thoughts, response, or behavior as a result of practice, experience, or intuition. In a sense it is knowing what was unknown before. *Attitude* is used to mean a broad group of learned predispositions to behave in a certain way.

There is a simultaneous interaction between the basic determinants. An example can aid in clarifying the differences. Such an example is shown in Table 1-2.

A person has a basic body requirement for food but may only become willing to act when sufficiently motivated by the physical discomfort of hunger. The consumer has learned from previous experience that both steak and quiche satisfy hunger. The consumer has also learned that, to him or her, steak tastes better. This learning experience becomes internalized in the consumer as an attitude—that steak is preferred over quiche. Thus in any choice between steak and quiche, the consumer has a predisposition to select steak. The consumer's perception is that quiche is a frivolous food. The consumer will probably act on his or her preference; we see that the consumer's solution to the need for food is to purchase and eat a steak. Each internal variable plays a part in the consumer's decision, and all four interact to condition the specific action taken.

Table 1-2
Example of Basic Determinants

Basic Determinant	Example
Need	Food
Motive	Hunger
Personality	Inclined toward direct action
Learning	Both steak and quiche satisfy hunger
Attitude	Steak is preferred over quiche
Perception	Quiche is a frivolous food
Consumer decision: Purchase and eat steak	

Environmental Influences

Consumers do not function in a vacuum; the individual is continually influenced by the environment. There are five broad environmental determinants of consumer behavior: (1) family influences, (2) social influences, (3) business influences, (4) cultural influences, and (5) economic infuences. These important variables of consumer behavior require further explanation. *Family influences* come from household members. *Social influences* result from all personal contacts other than family or business. Social influences arise from workplace, church, neighborhood, school, friends, and peers. *Business influences* refer to the direct contact, either at the store or through personal selling, sales promotion, and advertising, that the consumer has with business firms. *Cultural influences* are the innate beliefs and sanctions developed over time by the social system. *Economic influences* are the constraints placed on the consumer by money and related factors.[11]

The *family* usually has the greatest total influence on a consumer. Social and business influences rate close behind the family in total impact. These three external influences comprise the individual's contact with other people.[12] Ultimately, of course, all consumer activity results in interaction with businesses either in the form of shopping or actual purchasing. The cultural, ethnic, and religious variables, taken together, constitute a system of sanctions, biases, mores, and life-styles that become a part of the person, but these variables are manifested through human contact.

We cannot view the basic determinants and external influences separately. They interact simultaneously and continuously. Furthermore, there is interaction between the individual's needs, motives, personality, learning, attitudes, and perceptions. Each influences the other, and every individual decision is influenced by all six factors.

Communication

It is not proper to leave a discussion of the model of consumer behavior without mentioning communication. It is through communication that people develop as individuals over time. This is true because individuals learn about themselves and their environment through communication; communication connects the individual and the environment. Communication is the unifying factor in the entire model of consumer behavior, pervading all the sections.

Everything one does communicates data. The consumer takes in data, sorts it, and relates it to personal needs, motives, perception, and attitudes. The consumer can react to external data by:

1. Consciously synthesizing the data into his or her frame of reference.
2. Consciously rejecting the data.
3. Unconsciously synthesizing the data.
4. Unconsciously forgetting the data.

In actuality, the external environment cannot be separated from the individual. The environment influences every decision the individual makes. It is not a case of the consumer making up his/her mind on a product and then having the environment influence this decision, because the environment also influences the initial decision.

MARKETING STRATEGY DEPENDS ON CONSUMER KNOWLEDGE

Marketing effort is directed, in part, at satisfying consumer needs, wants, and desires. Marketing managers know that knowledge of the consumer decision-making process aids them in making better marketing decisions and designing more effective policies that affect the firm's profit position.

Marketing and Marketing Strategy

Contemporary texts limit the objective of marketing to the satisfaction of consumers (a consumer orientation). While such an attitude gives increased importance to consumers, it is inconsistent with the real world. A broader definition of marketing, in which several groups are satisfied along with consumers, is used in this book.[13] For our purposes *marketing* is defined as:

> *those policies managing an exchange between the firm and its environment to provide products that are profitable, wanted by consumers, legal, competitive, socially justified, and efficient in resource use.*[14]

Marketing strategy is the overall plan developed by marketing executives to achieve company goals. Marketing strategy has two steps:

1. *Identify marketing targets* — The marketing targets are a combination of selected persons from all external groups who have a common want or interest toward which marketing can direct an appeal. Includes identified consumers, government officials, competitive management, special interest groups, and suppliers of land, labor, and capital.
2. *Develop a marketing mix* — Select and coordinate the policies to satisfy the wants and/or interests of marketing targets.

Of course, any firm may be attempting to satisfy more than one target market at a time.

Marketing is directed at satisfying the common wants or interests simultaneously of selected persons in five major groups which make up the target plus the firm. (See Illustration 1-2.) Marketing does this by providing products that: (1) help the organization to achieve its goals (firm's internal satisfaction); (2) are wanted (consumer satisfaction); (3) are legal (government satisfaction); (4) are competitive (satisfaction of business efficiency); (5) socially beneficial (satisfaction of special interest groups); and (6) are efficient in resource use (supplier satisfaction). Of course the marketer is often faced with a conflict of interest among the five groups in which satisfying one group leaves another group partially satisfied. The product actually distributed is a compromise resulting from the combined wants of all groups. For example, the desire of some consumers for cigarettes overrides special interest groups' objection to tobacco. Government requirements that business supply financial information may lead to some inefficient use of resources, while government standards placed on products may limit some consumer choices.

Marketing managers attempt to satisfy their target markets by developing a coordinated marketing mix. This marketing mix consists of product, price, promotion, and distribution. *Product policy* consists of decisions related to developing and maintaining product types, brands, packages, and lines. *Price policy* consists of those decisions pertaining to determination of product price, discounts, and terms of sale. *Promotion policy* consists of decisions that communicate organizational and/or product features to consumers. *Distribution policy* includes those decisions of design and location of facilities along with transporting and storing products.

Marketing is *situation-oriented,* which means that:

> *the marketer responds to the common interests of identified persons within each of the five external groups in proportion to the importance of the group to the decision.*

The target group shown in Illustration 1-2 is composed of identified persons from among each of the five groups. *The target always includes all five external groups,* and it is a composite of a limited number of persons from within these groups. It is a function of managers to identify who makes up these identified persons. Specific persons from the five external groups move into and out of the target according to the decision considered. It follows that the composition of the marketing target may differ somewhat with each executive decision. Consumers may be more important for one decision, while competitors, suppliers, or some other group may be more important for another decision. However, all five

Illustration 1-2
Components of marketing

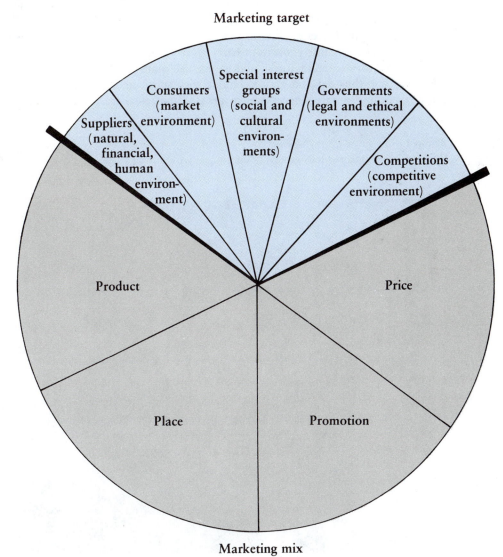

Chapter 1 – The Nature of Consumer Decision Making   **15**

groups must be satisfied with each decision because the appeal is to a common want or interest. It is this emphasis on a common interest that makes the marketer's task manageable in a complex environment.

Marketers attempt to achieve organizational goals by influencing the attitudes and/or behavior of suppliers, consumers, governments, competitors, and special interest groups.[15] The marketer supports behavior of external groups that is consistent with organizational objectives and attempts to influence behavior that is not. Each factor in the external environment can be identified with specific groups of people as shown in the diagram. Marketing strategy is directed toward people, not toward things or ideology. Marketers attempt to induce people to purchase their brands; they try to affect laws through the people who run government agencies; they develop alternative policies to counter the managers of competing firms.[16] If marketers could not affect the environment, business success would be hit-or-miss at best.

Even the physical environment can be influenced through people. For example, marketers purchase protection from insurers against natural disasters; they hire contractors to build stores and to enclose malls as protection against the weather; and they develop good relations with suppliers to assure a continuing flow of natural resources necessary to operate. Marketers are not interested in the

Photo 1-4
Markets are segmented into groups of consumers with like characteristics.

Part 1 – Overview of Consumer Decision Making

weather per se. They are interested in getting people into the store when it's raining.

While consumers are only one of the external groups that make up the marketing target, they are vital to the success of every marketing strategy. Consumers affect every marketing decision, and consumer needs, wants, and desires must be satisfied (along with the other groups' wants) if the marketing program is to succeed. It follows that the manager can never afford to slight the consumer when establishing policy. Let us consider some of the specific ways that consumer decision making affects marketing strategy.

Market Segmentation

All consumers share the need for sufficient food, clothing, and shelter to sustain life. Once these basic requirements are satisfied, consumers reach for an unlimited number of psychological wants or desires related to safety, belonging, esteem, self-actualization, curiosity, and esthetics. Every need, want, or desire that consumers have is a problem to which an acceptable solution must be found.

Marketers find their opportunities in satisfying consumer problems. Market segmentation is the tool used to relate the firm's abilities to individual problems. *Market segmentation* is dividing heterogeneous markets into smaller groups of customers having relatively homogeneous characteristics. Marketers must segment because, even when consumers have the same wants, their problems vary due to differences in location, climate, age, sex, income, occupation, education, religion, race, nationality, social class, psychological makeup, etc.[17] Marketers segment by grouping persons with relatively homogeneous characteristics together and attempting to satisfy their common needs, wants, and desires. For example, one business may satisfy a northern market segment's need for warmth with heavy coats. Another firm may satisfy the southern segment with light sweaters. The firms may further divide segments by income, sex, or age.

Segmentation lies at the heart of all marketing strategy. The marketing manager must be able to identify common problems among consumers before deciding how best to satisfy these persons. It follows that marketing executives spend considerable time studying consumer problems.

Product Policy

Product policy is the first policy area of the marketing mix to be discussed. Product policy, like all marketing mix decisions, is partly a response to the particular market segment included as part of the marketing target. In other words, marketing management must tailor the design and development of product types, brands, and lines to the specific wants of consumers. Marketers were happy to furnish one-speed bikes until consumer interest in physical fitness created demand for a more complex bike and led to the development of ten-speed bikes. There is now a new segment for bikes, consisting of consumers who want an all-terrain multi-speed bike. The point is that every feature of the one-speed, the ten-speed, and the all-terrain multi-speed bike is there to solve some problem for consumers. The same is true of vacuum cleaners, toilet papers, shirts, colognes, and pizzas. When the consumer's problems change, so do the products.

Marketers attempt to differentiate their products from those of competitors according to identified customer problems. For example, a Nissan Sentra is an entirely different automobile from a Ford LTD. The Sentra appeals to customers interested in passenger comfort, short-distance travel, gas economy, ease in parking, and low initial cost. The LTD solves problems related to more comfort, long-distance travel, greater trunk space, capacity for six, and prestige. Two competitors can each be successful by appealing to LTD type buyers and Sentra type buyers.

Distribution Policy

No marketing manager is comfortable deciding on a distribution policy without knowledge of the search patterns of consumers. When locating a particular store, marketing management wants to know, if buyers prefer downtown, suburbs, string streets, strip shops, or isolated locations. For example, department stores tend to locate downtown or in major shopping centers and near competitors because customers like to shop and compare products these stores sell. Grocery stores locate in smaller shopping centers near subdivisions because people don't like to travel long distances to purchase groceries. Motels conveniently locate near major intersections to accommodate user search patterns. Specialty stores with unique offerings can locate in out-of-the-way places because customers will seek them out.

The design of the store also reflects internal search patterns of consumers. Entrances are made to tempt individuals to enter the store. Counters, walls, colors, and merchandise placement are designed to make shopping a pleasure. Attempts are made to have the product as accessible as possible for inspection. Department store layout is designed to induce the customer to look around because the business emphasizes shopping goods for which comparisons are made before purchasing. Grocery stores place meat at the rear because management knows customers must pass other items which may be purchased on impulse. All stores place featured products at the end of aisles and up front to attract attention.

The number of products the store must carry in inventory and the type of transportation follows from store location and layout. Stores located farther from suppliers require more inventory to meet customer needs. Transportation must use carriers that assure little interruption in customer service. If customers change their search patterns, then management must modify its distribution policy. For example, the movement of people to the suburbs after World War II led to the development of planned shopping centers. These suburban shoppers resisted trading downtown because of the inconvenience. The same desire to provide convenience has prompted marketing managers to add techniques such as direct selling and telemarketing to their distribution policy.

Promotion and Price

Promotion and price are the final two policy areas related to the consumer purchase process. Promotion includes personal selling, sales promotion, advertising, and publicity which communicate to consumers information about the organization, its stores, its products, and its services. Price communicates the value or worth of the product to the consumer. Marketing management uses promotion to inform prospective buyers about their problems and their need to seek out solutions. Promotion presents the organization and its offerings as the best solution to these problems. Promotion, combined with price information, attempts to lead the consumer to make choices that are consistent with the firm's objectives. Marketing management also wants to assure customers that the decision to purchase the company's offerings is a sound one and that they could purchase them again when the problem arises. The more marketing managers know about consumer choice behavior and the types of choices that have been made previously, the better the odds that promotion and price policies can be tailored to achieve organizational objectives.

CONSUMER DECISION PROCESS

We explained earlier in this chapter that consumer purchase decisions are based on the individual's internal makeup and relevant environmental influences.[18] The thought process that consumers go through to arrive at their decisions is known as the *consumer decision process*. This decision process has five recognizable steps. They are: (1) problem recognition, (2) search for market related information, (3) evaluation of alternatives, (4) decision on alternatives, and (5) assessment. At this point, we want to explain the steps in the consumer's decision process and demonstrate how each step involves one or more of the basic determinants (internal) and environmental (external) influences. For the sake of convenience in discussion consumer evaluation and decision are treated together. This combination can be done because the two steps are so closely related. The combination is used throughout the book except where a separation aids in making a point.

Illustration 1-3 demonstrates that the decision process encompasses the basic and environmental determinants. These influences have an effect on each step in the decision process. These points are illustrated in the following discussion.

Problem Recognition

The first step in the consumer decision process is problem recognition. A *problem* exists any time the consumer has some purchase goal and is uncertain about how to achieve it. *Problem recognition* is understanding that there is uncertainty about the goal, its achievement, or the outcome.

Consumers can have problems related to all five facets of decision making. For example, there are problems related to *whether* (do I need a computer or not?), *what* (do I prefer a RCA or a Zenith television?), *where* (should I buy my cookies at K-Mart or Krogers?), *when* (should I shop today or put it off until tomorrow?), and *how* (should I pay cash or charge it?) to purchase. Most people face these or similar problems every day. Table 1-3 summarizes how all the factors affect problem recognition.

Of the basic determinants, needs, perception, and motives have the most direct effect on problem recognition. Problems are founded in consumer needs, wants, or desires. However, problem recognition is perceptual because it depends

Illustration 1-3
Consumer decision process

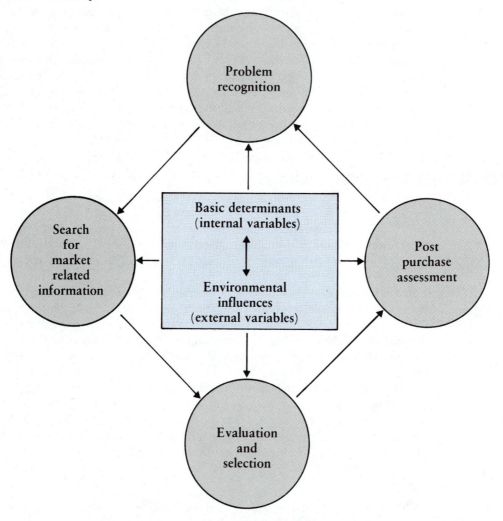

on the consumer's interpretation of things and situations. Two individuals may both be exposed to the advertisements of a microwave oven, yet only one of them may see the microwave as a solution to a problem. The one individual may see it as an unnecessary luxury and expense, while the other individual may see it as a necessity to solve the problem of not having enough time to cook.

The environmental variables are less directly involved but no less important to problem recognition. In our four-step decision process, a problem must exist before the consumer begins seeking external information. We recognize that a person's current needs, motives, personality, learning, attitudes, and perceptions have already been affected by the environment. This interaction and relationship are developed later in the book.

Table 1-3

Consumer Decision Making: Problem Recognition

	Problem Recognition	Search	Evaluation and Decision	Post-Purchase Assessment
Individual	Person understands that a problem exists			
Family	Family members help clarify problem and relate it to family goals			
Social and reference groups	Group expresses opinions about problem and relates it to group goals			
Culture	Individual and groups determine moral and ethical rewards and sanctions related to the problem			
Economic	Person decides income advantages and constraints associated with the problem			
Business	Firm determines products (with design features) available to solve problems			

Source: Developed in conjunction with Jagdish N. Sheth.

Search for Market-Related Information

The second step in the consumer decision making process is the search for information. *Consumer search* is:

the mental and physical activities undertaken by consumers to provide information on recognized problems.

Table 1-4

Consumer Decision Making: Search

	Problem Recognition	Search	Evaluation and Decision	Post-Purchase Assessment
Individual	Person understands that a problem exists	Person uses experience as a basis for seeking a solution to the problem		
Family	Family members help clarify problem and relate it to family goals	Family suggests advantages and disadvantages of known locations		
Social and reference groups	Group expresses opinions about problem and relates it to group goals	Group suggests preferences for available locations for the product		
Culture	Individual and groups determine moral and ethical rewards and sanctions related to the problem	Individual and groups decide moral and ethical rewards and sanctions associated with each location		
Economic	Person decides income advantages and constraints associated with the problem	Person decides cost/satisfaction outcomes associated with more or less search		
Business	Firm determines products (with design features) available to solve problems	Firm establishes distribution system (locations and product assortments) to aid individual's search		

Source: Developed in conjunction with Jagdish N. Sheth.

Consumer search is essentially a learning process by which the consumer identifies alternative products or brands, specific stores, trade areas, prices, terms of sale, and services. Consumer search sets the stage of evaluation by providing necessary information used in evaluation. For example, it is search when an individual checks the phone book for the number and location of barbers or banks.

It is search when the consumer visits downtown stores or a shopping center to compare specific products. It is search when a consumer compares price and/or features of two different brands observed in television commercials. Table 1-4 summarizes the consumer search process.

Consumer search may be internal or external. *Internal search* concerns data from the individual's experience as stored in the memory. It is most directly involved with the basic determinant of learning. The recall of previous experiences with a product, treatment by a salesperson, parking problems once encountered, and prices paid for an item all constitute internal search based on learning experience.

External search occurs when consumers consult sources outside their own experience to obtain information needed for decision making. Obtaining information from external groups (family, reference groups, culture, economic and businesses) is external search. It is external search when a person reads an advertisement in the paper, notes an effective store display, asks a friend's advice about shopping at a store, or consults with a family member about some product. Of course, some consumers engage in more search than others and some problems require more search for information than others.

Evaluation and Decision

The third step in the consumer decision process is evaluation and decision. *Consumer evaluation* is:

> the activity of identifying alternative solutions to a problem and determining the relative merits of each.

Consumers compare product features and/or store characteristics to preestablished evaluation criteria when comparing alternatives. *Evaluation criteria* are the acceptable limits set by the consumer when searching for a solution to their problem.[19] For example, an individual may realize a problem with the number of phones he or she has. If the individual determines purchasing an additional phone would be the solution, the purchase would be based on evaluation criteria. The individual may conclude that the desired phone must be tan, cordless, lightweight, touch tone, and below $100.00 in cost. These limits are the evaluation criteria. It must be noted that each consumer uses different criteria when evaluating products and stores. Also the evaluation criteria can change depending on the situation or environment.

Consumer decision is the outcome of evaluation, so we do not consider it a separate step in the decision process. *Consumer decision* is the mental process of choosing the most desirable alternative. The most desirable selection is the one that more closely measures up to the evaluation criteria established. It is the information provided by search that forms the basis for evaluation and decision. If the information is inadequate then the decision is likely to be faulty also.

Table 1-5 provides an overall view of the evaluation and decision process.

The basic determinants of personality and attitudes are very important to consumer evaluation and decision. Consumers purchase those items toward which they have favorable attitudes and which are consistent with their personali-

Photo 1-5

In her post-purchase assessment, how does this woman feel about her purchase of beauty services?

ty. Seldom does a person make a purchase that is inconsistent with these two internal variables. However, it would be a mistake to assume that the other internal variables and the external variables have no effect on consumer evaluation and decision. They do. Their effect is felt through attitudes and personality. Needs, perceptions, learning, and motives are important in shaping one's current attitudes and personality. What the consumer is as a person evolves out of these basic determinants.

The environmental variables also affect personality and attitudes because new and/or different information affects our basic determinants. In other words, the external determinants provide the impetus for changes in our attitudes and personality over time. In this text, attitudes and personality are viewed as encompassing the other variables. These other internal and external variables are discussed, along with attitudes and personality, where they add to the explanation.

Post-Purchase Assessment

The fourth and final step in the consumer purchase process is post-purchase assessment. *Post-purchase assessment* is:

the consumer's perception of the outcome of the purchase process.

Table 1-5

Consumer Decision Making: Evaluation and Decision

	Problem Recognition	Search	Evaluation and Decision	Post-Purchase Assessment
Individual	Person understands that a problem exists	Person uses experience as a basis for seeking a solution to the problem	Person considers criteria and product preferences to solve problem	
Family	Family members help clarify problem and relate it to family goals	Family suggests advantages and disadvantages of known locations	Family members modify their own positions to accommodate group preferences	
Social and reference groups	Group expresses opinions about problem and relates it to group goals	Group suggests preferences for available locations for the product	Person modifies personal position to accommodate group preferences	
Culture	Individual and groups determine moral and ethical rewards and sanctions related to the problem	Individual and groups decide moral and ethical rewards and sanctions associated with each location	Individual and groups consider moral and ethical positions relative to alternatives identified	
Economic	Person decides income advantages and constraints associated with the problem	Person decides cost/satisfaction outcomes associated with more or less search	Person relates preferred solutions to income opportunities and constraints	
Business	Firm determines products (with design features) available to solve problems	Firm establishes distribution system (locations and product assortments) to aid individual's search	Firm uses promotion to push product, price, and terms to aid person's decision	

Source: Developed in conjunction with Jagdish N. Sheth.

The result of purchasing can be either satisfaction or dissatisfaction. Satisfaction occurs when the product, brand, or store, etc., and the conditions surrounding its purchase, conform to the buyer's expectations. The outcome of purchasing is dissatisfaction if the product, brand, or store, or conditions surrounding its purchase do not conform to the consumer's expectations.

Table 1-6
Consumer Decision Making

	Problem Recognition	Search	Evaluation and Decision	Post-Purchase Assessment
Individual	Person understands that a problem exists	Person uses experience as a basis for seeking a solution to the problem	Person considers criteria and product preferences to solve problem	Person evaluates personal satisfaction with the product decision made
Family	Family members help clarify problem and relate it to family goals	Family suggests advantages and disadvantages of known locations	Family members modify their own positions to accommodate group preferences	Family conveys to buyer its evaluation of the success of the decision
Social and reference groups	Group expresses opinions about problem and relates it to group goals	Group suggests preferences for available locations for the product	Person modifies personal position to accommodate group preferences	Group expresses its evaluation of the decision's enhancement of person's group position
Culture	Individual and groups determine moral and ethical rewards and sanctions related to the problem	Individual and groups decide moral and ethical rewards and sanctions associated with each location	Individual and groups consider moral and ethical positions relative to alternatives identified	Individual and groups evaluate the moral and ethical results of the decision
Economic	Person decides income advantages and constraints associated with the problem	Person decides cost/satisfaction outcomes associated with more or less search	Person relates preferred solutions to income opportunities and constraints	Person evaluates whether outcome was worth the price paid
Business	Firm determines products (with design features) available to solve problems	Firm establishes distribution system (locations and product assortments) to aid individual's search	Firm uses promotion to push product, price, and terms to aid person's decision	Firm employs service to enhance soundness of the decision or to correct any dissatisfaction

Source: Developed in conjunction with Jagdish N. Sheth.

Post-purchase assessment is always the result of the buyer obtaining new information as illustrated in Table 1-6. The new data may come from experience with the product, the store or the method of buying. New information may also come about as a result of contact with external groups after the purchase. Thus both the basic (internal) determinants and environmental (external) influences affect post-purchase assessment. For example, on the way home from work a consumer purchases produce from a roadside stand. The consumer is satisfied with the price but becomes more satisfied when learning from friends that it was an excellent price compared to the prices at a local store. Or a consumer is happy with his or her new Nissan Stanza, but dissatisfaction sets in when the cruise control doesn't work or the car goes on sale a month after the purchase. A consumer remembers a bad purchase experience as clearly as an auto accident, and marketers must take steps to ensure a good purchase experience. These consumer reactions reflect attitudes and learning as affected by new information.

Although post-purchase assessment is the last step in the purchase process, it is not necessarily the end. The information gained as a result of purchasing and post-purchase assessment is stored at this stage. It becomes a part of the experience contained in the individual's memory. As Illustration 1-3 shows, the consumer could recall this information when entering into another purchase decision. Thus the purchase is, in one sense, a continual process. The end of one purchase decision is the beginning of another.

PLAN OF THE BOOK

This book is organized around the consumer decision process (problem recognition, search for information, evaluation and decision, and post-purchase assessment) that is presented in Illustration 1-3. Each decision stage is a major section of the book, except that assessment and selection are combined. This combination was made for convenience in presentation. There is also a section at the end of the text dealing with special topics of consumer behavior. These are important subjects related to consumer decision making, but because of their nature they do not fit conveniently under any single decision step.

Three types of information are explained under each decision step in the text. First, the consumer decision step under consideration is carefully explained. This typically is done in the introductory chapter to each section. Second, the basic and environmental determinants of consumer behavior are explained and related to the decision step. Typically one or more chapters are devoted to this subject. Third, the decision step under consideration is related to marketing decision making. This relationship is established in two chapters at the end of each section. The subjects of segmentation, product policy, distribution policy, promotion policy, and price policy are discussed. We demonstrate how the development of marketing strategy is directly dependent upon the consumer decision process. The emphasis in these chapters is on the relationship and not on explaining what product, distribution, promotion, and price are.

QUESTIONS

1. Explain the benefits you can obtain by studying consumer behavior.
2. Identify the interrelated activities involved in the consumption process and

the terms for those who engage in consumption. Give examples of each.

3. Distinguish between a consumer and an influencer in relation to the consumption process. Give examples of each.

4. Define and discuss the terms "potential consumer" and "realized consumer." Give an example of each type of consumer.

5. Describe the major types of markets to which a consumer belongs.

6. Discuss the questions involved in a purchase decision.

7. Describe internal and external determinants (variables). How do the basic determinants interact with each other?

8. Name and briefly discuss the environmental determinants of consumer behavior. Give examples.

9. Identify a product you recently purchased and describe the process you went through to make the purchase. Did you go through all the steps? Discuss why or why not.

10. What basic determinants have the most direct effect on problem recognition? Give examples.

11. For most of your purchase decisions do you use an internal search or an external search? Explain your answer.

12. In Illustration 1-3, why do you think the marketing policy focuses on the marketing target?

13. Discuss the statement: "The consumer is always right."

14. The marketing mix is made up of the product, place, promotion, and price. Which of the four elements do you think is most important? Discuss your answer.

15. How does a consumer's search pattern affect marketing managers' planning decisions? Give examples.

NOTES

1. Betsy D. Gelb, Gariel M. Gelb, and Richy W. Griffin, "Managing With the Consumer's Help," *Business Horizons* (April 1976), pp. 69–74.

2. Sandra Kresch, "The Impact of Consumer Trends on Corporate Strategy," *Journal of Business Strategy,* Vol. 3 (1983), pp. 58–63.

3. Thomas V. Bonoma, "Major Sales: Who Really Does The Buying," *Harvard Business Review,* Vol. 60 (May–June 1982), pp. 111–19.

4. Yoram Wind, "Preference of Relevant Others and Individual Choice Models," *Journal of Consumer Research,* Vol. 3 (June 1976), pp. 50–57.

5. Ibid., pp. 50–51.

6. Russell W. Belk, "Situational Variables and Consumer Behavior," *Journal of Consumer Research,* Vol. 2 (December 1975), pp. 157–64.

7. George W. Wynn and Charles W. Hubbard, "Purchase Decision Classification: Is Industrial Versus Consumer Antiquated?"in John C. Crawford and Barbara C. Garland, eds., *1985 Proceedings Southwestern Marketing Association Conference,* (North Texas State University and Southwestern Marketing Assn., 1985), pp. 131–24.

8. John Douglas, George A. Field, and Lawrence X. Tarpey, *Human Behavior*

in Marketing, (Columbus: Charles E. Merrill, Inc., 1967) and Rom J. Markin, Jr., *Consumer Behavior: A Cognitive Orientation,* (New York: Macmillan Publishing Co., Inc., 1974), pp. 55–56.

9. M. Joseph Siegy, "A Conceptualization of the Consumer Behavior Discipline," *Journal of the Academy of Marketing Science,* Vol. 13, (Winter 1985), pp. 104–21.

10. Morris B. Holbrook and Elizabeth C. Hirschman, "The Experimental Aspects of Consumption: Consumer Fantasies, Feelings, and Fun," *Journal of Consumer Research,* Vol. 9 (September 1982), pp. 132–40.

11. A. Ben Oumlil and C.P. Rao, "Income Effects on Consumer Store Choice Behavior Under Changed Economic Environmental Conditions," in John C. Crawford and Barbara C. Garland, eds., *1985 Proceedings Southwestern Marketing Association Conference* (North Texas State University and Southwestern Marketing Assn., 1985), pp. 54–60.

12. Ishmael P. Akaah, Edward A. Riordan, and David L. Williams, "Effects of Group Influence on Decision Strategy: A Reexamination of Stafford's Hypotheses Via Conjoint Methodology," in David M. Klein and Allen E. Smith, eds., *Marketing: The Next Decade,* (Boca Raton, Fla., and Southern Marketing Assn., 1985), pp. 58–62.

13. David Keley, "Critical Issues for Issue Ads," *Harvard Business Review,* Vol. 60 (July–August 1982), pp. 80–87.

14. C. Glenn Walters, Wayne Norvell, and Sam Bruno, "Is There a Better Way Than Consumer Orientation," in Henry Nash and Don Robin, eds., *Proceedings of the Southern Marketing Assn., 1975* (Mississippi State University and Southern Marketing Assn., 1975); C. Glenn Walters, Wayne Norvell, and Sam Bruno, "Situational Orientation to Marketing," *Pittsburgh Business Review,* (Summer 1978), pp. 7–10; C. Glenn Walters and Ron D. Taylor, "Contingency Marketing and Marketing Management: A Comparison," in Bill Pride and O.C. Ferrell, eds., *Conceptual and Theoretical Developments in Marketing: 1979* (Phoenix: American Marketing Assn., 1979); and C. Glenn Walters, John Darling, and Ron D. Taylor, "Situational Orientation to Marketing Management," *Finnish Journal of Economic Science* (1980), pp. 4–14.

15. John Naisbitt, *Megatrends: Ten New Directions Transforming Our Lives* (New York: Warner Books, Inc., 1984).

16. Bruce D. Henderson, "The Anatomy of Competition," *Journal of Marketing,* Vol. 47 (Spring 1983), pp. 7–11.

17. Alan J. Greco, "Linking Dimensions of The Elderly Market to Actionable Market Segmentation," in David M. Kline and Allen E. Smith, eds., *Marketing: The New Decade, 1985* (Boca Raton, Fla. and Southern Marketing Assn., 1985), pp. 127–34.

18. Girish N. Punj and David W. Stewart, "An Interaction Framework of Consumer Decision Making," *Journal of Consumer Research,* Vol. 10 (September 1983), pp. 181–96.

19. James B. Wiley, "Toward Upgrading the Quality of Consumer Decision-Making," *Journal of the Academy of Marketing Science,* Vol. 12 (Winter 1984), pp. 1–10.

PART 2

CONSUMER PROBLEM
RECOGNITION

SECTION A
CONSUMER PROBLEMS
AND RESULTS

2. Introduction to Consumer Problem
   Recognition
3. Consumer Problems Founded in Needs
4. Problem Recognition Leads to Motivation

CHAPTER 2

Introduction to Consumer

Problem Recognition

CHAPTER OUTLINE

I. NATURE OF CONSUMER PROBLEM RECOGNITION

II. SEQUENCE OF PROBLEMS

III. WHO IDENTIFIES CONSUMER PROBLEMS
  A. Problem Recognition by Individuals
  B. Family Problem Recognition
    1. *Wife as Purchasing Agent*
    2. *Everyone Identifies Problems*
    3. *Responsibility for Problem Recognition Varies*
    4. *Selection of Family Purchasing Agent*

IV. CONSUMER PROBLEMS RESIDE IN PRODUCT ASSORTMENT
  A. Nature of Consumer Assortments
  B. Assortment Composition Generates Problems
  C. Different Assortments: Different Problems
  D. Structure and Status Affect Problems
  E. Problems Reflect Assortment Closure

V. PROBLEMS IDENTIFIED BY INVENTORY
  A. Conditions That Signal Problems
    1. *Routine "Out" Condition*
    2. *When Expanding the Assortment*
    3. *When Deleting Products*
  B. Partial and Complete Inventory
  C. Casual and Formal Inventory
  D. Long- and Short-Run Assortments

VI. DEGREE TO WHICH PROBLEMS SPECIFIED

CHAPTER OBJECTIVES

After completing your study of Chapter 2, you should be able to:

1. Discuss the nature of consumer problem recognition.
2. Describe the sequence of problems.
3. Discuss who identifies consumer problems.
4. Explain how consumer problems affect product assortments.
5. Discuss the relationship between inventory and problem identification.
6. Discuss the degree to which problems can be specified.

The first step in the consumer's purchase process is problem recognition. Problem recognition is the trigger that sets into motion all consumer behavior, and there can be no purchase without recognizing that a problem exists.[1] If marketers are to have an effect on the purchase, especially the purchase of a firm's specific brand, then they must understand problem recognition. Although problem recognition is but one step in the total purchase process, it is a complete operation of its own. The marketer must understand what problems are, how they arise, what factors are involved in problem recognition and the results of understanding that a problem exists.[2] In this chapter we present an overview of problem recognition to serve as the basis for the remainder of the section.

NATURE OF CONSUMER PROBLEM RECOGNITION

The consumer faces many problems when acquiring the goods and services necessary to sustain life or to make living really worthwhile. Since personal satisfaction comes from acquiring benefits contained in products, a lack of products can cause dissatisfaction or discomfort. It follows that the lack of some specific good or service is the stimulus causing the consumer to engage in market activity.

A problem has been viewed broadly as either any question to be considered or as any indecision related to action. For our purpose a *consumer problem* is defined as:

> *any market-related situation where there is a significant difference between what the individual desires and what actually exists.*

There is a difference between the actual and the desired situation anytime a consumer has an unfulfilled want or desire for a good or service.

The consumer cannot act on a problem until there is sufficient dissatisfaction with the present state to cause the individual to seek change. A person may be out of Tylenol but take no action until there is a headache. Thus problem recognition is primarily a perceptual state. We define *consumer problem recognition* as:

> *an awareness of wanting to change the existing market to conform to the desired state.*

Illustration 2-1 illustrates how problem recognition occurs.

Illustration 2-1
Problem recognition by consumers

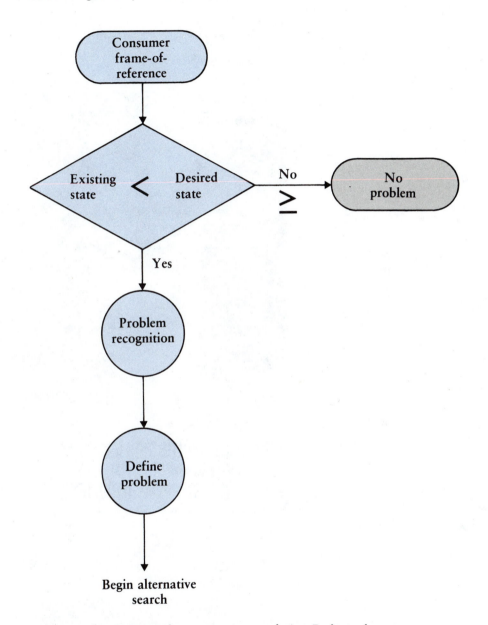

Assume the consumer has some want or desire. Perhaps the person wants a new bass boat. This desire is contained in the person's frame of reference as a result of past experience and contact with external groups. The consumer compares his or her existing state with the desired state. If the consumer already has a boat equal to or better than a bass boat, then there is no problem. If the person perceives that she or he has no bass boat (existing state) and wants a bass boat (desired state), then a problem is understood to exist. The consumer then defines the problem and begins a search for alternative ways of obtaining a bass boat to solve the problem.

Figure 2-1
Helping the consumer recognize a problem

Advanced Care Products, Division of Ortho Pharmaceuticals Corp.

Part 2 – Consumer Problem Recognition

Some information is always necessary before a problem is recognized. Figure 2-1 is an example of an ad that provides information to help the consumer recognize a problem. It is often assumed that all problems arise out of a lack of information, but this assumption is an oversimplification. It is true that the consumer has a problem when there is insufficient information to select a course of action. However, to recognize a dissatisfaction, one must have at least enough information to indicate that there is a difficulty or some possible solution. So long as one knows nothing, there is no doubt—and no problem. Doubt arises when there is enough information to act but not enough information to know how to act.

SEQUENCE OF PROBLEMS

We cannot assume that consumers deal with one problem at a time. In fact, one problem may lead to another as the consumer decides whether, what, when, where, and how to purchase. In many instances the consumer must deal with a sequence of related problems, as demonstrated in Figure 2-1. The reader should keep this in mind as we progress through the different sections of this text dealing with the decision process.

Illustration 2-2 shows three related problems. The consumer has the problem of which watch to purchase. Then there are the related problems of when and where to purchase the watch. Notice that each of these problems has its own complete decision process involving search for alternatives, evaluation and decision, and post-decision dissonance (not shown in the illustration). Problem recognition changes the consumer's awareness. Knowing that a problem exists and making the resulting decisions must contribute to the consumer's general education. Many types of changes in the consumer are possible. As the consumer identifies new problems, acquires information, and arrives at solutions, he or she can become more conscious of his or her environment. In the process, the consumer becomes a more experienced buyer. Poor problem recognition or inferior solutions make some consumers despondent or callous. Too many problems can cause consumers essentially to give up in their desire for specific products or a better life.

WHO IDENTIFIES CONSUMER PROBLEMS

The previous discussion indicates that problem recognition is a more complex subject than might be suspected. It is also no simple matter to determine consumer responsibility for problem recognition. Consumers, like businesses, handle problem recognition in different ways. Responsiblity varies with the type of family unit and the situation.[3]

Problem Recognition by Individuals

For a male or female living alone, problem recognition is relatively uncomplicated. The person has to provide food, clothing, and shelter but does not have to consider the wants or opinions of family members. Although less complicated, problem recognition and the resulting purchase may be just as important

Illustration 2-2
Problems occur in sequence.

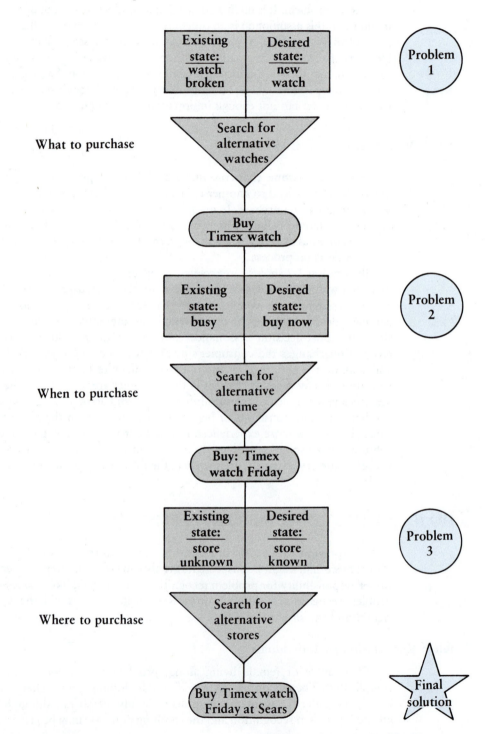

What to purchase

When to purchase

Where to purchase

for the single person as for anyone else. Any person who must maintain a certain standard of living on a limited income has difficult problems and significant decisions to make. The individual can be selfish because there is no one else to think of, and no one else is harmed if the solution is a bad one.

Family Problem Recognition

In a business, problem recognition is dealt with in two ways. First, a department may identify its own product problems and seek its own solution by direct negotiation with suppliers. Second, the business may employ purchasing specialists to deal with problems. The using department may identify its product requirements but allow the purchasing agent to seek the solution. It is also possible for the purchasing agent to identify the using department's product requirements and negotiate with suppliers for the firm as a whole.

Multi-member family units function much like a business when it comes to problem recognition. Family members may determine their own product requirements and do their own purchasing.[4] The family may also have a purchasing agent who acts on problems presented by individuals or who identifies problems and solutions for the family as a whole.

Who the family purchasing agent is has a direct bearing on problem recognition. For example, a mother may not perceive a son's desire for new track shoes as a problem. The son may view a lack of the shoes as a serious problem. A daughter may not consider a lack of loyalty to a particular store as a problem, but the father may disagree. A mother may understand the urgency in purchasing a daughter's party gown, but the father may not. The point is that personal biases and preferences have a lot to do with how problems are perceived within the family.

There are two important differences between a family purchasing agent and a business buyer. First, families, unlike businesses, do not permanently designate one single person as the purchasing agent. Responsibility varies over time depending on the type of product involved, the situation, and the family's life-style. Kids go to the store to purchase candy, mom picks up a six-pack on the way home from work, dad purchases mom flowers while grocery shopping, or dad meets mom downtown after she gets off work to consider dining room furniture. Another major difference is that the family purchasing agent often acts without explicit direction from the person with the need. A parent may purchase children's clothing or groceries without specifically asking what is desired. For many types of purchases, the purchasing agent just knows what is required.

Wife as Purchasing Agent. There is no doubt that in multi-member families, individuals make a significant number of purchases. Men, women, and children each tend to purchase most of their personal consumption items such as perfume, books, sports equipment, fashion clothing, toys and toiletries. These items constitute significant markets for specific businesses. However, in most families today, the majority of purchases still are concentrated in one person. Typically, this person is the wife, and she easily wins the title of family purchasing agent. This fact is true even when the woman is holding down a full-time job along with her household responsibilities (see Figure 2-2).

Wives purchase nearly all family groceries, and this item alone accounts for about 16 percent of consumer expenditures according to the latest Census. Wives purchase most work clothing, underwear and accessories; this accounts for another 5 percent of expenditures. Furthermore, the wife buys most gift items and a significant part of the household furnishings. It is easy to see why it has been estimated that wives do the buying of for a majority of all family items. No other single family member comes close to this figure.

Everyone Identifies Problems. It would be a mistake for business managers to concentrate their sales effort on women because they are the family purchasing agent. The fact is that the purchasing agent is not always responsible for recognizing the problem, and business is as interested in who determines the purchase as who actually makes it. In a majority of cases, the purchasing agent is acting at the direction of one or more family members who have specific wants. The purchasing agent may make final decisions on brand or box size, but the one with the want determines the need.

Evidence indicates that every member of the family has a say in the purchase of products that are jointly used by the family.[5] Table 2-1 shows who is responsible for problem recognition under different family situations. The husband is more likely to recognize a need for insurance and transportation. The wife

Figure 2-2
Wife as purchasing agent

Courtesy of Whirlpool Corporation

Table 2-1

Responsibility for Problem Recognition

Husband dominant	Wife dominant	Either party dominant	Joint responsibility
Life insurance	Cleaning products	Cosmetics	Children's toys
Other insurance	Kitchenware	Drugs	Living room
Automobile	Child's clothing	Appliances	furniture
	Wife's clothing	Husband's	Outside entertain-
		clothing	ment
	Food	Housing upkeep	Vacation
	Furnishings	Alcoholic beverages	Housing
		Garden tools	School
		Savings	
		TV/stereo	

recognizes problems associated with maintaining the home. Personal items tend to be recognized by the individual, but major problems associated with school, vacations, entertainment, and housing are jointly recognized.

Individual suggestions to the purchasing agent about a problem may be specific to a particular purchase, as when one spouse tells another, "Pick up some beer while you are at the store." The suggestion may come in the form of typical or usual wants expressed to the purchasing agent at times other than when in the act of purchasing. For example, one spouse may know not to buy liver because the other has regularly refused to eat it. The purchasing agent can make many purchases based on this typical information without even having to consult with the individual about the problem. However, it is still the individual who recognized the problem and not the purchasing agent.

Responsibility for Problem Recognition Varies. In a family, responsibility for problem recognition varies with time and the situation.[6] As children mature they begin to assume more responsibility for recognizing and solving their specific problems. Spouses left alone, for whatever reason, assume more problem recognition both for themselves and for children who are still at home. Single parents may learn to anticipate children's need for school supplies, or the need for routine car maintenance. If an individual marries or remarries, the responsibility for problem recognition has to be worked out over time, and the results may be different than either experienced while single. For example, one spouse may not want to give up responsibility for making routine household payments because it is a threat to his or her independence. Even the fact that the physical and emotional makeup of husband and wife change over time can lead to different patterns of problem recognition. Certainly, it is clear that this step in the purchase process can never be taken for granted.

Selection of Family Purchasing Agent. The family purchasing agent is not typically selected by formal appointment, as in a business. Neither is the job a result of formal balloting, as with government officials. In a family, it often happens that the individual becomes purchasing agent by default. No one else wants the job. Certain roles within the family tend to be perceived as carrying specific purchase responsibility.[7] Problem recognition is included as part of this role. For example, everyone may agree that one spouse handles problems related to paying bills, the other takes care of automobile repairs, and each spouse handles his or her own clothing problems.

Convenience is the most important factor in deciding who acts as the purchasing agent of staples. One spouse may frequently purchase groceries and drugs, while the other may pick up cigarettes or gasoline. The reason is that each has the necessary information, and it is relatively easy for each to act. The type of product is also important. In many families, search and purchase is divided along product lines. For example, one spouse may handle groceries, children's clothing, appliances, lamps, and car care while the other may handle monthly expenses, sports equipment for the children, automobile repairs, and yard equipment. Such items as haircuts, gifts, personal hygiene, and entertainment can only be sought by the user.

The importance of the purchase is a major factor in deciding who becomes the purchasing agent. Importance can be measured by the size of expenditure or the number of family members affected. Nearly everyone in the family may seek information and state opinions about the purchase of an automobile because of its psychic importance and the size of the expenditure. Family organization refers to how consumer search and purchase have previously been handled. This factor explains why the wife acts as the family purchasing agent 90 percent of the time in one family and only 10 percent in another.

Purchase competence is important to the selection of the purchasing agent

Photo 2-1
No two families assign the purchasing task the same way.

Part 2 – Consumer Problem Recognition

because it means that the person most capable of handling search and decision is given the task. For example, the person driving the car, eating the meat, cleaning the home, and performing the yard work typically has more pertinent information on these activities. The final factor concerns willingness to act as purchasing agent. One spouse may have to pay the monthly bills because the other refuses to accept the responsibility. A reluctant purchasing agent may perform poorly until it is better for another family member to undertake search and purchase.

The fact is that no two families act just alike when assigning the purchase task. Who is to act as purchasing agent is either implicitly or explictly negotiated among the family members. It is possible to have effective buying with either the wife or the husband taking on search and purchase responsibility. Of course, in most families these activities are shared on some reasonable basis. The important point is that every family must have some organization for handling search and purchase decisions.

CONSUMER PROBLEMS RESIDE IN PRODUCT ASSORTMENT

Consumer behavior would be much simpler if the individual could deal with one product need at a time. In practice, this situation is never found. Product problems do not occur in a vacuum. Rather, each product problem must be evaluated in relation to other product needs. When a person with limited income purchases one product it typically means that they either cut down on, or eliminate, the purchase of some other product. Consumers must plan purchases of individual items to satisfy their most urgent problems. It follows that consumer problems arise out of the assortment of products held by persons. In order to understand consumer problem recognition, we must understand assortments.

Nature of Consumer Assortments

Over the years, consumers accumulate large numbers of different types of products which we refer to as assortments. A *consumer assortment* is defined as:

> *that combination of goods and services recognized by the individual or family as necessary to maintain or improve the standard of living.*

The assortment is a particular combination of goods and services. This means that every consumer assortment is an individual one. The assortment of no two consumers is likely to be exactly the same. Since each consumer is an individual and each has a different assortment, it follows that each consumer has different needs and wants in the marketplace.

All consumer problems arise out of a need to meet some assortment goal—to replace goods routinely used up, to modify assortment makeup, or to increase product holdings in the assortment.[8] In fact, one can think of the assortment as a physical manifestation of a consumer's physiological and physical requirements. A consumer's ideal of a consumer assortment is the basis for the consumer's understanding of product deficiencies.

The consumer assortment is as much a mental condition as it is a physical fact. The consumer acts on the basis of what he or she believes the assortment is or ought to be as much as on the basis of what it actually is. Few consumers have an accurate inventory of their total product holdings, but most people can tell you whether they perceive that their standard of living is being met. They can also explain what product priorities are necessary to improve that standard of living. How a consumer perceives his or her assortment relative to those of others affects self-perceptions. If we perceive other persons to have more, we have a problem.[9] If we perceive ourselves to have more, we are happy no matter what the actual standard of living involved.

An assortment exists to satisfy consumer desires and to meet contingencies. However, few consumers obtain any real satisfaction just from having physical goods in their possession. Some people may want to possess things for their own sake, but even this type of satisfaction is usually related to the envy of others. That is the point. Physical goods exist for what they can do and not for what they are. Consumers buy and own physical goods because of the real or potential satisfaction seen in those goods. People do not want an automobile that does not run or a cake mix that makes sour cakes. The goal of consumers in developing target assortments is satisfaction. No matter how noble the idea, how appropriate the materials, or how well designed the product may be, it is not bought for an assortment unless it satisfies some desire held by a consumer.

Assortment Composition Generates Problems

Knowledge of the makeup of consumer assortments is an integral part of problem recognition. Without knowledge of what products one has, there is no sound basis for determining what products one is out of or which new products can solve some unsatisfied want. The makeup of an assortment has three attributes. They are width, variety, and depth. Consumer problem recognition is based on a knowledge of these attributes of an assortment.

The *width of assortment* is defined as the major categories of products that make up the consumer's holdings. Table 2-2 illustrates assortment width as transportation, home and home furnishings, food and clothing. The consumer has a problem if the existing product categories differ significantly from what he or she desires. For example, in the illustration there is no category for entertainment, education, or health. These categories would be perceived as deficiencies by some consumers but not by others. Figure 2-3 could be an ad directed at identifying deficiencies in the entertainment category.

The *variety of assortment* refers to the number of different product types that are contained within each major category. In our example, food has considerable variety, since it requires canned goods, fruits, vegetables, drinks, meat, paper containers, bread, and a large number of unspecified items. Variety is less for transportation because it involves only automobiles. If the consumer is deficient in any item considered necessary to maintain or improve the assortment variety, then there is a problem. For example, if one of the cars breaks down, there is a problem. There is also a problem if the family perceives the need for a vacation home.

The *depth* of assortment refers to the number of individual items of each type carried under each category. Table 2-2 lists five kinds of fresh meat, four suits,

Table 2-2
Assortment Grid for Consumer A

Transportation	Home and Home Furnishings	Food	Clothing
2 automobiles	1 house	30 units of canned goods	9 sets of bed linen
	2 davenports	6 items of fresh fruits and vegetables	4 suits
	5 chairs	5 kinds of fresh meat	10 ties
	6 tables	3 loaves of bread	3 pr shoes
	1 dining room set	40 items of assorted other foods	15 pr socks
	3 bedroom sets		30 sets of underwear
	30 items of miscellaneous furnishings		12 shirts
			50 pieces of other assorted clothing

five chairs, and twelve shirts. These amounts are the depth of assortment. The consumer has a problem any time item quantity drops below the required amount or any time there is a need to add to the total amount carried. Any change in a consumer's assortment is a change in its width, variety, or depth.

The assortment grid shown is hypothetical, and it is not intended to be definitive. The amount of detail any specific consumer would ascribe to his or her assortment depends on the thoroughness of the consumer in defining requirements. A more complete grid may show the specific items desired, and they could even be listed by brand. Some boxes shown in Table 2-2 are vacant. These empty boxes represent the individual's reservations about changing or expanding the assortment at some future time. You could say that the empty boxes represent the consumer's expectation.

Different Assortments, Different Problems

Individual consumers have different assortment compositions and their purchase problems vary accordingly. Compare the assortments of the consumers in Tables 2-2 and 2-3. These differences may range from minor to great. Perhaps Consumer A lives in the suburbs, has a family, and commutes to work each day. Consumer B lives in an apartment, is single, lives downtown, and walks to work— Consumer B has a completely different life-style from Consumer A.

Table 2-3
Assortment Grid for Consumer B

Transportation	Home and home furnishings	Food	Clothing
	2 rugs	25 kinds of snack foods	10 suits
	1 liquor bar	8 bottles liquor	30 shirts
	25 etchings	1 qt. milk	8 pr shoes
	1 love seat	3 bottles aspirin	20 pr shoes
	1 bed		25 ties
			40 sets of underwear
			60 items of other clothing

Each consumer needs many products in varying quantities to maintain her or his standard of living. A review of the two hypothetical assortment grids demonstrates that people do have rather definite product requirements at any given point in time and that they tend to maintain these products at levels sufficient to meet basic needs and provide for contingencies.

Consumer B's assortment has fewer product categories than Consumer A's, since B does not use private transportation. The assortment of B is restricted in variety compared to A for all types of products except clothing. Both assortments may be quite satisfactory for the individual involved, but there are obvious differences in how the consumers view their product needs. The differences lie in the personal characteristics, life-styles, responsibilities, and economic conditions of the two consumers. The difference is certainly not due entirely to economic aspects, because Consumer B may have twice the income of A. Consumer B may spend extra income outside the house or may save a large portion. The market behavior of A and B will differ due to the differences in their assortment needs.

Structure and Status Affects Problems

We can define two important characteristics of assortments based on our previous discussion that affect consumer problem recognition. Assortments have a definite structure, and products within assortments have status. The structure of assortments is determined by width, variety, and depth, as previously explained. Products that are vital to maintaining assortment structure are more readily perceived as problems by consumers than are those that are not vital. For example, if transportation is considered vital, then the consumer will more readily perceive a problem any time there is an interruption in transportation.

Consumers assign different degrees of status or importance to different products within their assortments. An important product is more likely to be perceived as a problem by the consumer than an unimportant product. For example, among food items, one consumer may assign higher status to canned goods than to fresh vegetables. Among the canned goods, soups may be more important than canned vegetables. Among canned soups, the consumer may consider Campbell's

Figure 2-3
Identifying deficiencies in the entertainment category

Sony Corporation of America

to be higher status than a private brand. Status does not alone determine expenditure—a consumer may part with a second car before greatly reducing food consumption. But it is fair to say that generally consumers will pay more for high-status products than for low-status products.

It was pointed out earlier that there is no reason for assortments except to satisfy wants, and consumers do not enter the market for unwanted products. However, consumers do make mistakes, purchasing products they later realize are unwanted. Such products tend to remain in the assortment indefinitely. Consumption is slow if it occurs at all. It is also true that products once desired that are no longer needed sometimes remain in the assortment. Many people hang onto possessions long after any possibility of their being used has disappeared.

Problems Reflect Assortment Closure

Consumer assortments can be described as open or closed depending upon whether some products normally on hand are depleted or not. An *open assortment* is one with some type of deficiency. The deficiency may be an item that is routinely replaced or an extension or shift in the holdings of the present assortment. A *closed assortment* is one which contains all the products required by the consumer and the assortment structure is complete. The reader may remember the vacant boxes in the assortment grids presented earlier. These boxes show that these illustrative grids were open assortments.

When the assortment is closed, the consumer has no problem and there is no need to enter the market. On the other hand, when the assortment is open, it does not necessarily mean that the consumer must enter the market to buy. Assortments are flexible. It is very capable of adjustment and reorganization. Most consumers seek to close their assortments, but they can operate at a reduced standard of living until that condition is achieved. In practice, it seldom, if ever, happens that the household assortment is completely closed.

It is normal that a given consumer's assortment is open with respect to several products at the same time. The children need new shoes, mother wants a dress, it's grocery shopping day again, and the car's radiator needs repair. Over any extended period of time, the entire assortment has to be replaced. Besides the more or less frequent and routine purchases of food and clothing, the family will, over time, need a paint job for the house, a fourth bedroom, a second car, two new television sets, bedroom furniture, and a gall bladder operation for father. One basic question individuals in a family face is how to establish some order to the purchase of all these different needs.

PROBLEMS IDENTIFIED BY INVENTORY

In a practical sense consumers identify their problems just as businesses do by inventory. A *consumer inventory* is a count of the number and types of products in the consumer's assortment. This consumer inventory points to "out" conditions and suggests opportunities to add items to or delete items from the assortment. The consumer becomes aware of problems by comparing their inventoried holdings to their wants. An understanding of the consumer inventory involves discussion of conditions that signal problems, partial or complete inventory, formal and casual inventory, and long- or short-run inventory. We turn our attention to these points.

Conditions That Signal Problems

There are three conditions that signal problems in the individual consumer's assortment, and they are all related to the inventory of holdings. These conditions are:

1. An "out" condition in the present assortment.
2. Wanting to add to present holdings.
3. Deletions that create new opportunities.

Any of these conditions can signal that a product is a candidate to solve a consumer problem by inclusion in the assortment.

Routine "Out" Condition. The first and most important signal of a problem is the "out" condition.[10] The assortment is in an "out" condition any time the consumer lacks products normally included in the assortment. When consumers casually or formally compare present assortment holdings to normal holdings, they frequently encounter shortages. Most deficiencies are of this type. An "out" condition can concern routine purchases or special purchases. Most impulse pur-

Photo 2-2
Families also face less routine needs, such as wedding purchases.

chases are quickly made decisions on products perceived as out-of-stock by the consumer, while shopping in the store. Routine "out" conditions refer to regular, frequent, and low-cost purchases. Groceries, light bulbs, staple clothing, etc., are routine purchases. Some "out" conditions are not routine, such as the replacement of a wedding ring, a couch or bedroom suite, or a fishing rod.

When Expanding the Assortment. A consumer can also have a problem when he or she wishes to expand the assortment. The consumer may wish to have products that are not now, and have never been, a part of the assortment. In this case, the present assortment is only "out" in the sense that it does not measure up to expectations. The purchase by a family of its first dining room suite or a storage shed are examples of products that consumers may seek to add to their assortments. Such additions increase the number and variety of product holdings. The consumer is likely to consider product additions when he or she has: (1) new or different information, (2) expanded desires, (3) expanded means, or (4) changed expectations.

New information is introduced to the individual by external sources, and it causes the person to question the performance of some product normally used. An example is information about aerosol drain openers that is causing many consumers to reassess their use of granulated drain openers. Pressed potato chips in a can have caused a re-evaluation of traditional potato chips. It often happens that the consumer gets into a habit of purchasing the same product, and it takes some new or different information to shake her or him out of this pattern. The source of new information may be a friend or acquaintance, business salesperson, or an advertisement.

The assortment may be expanded any time the consumer experiences increased desires. Expanded desires come from within the indivdual but may be influenced by the family, reference groups, or business firms. The result is that consumers no longer perceive their needs the same as previously. The expansion in desires may be for products of a different type or for better products of the same type.

"Improved means" simply refers to an increase in income that can be used to purchase products. That consumers can afford new or different products causes a dissatisfaction with their present situation. Consumers perceive opportunities that were previously closed and seek to improve their standard of living by adding to the assortment.

Not only do individuals' internal desires affect their willingness to expand the assortment, but their expectations have a similar effect. One's expectations are usually less than one's desires because expectations imply the possibility of achievement. Nevertheless, any change in one's expectations for income, product "out" conditions, needs, etc. may induce the consumer to enter the market. Changed expectations can result from business advertising, purchase displays, personal selling, or conversations with friends or acquaintances.

The evidence is that consumers with one or more of the following demographic attributes tend to experiment with new or different products: high income, education, and social standing. Personality attributes that lead to product additions include a positive attitude toward innovation, achievement, and group participation; wide interests; high motivation; and a tendency to be opinion leaders. One final factor is communication. People who are quick to purchase new products have wide exposure to communication sources—particularly mass communication.

When Deleting Products. The deletion of products presently in the assortment can lead to expansion or change in the assortment. When products presently in the assortment are deleted, they make room for new or different types of products. Someone may eliminate the early American furniture in the family room and replace it with contemporary. On the other hand, a family may eliminate one car as the children grow up, and they may begin to compensate with better food. It is also true that products deleted may not be replaced at all. This condition can occur when the consumer is cutting down on consumption in general, or when the consumer is obtaining an improved or different product. This decision is usually also related to that consumer's expectations.

Partial and Complete Inventory

The reader should remember that every consumer has an assortment whether that consumer knows what is contained in it or not. The amount of knowledge that the consumer has about his or her assortment depends largely on the extent to which that assortment has been inventoried.[11] One major difference in the efficiency of individual consumers is their knowledge of product holdings. The consumer has a *complete* inventory when everything the household owns is known. A complete inventory of one's assortment is not inconceivable, but it probably occurs only in cases where a relatively few products are involved or where someone in the family keeps very careful records. The author knows of a student who can name all his possessions. Of course, this student's accumulated goods consist of a well-chosen selection of clothes, expensive stereo equipment, and a Chevrolet van.

Most consumers are not conscious of all their possessions. Instead, they have a partial inventory. A *partial inventory* exists when the consumer has knowledge of only a portion of the household's belongings. A partial inventory can exist in several ways. Remember, an assortment displays the characteristics of width, variety, and depth. A consumer may know all the major categories of possessions, such as furniture, automobile, clothing, appliances, etc., but not be aware of the variety or the depth within each category. A consumer may be aware of all the specific items under one category, such as stereo equipment, but not be aware of complete width or depth. The consumer may be aware of how many pairs of pants are owned, but not know the variety of clothing or the total width of products held. The consumer may know some of the items of width, variety, and depth but not have full knowledge of any category.

Most individual consumers do have at least a partial knowledge of their possessions. For example, the average homemaker can recall at least a majority of the possessions of his or her home upon request. This ability to recall indicates a type of prior inventory in the sense that it exists before the actual need. However, a prior inventory is not necessary for the consumer to function. Most people, consciously or unconsciously, follow the principle of management by exception. That is, they make a partial inventory of products when the need arises. A consumer with a pair of shoes asks if a new pair will fit into the monthly budget. A consumer checks the supply of canned goods, laundry detergent, and toothpaste before leaving for the grocery store.

Casual and Formal Inventory

When the consumer takes an inventory of product holdings, it may vary all the way from very casual to highly formal, just as would be the case for a business. A *casual inventory* is defined as one where the consumer uses mental impressions or observation to determine the products currently owned. This can mean that almost no effort is made to survey product holdings. The consumer may assume that daily observation has led to a satisfactory understanding of possessions. Although most consumers could not give a thorough inventory from memory, consumers continually observe their home and become generally familiar with its contents. Someone may be aware of a missing dining room suite each time he or she passes that room. Someone else is reminded, each time she or he cuts the back yard, that there is no shed in which to keep tools and lawn equipment.

With a casual inventory, the individual can even mentally count holdings while miles from home or in some store shopping. It should be obvious that consumers who depend on a casual inventory make many mistakes in buying. For example, hardly a week passes that the average shopper doesn't come home either with some grocery item already owned in quantity, or without some needed item. The number of special trips made to obtain items forgotten at the chain grocery store has helped make a thriving business of convenience grocery stores. In spite of its faults, a casual inventory can be quite efficient for many consumers. It is the most common type of inventory.

A *formal inventory* consists of making a list, much as would a business, based on a firsthand check of household holdings. Consumers seldom undertake a complete list of the assortment. When they do, the list is usually associated with some other need such as home protection insurance or the layout of items on a home plan. A partial listing of assortment items is not uncommon. Consumers often make a list of their jewelry in case of theft. Other lists include items placed in a safety deposit box, in storage, or in the attic and landscape plans. The monthly budget kept by many consumers is a partial list of holdings, since the list represents regular payments for goods or services. Consumer do not necessarily adhere to casual or formal lists of holdings when purchasing. As we have already observed and will continue to indicate, a great many factors influence consumer problem recognition. The existence of some assortment inventory probably does add a degree of precision to problem recognition.

Long- and Short-Run Assortments

It is a mistake to consider the individual consumer's assortment in the same short- and long-run terms as a business assortment. A business consciously puts together and maintains a particular group of goods necessary to manufacture or distribute a finished product to consumers. Most consumers do not say, "I have certain short-run assortment goals and certain long-run assortment goals." Consumers do not think this way, or if they do, it is only in the vaguest of terms.

Figure 2-4
Long or short run decision?

Courtesy of Home Planners, Inc., Farmington Hills, MI

Nevertheless, the idea of short- and long-run assortments does apply to the development of consumer product holdings. There are two ways in which long-and short-run considerations can be applied to consumer assortments.

First, one can compare expectations versus immediate consumption plans.[12] Since expectations concern future consumer desires, it follows that expectations about desires can be considered a part of long-run assortment determination. Immediate purchase plans are taken to be short-run assortment decisions. By immediate purchase plans is not meant necessarily only today's buying. One may consider normal weekly or monthly purchases as short-run, and future expectations for a new home, automobile, furniture, etc., for which there is no specific time to buy as long-run. Are the items shown in Figure 2-4 parts of a long-run or a short-run assortment?

Second, one can consider the total assortment as long-run and any specific purchase requirement as short-run. That is to say, the maintenance of width, depth, and variety of assortment in a proper balance occurs over a long period of time. The purchase of any specific product or products immediately needed to meet balance requirements is a short-run assortment decision.

Furthermore, it should be pointed out that short- and long-run are terms that can be applied to different parts of the same assortment at the same time. A person may plan to replace an air conditioner compressor about every eight years, but this same consumer may replace groceries approximately four times per month. Thus such items as groceries, gas for the car, and haircuts are short-run needs within the assortment because they require frequent replacement on a relatively short time sequence. Within the same assortment, seed for the lawn, the new carport, and a television replacement are long-run assortment decisions because of their being either infrequent purchases or one-time purchases.

DEGREE TO WHICH PROBLEMS SPECIFIED

In even the smallest business enterprise, the management can tell with a high degree of accuracy which products are needed to meet customer wants. The average store can not only tell the specific brand but also the features, price, service, location of the buyer, and how long it will take to receive delivery. Businesses establish elaborate inventory methods to accomplish this degree of precision.

Unfortunately, the same cannot be said for the average American consumer. The evaluation of assortments and the determination of problems is a highly inexact business with consumers. All too often, it is more an emotional experience than a cold-blooded business decision. Many individuals enter the market with no real conception of the products needed. Let us use groceries as an example. One would think that, of all assortment problems, grocery needs would not be left completely to chance. Yet, single persons often go grocery shopping with nothing more in mind than buying what looks good. The purchase is made for only one or two meals in advance, and there is little planning for the future. Most consumers give their purchases of groceries a little more thought than that. Nevertheless, many people go grocery shopping with only the vaguest idea that they need meat, vegetables, and canned goods.

It is possible to specify five degrees to which product deficiencies are recognized in advance of market-related action by the consumer. These possibilities are listed below.

1. Unbranded product known.
2. Product and brand known.
3. Product, brand, and price known.
4. Product, brand, price, and service known.
5. Product, brand, price, service, and location known.

Of course, the information does not have to be known in the order listed. For example, a person may know the product, brand, and location. In most cases the consumer does not have full knowledge of deficiencies when entering the market. What is perhaps more normal is for the consumer to have a good idea of the un-branded product desired, a fairly good indication of the brand, or perhaps knowledge of the general price level. Many other decisions related to the purchase are made on the spur of the moment or after the consumer enters the market.

QUESTIONS

1. Define and differentiate between a consumer problem and consumer problem recognition.
2. Discuss some of the possible problems a consumer may experience in a decision making process. What are some of the consequences?
3. Compare and contrast how a multi-member family unit can function like a business when it comes to problem recognition.
4. Briefly discuss consumer assortment and the self-perception associated with it by the consumer.
5. The makeup of an assortment is composed of three attributes. Explain and relate them.
6. Give an example of different problems faced by individual consumers with different assortment compositions.
7. Discuss the relative importance of status and structure in relation to products within assortments.
8. Explain the concept of assortment closure and why it seldom occurs.
9. Describe the method that enables consumers to become aware of the problems in their personal assortments.
10. State the three conditions that allows the consumer to identify problems.
11. Why would a consumer decide to make product additions to his or her assortment?
12. Explain the alternatives that exist when considering the deletion of products from an assortment.
13. Discuss the term "partial inventory." Could you obtain a partial inventory of your assortment? A complete inventory?
14. How are short- and long-run considerations related to consumer assortments?
15. State and discuss the five degrees to which assortment deficiencies can be specified.

NOTES

1. Terence A. Shimp, "Perception of Time in Consumer Research: Comment," *Journal of Consumer Research*, Vol. 9 (June 1982), pp. 116–18; Robert J. Graham, "Perception of Time in Consumer Research: Rejoinder," *Journal of Consumer Research*, Vol. 9 (June 1982).
2. "Forget Wants, Needs, Listen to Consumers' Problems: Dillon," *Marketing News*, (June 2, 1978), p. 6.

3. Oswald Mascarenhas and Ramanujam Desavan, "Family Decision Making Behavior: A Systems Approach to Its Process Dynamics," in Paul C. Thistlethwait, Dorrie M. Gorman, Lynn J. Loudenback and Jim L. Grimm, eds., *Evolving Marketing Horizons: 1984 Style* (Western Illinois University and the Midwest Marketing Association, 1984), pp. 112–28.

4. George J. Szybillo, Arlene K. Sosanie, and Aaron Tenenbein, "Family Member Influence in Household Decision Making," *Journal of Consumer Research*, Vol. 6 (December 1979), pp. 312–16.

5. C. Whan Park and Easway Iyer, "An Examination of the Response Pattern in Family Decision Making," in Kenneth Bernhardt et al., eds., *Proceedings of the American Marketing Association Educator's Conference*, Series No. 47 (1981), p. 148.

6. Pierre Filiatrault and J.R. Brent Ritchie, "Joint Purchasing Decisions: A Comparison of Influence Structure in Family and Couple Decision-Making Units, *Journal of Consumer Research*, Vol. 7 (September 1980), p. 139.

7. Mary Lou Roberts and Lawrence H. Wortzel, "Role Transferal in the Household," in Andrew Mitchell, ed., *Advances in Consumer Research*, Vol. 6 (Ann Arbor: Association for Consumer Research, 1982), p. 264.

8. John S. Berens, "Assortment Prepotency — A Conceptual Note on the Process of Assortment Building," *Evolving Marketing Horizons Midwest Marketing Association, 1983*, (Southern Illinois University at Carbondale and Midwest Marketing Association, 1983), pp. 139–42.

9. Morris B. Holbrook and Michael J. Ryan, "Modeling Decision-Specific Stress: Some Methodological Considerations," *Administrative Science Quarterly*, Vol. 27 (Spring 1982), pp. 243–58.

10. James L. Heskett, *Marketing* (New York: Macmillan Publishing Co., Inc., 1976), p. 596.

11. David W. Cravens, "Marketing Strategy Positioning," *Business Horizons* (December 1975).

12. James L. Heskett, *Marketing*, p. 596.

Consumer Problems

Founded in Needs

CHAPTER OUTLINE

I. CONSUMER NEEDS
    A. Needs Are Body Requirements
    B. Terms Used to Describe Consumer Needs

II. CONSUMER PROBLEM IS TO SATISFY NEEDS
    A. Needs Are Innate and So Are Problems
    B. A Need Is Not Necessarily a Deficiency
    C. Need-Related Problems Associated with Products

III. NEEDS THAT REQUIRE SATISFACTION
    A. Physiological Needs
    B. Safety Needs
    C. Belonging Needs
    D. Esteem Needs
    E. Self-Actualization Needs
    F. Need to Know
    G. Esthetic Needs

IV. OTHER PERSPECTIVES OF NEEDS

V. PROBLEM VARIES WITH IMPORTANCE OF NEED
    A. Hierarchy of Needs
    B. Factors Affecting Need Hierarchy
        1. *Accumulated Wealth*
        2. *Discretionary Buying Power*
        3. *Attitude Toward Work and Leisure*
        4. *Need Conflict*
        5. *Influence of Others*
    C. Evaluation of Need Hierarchy

VI. CONSUMER PROBLEM OF UNSATISFIED NEEDS
    A. Repression of Need by Consumer
    B. Consumer Needs Resolved Through Fantasy
    C. Consumer Rationalization of Needs

CHAPTER OBJECTIVES

After completing your study of Chapter 3, you should be able to:

1. Discuss how consumer problems are founded in needs.
2. Identify the terms used to describe consumer needs.
3. Discuss how the consumer problem is to satisfy needs.
4. Describe the needs that require satisfaction.
5. Discuss the other perspectives of needs.
6. Discuss how problems vary with importance of needs.
7. Explain the consumer problem of unsatisfied needs.

This chapter discusses needs and the part they play in consumer problem recognition. The concept of a need is defined. Needs are explained as the basis for consumer problems, and the types of needs that must be satisfied are presented. The order in which consumer needs are satisfied and the reasons for this order are presented. The chapter ends with an explanation of how consumers deal with unsatisfied needs.

CONSUMER NEEDS

No discussion of problem recognition can proceed very far without introducing the part played by consumer needs.[1] Needs are the cornerstone upon which all consumer decision making is based.

Needs Are Body Requirements

The term "need" refers to something physical or psychological that the body must have to function and develop. More specifically, a *need* is defined as:

any requirement or ability upon which human performance, efficiency, and growth depends.

Needs underlie all human action. Needs cause us to replace body cells, to seek companionship, to think, or to flex our muscles. All needs do not necessarily lead to consumer behavior. For example, the need to flex our muscles or to blink the eyes are not directly associated with the use of any product. On the other hand, food is required to replace body cells, and one may either purchase products to cook at home or eat out. The need for companionship can lead to the purchase of many types of products such as clothes acceptable to others, theater tickets to share, or the taxi fare necessary to visit a friend. Our concern is not with needs in general, but with those needs that begin the consumer purchase process.

Terms Used to Describe Consumer Needs

We use the term "need" when referring to any human requirement. However, in the literature there are a variety of terms used when referring to particular kinds of requirements. These terms include basic needs, wants, desires, necessities, and luxuries. Let us identify these terms and place them into context with the broader concept of needs.

A *basic need* can be described as any body requirement without which life cannot be sustained in the short run. Basic needs consist of minimal food, clothing, shelter and medical care. Basic needs are sometimes referred to as *necessities*. Basic needs are not learned; the individual feels them automatically. One does not have to learn hunger, but one may learn to prefer steak to spinach for satisfying hunger. The same can be said of clothing and shelter. Marketers can make an appeal to basic needs even when consumer income is very limited. Consumers tend to satisfy such needs first.

Wants are requirements that one learns through experience. Wants spring more from anticipated pleasure than from the necessity to sustain life. Thus, a consumer needs food but wants a candy bar. The consumer needs affection but wants a steady diet of sex. The consumer needs warmth but wants a mink coat. Wants are sometimes referred to as *luxuries* because they entail purchases of products above the subsistence level. It follows that a want can more easily be put off because of its nonessential nature. However, it would be a mistake to think that a want does not have the power to drive the consumer to purchase in the same way that basic needs do. In the proper circumstance, wants can be as compelling on the individual to enter the market as basic needs.

A *desire* pertains to the consumer's market aspirations. A basic need or want

Photo 3-1
Wants and desires also have the power to drive a consumer to purchase.

Photo Courtesy of Princess Cruises

is a current requirement, while a desire is a forecasted requirement. It is, by nature, not presently being satisfied. In fact, the consumer may lack the means to satisfy a desire in the short run. Desires are related to a consumer's dreams and long-range goals. For example, a consumer has a comfortable house and is presently satisfied with it. However, this consumer realizes someday the house will become old and family income will increase. Thus, the consumer desires to replace the present home with a bigger and better one in the future.

We use needs, wants and desires interchangeably because, in practice, it is difficult to tell where one leaves off and the other begins. What is one person's necessity is another person's luxury. Each person views his or her present standard of living as necessary to well-being. Most persons do not generally recognize that they own luxuries. For example, most Americans feel that they could not get along without their refrigerator, automobile, vacuum sweeper and freezer. They are probably correct in this assessment. American courts have upheld the view that necessity is what the person *views* or *perceives* as essential. That these items would be gross luxuries to a less fortunate person does not change the dependency. Furthermore, there are differences among nations and regions of nations as to what constitutes a basic standard of living. Our definition identifies needs, wants and desires as requirements because they relate to good physical or emotional health. Marketers can make appeals to all types of these requirements.

CONSUMER PROBLEM IS TO SATISFY NEEDS

People have problems related to every aspect of their living. There are problems associated with work, marriage, child rearing, and growing older, just to name a few. However, not all human problems are consumer problems. When functioning as a consumer, a person has just one overriding problem. That problem is how to satisfy needs, wants and desires.[2] There may be any number of related subproblems such as how to select a store, which route to take to market, which brand is the best buy, or how to deal with salespersons. Everything discussed in this text involves how consumers engage in satisfying their needs, wants and desires. This is the reason we say that consumer problems are founded in needs.

Needs Are Innate and So Are Problems

All human needs are innate in the sense that individuals are born fully equipped. People do not have to learn how to need, and marketers cannot create needs in individuals. Marketers can only create awareness of the innate needs already possessed by these persons. A child is born with the need for body movement, elimination, food, water, sex, affection, acceptance and achievement. However, the child may become aware of some needs later than others as she or he matures. In what sequence do you think awareness occurs? Anyone who has watched a child develop through walking, talking, choosing a mate and growing old cannot doubt that needs are innate and that they develop at the appropriate time.

Because needs are innate, consumer problems are also innate. There is a potential problem associated with every consumer need, whether that need is recognized or not. It is a basic task of all marketers to cause consumers to become aware of their innate needs. A great deal of business promotion is directed to this end.

Innate needs are not learned, but consumers do learn to recognize problems in a particular way. For example, a person innately needs food but may perceive the problem as a lack of steak and potatoes or some other specific meal. One may also perceive the problem as "how to obtain a meal without eating spinach." Experience has shown the consumer that spinach is not a palatable solution to the need for food. Persons recognize problems not in general terms but with reference to their specific desired state. Marketers spend a lot of time and effort in getting consumers to perceive their products as specific solutions to the individual's problems.

A Need Is Not Necessarily a Deficiency

It is important to remember that a need is a requirement and not a deficiency. A deficiency is the lack or absence of something, but the body has the same needs whether or not some needs are currently deficient. For example, the body needs nourishment, air, water, and comfort; even if the body has enough of each, this does not change the fact that they are requirements necessary to sustain life. The body's requirement for air is just as real when it is ample as when it is deficient. For this reason, you should not consider needs to be deficiencies. Obviously, if a person's needs are filled, that person has no problem. He or she is content that the existing situation and the desired situation are compatible.

Need-Related Problems Associated with Products

Specific consumer needs are identified in products (goods and services) made available by businesses.[3] Illustration 3-1 illustrates the relationship. The automobile is a product supplied by a business and used by the consumer. Management perceives the bundle of benefits built into the car as the basis of an appeal that can result in profits. The consumer perceives the autombile as a bun-

Illustration 3-1
Consumer needs: business benefits

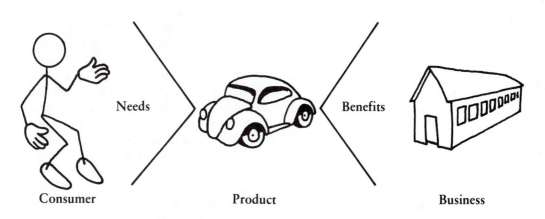

Consumer   Needs   Product   Benefits   Business

dle of features with the ability to satisfy some of his or her specific needs. Needs and benefits are simply two sides of the same coin, and both the consumer and the business are satisfied by the product exchange because the expectations of each differ. If the firm changes the features of the product, it appeals to a different market because different need satisfactions are involved. For example, if the car is made smaller and uses less gas, it may appeal to an economy market. If the car is made more luxurious, it appeals to a higher income market.

The degree to which needs or wants are satisfied by products is a measure of the consumer's well-being. Consumer need satisfaction can range all the way from low, where few needs are satisfied, to high, where many needs are satisfied. There can even be variations within the range. For example, one consumer may own products that satisfy most basic needs and some luxuries fully, while others are partially satisfied.

NEEDS THAT REQUIRE SATISFACTION

Everyone knows that consumers have rather specific needs that require satisfaction. The problem is that there is no single list of needs accepted by everyone. There are two reasons for this fact: (1) there are too many different needs that individuals attempt to satisfy, and (2) different lists serve specific purposes. We follow the rule that a list should be inclusive enough to illustrate the nature of consumer needs without unnecessarily confusing the issue.[4]

Nearly everyone agrees that there are two broad types of consumer needs. *Physiological needs* are associated with the consumer's biological functions, and *psychological* or *emotional* needs are associated with one's mental or emotional state. Abraham Maslow was one of the earlier scholars to work with the identification of human needs.[5] His original list included physiological needs and four psychological needs which were safety, belonging and love, esteem, and self-actualization. Other scholars have added the need to know and esthetic needs. Thus we have seven needs, and six of them are psychological. Each type of need is discussed below.

Physiological Needs

We have said that *physiological needs* are associated with the body's physical performance. These needs include food, water, sex, sleep, warmth, body elimination, blinking, temperature control, regeneration of tissue, and muscular activity. There is a tendency to believe that physiological needs do not involve feelings, but this is inaccurate. For example, sex is as much an emotional experience as it is a physical one. Hunger, thirst and sleep all involve feelings related to satisfaction or dissatisfaction. So it is with every physiological need. Some physical needs such as tissue regeneration and blinking occur automatically, but others like sex, sleep and food intake can be partially controlled by the mind. Where there is mental control over physical functions by the consumer, there is greater opportunity for the marketer to exert influence.

It is true that physiological needs are basic to life. However, it is not true, as some persons believe, that each need has the same importance. Some physical needs are more basic than others, and they cannot be treated by marketers as a homogeneous category. For example, the body can last only minutes without air, it can survive a few days without water, and it can last a few weeks without food. A minimum of physical activity can support a person for years, and rumor has it that sex can be put off indefinitely.

Some important products associated with physiological needs include water, basic food, staple clothing, shelter, contraceptives, sleep aids, glasses, toilet paper, aspirin, soap, deodorant, and exercise classes. It is important for the marketer to realize that while physical needs are basic, many of the associated products are not. A consumer may require: (1) sleep but not sleeping pills, (2) shelter, but not a private home or motel, or (3) exercise but not fancy gym equipment. The point is that marketers may have to work just as hard to promote products associated with physical needs as with any of the psychological needs explained below.

Safety Needs

Safety needs are the first of the psychological requirements, and they concern personal security. Safety needs include freedom from both physical and emotional insecurity. Like physiological needs, they relate to the total person. Personal safety is associated with freedom from physical pain, security of the home, order in one's daily life, certainty that certain events such as eating, sleeping, and working will occur, and freedom from threat or coercion.

Products related to safety needs include: hospital care, insurance, smoke detectors, safes, bank services, retirement plans, seat belts, burglar alarms, social security, government services, locks, indoor sprinkler sytems, and safety mats in bath tubs. Safety takes in a wide variety of both physical and service products. Personal safety and security may be as important to the individual as the physiological needs of food and drink. The sale of safety-related products is a very large and growing industry in the United States. Like physiological needs, the necessity to maintain personal safety and security is continual. Products are promoted and sold on a regular and recurring basis.

Belonging Needs

The need to *belong* is a psychological requirement associated with caring and relating harmoniously with others. These needs include love, friendship, affection, acceptance, and commitment. Thus belonging is a fundamental need that affects almost everything one does. Marriage grows out of a need to belong. Gift giving is a manifestation of belonging. Childbirth and development could not occur without the need to belong. Some persons place belonging before physical needs. For example, persons have laid down their lives for a friend, and soldiers fight because of a sense of belonging to their country. Rejection sometimes causes one to lose appetite or to withdraw from sexual or other physical functions.

Some important products and services associated with belonging include: weddings, jewelry, personal grooming products, theaters, fashion clothing, party gowns, picnic baskets, television, hotels, eating out, gift items, and greeting cards. Nearly all products associated with belonging relate to personal interaction

Figure 3-1
Advertisement relating a need to belong

Five things you can do for 72¢ or less...

1 Enjoy a cup of coffee...

2 Pick up a newspaper...

3 Buy a few stamps...

4 Have a soft drink...

 Or make a lasting difference in the life of a child and family overseas through Foster Parents Plan.

Here at home, 72¢ is the kind of pocket change you spend every day without thinking much about it. But for a child overseas, born into a world of desperate poverty, it can lead to a future full of promise and achievement.

Your spare change can change the life of a child. Forever.

As a Foster Parent, you'll be helping a needy child in the most critical areas of development. Like education. Better nutrition. Improved health. At the same time, your help will give your Foster Child the gift of hope.

It's hope that springs from Foster Parents Plan's comprehensive programs, built on your support combined with the hard work and determination of your Foster Child's family to help themselves. Programs that produce ways to make a better living. That build confidence and self-sufficiency, and that result in long-lasting improvements for *all their lives.*

What's more, you'll be able to share in these accomplishments through photographs, progress reports and letters about your Foster Child and family.

Don't wait—a child needs your help now.

Think about all the good you can do for just 72¢ a day, the cost of a morning coffee break. Then send your love and support to a child and family overseas, who need a chance for a better life. Please, do it now.

To start helping even faster, call toll free:

1-800-225-1234

Detach and mail or call toll free today.

Send to:
Kenneth H. Phillips, National Executive Director
Foster Parents Plan, Inc., 157 Plan Way, Warwick RI 02886

I want to become a Foster Parent to:

☐ **The child who has been waiting the longest,** or as indicated:

☐ Boy ☐ Girl ☐ Either

☐ Any Age ☐ 6–8 ☐ 9–11 ☐ 12–14

☐ Colombia	☐ Sri Lanka	☐ Mali
☐ Guatemala	☐ Thailand	☐ Sierra Leone
☐ Kenya	☐ Ecuador	☐ Sudan
☐ Philippines	☐ India	☐ Zimbabwe

☐ Enclosed is a check for $22 for my first month's sponsorship of my Foster Child. Please send me a photograph, case history, and complete Foster Parent Sponsorship Kit.

☐ I am not yet sure if I want to become a Foster Parent, but I am interested. Please send me information about the child I would be sponsoring.

H313

☐ Mr.   Mrs. ☐
☐ Miss   Ms. ☐

_____

Address _____ Apt. #

City _____ State _____ Zip

Founded in 1937, Foster Parents Plan is the leader in combining family assistance programs, community development, and personal communications between Foster Parent and Foster Child. These comprehensive programs provide long-term solutions to the unique problems facing Foster Children and their families. As a non-profit, non-sectarian and non-political organization, we depend on Foster Parents to make our work possible. A copy of our financial report, filed with the New York Department of State, is available on request. Your sponsorship is tax-deductible.

Foster Parents Plan.
Help so complete, it touches a child for life.

Foster Parents Plan

or commitment. Many products such as gifts, eating out, and personal grooming are highly emotional and marketers must adjust their presentation of these products accordingly. Figure 3-1 shows an advertisement directed toward the belonging need.

Esteem Needs

Esteem needs are the psychological requirements of maintaining a favorable image or impression of one's self. Esteem needs relate to (1) self-acceptance and (2) acceptance by others. Self-acceptance can be apparent in how we dress, carry ourselves, relate to others and work. Esteem is demonstrated by others in the form of prestige, fame or recognition, and status. Products associated with esteem needs are fashion clothing, furniture, cars, liquor, paintings, hobbies, club memberships, home ownership, education, and grooming products. There is perhaps no greater manifestation of esteem than "keeping up with the Joneses." Figure 3-2 shows an advertisement based on an esteem need. Is it an appeal to an external or an internal need?

Self-Actualization Needs

The *self-actualization needs* are psychological requirements involving personal ambition and fulfillment. It refers to the individual's desire to achieve up to his or her potential. Wilma Rudolph's overcoming personal tragedy to win a gold medal at the Olympics is an example. A writer may strive to produce the "great American novel," a businessperson may seek to build an empire like Henry Ford, or a humanitarian such as Helen Keller may seek to reduce human suffering. Although self-actualization is not limited to creativity, it is likely to take that form in creative persons, whether artists, writers, businesspersons, inventors, or statespersons.

In some persons self-actualization can be one of the strongest needs while in others it can be very weak. A lot depends on the type of person involved. Some products associated with ambition or seeking fulfillment are advanced educational degrees, health clubs, sports cars, tailor-made suits, office furniture, inspirational books, artist supplies, sports equipment, and expensive shoes. It should be noted that ambitious people display some of the same traits and purchase many of the same products associated with esteem needs. Many persons believe the old saying, "to be successful, one must look successful." Marketers should note that although esteem and self-actualization may lead to similar purchases, the reason for buying may be entirely different. For example, an ambitious person doesn't want to keep up with the Joneses, he or she wants to be a Jones! Thus different appeals may be necessary to make the sale.

Need to Know

The *need to know* should not be confused with education. Instead the need to know refers to curiosity or the desire to be informed about any subject, and it is a psychological need. It can be associated with seeking the truth in any situation.

Figure 3-2
Maintaining a favorable image is important to the consumer

"May I offer you a complement?"

In five highly complementary colors. Tura 240.

Complements of Tura

Tura, Inc.

Of course, education is a part of that process, but the education is not always the formal type found in schools. Most persons display some curiosity, and this is a most universal need. It can be observed in children learning to walk or talk. Inventors and creative persons display the need to know. Consumers who shop and compare before purchasing also demonstrate this need.

There are many products associated with the need to know. Some of the obvious ones include educational toys, newspapers, magazines, paperback books, television, radio, travel, counseling services, investment brokers, and vacations. Figure 3-3 is an example of an advertisement to satisfy our need to know. Any appeal that deals with the unusual, unknown, or uninitiated can be effective in promoting these products. Notice, however, that curiosity has its practical side. Business executives need to know about markets and competition, and consumers need to know what is a good buy. Thus practical appeals related to the specific problem are also effective.

Figure 3-3
Advertisement directed at the need to know

At Waterford, we take 1,120 times longer than necessary to create a glass.

While a machine can churn one out in only 45 seconds, we take over 14 hours to mouth-blow and hand-cut a single glass. But then, our goal is not efficiency, but beauty.

Waterford
Steadfast in a world of wavering standards.

Waterford-Wedgwood U.S.A.

Esthetic Needs

The last psychological need is the *esthetic need,* which concerns the requirement for beauty and order in our world. Figure 3-4 is an an advertisement

Figure 3-4
Advertisement appealing to the esthetic need

Princess Cruises to the Caribbean. Fly Free.

Sail the Sun Princess or Pacific Princess for 7 sun-filled days on the newest cruises in the Caribbean. Visit all the best ports. French Martinique. Dutch St. Maarten. Duty-free St. Thomas. A private beach party on Mayreau. And, enjoy Princess luxury all the way. Fabulous food. Charming British officers. And terrific entertainment. Cruises depart Saturdays. Call now. And make your date with Princess.

The most famous name in cruising.

"There's no better way to see the Caribbean than with Princess."
Gavin MacLeod in Martinique

British Registry

PRINCESS CRUISES
Caribbean · Transcanal · Mexico · Alaska · The Orient · South Pacific · Europe

---

TRAVEL AGENT NAME AND ADDRESS HERE

Please send me more information on Princess Cruises' 1987/88 Caribbean Cruises.

Name _____
Address _____
City _____
State _____ Zip _____

CANADIAN VERSION

Please send me more information on Princess Cruises' 1987/88 Caribbean Cruises.

Name _____
Address _____
City _____
Province _____ Code _____

Courtesy of Princess Cruises

directed at our aesthetic needs. Symmetry, order, progression, and balance are also ideas associated with esthetics. Most people like some beauty and excitement in their lives. It is not enough for these persons to be physically sound, successful, or appreciated. People seek beauty along with these other needs, and in some persons it is a powerful need. Pictures purchased for the home, haircuts, home cleaning products, house design, automobiles, and fashion clothing are products purchased wholly or partially because of their beauty. The appeal made by marketers is a direct one to the esthetic quality of the product. Most often esthetic appeals are combined with others when presenting products. Of all the needs which consumers have, this one is least likely to stand alone as the deciding factor in a purchase. It is an added reason to buy a product with some specific function for the consumer.

OTHER PERSPECTIVES OF NEEDS

Although A.H. Maslow's concept of needs is the most recognized, it is not the only perspective. However, most of the other lists are limited to psychological needs. Douglas McGregor describes *social needs*—those concerning a person's relationships with others; *ego needs*—those associated with self esteem, achievement, knowledge and recognition; and *self-fulfillment needs*—those related to achieving one's potential for development.[6] James A. Bayton also has three types of needs. *Affectional needs* are those dealing with harmonious satisfying relations with others. *Ego-bolstering needs* concern the personality—to achieve, gain prestige or recognition and to satisfy the ego. *Ego-defensive* needs relate to avoidance of physical and psychological harm.[7]

Henry Murray has presented one of the more complete lists of human needs. Table 3-1 shows these needs. A careful look at each of these need concepts shows a common thread. The basic differences are in the manner of grouping. Each list is consistent with Maslow, and one could redefine Murray's list under the seven items presented by Maslow. For this reason we tend to concentrate on Maslow's concept.

PROBLEM VARIES WITH IMPORTANCE OF NEED

Consumer problems are related to needs, but these needs are not equally significant to individual consumers. It is necessary to deal with this point because the more important needs underlie the type of problems that are handled first by consumers.

Hierarchy of Needs

Maslow suggested that some needs are more basic than others, and these needs tend to be satisfied first. Illustration 3-2 demonstrates this point. The need to know and esthetic needs have been added to Maslow's list, as previously discussed.

The idea is that basic physiological needs are recognized by consumers first. Once physical life is assured, and psychological development proceeds, the consumer recognizes a succession of psychological needs. These needs begin with safety and end with esthetics. As soon as a lower order need is reasonably satisfied, the consumer recognizes a more advanced need. A higher order need

Table 3-1

Murray's List of Psychological Needs

Type of Need	Description
Abasement	To become resigned to one's fate
Affiliation	To remain loyal to a friend
Achievement	To compete and surpass others
Aggression	To overcome, get free, or attack another
Counteraction	To have self-respect and pride
Autonomy	To be independent
Defendance	To defend the self or deal with failure
Deference	To conform to custom or yield to influence
Dominance	To control one's human environment
Exhibition	To make an impression or entice others
Harm avoidance	To avoid pain or injury
Infavoidance	To avoid humiliation by no action
Nurturance	To give sympathy or help others
Order	To achieve neatness, balance or precision
Play	To act only for fun
Rejection	To exclude, abandon, or be indifferent to others
Senience	To seek and enjoy sensuous things
Sex	To have erotic relationships
Succorance	To be nursed, supported, protected
Understanding	To ask or answer questions

Source: Desmond F. Cartwright, *Theories and Models of Personality,* (Dubuque, Iowa: William C. Brown, 1979), pp. 2–25.

must have peaked in satisfaction before the next need on the hierarchy can become dominant. An individual is actually in the process of satisfying most of his or her needs at the same time, but some needs are always more satisfied than others. Of course, the consumer's problem is proportional to the place of the need on the hierarchy and the degree to which needs have already been satisfied.

Factors Affecting Need Hierarchy

There are several factors that have a bearing on the importance of specific needs and resulting problem recognition. They are accumulated wealth, discretionary buying power, attitudes toward work and leisure, need conflict and influence from others.

Accumulated Wealth. The accumulated wealth of consumers and how they use it has a direct bearing on the ability to satisfy needs. Individuals and families tend to accumulate wealth over time. This wealth occurs in the form of savings, homes, furniture, cars, clothing, etc. The wealth that a person has reflects past needs that have been reasonably satisfied. Each instance of need satisfaction reduces some consumer problem. Since some persons accumulate more wealth than others, we use this fact to distinguish between those who are "well off" and those who are "poor." It follows that there is a correlation between wealth and the number and types of consumer problems.

Wealth alone cannot satisfy consumer needs. Needs are insatiable, and satisfaction of one causes another to be recognized. Since wealth is always limited, a problem arises with the consumer on how to allocate wealth among recognized needs. One must be careful when evaluating the effect of money on these problems. For example, some wealthy persons have problems in human relations that money cannot solve, and some wealthy persons are relatively poor consumers because so much of their income goes toward savings or investments. Some low income individuals may have many different needs requiring attention, but their aspirations may be reduced by poverty, and they do not act. Many of their needs go unsatisfied.

Discretionary Buying Power. Discretionary buying power affects problems. *Discretionary buying power* is defined as that part of one's personal income left after paying taxes and providing for basic necessities. Expenditures for taxes and necessities are largely predetermined. One must pay the rent, purchase necessary food, and meet clothing needs, but any income left over can be spent at the discretion of the consumer. Thus the name "discretionary buying power." The consumer's purchase of a vacation, higher-priced food, or a fancy automobile depends on income left after basic needs are provided for. A natural problem arises between the allocation of expenditures for necessities and discretionary expenditures. A consumer who can skimp on food, for example, may be able to afford theater tickets. It is also true that discretionary purchases come into con-

Illustration 3-2
Hierarchy of needs

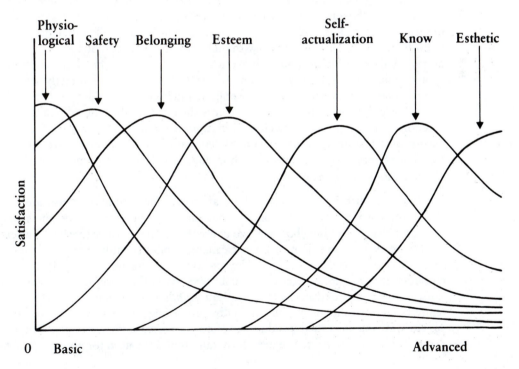

flict. The consumer may have to decide between a Caribbean cruise and a better automobile (see Figure 3-5).

A low income person who has satisfied few needs may encounter some different types of problems. So many unsatisfied needs can lead to many conflicts. A person who has funds will attempt to satisfy some needs. An individual without sufficient funds may find it necessary to accept the low state of need satisfaction. In the latter case, persons with low discretionary income may not be important buyers for some categories of products. Thus, while low income consumers may have many needs, they may not be important consumers of many products for which satisfaction is low. Not only are the low income consumer's funds insufficient, but there is evidence that the purchase of basic requirements costs more; this further limits buying. Business managers argue that they must charge more to cover the risk of selling in undesirable areas.

Attitudes Toward Work and Leisure. The amount of leisure available for most Americans is on the increase. At the same time, Americans have feelings of uneasiness with respect to leisure. Although individuals have a need for both work and leisure, problems develop because of our psychological attitudes toward each. Because we have been reared in a culture which frowns upon idleness, our leisure tends to be of the active variety.[8] We participate in golf, boating, camping, and gardening. As American income increases, this creates pressure for more time in which to spend the additional money. There is always the difficulty of balancing the time to do with the money to do it. Higher productivity leads to more money, and more money creates a need for more leisure. More leisure puts the pressure back on a need for money to utilize the time better.

American business executives have considerable amounts of discretionary money but much less discretionary time than other groups. The balance is the opposite for many elderly citizens with more time than money. Some products require a balance of time and money, for example, travel, bowling, spectator sports, camping, and do-it-yourself activities. Other products, indirectly affected by this balance, are certain foods, beverages, and home entertainment items. The important point for marketers to consider is the fact that they must literally compete for discretionary time as well as discretionary money.[9] The pressure for more leisure time has made some consumers less patient with shopping around; the trend is toward quick, convenient shopping, which gives the merchant fewer chances at a given consumer.

Need Conflict. The need hierarchy is affected by need conflicts. Illustration 3-3 illustrates the three types of conflict that may develop. First, consumers may have a problem in choosing between two desired needs that must be satisfied. The examples are exercise and sleep or home cleanliness and a beautiful home. The more equal the two needs appear to the person, the greater the conflict. The consumer may act on the needs in sequence (exercise, then sleep), or one act may satisfy both recognized needs (a clean house adds to its beauty). Managers attempt to take advantage of such conflict by promoting one product over the other by emphasizing that their product satisfies both needs. For example, Total, a cereal, makes an appeal to the need for vitamins and the need for good taste. An-

Figure 3-5
Discretionary buying power

Courtesy of the Pontiac Division of General Motors

tibacterial soap provides physical safety from infection and reduces the emotional fear of offensive body odor.

Second, the consumer may have a problem in choosing between something desired and something to be avoided. For example, a person may want to be professionally recognized and also want to avoid personal failure. A young person

Illustration 3-3
Conflict within need types

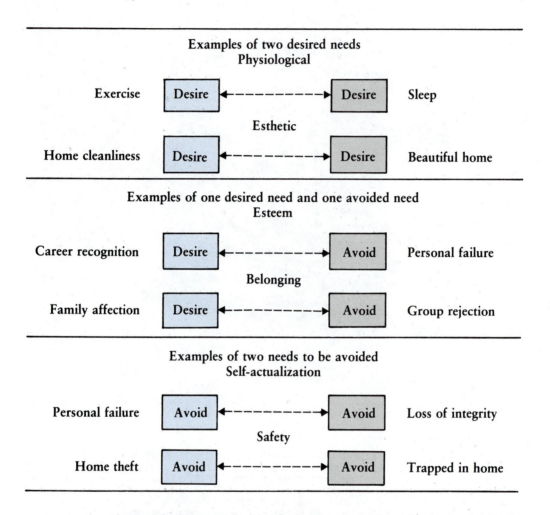

Examples of two desired needs
Physiological

Exercise | Desire ←--------→ Desire | Sleep

Esthetic

Home cleanliness | Desire ←--------→ Desire | Beautiful home

Examples of one desired need and one avoided need
Esteem

Career recognition | Desire ←--------→ Avoid | Personal failure

Belonging

Family affection | Desire ←--------→ Avoid | Group rejection

Examples of two needs to be avoided
Self-actualization

Personal failure | Avoid ←--------→ Avoid | Loss of integrity

Safety

Home theft | Avoid ←--------→ Avoid | Trapped in home

may be torn between conforming to family standards or group standards when the two differ. Typically, the decision is made to act on the need that is more important. Business managers attempt to stress the positive side of needs when making appeals to this type conflict. For example, health clubs stress health and feeling good and not the fact that you are fat. Insurance salespersons stress peace of mind rather than the fact that you are going to die.

Third, consumers may have a problem in deciding which of two negative needs to act upon. The examples in Illustration 3-2 are: personal failure and loss of integrity or home theft and being trapped in the home. A person may want to place multiple locks, alarms, window bars and burglar-proof doors through the house to ward off intruders, but show concern over the inability to escape quickly should the house catch on fire. The consumer may favor the avoidance need that causes the greatest concern, or the consumer may attempt a compromise solution.

For example, our consumer above may provide reasonable burglar-proofing to the house but leave avenues of quick escape. Marketers typically stress the relief from discomfort or fear when appealing to these negative need conflicts. For example, the Sears maintenance contract on their washers stresses lack of fear of a major breakdown. This lack of fear is also the appeal of the Fram oil filter slogan, "Pay me now, or pay me later." Deodorant and mouth wash ads play up the fear of not being sexy or appealing to the opposite sex.

Influence of Others. Need-related problems are affected by other persons with whom the consumer interacts. Family members, friends, coworkers, club members, and classmates all express opinions about the consumer's likes and dislikes. Where the consumers have need conflict, these persons state their preferences for products and stores. They indicate which course of action the buyer should take, and they indicate their approval or disapproval of actions taken by the consumer. How much influence the outsiders have on the consumer depends on many things including trust in the source, desire to be a part of the group, agreement with opinions expressed, and consequences of going against the wishes of others. We will have more to say about the effect of external persons on the consumer in later chapters.

Evaluation of Need Hierarchy

Maslow's hierarchy of needs is intended as a general guide to problem recognition. It is not an inviolate principle of consumer behavior. Numerous examples demonstrate that individuals may have a different hierarchy. Some persons place fame and recognition before belonging or even personal safety. We all know of instances when an individual has given up his or her life (safety need) for their comrades (belonging). Nevertheless, the hierarchy is a good general guide of how consumers perceive problems based on the importance of the needs involved.

CONSUMER PROBLEM OF UNSATISFIED NEEDS

Even though consumers attempt to deal with their problems by goal-directed behavior, often external barriers, personal defects, or conflicting needs are such that the problem cannot be solved. We noted in the above discussion that some problems are not solved and others are only partially solved. When the problem cannot be dealt with effectively, there is frustration. This frustration may cause the consumer to try even harder to find a satisfactory solution by modifying some aspect of behavior. On the other hand, one way out of frustration is to adjust to it. Adaptive processes by which the individual may reduce the frustration of unsolved problems are repression, fantasy, and rationalization. Because problem recognition is directly influenced by these adjustments, it is necessary that marketers have some understanding of them.

Repression of Need by Consumer

There are three types of thought repression. The first is *primal repression*, the denial of entry into the conscious mind of any thoughts related to the need or desire. Primal repression occurs when a consumer does not admit that the need exists. The young person without money for party clothes may put the party out of his or her mind.

Second, there is *forgetting*. We have a case of forgetting when thoughts are pushed back into the unconscious recesses of the mind that were once a part of the conscious mind. Someone discovering a lack of aptitude for sports may simply forget her or his need to excel in athletics.

Third, repression of needs occurs in the form of *inhibition*. Inhibition develops as a result of association. Let's say some event occurs simultaneously with feelings of shame or guilt, and the two become connected in the mind of the consumer. Since most people are conditioned to avoid shame or pain, the individual may also avoid the events associated with such feelings. Inhibition is accomplished by inhibiting recall; consciously avoiding stimuli associated with the shame, pain, or guilt feelings; and making substitute responses.

The goal of every sort of repression is entirely to eliminate any necessity for effective action relative to the need. One problem is that learned behavior can be more easily repressed than instinct. The elimination of an instinctive need, such as sex, is seldom attained. The interest in sex still influences consumer purchases, but at a different and less apparent level.

Several conditions are usually present that lead to a repression of needs. Among the needs most likely to be repressed by consumers are (1) needs based on ideas damaging to one's ego; (2) needs that are in disagreement with the individual's moral, cultural, and social code; and (3) needs based on ideas associated with conflicts or guilt feelings. Neither men nor women found midi-length dresses attractive, so this style failed, but both sexes have accepted blow dryers for the hair. In one case, the product did not enhance the ego and in the other case it did. Therein lies the reason for acceptance or rejection of the product.

Motivational research suggests that advertising, to be effective, must appeal to people in such a manner as to give moral permission for them to have fun without guilt. Particular examples of guilt feelings which arise from the purchase and use of certain products are evident. Cigarettes, liquor, and candy are purchased by a major part of the American public, yet some people consistently worry and feel self-indulgent and guilty when they use these products.

Consumer Needs Resolved through Fantasy

Most everyone has engaged at one time or another in daydreaming. The flight into fantasy allows a consumer to resolve needs temporarily by imagining something other than actuality. Each of us at times has a "secret life." We may image that we are a millionaire, a great athlete, or an outstanding scholar. Certain products, such as the movies, television, and stage shows, provide the consumer with ready-made fantasy. They allow the purchaser to escape temporarily and to capture a vicarious experience. Advertising for diamonds and perfume often appeals to fantasy in both the layout and the copy. A woman's dreams of male adoration are used to sell certain cosmetics, jewelry, perfumes, furs, and automobiles. Men respond to similar appeals from advertisers who show the fellow with the proper cologne or hair cream surrounded by attractive women.

Consumer Rationalization of Needs

Closely akin to repression is rationalization. Consumers sometimes find themselves attempting to justify purchasing decisions by searching for reasons for them after the decisions have been made. This is rationalization. Homeowners may purchase expensive furniture for reasons of status but do not readily confess this. Instead, they prefer to justify the purchase on the basis of the more acceptable reasons that the present furniture is wearing out and that the new furniture has been chosen for its durability.

QUESTIONS

1. Distinguish between a basic need, a want, and a desire. Give an example of each.
2. American courts have upheld the view that necessity is what the person views or perceives as essential. Give examples of products that you receive as necessary that someone else may not. Explain why there is a difference.
3. List some products related to a safety or security need. Do you perceive the sale of safety products to increase or decrease? Explain your answer.
4. Distinguish between esteem needs and self-actualization needs. Give examples of each.
5. Discuss the relationship between discretionary needs and purchases.
6. Explain how Maslow's hierarchy of needs can aid a marketing manager. Give examples.
7. Discuss how an individual can reduce frustration of unsolved problems.
8. Discuss with examples how the attitudes toward work and leisure can affect consumer purchase decisions.
9. Identify and give examples of the types of conflict that may develop in your needs.
10. Identify the individuals and groups that have the greatest influence on your needs. Are they the same for all needs? Discuss your answer.
11. Is it possible for different individuals to have different need hierarchies? Explain why.
12. Explain why a need is not necessarily a deficiency.
13. Explain how innate needs are related to problems. Give example.
14. What type of need is the need to know? Explain your answer.
15. Do you think marketing managers can influence the needs of an individual? Explain your answer.

NOTES

1. Melanie Wallendorf and Gerald Zaltman, *Readings in Consumer Behavior,* Section VII (New York: John Wiley and Sons, 1984), pp. 219–21.
2. Ernest F. Cooke, "A General Theory of Need Satisfaction," in John Summey, R. Viswanathan, Ronald D. Taylor, and Karen Glynn, eds.,

Marketing: Theories and Concepts for an Era of Change (Southern Illinois University at Carbondale and Southern Marketing Assn., 1983), pp. 96–98.

3. James U. McNeal and Stephen W. McDaniel, "An Analysis of Need-Appeals in Television Advertising," *Journal of the Academy of Marketing Science,* Vol. 12 (Spring 1984), pp. 176–90.

4. Richard W. Olshavshy, "Maslow's Hierarchy of Needs: Six Difficulties," in Carol H. Anderson, Rajinder Arora, Blaise J. Bergiel, Sion Raveed, and Ronald L. Vaughn, *Midwest Marketing Association 1981 Conference Proceedings* (Southern Illinois University and Midwest Marketing Assn., 1981), pp. 13–18.

5. A. H. Maslow, *Motivation and Personality* (New York: Harper and Bros., 1954), pp. 80–98.

6. Douglas M. McGregor, *The Human Side of Enterprise* (New York: McGraw-Hill Book Co., 1960), pp. 36–39.

7. James A. Bayton, "Motivation, Cognition, Learning—Basic Factors in Consumer Behavior," *Journal of Marketing,* Vol. 22 (January 1958), pp. 282–89.

8. Perry Bliss, *Marketing Management and the Behavioral Environment* (Englewood Cliffs: Prentice-Hall, Inc., 1970), pp. 28–29.

9. Lawrence A. Mayer, "The Diverse $10,000 and Over Masses," in Taylor Meloan, Samuel Smith, and John Wheatley, eds., *Managerial Marketing Policies and Decisions* (Boston: Houghton-Mifflin Co., 1970), pp. 67–69.

CHAPTER 4

Problem Recognition
Leads to Motivation

CHAPTER OUTLINE

I. CONSUMER MOTIVES

II. CONSUMER DECISIONS ARE MOTIVATED
- A. How Motives Arise
- B. Motivated Consumer Behavior
    1. *No Response to Motivation*
    2. *Reflex Response to Motivation*
    3. *Learned Response to Motivation*
- C. Motivation Involves Risk
- D. Satisfaction Reduces Motivation

III. TYPES OF CONSUMER MOTIVES
- A. Physiological and Psychological Motives
- B. Primary and Secondary Motives
- C. Conscious and Unconscious Motives
- D. Patronage and Selective Motives
- E. Positive and Negative Motives

IV. CONSUMER MOTIVATION DIFFERS
- A. Differences in Consumer Needs
- B. Variation in Consumer Means
- C. Motive Importance Varies with Consumers
- D. Consumers Have Multiple Motives
- E. Resolution of Motive Conflict
- F. Consumer Expectations Differ

V. CONSUMER ACTIONS WHEN MOTIVATED
- A. Defer Action on Problem
- B. Assign Priority to Problems
- C. All-or-Nothing Solution
- D. Single Solution for Problems
- E. Partial Solution to Problems

VI. CONCLUDING NOTE

CHAPTER OBJECTIVES

After completing your study of Chapter 4, you should be able to:

1. Define and discuss consumer motives and motivation.
2. Discuss how motives arise.
3. Explain how motivation involves risk.
4. Describe the different types of consumer motives.
5. Discuss why consumer motivation differs.
6. Describe the consumer actions when motivated.

The existence of some need is only a prior condition for consumer decision making. That the consumer has a need in no way assures that he or she will enter the market to seek satisfaction. Before there is action, the consumer has to want to do something about the need. In a general sense, this desire to act is called motivation, and that is the subject of this chapter.

CONSUMER MOTIVES

The word *motive* derives its meaning from move, and a motive is that thing within a person that causes him or her to act, move, or behave in a goal-directed manner. A motive is a reason for action. The attempt of consumers to gratify wants through market activities is motivated behavior. Motives act as governors for our system of responses to environmental change. Thus, by definition, consumer behavior based on motives is purposeful; it is directed at achieving goals by engaging in market activities. Motivation is the condition of being motivated. *Motivation* is defined as an active, strong driving force or a perceived necessity to reduce an existing state of internal human tension. Two conditions must exist for any consumer to be motivated.

First, there must be some *energy mobilization* that causes the consumer to want to do something about her or his tension. This energy mobilization is strictly internal and comes from the self. Second, there must be some *perceived goal* toward which the consumer's energies are directed. The goal, or at least the means to the goal, usually is in the form of products offered by business establishments. As we shall see, both of these conditions are necessary for motivation to occur. A consumer may have a need because his or her only suit is worn out, but it may take a friend's remark about the shabby condition of the suit to mobilize energy toward positive action. Even when a requirement is present and energy is mobilized, the consumer cannot take action until the goal is clear. The consumer must consider all the market related decisions of brand, store, and method of purchase necessary to buy a specific suit. Thus, motivation is a state of mind that directs the consumer's energy mobilization toward a specific market goal.

CONSUMER DECISIONS ARE MOTIVATED

Consumer motivation can be considered one of the central issues in consumer decision making. It concerns how the individual is moved to deal with market related problems. Unless the consumer is motivated in some way to act on problems, there is no search or decision making leading to a purchase.[1] For example, the body needs nourishment, but it is hunger, that gnawing sensation, that causes one to seek food. Without the hunger motive, there is no reason to believe the person would be aware that body cells require replacement. In Figure 4-1, the ad would have little effect unless the hunger motive was present. Thus motives are the link between all needs and consumer behavior.

Figure 4-1
The hunger motive

Courtesy of Pet Incorporated

How Motives Arise

To understand motives fully, we must know how they come about. Until now we have just assumed that motives exist. In fact, motives arise out of some deficiency in consumer needs. The consumer always has needs because they are innate. So long as there is no deficiency or inconsistency with these needs, *cognitive consistency*, or equilibrium, prevails with the consumer. The consumer's mind is satisfied and at peace. Indeed, the consumer may not even be aware of many needs during cognitive consistency. This condition exists toward nourishment just after a meal, toward sleep upon awakening, and toward fulfillment just after successfully completing some task.

Any deficiency in one or more needs shakes the body out of its equilibrium. The deficiency may be emotional (esteem, safety, belonging) or physical (water, sex, activity). The deficiency automatically sets into motion mental dissatisfaction, tension, or inconsistencies which we call *cognitive dissonance*. Cognitive dissonance is another term for doubt or inconsistency, and it leads to an attempt to regain cognitive consistency. Said another way, motivation arises out of the body's attempt to achieve or maintain equilibrium (cognitive consistency) by seeking satisfaction or avoiding dissatisfaction (cognitive dissonance) resulting from a need deficiency. We will have more to say about cognitive dissonance when we discuss attitudes and attitude change.

Motivated Consumer Behavior

Just because a consumer is motivated does not necessarily mean that a purchase will result. Three possibilities exist which are discussed below.

No Response to Motivation. A consumer, even though motivated, may elect to do nothing about the problem. We call this nonbehavior. The consumer will take no action when: (1) the need cannot reasonably be satisfied, (2) the need is not sufficiently strong for action, or (3) the need can be satisfied without taking action. For example, a consumer may perceive a need for a Rolls Royce or a mink coat but never have the money to act on the wish. The consumer does not act on the motive. A consumer sitting at home may feel the urge to have a beer, but it is just too much trouble to go to the store to purchase it. The consumer's motive is not strong enough for action. A motive long denied can cease to function. In fact, it is quieted without action. It is said, for example, that people have starved to death in relative comfort, because, after a period of intense pain, the hunger motive ceases to remind them that they are in need of nourishment.

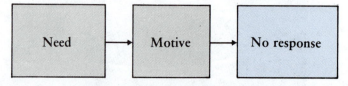

Reflex Response to Motivation. Several types of consumer behavior are not learned in the sense that they require no particular thought or previous experience for the action taken. We refer to such actions as reflex behavior. Reflex behavior is instinctive, and it would include blinking of eyes, heartbeat, sneezing, coughing, and knee jerking. At one time consumers were thought to have many instincts, but most have been proven false. For example, breathing is a reflex, but adapting breathing to an Aqua-lung is learned. It may be instinctive for a baby to cry, but crying to get a new toy is learned.

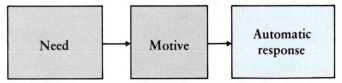

One type of instinctive consumer response is *habitual purchasing*. Let us say a young man purchases a Van Heusen shirt and likes it so much that he buys the same type of shirt each time he needs a new one. This is habitual behavior; although the original purchase was thought out, the others were not. Repeat purchases without shopping around are a type of reflex response. Another type of reflex consumer behavior is *impulse purchasing,* where no real thought is given to the item and no comparison shopping is carried out. It is "monkey see, monkey do." A great many consumer purchases have at least some aspect of reflex response connected with them.[2]

Learned Response to Motivation. Motivation leads to a learned response any time the consumer engages in serious thought leading to problem solving. This is the most common type of consumer behavior, and it is also the most complex and least predictable. A consumer needs nourishment but learns to prefer steak over spinach. A person may need liquid but learns to travel to convenience stores for a soft drink. There is learned behavior any time the consumer selects one grocery store over another, experiences indecision over which type of canned corn to purchase, or decides to pay cash rather than write a check.[3] It is important to note that just because consumer behavior is learned is no guarantee that it is more successful than reflex action. A consumer can be just as satisfied with a pack of chewing gum bought on impulse as with the new Buick which was thought out over several weeks.

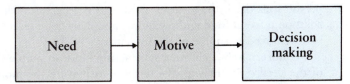

Motivation Involves Risk

Motives direct consumer behavior, and therefore motives involve risk. There is the normal risk of being wrong that is involved in every act or purchase. No one can escape this kind of risk. There is also "perceived risk."[4] Perceived risk is not limited to dollar outlay but includes all disadvantages present in a purchase situation. Perceived risk may involve the consumer's inconvenience, poor product performance, or a threat to social standing that can result from the purchase. The purchase of cologne does not require a large expenditure, but the risk of facial blemish, offending odor, and loss of status are very real.

Even the slightest expenditure may have risk associated with it, but the amount and type of perceived risk present in purchasing decisions does differ among individuals.[5] For example, the period of deliberation over higher-priced durable goods is more extensive for middle-income customers than for lower-income customers. There are two possible reasons for this difference in behavior. First, it may be that the middle-income customer perceives the risk of purchase to be greater than that perceived by the lower-income customer because of a greater investment in career, social standing, and personal property. The middle-income consumer may believe that he or she has more to lose from a faulty decision. Second, the lower-income consumer has less time for deliberation because he or she may be replacing a durable good that is completely worn out.

A relationship exists between the perceived risk of buying certain products and the frequency with which these products are ordered by telephone for delivery. Items perceived as having a high risk associated with them are purchased much less frequently than those perceived as having low risk. Among high-risk items are handbags, appliances, and furniture; examples of low-risk items are bed linens, men's and women's stockings, and underwear.

The consumer may rely on several strategies in an attempt to reduce uncertainty or risk in the purchase. An objective criterion of value may be established by referring to independent source material; purchasing decisions can be made on this basis with reduced risk. Many consumers feel that relying on *Consumer Reports* or some independent seal of approval will reduce risks. Support acquired from friends to substantiate a purchasing decision is another means of coping with risk. The consumer may also turn to the company to reduce risk by looking for guarantees (see Figure 4-2).

Satisfaction Reduces Motivation

The purpose of motivation is to reduce dissonance by eliminating the cause of the problem. The assumption is that there is a direct relationship between need deficiency and satisfaction. Since it is a need deficiency that causes motivation, it is the elimination of this deficiency that results in satisfaction. For example, if a person feels tired, the solution is to rest; if a person is deficient in vitamins, the solution is to eat food with vitamins; and if a person feels threatened, the solution is to remove the source of the insecurity.

Unfortunately, achieving satisfaction is not so simple. The consumer is aware of the need only through the tension created by the motive. In the consumer's mind, the motive, not the need, causes the problem. Therefore, consumers nearly always attempt to reduce dissonance by satisfying the motive rather than the need. Consumer needs are satisfied only to the extent that handling the motive also satisfies the need. For example, a person needs water, but it is thirst that the consumer acts upon. Thirst can be satisfied with soft drinks, water, juices, or alcohol. A person requiring rest is motivated by tiredness, and this can be satisfied by sleep, pep pills, or a change of activity. A person needing to belong is motivated by feeling unloved, which can be satisfied with drink, paid companionship, family participation, or religion. Notice that in every case some of the solutions relieve the problem while others only relieve the symptom.

TYPES OF CONSUMER MOTIVES

There are several recognizable consumer motives. Each type has a direct bearing on consumer decision making. The types are presented below.

Physiological and Psychological Motives

Consumer motives, like consumer needs, can be classified as physiological or psychological. This classification recognizes the close relationship between needs and motives. *Physiological motives* stimulate action relative to basic body functions, and *psychological motives* stimulate mental, or emotional, activity. The classification points to the fact that motives arise out of needs, and they cannot

Figure 4-2
Company reduces risk

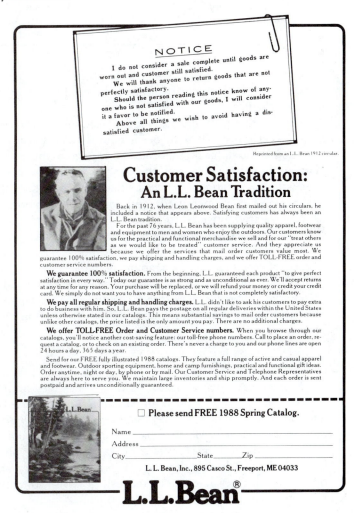

L.L. Bean Inc., Freeport, ME

Table 4-1

Motives That Arise out of Needs

Type of Need	Type of Motive
I. Physiological needs	**I. Physiological motives**
Food	Hunger
Water	Thirst
Sex	Unrest, yearning
Sleep	Fatigue, drowsiness
Warmth	Coldness, skin tension
Elimination	Bloatedness, physical pressure
Activity	Muscle pain, physical tension
II. Psychological needs	**II. Psychological motives**
Safety	Mental tension, insecurity
Belonging	Ignored, unloved, abandoned
Esteem	Embarrassed, ostracized, self hate
Self-actualization	Unfulfilled, inferior
Know	Curiosity, uninformed
Esthetic	Unsymmetrical, drab, unexciting

stand alone. As Table 4-1 demonstrates, there are one or more motives for every need. The table is organized around the needs as identified by Maslow in the previous chapter.

Physical and psychological motives lead to behavior designed to satisfy some need. For example, the body needs nourishment, but it is hunger, that gnawing sensation in the stomach, that causes one to go to the grocery store or restaurant. Without the motive of hunger, the person has no awareness that body cells are being destroyed, creating a deficiency that must be satisfied. Thus motives are the link between consumer needs and consumer behavior. We satisfy our needs because we are motivated to do so.

Any business representative who can correctly identify a prospective customer's need and relate it to a specific motive has a good chance of making the sale. This accounts for the amount of time salespersons spend studying their customers. This customer analysis continues even as the salesperson is making the presentation. The difficulty is that customers are so complex that one can never fully understand their motivation. This is the reason we say marketing is an inexact science.

Primary and Secondary Motives

Motives are often classified as to whether they are primary or secondary. *Primary motives* are founded on basic physiological needs as explained earlier. They include food, water, sleep, and sex. *Secondary motives* arise out of social and psychological needs such as safety, belonging, and esteem. In the broad sense, secondary motives become operative only after physiological needs have been satisfied at least minimally. In practice, primary and secondary motives operate on the consumer simultaneously. Even so, the primary motive tends to take precedence over the secondary motive.

Let us illustrate how primary and secondary motives work. A consumer requires activity, and the related physical discomfort is a primary motive. Now, how the consumer goes about satisfying the need for activity can involve secondary motivation. For example, the person can work out at the gym, take a friend to the movies, cook a meal for the family, or work in the garden. All these activities involve secondary motives related to self-actualization, belonging, or safety. A person talking to a friend at the grocery store and drinking a Pepsi satisfies the primary motive of quenching thirst and the secondary motive of belonging. If the thirst is not too great, this person may even feel that the association is more important than the drink. At some later date, the individual may purchase a Pepsi and enjoy it more than usual because of its association with the previous pleasant encounter with the friend.

Conscious and Unconscious Motives

Motives can be conscious or unconscious. The consumer is aware of the effect on their decision making with *conscious motives*, but *unconscious motives* work below the level of awareness. Both types of motives are important to consumer decision making and probably play a part in all consumer behavior. However, a given decision may be dominated by either conscious or unconscious motives.

Few people are fully aware of their purchase motives—a fact that makes motivation research difficult. Typically, a given need is associated with several motives, and the consumer may be aware of only one or two of these motives at any one time. Individuals may also not be aware of their true motives. We all rationalize our behavior to conform to what we want to be true. Take a consumer considering a new suit. The consumer may be aware that the material is good, the price is right, and the suit will be flattering. The consumer may not recognize equally real feelings that his or her spouse may not like the suit or that the purchase is intended to show up a neighbor.

Much of the promotion done by marketers operates *subliminally* because it uses stimuli that affect the unconscious mind. Experiments have been conducted in movie houses, where messages about popcorn and soft drinks were flashed on the screen during the show for a period too short for the conscious mind to comprehend. The results, though inconclusive, suggest that an increase in sales resulted. This is what one may expect from any advertising to persons who have a desire for food or drink. It can be suggested that most promotion operates subliminally because the person does not consciously see the ad in the book or newspaper, is not paying attention to the salesperson or television announcer, or sees the billboard along the road for too short a time for it to register. Subliminal promotion may, in fact, be the most effective on consumers because they are not completely aware of the effect that the marketers' appeal is having.

Patronage and Selective Motives

Patronage and selective motives relate directly to the consumer in the act of buying. *Selective motives* explain why a consumer purchases a particular type of product or brand. It may be because the color pleases one's esthetic sensibilities or because the function satisfies a need for warmth, sleep, or activity. Ask yourself what factors influenced you in your purchase of your last pair of shoes, candy bar, or meal. Much of the advertising and personal selling of marketers is directed at selective motives.

Patronage motives explain the consumer's choice of a particular store. The

Figure 4-3
Appealing to positive motives

Prince Matchabelli, Inc.

Part 2 – Consumer Problem Recognition

decision may be based on locational convenience, width of product line, services offered, or attention of store personnel. All these factors are involved with physical or emotional needs. It may be assumed that the consumer decides on a product first, then the store, but evidence does not support this position. In practice, the consumer may decide to purchase a product, say a Ford automobile, and seek out only those stores that stock this product. In other instances, the consumer may decide to trade at a specific store, say Sears, and purchase a dress from the selection that is available at that particular store.

Positive and Negative Motives

The polarity of motives refers to whether they are positive or negative. All motives signal a problem in that some body need requires attention. It is how one attends to the situation that determines whether the motive is positive or negative.

A *positive motive* is a cause for action where a specific satisfaction or release is sought because of the resulting pleasure. Probably most motivation is of this type. The anticipation of a fine meal, the joy of running, or the anticipation of seeing one's boyfriend or girlfriend are examples of positive motivation. Marketers seek to appeal to positive motives whenever they can in the products they sell (see Figure 4-3). That is why dresses are pretty, automobiles fun to drive, and pastries pleasing to the taste. Most marketers prefer to make positive appeals. Selling pleasure is easier than selling pain, and positive appeals are in line with what the consumer wants to do anyway.

A *negative motive* is a cause for action based on the avoidance of discomfort, pain, or some adverse psychological tension. When the eyes blink, ice is placed on a bruise, or if one coughs there is negative motivation involved. Negative motives are more widely used by marketers than one may realize. All "fear appeals" are based on negative motives. For example, deodorants, soap, and perfumes are sold to dispel the fear of body odor. Tooth brushes and toothpaste are sold to overcome the fear of cavities and bad breath. All life and health insurance base their appeals on the fear of accident or death. Other products associated with fear appeals include first aid items, douches, eye glasses, raincoats, and education.

Negative and positive appeals are often combined in the promotion of products. Figure 4-4 is an example. The Curél lotion advertisement appeals to the positive motive of beauty and comfort and the negative motive of avoiding dry, rough skin. The combination of positive and negative appeals can result in very strong buying inducements. It should be obvious that negative motives are involved in buying more often than one may imagine. Can you think of other examples of their use?

CONSUMER MOTIVATION DIFFERS

No two consumers are motivated exactly the same way even though they may purchase the same product. To know more about consumer decision making, managers must understand these differences in motivation.[6] When selling a product, appeals must be sufficiently broad based to reach most of the various motives held by prospective customers.

Figure 4-4

Appealing to both positives and negative motives

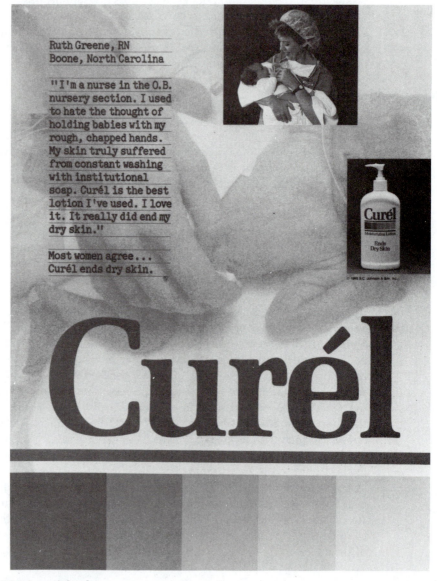

Ruth Greene, RN
Boone, North Carolina

"I'm a nurse in the O.B. nursery section. I used to hate the thought of holding babies with my rough, chapped hands. My skin truly suffered from constant washing with institutional soap. Curél is the best lotion I've used. I love it. It really did end my dry skin."

Most women agree...
Curél ends dry skin.

Curél

S.C. Johnson & Son, Inc.

Differences in Consumer Needs

Consumers are often motivated differently because of variations in their needs. All consumers have the same general types of needs (physical and psychological), but differences in the persons cause variations in the needs. For

Photo 4-1

Motivation varies due to placement along the needs hierarchy. This girl is meeting basic pet-care needs.

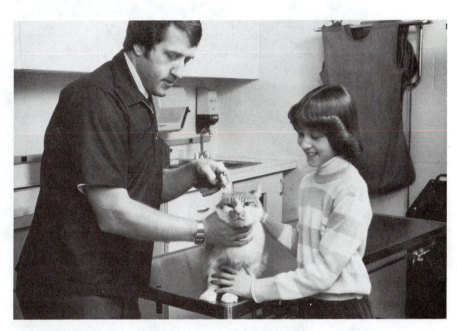

Flournoy and Gibbs, Inc.

example, in our society, the needs of a female consumer are not perceived as the same as those of a male. We assume that there will be a vast difference in how these two consumers are motivated. While males and females both require affection, a female may seek it in providing for the family by working outside the home, while a male may be motivated to create a loving atmosphere in the home. In the same way the needs of a farmer are not the same as those of a city worker. The needs of a tall person are not the same as for a short person, and the needs of an outgoing person are not the same as those of an introvert.

Motivation also varies due to placement along the need hierarchy. One consumer may just be meeting the body's basic physical requirements, while another may have satisfied all but the highest order of psychological needs. For example, there is a vast difference between the perceived needs of a ghetto consumer and those of a middle class suburban consumer. Their motivation varies in accordance with these differences.

Variation in Consumer Means

Even consumers with the same need are often motivated differently because of variations in their means to act. Said another way, motivation is tempered by income. Consumers tend to interpret how to act on needs in accordance with

Photo 4-2
There are also non-essential pet-care needs. How do different people meet pet care needs?

their ability to purchase. For example, a middle-income consumer may desire status but because of his or her need for warmth will more likely purchase a fancy garment than a piece of jewelry. A more affluent consumer is more likely to buy the jewelry. Furthermore, the source of income affects how consumers are motivated. For example, blue-collar workers tend to read *Popular Mechanics*, *Reader's Digest*, and *Ladies' Home Journal,* while white-collar workers tend toward *Time*, *National Geographic*, and *Fortune*. Blue-collar workers tend to spend more on personal consumption items like televisions, clothes, and radios, while white-collar workers spend more on their homes, cars, and insurance. Thus the amount and source of income is very important to consumer motivation.

Motive Importance Varies with Consumers

The power of consumer motives is not uniform among individuals. Motives vary in importance at different times and under different circumstances. The desire for new clothes may be greater at the beginning of each fashion season for one consumer and at the end of the season for another. More consumers tend to eat out on the weekend, but some prefer weekdays. It is interesting to observe a child around Christmas. One day he or she wants a new bicycle, the next day a tent, and the day after something different. The desire to visit a hairdresser may be stronger on the day before a business meeting than on any other day. Marketers often lose sales because they fail to take into account this variation in the intensity of consumer motives. An enthusiastic customer today may not be as enthusiastic after thinking over the situation.

Consumers Have Multiple Motives

The same motive does not have an identical effect on different consumers. A desire for security may cause one consumer to spend more on entertainment in order to be with other people. Another consumer may find security by staying at home and saving money. The desire for affection may have diverse effects on consumers. A person seeking affection may buy flowers or gifts, entertain, buy more clothes, or buy an engagement ring. There is no way to predict the effect that a given motive may have on a consumer.

Just as one motive can lead to many effects, so one effect can come from several different motives. It is not possible to determine the consumer's motive to any purchase with certainty by observing the effect. One person goes to a movie to see the show, another enjoys the company of a date, a third person is bored and wants to kill some time, and a fourth person seeks relaxation after a difficult examination. Each consumer's behavior is essentially the same, but the motives are vastly different.

Some consumer motives are founded on habit, and habit varies among consumers. A shopper may have purchased from a particular grocery store initially because it was located close by and continues to go to the same store out of habit even when many aspects of its operations are displeasing. This same shopper may get into the habit of buying certain canned goods each week. Daily meals may vary but not the type of food served over a given period of time. Another consumer may have a different pattern of habitual behavior.

Resolution of Motive Conflict

We recognize from previous discussions that there is typically more than one motive at work on the consumer in any decision situation. It is not realistic to expect that these motives are always in harmony. In fact, motives, like needs, are often in conflict. For example, a boy may desire to buy a candy bar, but conflict arises because his parents forbid eating before dinner. A family may have a conflict between taking a vacation or purchasing a new car; buying a computer or saving the money. Consumers can even experience multiple conflicts. For example, a consumer may be motivated to watch a particular television show, go shopping with a friend, and pay the monthly bills. There can be no question but that different individuals will perceive and deal with these motive conflicts in a variety of ways. The deciding factors are direction, strength, and number of supporting motives on each side of the conflict.

Consumer Expectations Differ

Consumer expectations may be described as the person's subjective notions about the future. Expectations are our estimates of the chances we have to satisfy

Photo 4-3

Products may serve more than one need. In this purchase, both fashion and practicality needs are met.

our future needs.[7] The expectations consumers hold are influenced by feelings, attitudes, beliefs, personality, reference groups, as well as by the present sense of satisfaction or dissatisfaction. These expectations influence how different stimuli are perceived as well as how we purchase. Individuals' expectations about their personal financial situation and the general economic outlook also influence purchasing behavior, purchase motives, and purchase aspirations.[8]

The purchase of products and services today is partly a function of our expectations for tomorrow. Our optimism or pessimism as to what the future holds may be the most important variable in the purchase decision. Even though most consumers are not sophisticated about the workings of our economy, they do have a feeling for what is going on. A college senior, three months before graduation, may purchase a new two-door hardtop priced at $12,500 with a minimum down payment and no present income. Such a decision is not based upon the present situation; it is based on the senior's expectations. It may be that she or he has accepted her or his first job, is to be commissioned in the Armed Forces, or will come into an inheritance upon receipt of the degree. The purchase decision is more influenced by expected income than that presently available. What might appear to the outside observer as "over-buying" in respect to income might not be in consideration of the future situation.

Seldom do individuals methodically observe prepared budgets in their purchase patterns. However, even though a written budget may not exist, consumers do allocate their income among various items. The house holder may not have the budget ordered with computer-like efficiency, but is well aware that $850 must be allocated each month for food and rent. The spend-save patterns of an individual may depend on price movements, availablility of credit, stock upturns or downturns, taxes, and the general economic conditions are interpreted.

CONSUMER ACTIONS WHEN MOTIVATED

Consumers are always motivated in some specific direction—toward some specific goal. Motivation, because it is directional, is never vague in its intent. Consumers are not motivated to "do something about my unrest." Rather, consumers are motivated to take care of the unrest by eating out, or going shopping, or taking a trip, or buying a new pair of shoes. Even when motives are in conflict, it is always a conflict over specific courses of action.

Although motives are directional, they do not necessarily lead to healthy or desirable behavior. Since all motives are filtered through the mind, they have an emotional base. Thus one can be motivated toward what is desirable and socially acceptable, or toward what is undesirable and not socially acceptable. For example, a consumer may spend money on tropical fish when the family is heavily in debt and the money might be better employed to pay off the loans. The discussion to follow presents some of the actions that consumers can take when motivated.

Defer Action on Problem

Many times consumers defer taking any action on a recognized need-related problem. That is to say, the consumer does not give up on ever satisfying the need, but action is put off for future consideration. The essential factors in deferment are that (1) there is no specified time for acting on the need, and (2) action is not related to the purchase of any other product. For example, deferment is not the same as a priority.

Deferred actions are often associated with insufficient money. Some products often associated with deferred needs include such expensive items as homes, automobiles, furniture, boats, fashion clothing, and vacations. However, even inexpensive staple items can be deferred because of a lack of money. For example, the consumer may put off purchasing a haircut until payday, or repairing a watch until the next trip into town. Some of these deferred problems will be handled in the near future, but others may be deferred indefinitely.

Inconvenience is a reason for deferring action on a problem. A busy parent puts off grocery shopping because of a prior engagement or a teenager postpones the purchase of a pair of jeans in order to visit a friend for the weekend. These items can be bought almost any time, and if the need is not urgent, there is no harm in the postponement.

An individual's aspirations often can lead to the deferring of action on need-related problems. An individual may desire a Mercedes automobile because of a need for prestige or recognition. Although economy may regularly dictate that the person purchase a Chevrolet or a Honda, the promise is made that someday he or she will own the Mercedes. Who knows? It could happen. Of course, we recognize that other things may intervene, and the postponement of action on a need may become permanent. In any case, deferment is a conscious choice that the consumer has when dealing with needs.

Assign Priority to Problems

Another method for handling need-related problems is to assign priorities to them. Because of barriers, such as income limitations, lower-priority needs may have to go unsatisfied at the expense of satisfying needs of a higher priority. A consumer purchasing his or her first new home might prefer a certain neighborhood and style of home that represent spaciousness and refined and dignified surroundings. However, because the dollars to finance the purchase of such a house cannot be obtained, the consumer may compromise and buy a smaller and more functional house in a less desirable neighborhood. In this case, the consumer's purchasing behavior is an attempt to satisfy the high-priority need for shelter at the expense of the low-priority needs for more space and a higher-status neighborhood. One can think of numerous situations where the conflict present between needs is resolved in this manner. Furniture, automobiles, and appliances are but a few of the products where the make and model purchased is determined by the priority given to various needs.

All-or-Nothing Solution

There are rare cases when a consumer may, in effect, "place all his or her eggs in one basket" by anticipating action on one problem to the exclusion of others. Of course, every consumer must deal with the basic necessities at some point in time. Thus, the all-or-nothing approach applies more to wants than to basic requirements. A person in the military service who has all his or her basic requirements taken care of may spend almost all his or her paycheck on entertainment. This person may literally have little money left over for savings, for the purchase of a car, furniture, or civilian clothing. A senior citizen, living on a fixed income, may forego better food, new clothing, or better housing because of the need to pay medical bills. Some college students have been known to sacrifice everything except necessities in order to pay for their education. The all-or-nothing approach is seldom inclusive of all needs; rather, it is more likely to apply when the consumer is dealing with a particular category of needs. Furthermore, the all-or-nothing approach is typically used by consumers only in the short run. Over the long haul, consumers must deal realistically with all their known needs.

Single Solution for Problems

It is often possible for a consumer to deal with several recognized problems with a single approach. For example, a single product may serve to satisfy multiple needs. The purchase of items of apparel satisfies more than the basic need for warmth. Clothes can also relate to affection by appealing to a mate; to prestige by appearing well-groomed at a party; to the ego by providing a good feeling due to increased confidence. The use of a single approach to multiple problems is associated with efficiency, because the consumer has made one product accomplish several goals.

The single approach solution may result in some compromise of need satisfaction. For example, a hamburger quickly eaten with a friend on the way to the beach may better serve social needs than the need for nourishment—especially if one does not like hamburgers. If a consumer plans a vacation and knows the money spent on a dress will cut short planned recreation along the way, there is a compromise. On the other hand, it is not necessary that one compromise needs when taking the single approach to multiple problems. A sport coat and slacks can serve to satisfy a person's need for warmth, sociability, and ego needs. Dinner out may be equally satisfying for nourishment, relaxation, and beauty. It is probably safe to say that most products purchased by consumers serve more than one need. This is normal because the needs themselves are not always mutually exclusive.

Partial Solution to Problems

When dealing with needs, the consumer may recognize that it is impossible to obtain complete satisfaction. The consumer may have to accept a partial solution to a need-related problem. Satisfaction may be incomplete for a single need or for several needs approached together. For example, a person may accept an economy washing machine due to cost constraints when the deluxe model would more completely satisfy the need for clean clothes, energy conservation, and beauty. High interest rates may cause one to build or purchase a smaller house than one's prestige and ego needs would prefer.

When a consumer has several needs in conflict, he or she may attempt to satisfy each one partially. This position may be preferred to satisfying one or two needs completely while having others go unsatisfied. For example, a family may purchase a smaller home than desired in order to have a more prestigious car or higher-quality home furnishings. The hatchback compacts such as the Toyota and Datsun partially satisfy some person's desire for a sports car and practical family car.

CONCLUDING NOTE

All these approaches to handling consumer need-related problems are used by consumers at different times. It is impossible to specify the situations in which each approach applies. Every consumer is different from every other consumer. Some people purchase products to satisfy needs that to another person may not be a need at all. The need and the problem exist, but problem recognition is incomplete at best. This inability to pinpoint the source of the deficiency makes problem recognition very difficult for the consumer with unconscious needs. It often leads to inconclusive purchasing which does not relieve the situation. The consumer may enter the market repeatedly in a vain attempt to deal with an unspecified deficiency.

It is equally difficult for a manager to appeal to consumers with unconscious needs. Without sure knowledge of the deficiency, the sales person does not know which product to promote, which product features are more appropriate or which sales approach to use. Furthermore, the customer is incapable of providing clues to aid the marketer. Thus, there can be indecision and inefficiency on the part of both the buyer and the seller.

QUESTIONS

1. Discuss the two conditions that must be present for a consumer to be motivated.
2. Explain the terms "cognitive consistency" and "cognitive dissonance." How do these terms relate to motives?
3. Discuss the various kinds of risk involved in the motivation of consumers.
4. Explain how satisfaction might reduce motivation. Include an example in your answer.
5. Define physiological motives and psychological motives and discuss advertisements that are directed at these motives.
6. Explain how the source and amount of income affects how consumers are motivated.
7. What factors influence your expectations as a consumer?
8. Discuss some of the reasons different individuals may react differently to the same problem.
9. Why is it unreasonable for a consumer to use the all-or-nothing approach in the long run for solving problems?
10. Discuss some of the benefits obtained from assigning priorities to problems.
11. State an example of a single solution and a partial solution to a problem.
12. Briefly explain how business leaders can be more interested in consumer motives than needs of the consumer.
13. Give an example of an advertisement where a positive appeal is present and an example where negative appeal is present.
14. Define with examples patronage motive.
15. Discuss why a primary motive tends to take precedence over a secondary motive.

NOTES

1. Ernest F. Cooke, "A General Theory of Need Satisfaction," in John Summey, R. Viswanathan, Ronald D. Taylor, and Karen Glynn, eds.,

Marketing Theories and Concepts for an Era of Change (Southern Illinois University and Southern Marketing Assn., 1983), pp. 96–98.

2. Peter Weinberg and Wolfgang Gottwald, "Implusive Consumer Buying as a Result of Emotions," *Journal of Business Research,* Vol. 10 (March 1982), pp. 43–58.

3. L. Rothschild and W. C. Gaidis, "Behavioral Learning Theory: Its Relevance to Marketing and Promotions," *Journal of Marketing,* Vol. 45 (Spring 1981), pp. 70–78.

4. Charles M. Schaninger, "Perceived Risk and Personality," *Journal of Consumer Research,* Vol. 3 (September 1986), pp. 95–100.

5. J. Paul Peter and Michael J. Ryan, "An Investigation of Perceived Risk at the Brand Level," *Journal of Marketing Research,* Vol. 13 (May 1976), pp. 184–88.

6. Leigh McAlister and Edgar Pessemier, "Variety Seeking Behavior: An Interdisciplinary Review," *Journal of Consumer Research,* Vol. 9 (December 1982), pp. 311–22.

7. A. H. Maslow, "A Theory of Human Motivation," *Psychological Review,* Vol. 50 (1943), pp. 370–96.

8. Eugene J. Kelley and L. Rusty Scheewe, "Buyer Behavior in a Stagflation/Shortages Economy," *Journal of Marketing,* Vol. 39 (April 1975), pp. 44–50.

SECTION B
BUSINESS RESPONSE
TO CONSUMER PROBLEMS

5. Target Identification Based on Problem
   Recognition
6. Product Development To Solve Problems

CHAPTER 5

Target Identification Based
on Problem Recognition

CHAPTER OUTLINE

I. MARKETING TARGET: RELATIONSHIP TO CONSUMERS

II. DECIDE FIRM'S ABILITIES: CONSUMER IMPLICATIONS

III. GROUPS MAKING UP THE MARKETING TARGET

    A. Segment Consumers by Needs and Motives

        1. *Location Needs Used to Segment*

        2. *Segments Based on Demographic Needs*

        3. *Psychographic Motives Make Segments*

        4. *Benefits Used to Segment*

        5. *Segments Based on Preferences*

        6. *Relate Consumer Segment to Firm's Abilities*

    B. Identify Governments by Needs and Motives

    C. Identify Competitors by Needs and Motives

    D. Identify Special Interest Groups by Needs and Motives

    E. Identify Suppliers by Needs and Motives

    F. Determine Makeup of the Single Target

IV. CAN THE TARGET BE REACHED?

V. DEVELOP STRATEGY FOR EACH TARGET

    A. Single Target Approach

    B. Segmented Target Approach

    C. Multiple Targets

VI. CONSUMERS ARE BASIC TO MARKETING STRATEGY

CHAPTER OBJECTIVES

After completing your study of Chapter 5, you should be able to:

1. Discuss how target identification is based on problem recognition.
2. Discuss the relationship between consumers and marketing targets.
3. Describe the relationship between firm's abilities and marketing targets.
4. Explain the importance of combining groups into marketing targets.
5. Discuss how to segment consumers by needs and motives.
6. Discuss the importance of deciding targets feasibility.
7. Explain the importance of developing strategy for each target.
8. Discuss why consumers are basic to marketing strategy.

In the previous chapters, we gave reasonable decisions that the business manager can make, and we gave specific examples of how consumer needs and motives relate to business. It is also necessary for the reader to understand how consumer decision making relates to the development of overall strategy by the businessman.

The two major components of marketing strategy were presented in Chapter 1. They are the selection of a marketing target toward which the firm directs its efforts and the development of a marketing mix to satisfy persons in these targets. In this chapter, we demonstrate the importance of consumers to managers when selecting the marketing target. In later chapters we demonstrate how consumer's knowledge affects marketing decision making relative to the components of the marketing mix.

MARKETING TARGET: RELATIONSHIP TO CONSUMERS

The temptation is great, especially in a consumer behavior text, to state that all business policy is directed at satisfying consumers. However, we know that there are five groups in every firm's environment that make up the marketing target. Given this lead, we can define a *marketing target* as:

> *Persons identified together from among suppliers, consumers, special interest groups, competitors, and governments having a common problem which the firm can satisfy to achieve organizational objectives.*

The target consists of some persons within each group, but not all persons within any group, who have a common want or interest in the firm's products, services, or manner of operation. Managers respond to this target with policies designed to provide products that are (1) competitive, (2) wanted, (3) profitable, (4) legal, (5) resource efficient, and (6) socially acceptable. In this way, the firm meets the interests of each group in the target.

Consumers make up one-fifth of the groups comprising the marketing target, but their importance varies with the decision. This is true of each group making up the target. For example, consumers in the target may receive 40 to 70 percent of management's attention on such decisions as developing a new advertising appeal, researching the market, designing benefits into a product, or indoctrinating sales personnel. The consumer may receive only 5 to 15 percent of management's attention when the firm lobbies for repeal of an unfair tax, attempts to counter a competitor's superior policies, or must meet with pressure groups seeking safer products and more responsible managers.

But consumers can never be ignored when management is developing marketing strategy. In fact, consumers are never more important than when management is defining the marketing target itself. Figures 5-1 and 5-2 demonstrate one company's identification of two marketing targets. There are four important steps in the process of selecting marketing targets, and consumers are important to every step. The steps are:

1. Determine the firm's abilities
2. Combine groups into a single target
3. Decide the target's feasibility
4. Coordinate the target to the firm's abilities

The remainder of this chapter demonstrates the consumer's importance to each of these steps in selecting a marketing target. We cannot explain the marketing target without bringing into the discussion all the groups that make up this target. However, our emphasis in this text is on consumers, and the other groups are important only to the extent that they are necessary to complete the explanation of marketing targets.

DECIDE FIRM'S ABILITIES: CONSUMER IMPLICATIONS

The first step in selecting the marketing target is to lay out the firm's assets and liabilities. Before the firm can identify who has wants and interests that it can satisfy, it must recognize its own abilities. In short, the firm must determine which problems it can solve before it attempts to locate persons in the environment who have those problems. It is fundamental to target selection that the firm be able to match its abilities to the wants and interests of specific persons in external groups.[1] Thus it is logical to begin the selection process with some understanding of what kinds of things the firm can satisfy and what types of advantages it may have when undertaking that satisfaction.

The marketing audit, which is an evaluation of every aspect of the firm's operations, is the device used to identify its abilities.[2] Specifically, a *marketing audit* is a systematic examination of the firm's objectives, strategies, organization and performance. It lists each unit being evaluated by name, location, and who is in charge. Then for the unit, the marketing audit should:

1. Enumerate and describe current activities related to sales, cost, prices, profits, and other performance factors.
2. Contain information on customers, competitors, governments, suppliers, and special interest groups that affect the firm's operations.
3. Indicate opportunities and alternatives for improvement of operations and strategy.
4. Provide an overall database to be used for planning and evaluation.

Figure 5-1
Advertisement directed to the female marketing target

Caroline Richard Student. Age: 21 My boyfriend refuses to discuss the philosophy that I'm studying. He's a great believer in Eastern thought, and thinks that Kirkegaard is absurd. AIDS is a dreadful problem, and it's especially sad for kids to be confronted with such a thing, when they don't even understand their sexuality yet. I like to spend time alone just sitting in my favorite cafe drinking coffee. My one greatest wish is to have children.

Esprit de Corp./Photos Olivero Toscani

Classics

The Classic group is really the starting point for the whole Esprit Jeans collection. The styles in this group are based on traditional, classic jeans design. The classic proportions never go out of fashion, and are adaptable to anyone's personal style. All the jeans, skirts and jackets in the Classic group are produced only in Esprit Stone Wash — what many of us have come to think of as the true color of denim.

Esprit de Corp./Photos Olivero Toscani

Like an accounting audit, a marketing audit should be conducted regularly. It may focus only on a few activities, or it may encompass the entire operation of the firm.

Consumers affect the marketing audit in several ways. Many of the activities performed by the firm are to satisfy consumers, so management wants to know if these operations are efficient. Consumer knowledge may point the way to improvement in several aspects of the firm's operations. Changes in consumer wants may necessitate a new audit, which, in turn, may indicate operational modifications. No marketing audit should be undertaken without relating it to consumers.

The marketing audit becomes the foundation upon which the remainder of target identification rests.

GROUPS MAKING UP THE MARKETING TARGET

The second step in identifying the marketing target is to combine competitors, consumers, special interest groups, governments, and suppliers into relatively homogeneous categories. This step involves identifying persons in each group that have needs or motives that relate to the firm's abilities as defined above. At this step, persons in each group are identified together by some related want or interest in the firm that they each have in common. Consider an automobile manufacturer. State and federal government agencies are interested in whether it meets Environmental Protection Agency emission and other performance standards; special interest groups are interested in safe seat belts; consumers are interested in performance; and suppliers are interested in the automobiles being built with their products or services. Thus the automobile manufacturer can identify all these groups together into a common target because of their special interest in the automobile. We discuss the identification of each group below, beginning with consumers.

Segment Consumers by Needs and Motives

At some point in the identification of the marketing target, it is necessary to group consumers into markets and segments.[3] In this section we define consumer markets and consumer market segments. We also discuss the basic methods of consumer segmentation and how each method relates to consumer wants and motives.

A market can be defined in several ways. It can be a store, like a supermarket; a place, like the western or southern markets; or a meeting place, like the farmer's market. For our purpose, a *market* is defined as people with income and an inclination to buy. We like this definition because it focuses on consumers. People have needs and are motivated to purchase in accordance with their income and basic inclination. Thus consumers lie at the heart of any market, and they are extremely important to the definition of any target. A segment is any part of a whole, thus a *market segment* is:

> *any group of persons possessing similar wants, desires, or interests that differentiate their specific product requirements from the generic demand of the market as a whole.*

Just as a market is part of the marketing target, so a marketing segment is a part of a market.[4] *Market segmentation* is:

> *dividing the heterogeneous market into smaller customer divisions having certain relatively homogeneous problems that can be satisfied by the firm.*

For example, purchasers of paint, stain, and wallpaper can be considered as separate segments of the market for wall coverings. Their problems are similar but their solutions vary. Consumers of liquid detergent, hand soap, and powdered detergents can be considered as separate segments of the soap market. Every marketer must have knowledge about the firm's market and market segment as a sound basis for developing policies to reach the potential. No aspect of the target is more important than this identification of consumers.

Many of the needs and motives associated with consumer problem recognition have their basis in the consumer's physical and mental makeup, location, preferences, or life style.[5] There exists a large number of these consumer characteristics upon which market segmentation can be based. Table 5-1 summarizes the major types of consumer characteristics, which relate to needs and motives, that are most often used to segment markets.[6] Each characteristic is related to consumers below.

Location Needs Used to Segment. Geographic area refers to the physical placement of customers.[7] Many consumer needs and wants are based on location, and most market segments use placement at least as a partial basis for segmentation. Persons located close together tend to have similar customs, mores, and habits that serve as a basis for sales.[8] Thus they are classified into the same market segment. For example, Southerners can get by with lighter topcoats than Northerners. Southerners tend to eat lighter foods, such as salads, because they do not need to generate so much heat. Homes in the West tend to be more varied to take advantage of the landscape and scenery. Consumers located near the East Coast tend to eat more seafood than those located inland due to the availability of the product.

Location tends to create some natural market segments. Geographic proximity can be important for attracting customers. Manufacturers, for example, may draw customers nationally, but there is evidence that some types of local retailers attract a majority of their clients from less than ten miles. Many national sellers regionalize their products because of this factor of customer location. Chain grocery stores and department stores adjust their product lines to reflect local tastes. Grits, boiled peanuts, and turnips sold in southern grocery stores are not found in other areas of the nation. Major oil refineries localize their gasoline for temperature and humidity. Many magazines regionalize their publications to the liberal or conservative taste of persons in specific locations. The *Farm Journal*, *Playboy*, and *McCall's* all have regionalized issues. They appeal to specific market segments based on location.

Segments Based on Demographic Needs. Demographic factors deal with the vital statistics of the population.[9] No aspect of consumer behavior is more used by managers throughout the business than demographic factors. The reason is that so many facts are published relating to market size, attitudes, income, race, sex, education, and occupation.[10] Market segmenting involves placing persons with similar characteristics in the same segment. Thus we may identify male segments, segments for tall persons, segments by occupation, and income segments. Most government sources, such as the *Census of Business*, *Census of Population*, and *Statistical Abstracts*, provide a variety of demographic information as well as buying patterns which can be used as a basis for segmentation. Some private publications such as *Sales Management* and *Purchasing* use demographics to classify consumer information.

Certain products, such as women's clothing, men's clothing, Catholic Literature, toys, and diapers, can clearly be identified with a specific segment of the total market. They can also be associated with specific needs. Children want toys

Table 5-1
Household Characteristics

Basis for Segment	Classification
I. Geographic Area	
Region	Northeast; South Central; South; West
County	A; B; C; D by population size
City Size	10,000–25,000; 25,000–50,000; 50,000–100,000; 100,000–250,000; 250,000–500,000; 500,000–1,000,000; 1,000,000 or more.
Location	Suburbs; Rural
II. Demographic Factors	
Age	1–19; 20–34; 35–64; 65 over
Sex	Female; Male
Marital Status	Married; Single; Other
Children	None; 1–2; 3–4; 5 over
Occupation	Professional; Managers; Farmers; Clerical; Sales; Craftsmen; Operatives; Laborers; Service
Education	Grade school; high school; some college; college graduate
Income	Under $5,000; $5,000–9,999; $10,000–14,999; $15,000–19,999; $20,000–24,999; $25,000–34,999; $35,000–49,999; $50,000 and over
Nationality	American; British; German; French; Chinese; etc.
Religion	Protestant; Catholic; Jewish; Other
Race	White; Black; Oriental; Indian; Other
III. Psychographic Traits	Aggressiveness; Cooperativeness; Outgoingness; Self Assurance; Achievement; Leadership; Independence; Conservatism; Autonomy; Ambition; Activity; Impulsiveness; Loyalty; Self-Indulgence.
IV. Benefits Sought	Quality; Price; Efficiency; Economy; Dependability; Convenience; Service; Prestige; Security; Acceptance; Fulfillment; Self-expression; Esteem; Safety; Affection
V. Product Preferences	
Expenditures	None; Medium; Heavy
Product Awareness	Unaware; Partially Aware; Aware
Loyalty	None; Recognition; Preference; Insistence
Usage	Never; Seldom; Occasionally; Regular

Characteristics presented are consistent with those used in government publications, although some scales were collapsed to aid presentation.

Source: C. Glenn Walters, Wayne Norvell, and Sam Bruno, *Basic Marketing: A Situational Orientation* (Bessemer, Ala.: Colonial Press, 1988).

to keep them amused and to learn. Diapers are needed by parents to protect their children. Women's clothing and men's clothing are needed for protection and to maintain appearance. It is not so difficult to specify the nature of the market segment that is associated with some of these products. However, it may not be so simple to decide which part of a particular market segment will purchase a specific product. Thus segmentation by demographics may appear more simple than it really is.

The needs associated with some products are not so easily identified, nor is the market segment. For example, bricklayers and college professors may earn similar incomes, but they do not read the same magazines, live in the same type of homes, or seek the same type of recreation. It is often assumed that persons of a given nationality, race, and education have some common wants because of social interaction and culture. In fact, this assumption is often incorrect. Many Italians may like pasta, particularly if they are recent arrivals in the United States, but their taste in cars or clothing may be more associated with the neighborhood in which they live. Nevertheless, no good marketing executive would neglect demographics when segmenting the market.

Photo 5-1
Location is a factor in market segmentation. Many customer needs and preferences are regional in nature.

Photo 5-2

No aspect of consumer behavior is more used by managers throughout the business than demographic factors.

H.U.D.

Psychographic Motives Make Segments. Market segmentation based on psychographic factors of consumers that lead to specific types of motivation is of relatively recent origin. It groups customers according to their psychological reactions to the environment around them.[11] Persons who react in similar patterns are classed together. In one sense, psychographic segmentation deals with the total life-style of the individual or group.[12]

A low-income family is not going to have the same outlook toward garbage disposals or pest control that a middle class suburban dweller has. A conservative person wears different clothes, eats differently, and furnishes the home differently than a liberal person. Both types can be classed into meaningful market segments. A cautious individual may spend twice as much time shopping as one not so cautious. This fact certainly has a bearing on how marketers locate their businesses.

Psychographic segmentation is more difficult for managers to use because it deals with the mind. Managers must be very careful when identifying persons this way. A particular advantage of psychographic segmentation is the fact that it does not depend on physical characteristics. It recognizes that persons with different psychological characteristics may, in fact, have similar problems and thus similar wants. Psychographics attempts to discover why buyers act the way they do, segment on this basis, then make an appeal which is meaningful.

Benefits Used to Segment. When consumer segments are based on benefits it refers to grouping persons according to some common satisfaction they perceive in the product.[13] Benefit segmentation is founded on the marketing idea that people purchase solutions to problems rather than physical things.[14] We purchase because of what products can do for us.[15] Thus, a segmentation scheme that can group customers together, who desire specific product benefits is conceptually superior to most other means of segmentation. The problem with the method is that it is very difficult to ascertain which benefits persons perceive in the product, and it is equally difficult to determine which person seeks the same benefits.

The influence of consumers on the segmentation process is perhaps greatest when benefit segmentation is used. It involves more than simply counting noses, as with location and demographics. It involves more than simply identifying psychological traits, as in psychographics. Benefits segmentation involves discovering how mental attitudes are specifically related to attitudes toward the product. For example, we recognize three segments for watches based on benefits perceived. They are: (1) price-conscious, (2) quality-conscious, and (3) prestige-conscious. The problem is discovering how many persons in the firm's market perceive each of these benefits.

Segments Based on Preferences. The use of product preference to segment the market involves grouping consumers by known market behavior. Consumer influence on marketing strategy is to discover how consumers solved problems in the past and concentrate marketing strategy on their preferences. Consumers with similar purchase habits, tastes, or shopping patterns are grouped together into a market segment.[16] The concept is simple, but it is more difficult to carry out. Some preferences, like demographics, are easily obtained. There is no better indicator of buying preferences than expenditure patterns. Expenditures for many products are readily available from such government publications as the *Census of Business*, *City County Data Book*, and *Statistical Abstracts*.

Other preference patterns can be determined by observation. For example, one can count the number of persons visiting a store or trade area. Product usage, product or brand awareness, and brand loyalty are also good indicators of customer wants.[17] These data are more difficult to obtain. It may be necessary to use a questionnaire to obtain the desired information. The major problem with segments based on preferences is that they are grouped by historical data. Just because a consumer acted in a certain way previously does not necessarily mean that the customer will act that way again.

Relate Consumer Segment to Firm's Abilities. Once the basis for segmentation has been established, management can relate the segment to the firm's abilities previously established. The relationship is shown in Illustration 5-1. It is common when segmenting to combine several consumer characteristics rather than to use only one.[18] This combination of consumer characteristics is shown at the top of the figure, and the abilities of the firm are shown down the side. The

Illustration 5-1
Market segmentation grid: seller of desks

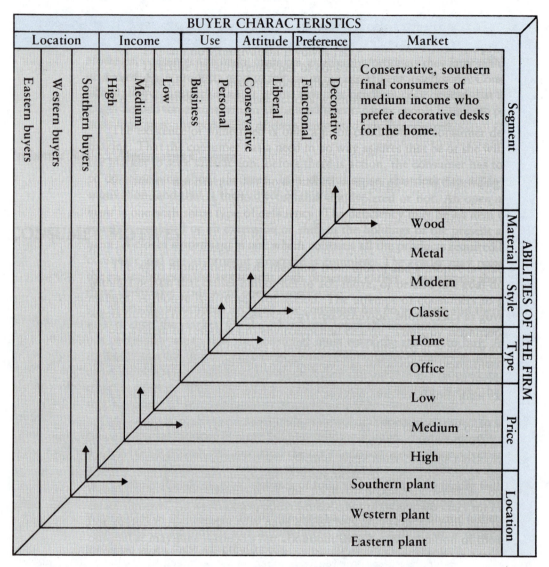

Source: C. Glenn Walters, Wayne Norvell, Sam Bruno, *Basic Marketing: A Situational Orientation,* (Bessemer, Ala.: Colonial Press, 1988).

arrows relate what the firm can do to consumer characteristics. For example, the firm makes wood furniture which appeals to consumers who want decorative rather than functional furniture. The firm makes classic furniture which appeals to conservative consumers. The upper right corner of the figure summarizes the firm's typical customer as "conservative, southern, final consumers of medium income who prefer decorative desks for the home."

The segmentation grid is only illustrative, and it is an aid to judgment. It can be as detailed as management desires. It could be expanded to show interaction where one company's ability relates to two or more customer characteristics or vice versa. A southern plant may reach both southern and midwestern consumers. Wood furniture may be both decorative and functional. The grid does tend to assure that all factors in the segmentation process are considered by management.

Identify Governments by Needs and Motives

We discussed consumer segmentation first as part of the marketing target, but in fact the order in which management considers groups in the target is of no particular importance. They must all be considered at some point. We now turn our attention to government agencies in the marketing target.

At some point in identifying the marketing target, government agencies that have a need or interest in the operation of the business must be taken into account. It is entirely appropriate to identify government agencies by these needs and interest. Table 5-2 has data on some of the important methods of identifying government agencies that affect the firm's marketing target.

Government needs and motives tend to relate to the manner of operation of the business. Government agencies need to collect taxes, they are motivated to arbitrate the fairness of competition, and they are required to see that rules and regulations are obeyed. Thus every one of the classes in Table 5-2 represents a need or motive that can be the basis for identifying government agencies that affect the firm. A local food store would only be interested in identifying local government agencies in its target, but a grocery chain may have to deal with government at the local, state, and national levels. The local grocery may identify tax and public service agencies such as the water works and electric company as important to it. The grocery chain may be involved with all types of government agencies.

Both the local grocery and national chain may be faced with governmental issues relating to environmental protection, business ethics and product quality. Government agencies, at all levels, would employ laws, taxes, contracts, regulations and threats to achieve compliance with their point of view.[19] The firm must identify which of these enforcement methods are important to its operations and then develop a way of dealing with each. The government agencies involved may have a probusiness, antibusiness, or neutral stand toward the firm, and its involvement may be intense or low. The firm would institute different policies in each of the latter two cases. The important point is that the firm identify all government agencies that have an effect on the firm's operations and develop specific policies to deal with each type of influence brought to bear by the government agencies involved.

As with consumers, the characteristics of government agencies affecting the firm must be related to the firm's abilities. Which government agencies can regulate the firm? Does product quality measure up to government standards, and does management have adequate quality testing? Does the firm comply with all licensing, zoning, price, and other regulations? Can management deal adequately with government agencies? The match must be sufficiently close that the firm can deal effectively with government agencies as a part of their daily routine.[20]

Table 5-2
External Groups' Characteristics

Type of group	Characteristic	Basis for Classification
Competitors, Governments, Special Interest Groups	I. Type of Issue	Public safety, Environmental protection, Minority rights, Business ethics and morality, Social change and innovation, Product quality, Fair prices, Business image, Product image, Public disclosure, Business responsibility, Lawful operations, Consumer protection, Fair competition, Allocation of resources, Efficiency, Public safety
	II. Type of organization	Government agencies (tax, police, public service, commissions, regulatory) Political parties, NAACP, Sierra Club, National Organization of Women, Klu Klux Klan, Audubon Society, Friends of the Earth, Common Cause, Moral Majority, Illinois Public Interest Research Group, Wilderness Society, Consumer groups, Better Business Bureaus, Women's Clubs, Educational Institutions, Churches, Minorities (youth, Blacks, senior citizens, women, men, gays), Firms, Labor Unions.
	III. Methods used	News releases, Magazine and Journal articles, Boycott, Threat, Public disclosure, Complaints, Letters to the editor, Letters to businesses. Newsletters, Public rallys, Sit-ins, Marketing, Laws, Taxes, Contracts, Regulations, Policies, Promotion Services
	IV. Type of activity	Political, Social, Economic
	V. Position taken	Pro-business, Anti-business, Neutral, Industry oriented or Individual Firm oriented
	VI. Involvement	Intense, Moderate, Low Violent or Nonviolent
	VII. Geographic	National, Regional, State, Local, Worldwide

Source: C. Glenn Walters, Wayne Norvell, Sam Bruno, *Basic Marketing: A Situational Orientation,* (Bessemer, Ala.: Colonial Press, 1988).

Identify Competitors by Needs and Motives

Competitors are an important part of the business marketing target. Management has about as much direct or indirect contact with competitors as it does with consumers. The fact is that almost every decision made by the organization's management impacts on competitors who will retaliate in some fashion.

Figure 5-2 shows some of the ways that competitors can be identified and classified by needs and motives. Competitors are other firms, and the business typically finds its competitors operating in the same geographic area as its own operations. Competitors always work against each other, but their involvement may be intense, moderate, or low. Competitors compete with similar or different policies that are designed to make them more efficient than your firm. These competitors may affect your firm through issues as product price, innovation, product image, product quality, allocation of resources, and management efficiency.

The identification of competitors is not too difficult in most cases. Management can simply visit competitive stores, talk to customers, read competitors' advertisements in the paper, talk to competitor salespersons, or even discuss issues with competitive managers at public gatherings. In this way, the number of competitors and their policies can be determined. It goes without saying that to a considerable degree, the success of the firm depends on how well competitors are identified and countered.

The firm is seeking some advantage when matching its abilities to competitor characteristics. Who are our competitors? How does our management stack up to competitive management? Is our product better, different, or lower-priced? How do our services compare to the competitors' services? What is our company image? It is in the matching that these and similar questions can be answered and included in our marketing strategy.

Identify Special Interest Groups by Needs and Motives

Special interest groups stand for the social and cultural environment in our society. Social and cultural issues are taken up by certain special interest groups and promoted by these groups. Figure 5-3 is an ad for a special interest group. In this way the needs and interests of the social and cultural environment are directly brought to the attention of business managers.

Special interest groups are perhaps the simplest and easiest to identify as part of the marketing target. That is because the group typically adopts a name associated with its issue and it publically pronounces what it wants from business. Special interest group identification is complicated because these groups often promote coalitions with government agencies, competitive businesses, and other special interest groups.

Most of the groups listed under type organization in Table 5-2 are special interest groups. Once you know the name of the group, it is not difficult to determine their needs, motives, and method of operation. Most of these organizations make such information public as a means of fostering their goals. Some are local but most are national. Most involve at least moderate to intense involvement with their particular issue, and some business managers tend to feel that they are anti-business. They use all means of political, social, and economic activity to promote their interests, and the methods they use include nearly all those listed in Table 5-2.

Matching special interest groups to the firm's abilities is not difficult, but it must be done with care. It is a matter of determining how these organizations' objectives match operations. Is our product socially acceptable? Does the firm use resources effectively? Does management relate well to people who represent special interest groups? Is management socially responsible without outside inducements? If the match is not sound, then the firm must either change to a better match or risk intense pressure from speical interest groups.

Figure 5-3

Special interest groups cannot be ignored in developing marketing targets

JAMESON PARKER: Husband, Father, Actor, Hunter, Member of
the National Rifle Association.

"Until a few years ago, I had hardly touched a gun.
And I certainly didn't know much about the NRA. But when I
began hunting and target shooting, a gun store owner
told me, 'The first thing you ought to do is join the NRA.' Frankly,
I was hesitant. But he gave me some NRA literature
and I began to see the NRA isn't what I perceived it to be.

"I realized the NRA is a bunch of intelligent people
that stand for the positive aspects of gun ownership. They teach
gun safety. They represent the millions of law-abiding
hunters, gun collectors and competitive shooters in this country.
Thank God they do. I love guns. I love hunting. I believe
in my right to defend my home and my family. But I also accept
the responsibilities that accompany these freedoms.

"You can tell my image of the NRA has really
changed. With my membership, I hope I can change a few
minds, too, about who the NRA
really is. It's people like me." **I'm the NRA.**

The NRA's Hunter Services Division offers programs and publications
for hunter safety and education, including the comprehensive "Basic Hunter's Guide."
If you would like more information about our publications,
or would like to join the NRA, write Harlon Carter, Executive Vice President,
P.O. Box 37484, Dept. JP-20, Washington, D.C. 20013.
Paid for by the members of the National Rifle Association of America. Copyright 1985.

National Rifle Association

Identify Suppliers by Needs and Motives

Suppliers are those organizations that make goods and services available to your business. Suppliers provide such raw materials as coal, iron ore, bauxite, ball bearings, cloth, motors, or pulleys. Suppliers also include labor unions and individuals who supply labor to the business and financial institutions who provide capital.

When it comes to identification in the marketing target, suppliers are very similar to special interest groups. They are known and they deal directly with the management of the business, so their attitudes are not too difficult to ascertain. Most suppliers operate on a cooperative basis with the firm's management. Exceptions occur when management seeks to renegotiate a labor agreement, renegotiate a raw materials contract, or default on a loan from the bank. Then the two roles may become adversarial. Success of the business can very definitely depend on being able to identify suppliers, their interests, and ambitions.

Can you identify some typical supplier classes based on needs and motives shown in Figure 5-2? Suppliers are firms and labor unions; they may cover any geographic area; they are typically highly involved, using economic activity; and they embrace all the same issues as competitors and special interest groups. It goes without saying that the identification of suppliers can be critical to the marketing target. Their needs and motives must be recognized and dealt with realistically if the firm is to succeed in the long run.

Matching supplier characteristics to the firm's abilities is often overlooked by management. The result can be poor supplier relationships. Management needs to be aware if supplier products fit company needs. Are supplier prices in line with the firm's ability to pay? Does our firm have effective personnel relationships with suppliers? What type of frictions exist? Are supplier services in line with our firm's requirements? The fit must be continually re-evaluated if the firm is to use suppliers in the most effective manner to obtain its objectives.

Determine Makeup of the Single Target

Once all the groups making up the marketing target of any firm have been identified, it is necessary to associate them together into the single target. We are not dealing with five separate targets, but five parts of the same target. The problem then is to combine the five separate groups once they have been identified. Table 5-3 illustrates a hypothetical target. We observe that this target has a small consumer group, average semidifferentiated competition, abundant costly quality-oriented suppliers, unimportant special interest groups, and neutral government. Of course, given a specific situation, any combination of groups is possible.

CAN THE TARGET BE REACHED?

The third step in determining the marketing target is to establish the feasibility of the target, or targets, that the business has recognized. It makes no sense to attempt to enter, or to continue servicing, a target where some factor, or factors, makes success highly unlikely. Management needs to know the circumstance

Photo 5-3
Suppliers' needs and motives must be recognized if the firm is to succeed.

© *Richard Younker*

Table 5-3
Target Feasibility Illustrated

Groups Comprising Marketing Target	Target Composition 1	Target Composition 2	Target Composition 3
1. *Market Segment*	*Small* / *Mass*	Medium / Segmented	Large / Multiple
2. Competition	Prohibitive / Differentiated	*Average* / *Semi-differentiated*	Weak / Non-differentiated
3. Suppliers	Unavailable / *Costly* / *Quality*	Adequate / Average / Average	*Abundant* / Bargain / Nonquality
4. Special Interest Groups	Incompatible / Fair	Compatible / Mixed	*Unimportant* / Unfair
5. Government	Unfavorable	*Neutral*	Favorable

Italics = Selected Target
Source: C. Glenn Walters, Wayne Norvell, Sam Bruno, *Basic Marketing: A Situational Orientation* (Bessemer, Ala.: Colonial Press, 1988).

under which marketing policy is being developed and implemented. Table 5-4 can be used as a basis for illustrating how target feasibility is determined.

As a general rule:

if management determines that any single group in the target is prohibitive to success, management should seek its opportunities in other targets.

Management would not seek to enter, or to maintain, marketing target 3 in Table 5-4. It has a small market, intense competition, high-cost suppliers, unfavorable special interest groups, and unfavorable government. On the other hand, marketing target 7 is one to enter or to keep, because there is no prohibitive factor. Which of the other identified targets in the table would you consider feasible?

Just one prohibitive factor can keep a firm from entering or maintaining a target. For example, no new firms can enter the market for water and electricity because they are government designated monopolies. Microwave pancakes, pizza sticks, and flavored grits did not succeed as targets because there were too few customers. On the other hand, Hammond organs are sold nationally, partly because there is very little competition. There are seldom more than a few thousand competitors at a given time. Of these, only a relative few are actively engaged in attempting to gain a product advantage over Hammond based on quality. There are even fewer government agencies that are concerned with the specific issue of Hammond product quality or distribution.

A business can typically weather more special interest group antagonism than consumer, government, or competitor antagonism. However, there are situations where special interest groups alone can cause a business to fail. For example, in some towns pornographic book stores have been put out of business by very active church groups even though they are legal and desired by large numbers of buyers. Atomic power plant projects have been stopped by special interest

Table 5-4
Determining Marketing Target Feasibility

Markets

		Large	Medium	Small	
		1	2	3	

Competition	**Intense competition**	Large markets
		Intense competition
		Favorable government
		Favorable special
		  interest groups
		High-cost suppliers
			Medium markets
			Intense competition
			Neutral government
			Neutral special interest
			  groups
			High-cost suppliers
				Small markets
				Intense competition
				Unfavorable government
				Unfavorable special
				  interest groups
				High-cost suppliers
					High cost

		4	5	6	

	Medium competition	Large markets
		Medium competition
		Favorable government
		Favorable special
		  interest groups
		Average-cost suppliers
			Medium markets
			Medium competition
			Neutral government
			Neutral special interest
			  groups
			Average-cost suppliers
				Small markets
				Medium competition
				Unfavorable government
				Unfavorable special
				  interest groups
				Average-cost suppliers
					Average cost

		7	8	9	

	Weak competition	Large markets
		Weak competition
		Favorable government
		Favorable special
		  interest groups
		Low-cost suppliers
			Medium markets
			Weak competition
			Neutral government
			Neutral special interest
			  groups
			Low-cost suppliers
				Small markets
				Weak competition
				Unfavorable government
				Unfavorable special
				  interest groups
				Low-cost suppliers
					Low cost

		Favorable	Neutral	Unfavorable	

Suppliers (right side)

Government and Special Interest Groups

Source: C. Glenn Walters, Wayne Norvell, Sam Bruno, *Basic Marketing: A Situational Orientation* (Bessemer, Ala.: Colonial Press, 1988).

groups. It goes without saying that management must consider very carefully the feasibility of each marketing target. It is also clear that consumers can be critical to the successful entry and maintenance of any marketing target. Without sufficient customers, no firm can make a successful appeal.

DEVELOP STRATEGY FOR EACH TARGET

The final step in target identification is to coordinate the target to the firm's abilities as previously discussed. In the final analysis, a firm's abilities become embodied into a marketing strategy. We identified this marketing strategy in Chapter 1 as consisting of (1) marketing targets and (2) a marketing mix. Every strategy has a goal and a means to achieve that goal. The goal of marketing strategy is to satisfy the wants and interests of persons making up the target. The

Illustration 5-2
Single target approach

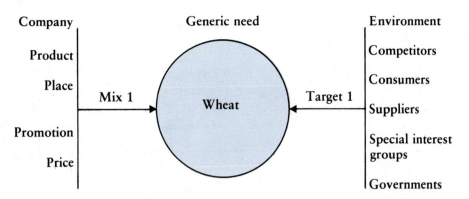

means to achieve this goal is the marketing mix (product, place, promotion, and price policies).

An appeal must be directed at satisfying the needs and motives identified with consumers, suppliers, special interest groups, competitors, and governments who make up the target. This appeal is made by relating product, place, promotion, and price policies to the needs and motives of the target. There are three approaches to this coordination process. They are the single target approach, the segmented target approach, and the multitarget approach. We shall observe that consumers are very important to each of these approaches.

Single Target Approach

The single target approach is used when the firm is distributing a generic product. The single target approach is illustrated in Illustration 5-2. The single target is characterized by mass markets (everyone has relatively homogeneous needs and motives), adequate suppliers, average competition primarily based on price, little government intervention, and indifferent special interest groups. Coordination is a matter of relating the firm's abilities that are embodied in the product, place, price, and promotion policies to the needs and motives held by suppliers, consumers, governments, special interest groups, and competitors. On the diagram we show mix 1 related to target 1 for the generic product wheat.

A completely generic single target probably does not exist in practice. However, the targets for such basic products as electricity, lumber, sugar, finger nail clippers, farm commodities, fresh fruit, and work clothes approach such targets. The consumer tends to be critical in these types of targets. Indeed, the entire question of whether to make an appeal to such targets may depend on whether there are sufficient consumers to support the firm. The other groups are not unimportant to the target, but the interests that they represent can be more readily dealt with.

The firm marketing to single targets tends toward the use of a single marketing mix, as illustrated. Although this mix affects all groups in the target, little

Illustration 5-3
Segmented target approach

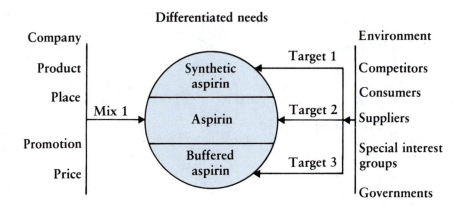

attention is paid to these groups, except for consumers, when management formulates the mix. The mix is simplified with minimal promotion directed at stimulating generic demand. Several marketing channels may be used to obtain the widest distribution. Price is important because with little to distinguish the product, the purchase decision is based on price. There is typically very little service in the sale of generic products.

Segmented Target Approach

Illustration 5-3 shows a segmented approach to coordinating marketing policy to the needs and motives of groups in different targets. This situation exists when the generic target can be differentiated by variations in basic needs and motives. The generic product show in the figure is pain suppressants, and the firm shown distributing to target 2 may be Bayer. A different firm that makes Tylenol may distribute to target 1, while a third firm, say the maker of Bufferin, may distribute to target 3. Other examples of segmented targets include private housing, fashion clothing, hardware, sports equipment, and ice cream.

A segmented target is characterized by smaller, more specialized markets, each with slightly different wants and motives. Competition is typically keen with more emphasis on special features of the product and quality than on price. Suppliers often sell across the entire generic market to all segments. Special interest groups and government agencies tend to take more interest in firms selling to segmented targets. Their interests range all the way from environmental protection to the establishment and enforcing of standards of manufacturer and sales.

The importance of consumers varies greatly in segmented targets—all the way from the most critical group to the least critical. One thing is sure, and that is that the consumer can never be ignored in segmented targets. For example, consumers are critical in the distribution of fashion clothing, canned foods, and furniture. The consumer and competition are about equal in importance for the sale of automobiles. It would be difficult to say whether consumers or government are more important to a firm distributing cigarettes. The firms have large markets in-

Illustration 5-4
Multitarget approach

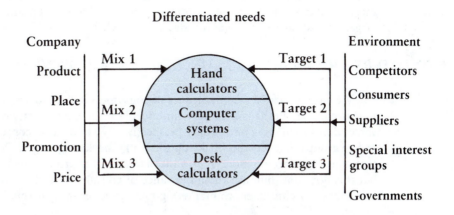

Differentiated needs

dicating the importance of consumers, but government restrictions placed on the sale of cigarettes greatly influence consumer buying.

A segmented approach to coordination means that the firm seeks to match its product, place, promotion, and price policies to the needs and motives associated with only one of the available targets. Specific attributes of the product are designed to influence persons within the five groups making up the selected target segment.[21] Price is important to the mix, but it may be higher or lower than competitor's depending on product quality. The marketing channel is highly specialized so that the product will reach specific customers.[22] Promotion is also personalized to fit the wants and interest of buyers, governments, special interest groups, suppliers, and competitors.

Multiple Targets

The multitarget approach to the coordination of target needs and motives to the abilities of the firm is the most complex of all. It is shown in Illustration 5-4. It involves separate marketing mixes directed at more than one target at a time.[23] In the illustration, we have a firm, perhaps IBM, that is making appeals to three separate targets within the calculator industry. The firm is using three different variations of its marketing mix to accomplish this end.

The characteristics of the multiple target is the same as that discussed for the segmented target. The only difference is that the firm is coordinating its abilities to several targets at the same time. Consumers have the same type of influence in this situation.

There may be problems with developing and implementing several promotional campaigns more or less simultaneously.[24] There can be increased pressure on marketing channels, particularly transportation and storage—there is a need to move and store more different types of products. Individual advertising campaigns must be developed for each target, and salespersons must be trained. It is unlikely that a single advertising campaign or sales training program will work for each product variation. These campaigns involve extra cost and have an increased chance of failure as problems become more complex. There is even increased pressure to change or modify the product more often and the cost associated with that. Of course, if sales and revenue increase significantly because of more products sold to more customers, then it is worth appealing to multiple targets. Most larger companies today are invovled with multitarget marketing.

CONSUMERS ARE BASIC TO MARKETING STRATEGY

We have indicated the importance of consumers in every discussion presented in this chapter. Perhaps it is now time to place the overall importance of consumer decision making into proper perspective. We know that consumers are one of five groups that together make up the firm's marketing target. Does this mean that consumers are no more important than the other groups? In a sense it does, but this does not diminish the importance of consumers. It does follow that the importance of consumers to marketing managers lies in their relationship to the target.

We know now that the marketing target is basic to all marketing strategy, and this strategy lies at the heart of marketing. The simple fact is that the marketing target can never be a viable entity without sufficient consumers to support it. We realize that sufficient consumers will not alone support a business, since any group making up the target may present a situation that makes success prohibitive. However, it also follows that a firm cannot be successful without a market. Thus, while consumers do not stand alone in the target, they are absolutely vital to it. Just as the target lies at the heart of marketing strategy, so consumers lie at the heart of the target. Everything undertaken by marketing managers must take into account the needs and motives of consumers.

No text on consumer behavior would be complete without demonstrating the connection between consumer decision making and the marketing mix. For this reason, each section of this text ends with one or more chapters relating consumers to the marketing mix. In the next chapter we take up the product as part of that mix. Later chapters deal with distribution (place), promotion, and price. We begin with the marketing target because of its essential relationship to the mix as a whole.

QUESTIONS

1. What is a marketing target? Explain.
2. Which group is most important to the marketing target? Explain.
3. Explain and relate briefly the steps involved in selecting the external group target. Are all these steps necessary? Discuss.
4. What is a market audit? In what way is this audit used in the selecting of external targets?
5. What is a market? Give some examples of markets.
6. Explain market segment. Explain market segmentation. How is a market segment related to a realized market?

7. What are the major consumer characteristics used to segment markets? Explain psychographic and benefit segmentation.
8. Use consumer characteristics to identify market segments for Swiss Colony Cheese and Beltone Hearing Aids.
9. Discuss how consumer needs relate to market segmentation.
10. Discuss how governments relate to the marketing target. How are relevant governments identified?
11. Explain how a marketing manager combines the five groups into a single target. Illustrate.
12. What is involved with determining the feasibility of the marketing target? Explain.
13. Use Table 5-4 to identify the target market for a basic marketing textbook. A pair of dress shoes. A set of radial tires.
14. What are the three approaches to coordinating marketing policy to marketing targets?
15. Contrast marketing policy for a segmented target and the multitarget approaches.

NOTES

1. Terrell Williams, Mark Slama, and John Rogers, "Behavioral Characteristics of the Recreational Shopper and Implications for Retail Management," *Journal of the Academy of Marketing Science*, Vol. 13 (Summer 1985), pp. 307–16
2. Alice M. Tybout and John R. Hauser, "A Marketing Audit Using a Conceptual Model of Consumer Behavior: Application and Evaluation," *Journal of Marketing*, Vol. 45 (Summer 1981), pp. 82–100.
3. Yoram Wind, "Introduction to Special Section on Marketing Segmentation Research," *Journal of Marketing Research*, Vol. XV (August 1978), pp. 315–16; Yoram Wind, "Issues and Advances in Segmentation Research," *Journal of Marketing Research*, Vol. XV (August 1978), pp. 317–37.
4. Johny K. Johansson, "Market Segmentation with Multivariate Aid," *Journal of Marketing*, Vol. 45 (Winter 1981), pp. 74–78.
5. Richard C. Becherer, "Using Marketing Segmentation to Develop Effective HMO Marketing Strategy: An Application," in David M. Klein and Allen E. Smith, eds., *Marketing: The Next Decade, 1985* (Boca Raton, Fla. and Southern Marketing Assn., 1985), pp. 219–22.
6. The types of characteristics presented are consistent with those used in government publications, although some scales were collapsed to aid presentation.
7. Charles A. Ingene and Robert F. Lusch, "Market Selection Decisions for Department Stores," *Journal of Retailing*, Vol. 56 (Fall 1980), pp. 21–40; Alan J. Greco, "Linking Dimensions of the Elderly Market to Actionable Market Segmentation," in David M. Klein and Allen E. Smith, eds., *Marketing: The Next Decade* (Boca Raton, Fla. and Southern Marketing Assn., 1985), pp. 127–30.

8. William O. Bearden, Jesse E. Teel, Jr., and Richard M. Durand, "Media Usage, Psychographic, and Demographic Dimensions of Retail Shoppers," *Journal of Retailing*, Vol. 54 (Spring 1978), pp. 65–74.

9. John J. Burnett, "Psychographic and Demographic Characteristics of Blood Donors," *Journal of Consumer Research*, Vol. 8 (June 1981), pp. 62–66.

10. Jagdish N. Sheth, "Demographics in Consumer Behavior," *Journal of Business Research*, Vol. 5 (June 1977), pp. 129–38.

11. Timothy Hartman and David Richmond, "Psychographics Segments of the Campus Beer Market," in Carol H. Anderson, Rajinder Arora, Blaise J. Bergiel, Sion Raveed, and Ronald L. Vaughn, eds., *Midwest Marketing Association 1981 Conference Proceedings* (Southern Illinois University at Carbondale and Midwest Marketing Assn., 1981), pp. 57–63.

12. See: Sadrudin A. Ahmed and Douglas N. Jackson, "Psychographics for Social Policy Decisions: Welfare Assistance," *Journal of Consumer Research* (March 1979), pp. 229–39; Richard C. Becherer, Lawrence M. Richard, and James B. Wiley, "Predicting Market Behavior: Are Psychographics Really Better?" *Journal of the Academy of Marketing Science* (Spring 1977), pp. 75–84; and William D. Wells, "Psychographics: A Critical Review," *Journal of Marketing Research* (May 1975), pp. 196–213.

13. Kenneth E. Miller and Kent L. Granzin, "Simultaneous Loyalty and Benefit Segmentation of Retail Store Customers," *Journal of Retail*, Vol. 55 (Spring 1979), pp. 47–60.

14. Kenneth D. Bahn and Kent L. Garnzin, "Benefit Segmentation in the Restaurant Industry," *Journal of the Academy of Marketing Science*, Vol. 13 (Summer 1985), pp. 226–47.

15. James H. Myers, "Benefit Structure Analysis: A New Goal for Product Planning," *Journal of Marketing*, (October 1976), pp. 23–22; Roger J. Calantone and Alan Sawyer, "The Stability of Benefit Segments," *Journal of Marketing Research* (August 1978), pp. 394–404.

16. Manoj K. Agarwal and Brian T. Tatchford, "Estimating Demand Functions for Product Characteristics: The Case of Automobiles," *Journal of Consumer Research*, Vol. 7 (December 1980), pp. 249–62.

17. Robert C. Blattberg, Thomas Buesing and Subrata K. Sen, "Segmentation Strategies for New National Brands," *Journal of Marketing*, (Fall 1980), pp. 59–66.

18. Zarrel V. Lambert, "Profiling Demographic Characteristics or Alienated Consumers," *Journal of Business Research*, Vol. 9 (1981), pp. 65–86.

19. George A. Steiner, "New Patterns in Government Regulation of Business," *MSU Business Topics*, Vol. 26 (Autumn 1978), pp. 53–64.

20. Fred Thompson and Larry R. Jones, "Fighting Regulation: The Regulatory Review," *California Management Review,* Vol. XXIII (Winter 1980), pp. 5–19.

21. Mark Moriarty and M. Venkatesan, "Concept Evaluation and Market Segmentation," *Journal of Marketing,* Vol. 42 (July 1978), pp. 82–86.

22. Michael Etgar, "Selection of an Effective Channel Control Mix," *Journal of Marketing*, Vol. 42 (July 1978), pp. 53–58.
23. Frederick W. Winter, "A Cost-Benefit Approach to Market Segmentation," *Journal of Marketing*, Vol. 43 (Fall 1979), pp. 103–11.
24. George S. Day, Allan D. Shocker and Rajendra K. Srivastava, "Customer-Oriented Approaches to Identifying Product Markets," *Journal of Marketing*, Vol. 43 (Fall 1979), pp. 8–19.

Product Development

To Solve Problems

CHAPTER OUTLINE

I. **IDENTIFICATION OF THE PRODUCT**
   A. Product as a Consumer Benefit
   B. Product Mix Addresses Multiple Consumer Wants
   C. Product Width and Depth Relate to Different Wants

II. **PROBLEM RECOGNITION DURING NEW PRODUCT DEVELOPMENT**
   A. Problem Recognition during Idea Generation
   B. Problem Recognition during Screening
   C. Problem Recognition during Development
   D. Problem Recognition during Test Marketing
   E. Problem Recognition during Commercialization
   F. Opposition to New Products
   G. Technology in Problem Recognition

III. **PROBLEM RECOGNITION OVER THE PRODUCT LIFE CYCLE**
   A. Recognition Most Critical at Introduction
   B. Recognition Increases during Growth
   C. Recognition Declines at Maturity
   D. Special Problem Recognition in Decline Stage
   E. Product Life Cycle and Problem Recognition

IV. **PROBLEM RECOGNITION AND PRODUCT DELETION**

V. **PROBLEM RECOGNITION OVER THE ADOPTION AND DIFFUSION PROCESSES**
   A. The Adoption Process Involves Recognition
   B. The Diffusion Process and Recognition
      1. *Innovators Have Unique Problems*
      2. *Early Adopters Are Quick to Recognize Problems*
      3. *Early Majority Follow in Recognition*
      4. *Late Majority Go with the Crowd*
      5. *Laggards Have Different Problems*
   C. Innovations Affect Adoption and Diffusion

VI. PROBLEM RECOGNITION RELATED TO PRODUCT ATTRIBUTE
A. Problem Recognition and Branding
B. Problem Recognition and Packaging
C. The Importance of Labeling to Problem Recognition
D. Supporting Services and Problem Recognition

CHAPTER OBJECTIVES:

After completing your study of Chapter 6, you should be able to:

1. Discuss how products are developed to solve problems.
2. Define a product.
3. Discuss the dimensions of a product.
4. Relate product recognition and new product development.
5. Discuss problem recognition over the product life cycle.
6. Explain the relationship of problem recognition to product deletion.
7. Discuss problem recognition over the adoption and diffusion processes.
8. Discuss how problem recognition is related to product attributes.

A day rarely passes in which a consumer does not recognize such problems as a gasoline tank approaching empty or the lack of proper shoes for an upcoming party. The unexpected breakdown of a major appliance like a washing machine or air conditioner creates problems that are more difficult to resolve. Some subtle problems, related to our desires, such as the decision to buy a home computer or microwave oven, may take longer to recognize. The kind of action consumers take in response to recognized problems relates directly to the available product.

The development of effective products by marketers begins with thoroughly evaluating the marketplace to identify consumer problems that the firm has the ability to satisfy. The basic hallmark of successful companies is identifying and meeting the problems faced by their consumers. Today product strategy is a high-risk marketing effort in an increasingly hostile environment. Yet, this vital activity, when the company successfully develops products to meet the consumer's problems, can win for the firm an increased market share, greater profitability, and survival.

IDENTIFICATION OF THE PRODUCT

It is important to identify the terms and concepts marketers use when discussing products and relating them to consumer decision making. At this point we need definitions of what is meant by the terms "product" and "product mix."

Product as a Consumer Benefit

Most consumers think they know what is meant by a product. Consumers understand that such physical items as shirts, potatoes, shoes, paper and blankets are products. Of course they are right, but products are much more than physical things. A hair cut, legal advice, and baby sitting are also products, as are accounting, travel, and banking consultants:

Broadly conceived, products are any physical or intangible benefits offered to consumers by profit or not-for-profit organizations.

Intangible services have become so important that they account for more of the consumer's income than tangible goods. Consumers now have greater choice when solving their problems between tangible products or intangible services. For example, if you were in need of a ladder, you could purchase it from Wal-Mart or rent it from Rent-All. Companies must now recognize these consumer options when developing new products or modifying old ones.

This broadened concept of a product, sometimes referred to as the *total product* concept or *extended product*, means that when we talk about products, two situations are possible.[1] We may have a physical good like a washer plus the service (delivery, repairs, installation) that surround it. We may also have a service product like a haircut and all the physical products (clippers, barber chair, tonics) that are necessary for its performance. The fact is that every product includes both physical and service components. We think of a haircut as a service

Photo 6-1
Intangible services now account for more of the consumer dollar than tangible goods.

Copyright © 1987, The Walt Disney Company

only because that is the most obvious component, and we think of a computer as a "thing" only because the physical component is the most obvious. Both the haircut and the computer are products, capable of satisfying a consumer's need or want.

Product Mix Addresses Multiple Consumer Wants

A company may use its knowledge of consumers multiple wants to group several products to satisfy their problems. This combination of individual items carried by a firm is its *product mix*. The product mix should always reflect consumer problems. For example, one company provides a mix of shampoos because consumers want different sizes, prices, and chemical makeup (oily, medium, dry hair). Cycle dog food was developed by General Foods in response to a segment of dog owners concerned about the health of their dogs and the nutrition they receive from dog food. There are four versions of Cycle: Cycle 1 — for puppies up to one year, Cycle 2 — for young adult dogs, Cycle 3 — for overweight dogs, and Cycle 4 — for older dogs. These were all developed because a significant number of consumers perceived that their dogs had different needs depending on age, amount of exercise, and physical makeup.

The *product mix* is made up of the *product item(s)* and the *product line* that a firm carries. For example, Gillette manufactures razors, cigarette lighters, writing pens, shaving cream, office supplies and appliances. Among its brands are Atra, Trac II, Cricket, Papermate, Flair, Foamy, Liquid Paper, and Supercurl, just to name a few.

A *product item* is a specific model, brand, or size of a product that the firm sells, such as an 11 oz. can of Foamy, 14¾ oz. can of Campbell's tomato soup, or a 4-door Cutlass. A product line usually is differentiated by characteristics such as price, size, or brand, and identified with its own stockkeeping number. A *product line* is a group of product items closely related either because they satisfy a class of needs, are used together, are sold to the same market, are marketed through the same outlets, or fall within given price ranges. For example, Gillette makes and markets Earth Born, Toni, and Silkience shampoos, Campbell sells many varieties of canned soups and products, and lawyers provide many different services (such as defense, wills, and divorces) for customers.

Product Width and Depth Relate to Different Wants

A typical retail store may have thousands of products in its mix, as illustrated in Table 6-1. *Width* of the product mix measures the number of separate product lines carried by the company. Table 6-1 shows that Gillette has a product width of four: lighters, razors, deodorants, and office supplies. The firm designs its width with major consumer problems in mind. Gillette deals with the problems associated with removing facial hair, eliminating body odor, creating fire, and routine office administration. Usually the *variety* of a product mix is measured by the number of different types of items offered to consumers in each product line. Variety assures the consumer that there is sufficient variation among similar products to express individuality and that there are sufficient items on hand so that

Table 6–1

Gillette Product Mix, Selected Products

	Product Width			
	Lighters	Razors	Deodorants	Office Supplies
Product Line, Variety, and Depth	100 Braun 150 DuPont 75 Cricket	200 Atra 30 Swivel 150 Trac II 80 Gillette 30 Daisy 100 Good News	500 Right Guard 300 Soft & Dri 150 Dry Idea	810 Liquid Paper

the consumer need not worry about availability. For example, Gillette has three types of lighters, each offered to satisfy a different target market. *Depth* is the number of items of each type carried. Depth is 100 for Braun, 200 for Atra, and 500 for Right Guard.

Some companies have a very narrow product mix. If a store sells only soup, carries only two brands, and has limited quantities of each, we say its product mix is both narrow and shallow; that is, the width and depth of the product mix is limited. On the other hand, if a company sells only soup, offers twenty brands, and has large quantities of each brand, we say it has a narrow product mix and the depth is considerable.

Specific items in a product line show the company's response to the different problems it perceives consumers to have. For example, Procter & Gamble's shampoo appeals to that part of the market concerned with dandruff, while Prell appeals to those who want a general-purpose family shampoo. Though the Audi Fox and Volkswagen Dasher are made by the same manufacturer, they appeal to different target markets because they are specific solutions to different consumer problems. Mechanically, the Audi and Volkswagen satisfy the same need for transportation, but they satisfy different psychological needs related to economy, power, styling, and trade-in value. As a result, they are distributed through different marketing channels using different promotion and pricing.

PROBLEM RECOGNITION DURING NEW PRODUCT DEVELOPMENT

Marketing efforts play a role in triggering problem recognition either by highlighting the ideal situation or by showing the inadequacies of the present situation. Nevertheless, the stimulation of problem recognition through any type of marketing activity is far more difficult than it might seem from the discussion thus far.

Management cannot always wait for consumers to recognize problems before they develop products to satisfy consumers. Most often product development by a firm is a response to perceived or anticipated problems that consumers have.[2] The amount of time required to get a new product to a market can be risky and extensive and so firms must be very careful during product development.[3] It took sixteen years to research and introduce the first automatic transmission,

Illustration 6-1

The new products development process

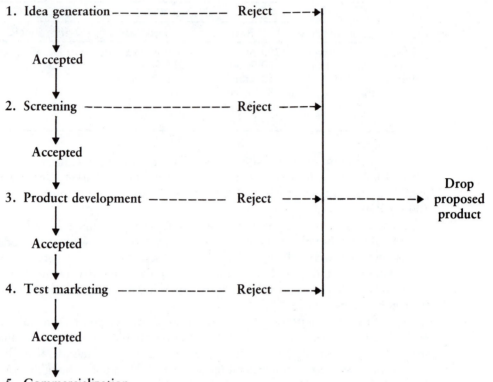

1. Idea generation ————————— Reject ———▶
   ↓
   Accepted
   ↓
2. Screening ————————————— Reject ———▶
   ↓
   Accepted
   ↓
3. Product development ———————— Reject ———▶ ————————▶ **Drop proposed product**
   ↓
   Accepted
   ↓
4. Test marketing ——————————— Reject ———▶
   ↓
   Accepted
   ↓
5. Commercialization

twenty-two years for instant coffee, and thirty-three years for fluorescent lights.[4] At supermarkets alone, over a thousand products are introduced annually. Depending on how one defines failure, the failure rate for new products ranges between 50 and 80 percent.

A new product designed to meet, or anticipate, consumer wants goes through the five phases of *New Product Development* shown in Illustration 6-1. They are: (1) idea generation, (2) screening, (3) product development, (4) test marketing, and (5) commercialization. The basic purpose of presenting this process is to show some of the events involved with planning and how problem recognition by consumers is considered in every phase of planning. Manufacturers typically begin the development process with idea generation, while retailers and wholesalers typically concentrate on screening finished products. It is important to remember that a proposed new idea or product can be rejected at any stage of the development process.

Problem Recognition during Idea Generation

Profit and not-for-profit organizations seek product and service ideas that help them achieve their objectives by solving consumer problems. *Idea generation* is the continuous, systematic search for new products or concepts with the potential to satisfy some consumer want. Idea generation is difficult, and only a few ideas are good enough to become commercially successful.[5] Pharmaceutical manufacturers estimate that only one out of every 6000 new drug ideas ever reaches the market. Chemical products manufacturers expect one out of 1000 to get to the marketplace. Overall, the failure rate of new products ranges between 50 and 80 percent. The reason for the high failure rate is that firms are anticipating solutions to consumer problems rather than responding to known problems. Many times these proposed products: (1) do not address a real consumer problem, (2) do not satisfy the problem or (3) cannot be successfully produced and marketed.

Idea generation requires that management keep close contact with consumers and understand their problems. It is necessary to delineate effective sources of new ideas and methods for generating them. Suggestions for new products are obtained from any source that has insights into consumer needs. These sources may be internal (employees, managers, consultants) or external (channel members, competitors, government, and consumers). Methods of generating new ideas include chance, formal research, and brainstorming where small-group sessions utilize open discussions to encourage a wide range of ideas.

New product ideas often start from internal sources. When a salesperson reports a consumer problem, a new product idea may be in the making. Large firms sometimes have research and development departments that employ scientists and engineers to identify consumer problems and develop interesting solutions. A Minnesota Mining and Manufacturing company engineer invented Scotch tape because consumers had a problem in bonding paper. DuPont scientists developed nylon in response to consumer needs for a strong light material. Any department in the organization can be a logical internal source of new product ideas. For example, advertising, marketing research, and production people might be able to see defects in existing products manufactured by a competitor. Ideas should be encouraged from all company personnel, from the top of the organization to the bottom.

Many new product ideas begin with external sources. Government and private sources are particularly fruitful. Many types of research are so expensive only the government can afford to engage in them. Consider all the products that have come out of space research by the government—including Teflon, computers, and worldwide television. The General Foods company discovered a valuable and unexpected idea when Johns Hopkins medical researchers found that when coconut oil is agitated in combination with other ingredients, it whips up very much like fresh cream. The researchers were trying to develop a coconut oil based plasma substitute.

Many of the most successful new product ideas begin with consumers. They answer the question: "How can the customer's needs be better served at a profit?" The importance of generating new product ideas cannot be overstated. Yet in bad economic times, research and development budgets and expenditures for consumer research are often the first to be cut back. The company that continues to spend in bad times is better able to enjoy good times.

Problem Recognition during Screening

Potential ideas that emerge from idea generation are forwarded to the screening stage. *Screening* is the evaluation of the feasibility of new product ideas in terms of workability, materials, cost, revenue, and ability to satisfy the consumer's recognized problem. Problem recognition is essential to this step because the broad aim of screening is to test product ideas against the consumer's recognized problem. *Preliminary screening* is carried out to separate ideas with greatest potential to solve consumer problems from those that do not. It is important to remember that the product must meet company objectives (i.e., profit) as well as solve consumer problems. If the product does not satisfy both the consumer and the company, it is dropped.

Final screening involves a comprehensive study of the consumer market for the new product. Final screening is a serious, critical step because the idea that survives is moved on into product development. Screening procedures are designed to identify the advantages and shortcomings of a product and what contribution it can make to the firm's success. The firm also checks to see that the product is compatible with its abilities, experience with advertising similar products or advertising to the same customers, a strong network of distributors, available capital, and manufacturing skills. In other words, when the consumer recognizes the problem, he or she should turn to the new product for satisfaction. Many ideas are discarded at the screening stage. Compared with other phases of the development process, the largest number of product ideas are rejected during screening.

Problem Recognition during Development

Once an idea has been screened and approved, it goes to the people responsible for research and development. Their job is *product development,* in which the idea is given a physical form designed specifically to satisfy the consumer's problem. This step typically involves building and testing a prototype product. The primary purpose of the development stage is to ascertain whether it is technically feasible to produce a product that can address the consumer's problems. Every feature of the product must be designed to satisfy the consumer's problem. One aspect of this consumer response is cost. The product must be produced at a cost low enough to attract a sufficient market. Style's effect on consumer satisfaction is considered at this point as well as alternative materials. Special consideration is given to consumer reaction to the physical product.[6]

The various ingredients that make up the marketing mix also must be developed for testing during the development stage. Copyrights, advertising copy, packaging, and labeling must be reviewed to determine legal ramifications. The promotional elements (i.e., sales promotion, personal selling) and distribution must be made at this time to ensure the effective integration of all elements in the marketing mix. Product development can be quite costly. Innovative consumer products often cost a million dollars or more for development. General Motors spent $2.7 billion in developing its "x-body" series of cars, which were subsequently named Oldsmobile Omega, Pontiac Phoenix, Chevrolet Citation, and Buick Skylark.[7]

In testing consumer reaction to the physical product, a method that is frequently used is called the consumer panel. A *consumer panel* consists of selected persons who are given samples of the product to test through use. The panel members keep a record of when they use the product and comment on its strengths and weaknesses. Among the problems with this method are that consumers tend to react favorably to all products they test, and they often make erroneous comparisons between the new product and one previously used. A variation on the consumer panel occurs when marketing researchers carefully select a sample of consumers and give them the new product together with a comparable competitive model for use or consumption during a specified time period. According to the reports of this panel, final refinements are incorporated in the design. If, after all the results have been taken into account, a decision is made to reject a product, the planning effort ends with this stage. However, if the product survives the product development stage, the firm moves on to the test marketing stage.

Problem Recognition during Test Marketing

The only way a firm can really know whether consumers will buy a product is to offer it for sale. *Test marketing* consists of offering the new product for sale in selected markets where actual purchase conditions are duplicated as near as possible. The consumer's product recognition is essential at this stage because the finished prototype product containing a bundle of satisfactions is tested against the consumer's specific recognized problem. Products that relate well are accepted for production. Test marketing involves all the distribution, pricing, services, promotion and other activities of marketing strategy — but on a small scale. Coca-Cola, for example, test marketed Mello Yello in Clarksburg, West Virginia, measured the advertising awareness level and the trial puchase rate, and decided to expand into a major portion of the country.

Test marketing enables the product to be analyzed in a real world setting. Rather than inquire about consumer intentions, test marketing allows actual consumer behavior to be observed. It considers whether the product is perceived as a satisfactory solution to the consumer's problem. The firm can also learn about competitor reactions and the response of channel members. On the basis of test marketing, the company can go ahead with its plans on a larger scale, modify the product and then expand its effort, modify the marketing plan and then expand its effort, or drop the product. Test marketing is used by companies of all sizes to minimize the risks of product failure. The dangers of introducing an untested product include undercutting already profitable products and (if the product should fail) losing credibility with distributors and consumers.

Although test marketing has been successful in many cases, some marketing executives now question its effectiveness and downplay this stage in the new product planning process.[8] They are dissatisfied with test marketing because it is expensive, it provides information to competitors, and it predicts national results based only on one or two test markets. The impact of external factors, such as economic conditions, weather, and interference by competitors during the test, can also affect the results. In the late 1960s Procter & Gamble test marketed in

Denver a new spray cleaner product called Cinch. The test results were very favorable because the leading competitor, Harrell International, had advance knowledge of it. Harrell withdrew all support from its Formula 409 brand in the Denver area, and brokers were discouraged from refilling the shelves when stock depletion occurred. Procter & Gamble based its decision to market Cinch nationally on sales projections derived from this test. As soon as Procter & Gamble began its national product introduction promotional effort, Harrell ran a special offer that allowed consumers to purchase a six-month supply of Formula 409. Cinch had to be withdrawn from the market less than a year after its "successful" test.[9]

Test marketing can allow nontesting competitors to catch up with the innovative firm by the time the product is ready for national distribution. Table 6-2 shows five cases, in which test marketing actually enabled competitors to reach the national market before the original firm did.[10]

If the product fails in the test market, the decision not to market the product is reasonable and the product is subsequently dropped. However, if the test market results indicate a good probability of success, the product becomes a candidate for full-scale production and introduction into the marketplace.

Table 6–2
Test Market Brands Beat Out by Competitor Brands

First Brand to Begin in Test Market	First Brand Introduced Nationally
Arm in Arm Deodorant (Helene Curtis)	Arm & Hammer Deodorant (Church & Dwight)
Cooking Ease (Clorox)	Mazola No-Stick (CPC International)
Prima Salsa Tomato Sauce (Hunt-Wesson)	Ragu Extra Thick & Zesty (Cheeseborough-Pond)
Maxim (General Foods)	Taster's Choice (Nestlé)
High Yield Coffee (Hills Brothers)	Folger's Flakes (Procter & Gamble)

Problem Recognition During Commercialization

The final step in new product development is commercialization. A product that has survived all the other steps is placed on the market at *commercialization.* This stage is the "test of the pudding." It is really quite simple to initiate. The company simply expands the implementation of the marketing mix, tested and adjusted during the test market, to the entire market. Of course, no test market ever exactly duplicates the real world. Therefore, those products that are successful may require some further adjustment in marketing strategy. It is a safe assumption that those products that are legal, competitive, consumer problem—oriented, socially justified and resource effective—will succeed in the marketplace.[11]

Opposition to New Products

Not all consumers, when recognizing a problem, desire new products or innovations. The Volkswagen is a case where consumers, for many years, preferred less change. The consumer tends to purchase the product that best satisfied their problem in the past instead of trying something new. The usual reasons given for desiring less change include the following.

First, most consumers simply resist change. People are conservative and feel comfortable with the known and understood. It typically takes considerable inducement to jolt them out of their habits. Second, consumer loyalty is a situation akin to a closed mind. The consumer is unwilling to consider any alternative. Third, the consumer may perceive that the manufacturer has perfected the existing product. They simply will not admit that another product can be better. They may also feel that, if improvement is possible, the manufacturer of their preferred product is the most likely to bring about a real improvement. Fourth, the opportunity to buy replacement parts or products may tie consumers to one product. This might be true if an individual is designing a room or stereo system. They want to know that they can get a replacement piece without changing the design. Of course, it is the marketer's place to jolt consumers out of their comfortable reliance on familiar products and make a change.

Technology in Problem Recognition

There has been a great deal of argument as to whether new products result from consumer pressures for change or from business pressures for sale. New product development invariably leads to product obsolescence. In fact, new products do frequently result from both business pressure to meet internal objectives and from recognized consumer problems.

Obsolescence takes several forms. *Planned obsolescence* is designed to meet the changes perceived as *wanted* by the consumer. It attempts to meet company objectives by satisfying the consumer. There are three types of planned obsolescence. *Technological obsolescence* is innovation in response to anticipated customer problems, and there has been some real and beneficial change in the product as measured by technical standards. This obsolescence is very similar to the concept of major innovation where some technological breakthrough results in a completely new product or idea (for example, where the company introduces a cassette stereo to replace the eight-track stereo). *Postponed obsolescence* is putting off technological improvements until the market recognizes the problem. For example, microwave ovens were being used for ten years by industry before the consumer recognized them as a viable alternative. Technology responds only to currently perceived consumer problem recognition.

Style or *fashion obsolescence* occurs when minor or superficial changes are made in the product in response to the need of many consumers for newness and novelty relative to others. The yearly modifications in high-fashion clothing, automobiles, and appliances fall into this category. *Built-in* or intentionally designed physical obsolescence is purposefully shortening the physical life of the product or one of its components. Built-in obsolescence can be introduced for several reasons. It can create a larger replacement market by introducing change in steps rather than all at once. Modification in materials may also create the impression of either improved quality or lower price as an inducement to consumers.

Consumers who favor change to satisfy a recognized problem also favor obsolescence. Technological and style obsolescence are most sought by American consumers, and built-in obsolescence is not far behind. Consumers opposed to change favor postponed obsolescence, but these consumers appear to be in a minority at the present time.

PROBLEM RECOGNITION OVER THE PRODUCT LIFE CYCLE

Few products last forever. Like living things, they are born, develop, and decline. A new product is introduced into the marketplace; sales increase, stabilize, and decline; and the product is dropped.[12] This series of events is called the product life cycle. As we shall see, there is a direct relationship between consumer problem recognition and the life cycle.

A *product life cycle* (PLC) consists of: the stages through which a product passes from its introduction to its "death" or abandonment. Some, like Gillette's Nine Flags cologne, have minimum market success; others, like Gillette's Trac II razor, are so successful that they spawn a flurry of competitive activity. Remember that our definition of a product focuses on both real and perceived benefits. Packaging, branding, labeling, pricing, and distribution techniques all affect the product life cycle, so the life cycles of products can be modified by marketers.

The life of a typical product can be divided into four major stages, based on rates of sales growth or decline and profit: (1) introduction; (2) growth; (3) maturity; and (4) decline. Illustration 6-2 shows a product life cycle for computers. The PLC is a concept that attempts to describe a product's sales, profits, customers, and marketing emphasis. Note that within an industry some products are at every stage in the PLC. This situation is typical for every firm with a multi-item product mix.

Problem Recognition Most Critical at Introduction

The *introduction* stage of the life cycle begins as the product is introduced to the market. We need not repeat our discussion of problem recognition at this point because all the points made about product development apply. In fact, the introduction stage of the PLC is product development. Profits are below zero because of the development cost, as explained earlier, which occur before any revenues are forthcoming. The sales of new products tend to start slow in the introduction stage. Consumers may not recognize a problem because they do not perceive a need.

In its introductory stage, a product often faces stiff market resistance or indifference. Especially subject to resistance are items that are not particularly new or distinctive or in which consumers perceive few meaningful attributes or benefits. Some products never pass successfully through the introductory stage. During this stage, potential buyers must be made aware of the product's features, uses, and advantages in relation to their needs. Heavy promotion expenditures relative to sales may be required to make potential customers aware that the product can satisfy a problem that has been recognized and to assure retailers that demand is substantial. Innovators who are willing to take risks, can afford to take them, and like the status of buying first are the first to turn to these products upon problem recognition.

Problem Recognition Increases During Growth

When sales of a new product accelerate and the firm begins to achieve a pro-

Illustration 6-2
Product life cycle

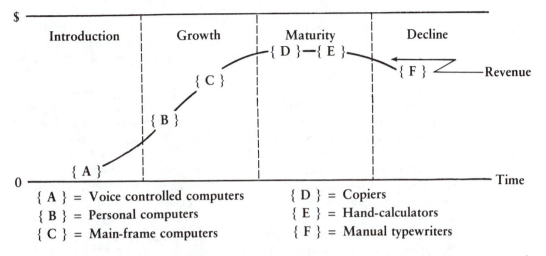

{ A } = Voice controlled computers   { D } = Copiers
{ B } = Personal computers   { E } = Hand-calculators
{ C } = Main-frame computers   { F } = Manual typewriters

fit, it has entered the *growth stage*. This stage occurs when business increases the number of consumers who recognize the product as a solution to their problem. Those products that show growth have the best fit with consumer's recognized problems. It is during this stage that profits peak, and start to decline. The growth stage is critical to a product's survival because competitive reactions to the product's success affects its life expectancy. If the product is successful in satisfying consumer needs, competitors enter the market. This competition drives prices down, creating the need for heavy promotional expenses. During the growth stage a firm tries to strengthen its market share and competitive advantage by identifying the product's benefits and emphasizing the benefits that satisfy the consumer upon problem recognition.

An example of an aggressive promotional pricing strategy during the growth stage can be observed in the policies of Texas Instruments. This business lowered its prices for electronic calculators almost monthly as many competitors entered and attempted to grab a share of the market. By adjusting its prices competitively, Texas Instruments was able to maintain its market lead during the growth stage. It was also able effectively to keep some firms from entering the market. It thus extended the life expectancy of its product far beyond that of marginal competitors.

Problem Recognition Declines at Maturity

During the *maturity stage*, sales of the product peak, and a period of relative stability follows. Most individuals have already recognized their need, and they are aware of the product's ability to solve their problems. Therefore, relatively few new customers are entering the market. It appears that some product classes never leave the maturity stage; most necessities, cars, and food products of many types, are good examples. This stage is characterized by severe competition as many brands enter the market. If the competitor's marketing strategy is really effective, its market share may even be greater than that of the originating firm. Also, competitors emphasize improvements and differences in their versions of the product. As a result, during the maturity stage, weaker competitors are squeezed out or lose interest in the product.

Operating costs are relatively low in this stage, but so are profits because of the squeezing effect of competition. This situation leads to reduced prices and to a search for ways to start sales climbing again. The marketing manager has several strategies to choose from in trying to respond to consumer problem recognition.

First, the firm may decide to try to increase the product's market share by actually investing more company resources in the marketing mix. For example, advertising that makes direct comparisons with other brands may lead the consumers of other brands to switch upon recognition. The manufacturer can persuade current customers to use and purchase more. The company can communicate to the users new ways to use their product. Arm and Hammer gives the consumer a variety of ways to use their product, and potato and rice producers suggest new recipes using their products. Figure 6-1 demonstrates how a company offers new uses for a product. Another way to increase market share (the proportion of total industry sales it obtains) is to attract nonusers of the product. Johnson & Johnson now sells baby oil, baby powder, and baby shampoo for use by adults. Second, the firm may decide to hold its market share at a consistent level, utilizing the marketing mix not to take the lead, but to remain competitive. Third, if the product's prospects appear dim, the firm may decide to reduce its market position (the way customers perceive a product) slowly by reducing its market share. This approach, called *disinvestment,* means gradually reducing expenses while increasing or maintaining present price levels. Disinvestment over a period of years may bring a very high contribution to profit from the product.

Special Problem Recognition in Decline Stage

There is nothing static in marketing. As time passes, there are changes in the business environment. Consumer needs and problems change, and new problems are recognized by consumers causing some products to decline. New technology or a new social trend may cause a product's sales to drop sharply as consumers recognize a better solution to an existing problem. In the decline stage, the product's decreased sales are making a smaller contribution to profit and expenses. For some products, profits have totally disappeared and the item is carried only for the convenience of the firm's consumers or to have a full assortment and a well-developed product mix.

The decline may be as sharp as the market growth was, or it may be quite slow. In the interest of efficiency and company objectives, a firm eventually must scrutinize a product carefully for possible deletion from the line. It simply does not solve the problem anymore for most consumers. Without sufficient customer interest, the costs of carrying the product or rejuvenating it are unwarranted. At the decline stage, consumers generally have recognized some new or different problem. They either consider the problem solved or the solution transferred to a competing firm. Thus problem recognition continues to be a serious problem for the business at this stage, as in every other stage.

Figure 6-1

New uses for a product

The Larsen Company

Product Life Cycle and Problem Recognition

It is apparent from Illustration 6-2 that for firms with a wide product mix, as one product is declining, other products are in the introduction, growth, or maturity stages of their life cycles. Product (A) is shown in introduction, (B) and (C) in growth, (D) and (E) in maturity, and (F) in decline. Many product life cycles are growing shorter, and marketing managers must deal with the dual problems of prolonging existing products or introducing new products. General Mills has prolonged the product life cycle of Bisquick, prepared biscuit mix, by systematically making improvements between its introduction in the 1930's and today. Other General Mills products such as Tuna Helper, Snackin' Cake, and Buc Wheats cereal have adjusted to satisfy changing consumers' preferences.

It is possible to change the growth rate of a product as indicated by (E) in Illustration 6-2. The dotted lines indicate that (E), while at the maturity stage, was given a new burst of sales, creating new growth. Such a change has to relate directly to the consumer's perception of problems. This change may have occurred because of a new product strategy which caused consumers to reevaluate their wants. In the case of hand calculators, the significant decrease in size, coupled with price reductions, led to a spurt in sales. The lesson is that management should only give up on a product after careful consideration.

The life cycle suggests that all firms must consider generating a continuous stream of new products in order to adjust to changing consumer wants. Such an action is necessary to maintain market position, solidify their company image, and hold profitability at desired levels. The product life cycle governs strategic marketing planning at all levels. This fact means not only product planning and development, but price, promotion, and distribution policies as well.

PROBLEM RECOGNITION AND PRODUCT DELETION

When the product no longer satisfies some recognized consumer problem, it must be considered for deletion. Product deletion is a special situation involving consumer problem recognition. A product deletion decision is seldom clear-cut. Effective product planning involves identifying items before they are ready for deletion, then deleting them on a systematic basis. In this way, the product can be gracefully removed, reducing marketing cost to the organization and minimizing inconvenience to the consumer.

Although some organizations drop weak products only after they have become severe financial burdens, a better approach is some form of review in which each product is evaluated periodically to determine its overall effectiveness in meeting consumer problems. The marketing executive must look at indicators in either the product's performance or in consumer acceptance. Normally, telltale signs indicate that the product is nearing the end of its useful life in the market. First, there may be a consistent decline in sales and profits. Every product's sales tend to rise and fall periodically. A poor product experiences a more consistent downward trend as consumers turn to more preferred solutions to their problems. Second, there may be the necessity for frequent price reductions. When other firms remove their unsuccessful products from the market, they generally reduce prices to clear out inventories. The marketing executive can pick up on possible weak products in the company line from these actions. However, one must be careful. Every reduction in price is not preparatory to removing the product from the market.

Third, there may be continued loss of market share. As a product loses its customer appeal to satisfy a problem, it also begins to lose market share. This is an important indicator of weakness. In a growing market the product's actual sales may remain steady and even increase. Yet a poor product might not be able to withstand the pressures of intense competition. Fourth, there may be an increasingly poor customer image. As the product's sales and market share decline, so does its image. When a consumer recognizes a problem, the product may be perceived as an unpopular, inferior, or outdated alternative. The marketing executive must carefully monitor the product's ability to satisfy consumer problems. Reviewing sales, profit records, and their trends and projections and evaluating a product's market share and the strength of its competitors, gives the marketing executive a clue to a product's strength. The marketing executive can use consumer research to assess attitudes toward the product and closely watch for any change in the product's ability to satisfy the consumer.

PROBLEM RECOGNITION OVER THE ADOPTION AND DIFFUSION PROCESSES

The introduction stage of the product life cycle is facilitated when customers accept the product rapidly. The acceptance rate and total sales level of new products rely heavily on two interdependent consumer behavior processes: adoption and diffusion.

The Adoption Process Involves Recognition

Marketers are especially interested in the stages that individual consumers go through when recognizing a problem and arrive at a decision of whether to adopt or not adopt a new product. The *adoption process* occurs at every stage in the product life cycle—indeed it occurs every time a consumer buys. When problem recognition occurs, the consumer will go through the following six steps in determining whether to adopt the product or not:

1. *Awareness*: The individual becomes aware of the product or brand as an option to satisfying a problem but has little or no information about it. Awareness for a product may cause the consumer to recognize a problem or a problem may make the consumer more aware of new or different product alternatives.
2. *Interest*: The individual is motivated to seek additional information about the problem or the product or their benefits. The amount of interest in a product is directly related to the seriousness of the consumer's problem.
3. *Evaluation*: The individual considers the product's benefits in relation to the perceived problem. It is often a comparison of alternative products. Products that the consumer perceives as more likely to solve the problem are evaluated more favorably.
4. *Trial*: The individual examines, tests, tries, or buys the product to determine its usefulness in satisfying the problem. The first purchase tends to be made to confirm the consumer's projected perception of the product's worth in satisfying his or her problem.[13]
5. *Adoption*: The individual buys the product on a regular basis to solve recurring problems. Adoption only occurs if the consumer finds the problem reduced or eliminated.
6. *Confirmation*: The individual looks for reinforcement and may reverse the decision if exposed to conflicting information.

The product adoption process has several implications for the marketing of products. First, in order to create widespread awareness of the product and its benefits, promotion is an important element of the marketing mix. Samples or simulated trials can be arranged to make consumers aware of both new and old problems. Marketing managers emphasize quality control and provide solid guarantees to reinforce buyers during the evaluation stage. Production and physical distribution must be linked to patterns of adoption and repeat purchases. Finally, follow-up by the firm occurs to reinforce the consumer decision to make the purchase.

It is important to remember that the product adoption process is only a model, and like most models it has some flaws. For example, if a consumer who buys on impulse or receives a free sample of the product may conceivably move through several of these stages simultaneously. The critics have also pointed out their concern with the sequence of the stages. The awareness stage may represent recognition of a problem or a felt need. Therefore, the product adoption process does not take into account that other events may precede awareness. Finally, the model does not adequately recognize that evaluation may not only occur at the evaluation stage, but it may occur throughout the decision making process.

The Diffusion Process and Recognition

The *diffusion of innovation* is the process by which new products or ideas are communicated within social systems over time. Some consumers quickly perceive innovative solutions to their problems while others must be shown the way. Some consumers may never adopt a new idea. Researchers have identified five categories of individuals based on the relative time when they adopted a given innovation.[14] The categories are rather arbitrarily partitioned on a time scale to represent unit standard deviations from the average time of adoption. Also, it should be noted that nonadopters are excluded.

What is most important is that the same behavior that causes the adoption and diffusion of new products is, in great measure, responsible for the product life cycle. Thus, if marketers understand diffusion and adoption of new products and if they are in any way able to control the process, they can better manage the revenues and profits flowing from their marketing strategies. Especially important are their product planning and development activities as they affect the life cycles of the firm's product line.[15]

Innovators Have Unique Problems. Innovators are extremely important to the success of new products or ideas even though they constitute only about 2.5 percent of the adopting market.[16] Innovators are individuals who recognize new problems or new products and can solve these problems before reinforcement and reward of being first. Innovators accept new products for their own satisfaction and not because of the attitudes of others. There is some evidence to suggest that innovators are markedly different in personality and life-styles. They are forerunners, often upscale (slightly above average in income for their age group), young, well-educated consumers. They tend to hold new values and are frequently opinion leaders, key figures in a network of personal and social influence. Innovators are likely to rely more on personal sources of information, including those external to their own social system, than on salespeople or other word-of-mouth sources.

Early Adopters Are Quick to Recognize Problems. Early adopters recognize problems and potential solutions ahead of the general public, but they are aware of the impact of their decisions on others. Early adopters make up about 13.5 percent of the market. They tend to be a more integrated part of a local social system. That is, whereas innovators are cosmopolites, early adopters are localites. Thus early adopters make excellent opinion leaders. They serve this function to a greater degree than any other adopter group. Television and movie stars are often early adopters, as are politicians, athletes, and professionals. They greatly influence the type of problems and solutions that affect the general public. Early adopters are greatly respected in their social system. While early adopters are not the first to adopt new products or ideas, if they receive a new product or idea coolly, this usually means it will have only limited market success. Sales-people are probably used more by the early adopters than by any other category, but advertising is quite effective on them.

Early Majority Follow in Recognition. People in the early majority category are the average consumer. They recognize problems and products in a more conservative way. They typically follow the lead of the early adopters, but they are not blind followers. They must be independently convinced of the soundness of a new ideas. They make up their own minds when buying. Thirty-four percent of all consumers are in the early majority category. They make up the first half of America's mass market and respond distinctly differently from the previous two groups. They are solid citizens, people who may be slight overachievers. They have good education, well-paying jobs, and spend their money for the good things of life. These are the individuals who validate the new products—make them an accepted part of the middle-class system of symbols. Unless the marketing executive has convinced the innovators and early adopters to buy, the early majority is not likely to recognize the problem or act. Without at least part of this market, the product probably cannot achieve sufficient sales volume to be especially profitable. To satisfy a problem, the members of this group rely quite a bit on advertisements, salespeople, and contact with early adopters. Business firms in this category are average-sized operations.

Late Majority Go with the Crowd. The more deliberately conservative group is the late group majority. This group also represents about 34 percent of the market. People in this category tend to be quite conservative in recognizing problems and skeptical of new products. They tend to follow the lead of the general public, accepting only what they perceive as already acceptable. This fact is true even though the product may be in relatively late stages of the product life cycle. Additionally, they tend to be very price-sensitive and are generally unwilling to buy until they are convinced that the price is at about its lowest point. They rely on their peers as sources of information. Advertising and personal selling are less effective with this group than is word-of-mouth.

Laggards Have Different Problems. This tradition-bound group—16 percent of the market—is the last to adopt an innovation to satisfy problems. Their point of reference is what was done in the past. Laggards are suspicious of innovations and innovators. They have little interest in the attitudes of opinion leaders and they purchase independent of the general population. They tend to see the same old problems followed by time tested and familiar solutions. Like innovators, they see their problems as individualistic and not group oriented. By the time laggards adopt something new, it may already have been discarded by the innovators, early adopters, and the early and late majority in favor of a newer problem or product. Laggards are older and tend to be at the low end of the social and economic scales. Therefore, price and quality are nearly always more important than fashion. They respond less to both advertising and personal selling when buying, but they do check the sales which stores promote.

Innovations Affect Adoption and Diffusion

The time required for a given innovation to be adopted may range from a few weeks to several decades.[17] Five characteristics of an innovation, as perceived by individuals to satisfy problems, seem to influence the adoption rate. One characteristic is *relative advantage* or the degree to which an innovation is superior to preceding ideas. Once a problem is recognized a relative advantage may be reflected in lower cost, higher profitability or some other measure. Another characteristic is *compatibility,* meaning the degree to which an innovation is consistent with the cultural values and experiences of the adopters. The degree of *complexity* of an innovation is another characteristic affecting adoption rate. The more complex an innovation is, the less quickly it will be adopted. *Trialability* is also a characteristic. This is the degree to which the new idea may be sampled on some limited basis. A central home air-conditioning system is likely to have a slower adoption rate than some new paint, which may be tried on a smaller scale. The characteristic of *observability* of the innovation affects its adoption rate. A diet plan where you lose one pound overnight can be accepted sooner than a plan that takes six weeks to work. The reason is that the latter—even though it may be a superior product—produces no immediate solution to the recognized problem.

PROBLEM RECOGNITION RELATED TO PRODUCT ATTRIBUTE

All the benefits that a product promises to deliver, both real (physical) and perceived (psychological), are part of the total product. Every product has many attributes that must be evaluated. While not all attributes can be treated in detail, the more important ones include branding, packaging, labeling, supportive services, and warranties. Depending on the particular item, any one or more of these product attributes may be more critical to the consumer upon problem recognition than the physical components of the product.

Problem Recognition and Branding

Branding is the procedure a firm follows in researching, developing, and implementing its brand(s).[18] Branding is a rather inclusive term, and the subject of considerable misunderstanding. A *brand* is a name, design, or symbol (or combination of these) that identifies the products and services of a seller or group of sellers. Everything on the can of soup in Figure 6-2 is part of the brand. This definition includes virtually all means of identification except packaging and product shape. *Trademark* is a brand name, brand mark, or trade character or combination thereof that is given legal protection. When it is used, a registered trademark is followed by ®. Notice the ® after Campbell's in the first sentence of the copy in Figure 6-2. That signifies that Campbell's is a trademark.

Figure 6-2
Registered trademark

NATURAL RESOURCES

When you sit down to enjoy a bowl of Campbell's® Vegetable Beef Soup, you get much more than delicious taste. You see, we've been very resourceful about nutrition, too.

Many of Campbell's Soups are a great way to get some of the important natural resources you've been hearing so much about today. Like vitamin A or fiber.

In fact, more and more is being learned every day about the important role vitamin A plays in helping to build up your body's resistance, as well as its role in maintaining healthy skin and good vision. Campbell's Vegetable Beef Soup has an abundance of vegetables that are a good source of vitamin A. Just one serving will give you 40% of your daily need for vitamin A.

Campbell's Split Pea with Ham and Bacon, Green Pea and Low Sodium Split Pea Soups are all a good source of dietary fiber, which so many people are giving high priority.

It's always been true that a bowl of warm, delicious Campbell's Soup, when part of a balanced diet, does a body good. Now you know why.

CAMPBELL'S SOUP IS GOOD FOOD

Fiber in a suggested serving: Split Pea with Ham and Bacon—6g; Green Pea—5g; Low Sodium Split Pea—7g.
Campbell's has a full line of low sodium soups for those people who are on a salt-restricted diet or have a concern about sodium.

Campbell Soup Company

The *brand name* is a word, letter, a group of words, or letters that can be spoken. Examples are Lite Beer, Lipton Cup-a-Soup, and Star-kist. The brand name in Figure 6-2 is limited to the word Campbell's wherever located in the ad. The brand makes it possible for consumers to identify a specific product with the solution of their problem. Thus it aids them in shopping and decision making.

When consumers face a problem without knowledge of a specific product to satisfy the problem, they tend to trust a favored or well-known brand name.[19] Consumers often think well-known brands are better for satisfying a problem because of perceived assurance of quality, dependability, performance, and service.[20] The following are several reasons why branding is important for aiding the consumer in recognizing a problem or identifying a preferred solution. It is easy to identify products. A customer can order a product or service by name instead of description. A brand name is substituted for a standard or specification. Brands provide quality assurance. Customers are assured that a product or service has a certain level of quality and that they obtain comparable quality if the same brand is reordered. Brands provide assurance of company responsibility. The firm responsible for the product or service is known. The producer of un-branded items cannot be directly identified.

Brands reduce price comparison as customers perceive brand distinctiveness. This is especially true when buyers attribute special characteristics to different brands. Brands aid buyer awareness. A firm is able to promote its products and services and associate a brand and its characteristics in the buyer's mind. Brands can add to the product's status. Product prestige is increased, as social visibility becomes meaningful. This is important if the perceived problem is social acceptance. Brands can reduce risk for the consumer. Consumers feel less risk when purchasing a brand with which they are familiar and toward which they have a favorable attitude. Branding helps segment markets and create a distinctive image. By using multiple brands, different market segments are attracted. For example, General Motors develops separate marketing programs built around its five brands—Chevrolet, Pontiac, Buick, Oldsmobile, and Cadillac.

When recognizing a problem, both consumers and sellers suffer in countries that do not use brand names. For example, in the past the absence of brands for television sets in Russia meant customers could not identify the factory that habitually produced "lemons." The sales of all television sets suffered as a result.

Problem Recognition and Packaging

Packaging refers to the activities related to designing and producing a container that both protects the product and enhances its marketability to satisfy consumer problems. The can shown in Figure 6-2 is the package for Campbell's soup. Consumers generally do not distinguish clearly between a product and its package. To consumers the package and product are part of an entity; the product is the package, and vice versa.[21] When consumers know little about competing products or regard them as being about equal in quality, the sales advantage may come from the package. Packaging assumed a selling role in 1899, when Uneeda biscuits appeared in a paper box that served both to protect the contents and to present a sales message. An increasing trend toward self-service merchandising has made packaging a $45 billion-a-year business today, and a product's package serves as the most important sales stimulant at the point of purchase.

The package is an important method of communication with the customer; it can even lead to consumer problem recognition. It identifies the brand, provides ingredients and directions, represents an image of the brand, and displays the product. It also serves as a promotional tool. The package is the final form of promotion the consumer sees prior to making a purchase decision. The package also serves a promotional purpose after a purchase is made, because a reusable package is a constant reminder of the product.

Photo 6-2
L'eggs is a classic example of successful packaging and display.

The Importance of Labeling to Problem Recognition

Labeling is closely related to packaging as a major product attribute that a consumer turns to when identifying problems. A label is that part of the product or the package conveying information about the product to the buyer. The label in Figure 6-2 is the paper covering on the can that contains the brand, brand name, trademark, and all other information.

Labeling is important for a variety of reasons. Legal requirements govern the disclosure of certain kinds of information about products. The marketing executive wants to ensure that the product is used for its intended purpose and in the manner prescribed. An informative label can reduce product misuse and help the consumer get satisfaction for the recognized problem. When problem recognition occurs, the labels also attract consumer attention in much the same manner as an innovative package. Since so many similar products are available, an attention-getting device or "silent salesperson" is needed to attract interest. The label is one of the most visible parts of a product, and it is an important decision in the planning of a product. The label, with proper design work and appropriate colors, can have a significant impact on the consumer during the problem recognition stage of the decision making process. Certainly the Levi, Campbell's, and Coors labels are widely recognized.

Supporting Services and Problem Recognition

Supportive services are those auxiliary services that assist the product in satisfying consumer problems and in doing so make the product more desirable. Marketing executives have increasingly turned to improving or expanding their customer services to better satisfy consumers and their problems. Some of the more common services follow.

First, many consumer products have become so advanced that buyers need instructions in learning how to use them properly. This service becomes more important as consumers turn to home computers and other high-technology products to satisfy their problems. Companies like IBM and Pillsbury have established consumer service telephone lines to help consumers upon problem recognition.

Second, companies have expended considerable effort in handling consumer problems and complaints. Many companies have established internal departments to facilitate better communications with the public. For example, Procter & Gamble Consumer Services have a hot line to provide consumers information about the company. They believe that once the facts are known, individuals will be reassured about the integrity of Procter & Gamble.

Third, despite the advances in technology, no product is designed to last forever. Marketing executives have begun to recognize the importance of having a good repair network, since poor maintenance has been a continuing source of consumer dissatisfaction and problem recognition. Companies like AT & T, Cross (Cross pens), and Texas Instruments are doing repair work directly by mail. Fourth, some consumers who recognize a problem also realize that they can not afford a solution. The "buy now, pay later" approach is no longer innovative, but it does allow potential consumers to purchase a product they otherwise would not be able to buy. For marketers of relatively expensive items, the offering of credit services allows a larger number of people to turn to them upon problem recognition, thus enlarging the market for the item. Fifth, a warranty specifies what the producer will do if the product malfunctions. Its most common purpose is to eliminate buyer uncertainty over the quality of the product, taking some of the risk out of the purchase decision. When the consumer recognizes a problem and has little personal capability to assess the quality or performance of a product, a warranty is especially important. By providing the warranty, the marketing executive at least partially removes one obstacle to the product's acceptance as an alternative to satisfy a consumer's problem.

While supportive services can be beneficial to the consumer during the problem recognition stage and be a powerful competitive weapon for the company, they are not without their drawbacks. One serious disadvantage is the high cost of developing and maintaining these programs. An additional detriment is that competitors can quickly offer similar services if they prove successful. Finally, unless the quality of the services is very high, it can lead to consumer dissatisfaction. Designed to assist the product in satisfying consumer problems, low quality supportive services can seriously damage the image and attractiveness of the product.

QUESTIONS

1. Discuss the statement: "There are no two identical products."
2. List the tangible and intangible attributes that a bottle of aftershave provides. Compare the benefits of aftershave with those of a service.
3. Discuss when a company should add product depth to its product mix and when should it add product width.
4. Identify and discuss with examples products that were developed before there was a consumer demand.
5. Define minor innovations and major innovations. Give examples of each.
6. During the test marketing stage of the new product development process, new products are offered for sale in selected markets. Would there be any time a company may decide not to test market its products? Discuss your answer.
7. Give examples of products that have made it to the commercialization stage and still have failed. Discuss why.
8. Discuss why consumers may be opposed to new products.
9. What is the major difference between planned obsolescence and built-in obsolescence? Give examples of each.
10. Draw the product life cycle with approximate dates of the different stages for a calculator.
11. Discuss the appropriate marketing mix strategy for a product in the maturity stage of its life cycle. Give some examples of such a product.
12. It has been said that some products within an industry can be profitable during the decline stage for the industry. Discuss why this may be possible and give some examples of products.

13. Why might a company be unable to delete an unprofitable product? Give several reasons.
14. Identify where you fall within the diffusion process. Is it the same for all products? Discuss your answer.
15. How does branding benefit an organization? The consumer?

NOTES

1. Michael F. Smith and Donald F. Dixon, "Consumers' Perceptions of Goods and Services," in John H. Summey, Blaise J. Bergiel, and Carol H. Anderson, eds., *A Spectrum of Contemporary Marketing Ideas* (Southern Illinois University at Carbondale and Southern Marketing Assn., 1982), pp. 65–68. 65–68.

2 Lee D. Dahringer, Virginia Langrehr, Philip E. Hendrix, and Norman Marcus, "Technology: Impact on Consumer and Marketing Implications," in John H. Summey, Blaise J. Bergiel, and Carol H. Anderson, eds., *A Spectrum of Contemporary Marketing Ideas* (Southern Illinois University at Carbondale and Southern Marketing Assn., 1982), pp. 226–28.

3. Hirotaka Takeuchi and Ikujiro Nonada, "The New New Product Development Game," *Harvard Business Review*, Vol. 54 (January–February 1986), pp. 137–46.

4. Tommy Greer, "Look for These Specialists in Better Mousetrap Building," *Marketing Times* (March–April 1978), p. 11.

5. Hirotaka Takeuchi and John A. Quelch, "Quality Is More Than Making a Good Product," *Harvard Business Review*, Vol. 61 (July–August 1983), pp. 139–45.

6. Jack Reddy and Abe Berger, "Three Essentials of Product Quality," *Harvard Business Review*, Vol. 61 (July–August 1983), pp. 153–59.

7. Pamela G. Hollie, "G.M. Previews Fuel Saving Car," *New York Times* (April 4, 1979), p. D5.

8. Ted Karger, "Test Marketing as Dress Rehearsals: Bundle Tests and Test Market Diagnostics," *The Journal of Consumer Marketing*, Vol. 2 (Fall 1985), pp. 49–56.

9. Joe R. Evans and Barry Berman, *Marketing* (New York: MacMillan Publishing Co., Inc., 1982), p. 256.

10. Geoffrey E. Meredith, "Test Markets Succumb to the Defense," *Advertising Age* (February 4, 1980), pp. SS-24-S-a25.

11. William D. Smithburg, "The Development and Marketing of New Consumer Products: Some Successes and Failures," *The Journal of Consumer Marketing*, Vol. 2 (Summer 1985), pp. 55–58.

12. Michael F. Petruny, Sharon A. Grimes, and Jaime Agudelo, "The Use of Accounting Information to Identify Product Life Cycle Stages," in John Summey, R. Vishwanathan, Ronald D. Taylor, and Karen Glynn, eds., *Marketing: Theories and Concepts for an Era of Change* (Southern Illinois University at Carbondale and Southern Marketing Assn., 1983), pp. 32–35.

13. Robert E. Smith and William R. Swinyard, "Attitude-Behavior Consistency: The Impact of Product Trial Versus Advertising," *Journal of Marketing Research*, Vol. XX (August 1983), pp. 257–67.

14. Everett M. Rogers, *Diffusion of Innovations,* 3rd ed. (New York: The Free Press, 1983), chapter 6.

15. Vijay Mahajan and Eitan Muller, "Innovation Diffusion and New Product Growth Models in Marketing,"*Journal of Marketing*, Vol. 43 (Fall 1979), pp. 55–68.

16. Mary Dee Dickerson and James W. Gentry, "Characteristics of Adopters and Non-Adopters of Home Computers," *Journal of Consumer Research*, Vol. 10 (September 1983), pp. 225–35.

17. Elizabeth C. Hirschman, "Innovativeness, Novelty, Seeking and Consumer Creativity," *Journal of Consumer Research*, Vol. 7 (December 1980), pp. 283–95.

18. Gerald A. Schorin and Bruce G. Banden Bergh, "What's in a Brand Name," in Nancy Stephens, ed., *Proceedings of the 1985 Conference of the American Academy of Advertising* (Arizona State University and American Academy of Advertising, 1985), pp. 28–31.

19. Meryl Paula Gardner, "Does Attitude Toward the Ad Affect Brand Attitude Under a Brand Evaluation Set?" *Journal of Marketing Research*, Vol. XXII (May 1985), pp. 192–98; Roger Calantone and Robert G. Cooper, "New Product Scenarios: Prospects for Success," *Journal of Marketing,* Vol. 45 (Spring 1981), pp. 48–60.

20. Joseph A. Bellizzi, Harry F. Kruckeberg, John R. Hamilton, and Warren S. Martin, "Consumer Perceptions of National, Private, and Generic Brands," *Journal of Retailing*, Vol. 57 (Winter 1981), pp. 56–70.

21. Walter Stern, "Design Research: Beauty or Beast," *Advertising Age* (March 9, 1981), p. 43.

PART 3

CONSUMER SEARCH
FOR INFORMATION

SECTION A
PATTERNS OF
CONSUMER SEARCH

7. Introduction To Consumer Search
8. Internal Consumer Search
9. Family Information Sources
10. Social Groups As Information Sources
11. Cultural Values Guide Consumer Search

CHAPTER 7

Introduction To
Consumer Search

CHAPTER OUTLINE

I. **THE NATURE OF CONSUMER SEARCH**

II. **THE IMPORTANCE OF CONSUMER SEARCH**

III. **CONSUMER SEARCH REQUIRES COMMUNICATION**
   A. The Communication Process
   B. One-Way or Two-Way Communication
   C. Two-Step Flow of Communications
   D. The Importance of Opinion Leaders
   E. Who Are Opinion Leaders?
   F. Noise in the Communication Process

IV. **INTERNAL AND EXTERNAL CONSUMER SOURCES**
   A. Internal Search Uses Personal Experience
   B. External Reference Group Sources
   C. External Business Sources

V. **DETERMINANTS OF SOURCE SELECTION**
   A. Type of Information Desired
   B. Confidence in the Source
   C. Source Effectiveness

VI. **THE AMOUNT OF CONSUMER SEARCH**
   A. Value of the Product
   B. Availability of Information Without Search
   C. Satisfaction Derived from Search
   D. Perceived Consequences of Search
   E. Usefulness of the Information

VII. **PATTERNS OF CONSUMER SEARCH**
   A. Active and Passive Search
   B. Continual or Intermittent Search
   C. Casual or Formal Search
   D. Local or Extended Search
   E. The Time to Shop
   F. The Number of Stores to Visit

CHAPTER OBJECTIVES

After completing your study of Chapter 7, you should be able to:

1. Discuss the nature of consumer search for information.
2. Discuss the importance of consumer search for information.
3. Discuss the importance of communication in consumer search.
4. Describe the internal and external consumer sources of information.
5. Discuss the determinants of source selection.
6. Discuss the factors that affect the amount of consumer search.
7. Discuss the patterns of consumer search.

Once a consumer problem is recognized, something must be done about it. This is where consumer search, the second step in the decision process, begins. In the search for information, the individual begins to act to correct the situation or solve the recognized problem. No step in the decision process is more important than consumer search. This chapter provides an overview of the search process that is the basis for the remaining chapters in this section of the book.

THE NATURE OF CONSUMER SEARCH

In a broad sense, search for information is the activity undertaken to provide data to be used for the decision making.[1] All decisions that are not made intuitively involve some search. *Consumer search* is a distinctive type of search, and it can be defined as:

The mental and physical activities undertaken by consumers to provide information on products and store alternatives.

Searching is a specific type of activity. Its object is to collect information; it does not include organizing information or selecting alternatives. Although consumer search is initiated by some recognized or anticipated product deficiency, consumers search for a much wider range of data than which products are available. Consumer search also includes data on brands, prices, store location, product quality, and store services. It stands to reason that consumer search is one of the more important steps in the purchase process.[2] It underlies both the ordering of product preferences and consumer decision to be discussed in coming chapters.

Consumer search may be either internal or external. *Internal search* involves recalling information, attitudes, and needs already stored in the mind. This type of search can be accomplished anywhere, and it usually occurs immediately after the problem is recognized.[3] *External search* is consulting friends, relatives, associates, and marketers to obtain information not already accessible.[4] For example, a consumer may have general internal information about how a car works but may consult several people about the features of a particular model before buying. While external search can also be done at home, it always involves seeking some information from outside the home. Search can even be unintentional;

consumers glean much information from advertisements, observations in store windows, and casual conversations that do not have to do with immediate product needs. The information is simply stored or forgotten until a situation arises where it is needed.

THE IMPORTANCE OF CONSUMER SEARCH

How nearly persons come to maintaining their standard of living depends significantly on consumer search. When search is effective, the products bought fit the consumer's wants, and these products are obtained with relatively less expenditure of time, effort, and money. Poor consumer search can mean that the individual spends more yet satisfies fewer household requirements. It follows that a knowledge of search behavior is important to both the consumer and the marketer.

Our principal interest is in consumers, and they can benefit from a knowledge of search in several ways. First, a knowledge of the forces helping shape market entry, such as advertising and personal selling, can make consumers more competent in reacting to these forces. Second, a knowledge of the search process can make consumers more astute shoppers. Third, the planning that underlies search and market entry can help make consumers aware of problems, alternatives, and methods of countering sales attempts made by business executives. When the consumer is a more thoughtful buyer, marketers must become more thoughtful sellers, and everyone benefits.

There are important ways that marketers can benefit from a knowledge of consumer search patterns. First, tactical knowledge is useful for determining marketing targets. Knowledge of the products sought, stores visited, services requested, method of transportation, distance traveled, etc., can help the marketer account for these patterns when appealing to particular customer groups. Second, a knowledge of the consumer's search pattern provides clues to the type of appeals that the marketer can make. A study of these activities can also point out ways of meeting specific objections to buying. Finally, a knowledge of consumer search is useful for market analysis. Various types of customer analysis comparing before and after search behavior is useful for market planning. The marketer can also compare customer types based on search characteristics. Much of consumer search is easy to observe, which makes collecting data easier than it is for some other steps in the purchase process.

CONSUMER SEARCH REQUIRES COMMUNICATION

All consumer search is based on the communication of information. One must find out what one does not know about a market or the products offered there, and one must review what one already knows to see if it applies to the decision. We must understand communication to understand consumer search.

Communication is not easy to define. Communication is really a synonym for social interaction, since all social interaction takes the form of some communica-

Figure 7-1
Information communication is conveying facts to the marketing target

Help Yourself.

South Central Bell's Customer Guide gives you the information you'll need. Right at your fingertips.

Who to call to get new phone service. How to solve billing problems. Who to call to get service repaired. How to handle harassing phone calls. Who to call in an emergency. Even how to use Custom Calling Services.

For answers to these and many other important questions about your phone service and your community, help yourself.

Because all this useful information—and much more—is just inside the cover of your phone book. Literally. It's in your Customer Guide, beginning on Page 1 of your South Central Bell directory.

The Customer Guide is the first place to turn when you need to know who to call or how to call. It's fast and easy. With a quick reference contents page right in front. So, when you need a number or information about your telephone service, you can find it—quickly and easily.

After all, what good is a Customer Guide if the customer can't use it?

So please, use it. Help yourself to the wealth of information in your Customer Guide. From South Central Bell.

Call On Us.

South Central Bell
A *BELLSOUTH* Company

Used with Permission of the South Central Bell Telephone Co.

tion. "Communicate" is sometimes used to mean to send or transmit information, but it actually means to make common or to share. Following these leads, we define *consumer communication* as:

an exchange of any type of market-related information between two or more persons.

In other words, consumer communication is the result of any action that conveys meaning about consumption problems. This information can then be used to aid in solving the problems.

There are several meaningful ways that communications can be classified. First, communications can be classed by *type of coverage* into personal or mass communications. Personal communications take place between two individuals, or between a business and an individual, and mass communications are designed to reach the general public.

Second, classed by *method of communicating*, there are written, verbal, and physical communications. Verbal communication is spoken while written communication uses visible symbols. Physical communications include body movements, odor, and clothing—in short, all things communicate, but they communicate different things to different people.[5]

Third, communications can be classed by *purpose* into casual, informative, persuasive, or reminder. Casual communication is the backyard variety, usually indulged in to pass the time. Some of the most important communications are casual. We normally associate casual communication with friends and relatives. Informative, persuasive, and reminder communications are typically associated with businesses. They are designed to affect the consumer's attitudes or behavior. Informative communication has the principal purpose of conveying factual data to evoke a decision favorable to the firm (see Figure 7-1). Persuasive communication is designed to affect some change in the consumer's attitudes or behavior of the consumer that are favorable to the firm. Reminder communication lets consumers know the product is still available to satisfy their problems.

The Communication Process

The very idea of communication is the establishment of some common ground of understanding—to share feelings or attitudes.[6] The process of sharing is illustrated in Illustration 7-1.[7] The communications process consists of two basic components, three activities, and one result. These elements are defined below:

Components
  Sender—the person or group of persons who have some thought, idea, or concept to be transmitted to others.

  Receiver—the person or persons who are the target of the thought that is transmitted.

Activities
  Encode—to translate what the source wishes to communicate into effective symbolism for transmission.

  Decode—to interpret the symbolism transmitted for the receiver.

  Transmission—conveyance of the thought or idea through some effective channel between the sender and the receiver.[8]

Result
  Message—the thought, idea, or concept which is transmitted between components.

Illustration 7-1
Communication process

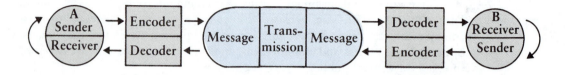

Communication is typically a push-pull process in which a message is sent and some response, called feedback, is evoked. This *feedback* is just reverse communication, and no special device is needed to demonstrate it in the illustration.[9] Feedback contains all the elements of the original communication. In the illustration, individual A has some thought to transmit to individual B concerning a product recently observed. Individual A translates (encodes) the thought into a message and transmits it via a channel such as the air or a note. Individual B interprets (decodes) the message and internalizes it. One complete communication has occurred at this point.

Let's say that A has informed B about a sale taking place at J.C. Penney's. Should B wish to respond to A's message, which is fairly typical in cases of social interaction, then the roles of the parties are reversed. Assume that B wants to inform A that B intends to visit Penney's tomorrow to check the product on sale. This is feedback; B becomes the sender and A the receiver.

In execution, this reverse communication is exactly like the original. However, it is generally called feedback because the message is made in response to a previous communication. In practice, the two parties may communicate for some time, alternately reversing their roles in the communication process.

One-Way or Two-Way Communications

Communication can be either one-way or two-way. *Two-way communication* occurs in a person-to-person relationship, such as a personal purchase. There is typically one sender and one receiver, with immediate feedback between the two. The feedback can occur in several forms — sight, sound, smell, and so on. Feedback is immediate and thus continuous. This type of communication offers opportunities for improved understanding between the sender and receiver. It accounts, in part, for the effectiveness of personal selling.

One-way communication occurs between a sender and a mass audience. Feedback is nonexistent or delayed, and the sender has difficulty determining how much of the message was actually received. One-way communication can reach many more people at reduced cost per person reached, but the ability to cause action, as in the case of advertising, is low. The sender must anticipate needs, appeals, messages, and objections. The chances for misunderstanding are great.

A question arises as to when actual communication has taken place. Is there communication when a message is received or is understanding or agreement necessary for communication? The attitude taken here is that communication requires more than simply receiving the message. Some degree of understanding is necessary, but it is not necessary that there be agreement on the ideas communicated. If there is no agreement, the sender may consider the communication ineffective—but it is still communication if it was understood. Thus, the effectiveness of communications depends on the goal sought. If an advertiser attempts to create a quality brand image, but the consumer associates the brand with lower quality and still buys, has there been communication? The answer is that there has been communication, and if the goal is sales, then the communication was effective. If the goal was a favorable consumer frame of mind toward the quality of the product, then the communication was ineffective.

Two-Step Flow of Communications

Until now we have discussed influence as if it always resulted from direct communication between a sender and a consumer. However, influence is seldom that simple. Communication is often direct, but it occurs in two steps, with an intermediary between the original source and the final destination.

Illustration 7-2 shows the basic nature of the two-step-flow concept. Influence tends to flow from the mass media to opinion leaders (1st step) who are receptive to the idea presented, and from these opinion leaders to the general public (2nd step). The contention is that union leaders influence others as a result of their interest and placement in the communication network. In other words, if the firm can sell the opinion leaders, they will in turn sell the public. It was also felt that opinion leaders exerted pressure on the masses to conform to the leaders' preference for products, services and ideas. While evidence exists to support this first position, there is considerable doubt about the ability of opinion leaders to exert pressure on the group.

The market is composed of relatively few active information seekers and a

Illustration 7-2
Two-step flow of communication

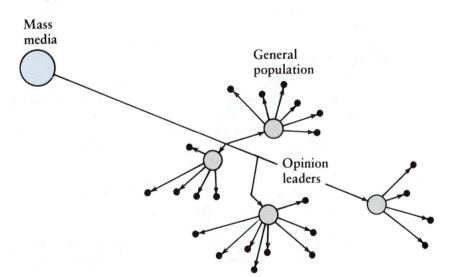

Mass media

General population

Opinion leaders

Photo 7-1

Communication is a two-way relationship in a personal selling situation.

large number of passive information receivers.[11] The information seekers may be different from innovators; they may seek information only about the product or service that interests them. The opinion leader may be conservative in all other respects. Innovators, on the other hand, seek change for its own sake. The influence of opinion leaders can be horizontal as well as vertical.[12] A *vertical flow* is from high-status, socially elite individuals to the average consumer. A *horizontal flow* occurs between peers. There is a growing feeling that a horizontal, two-step flow is more important than the vertical type. Consumers tend to be influenced by their peers.

The Importance of Opinion Leaders

The significance of group influence on consumer behavior cannot be overestimated. The opinion leader is a trendsetter who accepts the risk and uncertainty of new products, services, and market innovations. This is true whether the instigator is a political figure, a movie star, or the next-door neighbor. The opinion leader interprets, evaluates, and guides the general acceptance by other consumers of new ideas. Personal influence has been shown to have more effect in purchasing new products and in switching stores.[13] Even so, one cannot discount the influence of the mass media; they influence consumers and opinion leaders. For example, the pattern of purchase by families in an apartment building tends to follow the patterns of social contact in the apartment. If one family in the building purchases an air conditioner, others will follow their pattern—even to the brand of air conditioner purchased. However, once a critical

Illustration 7-3
Noise in the communication process

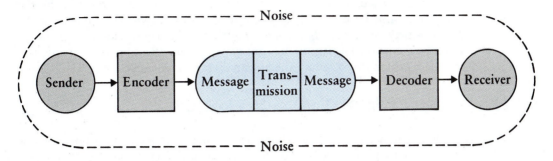

number of units have been purchased, the pattern breaks down as it becomes fashionable for everyone to purchase an air conditioner.

The automobile industry provides a good example of the failure to recognize the importance of opinion leaders. In the 1950s, the industry considered the owners of small foreign cars as strange and unworthy of notice. Unfortunately for the auto makers, these consumers turned out to be opinion leaders, and the small car caught on. As a result, Detroit had difficulty cracking the small-car market.

Who Are Opinion Leaders?

The term "opinion leader" can be misleading, because it assumes that someone has control over others who must follow.[14] We tend to think of opinion leaders as prominent people. Indeed, for certain products—such as fashion clothing, jewelry, and shoes—politicians, movie stars, presidents and their spouses, and athletes make excellent opinion leaders. These persons have a lot at stake in keeping up with fashions. However, anyone can dictate fashion and other product trends. Some of the more lasting consumer trends have been established by quite ordinary persons. For example, high school students tend to set the fashion for music; college students are important in men's clothing fashion; and young adults greatly influence the fashion in small sports cars.

The most important characteristics of opinion leaders are venturesomeness and social mobility, although participation, financial standing, and interest outside the community were also important.[15] In any case, it is clear that a variety of persons can be product innovators, depending on the product and the situation.

Noise in the Communication Process

Noise is used to mean any type of interference with communication.[16] Illustration 7-2 did not show noise as an element of communication because it is usually disruptive, not constructive. Interference can occur anywhere in the process where there is interaction. The major points are shown in Illustration 7-3. Several types of noise are possible in the communication.

One kind of noise occurs when the sender and receiver have completely different environments. A non–French-speaking consumer who attempts to purchase wine in France can have great difficulty. A poor person has difficulty appreciating the pitch of a condominium salesperson. Feedback can sometimes alleviate either situation. Noise can occur because the idea presented by the sender may not be clear, the thought may not be properly encoded, or the decoding may be at fault. Noise may result from channel selection, since a consumer may miss the message or may not pay sufficient attention to register it. The net effect of noise is to reduce the effectiveness of communications.

INTERNAL AND EXTERNAL CONSUMER SOURCES

We have determined that almost every consumer search uses both internal and external sources. The remainder of this chapter focuses on these two important sources of consumer information. We begin here by identifying the types of internal and external sources available to the consumer.

Internal Search Uses Personal Experience

Personal experience is the consumer's history. It encompasses the individual's previous product problems, success in obtaining information, comparisons made, solutions discovered, and successes or failures encountered. All the market experience of the individual, both conscious and unconscious, is stored in the mind to be called upon as the consumer requires it. Thus personal experience is an internal source of information. The person does not have to engage in any overt activity in order to obtain the information, but the successful use of personal experience is directly related to the individual's ability to recall.

Personal experience, since it comes from the memory, provides the consumer with a good deal of information.[17] It is also generally available when the consumer wants it. The information is low in cost, trusted, and easily obtainable. The major problems with personal experience are that the information is often incomplete, it may be incorrect, and it may reflect a narrow perspective on the market situation.

External Reference Group Sources

Reference group sources of consumer information are based on social contacts the consumer has with others. These contacts may be in family relationships, at work, in community projects, in government agencies, and in entertainment groups. The opinion of others plays an important part in consumer search activities. There are several advantages for the consumer when using reference group sources of market information. There is a variety of information typically available from several different reference groups. The information is generally trusted, it is easy to obtain, and it is low in cost.[18] Furthermore, the consumer has the opportunity to select relevant data from the great variety available.

There are problems with reference group information. Although the consumer may trust the data source, the information may still be incorrect or based on incomplete or false impressions. Individuals in reference groups often have their own biases that are reflected in the information they provide. The information is intermittent, and the consumer may have to seek the information out. Reference group information is often insufficient to make a sound judgment. It follows that consumers should use reference group data with care.

External Business Sources

Consumers obtain business information from door-to-door salespersons, mass media, and visits to retail stores. The primary source of business information is the retail store. A visit to a retail store is essential in the purchase of most consumer products.[19] The principal contact within the store is the retail sales clerk, who provides almost any information about the product including function, price, services, warranty, and performance record. It is a primary source of information for most consumers.

Advertisements supply consumers with a variety of information, including brands, price, sales, product features, location, and store name. Consumers typically use advertisements to gain an overall impression of the product and the store. Advertisements have the following rank of importance as an information source to consumers: (1) in-store displays, (2) newspaper ads, (3) TV commercials, (4) ads in women's magazines, (5) articles in women's magazines, and (6) newspaper articles. The reader may be surprised at the high rank of in-store displays.

Door-to-door salespersons are used much less often. Insurance, cosmetics, brushes, tree surgery, and books are products sold door-to-door. Door-to-door salespeople provide the same types of information as retail store clerks.

The advantages of business sources of information for consumers are the variety of information available, the low cost of information, the availability of specific data, and the ease with which the information is available. There is perhaps no better source of specific data on the product. However, there are problems with business sources. The information is always favorable to the business. Some information may be withheld, and some may be slanted so as to be incorrect. As a result, consumers are generally skeptical of business information. Consumers often obtain information from business sources and check its reliability with family and reference groups.

DETERMINANTS OF SOURCE SELECTION

There are three principal determinants used by consumers in selecting information sources.

Type of Information Desired

Consumers place different importance on sources, depending on the type of information desired. The tendency is to obtain a variety of information from the mass media and check its validity from personal sources. Consumers tend also to obtain more general information from the mass media and specific facts from company salespeople or personal sources. If the information is crucial to the decision, the consumer may seek more trusted personal sources.

Information about the criteria used to select from among alternatives tends to come from personal experience. Performance information tends to come from business sources, but it is checked with persons who have had experience with the product or store. Consumers pick up much information accidentally; they see and hear things when they are not specifically looking for information and may not even be in the act of purchasing. This information is internalized to be used later if needed.

Confidence in the Source

A consumer has confidence in a source when he or she believes the information it supplies. If the consumer has had good results with products recommended by the source, he or she is likely to use it again. If a consumer has received unreliable information from some reference group source, such as a friend, that source may not be trusted in the future. However, credibility does not just apply to reference group sources. Often consumers have lasting relationships with salespersons, and they believe what these persons tell them. Consumers also develop identification with specific firms or their advertising, and they tend to have confidence in those firms with which they have a positive identification.

Some external sources can be relied on more for one type of decision than for another. It is not always sound to ask a merchant an honest opinion of a competitor's product. This same merchant may be perfectly candid in explaining the performance of his product. A personal friend may give you an honest opinion about a merchant but stretch the truth about some product that he or she owns. After all, the friend does not want it known that he or she purchased a poor product.

It may be that the credibility of the seller of some products can be increased by disclaiming superiority of some product features. This result was discovered in a study using a ballpoint pen, watch, blender, camera, and clock radio. A statement was made that the product had been compared to the industry leader, and several features were listed. Some questionnaires claimed superiority of all features and some did not. The results demonstrated greater confidence in the latter. Consumers apparently regard consistent claims of superiority for all product features to be too good to be true.

Source Effectiveness

Sources of information selected by consumers can be classified into those that have decisive effectiveness, partial effectiveness, and ineffectiveness. A source is *decisive in effectiveness* when it is the most important determinant of the purchase. A source has *partial influence* so long as it plays some part but is less than decisive. This class can obviously be divided into several subclasses. A source is *ineffective* when it plays very little or no part in the decision. Information may be obtained, but it is either ignored or disregarded for the purchase decision. Consumers utilize multiple sources of information. In a given decision, one or two sources may be decisive, several may be partially effective, and some may have very little effect.

THE AMOUNT OF CONSUMER SEARCH

Consumers seeking market-related information do not all behave alike. We know from experience that some consumers seek more information than others, even when consulting the same types of sources.[20] Nearly all consumers engage in more search for some types of products than for others. These points naturally lead to the question, "How much search is necessary?" The answer depends on the value of search and the factors affecting the amount. These points are discussed below.

The search for consumer information is costly, but its results are valuable.[21] The values center around the fact that more information can lead to sounder decisions. It can result in lower prices or more suitable products. The costs involved in information seeking are both financial and psychological. It is not possible to make a definitive list of values and costs because they mean different things to different consumers. For example, the time necessary to search and compare products is an advantage to a consumer who wants a more suitable product or lower price. Time is a disadvantage to a consumer who wants the convenience of a quick purchase. To one consumer shopping is fun, but to another it is mental anguish.

Although values and costs cannot be generalized, it does follow that for an individual consumer, the amount of search is determined by balancing the values and costs of information seeking. This balancing is not easy because of the number of variables the consumer must consider. We now look into these variables, remembering that any one can be a value or a cost to the individual.

Value of the Product

The more valuable the product, the greater the amount of search the consumer is likely to undertake.[22] A product's worth to a consumer can be measured in several ways: financial worth, worth in terms of the consumer's needs and motivation, and worth as indicated by placement in the consumer's target assortment. For example, more costly products get more attention than less costly products, and products that are fundamental to a consumer's needs or motivation get more attention. Price, convenient location, and services are the most important reasons a person trades with a particular retailer store, and changes in price affect purchase patterns.[23]

Availability of Information Without Search

If the consumer can obtain information without a physical search, so much the better. A great deal of information is available to consumers through the mass media. The consumer often obtains this information whether it is wanted or not. Once obtained, it becomes a part of personal experience. Newspapers, television, and radio constantly provide consumers with market information that can help solve current problems without physical search. If the amount of information is not sufficient, search is necessary. Not all experience applies to a given problem.

Experience is suitable if it contributes to understanding the problem at hand. The problem may be similar to a previous problem, or some anticipated satisfaction may be similar to past satisfactions. A previous solution may be transferable to the present situation. It also follows that if experience cannot be recalled, then search is necessary to fill in the gaps.

Satisfaction Derived from Search

Among considerations that can lead to search satisfaction are convenience, better information, pleasure from shopping, and social satisfaction.[24] Search can be convenient because more search can lead to better information for deciding, or less search can save time. Better information can lead to more suitable products, lower prices, or both. Search may be enjoyable to some consumers, rendering direct satisfaction. A consumer who enjoys shopping is likely to do more of it. A consumer who does not like shopping is likely to make do with less information. Social values pertain to the psychic satisfactions derived from search — the enjoyment of owning the perfect garment, social acceptance into a particular group, and so on.[25] A consumer placing great value on these psychic considerations may seek more information before deciding on a product.

Perceived Consequence of Search

The perceived consequence of search refers to the outcome the consumer expects. Important consequences that affect the amount of search are product satisfaction, financial outlay (price and time of payment), social risk, risk of being dissatisfied, and inconvenience. More search is necessary to obtain the correct product, to save money, to avoid social risks, and to reduce inconvenience or the risk of product dissatisfaction.[26]

Usefulness of the Information

The consumer is more likely to engage in search when the information is expected to make a significant contribution to the decision.[27] Consumers are more likely to seek information about a product's quality or performance than about product color or materials. Shoppers frequently seek information concerning competitive brands, price, and warranty. They are also interested in the availability of service for those products that require it. It follows that technical products are more likely to be searched than convenience products.

PATTERNS OF CONSUMER SEARCH

The specific patterns for seeking market information vary considerably among consumers. Some individuals but not others actively seek facts; some but not others search continually until the problem is solved. Furthermore, some consumer problems are such that the entire family becomes involved in the search, while other problems involve only the individual.

Photo 7-2

Some consumers enjoy shopping more than others. Consumers who enjoy shopping will search longer.

Active and Passive Search

All consumers seek product and store information at times, but we can distinguish active searchers from passive searchers. *Active searchers* seek market information for its own sake.[28] They enjoy the physical activity involved with external search, and they engage in it even when there is no immediate problem. These consumers often shop simply to keep abreast of what product and store alternatives are available. They ask about the new products that they see their friends and neighbors using. They read ads and inquire among reference groups about new ideas observed in the various media. Active searchers tend to be inquisitive persons. They participate in many activities outside the home, are receptive to new and different products, are interested in themselves and their community, and like to be well-thought-of by others. These consumers store market data for use when a specific problem arises.

Passive searchers are not willing to expend much effort in seeking product and market facts. These consumers are not uninterested in making effective decisions. They usually perceive themselves as too busy or feel that they have sufficient facts or that the search is not likely to be worthwhile. Passive searchers seek market information only when it has specific and immediate use. These consumers tend to use external sources, such as television, radio, newspapers, magazines, catalogs, and pamphlets that are available without much external search. Passive searchers visit the store primarily to purchase; often their mind is essentially made up when they take action. Passive searchers are frequently introverted and preoccupied with work or family. They tend to prefer family-oriented leisure, they frequently purchase by habit, and they are not inquisitive about new ideas. Of course, most consumers do not fit either extreme. It is typical to engage in both active and passive search.

Continual or Intermittent Search

Consumer search can be continual or intermittent. A consumer who engages in *continual search* seeks information systematically and regularly until a definitive basis for action is established. Someone who makes several shopping trips in the space of two weeks before buying a garment is engaging in continual search, as are a husband and wife who visit several automobile dealers, collect and compare dealer literature, and discuss different cars with their friends over a month. *Intermittent search* refers to sporadic information seeking that continues until a course of action is chosen. After some period of inconclusive or unsatisfactory search, the individual may cease looking, only to begin again later. A person who types at home may periodically check the want ads for a used typewriter. A poor child may check the Sears catalog all summer, dreaming about the one or two toys that may be possible at Christmas.

The types of action are the same whether consumer search is continual or intermittent. The three possibilities are: (1) abandonment of the search, (2) storage of the facts discovered, or (3) purchase of a product. Abandonment may occur because the consumer loses interest in the product, because the search is unsuccessful, or because the facts indicate that the consumer should not purchase. Facts may be stored until the consumer has the money to buy or until a more appropriate time for purchase presents itself. Intermittent search is often associated with unsuccessful search, but it can also occur for other reasons. Active seekers, mentioned previously, often engage in intermittent search to check the market. A consumer may engage in intermittent search when the product need is not urgent. Intermittent search may precede the purchase of major durable goods such as a home or furniture.

Either continual or intermittent search may begin with the individual aware or unaware of a specific product need. The consumer may become aware of a product need while shopping and may engage in continual search until a purchase is made. The consumer may have a generic product in mind but may engage in intermittent search until the specific item or brand is discovered. It often happens that a consumer cannot afford the time for continual search even though the specific product is known, so the consumer searches sporadically when an opportunity presents itself.

Casual or Formal Search

Another important pattern of consumer search concerns the seriousness with which the consumer approaches the task. Consumer search is casual when it is incidental to another activity of the individual. A nonshopper may inquire about a product observed while accompanying a friend downtown. A TV advertisement may spark the individual's interest. Casual search is more likely to be undertaken when the product is of small unit value, unimportant, routinely purchased, or nontechnical. Convenience products and impulse purchases are often based on a casual search.

Consumer search is formal when the primary purpose of the activity is to obtain decision information about products, stores, or market conditions. Formal search typically involves more careful consideration, thought, and effort than does casual search.[29] Products that are highly technical, durable, and expensive and that require service typically receive serious attention. Shopping products and long-term investment products such as houses, furniture, or insurance are searched more formally. However, it would be a mistake to assume that formal search is automatically better or more successful than casual search. Either type can result in effective market behavior. The type of search employed depends on the reason for search and the situation.

Local or Extended Search

Shoppers have the choice of purchasing products locally or extending their search to more distant shopping centers, trade areas, or towns.[30] Two generalizations can be made relative to which course of action is followed.

First, all types of consumers tend to resist traveling in their search for products. Most consumers will travel further for shopping products than for convenience products. Even so, a round trip of approximately five miles is the limit of search for the vast majority of consumers. The decentralization of retail trade in larger cities has brought a great many product alternatives close to the consumer's residence. There is no need for most shoppers to travel great distances to find desired products.

Second, the size of the town has impact on customer willingness to travel. Persons in relatively smaller towns tend to travel to larger towns to shop—no matter what the actual size of the towns. Extended travel costs more, but the perception of greater product selection, better prices, and status associated with the larger town attracts consumers.

Consumers also travel from larger cities to smaller ones to shop. They feel that the smaller city, because of less demand, must make a price appeal in order to compete with nearby larger cities. It is entirely possible that this perception is false, but it does persist. A wide range of products are purchased out of town. Some of the more common ones include carpets, men's and women's clothing, curtains, and housewares. Automobiles, furniture, appliances, and jewelry are not purchased as often out of town.

The Time to Shop

Even when purchasing the same type of products, consumers visit stores at different times.[31] Both the time of day and the day of the week are important.

First, let us look at the time of day. The afternoon hours are generally most popular for shopping, with early evening next most popular. The early morning hours are less popular for most stores, although grocery stores do a good business

Photo 7-3
People perceive some items to be cheaper away from the city.

USDA Photo by David Warren

at these times. Generally, homemakers like to do housework in the morning and shop in the afternoon. There is a greater likelihood that couples can shop together in the afternoon or early evening, because both can leave work.

Second, consider patterns of shopping by days. The popularity of shopping days varies by product, type of store, and circumstances. Friday and Saturday are popular for many types of durable goods. Grocery stores find Friday the most popular shopping day, followed by Thursday and Saturday. Shopping on Sunday is increasing in popularity because of the inability to enforce Sunday closing laws. Monday is the least popular day to visit most stores. Many customers deliberately pick the morning hours and the slow days to do their shopping in order to avoid congestion. Also, many customers like to take advantage of specials and sales which firms use to attract customers on the "off days." The importance of Thursday specials in the grocery industry is well known. White sales and special holiday sales often draw large numbers of customers. Christmas is still the single largest selling season for most stores.

The Number of Stores to Visit

The number of store visits is important to search. Some customers engage in multiple purchases from a single store, while others shop at several stores or even different trade areas before purchasing a single product.[32] Even grocery stores, which sell primarily convenience goods, report that customers use other stores. One study indicated that customers, on the average, visited two other supermarkets.[3] Multiple purchases at one store save the consumer time and shopping trips. Shopping at several stores or trade areas may insure a more successful purchase.

The pattern of store visitation affects the manner of transportation. The automobile is the single most used transportation means, but it is particularly important when shopping at several stores because of its speed and flexibility of movement. About 50 percent of consumers use the automobile, 30 percent walk, and 19 percent use public transportation or taxis when shopping.[34] The average grocery shopper makes approximately 2.28 trips to the store per week.[35] The number of shopping trips is less for durable and fashion products.

QUESTIONS

1. Is it possible that once a consumer recognizes a problem he or she would skip the search step of the decision process? Discuss your answer.
2. Discuss the important ways that marketers can benefit from a knowledge of consumer search patterns.
3. Communications can be classed by purpose into casual, informative, persuasive, and reminder. Find advertisements that represent each of these purposes.
4. Can marketing managers be assured their communications are complete without feedback? Explain your answer.
5. Sales are often used to measure the effectiveness of one-way communications. Is this a reliable measurement? Explain your answer.

6. What are the advantages and disadvantages of two-way communications?
7. The influence of opinion leaders can be horizontal as well as vertical. Is this true for all types of products? Discuss your answer.
8. Do you perceive opinion leaders to be a more reliable source of information than advertisements? Explain your answer.
9. Identify the types of noise you may encounter when reading an advertisement in the newspaper.
10. What are the advantages of personal experience over reference group sources and the advantages of reference group sources over personal experience?
11. Identify the types of magazines an active searcher would read. Why?
12. Identify products for which you would engage in continual search for information and those for which you would engage in intermittent search for information. Why the difference?
13. When are you more likely to conduct a casual search for information? A formal search for information?
14. Take the following products: shoes, sweater, and a radio. Compare these products at a store in a mall and a store downtown. Where can you find the best price, selection, and information about the product?
15. Grocery stores find Friday to be the most popular shopping day. What do you think are the reasons for this?

NOTES

1. Geoffrey C. Keil and Roger A. Layton, "Dimensions of Consumer Information Seeking Behavior," *Journal of Consumer Research*, Vol. XVIII (May 1981), pp. 233–39.
2. Joseph W. Newman and Bradley D. Lockeman, "Measuring Prepurchase Information Seeking," *Journal of Consumer Research,* Vol. 2 (December 1975), pp. 216–22.
3. Gabriel Biehal and Dipankar Chakravarti, "Information Accessibility as a Moderator of Consumer Choice," *Journal of Consumer Research,* Vol. 10, (June 1983), pp. 1–14.
4. Patrick Dunne, "Some Demographic Characteristics of Direct Mail Purchasers," *Baylor Business Studies* (May, June, July 1975), pp. 62–73; Arch G. Woodside and M. Wayne Delozier, "Effects of Word of Mouth Advertising on Consumer Risk Taking," *Journal of Advertising*, Vol. 5 (Fall 1976), pp. 12–19.
5. Patrick L. Schul and Charles W. Lamb, Jr., "Decoding Nonverbal and Vocal Communications: A Laboratory Study," *Journal of the Academy of Marketing Science,* Vol. 10 (Spring 1982), pp. 154–64.
6. Rashi Glazer, "Multiattribute Perceptual Bias as Revealing of Preference Structure," *Journal of Consumer Research*, Vol. 11 (June 1984), pp. 510–21.
7. George Katona and Eva Mueller, "A Study of Purchasing Decisions," in Lincoln Clark, ed., *Consumer Behavior: The Dynamics of Consumer Reac-*

tion (New York: New York University Press, 1955), p. 45.

8. Japhet H. Nkonge, "How Communication Medium and Message Format Affect Corrective Advertising," *Journal of the Academy of Marketing Science*, Vol. 12 (Winter 1984), pp. 58–68.

9. Leo Bogart, B. Stuart Tolley, and Frank Orenstein, "What One Little Ad Can Do," *Journal of Advertising Research*, Vol. 10 (1970), pp. 3–13.

10. Gordon L. Wise, "Impact of the Gasoline Price War on Consumer Patronage Motives," *Journal of Retailing*, Vol. 48 (Summer 1972), pp. 64–66, 91.

11. Laurence P. Feldmand and Alvin D. Star, "Are Active Shoppers Different?" *Business Ideas and Facts*, Vol. 7 (Winter 1974), pp. 15–23.

12. Fred D. Reynolds and William R. Darden, "Intermarket Patronage: A Psychographic Study of Consumer Outshoppers," *Journal of Marketing*, Vol. 36 (October 1972), pp. 50–54.

13. Arieh Goldman, "Do Lower-Income Consumers Have More Restricted Shopping Scope?," *Journal of Marketing*, Vol. 40 (January 1987), pp. 46–54.

14. John R. Thompson, "Characteristics and Behavior of Out-Shopping Consumers," *Journal of Retailing*, Vol. 47 (Spring 1971), pp. 70–80; William R. Darden and William D. Perreault, Jr., "Identifying Interurban Shoppers: Multiproduct Purchase Patterns and Segmentation Profiles," *Journal of Marketing Research*, Vol. 13 (February 1976), pp. 51–60.

15. Converse used the formula below to predict the flow of trade to two cities from towns located in between:

$$\frac{Ba}{Bb} \quad \frac{Pa}{Pb} \quad \frac{Db}{Da}$$

where

Ba is the proportion of trade to city A

Bb is the proportion of trade to city B

Pa is the population of city A

Pb is the population of city A

Da is the distance to city A

Db is the distance to city B

Paul D. Converse, "New Laws of Retail Gravitation," *Journal of Marketing*, Vol. 13 (October 1949), pp. 379–88.

16. Ernest F. Larkin and Gerald L. Grotta, "Consumer Attitudes Toward and Use of Advertising Content in a Small Daily Newspaper," *Journal of Advertising*, Vol. 5 (Winter 1976), pp. 28–31.

17. Gabriel J. Biehal, "Consumers' Prior Experiences and Perceptions in Auto Repair Choice," *Journal of Marketing*, Vol. 47 (Summer 1983), pp. 82–91.

18. Johan Arndt and Frederick E. May, "The Hypothesis of a Dominance Hierarchy of Information Sources," *Journal of the Academy of Marketing Science*, Vol. 9 (Fall 1981), pp. 337–51.

19. Marsha L. Richins, "An Analysis of Consumer Interaction Styles in the Marketplace," *Journal of Consumer Research*, Vol. 10 (June 1983), pp. 73–82.

20. Girish N. Punj and Richard Staelin, "A Model of Consumer Information Search Behavior for New Automobiles," *Journal of Consumer Research*, Vol. 9 (March 1983), pp. 366–80.

21. John D. Claxton, Joseph N. Fry, and Bernard Portis, "A Taxonomy of Prepurchase Information Gathering Patterns," *Journal of Consumer Research*, Vol. 1 (December 1974), pp. 35–42.

22. Roger Dickinson, "Search Behavior: A Note," *Journal of Consumer Research*, Vol. 9 (June 1982), pp. 115–16.

23. Gordon L. Wise, "Impact of the Gasoline Price War on Consumer Patronage Motives," *Journal of Retailing,* Vol. 48 (Summer 1972), pp. 64–66, 91.

24. Edward M. Tauber, "Why Do People Shop?" *Journal of Marketing,* Vol. 36 (October 1972), pp. 46–49.

25. David F. Midgley, "Patterns of Interpersonal Information Seeking for the Purchase of a Symbolic Product," *Journal of Marketing Research*, Vol. XX (February 1983), pp. 74–83.

26. Luis Dominguez and Richard W. Olshavshy "Information Processing Analysis of a Stochastic Model of Brand Choice," *Journal of Business Research,* Vol. 9 (1981), pp. 39–48.

27. Geoffrey P. Lantos, "The Influences of Inherent Risk and Information Acquisition on Consumer Risk Reduction Strategies," *Journal of the Academy of Marketing Science*, Vol. 11 (Fall 1983), pp. 358–81; James B. Wiley, "Toward Upgrading the Quality of Consumer Decision-making," *Journal of the Academy of Marketing Science*, Vol. 12 (Winter 1984), pp. 1–10. pp. 1–10.

28. Laurence P. Feldman and Alvin D. Star, "Are Active Shoppers Different?" *Business Ideas and Facts*, Vol. 7 (Winter 1974), pp. 15–23.

29. Jacob Hornik, "Subjective vs. Objective Time Measures: A Note on the Perception of Time in Consumer Behavior," *Journal of Consumer Research,* Vol. 11 (June 1984), pp. 615–18.

30. Fred D. Reynolds and William R. Darden, "Intermarket Patronage: A Psychographic Study of Consumer Outshoppers," *Journal of Marketing*, Vol. 36 (October 1972), pp. 50–54.

31. Jacob Hornik, *op. cit.,,* pp. 615–18.

32. R. Eric Reidenback, M. Bixby Cooper, and Mary Carolyn Harrison, "A Factor Analytic Comparison of Outshopping Behavior in Larger Retail Trade Areas," *Journal of the Academy of Marketing Science*, Vol. 12 (Spring 1984), pp. 145–58.

33. "Consumer Behavior in the Supermarket," *Progressive Grocer*, Vol. 54 (October 1975), pp. 37–59.

34. Daniel J. McLaughlin, "Consumer Reaction to Retail Food Newspaper Advertising in High and Low Income Areas," *Business Ideas and Facts,* Vol. 7 (Fall 1984), pp. 21–24.

35. Robert Dietrick, "They've Changed Their Ways of Shopping," *Progressive Grocer*, Vol. 53 (April 1974), pp. 45–47.

CHAPTER 8

Internal Consumer Search

CHAPTER OUTLINE

I. **INTERNAL CONSUMER SEARCH INVOLVES ATTITUDES**

II. **FUNCTIONS OF ATTITUDES IN INTERNAL SEARCH**
   A. Adjustment Function
   B. Value Expressive Function
   C. Ego Defensive Function
   D. Knowledge Function

III. **INTERNAL SEARCH DEPENDS ON LEARNED ATTITUDES**
   A. What Consumers Learn
   B. Learning Theories
   C. How Consumers Learn Attitudes
   D. The Learning Curve
   E. Effects of Forgetting on Attitudes
   F. Patterns of Consumer Forgetting

IV. **WHAT INTERNAL SEARCH REVEALS ABOUT ATTITUDES**
   A. Attitudes Provide Appropriate Responses
   B. Attitudes Provide Polarity to Responses
   C. Attitude Intensity Affects Responses
   D. Attitudes Are Transferable
   E. Attitudes Are Not Always Reliable

V. **CONSUMER ATTITUDE STABILITY**
   A. Structure of Attitudes Provides Stability
   B. Casualty of Attitudes Affects Stability
   C. Congruence Conditions Attitude Stability

VI. **CONSUMER ATTITUDE CHANGE**
   A. Conflict of Attitudes Affects Change
   B. Traumatic Experience
   C. Change in the Product
   D. Perceptual Change
   E. Strength of the Attitude
   F. Store of Information

CHAPTER OBJECTIVES

After completing your study of Chapter 8, you should be able to:

1. Explain how internal consumer search involves attitudes.
2. Discuss the functions of attitudes in internal search.
3. Discuss how internal search depends on learned attitudes.
4. Discuss what internal search reveals about attitudes.
5. Discuss consumer attitude stability.
6. Discuss consumer attitude change.

It was pointed out previously that consumers can search out information internally and externally from their environment. Internal search is a mental process of assessing what one already knows, and external search is acquiring new information by communicating with persons in the environment. This chapter is concerned with internal search. The next three chapters deal with external search.

INTERNAL CONSUMER SEARCH INVOLVES ATTITUDES

Consumers react to the market environment by forming attitudes toward products, businesses, and methods of purchase. A *consumer attitude* is defined as:

the readiness to act in a predetermined manner toward some specific market-related stimulus.

Internal search involves attitudes because it is the recall, from memory, of one's predispositions. When a consumer sees a box of Quaker Oats and thinks, "I haven't enjoyed that for quite a while," there is internal search. When a consumer attempts to remember the store where he or she saw an item, there is internal search.

Such words as *beliefs, feelings, opinions, inclinations,* and *biases* are often used to depict attitudes. While an attitude is any predisposition, each of the above terms denotes a particular type of attitude. Of course, any type of attitude may be conscious or unconscious. We detect shades of difference in personal predispositions according to what individuals do or say. However, the attitude itself is a combination of cognitive processes (such as thought and memory) and motivational processes (involving emotion and striving).

Opinions, beliefs, and feelings are usually thought of in relation to a person's preference for one viewpoint in matters which are controversial or on which there is more than one side. Store loyalty, brand preference, store atmosphere, product quality, and prices are subjects on which consumers often have beliefs and opinions. However, the types of predispositions differ among consumers and situations in several important respects.[1] The most important differences relate to their duration and intensity.

Beliefs are predispositions accepted as truth and supported by strong facts or other information. Most beliefs are reasonably permanent, but they may, or may not, be important. For example, a consumer may have strong beliefs about a Kenmore washer and Borden's milk, but they are not equally important. *Opinions* are predispositions not based on certainty. There may be some facts, but they are only suggestive of the conclusion drawn by the consumer. Opinions tend to relate to current questions, and they are relatively easily changed. Nearly everyone had an opinion on the reason for the energy crisis in the 1970s, but a few facts could change many minds. *Feelings* are predispositions of a basically emotional nature. They can be quite durable and deep-seated, but they are not usually supported by relevant facts. The feelings that a woman's place is in the home or that men who shop with their wives are sissies are deeply entrenched in many minds. We can think of feelings as sentiment, opinions as impressions, and beliefs as values. Attitudes, then, can be any type of conviction—weak or strong, permanent or temporary—based on fact or emotion.

Inclinations and bias can refer to any type of attitude. An *inclination* is a partially formed attitude when the consumer is in an essentially undecided state. For example, between Phillips 66 and Exxon a buyer may be inclined toward Phillips 66 because of the reputation of the dealer, but still undecided because of a preference for Exxon's brand. *Bias* is a mental prejudice believed in spite of the fact that there is evidence to the contrary. A consumer may have biased feelings, opinions, or beliefs. Bias can work for or against a retailer. For example, product preference is a type of bias.

FUNCTIONS OF ATTITUDES IN INTERNAL SEARCH

Attitudes perform several functions that relate to consumer internal search. They are: (1) the adjustment function, (2) the value expressive function, (3) the ego defensive function and (4) the knowledge function. Each of these functions relates to the individual's predisposition toward products, stores, or methods of purchase. Internal search relates these functions to the external stimulus.

Adjustment Function

Attitudes designed to maximize perceived rewards in any market situation and to minimize punishment serve an *adjustment function*. Internal search brings out perceived rewards and punishments that apply to a given market situation. In a general way, consumers develop favorable attitudes toward products and stores that satisfy and unfavorable attitudes toward products and stores that displease.

Marketers can make appeals to the adjustment function of attitudes. The ad in Figure 8-1 plays on both rewards and punishment. What we have here is an adjustment or accommodation to the situation.

Value Expressive Function

The *value expressive function* allows the consumer to demonstrate positively his or her basic values. A consumer can express strong feelings about health by riding a bicycle, eating health foods, and quitting smoking. The consumer who always purchases the least expensive product is exercising the value expressive

Figure 8-1
Appealing to the adjustment function

Cancer attacks more than the body.

It attacks the minds of cancer patients and their families. Imagine telling a six-year old child, "Mommy has cancer." For the cancer patients and their families, that's just the beginning. Some people find great strength when faced with serious problems. But for others, the onset of cancer can be psychologically devasting. That's why there's CANCER CARE.

CANCER CARE counsels cancer patients and their families in dealing with the psychological threat as well as physical problems. It's people helping people, giving hope and strength for the troubled times ahead. They're professionals who help them know that living doesn't have to end when cancer begins. It helps cancer patients and their families to continue.

CANCER CARE also refers cancer patients and their families to available services that can ease the burden and pressure of a very shocking discovery.

CANCER CARE. It's people helping people to continue.

CANCER CARE
people helping people

Cancer Care, Inc., 1180 Sixth Avenue, New York 10036, (212) 679-5700

Cancer Care, Inc.

function. The Coca-Cola slogan "It's the Real Thing" expresses life-styles with which many consumers can identify. Value expressive attitudes give consumers an opportunity to show how they feel about the world around them. The marketer's task is to identify with these attitudes.

Ego Defensive Function

The *ego defensive function* aids the consumer in dealing with inner conflict by protecting the self-image from hostile elements in the environment. Consumers rarely behave in ways that damage their positive self-image. The consumer builds up defense mechanisms, rationalizes, and avoids criticisms that damage the ego. Internal search identifies these defenses and brings them into play in buying situations. The cigarette smoker avoids all literature that condemns smoking and refuses to believe medical claims. Other products that have aspects of enhancing the self include grooming aids, fashion clothing, and hairpieces.

Knowledge Function

The knowledge function of attitudes serves to give order and meaning to the person's environment. It is an information filter by which internal search can determine what one feels about a person or situation as well as what one will believe.[2] For example, when one approaches a salesperson in a retail store, the knowledge of previous encounters with salespersons establishes expectations. The recall of previous attitudes allows one to know that one prefers Calvin Klein jeans, Toyota automobiles, rock music, or price appeal stores. Thus, the consumer does not have to re-examine her or his preferences, habits, life-styles, or values for each new buying situation. Internal knowledge easily recalled thus simplifies our interaction with the world around us. No function of attitudes is more important than the knowledge function.

INTERNAL SEARCH DEPENDS ON LEARNED ATTITUDES

Internal search is acquiring or recalling information already contained in the mind about a market-related situation. It calls to mind existing attitudes that make external search unnecessary. The consumer's internal knowledge must be gained by some means. It is not acquired automatically. Therefore, internal consumer search is involved with learning and how learning provides for attitudes.[3]

Like most ideas, learning can be viewed in more than one way.[4] Psychologists generally consider *learning* to be:

any change in an individual's response or behavior resulting from practice, experience, or mental association.[5]

To some, learning is the change that results, and to others, it is the process of arriving at the change through practice, experience, or mental association.[6] Actually, learning implies both. The difficulty is that the learning process cannot be observed — only the results of learning or of what has been learned are observable. We see that a consumer is continually drawn to a single brand of watch (brand loyalty) or that after watching several TV commercials, a consumer changes his or her habit of purchasing a certain brand of dog food. We cannot observe the actual learning that led to these behavior patterns or to changes in them, only the behavior itself.

What Consumers Learn

Consumer decision making involves learning at two different levels, one essentially mental and the other essentially physical.[7] On the first, and more basic, level, the consumer must learn thought processes. These thought processes involve the consumer's beliefs, preferences, feelings, opinions, and mental associations that relate to attitudes.

1. A consumer learns to associate a question mark with a pair of jeans.
2. A consumer learns that one department gives efficient service and another doesn't.
3. A consumer learns to prefer Manhattan shirts.

On the other level, the consumer learns attitudes toward specific physical behavior. This behavior may be in the form of a direct action to satisfy an inner desire or a specific reaction to unforeseen market stimuli. Thus, learned physical behavior always involves previously learned attitudes:

1. A consumer learns that one route to the shopping center is faster than another.
2. A consumer learns that one haggles over the price of furniture in one store but not in another.
3. A consumer learns a specific reaction to an advertisement for a detergent.

Nearly all consumer behavior involves learning at both levels, but the learning does not necessarily occur at the same time. Actions may be learned long after the attitudes have been formed. New attitudes may be formed as a result of specific behavior. For example, a young woman requires both types of learning for the purchase and use of makeup. She learns attitudes toward the use of makeup, attitudes toward particular brands, specific actions in applying makeup, and specific actions in obtaining the makeup.

Whether dealing with thought processes or behavior, the consumer learns both what is right or acceptable and what is wrong or unacceptable. We often think of learning as positive, perhaps because of its association with school. However, we can just as easily learn *avoidance* thoughts or behavior as *seeking-out* thoughts or behavior. Consumers learn, often by trial, to avoid certain clerks in a store. They learn that specific brands are not suited for their purposes, and they learn to avoid certain stores.[8] Consumers also learn to avoid shopping during the rush hour, to avoid putting off the payment of bills, and to avoid unlawful market activity.

Learning Theories

Several theories have been advanced to explain the learning process of consumers. While it is not our major task to explain learning, it is important to know the general way in which consumers learn. Table 8-1 summarizes the important types of learning theories. The fact is, as demonstrated in the next section, some or all of these theories may be involved in the same consumer decision. That is to say, they are not necessarily exclusive.

How Consumers Learn Attitudes

Consumers use a combination of classical conditioning, experience, problem solving, and pleasure-pain theories to learn the attitudes that guide their internal search. The first element in the learning process is some *perceived object* that is capable of stimulating consumer thought or action. This stimulus object is the learning goal. For example, the object may be a hand calculator, a meal at McDonald's, or an anticipated trip to the mall. In any case, the object stimulates perceived satisfaction. The consumer may anticipate the satisfaction of better grades by using the calculator, the pleasant taste of the meal, or the fun of shopping by going to the mall.

The second element in the learning process is the *response*—any action, reaction, or state of mind the observed object evokes. If the consumer has knowledge of the object (experience theory), he or she may know immediately whether to purchase or not.[9] A part of that experience may be the satisfaction or dissatisfaction (pleasure-pain theory) from previous use of the product or shopping trip. The consumer may have perceived a need for the calculator, meal, or shopping trip on many other occasions. Each time the result was satisfactory. These repeat performances are known as *reinforcement*, and each positive reinforcement tends to assure the same reaction next time.[10] If so, the consumer may have been set up to purchase (classical conditioning), and he or she may act more or less out of habit in similar future buying situations.

If the consumer is not familiar with the product, then a problem exists (problem-solving theory). The consumer may have to engage in both internal and

Table 8–1
Learning Theories of Consumer Behavior

Connectionist Theories	Cognitive Theories
A person can be trained, by repetition, to respond the same way each time a specific stimulus is given.	People have the ability to think and associate facts to solve problems. These theories discount repetition in favor of insight.
1. Classical Conditioning. Two completely unrelated ideas can be related by repeated association with a reward. The famous experiments by Pavlov demonstrated that by associating the ringing of a bell with food, a dog could be taught to salivate at the ringing of the bell alone. By associating repeated satisfaction with a product, a consumer can become loyal to that product.	1. Problem-solving Theory. Faced with a market-related problem the consumer is capable of thinking logically to arrive at a solution. The reward may come by solving the problem or from satisfaction that results from solving the problem. A consumer, new to a city, uses problem solving to decide on preferred doctors, lawyers, automobile mechanics, and grocery stores.
2. Instrumental Conditioning. People seek pleasure and avoid pain. Individuals learn by association which things give pleasure and which result in pain. A consumer may give in to a salesperson and buy because it is uncomfortable to argue further.	2. Experience Theory. The idea is that when faced with a problem, the consumer applies previous methods or solutions to that problem. Trial and error are used until a satisfactory solution is reached. Insight is used to make the connection that some known solution to a problem can be applied to a different problem. A consumer recognizes a product as desirable because of experience with the brand, or experience with Delco batteries may be sufficient to convince a consumer that other Delco products are satisfactory.

Photo 8-1
These consumers are anticipating the satisfaction they will receive from a planned purchase.

external search in order to obtain facts about the problem necessary for making a decision. Suppose the consumer has no knowledge of hand calculators. Internal search may indicate confidence that they work, knowledge that others have used them with success, and a vague identification of a few brands. External search may provide data on price, quality, service, and other facts to be used for comparison. Then the application of logic to this information can lead the person to purchase a Texas Instruments calculator for $6.95 from the local Wal-Mart store.

The third element in the learning process is the *reward,* which relates to the success or failure of the market action. Learning—retaining the experience—occurs because the reward is desired. If there were no reason to file the knowledge in the memory, there could be no learning. No matter how the learning occurs, the attitudes formed toward products, stores, and methods of purchase become part of the consumer's mind. Internal search can bring forth these attitudes in future buying situations.

The Learning Curve

What we refer to as learning does not usually take place all at once. Learning is an incremental process. That which we learn increases with the number of experiences or trials. Illustration 8-1 shows this process. This graph is known as the learning curve. The number of trials is plotted on the horizontal axis, and the probability of a given response is plotted on the vertical axis. The learning curve may apply to a product, a service, a store, or anything that is capable of being learned.[11]

If we assume that the curve refers to the purchase of a particular brand of merchandise, then we find that, after three trials, there is about an 0.62 probability that the person will buy the same brand on the next purchase. The probability of a repeat purchase of the brand is about 0.76 on the sixth trial. By the time we reach the upper limit of the curve, behavior is instantaneous. The rate of learning is small.[12]

The curve is divided into three phases. Phase I is the trial phase. The consumer is solving problems. More time is taken with the decision, and the outcome is less sure. In phase II, decision time has been reduced, and the probability of repeat purchase is greatly increased. At phase III, learning is almost complete, and repeat purchases are automatic and based on habit.

Illustration 8-1
Learning curve

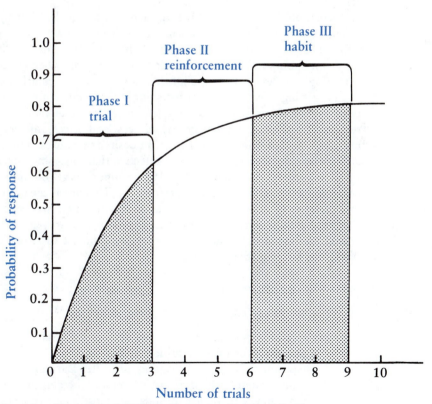

Adapted from John A. Howard, *Marketing Management: Analysis and Planning,* rev. ed. (Homewood, Ill.: Richard D. Irwin, Inc., 1986), p. 36.

Effects of Forgetting on Attitudes

Learning and forgetting go hand in hand. *Forgetting* is the loss, or extinction, of a thought process once held in the mind. A particular purchase pattern, once the consumer learns it, can never be unlearned, but it can be repressed into the unconscious mind.[13] This repression of thought is essentially what we mean by forgetting. That thoughts are never completely lost to the mind is indicated by the ability of persons to remember things forgotten with vivid clarity under hypnosis.

Forgetting serves a useful purpose in consumer behavior. It is difficult to imagine the effect on a person of total recall. The mind would be continually cluttered with useless or unnecessary information about products, stores, buying experiences, etc. Furthermore, it would be almost impossible for a person to face up to the constant reminder of all pleasant, embarrassing, desirable, or painful market experiences. Forgetting allows the mind to file away unneeded or unwanted information, thus making room for new experiences, current experiences, or relevant experiences. It focuses the person's mind on anticipating the future rather than re-living the past. This is an altogether healthy situation. Of course, forgetting works both ways. If one can forget what is unpleasant, one also forgets what is pleasant. The knife cuts both ways.

Frequently, information that has been forgotten can be brought back by careful, intense concentration. Thus, ideas about products, stores, advertisements, etc., that have been forgotten can be recalled when the need arises again. Sometimes forgotten information is brought back to the conscious mind without further experience or effort. This unaided recall is called *spontaneous recovery*. Spontaneous recovery can occur at any time when the consumer is least expecting it, or even when the information is not particularly needed.

Forgetting affects consumer behavior in three important ways. First, it makes purchase reinforcement necessary. Because consumers do not automatically remember products, brands, stores, services, and prices, information or rewards must be repeated over and over to effect desired responses. This is why repetitive advertising can sometimes be more effective than one-time advertising. Second, forgetting fosters consumer change.[14] Consumers forget old brand loyalties, purchase strategies, and assortment preferences. This opens the door for new brands and preferences. Third, the fact that consumers forget makes continuous repetition necessary, at least on a periodic basis. This is true even where the consumer is sold on the store, brand, price, or service. The use of reminder advertising is based on this principle.

Patterns of Consumer Forgetting

Four points are important concerning forgetting.[15]

1. Consumers forget information at about the same rate no matter how important or meaningful it may be.
2. Consumers forget very rapidly just after learning.
3. Understanding the information retards the consumer's forgetting.
4. Consumers recognize brands, slogans, sales appeals, and so forth, easier than they can recall this information.

These facts help explain why consumers sometimes cannot recall advertisements or other information just perceived. These points also add weight to the use of reminder advertising; presentation of nonsense slogans, brands, and jingles, courtesy calls by salespeople; use of increased shelf space; catchy brand names; and unusual layout in their ads (see Figure 8-2).

Figure 8-2
Layout can help in getting the consumer to remember the advertisement

Keebler Company, Ready-Crust®

WHAT INTERNAL SEARCH REVEALS ABOUT ATTITUDES

Internal consumer search can be very useful especially since no overt action is necessary before taking a position. Let us consider what internal search can mean for consumer decision making.

Attitudes Provide Appropriate Responses

In some ways, consumer attitudes are like the trigger of a pistol. Just as the trigger sets the reaction of the pistol into motion, so attitudes initiate the reaction of consumers.[16] Attitudes simplify consumer behavior. The mind cannot process, categorize, and evaluate all the necessary market information that leads to logical purchases in every situation faced. Attitudes provide the consumer with an immediate and appropriate response that bypasses much of the learning and thinking process.[17] Consumer attitudes function somewhat as a program functions for a computer. A computer acts as it is programmed to act. Consumers, through their attitudes, also act according to how they are "programmed." Attitudes are learned over a long period of time. Not only do attitudes make the consumer's market reactions simpler and less time-consuming, but they also reduce the amount of information that has to be learned. Because consumers have formed attitudes, they do not need to re-learn how to react to each market situation.

Attitudes Provide Polarity to Responses

The position taken toward a market problem can be based on positive or negative attitudes. *Positive attitudes* predispose people to act or react favorably to products or stores. *Negative attitudes* predispose people to avoid some situation by market action, but it does not preclude purchasing.[18] A consumer with a negative attitude toward burnt orange is not likely to purchase a sweater of that color. A consumer may have a positive attitude toward a pair of shoes and a negative attitude toward the item in Figure 8-3 because it is unpleasant to think about accidents. The consumer may purchase in both cases. Thus, a negative attitude can act as a stimulus to buy in the same way as a positive attitude. It is difficult to determine the difference between a surface annoyance and deeper, more meaningful attitudes. A consumer may be annoyed by a particular door-to-door salesperson, but the annoyance is not deep. However, if the person is predisposed to hate all salespeople, then an attitude is involved. A merchant can overcome a negative annoyance fairly easily, but to change the attitudes held by customers is difficult.

Attitude Intensity Affects Responses

There are degrees of feeling involved with consumer attitudes, no matter which *direction* the attitude takes. Consumers can evaluate their attitudes toward a product as very positive, slightly positive, or positive, and the same type of evaluation can be made for negative attitudes. Actually, consumer attitudes can be visualized to lie somewhere along a continuum such as the one shown below.

Very positive   Neutral   Very negative
I_____I_____I

The number of predispositions a consumer can hold along the continuum is infinite. Notice that some predispositions may tend toward neutral. That is to say, the consumer has no strong predisposition. Although it is virtually impossible to measure precisely the degree to which an attitude is favorable or unfavorable, it is possible to determine its relative position in the scale.

Attitudes Are Transferable

Consumer attitudes play an important part in simplifying consumer decision making. One way that this simplifying occurs is by *attitude transfer,* where an attitude toward one situation can be applied to another situation. Although a consumer may have thousands of stimuli, the attitude that one feels toward one purchase situation is often quite similar to that felt toward another. For example, a person who is conservative in dress is likely to be conservative in the choice of an automobile, eating habits, recreation, and furniture. Thus, one attitude affects several purchase situations. It follows that management may find clues about

Figure 8-3
Advertisement dealing with unpleasant subject

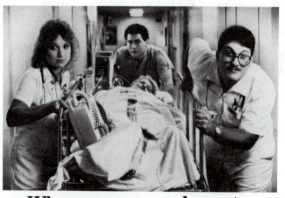

Courtesy of Our Lady of Mercy Hospital, Cincinnati, Ohio

how a consumer may purchase one product, say a suit, by observing that person's purchase of another product, say shoes.

Attitudes Are Not Always Reliable

Consumer attitudes tend to show a property that may be called *completeness*. It sometimes happens that consumers base their attitudes on insufficient information.[19] In spite of this fact, the consumer assumes that the attitude is accurate and acts on it. For example, a consumer may, because of one poor performance, consider a television repairperson to be incompetent or dishonest. Because of the tendency toward completeness, this attitude may well carry over to the store and management that hired the repairperson. A consumer develops an attitude toward a particular brand of television as well-made and dependable. This consumer may transfer this attitude to all products made by the manufacturer of the television set. People do not like things incomplete. They tend to fill in the missing details, and this is true of attitudes.

CONSUMER ATTITUDE STABILITY

The attitudes that consumers have do not just happen. Consumers are not born with all their attitudes established, although many are formed very early in life. Yet, once formed, attitudes have a tendency to persist until something happens to jolt the person out of the established pattern. Let us consider some of the important factors of attitude stability.

Structure of Attitudes Provides Stability

It was pointed out earlier that consumers hold similar attitudes toward products or market situations that they consider to be in the same class. Consumers, in their acceptance of new products, are often reflecting the structure of their attitudes toward the product class rather than the new product.[20] A consumer may reject a new cold-water detergent because of negative attitudes toward all cold-water detergents, even though the new product may be superior to any the consumer has used. Consumers tend to find a balance in their beliefs about various products. When consumer attitudes are in balance, they tend to be stable. We can say that where balance exists, attitudes tend to reinforce one another; there is a tendency to resist change. Furthermore, the consumer has more at stake when several beliefs are at stake rather than one. The consumer tends toward self-protection by holding on to personal attitudes. A consumer's attitudes toward products or stores of the same class affect each other if they are strengthened or weakened. If the consumer's attitude toward the new cold-water detergent product is weakened by new information, the attitude toward all other detergents in the same class may be changed in either of two ways. The attitude toward all cold-water detergents may be weakened or the consumer may disassociate this product from all others in the class. In the latter case, the consumer has reorganized the perceived class of objects.

Photo 8-2

Your attitude toward a business may be based on your attitude toward the salesperson. How might it differ with these two clerks?

Casualty of Attitudes Affects Stability

If consumers view something as having been the cause of something else, they associate the cause and effect through attitudes. A husband who feels very strongly that grocery prices are unjustifiably high may carry his negative attitude over to trading stamps or other merchandising techniques. In addition, consumer attitudes toward certain means resemble consumer attitudes toward the ends to which they apply. Cause-and-effect relationships tend to strengthen and stabilize our attitudes because we can observe direct relationships. A consumer's attitude toward a business is likely to be the same as that toward the salesperson who represents the business.

Congruence Conditions Attitude Stability

Congruence means agreement or harmony of the attitudes of the individual consumer with those of others.[21] Consumers compare attitudes toward the same products or market situations in the same way that they compare other things. Since all consumers justify their own attitudes, it reinforces their opinions to find other consumers in basic agreement. Thus, the attitude tends to be stabilized. Individuals perceive the person who is in agreement with their attitudes as being compatible.[22] This is of particular importance in personal selling, where the situation dictates agreement between the customer and salesperson if the sale is to take place. It also holds for customers' choice of store or trade area.

CONSUMER ATTITUDE CHANGE

Even though consumer attitudes are relatively stable in the short run, changes do occur.[23] Actually, some consumer attitudes are always changing. When we refer to stability, we mean only a tendency for most consumer attitudes to remain stable in the short run. Thus, we actually find a kind of stability in the midst of constant change. It is time to consider some of the causes of these changes.

Conflict of Attitudes Affects Change

Consumers have many attitudes, and every individual is a bundle of contradictions. That is to say that, in the thousands of attitudes a person holds, there is never complete consistency. A consumer may have a very favorable attitude toward the color blue but may not like blue on his or her spouse. When attitudes are in conflict, the consumer may have to make compromises. It is a question of which attitude is more important. A man may buy a convertible in spite of an attitude against this style. We would be hasty to conclude that the person was going against his attitudes. We seldom really go against our attitudes. What probably happened to this consumer is that the person, a father, also had a favorable attitude toward his family, and the family members wanted the convertible. In this case, the father compromised the two attitudes in favor of pleasing his family. He still bought a car, but his attitude toward the family determined the type of car. A consumer may favor expensive clothes; but this consumer may purchase more modest clothes because of an attitude toward thrift.

Traumatic Experience

Attitudes may develop quickly as a result of some traumatic experience involving a great deal of emotion. The attitude one has toward seat belts can be changed very quickly from neutral to positive as a result of an accident. Unexpected good treatment by a sales clerk can create a positive attitude toward a store. Normally, the formation of attitudes is not so quick but depends on repeated exposure. Attitudes that result from traumatic experience often are not as lasting as those that develop more slowly.

Change in the Product

If a product itself is changed and consumers learn about the change, their attitudes may be affected. Often this is the simplest and easiest way to get people to change their attitudes. A slight change in the packaging of a consumer product may quite literally be ten times as effective as all other advertising or personal selling efforts. A change in the properties of the product is readily observable, and sellers do not have to rely as much on persuasion and argument to convince the customer that something is different from before. There are many things a seller can change besides the product. The seller can change service, the attitude of

Photo 8-3
A change in service or the layout of the store may change consumer attitudes about the store.

salespeople, or prices. It is often very effective to change the physical appearance or location of a store. Modernizing can create to a completely new attitude on the part of the customers.

Perceptual Change

There are many instances where attitude change can be brought about by new perceptions even though the product or store remains the same. New information may modify consumer attitudes because it changes perception of the properties of the product or the situation.[24] A change in price or content can cause the consumer to re-evaluate his or her conception of the product. A change in promotion can also be effective. For example, many marketers have been concerned about the effect of putting blacks in advertisements. The worry was that the whites, who comprise the bulk of the market, would reject products that use blacks in their appeal.

The subjective characteristic of perception may lead to a change in attitude even though there is actually nothing new in the situation. The important thing is that the consumer believes that the situation has changed. New information that does not fit well with our attitudes may be ignored or misinterpreted. Thus, attitudes may not change even when appropriate. An effective sales or advertising campaign can lead to a perceived change in a company's operations whether such a change has actually occurred or not.

Strength of the Attitude

Weak attitudes are more susceptible to change than strong or extreme attitudes. A weak consumer attitude may be either positive or negative. The weakest attitude is a neutral feeling. Persons with either strong favorable or unfavorable attitudes undergo the least change in their original position when they receive new information. Those persons without strong favorable or unfavorable attitudes and relatively weak attitudes toward the topics undergo the greatest change. Even a strong attitude can be changed if it is systematically attacked. It may be necessary to give a strong, but sound, reason for the change. Repetition is also effective for changing strong attitudes. The attitude is chipped away a little at a time.

Store of Information

Consumers having a limited amount of information about the product or firm are more susceptible to a change in attitude than are those with a greater store of information.[25] Contradictory information is more likely to bring about an attitude change in consumers who have little information than in consumers with a large amount of information. Marketers are well aware of the difficulties involved in breaking into a market where large doses of effective informational advertising have caused brand preference. The attitudes of children and poorly educated persons are more easily influenced with respect to certain attitudes than are those of adults or people with higher education. Children are exposed to different types of information, to some degree, than adults. Children's responses to advertising provides the following results:

1. Children aged five to nine years watched more children's programs, movies, and family programs. Children aged nine to twelve watched more adventure, education, and sports programs.
2. The younger children were exposed to more food, gum, and toy commercials, while older children viewed more drug, patent medicine, and all other types of commercials.
3. Both groups gave full attention to the television before the commercial, but only about 39 percent of the older children continued to give full attention during the commercial. Younger children tended to continue giving full attention during the commercial.
4. About 20 percent of older children, compared to many fewer younger children, expressed a negative reaction to commercial onset.

Children are usually brought up to respect their elders' judgment, because these children have little information with which they can evaluate many objects. Thus, the effects of advertising vary due to the educational level of the appeals used in the ads.[26] The amount of information present is not only limited by age and education. Even highly educated persons may revise their attitudes when given new information. Certainly, this accounts for much of the brand switching that goes on in the market.

QUESTIONS

1. Consumers react to the market environment by forming attitudes toward products, businesses, and methods of purchase. What comes first, attitudes or behavior? Discuss your answer.
2. Give examples where consumers may purchase a product or buy from a store even if they have unfavorable attitudes toward the product or store.
3. Find several advertisements that express life-styles with which many consumers can identify. Discuss how the advertisement reflects the different life-styles.
4. Discuss and explain the statement: "No function of attitudes is more important than the knowledge function."
5. Discuss why some things are easier to learn than others.
6. Take the classical conditioning theory of learning and apply it to a purchasing situation.
7. What methods or tools can a marketing manager use to provide positive reinforcement to a consumer after a purchase?
8. Of what benefit is it to a marketing manager to know that trial is necessary before learning takes place?
9. What can marketing managers do to overcome the problem of consumers forgetting?
10. Is consumer forgetting always bad? Discuss your answer.

11. Discuss some possible ways marketing managers can overcome negative attitudes toward their products or services.
12. Give examples of how a marketing manager can take advantage of the fact that attitudes are transferable.
13. Individuals perceive people who are in agreement with their attitudes as being compatible. Discuss how this fact can be used to influence consumer decisions.
14. Identify the sources that influence your attitudes. Are they the same for all situations? Discuss your answer.
15. Is there always a direct relationship between attitudes and consumer behavior? Discuss your answer.

NOTES

1. Milton Rokeach, *Beliefs, Attitudes, and Values* (San Francisco: Jossey-Bass, Inc., 1968).
2. Morris B. Holbrook, Robert W. Chestnut, Terence A. Oliva, and Eric A. Greenleaf, "Play Is a Consumption Experience: The Roles of Emotions, Performance, and Personality in the Enjoyment of Games," *Journal of Consumer Research,* Vol. 11 (September 1984), pp. 728–39.
3. Michael L. Rothschild and William C. Gaidis, "Behavioral Learning Theory: Its Relevance to Marketing and Promotions," *Journal of Marketing,* Vol. 45 (Spring 1981), pp. 70–78.
4. George P. Moschis, "Patterns of Consumer Learning," *Journal of The Academy of Marketing Science,* Vol. 9 (Spring 1981), pp. 110–26.
5. Jack A. Adams, *Learning and Memory: An Introduction* (Homewood: The Dorsey Press, 1976), p. 6.
6. Richard A. Winett and John H. Kagel, "Effects of Information Presentation Format on Resource Use in Field Studies," *Journal of Consumer Research,* Vol. 11 (September 1984), pp. 655–67.
7. Rom J. Markin, Jr., *Consumer Behavior: A Cognitive Orientation* (New York: Macmillan Publishing Co., Inc., 1974), pp. 152–53.
8. Joseph W. Newman and Richard Staelin, "Purchase Information Seeking for New Cars and Major Household Appliances," *Journal of Marketing Research,* Vol. 9 (August 1972), pp. 249–57; Leo Bogart and Charles Lehman, "What Makes a Brand Name Familiar?" *Journal of Marketing Research,* Vol. 10 (February 1973), pp. 17–22.
9. Eric J. Johnson and J. Edward Russo, "Product Familiarity and Learning New Information," *Journal of Consumer Research,* Vol. 11 (June 1984), pp. 542–50.
10. Frances K. McSweeney and Calvin Bierley, "Recent Developments in Classical Conditioning," *Journal of Consumer Research,* Vol. 11 (September 1984), pp. 619–31.
11. John A. Howard, *Marketing Theory,* (Boston: Allyn Bacon, Inc., 1965), pp. 100–12.
12. Ibid.

13. Chester R. Wasson, *Consumer Behavior: A Managerial Viewpoint* (Austin: Austin Press, 1975), pp. 96–97.
14. Edward E. Smith, Susan E. Hariland, Lynne M. Reder, Hiram Brownell, and Nancy Adams, "When Preparation Fails: Disruptive Effects of Prior Information on Perceptual Recognition," *Journal of Experimental Psychology,* Vol. 2 (May 1976), pp. 151–61.
15. Benton J. Underwood, "Forgetting," *Scientific American,* Vol. 210 (March 1964), pp. 91–92.
16. A. Oaker and G. S. Day, "Dynamic Model of Relationships Among Advertising, Consumer Awareness, Attitudes and Behavior," *Journal of Applied Psychology,* Vol. 59 (June 1974), pp. 28–86.
17. Calvin P. Duncan and Richard W. Olshavshy, "External Search: The Role of Consumer Beliefs," *Journal of Marketing Research,* Vol. XIX (February 1982), pp. 332–33.
18. Michael B. Maxis, Robert B. Settle, and Dennis C. Leslie, "Elimination of Phosphate Detergents and Psychological Reactance," *Journal of Marketing Research,* Vol. 10 (November 1973), pp. 390–95.
19. Robert J. Meyer, "A Model of Multiattribute Judgements Under Attribute Uncertainty and Informational Constraint," *Journal of Marketing Research,* Vol. XVIII (November 1981), pp. 428–41.
20. Gerald J. Gorn and Charles B. Weinberg, "The Impact of Comparative Advertising on Perception and Attitude: Some Positive Findings," *Journal of Consumer Research,* Vol. 11 (September 1984), pp. 719–27.
21. Paul E. Green, Yoram Wind, and Arun K. Jain, "A Note on Measurement of Social-Psychological Belief Systems," *Journal of Marketing Research,* Vol. 9 (May 1972), pp. 204–08.
22. Richard F. Yalch and Rebecca Elmore Yalch, "The Effect of Numbers on the Route of Persuasion," *Journal of Consumer Research,* Vol. 11 (June 1984), pp. 522–27.
23. George S. Day and Terry Deutscher, "Attitudinal Predictios of Choice of Major Appliance Brands," *Journal of Marketing Research,* Vol. XIX (May 1982), pp. 192–98.
24. Richard E. Petty, John T. Cacioppo, and David Schumann, "Central and Peripheral Routes to Advertising Effectiveness: The Moderating Role of Involvement," *Journal of Consumer Research,* Vol. 10 (September 1983), pp. 135–46.
25. Vithala R. Rao, "Changes in Explicit Information and Brand Perceptions," *Journal of Marketing Research,* Vol. 9 (May 1972), pp. 209–13.
26. Glen Riecken and A. Coskun Samli, "Measuring Children's Attitudes Toward Television Commercials: Extension and Replication," *Journal of Consumer Research,* Vol. 8 (June 1981), pp. 57–61.

CHAPTER 9

Family Information

Sources

CHAPTER OUTLINE

I. FAMILY AND HOUSEHOLD
   A. Family Formation
   B. Family Function

II. FAMILY ORGANIZATION AFFECTS INFORMATION SHARING
   A. Family Composition
   B. Family Compatibility

III. IMPORTANCE OF ORIENTATION ON INFORMATION
   A. Family-Centered Family
   B. Career-Centered Family
   C. Consumption-Centered Family
   D. Combination Family

IV. INFORMATION FLOW PARALLELS FAMILY ROLES
   A. Instrumental and Expressive Roles
   B. Purchase Involvement and Role
   C. External and Internal Roles
   D. Husband-Wife Purchase Roles
   E. Changes in Men's and Women's Roles

V. INFORMATION SHARING CHANGES WITH LIFE CYCLE
   A. Bachelor Stage
   B. Newly Married Couples
   C. Full Nest I: Young Children
   D. Full Nest II: Older Children
   E. Full Nest III: Dependent Children
   F. Empty Nest I: In Labor Force
   G. Empty Nest II: Retired
   H. Solitary Survivor I: In Labor Force
   I. Solitary Survivor II: Retired

VI. LIFE-STYLE UNDERLIES INFORMATION SHARING
   A. Life-Style Concept
   B. Life-Style Profiles
   C. Regional Life-Styles

CHAPTER OBJECTIVES

After completing your study of Chapter 9, you should be able to:

1. Discuss family information sources.
2. Discuss how family formation and function affect information sources.
3. Explain how family organization affects information sharing.
4. Explain the importance of orientation in information.
5. Discuss how information flow parallels family roles.
6. Discuss how information sharing changes with life cycle.
7. Explain how life-style underlies information sharing.

The most basic of all external sources of consumer information is the family. Most individual associations revolve around the family, and the family is the home base from which individuals reach out into the world. Therefore, it is appropriate that we begin our discussion of consumer search with the family. Later chapters in this section deal with other types of reference group sources of consumer information for decision making.

The basic spending unit in any society is the family. This statement means that everything consumers purchase is either bought for individuals within a family or for the family as a unit. A daughter who purchases a new dress with money she earned is an example of the former situation, while a husband purchasing the week's groceries is an example of the latter. It follows that in the normal pursuit of buying, other family members constitute the primary source of information about wants and preferences for products and stores. In this chapter we discuss the family as a source of information.

FAMILY AND HOUSEHOLD

The terms "family" and "household" are used somewhat interchangeably to denote the basic spending unit, although there are differences in the terms. Family is the more traditional term. A *family* is:

a group of persons related by blood, marriage, or adoption who function together for member security and perpetuation of the unit.

In most societies, families are formalized through the institution of marriage, and they display well-developed systems of rules, roles, language, and rituals. The security referred to in the definition can be either physical or economic, and it comes from the support, social interaction, and group cooperation made possible through the unit. Perpetuation of the unit is primarily the result of procreation and child rearing.

The term household is broader in concept than the term family. *Household* means:

all individuals living alone, or persons living together, and functioning as a social and economic unit.

"Household" encompasses families but also includes unmarried persons living together, boardinghouses, fraternities and senior citizen homes which function as a unit. A great deal of government information uses the household as the basic spending unit. It is the most important spending unit from the point of view of consumer behavior. In this book, family and household are used interchangeably except when a distinction is necessary.

Family Formation

The process of family formation is of vital interest to marketers, and communication about the likes and dislikes that underlie purchasing are directly involved in this process. Illustration 9-1 demonstrates the relationship between family formation and consumer behavior. Family formation has five steps: meeting, getting acquainted, developing attachment, being in love, and forming a partnership. This process can be described as one of increasing involvement and commitment between the two persons and of developing comfortable roles.

Products associated with meeting relate to appearance and socialization. One must socialize in order to meet people, but appearance, personality, and outlook are the factors that attract initially. Getting acquainted involves products associated with initial dating. When developing attachments, the couple begins to purchase more personalized products related to serious dating and informal companionship. The products associated with being in love revolve around planning a life together and demonstrating commitment. Once a partnership is formed, the couple begin to use products necessary to operate the family on a daily basis.

Of course, the reader must understand that there is considerable overlap in the use of products between steps in the family formation process. For example, one does not neglect personal grooming after meeting a prospective partner, and the couple may continue to date throughout the process. Products are included only when they first enter the process of family formation.

Family Function

Every household performs an economic and a social function. The *social function* establishes the interaction that is the basis for household roles and behavior. The *economic function* results in income necessary to sustain the household. Families carry out these two functions, plus one more—procreation, or the birth and child-rearing function.

Each of these basic functions of the family can be associated with consumer products and information sharing.[1] Families regularly share information regarding their relationships, their economic status, and their children. Sex and procreation affect nearly all consumer behavior. There are, of course, products to aid procreation and products to interfere with it. Of more importance are the indirect effects of sex on consumer behavior. The desire to attract and hold a mate directly affects the consumer's choice of clothes, jewelry, perfume, hair preparations, food, and recreation (see Figure 9-1). Thus, much consumer advertising has some sexual connotation. Child rearing and social activities are almost as important as sex to consumer behavior. The consumer's home, mode of dress,

Illustration 9-1
Family formation

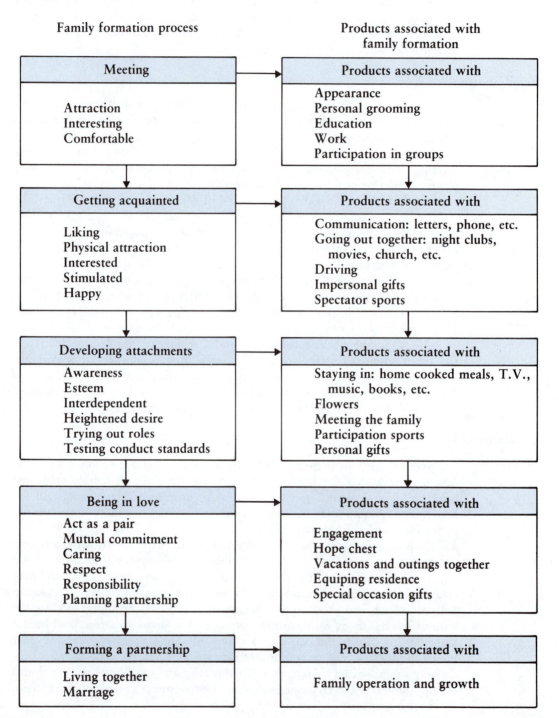

Family formation process

Products associated with
family formation

Meeting	Products associated with
Attraction Interesting Comfortable	Appearance Personal grooming Education Work Participation in groups

Getting acquainted	Products associated with
Liking Physical attraction Interested Stimulated Happy	Communication: letters, phone, etc. Going out together: night clubs, movies, church, etc. Driving Impersonal gifts Spectator sports

Developing attachments	Products associated with
Awareness Esteem Interdependent Heightened desire Trying out roles Testing conduct standards	Staying in: home cooked meals, T.V., music, books, etc. Flowers Meeting the family Participation sports Personal gifts

Being in love	Products associated with
Act as a pair Mutual commitment Caring Respect Responsibility Planning partnership	Engagement Hope chest Vacations and outings together Equiping residence Special occasion gifts

Forming a partnership	Products associated with
Living together Marriage	Family operation and growth

Figure 9-1
Use of affection to attract attention

Photo Courtesy of Levi Strauss & Co. "Levi's®

recreation, and eating habits are influenced by social contacts. Furthermore, the children in the family have their own needs.

FAMILY ORGANIZATION AFFECTS INFORMATION SHARING

Products are bought for individual members of the family or for the group. Each member, by sharing information, exerts some influence over the other members for most products purchased. The type and amount of this influence is directly related to the organization of the family.

Family Composition

Most Americans are members of two families—the family they are born into and the family they help to establish. The flow of information depends on what combination of members are present within the family at a given time. We can identify three types of families based on their composition. They are shown in Table 9-1.

The number and types of products required to maintain a family are directly

Table 9–1

Types of Families

Nuclear	Extended	Compound
This is the basic and most elemental family type in our society. It consists of husband, wife, and children, if any, living together.	This family is larger, consisting of the nuclear family plus other relations such as grandchildren, grandparents, uncles, and cousins living together.	The compound family exists when a husband has more than one wife or when a wife has more than one husband. This type of family is not important in our society because our laws and customs forbid it. However, in some cultures it is essential for economic reasons.

related to the number and types of individuals that make up that family. The information flow concerning these products becomes more complex as the family unit becomes larger.

Several generalizations can be made concerning the flow of information in American families. First, the formation of new families through marriage tends to increase communication between parents concerning product requirements, while communication between parents and children declines. As parental influence decreases, children become more independent in their use of products.

Second, American families are kept relatively small because children do not typically continue to live with parents after marriage. These extended families are more common in many European countries. American families average only 2.4 members. Most products reflect this family size. For example, homes have three bedrooms, cars increasingly are made to carry four persons, refrigerators and washers are designed for the small family, and food cartons contain the amount that a family of three or four can use.

Third, new family formation leads to new patterns of authority. It is necessary for the family leaders to communicate and establish roles. The overall responsibility for the purchase of products is worked out in the process. It is not so important which spouse has the authority, but the purchase role must be clearly understood by both parties.

Fourth, the change from a child in the nuclear family to the head of a newly established nuclear family is drastic in American life. There is no gradual transition, and there is increasingly less reliance on the experience of parents before or after the change. The new family must quickly work out its product and store preference so that it can function efficiently. Some families are more successful in this respect than others.

Family Compatibility

A compatible family is one characterized by a high degree of harmony. Love and affection are demonstrated, and arguments are not serious. An integrated family is one that is organized and functions as a unit. The members know their places, there is a large measure of agreement on actions and decisions, and family members seldom step out of place. Based on these concepts, we can describe four conditions of family compatibility:

1. Compatible-integrated.
2. Compatible-nonintegrated.
3. Noncompatible-integrated.
4. Noncompatible-nonintegrated.

The *compatible-integrated* family approaches an ideal. The members get along, and the family functions as a unit. Such a family is democratic. Members talk over purchase decisions, and goods are bought with considerable agreement. Members are willing to compromise on purchases and often bow to the judgment of other members who feel strong product needs.

The *compatible-nonintegrated* family is the sloppy family. There is a great deal of love, but the family isn't organized. The house may be unkempt, and family members exert considerable individuality in their friendships, behavior, and purchase habits. Purchases are not discussed as often, and there is less agreement on the course of action to take.

Noncompatible-integrated families show less affection. The husband and wife have little in common. It may be that the family is held together by the parents' feelings for the children. There is, however, outward unity. The husband and wife do not allow private feelings to interfere with normal household duties. This family functions as a unit but has no common bond of feeling. In private matters, the parents may seek separate identities. There is a great deal of agreement on all purchases related to household operations, but practically no agreement on products of a personal or recreational nature.

Noncompatible-nonintegrated families cannot long exist. This family has no common bond to hold it together. The purchase behavior of such a family, while it exists, is erratic. Of course, there are degrees of family compatibility that lie between the ones described.

IMPORTANCE OF ORIENTATION ON INFORMATION

Family orientation refers to the group's overall philosophy of life with respect to achieving its goals. It is possible to group families by this orientation into: family-centered families, career-centered families, consumption-centered families, and combination families. The orientation of a family underlies all exchanges of information because the data are presented and interpreted in the light of the family's goals.

Family-Centered Family

A family-centered group highly values family togetherness. Families exhibiting this orientation are sometimes called close-knit. The group shares a great deal of information, and product decisions typically take into account the wants and desires of the group as a whole. There is respect for the opinions of others.

Photo 9-1
A family-centered family is very close-knit throughout the generations.

The typical patterns for such families might be the following: Marriage occurs at a young age for both the male and female, and both spouses work for a short time. During this time, the family tries to accumulate some savings. Within a relatively short time, children are born, and the life of the family begins to center around the children. A strong child-centeredness continues for many years. Such a family tends to remain close over the years. The so-called generation gap is less pronounced in such families. An example is found in families from some Far Eastern cultures. These families tend to be very cohesive. Even after several generations of living in the United States, the close identification remains. In these families juvenile delinquency is very rare and because "face" is important, children do not do those things that reflect poorly on their parents.

A family-centered orientation is easily illustrated. The family curtails social activities rather than entrust the children to a baby-sitter. The family decides to move to the suburbs because it would be better for the children, allocates a large part of the family budget for educational insurance policies for the children, and selects a vacation spot acceptable to the children.

Career-Centered Family

Some families focus predominantly on success at a career. They are typically upwardly mobile. The parents spend most of their time, energy, and money on career enhancement. There may be considerable communication, but it is career-centered. Individual family members, particularly children, may be neglected.

Casual communication between husband and wife or between parents and children is reduced. There is little general discussion of products except those that enhance the career. Family members tend to make independent product decisions or consult peers. There is an almost inverse relationship between the career-centered and the family-centered orientations. Extreme examples of this preference would result in marriage being delayed and children postponed. Families of this type often emphasize a big new home appropriately located in a "proper" neighborhood, the "right" kind of car, membership in certain clubs, and products that symbolize status.

Consumption-Centered Family

A third family orientation is that which seeks the highest standard of living possible. The goal is to consume products that provide for the "good life." Figure 9-2 is an ad directed at the consumption-centered family. The consumption-centered family is typically easygoing and close knit, and communication is frequent among all members of the group. Since products are so important to this type of family, they often share information about products and tend to seek

Figure 9-2
A consumption-centered family

What other card lets you earn money on your next vacation?

Money back every time you use it. Real money.

All you have to do is pay for your vacation with the card that pays you back. The one that earns you a yearly

Cashback Bonus. Up to 1% based upon your annual level of purchases. Not enough to make you a millionaire, but then again,

how many other cards give you even a penny in real money?

You can credit your Cashback Bonus to your account. Or get it back in a gift certificate. Or, if you choose to add it to a Discover℠ Savers' Account, you'll double its value.

What other card pays you back for getting away from it all?

The Discover Card. **For people who expect value.**

And now you can use your Discover Card to purchase your tickets on Eastern Airlines.

© 1987 Greenwood Trust Company, Member FDIC

Sears Financial Network

advice from each other before purchasing. They spend a large proportion of their time and money on products and services associated with enjoying life and having a good time. Sports cars, extensive and expensive leisure activities, and frequent travel are typical of the expenditures of these families.

Combination Family

The orientations discussed above are not mutually exclusive. Most families display elements of all three perspectives, and the flow of information tends to also be mixed. The following combinations are possible.

1. *Family-career centered*. Both family and career receive equal emphasis in this mode of living. However, little emphasis is placed on consumption.
2. *Family-consumption centered*. A balance is struck between family and consumption. This is the family that enjoys life and doing things together. Little emphasis on a career is present.
3. *Career-consumption centered*. Little emphasis on family is present, as most activities and expenditures are directed toward career success and consumption for enjoyment.

In urban societies, a wide variety of orientations exist in varying degrees. Even in the combinations described above, it is possible for one to dominate more than another. A family can also have a broad enough orientation to include family, career, and consumption aspects. As one can see, the structure of families and their influence on purchases is a very complex subject.

INFORMATION FLOW PARALLELS FAMILY ROLES

The importance of family member roles to information sharing and consumer behavior cannot be emphasized enough. Roles define the responsibility for making certain decisions, including consumer decisions. Roles also define status within the group; this in turn affects who a family member asks for information and who is in a position to provide information.[2] Let's consider the effects of family roles on information sharing and consumer decision making.

Instrumental and Expressive Roles

A family member's *instrumental role* relates to activities or tasks to be performed, and they are primarily economic in nature. The spouse who prepares meals, works outside the home, cares for the children, or makes home repairs is performing an instrumental role. A family member's *expressive role* relates to the values they prize. Expressive roles typically involve emotions such as love, beauty, religion, and art. A spouse who demonstrates love for a child, attends a concert, or engages in gourmet cooking is performing an expressive role. The two roles are not completely exclusive in real life. For example, one can express love while performing the instrumental function of caring for a child.

Traditionally, the husband performed the instrumental role in the family and the wife performed the expressive role. This has changed, and we now recognize that either spouse may engage in both roles. In the purchase of furniture, for example, the interaction of instrumental and expressive values becomes apparent. One spouse may carefully check the colors and finish (expressive function) while the other observes more closely the joints, springs, and structure (instrumental function).

Persons in the family tend to have primary responsibility for products associated with their role.[3] For example, a spouse who normally does the cooking is responsible for purchasing groceries. If that same spouse is working outside the home, she or he may also be responsible for the upkeep of the car used for work. The responsible person tends to communicate with other family members concerning product responsibility. They seek new ideas, confirmation for the success of products previously purchased, and the solution to product problems. In this communication, one tends to satisfy instrumental values first, then expressive values. On the other hand, so long as a product performs satisfactorily, people tend to pay more attention to expressive values. Instrumental values tend to be taken for granted until something goes wrong. Then they become very important.

Purchase Involvement and Role

It follows that each family member is more involved in some product decisions than in others.[4] Role within the family has a bearing on this involvement and information sharing. Illustration 9-2 is a hypothetical *perceptual map* showing some of these relationships. The figure illustrates information sharing within a nuclear family. The basic roles that affect the situation are father, mother, son, and daughter. Four situations are possible.

First, there are *routine joint decisions*. The role of each family member is involved here, but most are passive. In this situation there is a lot of family involvement in the decision, but little information sharing. Information may have been shared when the original decision was made, but now the purchase is routine. For example, if the family purchasing agent knows individual preferences, then there is no need for consultation before each purchase of groceries. The car is used by all adults; whoever has the car at the time routinely buys gasoline. Second, there are *nonroutine joint decisions*. In this situation, there is considerable family involvement, but the involvement is necessary with each product decision. Roles may be extremely important here because the money involved may dictate care in the purchase. Information sharing is extensive for such products as automobiles, vacations, and furniture. For example, children may be allowed to select their own furniture within style and price ranges set by the parents.

Third, there are *routine personal decisions*. Only one or a few family members are involved and there is little information sharing. In this case, the individual buys according to her or his role. Highly personalized products such as shoes, underwear, and deodorant fit this category. The individual buys for self-satisfaction and has already thought out the choice and reduced the decision to routine.

Fourth, there are *nonroutine individual decisions*. In this case, the purchase is for an individual's sole use, but information may be necessary from others. This situation may exist when an individual is trying a new product or when one fami-

Illustration 9-2

Perceptual map of family purchase involvement

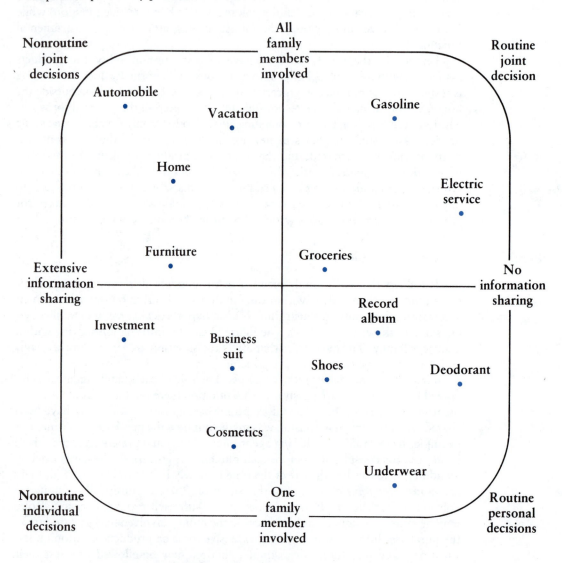

ly member is undecided between several products. Information may be selectively sought according to family member roles. For example, a child may seek a parent's counsel on an investment opportunity.

External and Internal Roles

Traditionally, husbands were more concerned with matters outside the family such as legal questions, license plates, income tax, the mortgage, insurance, and investments. They were considered excellent sources of information on such matters. The wife's role, historically, revolved around matters internal to the family

Photo 9-2
Men are often involved in decisions such as home decoration that were once thought of
as strictly women's decisions.

such as interior design, children's health and education, food preparation, and
house cleaning. It is in this realm of a homemaker that women were considered
expert providers of information useful in purchase decisions.

These roles used to be differentiated according to gender, but this division
becomes less and less important as women become more active outside the
home.[5] Working wives and social class differences will directly affect the degree
of importance this distinction has in any particular family. An example of such
overlapping of roles might be a situation in which both husband and wife share
an interest in home repairs (instrumental-internal), and the decision is one involving both members. Entertainment outside the home (expressive-external) is also
decided jointly. However, each spouse makes his or her own special contribution
to most purchase decisions. It cannot be simply stated that one or another makes
an independent decision, because a passive influence is present by the very nature
of the family structure.

Husband-Wife Purchase Roles

In every home there tends to be some role specialization that affects information flow and purchases.[6] Illustration 9-3 makes the point. Four possibilities are reported in this study.

Husband dominant: the male makes most decisions with little influence from the female.

Wife dominant: the female makes most decisions with little influence from the husband.

Autonomic: an equal number of decisions, each separate, is made by the male and female.

Syncratic: most decisions are made jointly by male and female.

This study found that husbands tend to dominate the purchase decision for insurance, while wives dominate for most clothing and household operation items. Joint decisions are made for furniture, vacations, school, housing, entertainment, and toys. The remainder of the decisions are made separately by either the husband or the wife.

Davis and Rigaux found that husband-wife influence varies over the decision process.[7] Although there was some change for every product, the sixteen circled items in Illustration 9-3 did not move out of its decision category over the decision process. Of those products that did change categories, there was a tendency for joint decision products (syncratic) to move toward more equal decision making (autonomic) between the problem recognition stage and the search stage. In the search stage, individuals seek independently to obtain more information for the final decision. Between the search and decision stages, there was a marked tendency for all products to move toward joint decision making (syncratic). Also, between these latter two stages, televisions, cars and savings tended to be dominated by the husband.

Changes in Men's and Women's Roles

The role of women in the American family has changed drastically in recent years. Women have become more independent. Within the family, they are increasingly making decisions normally reserved for the male. Today, women pay the bills, change the car's oil, mow the lawn, make major investment decisions, discipline the children, make career decisions, and exercise control over how their bodies are used.

Large numbers of women are now working outside the home. Women now make up over 60 percent of the American labor force. Not only are many women opting for careers in business, but they are increasingly going into jobs traditionally held by men. It is not uncommon today to observe women driving cabs; working around construction; performing as managers, doctors, and lawyers; operating heavy equipment; and managing computers.

Men have had to adjust to the changing role of women. Men have become more integral but less dominant family members. Men now change diapers, cook, wash dishes, sew, and clean house.

Illustration 9-3
Husband-wife purchase roles

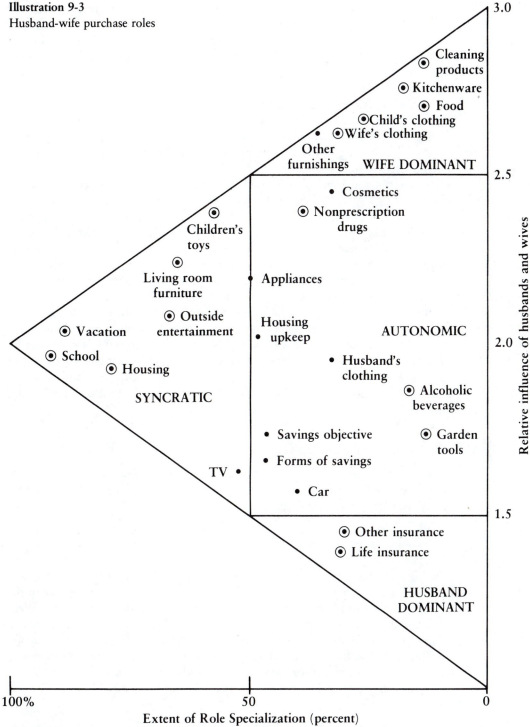

Source: Harry L. Davis and Benny P. Rigaux, "Perception of Marital Roles in Decision Processes," *Journal of Consumer Research,* June 1974, p. 54.

The overall result of these changes is that the traditional sex roles of men and women are merging. Women are taking on more responsibility, while some men are experiencing a loss of confidence and identity. More and more decisions in the family are being made jointly. Husbands are participating more in family recreation, but women are increasingly taking on leadership roles. These trends are likely to continue into the foreseeable future.

The changing roles of men and women are reflected in consumer decision making. There is more joint shopping and a greater sharing of information including preferences between husband and wife. Women are asserting their wants more so that such products as automobiles, insurance, housing, vacations, and entertainment reflect their opinions. The trend toward frozen foods, prepared foods, and fast-food outlets reflects, in part, the fact that women have less time to spend cooking. Interestingly, research suggests that nonworking wives have more appliances and convenience items in the home than working wives. It is suggested that nonworking wives spend less time on household operations with the use of appliances which leaves more time for family-oriented activities. Employed wives spend less time shopping, and they prefer shopping in the evening. When they buy, convenience and the extent of the assortment are the most important criteria for selecting a particular store.

Business is beginning to tailor advertisements specifically to the changing role of women. Clairol's slogan, "This I do for me," is an example. The Virginia Slims slogan, "You've come a long way baby," is designed to appeal to the emancipation of women. Nearly all businesses today have ceased to emphasize the traditional stereotyping of women in their advertisements. However, businesses do continue to use with success traditional sex roles; appeals to affection, sharing, convenience, quality, and giving still work.

INFORMATION SHARING CHANGES WITH LIFE CYCLE

Information sharing and consumer decision making varies over the family life cycle.[8] *Family life cycle* is a term used to denote the changing composition of a family over time, and it is defined as:

> the identifiable stages in a family's development based on marital status and the number and age of children.

This life cycle has been presented in several different configurations, but the most popular is shown in Table 9-2. Over 50 percent of American families are in the full nest stages of the life cycle. These stages roughly correspond to the nuclear family, and it is the largest single market. However, there are significant specialized markets for newly married couples, empty nest couples, solitary survivors, and the singles we have already discussed. Now let us consider the importance of each stage to consumer information sharing and decision making.[10]

Bachelor Stage

The first stage in the family life cycle is the bachelor stage. Earnings are typically low, but needs may also be low. The individual may be in college or just

Table 9–2
Family Life Cycle

	Stage	Description	Percent of U.S. Families
1.	Bachelor stage	Young, single persons not living at home	8.2
2.	Newly married couples	Husband and wife, young, no children	2.9
3.	Full nest I	Married couple, youngest child under six	24.2
4.	Full nest II	Married couple, youngest child six or over	13.2
5.	Full nest III	Married couple, older, with dependent children	14.7
6.	Empty nest I	Married couple, older, no children at home, head in labor force	5.5
7.	Empty nest II	Married couple, older, no children, head retired	5.2
8.	Solitary survivor I	Single or widowed, older, in labor force	0.2
9.	Solitary survivor II	Single or widowed, older, retired	2.0
	Not accounted for by the life cycle		23.9
	TOTAL		100.0

entering the labor force. There may be more communication with outside persons than with the family that the person has just left. The person is feeling his or her freedom. The individual has relatively few debts because he or she rents rather than buys a home and has little commitment to such durable goods as furniture and appliances. The person is recreation-oriented because she or he is young, there is time, and because some recreational activity is associated with seeking a mate. Young people tend to be fashion communicators, and many of them are very brand-conscious.

Bachelors tend to be good markets for personal consumption items such as clothing, cosmetics, shoes, and toilet items. Of course, many of these types carry throughout the life cycle. Bachelors need most household items necessary to live alone. They purchase basic kitchen equipment, and enough inexpensive furniture to get by. They are in the market for a new or used car. They buy equipment related to the mating game, and they are able to take regular vacations.

Newly Married Couples

Newly married couples are better off financially than they will be later when the children arrive. Both persons are probably working, and each has been in the labor force long enough for their income to begin to climb. They spend a lot of time together and they communicate with each other as part of the learning process of marriage. They may begin to reopen communications with their parents to obtain advice or to work out problems that occur with newlyweds. The process of testing and determining roles becomes involved with purchasing.

Even though earnings are on the rise with newly married couples, so are commitments. The couple needs everything for the home and building a life together. Therefore, this group is among the highest purchasers of durable goods such as cars, refrigerators, stoves, sensible and durable furniture, insurance, and white goods. There may be some savings, and since the couple is not tied down with children, they tend to continue taking vacations. Newly married couples are important purchasers of gift items and contraceptives. They may move into a larger, more modern apartment or purchase a small tract house or trailer.

Full Nest I: Young Children

The full nest I phase is one of the most critical. The relatively carefree unmarried and early marriage days are over as the arrival of children brings on increased responsibilities and leads to a drain on finances. Liquid assets become low, savings may be used up, and the couple becomes frustrated with their inability to stay ahead of the bills. The exchange of purchase information is primarily centered within the immediate family, but daily stress may cause friction and reduce communications for periods. Children begin to play an important part in purchase decisions.

Home purchasing is at its peak in the full nest I stage of the life cycle. This fact partly accounts for the drop in liquid assets. The family is becoming more integrated and independent, so members are interested in branded items and new products. They tend to rely more on advertised products. Some of the specific items frequently purchased at this stage are: washers, dryers, TVs, baby food, chest rubs, cough medicine, vitamins, dolls, wagons, sleds, skates, children's clothing, diapers, and children's furniture. The arrival of children greatly increases medical expenditures.

Full Nest II: Older Children

In this stage the family's financial position begins to improve. The income of parents is increasing rapidly while expenditures for baby items, furniture and household appliances tend to decrease. Liquidity is still a problem for the family, however. Family roles have been generally settled and communication is established on a routine basis. The family has achieved its identity, and there are more routine purchases of consumer products. Spouses who never worked, or those who had to leave the labor force while the children are small, begin to enter or re-enter the labor force.

Family members tend to be less influenced by advertising during the full nest II stage. Older children lead to the purchase of larger package sizes, more junk and snack foods, and candy. Multi-unit packages and deals are popular with the family purchasing agent. Some specific items purchased at this stage include a variety of foods, cleaning materials, a second car, bicycles, music lessons, and pianos.

Full Nest III: Dependent Children

The full nest III stage of the life cycle begins the "good years." The children are older and self-sufficient, many of the products necessary for home operation have been purchased, and income is reaching its peak. Income is high because the income earner or earners have had years of experience on the job and a spouse who has stayed at home may enter the work force. Many activities center on the children; communication follows this pattern. Parents find themselves spending a good deal of time transporting children. There is involvement in dating, school activities, and athletics. Parents find it increasingly difficult to have time for themselves. They see and communicate with each other less. They may begin to think of their lives as hum-drum.

Parents in the full nest III stage are hard to influence with advertising. They are worldly. Durable goods purchases begin to peak again, as worn furniture and appliances must be replaced. This is also the period when many families begin to upgrade the quality of their household goods. Expenditures increase for automobile travel, non-necessary appliances, boats, dental services, magazines, hospital insurance, and entertaining.

Empty Nest I: In Labor Force

The good life continues at this stage in the life cycle. Income has peaked, and some women even begin to leave the labor force. Communication is still routine between husband and wife, but interaction with children is greatly reduced. Joint purchasing tends to increase as the parents begin to spend more time together.

Home ownership is at its peak during the empty nest I phase of the life cycle. The couple is satisfied with its financial position, and savings increase. The parents' interests change in favor of more travel, recreation, and self-education. They begin to increase gifts and contributions to charitable organizations. Their interest in new products declines drastically as their tastes become more conservative. A larger portion of income is spent on vacations, luxury items, and home improvements. Medical expenditures also begin to climb at this stage.

Empty Nest II: Retired

The empty nest II is the second most critical phase of the life cycle. There is a rather drastic change in family roles, communication, and outlook that results from retirement.[11] There is a drastic cut in income, but it comes at a time when most family requirements other than food and clothing have been met. However, the erosion of purchasing power due to inflation is a serious worry to the family. The family tends to keep a home in this phase, but they may sell their original home in favor of a smaller retirement home. The couple may also consider moving to a warmer climate. There is an increase in medical costs, including doctor bills, medical insurance, and medical appliances. Other significant purchases include products which aid health, sleep, and digestion. Figure 9-3 recognizes the budget constraints of this group.

Solitary Survivor I: In Labor Force

The solitary survivor who works must adjust to living alone. Communication is greatly reduced, but the communication that exists is with outsiders rather than with immediate family. The individual may increase contacts with married children or grandchildren, but loneliness is a real problem. Income is still good, and there are even fewer demands than in the empty nest I stage. Savings may increase drastically as a result. The survivor may sell his or her home and move back into an apartment. This decision may be made because of the opportunity to meet people or to avoid keeping house with no one to appreciate it. Medical expenses continue to be high.

Figure 9-3
Advertisement aimed at senior citizens

Best Western International

Solitary Survivor II: Retired

There is little difference between the two solitary survivor stages except that income has been drastically reduced for the retired person. Persons at this stage need special attention, affection, and security. Most purchasing is greatly reduced and in some cases adult siblings have to make purchase decisions for the survivor.

LIFE-STYLE UNDERLIES INFORMATION SHARING

Another factor that affects information sharing within the family is its life-style. The discussion of family life-style was saved until last because it involves all the other factors of family information sharing and decision making. The family life-style helps to explain why families, even those with the same organization, orientation, or stage in the life cycle do not communicate and consume alike.[12]

Table 9-3
Life-Style Determinants

Activities	Interests	Opinions	Demographics
Work	Family	Themselves	Age
Hobbies	Home	Social issues	Education
Social events	Job	Politics	Income
Vacation	Community	Business	Occupation
Entertainment	Recreation	Economics	Family size
Club membership	Fashion	Education	Dwelling
Community	Food	Products	Geography
Shopping	Media	Future	City size
Sports	Achievements	Culture	Stage in life cycle

Source: Joseph T. Plummer, "The Concept and Application of Life Style Segmentation." *Journal of Marketing*, Vol. 38 (January 1974), pp. 33–37.

Life-Style Concept

Life-style is a type of philosophy by which to live.[13] Specifically, *life-style* refers to the particular manner in which a person, or group of persons, live. The most common means of measuring life-style is the AIO (activities, interests, and opinions) rating.[14] Table 9-3 shows the major AIO determinants of life-style. A questionnaire is administered with statements about a person's activities, interests, and opinions. Statements may include:

"I stay home most evenings."
"I enjoy television."
"I read a book most evenings."
"I usually have a drink before dinner."

There could be as many as 300 such statements on the questionnaire. The respondents are asked to agree or disagree with each statement. A profile can be determined by summing the responses and determining the patterns of preference.

Life-Style Profiles

It is possible to generalize some ideal life-style profiles. Table 9-4 shows some commonly accepted life-style profiles. These profiles were based on a study of 3000 persons. However, the reader is reminded that these male and female profiles only indicate tendencies. No person is likely to fit exactly a specific profile.

A person who is a loner will be a loner at every stage of the life cycle and no matter what the family life-style.[15] That person will seek less information when purchasing and show more independence in products selected no matter what other considerations are involved. If one's parents are thrifty with money, one will be thrifty at every stage in the life cycle. The major difference pertains only to how much can be saved with changes in income. Communication among members will center on the factors important to a particular family's life-style. Life-style is even important in determining family contacts; this in turn influences the amount and types of information received.[16] For example, a family with many external contacts has a wider range of information than one with fewer contacts.

Table 9–4

Profiles of Male and Female Life Styles

Male Life-Styles	Female Life-Styles
Herman (retired homebody). He has opinions that conflict with nearly everything in the modern world. He can neither change the world nor cope with it. His favorite meal is a hearty breakfast. He uses low-cholesterol products, and he is very concerned about high prices. He distrusts foreign-made products.	Thelma (old-fashioned traditionalist). She is a devoted wife, doting mother, and conscientious housekeeper. She has few interests outside her own family. She does not condone sexual permissiveness or political liberalism, nor can she sympathize with women's libbers.
Dale (devoted family man). He married early, fathered a family, and is happy. A blue-collar worker with a high school education, he is more interested in knowing what a product can do for him than what star endorses it and worries about excessive sex and violence on TV.	Mildred (militant mother). She married early, had children, and now wishes the women's liberation movement had happened in time to help her. She likes soap operas and lottery tickets because they help her escape into a fantasy world.
Ben (self-made businessman). He believes you get what you pay for, values his time, eats bacon and eggs despite his doctor's disapproval because "there's no substitute," and thinks government should keep its nose out of private industry.	Candice (chic suburbanite). She is an urbane woman, well-educated, probably married to a professional man. She is a prime mover in her community and is active in club affairs.
Fred (frustrated factory worker). He married young and is now unhappy and cynical. He likes to think that he is a bit of a swinger. He fantasizes and goes to the movies to escape from his everyday world.	Cathy (contented mother). She married early, had a big family, and likes it that way. She thinks women's liberation opposes biblical teachings, is trusting and relaxed. She buys only the cereals her children demand.
Scott (successful professional). He is much smoother. His speech is more confident and his manner sure. He carries three major credit cards and uses them primarily to pay for business travel.	Eleanor (elegant socialite). She says women's liberation is unnecessary if a woman has a man to take care of her. She spends little time preparing meals but spends a lot of time and money on cosmetics and high-fashion clothes. She thinks face creams are better if they cost more.

Source: Peter W. Bernstein, "Psychographics Is Still an Issue on Madison Avenue," *Fortune,* January 16, 1978, pp. 78–84.

Regional Life-Styles

Table 9-5 indicates some of the important regional differences in life-style for Americans. The table reflects statistics, not stereotypes, but it can lead to generalizations, which we summarize here. First, Easterners think of themselves as cosmopolitan. They are more likely to travel, have a cocktail before dinner, cook outdoors, prefer traditional marriages, use bank charge cards, and read the evening newspaper. Southerners tend toward a conservative life-style. They are likely to attend church, cater to children, and be active in the community. Many are poli-

Table 9–5
Regional Life-Style Profile

Item	Percentage agreeing					
	Total	East	South	Midwest	West	Southwest
Prefer a traditional marriage with the husband assuming the responsibility for providing for the family and the wife running the house and taking care of the children	52	39	52	59	45	61
When making important family decisions, consideration of the children should come first	52	49	62	51	48	50
Every vacation should be educational	48	49	54	52	38	47
I am considering buying life insurance	19	14	30	17	17	21
I nearly always have meat at breakfast	29	14	52	22	26	34
Went out to breakfast instead of having it at home at least once last year	57	57	42	61	71	61
Worked on a community project at least once during the past year	35	39	50	34	31	34
Attended church 52 or more times last year	28	23	37	31	20	30
I like to visit places that are totally different from my home	72	79	63	72	75	65
I would like to spend a year in London or Paris	33	40	36	27	38	24
Went on a trip outside the U.S. last year	14	24	8	12	19	15
Rode a bus at least once last year	32	49	26	28	40	24
It is hard to get a good job these days	77	82	83	77	65	80
Used a bank charge card at least once last year	43	52	43	41	52	50
Returned an unsatisfactory product at least once during the past year	65	67	52	70	65	64
Used a "price off" coupon at a grocery store	63	67	50	72	60	53
My days seem to follow a definite routine—eating meals at the same time each day, etc.	62	68	66	58	53	64
Cooked outdoors at least once last year	81	86	82	84	80	84
Went on a picnic at least once last year	75	78	65	79	79	73
Had wine with dinner at least once during the past year	60	70	38	62	72	49
Had a cocktail or drink before dinner at least once last year	70	78	59	75	77	53
I am interested in spice and seasoning	43	46	44	41	54	35
Visited an art gallery or museum from 1 to 4 times in the past year	30	29	27	32	40	34
Went bowling at least once last year	36	42	20	44	34	24
Went hiking at least once during the past year	46	49	47	43	59	45
Went backpacking at least once last year	6	8	7	4	16	5
Went hunting at least once last year	32	18	43	29	32	40

Source: Needham, Harper & Steers Advertising Inc., *Life Style Survey,* 1975.

tical conservatives. Midwesterners think of themselves as average. They are more likely to prefer popular music and bowling. They prefer traditional marriage, and are above average in reading the evening newspaper, and having a cocktail before dinner. They are also more likely to return unsatisfactory products. Southwesterners prefer traditional marriage, are less likely to drink before dinner, and desire less travel. They are above average in reading the morning newspaper, and in their preference for time-saving appliances. Westerners tend toward liberalism. They are above average in riding the bus, visiting art galleries, hiking, and backpacking. They are also above average in use of appliances, color TV, and charge cards. Westerners tend to feel secure.

Can you generalize some of the different patterns of communication and decision making that may result from these regional life-styles? How could this knowledge be useful to you as a marketer?

QUESTIONS

1. Define family and household. What is the difference?
2. Identify products and brands that you buy today because your parents bought them. Also identify products and brands that your parents would never buy. Why is there a difference?
3. Define and distinguish between the four conditions of family compatibility.
4. Is the so-called generation gap present in your choice of products and your parents' choice of products? Is this true for all products? Discuss your answer.
5. Would there be any difference in the decision making process between a family-career centered family and a family-consumption centered family? Discuss your answer.
6. Discuss how the increase in the number of working wives has influenced the instrumental role and expressive role of family members.
7. Design a perceptual map of your family's purchases.
8. Give examples of products or services that can be purchased under a non-routine joint decision and under a routine personal decision. Discuss the reasons why there is or is not a difference.
9. Discuss the role specialization in your family. Identify the types of products for which each person is responsible.
10. Do single and divorced individuals of the same age and sex demonstrate the same purchase behavior? Discuss your answer.
11. Discuss with examples how men have had to adjust to the changing role of women.
12. Business is beginning to tailor advertisements specifically to the changing role of women. Bring to class examples of advertisements that demonstrate this change.
13. The family life cycle is shown in Table 9-2. Give examples of promotional media that a marketing manager might use for each stage of the life cycle.

14. Give examples of how a marketing manager could use the AIO rating of their customers to satisfy their needs better.
15. What promotional tool would you use to provide information to each of the female life-styles listed in Table 9-4? Discuss your answer.

NOTES

1. Robert T. Green et al., "Social Development and Family Purchasing Roles: A Cross-National Study," *Journal of Consumer Research*, Vol. 9 (March 1983), pp. 436–42.
2. Peggy Osborne, "Methodological Issues Concerning Family Purchase Decision Processes: A Brief Examination," in David M. Klein and Allen E. Smith, eds., *Marketing Comes of Age, 1984* (Boca Raton, Fla.: Southern Marketing Assn., 1984), pp. 290–301.
3. Robert W. Cosenze, "Family Decision Making Decision Dominance Structure Analysis—An Extension," *Journal of the Academy of Marketing Science*, Vol. 13 (Winter 1985), pp. 91–103.
4. Mark E. Siama and Armen Tashchian, "Selected Socioeconomic and Demographic Characteristics Associated with Purchasing Involvement," *Journal of Marketing*, Vol. 49 (Winter 1985), pp. 72–82.
5. Pierre Filiatrault and J. R. Brent Ritchie, "Joint Purchasing Decisions: A Comparison of Influence Structure in Family and Couple Decision-Making Units," *Journal of Consumer Research*, Vol. 7 (September 1980), pp. 131–40.
6. Jack J. Kasulis and Marie Adele Hughes, "Husband-Wife Influence in Selecting a Family Professional," *Journal of The Academy of Marketing Science*, Vol. 12 (1984), pp. 115–27.
7. H. L. Davis and B. P. Rigaux, "Perception of Marital Roles in Decision Process," *Journal of Consumer Research* (June 1974), pp. 51–62.
8. David J. Fritzsche, "An Analysis of Energy Consumption Patterns by Stage of Family Life Cycle," *Journal of Marketing Research*, Vol. XVIII (May 1981), pp. 227–31; Janet Wagner and Sherman Hanna, "The Effectiveness of Family Life Cycle Variables in Consumer Expenditure Research," *Journal of Consumer Research*, Vol. 10 (December 1983), pp. 281–91.
9. Patrick E. Murphy and William A. Staples, "A Modernized Family Life Cycle," *Journal of Consumer Research*, Vol. 6 (June 1979), pp. 12–22.
10. Frederick W. Derrick and Alane K. Lehfeld, "The Family Life Cycle: An Alternative Approach," *Journal of Consumer Research*, Vol. 7 (September 1980), pp. 214–17.
11. Ganeasan Visvabharathy and David R. Rink, "The Elderly: Still the 'Invisible and Forgotten' Market Segment," *Journal of The Academy of Marketing Science*, Vol. 13 (Fall 1985), pp. 81–100.
12. Stephen C. Cosmas, "Life Styles and Consumption Patterns," *The Journal of Consumer Research,* Vol. 8 (March 1982), pp. 453–55.
13. Michael A. Belch, "A Segmentation Strategy for the 1980's: Profiling the

Socially-Concerned Market Through Life-Style Analysis," *Journal of The Academy of Marketing Science*, Vol. 10 (Fall 1982), pp. 345–58.

14. John L. Lastovicka, "On the Validation of Lifestyle Traits: A Review and Illustration," *Journal of Marketing Research*, Vol. XIX (February 1982), pp. 126–38.

15. Larry D. Kelly, Richard F. Beltramini, and Kenneth R. Evans, "Lifestyle Profile Analysis in Broadcast Media Planning," in Donald R. Glover, ed., *Proceedings of the 1984 Convention of the American Academy of Advertising* (American Academy of Advertising, 1984), pp. 86–91.

16. Anthony Bushman, Systematic Life Styles for New Product Segmentation, *Journal of the Academy of Marketing Science,* Vol. 10 (Fall 1982), pp. 377–94.

CHAPTER 10

Social Groups As
Information Sources

CHAPTER OUTLINE

I. REFERENCE GROUP SOURCES

II. INFORMATION BY TYPE OF REFERENCE GROUP
  A. Sources Classed by Function
  B. Sources Classed by Formality
  C. Groups Classed by Interaction
  D. Groups Classed by Type of Membership
    1. *Participation Groups*
    2. *Automatic Groups*
    3. *Anticipatory Groups*
    4. *Negative Groups*
  E. Groups Overlap

III. FACTORS OF REFERENCE GROUP INFORMATION
  A. Group Roles
  B. Status within the Group
  C. Conformity to Group Norms
  D. Strength of Group Influence

IV. SOCIAL CLASS SOURCES
  A. Properties of Social Class
  B. Indicators of Social Class
    1. *Occupation*
    2. *Income*
    3. *Education*
    4. *Achievement*

V. INFORMATION VARIES BY SOCIAL CLASS
  A. Upper Upper Class
  B. Lower Upper Class
  C. Upper Middle Class
  D. Lower Middle Class
  E. Upper Lower Class
  F. Lower Lower Class
  G. Other Concepts of Social Class
  H. Social Mobility and Information

VI. IMPORTANCE OF SOCIAL INFLUENCE

CHAPTER OBJECTIVES

After completing your study of Chapter 10, you should be able to:

1. Discuss how reference groups are a source of information.
2. Discuss information by the type of reference group.
3. Discuss the factors of reference group information.
4. Discuss social class sources of information.
5. Explain how and why information varies by social class.
6. Explain the importance of social influence.

Any association of an individual with persons outside the family, whether personal or impersonal, may be referred to as social interaction. Social groups are the second major type of external source of consumer information. All persons outside the family are members of one or more groups, and this affects any interaction they have with others. There are two broad categories of social groups whose information affects consumer decisions about products and stores. They are reference groups and social classes. We discuss reference groups first, then social classes.

REFERENCE GROUP SOURCES

The first major social group from which consumers receive information is the reference group. The term *reference group* is used to designate any two or more persons identified together by a common function or goal with which the individual identifies or interacts. The consumer does not necessarily have to be a member of the reference group, but the reference group does provide information which influences the person's decision making. In a general way, the consumer draws upon the group's frame of reference or value system to guide his or her decision making in the marketplace. The reference group can, in fact, be one in which it is impossible to become a member. A young girl cannot be a member of the Chicago Bears, but the information she receives from identifying with this team may lead her to collect player cards or purchase magazines with stories about the team. The often discussed but never identified "Joneses" with whom we are forever trying to keep up represent an intangible reference group. Testimonial advertising is often quite effective because an individual can identify with the reference group represented by the person in the ad. Witness the success of Jimmy Connors in identifying his brand of tennis equipment with the weekend player.

The consumer can identify with reference groups because of some specific or general knowledge about the group or individuals within the group.[1] This information may be gained by personally interacting with group members, by reading about the group, or by observing its behavior. The amount and accuracy of the information depend largely on the frequency and nature of the contact. However, influence on the consumer does not depend on the accuracy of the information about the reference group. The consumer behaves based on perceived knowledge of the group.[2] The consumer may purchase in a specific manner to achieve several purposes related to the reference group. The consumer may want to achieve the same goal as the group. A man may contribute to the poor because it is accepted practice in his church. A consumer may purchase in such a manner as to become a member of the group. We have all heard how some "nouveau riche" dress and entertain in the manner of "established rich" in hopes of being accepted into the group. The important point is to recognize that reference groups have a direct bearing on consumer decision making because of the amount and type of information they provide.

INFORMATION BY TYPE OF REFERENCE GROUP

Different reference groups provide different amounts and types of information to consumers.[3] Reference groups can be classified by function, formality, interaction, and membership.

Sources Classed by Function

Humans are social animals who seek out other humans for social, protective, and economic purposes. Reference groups can be classified according to these and other purposes. This classification includes such diverse groups as work groups, athletic teams, church groups, the Army, supper clubs, and fraternities and sororities. The development of these functional groups is inevitable; some develop on a voluntary basis and some out of necessity. The information exchanged among members of functional groups often relates to the purpose of the group. This is true whether the group is large or small. For example, a football team (small group) exchanges a good deal of information about offenses and defenses. The United States Army (large group) concentrates information on training and maintaining the moral and efficiency of soldiers. In both these groups, any exchange of market-related information is incidental to the overall function of the group. A small consumer group, on the other hand, has as its purpose the exchange of information relating to the purchase decision. In all cases individuals interact, and the individual is brought into contact with the group opinion. The consumer's purchase behavior is directly affected by these opinions.[4]

Sources Classed by Formality

Groups can also be classified by the extent of their formality—that is, the extent to which their purpose, structure, and roles are clearly defined. *Formal groups* have clear written purposes, specified structure with defined authority and responsibility, rules to guide behavior, and roles that are understood by the membership. Formal groups include the United States Congress, labor unions, universities, and businesses. Interaction and information follow the formal organization. For example, in a business, there is no more operational information exchange between secretaries and managers, and between levels of management, than between secretaries. However, even in formal organizations, there are informal exchanges of information which exert a good deal of influence on consumer behavior. A worker praises a new car or coffee or discusses a shopping mall on his or her side of town.

Loosely defined groups with little organization are called *informal groups*. The League of Women Voters is an informal group. The organization elects officers and meets regularly to discuss civic problems. Other examples include supper clubs, block parties, and alumni associations. These informal groups can be extremely important influences on consumer decision making. The primary purpose of many of these groups is the exchange of information. The group often has strong opinions which carry over into consumer behavior. For example, a supper club made up of conservative members is likely to dress conservatively.

Groups Classed by Interaction

Consumers do not interact to the same degree in all groups, so we can use interaction to classify primary and secondary groups. *Primary groups* are characterized by face-to-face associations and a high degree of cooperation among members. Primary groups are basic in forming the social nature of consumers, since it is within these groups that a person's most direct and frequent interaction takes place. Primary groups to which consumers are exposed include family, neighbors, bridge clubs, work groups, and golf foursomes. From childhood to old age, consumers find many of the everyday purchasing decisions affected by the opinions, experiences, and biases expressed by members of their primary groups. For example, Sue files for future reference Mary's statement that a certain deodorant caused her to break out in a rash. A fellow worker complains continually of car trouble, and this affects the consumer's attitude when the time comes to buy a new car.[5] Someone installs new carpeting, and neighbors suddenly realize that their own homes could use a little repairing.

The term *secondary group* refers to all those organizations with which the consumer has a casual, infrequent, and impersonal relationship. The consumer either does not consider the opinions of this group important, or they may be important only on a narrow range of topics relating to the specific group. Secondary groups come under the general heading of "special interest groups." Some secondary groups are the Democratic or Republican parties, the AFL-CIO, the church, and Delta Sigma Pi. Secondary group opinions can be very important to the consumer, especially if the information relates to the purpose of the group. For example, union members are careful not to purchase nonunion products. Individuals with strong religious beliefs may not use cosmetics, attend movies, or drink alcoholic beverages. However, since secondary group relations are not face-to-face, there may be a delay in feedback from communication within the group. This can affect the impact of the influence.

Groups Classed by Type of Membership

There are four types of group membership: (1) participation, (2) automatic, (3) anticipatory, and (4) negative.[6]

Participation Groups. The participation group is one in which the consumer actually takes part. These may be either large or small. Small face-to-face communication groups, such as the family or social organization, are examples of such groups. Direct associations between the members are the rule in small groups. In larger groups, there is less personal association, active participation, and face-to-face association. This is true of political party membership. Participation groups tend to affect consumer attitudes directly, and they usually affect attitudes having to do with the group. For example, standards of dress may be established in the group.

Automatic Groups. Automatic reference groups are those in which a person automatically belongs because of age, sex, marital status, race, education, and so on. Thus, mothers, teen-agers, college students, Americans, and millionaires constitute automatic reference groups. Membership in such groups may be loose and identification among members low, but one is aware of belonging to the group. The individual in an automatic reference group assumes the role that is expected of all those who belong to the group, and these roles affect consumer behavior. A newlywed, in his role as a homemaker, may wonder what other persons would do in a similar situation. The dominating influence of automatic reference groups results from the consumer's perception of society's expectations. These people's purchase behavior can be influenced by augmenting their role or increasing their feeling of belonging. A salesperson, for example, may point out to the young wife that the brand of cookware he or she is selling is preferred by most housewives.

Photo 10-1
Consumers in a group tend to make similar purchases.

H. Armstrong Roberts

Anticipatory Groups. The anticipatory group is one to which the consumer aspires but in which he or she does not presently hold membership. We can observe anticipatory group behavior in persons who wish to join the country club, move into a better neighborhood, or climb into the better social circles of the city. These people make comparisons with the anticipatory group when making purchase decisions. They are apt to adopt the standards of dress, talk, ethics, and entertainment followed by the anticipatory group.

Negative Groups. Negative groups are the opposite of anticipatory groups. A person avoids association with negative groups. A person may not wish to be identified with bums, hippies, the nouveau riche, the Ku Klux Klan, the NAACP, politicians, communists, or criminals. Notice that very often, but not necessarily, the attitude held toward a negative group is based on group biases of those outside the negative group. The negative reference group influences consumer decisions in that people do not take certain actions or purchase certain products that may identify them with these groups. The person may or may not actually belong to the group, but one's actions are nevertheless an attempt to dissociate oneself. The beer industry has had difficulty dissociating beer from the lower classes on order to persuade middle- and upper-class consumers to purchase more beer.

Groups Overlap

It should be apparent to the reader that the reference groups discussed above are not mutually exclusive. They usually overlap. A person can be a member of a functional, primary, and participation group at the same time. For example, the Democratic Party is a secondary, participation, formal group. The family is a primary, informal, automatic, participation group. Furthermore, a consumer can belong to several different types of groups at the same time. They all have influence on the consumer's decision making in varying degrees.[7] There can be, and often is, conflict among the positions taken by these groups. The consumer has to work out these differences.

FACTORS OF REFERENCE GROUP INFORMATION

The ways in which groups influence consumer behavior are many and varied. Groups affect immediate buying plans by influencing decisions. Groups affect future purchasing through aspirations by acquainting individuals with the lifestyles of others. Groups also provide the standard for measuring the social success and failure of purchase decisions because individuals compare their achievements to those of members of the group.[8]

We can group some of the important factors that affect the flow and acceptance of information by consumers. They are group roles, status within the group, and conformity to group norms. Each factor is explained below.

Group Roles

A *role* is a behavior pattern that an individual is expected to follow in a given social position. It is a part one plays. A person performing in a certain role, i.e., spouse, politician, teacher, or businessperson, is expected to display attitudes, values, and physical behavior that others perceive as consistent with the role. In a sales situation it is expected that the salesperson should be aggressive, knowledgeable, outgoing, and able to handle any situation. The consumer is expected to be defensive, wary of the salesperson, reserved, and uncommunicative. Of course, many salespersons and consumers do not fit their roles exactly. Nevertheless, it is easy to understand that the role played by each party affects the manager, amount, and believability of the information exchanged.

Roles can be identified as ascribed or achieved. An *ascribed role* is one the person was born with or acquires naturally. Roles associated with age, sex, and kinship are ascribed. An *achieved role* is adopted due to personal growth or attainment goals. Achievement roles include marital status, occupation, public service, and education. Many roles have elements of both. The important fact is that who you communicate with and how you communicate are greatly affected by the role you play. Everyone has an idea of how a millionaire and a garbage collector should behave when buying in a retail store. The millionaire and the garbage collector also have an idea about how they are expected to behave, and each acts accordingly.

Society's understanding of roles changes over time. It follows that the type and amount of communication also changes as a result. Some of the more important recent role changes in America are summarized below.

First, women are increasingly assuming the role of family decision maker in financial and career matters not related to managing the home. This change has resulted because women no longer see their role as cooking, cleaning, and raising children. As their responsibility has expanded, so has the number and variety of their interactions. Women are also increasingly assuming the role of family provider. This change has resulted from an increase in the number of single family heads who are women and from the large number of women moving into the work force. The women are now performing in the role of either employer or manager. How do you view the role of the woman in Figure 10-1? Do you feel she would have been presented this way twenty years ago?

Second, husbands are increasingly assuming the role of decision maker where family operations and childrearing are concerned. Men are spending more time at home and are more involved in housework, teaching children, discipline, and shopping. The husband's role as family financial manager has declined. In short, sex roles are becoming more similar.

Third, children have expanded their decision making role within the family. Reduced discipline has resulted in more freedom for children. This, coupled with the fact that more children are providing part of their spending money, has resulted in children playing the part of adult participator in family matters. Their influence has increased in relation to their expanded contact and interaction with others.

Fourth, black men and women have become better integrated into our society; this has modified their role.[9] Blacks are more accepted in social situations than they are in work situations, but the change in both is significant. As a result, blacks are assuming family, work, and social roles similar to those of whites. Their patterns of information flow have expanded proportionately. This tenden-

Figure 10-1
Advertisement emphasizing role of women and minorities

Everybody's somebody at Dean Witter.
Just ask Gwendolyn Kirkland.

For eight years, Gwendolyn Kirkland was an elementary school teacher in Chicago. Gwendolyn loved teaching, but her other ambition was to be part of the financial world:

"I wanted more of a challenge, more of an opportunity to excel. And I still wanted to guide and educate, but in money matters. So, I interviewed with Dean Witter. They understood my goals and gave me the opportunity I needed."

Gwendolyn now works as an Account Executive at the Dean Witter office in Matteson, Illinois—a suburb just south of Chicago.

"The people here are very supportive...the atmosphere is warm and comfortable. And our clients feel the same way."

Gwendolyn Kirkland, Account Executive. Just one other example of how everybody's somebody at Dean Witter.

A member of the Sears Financial Network
DEAN WITTER

AN EQUAL OPPORTUNITY EMPLOYER M/F WE ENCOURAGE APPLICATIONS FROM FEMALE, MINORITIES AND ALL OTHER PERSONS © 1986 DEAN WITTER REYNOLDS INC

© 1986 Dean Witter Reynolds Inc.

cy is likely to accelerate in the future. Observe how the black woman is portrayed in Figure 10-1. This portrayal is quite different from a few years ago. Fifth, minorities, such as blacks, homosexuals, environmentalists, and women are becoming increasingly involved in government. This involves playing the role of politician, and it exposes people to all types of involved communication patterns.

Status within the Group

Status is defined as the prestige associated with one's position within a social group relative to the placement of others. A manager has higher status than a worker, but top management has higher status than line managers. The leader of an informal group, such as a car pool, has higher status than others in the group. Status is often thought of in terms of the influence the person has on the attitudes and behavior of others. It follows that persons with high status act as role models for those with lower status. Information conveyed by persons of status tends to carry weight. It is considered a good thing to have status in any organization.

Persons within a group—such as the coffee club at work, the bridge club at home, or the altar society at church—tend to exchange more personal, opinionated, and informal information with those who have about the same status in the group. That is because persons of the same status tend to socialize more within the group. The information that flows between status groups tends to be

Photo 10-2
Income and status are based on occupation and education. In what status level is this career?

more formal. Managers give orders to subordinates. Subordinates pass on results to managers. Thus status limits the amount and type of information that passes between persons within the group.

Conformity to Group Norms

Group norms are the implicit rules of conduct or standards of behavior that groups expect of members. The group may have established norms of behavior, dress, and thought processes. These norms must be communicated to the members and reasonably enforced. Of course, not every member adheres to the group's norms in every case. Conformity refers to the percent of time that the group's members willingly behave in ways acceptable to the group.[10] In terms of consumer behavior, willing behavior can be purchasing acceptable clothing, trading with acceptable stores, dining out or entertaining in acceptable ways, and keeping members posted about new products or stores.

Conflict occurs when some members of the group do not perform in acceptable ways. The group can force compliance by (1) communicating that past behavior is unacceptable, (2) ostracizing persons who do not conform, and (3) expelling someone from the group. The latter is typically a last resort. People who value participation in the group typically conform most of the time. It is a general rule that persons with high status in the group can deviate from the norms to a greater degree than others.

There are three degrees of conformity that may occur within groups. Compliance, identification, and internalization describe these degrees. *Compliance* is conforming to group expectations in order to achieve a reward or avoid a sanction that the group can impose. The individual's fundamental values are not changed by compliance. For example, a person who is fundamentally against guns may join a gun club because of some political or social advantage. *Identification* is adopting group behavior in order to identify with some person or persons in the group. An example is the young person who identifies with a movie star and copies the star's style of dress, hair style, and walk. The person believes in his or her actions because of the effect of the role model. Identification is a more intense association with the group than compliance. *Internalization* is accepting the behavior of the group because it has been made a part of the individual's value system. Internalization represents the highest order of social influence. In this case, the individual behaves like the group automatically.

Strength of Group Influence

Group influence varies between consumers and over time. Group influence also varies by the type of decision the consumer is making.[11] For example, the influence may not be the same for decisions about product, brand, store, services, or method of purchase. Furthermore, the influence felt by the consumer relative to any decision may be either strong or weak. Illustration 10-1 depicts the different strengths of group influence on a consumer where product and brand are concerned.[12]

Four conditions can be described based on Illustration 10-1. The group may exert (1) strong product-strong brand influence; (2) strong product-weak brand

Illustration 10-1
Reference group influence on consumers

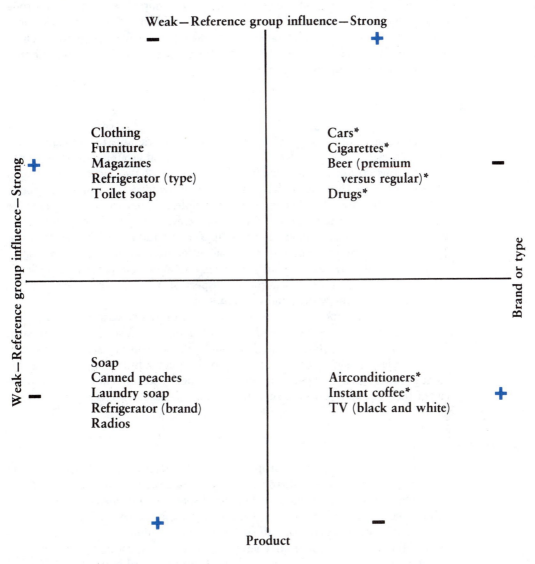

Weak — Reference group influence — Strong

Brand or type

Weak — Reference group influence — Strong

Clothing
Furniture
Magazines
Refrigerator (type)
Toilet soap

Cars*
Cigarettes*
Beer (premium
   versus regular)*
Drugs*

Soap
Canned peaches
Laundry soap
Refrigerator (brand)
Radios

Airconditioners*
Instant coffee*
TV (black and white)

Product

Source: Bureau of Applied Social Research, Columbia University.

Note: Products and brands of consumer goods may be classified by the extent to which reference groups influence their purchase. (The classification of all products marked with an asterisk (*) is based on actual experimental evidence. Other products in this table are classified speculatively on the basis of generalizations derived from the sum of research in this area and confirmed by the judgment of seminar participants.)

influence; (3) weak product-strong brand influence; or (4) weak product-weak brand influence. There are some types of products, such as cars, cigarettes, beer, and drugs, where the groups exert a strong influence on both the choice of product and choice of brand. Other products have only a small group influence on the brand choice but greatly affect the product choice. Such products as instant coffee, air conditioners, and television sets, fit this group. A weak product-strong brand influence by the group is found for such products as furniture, clothing, magazines, refrigerators, and facial soaps. Many conveniences goods such as canned goods, underwear, and so on, have both a weak product and weak brand influence by the group or consumer.

SOCIAL CLASS SOURCES

The second major source of group information available to individual consumers is social classes.[13] *Social class* is the hierarchical grouping of persons into distinct status groups so that members of each group have, more or less, equal status or prestige. Americans have traditionally avoided the concept of social class. As a nation founded on democratic principles, we like to think of all people as equal. The American dream of a land where everyone has an opportunity to rise to the top prevails. Rather than face up to a contradiction between the ideal of equality and the concrete fact of social difference, we look the other way. When we do this, however, we fail to recognize an important part of our society's way of life. Social class enters into every aspect of our lives—marriage, family, business, government, work, and consumption.

Social class is important to the study of consumer decision making because buying is frequently directly related to class. Individuals who identify with such classes as the working class or the upper middle class tend to have similar values and life-styles. They expose themselves to different advertising, purchase different product types, and patronize different types of stores. The manner and extent of their communication also varies among social classes as it relates to the market.

Properties of Social Class

There are three important properties that characterize social class and affect the flow of information. First, social class is *hierarchical;* groups can be ordered from higher to lower. Second, social class displays *homogeneity within classes* because there exist similar values, beliefs, and behavior by persons within the group. It follows that persons with such similarity communicate more and agree more on the shared information. Therefore, we would expect them to consume in similar patterns, and this is in fact what we find within limits. Third, there is *heterogeneity between social classes* in that significant differences in thought patterns and behavior exist. It is this heterogeneity that makes it possible to identify classes, but it also makes communication difficult across class lines.

Indicators of Social Class

Scholars have used a number of indicators to measure the different social classes. Some of the more important are occupation, income, education, and achievement. Some of these indicators are more measurable than others. It should be remembered that these indicators only stand for social class. The concept of social class involves our whole life-style, which is difficult to pin down quantitatively.

Occupation. In our society, some occupations have higher status than others. It is difficult to pin down the rank order of these occupations, but to some they are the single most important indicator of social class. Table 10-1 illustrates the results of one study on occupational prestige. University professors ranked first, and persons on welfare ranked last.

Occupations that require great skill or education tend to rank highest, and generally white collar workers rank higher than blue collar workers. Notice the placement of clergy, construction workers, and persons "on social security." Although we earn the right to be "on social security," it does not carry prestige. These results should be interpreted with care because occupational prestige changes over time, and individual ranks differ depending on who does the ranking and the type of scale used.

Table 10–1
Occupational Prestige Scale

Occupation	Rank	Occupation	Rank
University professor	78	Soldier	39
Physician	78	Post office clerk	39
Lawyer	71	Receptionist	38
Dentist	70	Telephone operator	38
Head of large firm	70	Machine operator	38
Accountant	68	Car salesperson	36
Executive	67	Model	36
High school teacher	64	Beautician	35
Veterinarian	61	Firefighter	35
Clergy	60	Plumber	34
Lives off property	57	Undertaker	34
Journalist	55	Sales clerk	34
Nurse	54	Truck driver	33
Secretary	53	Cashier	31
Flight attendant	50	Assembly-line worker	30
Real estate agent	49	On Social Security	30
Bank teller	48	Barber	30
Farmer	47	Factory worker	29
Construction worker	46	Taxi driver	28
Keypunch operator	45	Doorman	27
Office clerk	43	Gas station attendant	25
TV repairer	42	Janitor	21
Proofreader	41	Laborer	19
Police officer	40	Migrant worker	18
Cabinetmaker	40	On welfare	16

Source: Donald Treiman, "Occupational Prestige," *Human Behavior,* 1977.

Income. Historically, income was the most important indicator of social class.[14] To have money was to have prestige because of the ability to affect the lives of others. No doubt the association grew out of our early striving to succeed as a nation. Individuals who rose above their modest circumstance to succeed were highly thought of in our society. With our maturing as a nation, other factors such as occupation and education have eroded the importance of income as an indicator of social class. It is still important, however. In Table 10-1, occupational prestige generally, but not completely, follows income. The more prestigious occupations tend to be those with the highest income. A couple of notable exceptions include university professor, high school teacher, clergy, and nurse. Undertakers and car salespeople, who earn high incomes, do not rate high on the scale of occupational prestige.

Education. This factor is becoming increasingly important as an indicator of social status. Persons with higher degrees or more years of education tend to rank higher in social class. This fact explains the rank of university professors in Table 10-1. College professors, clergy, and politicians tend to be welcome in social circles that others, even with high income, cannot touch. A part of the reason for this fact is the effort involved in education and the relatively small number who succeed in reaching the higher educational levels.

Achievement. This social indicator overlaps all the others. For example, achievement can be viewed as improving income, education or occupation that leads to social status. However, we often associate achievement with the acquiring of possessions. In this sense, the person has achieved the most who has the largest automobile, the finest home, the latest fashions in clothing, and membership in the "right" clubs. As a nation, we have always revered achievement. We pull for the underdog who makes it, the immigrant who becomes a millionaire, the understudy who becomes the star. We appreciate material wealth, and we attribute social status to those who have it.

INFORMATION VARIES BY SOCIAL CLASS

Social class impedes communication because of real or imagined barriers between the classes. Very rich persons do not behave or perceive their world in the same way that the poor and unemployed do. There is more information flowing within social classes than between them. This tends to lead to consistent patterns of behavior in the marketplace for persons within a social class.[15] For this reason it is important that we understand social class as a factor of consumer decision making.

There are several methods of measuring social class, but the most important one was conceived by Warner. It has six classes, illustrated in Table 10-2. There may be persons in a social class that have attitudes and behavioral patterns that include aspects of two social classes. There may be persons in one social class who adapt the attitudes and behavioral patterns of persons in another because they identify with the other group. Therefore, any discussion of social class must be taken as an expression of tendencies. With this understanding in mind, let us consider each of Warner's social classes.

Upper Upper Class

The upper upper class is composed of a very small number of socially prominent persons in the community. They include merchants, financiers, or higher professionals who have inherited third- or fourth-generation wealth. They tend to be separated from the other members of the community. They communicate with their own group, although they may be highly conscious of human and community needs. Persons within this group provide community leadership. They are the principal supporters of civic, cultural, and welfare activities with both funds and personal involvement. They are the trustees of universities, colleges, hospitals, and charitable organizations.

Upper upper class people travel a good deal. They are knowledgeable about world affairs, fashion, politics, business, and the arts. However, because they communicate primarily within their own group, they are a poor source of information for others. They are seldom in the limelight, and they consider themselves above fashion. They tend to act without regard to what is accepted. In this sense they are nonconformists. They seldom visit stores to shop. Rather, they prefer to attend private showings or to have others perform this task for them. They are often catered to at home by barbers, beauticians, furriers, jewelers, automobile dealers, and real estate agencies. They serve as role models for persons in the lower classes who want to rise to the upper upper class.

Lower Upper Class

This class represents the new arrivals in the upper class—the "nouveau riche." They tend to identify more with the middle class than with the upper upper class; they have not yet learned the rules of the upper crust. The lower upper class is composed primarily of the executive elite; founders of large businesses; prominent doctors, lawyers, and professionals; politicians; and entertainers. Their money is first-generation, and their children will be more accepted into "society" than they.

Table 10–2
Warner's Social Class

Class	Percent of Population
Upper Upper Class } Lower Upper Class }	.9
Upper Middle Class	7.2
Lower Middle Class	28.4
Upper Lower Class	44.0
Lower Lower Class	19.5
	100.0

People in the lower upper class are highly visible to the classes below themselves. They are visible because of their occupations, use of money, method of living, or associations. They engage in conspicuous consumption as a symbol of their social advancement. Thus they are major purchasers of large homes, luxury automobiles, fashion clothing, exotic vacations, airplanes, boats and property. They hold extravagant parties.

Members of the lower upper class are often creative persons; this accounts for their recent success. They act as communicators of innovative ideas, fashions, and life-styles; thus they are an important source of consumer information. They tend to interact outside their class, and they are in the public eye. It may be fair to say that they are the single most important information source in our society for products and ideas related to change. People tend to associate this group with success and to emulate their attitudes and behavior.

Upper Middle Class

Members of the upper middle class include young, successful professionals, medium-sized business owners, middle managers, professors and politicians. They do not have great family status or wealth, but they are career-motivated. Most people in this group are college graduates, and many have advanced degrees. They become involved in community volunteer service, country clubs, athletic clubs, and informal groups of all kinds. They tend to be status-conscious but home- and children-centered.

The upper middle class live in moderate modern homes, drive good cars, and purchase fashion clothing. They take regular vacations, give parties, engage interior decorators, and purchase home improvements. They are also important purchasers of home stereos, cameras, clothing accessories, swimming pools, and expensive television sets. Because they are integrated into the community, members of the upper middle class tend to be effective communicators. Fashion leaders often come from this group. They do tend to be effective communicators because they are trusted. We tend to trust those persons with whom we associate and know intimately. This group probably has the widest range of associations than any other group. Since they serve as the role model for the classes below them, their influence on consumers is very great.

Lower Middle Class

The lower middle class is the second largest social class, consisting of about 30 percent of the total population. It includes nonmanagerial office workers, small business owners, and higher-paid blue-collar workers such as plumbers and factory workers. We might call this group "typical Americans." They tend to be characterized as striving, respectable, and conservative. They are comfortable and want things to remain the way they are.

Persons identifying with the lower middle class live in modest row houses or small suburban homes. They are family-oriented, and they want their children to be well-behaved. They vacation together as a family, go to church regularly, and join the Elks, Shriners, Masons, and Odd Fellows. They are major consumers of do-it-yourself products, television, conservative clothing, efficient and small cars, home furnishings, and appliances. They communicate within their circle of acquaintances. Few lower middle class consumers are trend-setters or communicators. They tend to purchase with care after consulting family members, friends, and visiting several retail stores.

Upper Lower Class

When we speak of the working class we have in mind the upper lower class. It is the largest single social class, with about 44 percent of the total population. Its sheer numbers make it important both as a source of information and as consumers. The upper lower class is made up of semiskilled workers and skilled workers; it is solidly blue-collar. Members of the upper lower class have low but adequate income. They perceive work as a means to provide enjoyment rather than an end in itself. They are pro-union and perceive union membership as a means to achieve security for themselves and their families. They are less likely to plan for their children's futures than the lower middle class. In a sense, they tend to live, consume, and plan only for today. Tomorrow will take care of itself.

Upper lower class members tend to spend impulsively, and they do not put aside savings for a rainy day. They spend less on their homes and appearance and more on leisure products, radios, inexpensive televisions, camping equipment, and durable clothing. They act as communicators primarily within family groups, but they are large consumers of information from other groups through advertising and visits to retail stores.

Lower Lower Class

The lower lower class lies at the bottom of the social strata. It consists of unskilled workers, unemployed, unassimilated ethnic groups, and those on welfare. Lower lower class members are large consumers only of staple domestic items. They do not own homes and their living quarters are generally substandard. If they have a car, it is old and in need of repairs. Lower lower class members tend to communicate mostly with each other; they do not tend to identify with other classes. Often they are, of necessity, too concerned with surviving to consider social climbing. That this group represents nearly 20 percent of the total population does not speak well for our society. If their economic situation could be improved, they would represent a significant potential consuming public.

Are the advertisements in Figures 10-2 and 10-3 directed at the same social class?

Other Concepts of Social Class

Warner uses six categories of social class. However, marketers do not agree on the precise number of categories, and the range varies all the way down to two. These differences are shown in Table 10-3. The difference in these concepts is primarily one of degree and detail. The important thing is to recognize the existence of social class and the impact it has on consumer decision making. The choice of how many categories to use depends on the amount of detail the marketer feels is necessary to the problem at hand.[16]

Figure 10-2
Advertisement illustrating inexpensive car for social class orientation

Subaru of America Inc.

Social Mobility and Information

A person's placement into a social class is not fixed. This fact is truer in the United States than in some other countries where birth and family history play a more important part in social classification. Our nation has placed more emphasis on achievement than on placement at birth. The classic Horatio Alger story of the underprivileged errand boy who rises to own the business is often used as a symbol in our society. Although the story is an exaggeration which does not happen nearly as often as we would like to believe, social mobility is a fact in modern America. Relatively large numbers do move from lower to higher social status over their lifetime. The reverse is also true; persons of higher status move into lower categories. We are all familiar with the story of the fallen angel.

Because of social mobility, higher social classes often act as anticipatory reference groups for persons who rank lower. These persons tend to emulate higher classes in an attempt to improve themselves and move up in society. These persons seek information from the higher classes, they attempt to identify consumer patterns of the higher group, and they condition their consumer decision making after the higher social group. Marketers take advantage of this fact in advertising and personal selling by providing the needed information. However, marketers must be careful that the symbolism used is not too far above the consumers they are attempting to reach. If consumers cannot identify with the sym-

Figure 10-3
Advertisement illustrating expensive car for social class orientation

Cadillac Motor Car Division

Table 10–3
Categories of Social Class

Two Categories of Social Class	Three Categories of Social Class	Four Categories of Social Class	Five Categories of Social Class	Warner's Six Categories of Social Class
1. White-collar and blue-collar	1. White-collar gray-collar, blue-collar	1. Capitalists white-collar, gray-collar, blue-collar,	1. Capitalists white-collar, gray-collar, blue-collar, underclass	1. Upper upper, lower upper, upper middle, lower middle upper lower, lower, lower
2. Upper and lower	2. Upper, middle, lower	2. Upper, upper middle, lower middle, lower	2. Upper, upper middle, lower middle, upper lower, lower lower	

bolism, they may be discouraged or fail to make the proper connection between the symbol and what the marketer wants to convey.

IMPORTANCE OF SOCIAL INFLUENCE

It was established that social groups, through communications, have decided influence on consumer behavior. This influence can be greater than the direct effect of business promotion.[17] It follows that businesspeople have a high vested interest in knowing about group influence. Business executives have several types of specific interest in knowing about groups.

First, business managers need to identify important groups in our society and communities. It is important to know why people join certain groups. What pattern of socio-demographic factors can be identified in these individuals that can give clues to selecting promotional appeals and methods of presentation to these consumers? How do they differ? How can they be reached in the market?

Second, business needs to understand the inner organization and operation of groups in general. This includes such considerations as how status is determined, the rewards and sanctions of belonging to specific groups, and how these rewards and sanctions are administered. Of particular importance to business management is how influence flows through the various types of social groups. We actually know little about the process of word-of-mouth communications between coworkers, neighbors, church and social groups, consumer groups, etc. How strong and in what directions are specific effects on individual consumers?

Third, business executives need to know who the opinion leaders are in various groups. Do these leaders vary from group to group? Do different opinion leaders exert influence in different ways? If business knew this it could direct some types of promotion to the masses and other types to the opinion leaders. The total effect of promotion would be much greater. Clues to opinion leaders might be found if business could determine how leaders obtain and maintain their position of influence.

Fourth, business managers need to know the effect of consumers belonging to several groups at the same time. What type of purchase conflicts arise and how does the consumer resolve them?[18] Which groups have the most influence on consumption patterns? How does the type of source affect consumer believability on matters pertaining to consumer behavior?

QUESTIONS

1. Identify individuals you feel are in your reference group. Discuss why.
2. Discuss the statement: "Coworkers are always in your reference group."
3. Identify a formal group you belong to and discuss its influence on your purchasing behavior.
4. Define participation groups and negative groups. Give examples of how they influence your purchasing behavior.
5. Which reference groups do you turn to for information when purchasing:
           a. a car?   b. clothing?   c. food?
   Discuss why.
6. What changes do you see in the future of the role of women? Why?

7. What role does a child play in the purchase decision of:
   a. a car?   b. food?   c. recreation?
8. Define and discuss the degrees of conformity that may occur within groups.

9. Give examples of products where a group could exert:
   a. strong product-strong brand influence
   b. strong product-weak brand influence
   c. weak product-strong brand influence
   d. weak product-weak brand influence

10. Scholars have used a number of indicators to measure the different social classes, such as occupation, income, education, and achievement. Which do you think is the least important indicator and why?
11. Using Warner's Social Class classification (Table 10-2), identify the types of print media that a marketing manager might use to provide information to each class.
12. It has been said that the lower classes generally pay more for their purchases than any other group. Discuss why this might be true.
13. Identify and discuss some of the reasons why the United States is considered a mobile society.
14. What effect, if any, does mobility have on culture? Discuss your answer.
15. Identify several individuals who you perceive to be opinion leaders. What characteristics do they have to make them opinion leaders?

NOTES

1. William O. Bearden and Michael J. Etzel, "Reference Group Influence on Product and Brand Purchase Decisions," *Journal of Consumer Research*, Vol. 9 (September 1982), pp. 183–94.
2. Alan J. Greco and Cristie H. Paksoy, "Reference Group Influence on the Elderly Consumer's Brand Choice Behavior," in David M. Klein and Allen E. Smith, eds., *Marketing: The Next Decade, 1985* (Boca Raton, Fla. Southern Marketing Assn., 1985), pp. 24–31.
3. Joel Rudd and Frank J. Kohout, "Individual and Group Consumer Information Acquisition in Brand Choice Situation," *Journal of Consumer Research,* Vol. 10 (December 1983), pp. 303–9.
4. William O. Bearden, "Reference Group Influence on Product and Brand Purchase Decisions," *Journal of Consumer Research,* Vol. 9 (September 1982), pp. 183–94.
5. M. E. Schnake, Michael Dotson, and Louis M. Capella, "The Formal Work Group as a Reference in Consumer Purchasing Decisions," in John H. Summey, Blaise J. Bergiel, and Carol H. Anderson, eds., *A Spectrum of Contemporary Marketing Ideas* (Southern Illinois University at Carbondale and Southern Marketing Assn., 1982), pp. 198–202.
6. Francis S. Bourne, "Group Influence in Marketing and Public Relations," in Rensis Likert and Samuel P. Hayes, Jr., eds., *Some Applications of*

Behavioral Science Research (Paris: UNESCO, 1957), pp. 217–24.

7. Richard D. Becherer, Fred W. Morgan, and Lawrence M. Richard, "Informal Group Influence Among Situationally/Dispositionally-Oriented Customers," *Journal of the Academy of Marketing Science,* Vol. 10 (Summer 1982), pp. 269–80.

8. Jeffrey D. Ford and Elwood A. Ellis, "A Reexamination of Group Influence on Member Brand Preference," *Journal of Marketing Research,* Vol. 17 (February 1980), pp. 125–32.

9. Lynn Weber Cannon, "Trends in Class Identification Among Black Americans from 1952 to 1978," *Social Science Quarterly,* Vol. 65 (March 1984), pp. 112–26.

10. Alan J. Greco, "Reference Group Influence on the Elderly Consumer's Brand Choice Behavior," pp. 24–31.

11. Mark Granovetter, "Economic Action and Social Structure: The Problem of Embeddedness," *American Journal of Sociology,* Vol. 91 (November 1985), pp. 481–510.

12. The table is only illustrative for products and brands. There is little empirical evidence concerning group influence on stores, services, and method of purchase.

13. Richard P. Coleman, "The Continuing Significance of Social Class to Marketing," *Journal of Consumer Research,* Vol. 10 (December 1983), pp. 265–280.

14. Charles M. Schaninger, "Social Class Versus Income Revisited: An Empirical Investigation," *Journal of Marketing Research,* Vol. XVIII (May 1981), pp. 192–208.

15. Paul S. Hugstad, "A Reexamination of the Concept of Privilege Groups," *Journal of the Academy of Marketing Science,* Vol. 9 (Fall 1981), pp. 399–408.

16. Luis V. Dominguez and Albert L. Page, "Use and Misuse of Social Stratification in Consumer Behavior Research," *Journal of Business Research,* Vol. 9 (1981), pp. 151–73.

17. Edward M. Tauber, "Why Do People Shop?" *Journal of Marketing,* Vol. 36 (October 1972), pp. 46–59.

18. Joseph T. Plummer, "Life Style Patterns and Commercial Bank Credit Card Usage," *Journal of Marketing,* Vol. 35 (April 1971), pp. 35–41.

Cultural Values

Guide Consumer Search

CHAPTER OUTLINE

I. **CULTURAL IDENTIFICATION**
   A. Culture and Subculture
   B. Sources of Culture
   C. Function of Culture

II. **CULTURE UNDERLIES ALL CONSUMER SEARCH**
   A. Culture Establishes Norms of Market Behavior
   B. Types of Norms
   C. Norms Operate through Rewards and Sanctions

III. **ATTRIBUTES OF CULTURE THAT AFFECT SEARCH**
   A. Culture Is Handed Down
   B. Culture Is Ideational
   C. Culture Is Adaptive
   D. Culture Is Integrative

IV. **CULTURAL CHARACTERISTICS AFFECTING SEARCH**
   A. Religious Belief
   B. Stress on Material Comfort
   C. Perception of Personal Equality
   D. Reliance on Behavioral Conformity
   E. Belief in Technology
   F. Humanitarianism

V. **RACIAL AND ETHNIC SUBCULTURES**
   A. Hispanic Subculture
   B. Black Subculture

       1. *Black Demographics*
       2. *Black Purchasing Patterns*
       3. *Attitudes of Blacks Toward the Media*

VI. **RELIGIOUS SUBCULTURES**

VII. SUBCULTURES BASED ON AGE AND MARRIAGE
 A. Adolescents
 B. The Teenage Group
 C. Young Adults
 D. Senior Citizens
 E. Singles

CHAPTER OBJECTIVES

After completing your study of Chapter 11, you should be able to:

1. Discuss cultural identification and the function of culture.
2. Discuss how culture underlies all consumer search.
3. Discuss the attributes of culture that affect search.
4. Describe the cultural characteristics that affect search.
5. Discuss racial and ethnic subcultures.
6. Discuss religious subcultures.
7. Discuss the subcultures based on age and marriage.

Culture is the third major group of external sources of consumer information. One may wonder what relationship can exist between culture and consumer search. What can a person's deep-seated values have to do with the process of acquiring such items as the week's groceries or a new automobile? The fact of the matter is that culture has a great deal to do with a consumer's search and selection of groceries, automobiles, and all the other products that one purchases. In this chapter we explain what culture is and demonstrate its importance to consumer search and decision making.

CULTURAL IDENTIFICATION

Every individual can be identified with some specific culture. Consumer decision, including search decisions, are affected by that culture. It is important to understand what is meant by culture and to distinguish between culture and subculture, since both types are important to the consumer's search processes.

Culture and Subculture

Culture is the thinking, feeling, and believing that binds people together. It is not limited to the fine arts, but embraces all the interactions involved with human activity. However, we are interested in consumers, so our definition of *culture* is:

the social heritage of a people, including such shared characteristics as values, customs, beliefs, morality, and ethics which regulate that society's consumer behavior.

Culture varies from nation to nation. Culture is the foundation upon which all social interactions rest. It consists of the historical rules by which present interaction takes place.

The term *subculture* is used to recognize group variations that exist within a culture. We define *subculture* to mean:

any group within a society that preserves the principal characteristics of that society's culture but provides values and beliefs distinguishable as its own.

It follows that a culture may have any number of subcultures.[1] However, a culture is more than simply a summation of all the subcultures of which it is composed. Some of the more common bases for identifying subcultures are regions, nationality, ethnic origin, religion, age and sex. Within the American culture, we can identify relatively homogeneous subcultures based on each of these classes. More is said about that later.

Sources of Culture

Culture is acquired from almost any source of social contact. It is not necessarily passed down from senior to junior citizens. However, in every society there are certain institutions that become the focal points of cultural accumulation. In primitive tribes, this function was often handled by the village elders; but as societies advanced, more complex institutions had to be developed to deal with cultural knowledge. Today, the primary sources of cultural knowledge are family, school, church, political institutions, and other institutions.

Photo 11-1
The family is a source of cultural and consumer values.

© *Jim Whitmer Photography*

Chapter 11 – Cultural Values Guide Consumer Search

It is difficult to pinpoint which institutions are responsible for which cultural values, because they all interact. However, some institutions do tend to take the lead where certain values are concerned. It can be helpful to identify some of these tendencies.

The basic institution of cultural accumulation in the American society is the family, followed by the school. The other institutions influence in varying degrees that are impossible to rank. The family is pervasive not only because family members begin their influence at birth when the individual is most susceptible, but also because most other cultural knowledge is filtered through the family. Every type of cultural value is influenced, to a substantial degree, by the family. The family is particularly important in establishing values of personal identity, pride, sharing, affection, honesty, social status, and biases.

The school also reaches the child at an early, impressionable age and greatly influences cultural values. The school is particularly important in shaping social values, sex values, work values, competition, achievement, and social reward and sanctions. Religion tends to affect a person's moral, ethical, and religious values, and this is true whether the person is an agnostic or avidly religious.[2] After all, rejecting one's religion is as much an effect as is accepting it. Political institutions augment social values, but they play a great part in creating the values of national culture such as pride in one's heritage, country, flag, and national achievement.

In a given society, and at a given time, the institutions of cultural knowledge vary in their importance. For example, the family used to be the major source of sex values in America; now schools and peers are increasing in influence. The family's effect on political attitudes has been greatly shifted to political parties, largely as a result of the mass media. The social graces, once taught in the home, are increasingly being shifted to social groups and schools. The result is a decline in family influence on cultural knowledge and an increase in the influence of schools and political groups. There is some evidence that religion, which has been out of favor for some time, is back on the rise as a cultural influence.

It is important to recognize the source of influences on cultural values. For example, the decline of church and family influences has profoundly affected people's attitudes toward marriage, family planning, and abortion. Products related to these issues have also undergone changes. The bias of schoolteachers at lower grades toward girls has been frequently cited. This bias not only affects the attitude of boys toward school, but could be a factor in the unisex trend and the tendency of males to accept more readily female-oriented products such as long hair and ornate clothing.

Function of Culture

The function of any culture is twofold. First, culture is the force which determines rules of behavior. Culture is the standard that people use for guidance when they are not sure which type of action or behavior is proper. How does a young girl behave on her first date? What is the proper role of a millionaire toward charity? What will be the neighbor's reaction if a consumer purchases a high-priced automobile? These and other questions can be partly answered on the basis of cultural standards. Second, culture functions as a type of enforcer of

Illustration 11-1
How culture operates to affect consumers

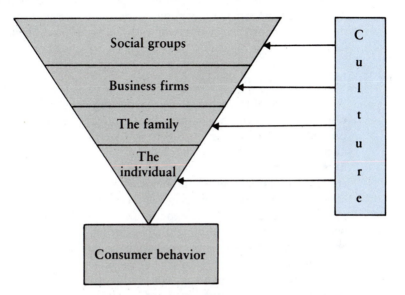

group standards; it tends to force prescribed types of behavior.[3] The often used phrase, "society's point of view," refers to this type of pressure. Society as a whole can both reward and punish, and this fosters individual conformity.[4] Obviously, some conformity is good and is needed in any group activity, but society can become oppressive. When culture becomes too formalized, it can stifle change and innovation. Some changes, as some standards, are needed for any social order to survive.

CULTURE UNDERLIES ALL CONSUMER SEARCH

All consumer search is conducted within the framework of society. Consumers begin to learn at a very early age what is acceptable behavior when seeking out products and what is not. The significance of this statement can be determined from Illustration 11-1. We recognize that the individual is the smallest unit of consumer behavior, and the pyramid rises from there according to the increasing size of the unit with which the individual identifies. Culture affects all levels of the society as shown.[5]

Culture operates on the individual consumer in many ways. For example, the individual knows that he or she must seek out and purchase needed goods rather than steal them. The consumer also knows, no matter what type of search is involved, that one is expected to honor all contracts, make payment, pay on time, register complaints in legitimate ways, observe rules, and assume responsibility for information seeking. We recognize these prescribed ways of doing business as cultural customs, beliefs, and ethics. No one has to tell us how to behave in the search process; it is a part of our nature.

Culture also affects consumer behavior by operating through the family, business firms, and social groups. First, culture directly affects each of these groups helping to shape the attitudes, feelings, biases, and opinions that the individual consumer may draw upon. Second, the various groups render rewards to the consumer for correct behavior and punish incorrect behavior. For example, jail may await the consumer who steals or does not honor contracts.

Culture Establishes Norms of Market Behavior

Culture establishes the standards, or norms, upon which all market behavior rests. A *cultural norm* is defined as an understood way of acting or behaving prescribed by the society as a whole. Norms sometimes change and are often unclear or ambiguous, but they exert a powerful influence that guides our daily lives. A norm can be any kind of social standard, but nothing is just or correct, ethical or moral, except what the norms of a society declare to be just or correct, ethical or moral. In some societies, a consumer is expected to haggle with the merchant over every purchase, but in the United States most purchases are made without bargaining. Although some prices are negotiated, our system is characterized as a one-price economy because the retailer sets the price and the consumer can accept or reject it.

Cultural norms serve to guide our actions as consumers. For example, in searching for products the consumer is expected to acquire sufficient information to make a sound judgment. Society prescribes that the seller may withhold information, but not lie about the product. Cultural norms come in pairs: they prescribe what is acceptable behavior and what is not. We are required to do one thing and are forbidden to do its opposite. We are required to drive on the right side of the road (prescribed) and forbidden to drive on the left (proscribed). Consumers are required to deal honestly and forbidden from dealing dishonestly.

Cultural norms are standards to judge behavior. Conformity is accepted and nonconformity is not accepted. We can judge our own behavior as well as that of others.

Types of Norms

There are many types of cultural norms that can be identified, but the most important are laws, mores, and customs.

Customs are traditional ways that people interact with each other. Observance of these customs is not required by law; their only enforcement is by the people themselves. People conform to them because they believe in them. We eat three meals a day, observe retail store hours, and purchase the latest fashions because we feel it is the right thing to do.

Mores are those customs or usages of a society that are regarded as being essential to its welfare and even survival. They include moral attitudes and are the more formal rules and customs prescribed by the society. Although there are no agencies to enforce mores, the penalties for breaking the rules can be severe. Whereas deviations from customs are not serious, deviations in moral conduct are considered a threat to the entire society. Thus, family responsibility, sexual behavior, and business ethics are considered very serious matters.

Laws are the most formal of all social norms and pertain to deviations from accepted conduct, some so serious that they cannot be tolerated by the society. In every culture there are some laws that are questioned by certain groups (see Figure 11-1). Laws are formally enacted by the courts or some duly authorized governmental body and may be enforced by various agencies such as the police, national guard, or army. The legal structure has a direct bearing on the operation of business. Laws prescribe many of the relationships between business and the consumer.

Figure 11-1
The legal structure has a direct bearing on business

#1 in a Series on Civil Justice Reform

Justice for all?

The right to sue is as essential to a free and fair country as any right guaranteed in the Constitution.

But when a woman riding in an automobile spills hot coffee on her lap, then sues the restaurant where she bought the coffee, something is wrong.

And when a man can drag a liquor company into court because he has become an alcoholic, something is wrong.

Americans have a strong foundation for resolving disputes. Our civil justice system has served us well for many years. But the system's original purposes have become distorted with the passage of time.

Our civil justice system was created to balance individual rights with society's needs. But it has strayed from this objective.

It used to provide an efficient way for the injured to be compensated. Now, too often, it is intolerably slow—and costly.

It used to make judgments primarily based on fault. Now, too often, it makes judgments based on who can pay when something goes wrong.

And the system used to compensate people fairly when they were injured by someone else's wrongful act. Now, too often, it can hand out big awards that have no logical relationship to the injuries suffered.

Our civil justice system is bloated with unnecessary costs and delay, played without clear rules, and capable of producing verdicts that truly offend the conscience. But Americans have a demonstrated capacity to fix things that go wrong. We've been doing it for 200 years.

We *can* restore balance to this system. Public demand has put this on the agenda for change in state after state. I hope you will join me in working for meaningful reform of our civil justice system.

William O. Bailey
Vice Chairman
Ætna Life & Casualty
Hartford, CT 06156

"Our civil justice system is bloated with unnecessary costs and delay, played without clear rules, and capable of producing verdicts that truly offend the conscience."

William O. Bailey

Courtesy of Aetna Life & Casualty

Norms Operate through Rewards and Sanctions

Norms of culture are enforced by the use of rewards and sanctions. *Rewards* are the favors that society can bestow in appreciation for conformity; *sanctions* are the penalties society can bring to bear on the nonconformist. Both can be effective in assuring a large measure of conformity, and both can be formally or informally structured into the system.

Formal rewards are such things as diplomas, awards, plaques, medals, and testimonials. Informal rewards usually take the form of approval by our friends—a handshake, a pat on the back, an acceptance of a dinner invitation, or flattery.

Formal sanctions result from the laws previously mentioned. These sanctions vary in form from money payments for minor deviations, such as parking violations, to long prison terms for more serious crimes, such as stealing. Informal sanctions are in the form of disapproval by our peers. The ostracized person, or the social outcast, knows informal sanctions. These sanctions may take the form of a look, a gesture, silence, or avoidance, and any one of these can be effective. People conform to norms for a number of reasons. First, norms bring a high measure of order into daily interactions. We know what to expect from the behavior of others because we conform to the same norms. Second, norms are a partial substitute for judgment. Because of established norms, we know what is right or wrong and what is acceptable behavior without worrying about it. Third, people like the approval of their peers that results from conformity to norms. Fourth, most people do not care for the disapproval that results when norms are broken. Finally, it is often easier to conform than not.

Norms affect market behavior because they apply to both buyer and seller. Such everyday business ethics as honoring contracts, offering honest service, and competing fairly are based on norms. Laws such as the Robinson-Patman Act, the Federal Trade Commission Act, the Pure Food and Drug Act, and the Truth in Lending Law place direct limits on the actions of business.

Other facets of marketing, such as the hours for opening and closing stores, are affected by mores and customs. The practice of closing on Sunday is partly custom and partly legal. In short, there is very little of business life that is not affected by norms.

The effectiveness of cultural norms should not be judged by the amount of formality associated with them. Mores are more formal than customs, and laws more formal than mores, but the degree of formality does not insure a degree of conformity. Laws act as deterrents on certain actions, but individuals break laws regularly. The real effectiveness of norms, therefore, lies in the willingness of people to conform to the standard. Prohibition did not keep consumers from drinking, just as chain grocery stores and discount houses grew in spite of formal opposition by traditional retailers.

ATTRIBUTES OF CULTURE THAT AFFECT SEARCH

There are four specific attributes of culture that directly affect the consumer search and decision process.

Photo 11-2
Culture and values are learned.

© *Loren G. Hosack/1988*

Culture Is Handed Down

Culture is handed down from one generation to the next. One generation understands what the previous generation considered acceptable social behavior. Culture differs from other learning in that it involves only the moral and ethical guides to behavior that transcend generations. When someone is told of a new product by a friend, that is learning; but when a father explains to his child why the family does not grocery shop on Sunday, that is cultural. It is also part of culture when religious and educational institutions interpret ethical and moral behavior for students.

Because culture passes between generations, it can be modified. The new generation adds its own perceptions and feelings to the previous understanding. Thus attitudes do change toward how far to travel when shopping, how to act if a seller returns you too much change, and what in-store behavior is expected.

Culture Is Ideational

Culture is ideational; the norms of culture are bigger than life. Cultural standards are ideals which most persons cannot live up to fully. A person may agree you should not steal but see nothing wrong with taking a towel from a hotel. Culture may prescribe that lying is unacceptable, but both the buyer and the seller may withhold information that the other could use. In most cultures it is understood that one can never meet the high standards of the culture. However, one is expected to try, and one should never overstep the bounds of what is permissible deviation from the norm.

Culture Is Adaptive

Culture adapts to the physical and social environment. Culture in the tropics dictates a slower pace for people because of the heat. Thus trade moves at a slower pace. Stores tend to be closed in the afternoon but open later at night. The consumer must adjust search patterns to these cultural considerations. In more temperate climates the pace is faster. American businesses have often found themselves in trouble overseas for paying bribes to business and government officials in order to obtain contracts. The problem is that our government applies the same standards of ethical and moral practice for our firms overseas as in this country. We do not recognize that bribery is culturally acceptable in some countries. If you do business there, you must operate in their culture; in this respect, Americans have been slow to adapt culturally.

Culture tends to borrow from its neighbors. As more and more interaction takes place, geographic areas and nations tend to become more alike culturally. Isolated cultures tend to be less susceptible to change.

Culture Is Integrative

Culture is integrative in that cultural norms form a consistent pattern of behavior. They constitute the rules of life, and what is acceptable in society generally is acceptable for consumers. Seldom, if ever, do the rules of culture contradict one another. Stealing is wrong, whether from a neighbor or from a business. The responsibility to keep oneself informed is the same when exchanging gossip and when seeking market information. Culture provides consistency to all market-related activity, and it is the foundation upon which all consumer search takes place.

CULTURAL CHARACTERISTICS AFFECTING SEARCH

Attempts have been made to define the basic cultural factors of all Americans. These attempts center on delineating the cultural attitudes of an average American. Such attempts are doomed to failure because there is no average American, nor is there any average American culture. What we are likely to get is a composite view of cultural perceptions; the facts may be quite different. Even so, the knowledge is useful, since we have established that individual consumers vary much in accordance with their perceptions.

American culture is characterized by the following basic values:[6] (1) religious belief, (2) material comfort, (3) equality, (4) conformity, (5) technology and innovation, and (6) humanitarianism.

Religious Belief

Americans perceive themselves to be religious. We may not go to church and we may not live up to the ideal, "love thy neighbor as thyself," but religious doctrine conditions our attitudes toward work, morality, other people, and consumption. We generally subscribe to the *Protestant ethic,* feeling that: (1) work is good, (2) good rewards industry and hates idleness, (3) one should strive for efficiency in all things, (4) a moralistic attitude is the only sound approach to life, and (5) one should save some of the fruits of labor for a rainy day.

This Protestant ethic partially explains our industry as a nation, our impatience with welfare recipients, our lack of faith in social class, our attitude toward possessing things (material wealth), and our preoccupation with striving to be better. Because of the Protestant ethic, consumers tend to seek only ethical information, they tend to search efficiently, they seek only necessary information for making the decision, and they consider successful purchasing their reward.

Stress on Material Comfort

Material comfort is an American way of life. A rising level of living is considered the reward for hard work. Whether correct or not, most Americans consider a lack of success to be related to laziness. As a nation we are not ashamed of the things we have, and we consider striving for material things to be good. This perception is summarized in the saying, "God helps those who help themselves." Thus a consumer is justified in owning whatever he or she can afford to buy. The only limitation is that in the search process, one should purchase prudently and deal fairly.

Perception of Personal Equality

Americans believe in the ideal of equality. We value achievement rather than birth, and we admire those who have achieved personal success. We honor individualism and the person's right to rise above his or her background.

We tend to dismiss the obvious inequalities around us as due to other considerations. We like to think that the poor or those on welfare have the same opportunity as the successful. They just have not done as much with their lives. We overlook the fact that blacks and women earn only about one-half as much as whites or males. Our perception of ourselves is that of the melting pot of the world where anyone has the opportunity to achieve up to the limit of their ability.

Reliance on Behavioral Conformity

Americans value conformity. Conformity is awareness of the group. How we live, what we buy, our attitudes toward leisure, and where we shop are conditioned by group awareness. This fact may explain the sameness of shopping malls and the products that they carry. A mall, and the stores within, is pretty much like any other mall. The only real difference lies in the size of the unit. In other words, larger malls have more stores and smaller malls have fewer stores, but within each group the types of stores are pretty much alike. All Americans conform to some degree, yet we all try to be a little different. This helps to explain the different patterns of search and purchase identified among consumers; consumers don't like buying the same dress or furnishing their homes the same way.

Belief in Technology

Americans prize technological advance and innovation. This is no contradiction of reliance on conformity. Americans seek innovation, but they tend to want to participate in the same innovation. We do perceive ourselves as constantly pressuring for more and better products. This explains to some degree why we are such an adaptive people. This drive helps explain why consumers seek out new stores and products. They want to be different—but only just so different.

Humanitarianism

Americans recognize the individual's responsibility to others. In spite of our impatience with failure, we recognize the need to help those who are less fortunate than us. We are one of the most generous nations on earth. One need look no further than the Marshall Plan after World War II, our willingness to accept Cuban, Mexican, and Vietnamese refugees, and our attitude toward relief programs around the world such as Ethiopia. This attitude affects the amount individuals have to spend in the marketplace. It can cause prudence in shopping and buying. We often purchase products for humanitarian reasons. Consider the purchase of religious products and the sale of products to help the poor.

RACIAL AND ETHNIC SUBCULTURES

Knowledge of the particularities of major subcultures helps in explaining differences in search and buying patterns among consumers.[7] In this section we deal with Hispanics and blacks.

Hispanic Subculture

There are a number of distinct groups within the Hispanic subculture. These include the Mexican-Americans, 61.2 percent, Puerto Ricans, 13.5 percent, and other, 25.3 percent.[8] These Hispanic subcultures are concentrated geographically along the southern states from California to Georgia. Over 75 percent of Hispanics live in the top 30 metropolitan areas, with about 40 percent living in New York.

Table 11-1 summarizes the characteristics of the Hispanic population of the United States. The majority of Hispanics are between the ages of fifteen and forty-four. About 28.4 percent have finished high school, with only about 7 percent unemployed. Over 35 percent of the Hispanics have a family income between $25,000 and $50,000. The figures show that 71.7 percent of Hispanics are married, and, of all the Hispanics, 28.4 percent are below the poverty level. Hispanics differ from whites in several ways.[9] On the average, they have lower income, less education, have larger families, are more likely to be city dwellers, and are less likely to be professional or white-collar workers.

In terms of buying patterns, Hispanics show a strong preference for branded products, and they display considerable brand loyalty.[10] They tend to maintain their Spanish language, and this causes some problems in purchasing. Some marketers such as Procter and Gamble, Chrysler, Pepsi-Cola, Carnation, and Bristol-Myers have penetrated the Hispanic subculture with Spanish language mass media appeals. The Hispanic families tend to be consumption oriented, with a large portion of their income going into personal and household purchases.

Black Subculture

The major racial subculture in the United States is that of blacks. They are the largest racial minority in the nation.

Black Demographics. Some important demographics on the black population of the United States are shown in Table 11-1. In terms of age, the black population has more young people and fewer older people than the general population. Blacks have fewer persons in college and they have a much higher proportion of unemployed (9.5 to 4.7 percent) than the general population. More black families have children than is true for the general population, and there is a much larger than average proportion of black families with female heads. The black population has been characterized as matriarchial.[11] The median income of blacks, $15,432, is almost half that of the general population, $26,433. In part, this reflects the high unemployment rate. Blacks are less likely to hold professional or white-collar jobs than others in the society.

Black Purchasing Patterns. It is not completely clear whether black purchasing patterns differ from those of whites. It has been suggested that blacks purchase like whites in order to become mainstream Americans. It has also been suggested that they purchase in distinct patterns in order to maintain their black heritage. It is clear that there are differences in how blacks purchase compared to whites. For example, there are many cases where the two groups have clear differences in their preferences for specific brands. Blacks tend to have a stronger brand preference than whites and to purchase disproportionately to their income some conspicuous consumables such as automobiles.

Some products, such as cameras and cigarettes, provide little or no differentiation specifically designed into the product to appeal to blacks. However, some of the ads for their products do have special appeals. On the other hand, blacks tend to be innovators in their purchase of clothing, and they are often trend-setters in music. Otherwise, there are similar preference patterns between blacks and

Table 11-1

Social and Economic Characteristics of the White, Black, and Spanish-origin Population: 1985

Characteristic	Number (1,000)					
				Spanish origin		
	Total population	White	Black	Total	Mexican	Puerto Rican
Total persons	234,066	199,117	28,151	16,940	10,269	2,562
Under 6 years old	17,958	14,610	2,699	1,809	1,205	271
6–14 years old	33,792	27,417	5,218	3,355	2,219	516
16–44 years old	110,948	93,852	13,590	8,550	5,160	1,333
45–64 years old	44,549	39,033	4,406	2,407	1,227	372
85 years old and over	26,818	24,205	2,238	819	428	68
Years of School Completed						
Persons 25 years old and over	143,524	124,905	14,820	8,455	4,755	1,241
Elementary: 0–8 years	19,893	16,224	3,113	3,192	2,062	417
High school: 1–3 years	17,553	14,365	2,851	1,210	700	248
4 years	54,866	48,728	5,027	2,402	1,243	347
College: 1–3 years	23,405	20,652	2,188	932	486	141
4 years or more	27,808	24,935	1,640	718	264	87
Labor Force Status						
Civilians 16 years old and over	178,206	153,679	19,664	11,528	6,670	1,594
Civilian labor force	115,461	99,926	12,364	7,448	4,469	835
Employed	107,150	93,736	10,501	6,664	3,983	719
Unemployed	8,312	6,191	1,864	785	487	116
Unemployment rate	7.2	6.2	15.1	10.5	10.9	13.9
Not in labor force	62,744	53,753	7,299	4,080	2,201	759
Family Type						
Total families	62,706	54,400	6,778	3,939	2,251	621
With own children	31,112	26,232	3,890	2,602	1,543	447
Married couple	50,350	45,643	3,469	2,824	1,703	323
With own children	24,210	21,565	1,822	1,892	1,207	218
Female householder,						
no spouse present	10,129	6,941	2,964	905	418	273
With own children	6,006	3,922	1,942	642	302	213
Male householder,						
no spouse present	2,228	1,816	344	210	130	25
With own children	896	744	126	68	34	16
Family Income, 1984						
Total families	62,706	54,400	6,778	3,939	2,251	621
Less than $5,000	3,144	2,057	999	383	173	128
$5,000–$9,999	5,894	4,433	1,300	618	350	143
$10,000–$14,999	6,780	5,607	1,014	591	377	83
$15,000–$24,999	13,520	11,775	1,472	937	559	118
$25,000–$49,999	23,481	21,324	1,597	1,145	658	129
$50,000 or more	9,889	9,207	396	263	136	20
Median income (dol.)	26,433	27,686	15,432	18,833	19,184	12,371
Persons below poverty level	33,700	22,955	9,490	4,806	2,904	1,106
Housing Tenure						
Total occupied units	86,789	75,328	9,480	4,883	(NA)	(NA)
Owner-occupied	55,845	50,661	4,185	2,007	(NA)	(NA)
Renter-occupied	30,943	24,667	5,295	2,876	(NA)	(NA)

Table 11-1 (Continued)

Characteristic	Percent Distribution					
				Spanish origin		
	Total population	White	Black	Total	Mexican	Puerto Rican
Total persons	100.0	100.0	100.0	100.0	100.0	100.0
Under 6 years old	7.7	7.3	9.6	10.7	11.7	10.6
6–14 years old	14.4	13.8	18.5	19.8	21.9	20.1
16–44 years old	47.4	47.1	48.3	50.5	50.3	52.0
45–64 years old	19.0	19.6	15.7	14.2	12.0	14.5
85 years old and over	11.5	12.2	7.9	4.8	4.2	2.7
Years of School Completed						
Persons 25 years old and over	100.0	100.0	100.0	100.0	100.0	100.0
Elementary: 0–8 years	13.9	13.0	21.0	37.7	43.4	33.7
High school: 1–3 years	12.2	11.5	19.2	14.3	14.7	20.0
4 years	38.2	39.0	33.9	28.4	26.1	28.0
College: 1–3 years	16.3	16.5	14.8	11.0	10.2	11.4
4 years or more	19.4	20.0	11.1	8.5	5.5	7.0
Labor Force Status						
Civilians 16 years old and over	100.00	100.0	100.0	100.0	100.0	100.0
Civilian labor force	64.8	65.0	62.9	64.6	67.0	62.4
Employed	60.1	61.0	53.4	57.8	59.7	46.1
Unemployed	4.7	4.0	9.5	6.8	7.3	7.3
Unemployment rate	(x)	(x)	(x)	(x)	(x)	(x)
Not in labor force	35.2	35.0	37.1	35.4	33.0	47.5
Family Type						
Total families	100.0	100.0	100.0	100.0	100.0	100.0
With own children	49.5	48.2	57.4	66.1	68.5	72.1
Married couple	80.3	83.9	51.2	71.7	75.7	52.0
With own children	38.6	39.6	26.9	48.0	53.6	35.1
Female householder,						
no spouse present	16.2	12.8	43.7	23.0	18.6	44.0
With own children	9.6	7.2	28.7	16.3	13.4	34.3
Male householder,						
no spouse present	3.6	3.3	5.1	5.3	5.8	4.0
With own children	1.4	1.4	1.9	1.7	1.5	2.6
Family Income, 1984						
Total families	100.0	100.0	100.0	100.0	100.0	100.0
Less than $5,000	5.0	3.8	14.7	9.7	7.6	20.6
$5,000–$9,999	9.4	8.1	19.2	15.7	15.6	22.9
$10,000–$14,999	10.8	10.3	16.0	15.0	18.8	13.4
$15,000–$24,999	21.6	21.6	21.7	23.7	24.8	19.1
$25,000–$49,999	37.4	39.2	23.6	29.0	29.2	20.7
$50,000 or more	15.8	16.9	5.8	6.6	6.0	3.3
Median income (dol.)	(x)	(x)	(x)	(x)	(x)	(x)
Persons below poverty level	14.4	11.5	33.8	28.4	28.3	43.2
Housing Tenure						
Total occupied units	100.0	100.0	100.0	100.0	(NA)	(NA)
Owner-occupied	64.3	67.3	44.1	41.1	(NA)	(NA)
Renter-occupied	35.7	32.7	55.9	58.9	(NA)	(NA)

Source: U.S. Department of Commerce, *Statistical Abstracts of the United States* (Washington, D.C., 1987), p.35.

Table 11–2
Black-Oriented Magazines

Black female		Black male	
Magazine	Read in last two months	Magazine	Read in last two months
Ebony	47%	Jet	40%
Jet	37	Ebony	38
Essence	22	Sports Illustrated	23
Better Homes and Gardens	18	Black Sports	15
Good Housekeeping	16	People	10

Source: Reprinted from "Minority Readership Poll," *Advertising Age,* September 22, 1980.

whites for fashion merchandise. Blacks are less innovative in purchasing home appliances, but they are more heavy consumers of milk, soft drinks, and liquor. The two groups spend about the same for recreation and leisure.

Attitudes of Blacks Toward the Media. Blacks show a marked preference for media that emphasize black models, themes, and life-styles. Table 11-2 shows a number of successful black-oriented magazines. This demonstrates the effective use of black-oriented media to reach black consumers. Blacks tend to listen to more radio than whites, so commercials placed there are effective, especially since they tend to have no color. Blacks also watch more television than whites. Perhaps more blacks integrated into TV commercials and more strategically placed

Table 11–3
Religious Bodies—Church Membership, 1960 to 1984, and Number of Churches, 1984

Religious Body	Membership						Number of Churches 1984
	1960	1970	1975	1980	1983	1984	
Total	114,449	131,045	131,013	134,817	140,816	142,172	344,410
Members as percent of population	64	63	61	59	60	60	(x)
Average members per local Church	359	399	393	401	416	409	(x)
Buddhist Churches of America	20	100	60	60	70	100	100
Eastern Churches	2,699	3,850	3,696	3,823	4,034	4,053	1,661
Jews	5,367	5,870	6,115	5,920	5,728	5,817	3,416
Old Catholic, Polish National Catholic, and Armenian Churches	590	848	846	924	1,150	1,024	427
The Roman Catholic Church	42,105	48,215	48,882	50,450	52,393	52,286	24,275
Protestants	63,669	71,713	71,043	73,479	77,254	78,702	313,411
Miscellaneous		449	372	161	188	190	1,120

Source: National Council of the Churches of Christ in the United States of America. New York, N.Y., *Yearbook of American and Canadian Churches, Annual.*

black commercials can be effective. There is some evidence that blacks preferred black models in point-of-sale advertisements in grocery stores, and that whites preferred ads with white models.

RELIGIOUS SUBCULTURES

There are more than 220 religious groups in the United States. Table 11-3 has figures on the major religious groups. About 55 percent of our population belongs to some religious order. Protestants are the largest religious group, followed by Catholics. These religious groups affect consumer search in two ways. First, they have a strong influence on consumer ethics and morality. Second, they have an influence through the sale of products that have religious symbolism, such as crosses, beads, statues, and incense, and products associated with religious holidays. Religion also affects consumer ability to purchase due to the amount of donations made to the various churches. Third, religion has a strong influence on search and purchase because of the association of buying with such holidays as Christmas and Easter. It is safe to say that while the effect of religion on consumer search is diffuse, it is also profound and highly significant.

SUBCULTURES BASED ON AGE AND MARRIAGE

Age and marriage are two very important subcultures in our society. Persons in these groups have an effect on how consumers search and decide about products. Table 11-4 demonstrates the changing age of the American population. Keep this table in mind for the following discussion.

Children Under Thirteen

The average family contains 2.4 members, and children are the recipients of a great deal of attention from adults. The smaller family size, combined with a relatively high family income, has meant more for everyone. Children are rewarded for passing from one grade to another in school, cleaning up their rooms, or going on errands. When accompanying parents on shopping excursions, the child receives consumer training by observing the parents. Children between seven and nine years old are asked questions by their parents with regard to household purchases.

Consumption patterns are beginning to be established by the age of five.[12] Five-year-olds make purchase suggestions, mainly for personal items, but a small percentage actually make suggestions about such family items as meat, canned goods, cake mixes, and other food products. Many of these suggestions are identified by brand name, and the child's principal source of information is television.[13]

By the age of seven, a child has taken on more attributes of older consumers. Income comes from the performance of small tasks and from a regular allowance. The seven-year-old makes independent selections of personal items and independent choices of such group products as cereal, frozen juices, cookies, and luncheon meat. The adolescent also makes a number of purchase suggestions to parents.

Many nine-year-olds are dissatisfied with parents' purchases made for them

Table 11–4
Projections of the Total Population by Race, Sex, and Age: 1990 to 2000

Age, Sex, Race	Lowest Series (series 19)			Middle Series (series 14)			Highest Series (series 9)		
	1990	1995	2000	1990	1995	2000	1990	1995	2000
Total population	245,753	251,876	256,093	249,657	259,550	267,955	254,122	268,151	281,542
Under 5 years old	17,515	16,193	14,942	19,198	18,615	17,626	20,615	20,815	20,530
5–17 years old	44,486	46,125	44,951	45,139	48,518	49,763	46,055	50,990	54,434
18–24 years old	25,547	23,347	24,157	25,794	23,702	24,601	26,137	24,233	25,326
25–34 years old	43,147	39,887	35,596	43,529	40,520	38,415	44,329	41,672	37,850
35–44 years old	37,570	41,500	42,972	37,847	41,997	43,743	38,229	42,870	45,128
45–54 years old	25,226	31,044	36,533	25,402	31,397	37,119	25,578	31,763	37,813
55–64 years old	20,910	20,655	23,326	21,051	20,923	23,767	21,189	21,190	24,212
65 years old and over	31,353	33,127	33,621	31,697	33,887	34,921	31,989	34,618	36,246
16 years old and over	190,198	196,242	203,526	191,819	199,188	208,185	194,035	203,249	214,597
Male, total	119,620	122,608	124,671	121,518	126,368	130,491	123,698	130,577	137,163
Under 5 years old	8,964	8,288	7,647	9,827	9,529	9,022	10,550	10,653	10,508
5–17 years old	22,745	23,586	22,989	23,082	24,815	25,458	23,549	26,074	27,842
18–24 years old	13,016	11,904	12,314	13,127	12,072	12,530	13,283	12,325	12,881
25–34 years old	21,722	20,155	18,009	21,892	20,443	18,384	22,281	20,959	19,044
35–44 years old	18,598	20,649	21,508	18,732	20,879	21,866	18,927	21,322	22,537
45–54 years old	12,268	15,152	17,903	12,350	15,327	18,196	12,441	15,518	18,563
55–64 years old	9,804	9,733	11,046	9,871	9,865	11,272	9,936	10,000	11,511
65 years old and over	12,503	13,143	13,255	12,637	13,440	13,762	12,751	13,725	14,277
16 years old and over	91,205	94,152	97,779	91,929	95,480	99,906	92,964	97,378	102,913
Female, total	126,133	129,268	131,427	128,139	133,191	137,464	130,424	137,574	144,379
Under 5 years old	8,551	7,906	7,295	9,371	9,086	8,604	10,065	10,161	10,022
5–17 years old	21,741	22,539	21,962	22,056	23,703	24,305	22,506	24,915	26,592
18–24 years old	12,632	11,443	11,843	12,667	11,630	12,071	12,854	11,908	12,445
25–34 years old	21,426	19,731	17,586	21,637	20,077	18,031	22,068	20,713	18,806
35–44 years old	18,971	20,851	21,465	19,116	21,119	21,877	19,302	21,648	22,591

Table 11–4 (Continued)

45–54 years old	12,958	15,891	18,630	13,051	16,071	18,923	13,137	16,245	19,251
55–64 years old	11,105	10,922	12,279	11,180	11,059	12,495	11,253	11,190	12,702
65 years old and over	18,850	19,984	20,366	19,061	20,447	21,158	19,238	20,893	21,969
16 years old and over	98,993	102,090	105,747	99,890	103,708	106,279	101,071	105,871	111,684
White, total	207,799	211,481	213,498	210,790	217,412	222,654	213,753	223,236	231,980
Under 5 years old	14,046	12,884	11,760	15,390	14,797	13,843	16,451	16,417	15,958
5–17 years old	36,028	37,062	35,876	38,523	38,941	39,667	37,149	40,716	43,061
18–24 years old	20,989	19,008	19,485	21,170	19,267	19,806	21,369	19,578	20,238
25–34 years old	36,027	32,867	29,009	36,289	33,312	29,590	36,768	33,998	30,442
35–44 years old	32,097	35,037	35,822	32,292	35,379	36,355	32,509	35,895	37,180
45–54 years old	21,868	26,822	31,239	21,994	27,077	31,662	22,090	27,286	32,071
55–64 years old	18,432	18,014	20,273	18,636	18,213	20,605	8,605	18,362	20,868
65 years old and over	28,313	29,787	30,032	28,596	30,424	31,126	28,810	30,984	32,162
16 years old and over	162,971	166,987	171,734	164,160	169,181	175,245	165,486	171,695	179,346
Male	101,518	103,352	104,369	102,979	106,266	108,879	104,460	109,175	113,536
Female	106,281	108,129	109,129	107,811	111,146	113,775	109,292	114,061	118,445
Black, total	30,836	32,506	33,957	31,412	33,651	35,753	31,974	34,730	37,602
Under 5 years old	2,948	2,771	2,620	3,215	3,165	3,079	3,440	3,525	3,570
5–17 years old	6,942	7,498	7,553	7,042	7,871	8,321	7,159	8,222	9,031
18–24 years old	3,766	3,495	3,715	3,798	3,542	3,773	3,849	3,620	3,865
25–34 years old	5,809	5,683	5,208	5,880	5,768	5,316	5,932	5,884	5,479
35–44 years old	4,254	5,096	5,701	4,295	5,169	5,811	4,339	5,281	5,954
45–54 years old	2,600	3,210	4,036	2,626	3,262	4,124	2,646	3,307	4,211
55–64 years old	1,978	2,035	2,292	1,998	2,073	2,355	2,013	2,103	2,407
65 years old and over	2,538	2,717	2,833	2,579	2,802	2,975	2,597	2,857	3,085
16 years old and over	21,922	23,230	24,996	22,138	23,618	25,613	22,372	24,055	26,317
Male	14,645	15,451	16,156	14,926	16,013	17,040	15,204	16,573	17,958
Female	16,191	17,055	17,802	16,485	17,638	18,714	16,769	18,207	19,644

Source: U.S. Department of Commerce, *Statistical Abstracts of the United States* (Washington, D.C., Bureau of the Census, 1987), p. 16

and prefer to buy their own personal items. It is common for the nine-year-old to make frequent trips to retail outlets, and the child is actively engaged in and aware of the marketing process. The child in this age group is aware of the differences in cost among products and has an acute awareness of TV commercials. When asked, the nine-year-old shows a preference for products that have prestige value.

The Teenage Group

The main source of income for most teenagers is an allowance. The allowance represents a bare minimum, as parents are almost always willing to supplement it with emergency loans or gifts. Money received from part-time or full-time jobs also represents a substantial source of income. Teen buyers represent a highly profitable market segment for certain producers, since most of their money is available for recreational, luxury, and impulse spending. Figure 11-2 is an ad designed for this group. Not having to pay for food, clothing, or shelter, teenagers spend money on goods they want.

Figure 11-2
Appealing to the teen market

Courtesy of Timex Corp.

There are several peculiarities common to the teenage market. It is extremely fluid, and things change so rapidly that products and fads can become obsolete almost overnight. The real problem when marketing to this group, however, is the danger of alienating its members. Not only are young people changing because of the constant flow into and out of the teenage group, but the youths themselves do not like to be figured out. The young often take pride in being different from their parents. It does not follow that selling the parents sells the teenager; a teenager may reject a product just because the parent uses it.

Young Adults

The young-adult market is made up of people from ages eighteen to twenty-five. This is really two market segments, comprising the college group and the young married group. It is estimated that nearly 65 percent of young people from ages sixteen to twenty-one are in college.[14] College students are big spenders on wearing apparel, furnishings, books, and recreational equipment. They are also among the heavier beer drinkers.

"More girls marry at 18, as a part of this youth market, than at any other age."[15] These young marrieds are better informed than their parents were. New families need more of all types of products, so it is reasonable to predict more spending by this group in the future. However, the need to increase spending comes at a time when earnings are low. The young family has not reached its peak earning capacity. Thus the young marrieds tend to be discriminating buyers. One way out for the newly married is for both spouses to work.[16] Dual-income families sometimes splurge on recreation, entertainment, travel, and eating out. The young married market can be further subdivided along product lines, such as for homes, clothing, food, and home furnishings.

Senior Citizens

In 1982, 20.7 percent of United States families had a head of household sixty-five years of age or over. This group is growing at a substantially faster rate than the population as a whole. While the total population is expected to increase by 31.7 percent between 1970 and 1990, the population sixty-five years of age and over will increase by 40 percent.

Senior citizens constitute a different but significant market for products.[17] Children have left the nest, income has declined to that of retirement level, and the senior citizen is often left alone. People in this group spend much of their time at home, frequently with a health problem. The senior citizen has already accumulated most of the products needed for home operation. These consumers require small homes, less transportation, and fewer clothes and accessories; but they need more insurance, recreation, medical care, and services. The tastes of senior citizens tend toward the conservative. This group is not so venturesome as teens or young adults.

The mere fact that a person reaches retirement age does not obviate his or her need for products and services.[18] In many cases, the senior citizen offers a better market for products and services that satisfy more complex psychological needs, such as social and self-fulfillment needs. This, however, is a difficult group to reach because of attitude and outlook. Products and appeals which single them out as a unique and special group may have negative results. Although they feel that more attention should be given to members of this age group, they tend to resent special marketing treatment, especially that which makes them feel inferior because of age considerations.

Singles

Table 11-5 has important information pertaining to the number of single people in the American society. These data show that singles are an important part of population, especially between the ages of twenty and twenty-four. The figures show that singles are 25.2 percent of the male population and 18.2 percent of the female population. This group is a relatively large market and has its own search and purchasing patterns.

Singles are now established in metropolitan areas, and they are rapidly expanding into the suburbs and small towns. The reasons are a tendency to put off marriage, the high divorce rate, and a tendency not to remarry so quickly after divorce. Singles tend to be more affluent than average. They are highly visible and range in age from the early twenties to the late thirties. They are frequently career-oriented rather than family-oriented. Some enjoy multiple short-term relationships.

Singles develop independence and responsibility very rapidly because there is no spouse or parent with whom to communicate. They must learn to deal with loneliness, and considerable time is spent "getting into circulation" or "getting back into circulation." Most singles must work.[19] This need to work is a special problem for widowed and divorced parents with small children. They must deal with the psychological problem of lack of personal contact with their children and the physical problems of obtaining care for their children when they are at work. Dating, and meeting people generally, is another problem for single parents. On the other hand, the time spent cooking and taking care of the house is greatly reduced among singles compared to the nuclear family. However, the single must become proficient at all household chores, as there is no division of labor. Singles are much more mobile than nuclear family members. They can change jobs, residences, and relationships much more readily and with fewer adverse consequences.

One of the first requirements for a single is housing. Young singles and divorced persons tend to think in terms of apartments or trailers. There is evidence that single college graduates consider a well-furnished, well-decorated apartment a strong statement about the owner's independence, ability to support oneself, and career progress. Thus rent is an important expenditure for singles. The "singles craze" has led to condominiums and apartment complexes designed to appeal to young singles. Similar complexes now exist in retirement areas for older singles.

Singles tend to spend more on clothes—probably because of the need to get out in public more and because of job demands. How one dresses is considered as important a statement about one's life as is one's residence. The manner of dress, as in the nuclear family, reflects the individual's age and type of occupation.

Food is an important problem for singles, but marketers are beginning to respond to their unique needs. Singles tend to eat more frozen and ready-to-eat meals than do nuclear families. Singles also tend to eat out much more, but they may frequent lower-cost eating places except when with a date. Canned goods, particularly

Table 11-5
Marital Status of the Population by Sex and Age: 1985

Sex and Age	Number of Persons (1,000)					Percent Distribution				
	Total	Single	Married	Widowed	Divorced	Total	Single	Married	Widowed	Divorced
Male	81,452	20,543	53,536	2,109	5,264	100.0	25.2	65.7	2.6	6.5
18–19 years	3,640	3,534	106	–	–	100.0	97.1	2.9	–	–
20–24 years	10,055	7,605	2,310	3	138	100.0	75.6	23.0	–	1.4
25–29 years	10,420	4,037	5,751	3	629	100.0	38.7	55.2	–	6.0
30–34 years	9,764	2,027	6,804	7	926	100.0	20.8	69.7	.1	9.5
35–44 years	15,333	1,444	12,254	54	1,581	100.0	9.4	79.9	.4	10.3
45–54 years	10,848	682	9,096	131	939	100.0	6.3	83.8	1.2	8.7
55–64 years	10,377	633	8,711	388	644	100.0	6.1	83.9	3.7	6.2
65–74 years	7,259	380	5,899	672	307	100.0	5.2	81.3	9.3	4.2
75 years old and over	3,755	200	2,604	851	100	100.0	5.3	69.3	22.7	2.7
Female	89,917	16,377	54,354	11,372	7,814	100.0	18.2	60.4	12.6	8.7
18–19 years	3,738	3,240	468	2	28	100.0	86.7	12.5	.1	.7
20–24 years	10,411	6,091	3,953	20	347	100.0	58.5	38.0	.2	3.3
25–29 years	10,686	2,824	6,963	57	843	100.0	26.4	65.2	.5	7.9
30–34 years	9,987	1,351	7,299	104	1,234	100.0	13.5	73.1	1.0	12.4
35–44 years	15,966	1,091	12,312	323	2,242	100.0	6.8	77.1	2.0	14.0
45–54 years	11,550	529	8,812	809	1,401	100.0	4.6	76.3	7.0	12.1
55–64 years	11,774	440	8,240	2,047	1,047	100.0	3.7	70.0	17.4	8.9
65–74 years	9,317	412	4,764	3,622	519	100.0	4.4	51.1	38.9	5.6
75 years old and over	6,487	400	1,543	4,390	154	100.0	6.2	23.8	67.7	2.4

Source: U.S. Department of Commerce, *Statistical Abstracts of the United States* (Washington, D.C., Bureau of the Census, 1987), p. 39.

soups, are important consumption items with singles. A single person does not need the large portions required by nuclear families. Marketers are packaging portions accordingly, as evidenced by Lipton's "Cup-A-Soup," single-portion canned goods, and small snack packages. Greeting cards, such as Hallmark, now appeal to singles.

Furniture and appliances are being designed with singles in mind. Examples are found in smaller dishwashers, washing machines, deep fryers, and coffee makers. Even furniture is being designed for singles. Of course, these product modifications are reflected in promotional campaigns. Many companies are now directing campaigns specifically toward singles.[20]

The media have had to respond to the increasing, and somewhat unique, wants of the singles subculture. More and more commercials depict both men and women in single roles. These advertisements show singles in much more favorable roles than was previously true. More different types of products, especially designed for singles, are currently advertised on television, radio, and the other media. This trend is very likely to accelerate in the future as singles become even more a part of our society.

QUESTIONS

1. Cultural differences can be found in almost every town. Identify and discuss the subcultures in your town.
2. Identify your primary sources of cultural knowledge. Which ones have had the greatest influence on you and why?
3. Identify the functions of culture and give examples of situations where they have applied.
4. Explain with examples how culture affects your purchasing decisions, both directly and indirectly.
5. Discuss the statement: "We should not worry about cultural norms because we cannot change them."
6. Identify and discuss some cultural norms that may be different in different parts of the United States.
7. If you had a choice, would you prefer formal rewards or informal rewards? Why?
8. What comes first, norms or laws? Discuss your answer.
9. Because culture passes between generations, it becomes modified. Discuss this and give examples of culture being modified.
10. Discuss, with examples, how different religious beliefs can have an impact on consumers' purchases.
11. Discuss the statement: "All Americans conform, yet they all try to be a little different."
12. What adjustment would marketing managers have to make if their town had several subcultures?
13. Identify the religious subcultures in your town. What are the implications of these subcultures to a marketing manager of a store in your town?

14. Identify a store in your town that caters to all age groups and a store that caters to a specific age group. What are the differences in the products and services they offer?

15. Interview two individuals of the same age and sex, one married and one single, to determine what differences and similarities they may have as far as preferences of magazines, newspapers, television programs, and radio programs.

NOTES

1. Michel J. Bergier and Jerry Rosenblatt, "Cross-Cultural Differences: Back to the Drawing Board," in John H. Summey, Blaise J. Bergiel, and Carol H. Anderson, eds., *A Spectrum of Contemporary Marketing Ideas, 1982* (Southern Illinois University at Carbondale and Southern Marketing Assn., 1982), pp. 164–67.

2. John K. Johansson, Susan P. Douglas, and Ikujiro Nonada, "Assessing the Impact of Country of Origin on Product Evaluations: A New Methodological Perspective," *Journal of Marketing Research,* Vol. XXII (November 1985), pp. 388–96.

3. Harold G. Grasmick, "Social Change and Modernism in the American South," *American Behavioral Scientist,* Vol. 16 (July–August 1973), pp. 913–33.

4. A. Fuat Firat and Nikhileash Dholakia, "Consumption Choices at the Macro Level," *Journal of Macromarketing,* Vol. 2 (Fall 1982), pp. 6–15.

5. Conrad M. Arensberg and Arthur H. Nichoff, *Introduction to Social Change: A Manual for Americans Overseas* (Chicago: Aldine Publishing Co., 1964), pp. 153–83; R. M. Williams, *American Society, A Sociological Interpretation* (New York: Alfred A. Knopf, Inc., 1951), pp. 388–442.

6. Ibid.

7. Robert E. Wilkes and Humberto Valencia, "A Note on Generic Purchaser Generalizations and Subcultural Variations," *Journal of Marketing,* Vol. 49 (Summer 1985), pp. 114–20.

8. *Statistical Abstract of the United States* (Washington D.C., U.S. Department of Commerce, 1986), p. 34.

9. Humberto Valencia and Danny N. Bellenger, "Ethnic and Income Influences on Hispanic Shopping Behavior," in John H. Summey, Blaise J. Bergiel, and Carol H. Anderson, eds., *A Spectrum of Contemporary Marketing Ideas,* 1982 (Southern Illinois University at Carbondale and Southern Marketing Assn., 1982), pp. 190–94.

10. Madhav N. Segal and Lionel Sosa, "Marketing of the Hispanic Community," *California Management Review,* Vol. XXVI (Fall 1983), pp. 120–34.

11. Peter K. Tat, "Social Class Differentials in the Fashion Buying Behavior of Black Working Women," in John H. Summey, Blaise J. Bergiel, and Carol H. Anderson, eds., *A Spectrum of Contemporary Marketing Ideas, 1982* (Southern Illinois University at Carbondale and Southern Marketing Assn., 1982), pp. 195–97.

12. Deborah L. Roedder, Brian Sternthal, and Bobby J. Calder, "Attitude-Behavior Consistency in Children's Responses to Television Advertising," *Journal of Marketing Research,* Vol. XX (November 1983), pp. 337–49.

13. Gerald J. Gorn and Marvin E. Goldberg, "Behavioral Evidence of Televised Food Messages on Children," *Journal of Consumer Research,* Vol. 9 (September 1982), pp. 200–5.

14. Helen Axel, *A Guide to Consumer Markets* (New York: The Conference Board, Inc., 1975), p. 66.

15. Ibid., p. 70.

16. Dowell Myers, "Wives' Earnings and Rising Costs of Homeownership," *Social Science Quarterly,* Vol. 66 (June 1985), pp. 319–29.

17. James R. Lumpkin, "Shopping Orientation Segmentation of the Elderly Consumer," *Journal of the Academy of Marketing Science,* Vol. 13 (Spring 1985), pp. 271–89.

18. Joseph O. Rentz, Fred D. Reynolds, and Roy G. Stout, "Analyzing Changing Consumption Patterns with Cohort Analysis," *Journal of Marketing Research,* Vol. XX (February 1983), pp. 12–20.

19. Don Bellante and Ann C. Foster, "Working Wives and Expenditure on Service," *Journal of Consumer Research,* Vol. 11 (September 1984), pp. 700–7.

20. James R. Lumpkin and Gemmy S. Allen, "Shopping Patterns of Single Head of Households: Segmenting the Singles Market," in Daniel R. Corrigan, Frederic B. Kraft, and Robert H. Ross, eds., *1982 Proceedings Southwestern Marketing Association Conference* (Wichita State University and Southwestern Marketing Association, 1982), pp. 256–69.

SECTION B
BUSINESS POLICY
AFFECTING SEARCH

12. Distribution Strategy Reflects Consumer Search
13. Promotion Influences Consumer Search

CHAPTER 12

Distribution Strategy

Reflects Consumer Search

CHAPTER OUTLINE

I. **DISTRIBUTION METHODS: GENERAL OBSERVATIONS**
   A. Use Appropriate Channels to Affect Search
   B. Plan Benefits into the Channel
   C. Relate Market Coverage to Consumer Search

II. **PRODUCT LINE INFLUENCES CONSUMER SEARCH**
   A. Limited-Line Stores
   B. Departmentalized Retailers
   C. Superstores

III. **SINGLE OR MULTI-UNIT STORES AFFECT SEARCH**

IV. **NONSTORE OPTION AFFECTS CONSUMER SEARCH**
   A. Direct Marketing
   B. Vending Machines
   C. Door-to-Door Sales

V. **STORE LOCATIONS AFFECT CONSUMER SEARCH**
   A. Unplanned Shopping Districts
   B. Planned Shopping Centers

VI. **EXTERIOR STORE DESIGN AFFECTS CONSUMER SEARCH**
   A. Store Architecture Creates Image
   B. Signs Influence Customer Search
   C. Windows Attract Customers

VII. **INTERIOR STORE DESIGN INFLUENCES CONSUMER SEARCH**
   A. Atmospherics Sets the Stage
   B. Layout Directs Customer Flow
   C. Merchandise Grouping Affects Search
   D. Department Location Affects Search

CHAPTER OBJECTIVES

After completing your study of Chapter 12, you should be able to:

1. Explain distribution methods.
2. Discuss how product line influences consumer search.
3. Explain how single or multi-unit stores affect search.
4. Discuss how in-home option affects consumer search.
5. Explain how store locations affect consumer search.
6. Discuss how exterior store design affects consumer search.
7. Discuss how interior store design influences consumer search.

Business managers develop strategies in response to how consumers search for information. The business strategy attempts to get the consumers to react favorably to the firm's product, service, and price offerings. No aspect of this business plan is more important than the marketing channel. The marketing channel allows the organization to provide products and services to locations favorable and convenient to consumers. In this way the firm attempts to induce consumers to buy from the store rather than from competitors.

In this chapter we discuss how companies use their knowledge of consumers' search patterns to aid in the planning of channels of distribution.

DISTRIBUTION METHODS: GENERAL OBSERVATIONS

The marketing channel is important to consumers because it determines the conditions under which the consumer must shop. Management plans its channels to influence the consumer's search.[1] The consumer's search for a bottle of Budweiser beer does not take long because it is available in many different types of stores and locations. It may take much longer for the consumer to locate and purchase Waterford crystal. It is a small miracle that you can buy "Bud" at thousands of places, considering that it is only produced in four locations. Yet the "miracle" is accomplished rather undramatically. Each Budweiser brewery sells cases of beer to hundreds of beer distributors. The beer distributor is a wholesaler whose operation depends on a large warehouse and a fleet of trucks. Each distributor sells cases of Budweiser to hundreds of retail outlets who, in turn, make the beer available to consumers. The process is essentially the same with the Waterford crystal.

The journey we have just described, which takes a bottle of beer from the place it is produced to its final consumption is an example of what we call a channel of distribution. Most of us have a fairly good idea of what channels of distribution are. The phrase itself is descriptive. *Channels* are routes, avenues, or pathways, suggesting movement or flow. *Distribution* means to proportion, disseminate, or spread about. Hence, we can define the *channel of distribution* as:

the movement of goods and services between the point of production and the point of consumption through organizations that perform a variety of marketing activities.

It is critically important that management understand the channels of distribution providing the consumer with better information, easy accessibility to products, and ease in shopping.

Use Appropriate Channels to Affect Search

A channel of distribution should be treated as a unit or a total system of action. Middlemen must understand that organizations are designed to maximize marketing effectiveness by meeting the needs of consumers and other groups in the firm's environment. Even to describe the major channels is risky because it may suggest an orthodoxy that does not exist. Nevertheless, what follows is an outline of the most frequently used channels for consumer products (see Illustration 12-1).

Channels of distribution may be long, intermediate, or short. These terms do not refer to distance but rather to the numbers of intermediaries within each channel. For example, in Illustration 12-1, channels 1 and 2 are basically short channels. Short channels get products to customers in less total time, but they tend to be more expensive for the manufacturer because there is little cost sharing. Channels 3 and 4 are of an intermediate length. That is, they contain a moderate number of channel members. Channels 5 and 6 are relatively long because of their rather large number of intermediaries. The longer channels are slower, but they tend to cost the manufacturer less because expenses are shared with more middlemen. Whether the channel of distribution is short or long, it still must aid the consumers in their search.

There are two types of middlemen in a marketing channel. *Merchants* take

Illustration 12-1
Channels of distribution for consumer products

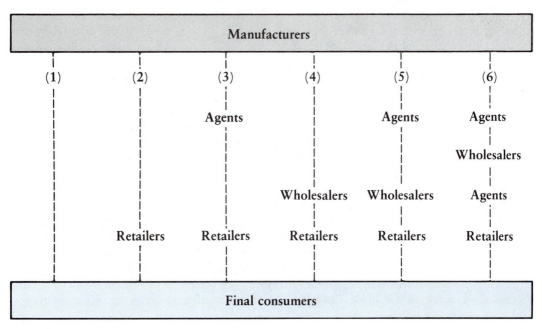

title to products and thus buy and sell in their own name. The retailer, wholesaler, and manufacturer are merchants. *Agents* or *brokers* do not take title to products but perform some service or function for their merchant principal. There are many types of agents, including advertising agencies, consultants, doctors, lawyers, and architects.

The first channel in Illustration 12-1 is a direct channel of distribution between the manufacturer and the final consumer. Direct channels include mail-order selling, catalog selling, or house-to-house selling. Avon cosmetics and Tupperware are products sold by manufacturers directly to final consumers. The second channel has one type of merchant called *retailers* because they sell only to final consumers. Channel 3 contains the retailer and an agent or broker. The fourth channel has retailers and wholesalers. A *wholesaler* is a middleman who sells to manufacturers, retailers, other wholesalers and nonbusiness institutions. Retailers and wholesalers can therefore be distinguished by the purpose for which they buy and accumulate inventories. Retailers plan to sell to satisfy the final consumers, whereas wholesalers buy for resale. Channels 5 and 6 both contain merchants and agents. The only difference between them is that channel 6 has agents between the wholesaler and retailer.

The M-W-R-C channel is considered to be normal since about 60 percent of all goods flow through such channels. However, few manufacturers use one channel consistently. Most manufacturers use multiple channels. For example, retailers regularly purchase through wholesalers, but when they need emergency orders they may go directly to the manufacturer.

Plan Benefits into the Channel

The overriding purpose of all aspects of store operations is to influence consumers during their search. Thus, the store image must convey the message that the store's operations offer desired benefits to consumers. Generally speaking, store operations can benefit consumers by adjusting the total product to customer wants, by making search for information convenient, or by providing psychic satisfaction.

One important benefit of channel operations is to adjust, in the mind of consumers, the total product more nearly to consumer wants. Few products are tailor-made for the individual, nor does every consumer want every possible service that can be associated with specific products. One consumer may want the product but not credit or delivery. Another person may desire credit and delivery. The desire for protection of the product, and for privacy and convenience in handling it, creates a need for packaging and wrapping. Every business, even those with essentially similar brands of merchandise, must successfully adjust to specific desires related to consumer search.

Another benefit of channels is to adjust the total cost of the product. The ability to communicate store personality makes a substantial contribution to customer convenience during the search for information.[2] How much and what type of a contribution depends on what the customer wants to make convenient. The rule is that every convenience offered by a firm has some cost connected with it. This cost may take the form of a product cost or a convenience cost. *Product cost* is the total price of the merchandise, including the cost of physical a product good and all the services that are included with it. For example, the cost of a razor is a product cost. Any payment for credit or delivery included in the price is also a product cost. *Convenience cost* is the monetary, physical, and mental expenditure necessary to overcome the separations of time and location in shopping.[3] The time spent shopping, the difficulty of finding a parking place, and wear and tear on the car are all convenience costs. Saving on convenience costs usually necessitates spending more on product costs. People who shop less reduce convenience costs but may miss a bargain that would cut the price of two products.

Marketing channels also provide psychic satisfaction. Some effects of store operations on consumers cannot be explained by any specific actions taken by the firm. The shopper may just feel comfortable in the store. This feeling may be associated with the colors on the wall, the friendly atmosphere created by salespersons, the ease of getting around in the store, or some similar factor. Even the consumer may not be sure why the feeling exists. We refer to this as *psychic satisfaction*. It is believed that everything the store does contributes to this feeling. Psychic satisfaction results from all those aspects of store operations that cause a pleasant shopping experience during the consumer's search.

Relate Market Coverage to Consumer Search

The number of different types of stores employed by a seller and their location is determined largely by the cost and the desires of the consumer. For example, if consumers expect to find a product only at exclusive shops in large cities, then the manufacturer would not want to have it carried by drugstores. In contrast, a product for which the consumer expects to spend little or no time searching should be sold through as many retail outlets as possible. The *intensity of distribution* refers to the relative availability of a product or service to the consumer. It consists of the number of different types of stores through which the firm sells (drugstores, department stores, discount houses, shoe stores) and the number of stores of each type used.

There are three types of distribution intensity: intensive, exclusive, and selective distribution. Each type is explained below.

Ordinarily the strategy of *intensive distribution* is used by companies which distribute convenience goods. *Convenience goods* are those for which consumers spend little time traveling or making comparisons for quality, price, or service. Management seeks maximum exposure coupled with considerable promotion about convenience goods. In fact, the firm attempts to saturate the market by placing the product in every conceivable outlet. Illustration 12-2 demonstrates an example of intensive distribution. Intensive distribution places most of the burden of promotion to the consumer on the shoulders of the manufacturer. Some products that use intensive distribution are chewing gum, snack foods, soft drinks, batteries, work clothes, and paperback books.

The opposite of intensive distribution is *exclusive distribution*, whereby a product is made available through one outlet in any one trading area. Generally, exclusive distribution is used with *shopping goods* where the consumer is willing to search for specific brands and compare prices and services. Illustration 12-3 shows an example of exclusive distribution. You may be most familiar with exclusive distribution as seen in the marketing of Ford automobiles, Rolex watches, Ethan Allen furniture, John Deere tractors, and Janzen bathing suits. Exclusive distribution reduces the choices available to consumers and may increase travel to find the product. On the other hand, it simplifies the choice, provides psychic satisfaction, and makes comparison easier.

The term *selective distribution* refers to limiting outlets in a given market to a small number of the stronger retailers. Illustration 12-4 shows an example of selective distribution. Products associated with selective distribution include GE appliances, Litton microwave ovens, IBM personal computers, and Elgin watches. Although employed for a wide variety of products and services, selective distribution is particularly appropriate when consumers can perceive, during search, a difference among brands. By selecting a few, better retail outlets and working more cooperatively with them, manufacturers may feel that they can create a more receptive climate for their merchandise.

PRODUCT LINE INFLUENCES CONSUMER SEARCH

The product line offered by a store can influence the consumer in his/her search. A firm can make an appeal based on any one of the three store types shown in Illustration 12-5. These three categories are used to simplify the vast array of stores. It is possible that stores you know would fall somewhere in between the three categories.

Illustration 12-2
Intensive distribution

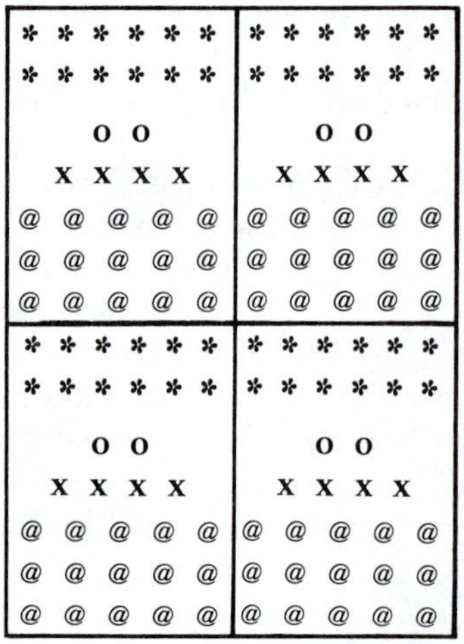

Illustration 12-3
Exclusive distribution

Illustration 12-4
Selective distribution

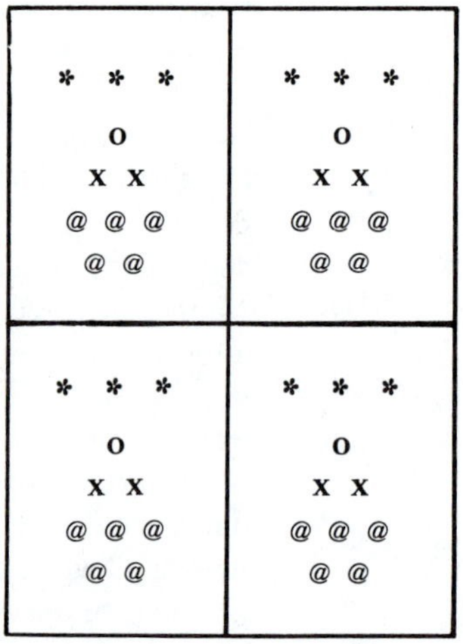

* – Drug store
o – Department store
x – Discount house
@ – Specialty store

Illustration 12-5
Classification of stores by product line

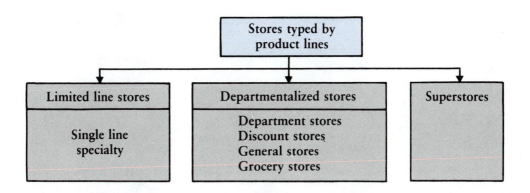

Limited-Line Stores

Limited-line stores restrict their offering to a narrow range of goods. The two basic kinds of limited-line stores are single-line and specialty stores. Although the distinction between these two forms of stores is frequently obscured, they do make specific appeals to consumers that affect search.

The *specialty stores* are generally small, full-service establishments that handle a narrow line of products. They frequently handle a wide range of complimentary products. One of the best examples of a specialty store is the dress shop that specializes in women's clothing but may also carry hats, handbags, gloves, scarves, and jewelry. Other examples include bookstores, convenience food stores, computer centers, camera shops, and maternity stores. Figure 12-1 is an ad for a product typically sold in a specialty card shop. Most service retailers—such as dry cleaners, theatres, and barber shops—are classified as specialty establishments.

Specialty stores possess certain advantages over other types of stores when the consumer searches for products. Because of their extreme specialization, these stores establish a close association with both their suppliers and their customers. They typically have great depth in the lines they carry, and they offer specialized services such as alteration, delivery, credit, gift wrapping, and personalized attention. In some instances these merchants may be the exclusive outlet in their market area for a supplier's merchandise so they may be one of the only sources of the product.

A broad array of merchandise within a particular line is offered by *single-line* stores. These establishments are generally identified by the most important line of goods they handle. Some of these stores, such as automobile dealers, lumber yards, hardware stores, and furniture stores, are quite large. Others, such as shoe stores, candy stores, jewelry stores, and health food stores, are much smaller.

By restricting the product line, a single-line store offers advantages to consumers. With fewer lines to handle, merchants are able to keep abreast of their markets and become merchandise specialists in their lines. They can handle all sizes, styles, or models and provide specialized services when necessary. Their

Figure 12-1
Products that can be found in a specialty card store

Hallmark Cards Incorporated

salespersons can become knowledgeable about the narrow line, thus serving customers better.

Departmentalized Retailers

Departmentalized retailers are just the opposite of limited-line retailers; they carry many categories of products organized into groups by departments. Administration, pricing, and services typically revolve around these departments. Types of departmentalized retailers are department stores, general stores, grocery stores, discount houses, and variety stores. The combination of product lines, prices, and services offered by these stores directly affects the consumer's search process. Consumers seek that combination of benefits best suited to their needs.

A *department store* is defined as a large retailing business unit with merchandise organized into departments under one management. They handle a wide variety of shopping and specialty goods that includes women's wear, men's wear, piece goods, small wares, and home furnishings. It is organized into separate departments for purposes of providing information, service, and control. Department stores have moderate variety and depth of products, and they are the most service-conscious of all retail stores.[4] The departments of the store are directed at different market segments to enable them to aid the consumer in the search for information. The record department, for example, may be geared toward teenagers and young adults, while the sporting goods department may emphasize merchandise and information for skiers, tennis players, and golfers.

Small, departmentalized establishments that are usually located in thinly populated rural areas are called *general stores*. Their departments are less identifiable, and their range of products is very broad but with very limited depth. They serve the needs and provide a source of information for the isolated markets by stocking a wide range of staple goods. A general store must serve and inform its customers between their occasional trips to the city. The advent of superhighways, the growth of regional shopping areas, and the desire by storekeepers for a better working environment have resulted in the slow demise of general stores. However, those that remain are still a valuable source of information for the consumers.

A *grocery store* sells a wide line of food and related products organized into departments under one management. These retailers are often called supermarkets. We all recognize Kroger, A&P, and Winn Dixie as important grocery store types. A single grocery store may carry as many as 10,000 to 25,000 items. Grocery stores do not tend to offer many services such as credit or delivery, and most are self-service operations. Grocery stores were among the first retailers to use self-service. They also employ effective store layout to draw customers through the entire store, thus increasing impulse purchases.

A *discount house* operates like department stores, offering wide lines of convenience and shopping items organized into departments under one management. However, department stores emphasize service, and discount houses emphasize low prices.[5] All items sold are advertised at a reduction from list price, which is what discounting is. Recognized discount houses are Service Merchandise, K-Mart, Wal-Mart, and Western Auto stores. Many other stores have picked up on discounting as a method of operation. Today many specialty shops such as Pay Less Shoes and self-service gas stations use the technique. This has caused a blurring of the lines among stores that discount.

A *variety store* sells convenience items which are organized into departments under one management. These stores were at one time called five and ten cent stores. The more notable examples are Kress, Woolworth's, and Lowes. They carry a wide line of convenience merchandise and offer no services. The appeal is primarily price.

The advent of the departmentalized store in the 1860s led to the concept of scrambled merchandising. *Scrambled merchandising* is selling lines of merchandise not normally thought of as being sold by that type of store — placing together incongruous items such as clothing and food, drugs and magazines, or housewares and food. Figure 12-2 shows a Lowes ad featuring ceiling fans, latex paint, a television set, and lime. Of course, once we begin to think of the items together, they are no longer scrambled. Department stores were the first scrambled stores,

Figure 12-2
Scramble Merchandising

and we now consider it normal to find clothing, furniture, garden supplies, and appliances in the same store.

Superstores

The newest and possibly the toughest innovative competitor of the conventional store is the *superstore*—also called a hypermarket. When consumers can search under one roof for information about discount products, food items, drug items, and whatever else they routinely purchase, they are probably in a superstore. A superstore is the combination of a huge discount store and a giant supermarket. The superstore provides consumers with a vast array of information and products, so the consumers can meet all their routine needs at a low price.

SINGLE OR MULTI-UNIT STORES AFFECT SEARCH

When considering how best to affect the search patterns of consumers, management must decide whether to use a single-store outlet or multiple stores, called chains.[6] Chains cover the market much better, thus appealing to consumers by reducing their search time. On the other hand, it is very costly to invest in all the buildings and equipment necessary to cover the market with multiple stores. Both single-store operations and chains have been successful.

All the businesses we have discussed were presumed to be single stores. Actually many specialty stores, department stores, grocery stores, and discount houses are chains. A *chain* is defined as four or more stores under one management offering similar lines of merchandise. An organization with two or more stores is a branch operation. All types of organizations, including specialty stores, department stores, discount houses, and others can be chains. Some well known chains include Sears, Waldenbooks, Ramada Inns, Firestone stores, A&P and Stuarts. Chains have the advantage of mass buying, mass merchandising, more complete market coverage, tailored services, and specialized personnel.

Another multi-store operation is franchising. *Franchising* occurs when an independent retailer agrees, by contract, to cooperate with either a manufacturer or wholesaler on matters of product line, pricing, and operating policy. The franchisor obtains low-cost outlets since no ownership of the retail store is involved. The retailer has the advantage of exclusive rights to sell the product in an identified area plus the specialized skills of the franchisor's personnel in such areas as accounting, production, and sales. Some noted franchises are Kentucky Fried Chicken, automobile dealers, Computerland, Holiday Inns, and Pizza Huts. Figure 12-3 is an ad designed to attract the attention of potential franchisors.

Figure 12-3
Attracting the attention of potential franchisees

Courtesy of Subway

Illustration 12-6
In-home buying options of consumers

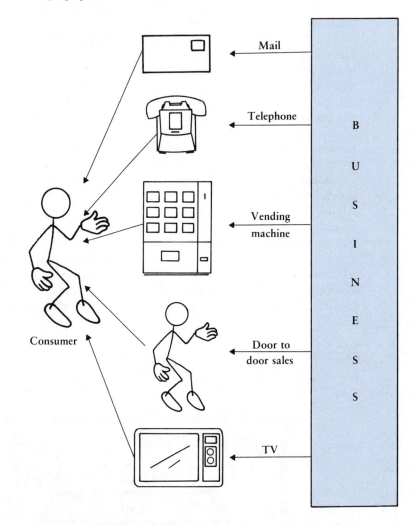

NON-STORE OPTION AFFECTS CONSUMER SEARCH

Our discussion of how retail managers develop policies to influence consumer search has concentrated on retail stores because a majority of retailing activity occurs in such stores. However, an alternative is to use *non-store* retailing, in which the manufacturer reaches the customer directly by means of mail, phone, vending, TV, or door-to-door salespersons.[7] (See Illustration 12-6.) All these methods reduce search time outside the home in specific retail stores for the consumer. They allow for relaxed shopping either within one's own home, or in other convenient locations. The problem is that the choice of merchandise and prices is limited. Furthermore, the buyer may not be able to shop at a convenient time.

Direct marketing or direct-response marketing is a redefinition of what was once called *mail-order selling* which involved having consumers place orders from a catalog to a central warehouse. Products are then delivered by mail. The new, broader technique uses the media to provide information about merchandise in addition to using direct-mail advertising through catalogs and brochures. Direct marketers take orders through the mail and by telephone, including toll-free 800 numbers, and merchandise can be charged to credit cards (see Figure 12-4). Merchandise may be shipped by any convenient means. This includes the U.S. Postal Service, United Parcel Service, and many other private freight lines. Sometimes merchandise may also be picked up at catalog stores. Some of the major retail stores, including Sears and J.C. Penney, have turned to direct marketing to aid the consumer in their search for information.

Direct marketing businesses originally were independently operated out of warehouses. Mail order has been increasing in importance because it has moved into the department stores.[10] Sears, Wards, and Federated Stores all have active

Figure 12-4
Direct marketing advertisement

Country Curtains

mail-order departments today. However, direct marketing techniques are used in the sale of most types of merchandise. It has the advantage of in-home ordering, which reduces physical search and lower prices. It is somewhat inconvenient because the buyer cannot inspect the merchandise. Other problems can also be caused by delivery—incorrect merchandise, damaged items, and delay in obtaining a product.

Direct marketing is especially effective in providing information to consumers over a wide market area.[8] The entire population of the United States is a potential market. Direct marketing rarely saves the customer money because of the expense of freight and postal charges. It does save customers time during their search, and it may be more convenient and pleasant than shopping through crowded stores.[9]

Vending Machines

Many manufacturers are using vending machines to remove most of the barriers between the customer and the merchandise. *Vending* utilizes a coin-operated machine, which can be located almost anywhere, to dispense merchandise directly to the consumer. The most important problem is the limitation on the types of merchandise that can be sold by vending. Since the 1920s this type of retailing has been used to reach the consumer and has grown steadily in volume and variety. Vending machines now offer refrigerated foods and foods that can be heated with microwave ovens provided nearby. Gasoline stations and motels frequently have vending machines that cater to the needs of the traveler, offering headache remedies, toothpaste and toothbrushes, combs, hosiery, and children's toys and games, among other products. Vending machines dispense insurance policies at airports, and some change paper money to coins so that the consumer may operate other vending machines. An interesting development in automatic merchandising is the automated bank teller, which can handle deposits or withdrawals twenty-four hours a day, seven days a week.

Door-to-Door Sales

The term *door-to-door* selling, in-home selling, or direct selling means management goes directly to the consumer's home to provide them with products. Door-to-door selling is one of the oldest retailing methods in history. Sometimes it simply involves house-to-house canvassing, without any advance selection of prospects. Most likely, however, there is an initial contact, or search for information, in a store or by phone, or a mailed-in coupon. Also, included in this category is *party-plan* selling. An individual invites friends to a party. These guests understand that a salesperson, say for a cosmetics or a housewares company, will be there to provide information and make a sales presentation at the party. The sales representative has a larger prospective market under more favorable conditions than if the guests were approached individually. The guests search for information and do their shopping in a pleasant, friendly atmosphere.

STORE LOCATIONS AFFECT CONSUMER SEARCH

Managers know that a store's location determines how convenient search is for the consumer.[11] As we might expect, retailers tend to follow population patterns so they can better respond to the search patterns of the consumer. Retail store locations fall into one of two classifications: unplanned (evolved) or planned (designed, built, and operated as a unit). (See Illustration 12-7.) These classifications recognize the geographic preferences of consumers.

Illustration 12-7
Classification of retailers by location

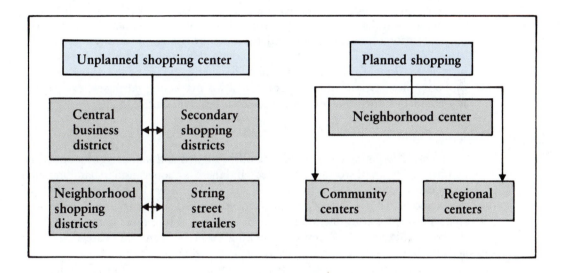

Unplanned Shopping Districts

There are several discernible types of unplanned shopping districts within every city. These constitute a retailing structure that has evolved in response to the needs of consumers. The hub of retailing activity has traditionally been the *central business district.* This unplanned shopping area developed because early horsecars and trolley cars were directed straight into and out of the central part of the city. There was almost no means of getting around the perimeter of the city. Even today, the central business districts of most cities have more retail stores with more products, price, and service options than any other single area. This affects consumer search patterns—many store managers prefer downtown locations for their stores.

The automobile made movement in all directions within the city possible. This weakened central business districts and led to the growth of suburban shopping centers. The many empty storefronts in the blighted downtowns of our cities is mute testimony to the shift of customers away from these areas.

In the older, larger cities, we often find an unplanned *secondary shopping district* with branches for downtown stores. Secondary shopping districts are formed by a cluster of stores at an intersection of one of the major streets that leads to the central business district. Retailer managers recognize that stores located in secondary districts make it possible to intercept customers before they reach the central district.

The strips of grocery, drug, clothing, and hardware stores along major thoroughfares in residential areas are known as *neighborhood shopping districts*. These stores are patronized mainly by neighbors.

Many cities have a major artery that is a *string street* of retail establishments. The tempo of traffic on these streets is increased by the flow of shoppers that move in and out of the numerous roadside businesses. Some streets may begin to specialize by product line, because new retailers want to be close to others who are already attracting consumers during their search. For example, some cities have an automobile row populated by the showrooms of automobile dealers. Many communities have franchise rows containing popular fast-food restaurants such as McDonald's, Burger King, and Pizza Hut. None of the above types of shopping districts is planned or controlled for marketing purposes, except that city planners sometimes restrict commercial development.

Planned Shopping Centers

Planned shopping centers are carefully designed and managed as a unit. The number and types of stores are planned, and there is cooperation in handling such joint costs as parking, advertising the center, and services. By offering a variety of stores and broad assortment of goods, these planned shopping centers have been able to influence consumers during their search and lure them away from older shopping districts.[12] Planned shopping centers can be categorized as neighborhood centers, community centers, or regional centers.

A *neighborhood planned shopping center* is composed of a group of approximately ten to fifteen convenience stores that serve customers who live within a few minutes of the center. This type of center often consists of hardware, drug, grocery, and clothing stores located on either side of the prime traffic generator, a supermarket. For many residents these small centers have replaced the older neighborhood stores as convenient places to shop and search for information.

A *community planned shopping center* is larger and consists of a cluster of fifteen to thirty stores that sell shopping goods as well as the type of convenience goods found in neighborhood shopping centers. The dominant store in this center is generally a large variety store, a department store, or a junior department store that emphasizes apparel and home furnishings. In numerous localities these carefully planned and located community shopping centers have drawn customers away from many of the older, unplanned, and randomly located secondary shopping districts.[13]

A *regionally planned shopping center* is the largest type of center. It includes two or more major department stores and sometimes more than 150 to 200 smaller stores. The smaller retailers are usually located between the major department stores, thus making consumer search easy. The regional shopping center is often a multilevel, enclosed, air-conditioned mall with every type of shopping and convenience product typical of a small to medium central business district. The regional shopping center aids consumers during their search by providing a vast array of goods and services in a pleasant surrounding.

EXTERIOR STORE DESIGN AFFECTS CONSUMER SEARCH

The exterior design of a store visibly reflects its image and can dramatically influence consumers during their search. Managers know this and plan accordingly. Many consumers appraise a store based on its outward appearance. Management uses store design to make optimum use of its location.

The store is the package that contains the merchandise offered to the consumer. Since any product package is important, retail managers should take special care in designing stores. If the store package does not attract or entice the customer into the store, the product will never be sold. A good store design helps to sell the product and a poor design does not.

Store Architecture Creates Image

The *architecture* of a store is management's first chance to induce the customer inside the store. The building should be in keeping with management's desired image. Notice how a bank building differs from a grocery store or a department store differs from a furniture store. Bank buildings give an image of stability, conservatism, and concern, while the grocery store reflects modern, efficient, economical operations.

For a chain organization, uniformity of architecture is important to aid the consumers in their search. Most K-Mart, J.C. Penney, and Hickory Farm stores can be easily identified in any city in the United States. Architecture, like that of McDonald's or Wendy's, is basically the same all over the world; this aids consumers in their search.

The overall exterior of a store must be eye-catching as well as functional. When planning the exterior, management must take into account its importance to customer search.[14] Several areas must be taken into account:

1. *Size* — the building conveys the size of the business and the range of merchandise and services offered by the store.
2. *Permanence* — the exterior projects trust and dependability.
3. *Nature of merchandise and customer* — everything about the store conveys the message that the store is what that particular target market is searching for.
4. *Store character* — the exterior conveys the appropriate store image.

Signs Influence Consumer Search

Store signs can instruct, signal, direct, and inform potential customers. To be effective, the sign should identify the store by name and type. The traditional three balls on a pawn shop sign have identified this type of store for hundreds of years. In more recent times, the McDonald's arch or Kentucky Fried Chicken's red and white striped bucket have signalled to the passing customer that fast food is available. Outside signs are also used to direct customers to specific stores or service centers in regional shopping centers and malls. They are also used to show store hours and the availability of parking lots.

Windows Attract Customers

Merchandise displayed in store windows gets customers' attention and triggers thoughts. These thoughts, in turn, induce customers to enter the store and continue their search. Window displays make the customer's searching task easier by indicating the assortment of merchandise and a price-quality level. Customers may judge whether a store's prices and assortments meet their requirements without having to make an inquiry. Because of its power to influence customers, window space at retail stores is valuable. The wise retailer uses window areas well by merchandising them carefully, keeping them neat and clean, and changing displays frequently to keep the store interesting to the customer.

INTERIOR STORE DESIGN INFLUENCES CONSUMER SEARCH

The interior design carries out the image that management started with exterior design. It makes search pleasant and puts customers in the mood to buy. First impressions are very important in retailing. The interior of a store is vital to such a business because sales and profits are generally made in the store.

Atmospherics Set the Stage

Atmospherics is defined as the conscious designing of space to create certain effects in buyers.[15] Creating the correct atmosphere in a store is vital to the success of the business. Such an atmosphere is generally created through the use of the various senses—smell, sound, touch, and sight—to the benefit of the retailer and the customer.[16]

Smell can be very important to the management's interior store planning. The interior design of a bakery should have baked goods up front for the passerby to smell. Fans may help distribute the pleasing odor. Another store may have perfume automatically dispensed into the air every few minutes in its cosmetic departments. An appropriate odor is advantageous, but a wrong odor can be a problem. A store that smells of stale cigarette smoke or musty carpet is not inviting. Also, what is good for one retailer may not be good for the store next door. The smell of popcorn would not sell designer clothing.

Management cannot overlook the effects of sound on customers. Music eliminates the "dead store" sound. It has been found that when music is playing in a store and then shuts off, customers become quiet and uneasy. Every noise seems louder. Sales personnel also seem to move slower. When the music is turned back on, everyone gets a psychological lift. This lift is believed to be so important that Muzak, a company that supplies music to stores, sets up its music with a break or silence every fifteen minutes. The beat of the music is also increased during the fifteen-minute period as it builds to the short period of silence. The music must be consistent with the overall store image. A teen shop selling clothes plays rock

Photo 12-1

Windows draw customers into the store. Companies spend time and money to make them appealing.

music for its customers. Likewise, a high-fashion conservative store has quiet, restful background accompaniment.

Music is very important for atmospheric considerations, but it is not the only important source of sound for the consumer. The sound of hamburgers frying sells hamburgers. The sound of a wind chime or a grandfather clock sells these items. A stereo or record playing for a customer or a person playing an organ can attract attention.

Touch is another important factor of interior design. The store layout should encourage touching. It was pointed out earlier that at the trial stage of the adoption process, the individual gains additional knowledge by using the product on a small scale. If the consumer cannot try the product, more than likely he or she will not buy it. Radios are meant to be played; the store that provides a place for customers to play the radios sells more radios. Some bookstores have their books on the wall from floor to ceiling. If the customer wants one high on the wall, he or she must ask for it; many probably never bother to ask. The secret to selling a new product is often to get the customer to touch it or try it.

Sight influences consumers to purchase. Shopping provides the customer with the attraction of actually seeing and comparing an assortment of offerings. In today's climate of intensified competition and rising costs, increased emphasis is being placed on *visual merchandising*. *Visual merchandising* is a combination of every factor that can affect the consumer's visual perception of the store. It utilizes every square inch of the store, inside and out, to sell the company and its product.[17]

When the consumer is searching, a product can often benefit greatly if it is given unusual display treatment that clearly sets it apart from competitors. Illustration 12-8 summarizes data discovered in one test concerning the results attributable to rather simple comparison of sales before and after using signs with the merchandise. The volume increased in each case, but the change associated with the use of the sign varied with the type of information provided.

Layout Directs Customer Flow

Management designs the interior layout so that customers are able to search efficiently and comfortably. Research on crowding and its effect on shopping behavior shows that shoppers may be affected by crowding.[18] It shows that shoppers may be affected by crowding in the following ways:[19]

1. Shopping time is reduced with crowding.
2. Conversations with employees and special requests are limited with crowding.
3. Certain purchases may be delayed with crowding.
4. Customers are delayed in leaving the store with crowding.

In the past, retailers believed that the longer customers remained in the store, the more they purchased. However, it appears that many shoppers want to finish shopping more quickly so that more time can be spent elsewhere.

Store management can adopt certain basic patterns for interior layouts. These include the rectangular or grid pattern, free flow, and boutique. Each type of

Illustration 12-8
Effects of shelf signs on sales

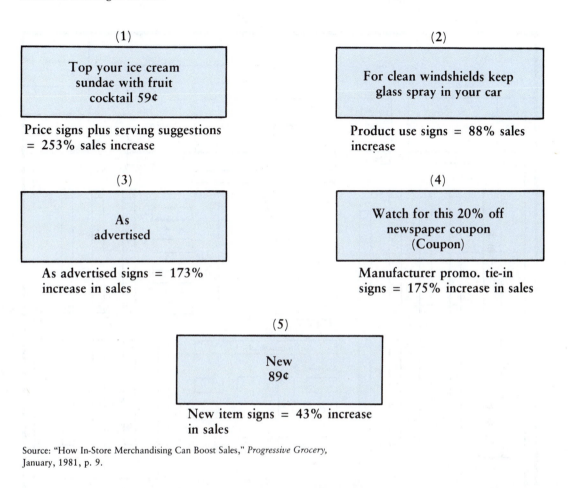

(1)

Top your ice cream
sundae with fruit
cocktail 59¢

Price signs plus serving suggestions
= 253% sales increase

(2)

For clean windshields keep
glass spray in your car

Product use signs = 88% sales
increase

(3)

As
advertised

As advertised signs = 173%
increase in sales

(4)

Watch for this 20% off
newspaper coupon
(Coupon)

Manufacturer promo. tie-in
signs = 175% increase in sales

(5)

New
89¢

New item signs = 43% increase
in sales

Source: "How In-Store Merchandising Can Boost Sales," *Progressive Grocery,*
January, 1981, p. 9.

layout tends to direct the customer through the store in ways that maximize the opportunity to purchase the store's products.

The *grid pattern* is much like a football field. This layout makes it possible to display the maximum amount of merchandise in the smallest space. It is relatively inexpensive to build and use. Stores with a grid pattern tend to have high sales per square foot. This pattern is typically used by specialty stores, grocery stores, and hardware stores. The A&P Futurestore in Baton Rouge, Louisiana, has a grid pattern, as shown in Illustration 12-9. It routes people from the front to back or across the store.

One of the most striking aspects of the Baton Rouge store's design is the use of nearly two hundred pictographs. Pictographs are used to help guide people to products. Cutouts of strawberries, bananas, and other fruits and vegetables rise above the rear of the produce cases. These signs are easy to see with the grid pattern layout. More than twenty-five representations of dairy products hang at

Illustration 12-9

Example of a grid-type layout

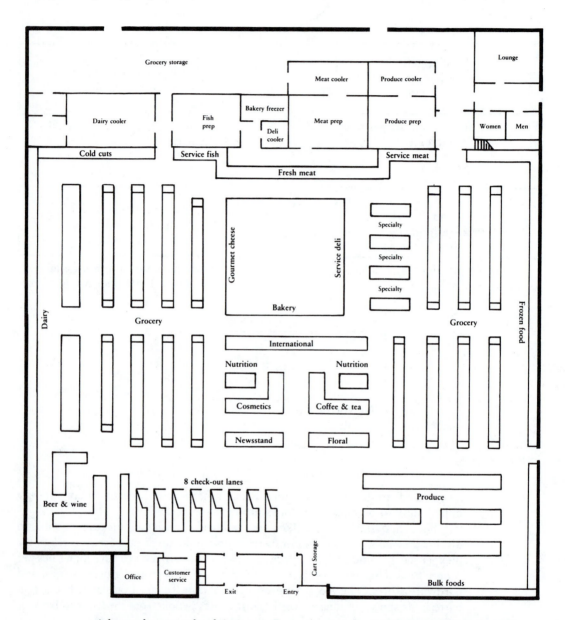

right angles over the dairy case. Even the grocery gondolas have pictographs attached to the shelving, showing cakes over the cake mixes, a cup of tea next to the tea bags and so on. The pictographs resemble the symbols used as international means of communication. Anybody can understand what each symbol represents. Each individual sign was given extensive thought to determine how it best describes the product merchandised near it.

Illustration 12-10
Example of a free-flow layout

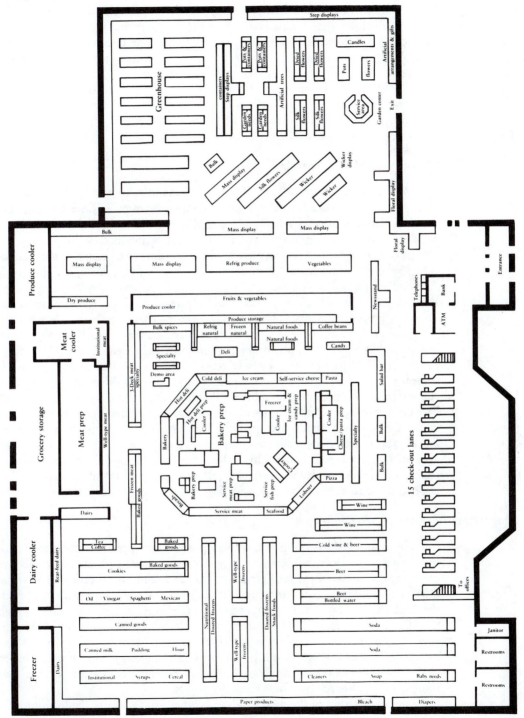

Another layout frequently used is the free flow. A *free flow* pattern uses fixtures and aisles to cause customers to browse throughout the store. Illustration 12-10 demonstrates a free flow pattern. Notice how persons are pulled from one department to another. The advantage of the design is that it exposes customers to a lot of merchandise by encouraging browsing. The disadvantage is that the cost of fixtures and equipment is very high. Department stores, some discount houses, and specialty stores use the free flow pattern.

The *boutique* pattern is used by specialty stores where different types of merchandise are placed in the same department. Customers with a particular life-style can find all their requirements in one department. The boutique pattern is designed to convey fashion and excitement.

Merchandise Grouping Affects Search

Management groups different lines of merchandise to aid consumers during their search. There are several ways of grouping the merchandise: generic, consumer preference, target market, and trade practice. These are mutually exclusive; retailers often use a combination of the grouping techniques.

Generic grouping places the merchandise according to its common characteristics. The usual arrangement of produce, meat, frozen food, dairy, and dry goods in a supermarket is a generic layout. Under the *consumer preference* arrangement, layout is based on the physical differences of products, on shelf space, or on servicing requirements. The *product group* or cluster is based on what the customer perceives it to be. Examples of this arrangement may be a gift department that has many physically different items such as cologne, playing cards, and candy. A *target market arrangement* results in the same items being placed at several different places in the store in order to appeal to different types of consumers. The most common example would be the duplication of merchandise in a basement or budget department which emphasizes price and in the more prestigious departments which emphasize quality. The basement and prestigious departments appeal to quite different customer types. Using *trade practice* arrangements, the layout is developed along the lines of layouts in use in similar stores. This provides a layout with which the customer will already be familiar. No effort is made to provide the store with any unique layout features under this plan.

Department Location Affects Search

The amount of effort that a consumer is willing to spend searching for a product often determines its placement in a store. Impulse items such as candy are placed at the points of the greatest traffic flow, adjacent to the entrance or at the intersection of major aisles. In stores with central checkouts, the space in front of the checkout is a powerful selling area for small impulse items that carry a high markup, such as razor blades and batteries. Because customers are willing to spend more time searching for shopping goods, such as suits and dresses, these items can be located away from the primary traffic areas of the store. Designer clothing and fine jewelry can be tastefully displayed in remote areas because consumers actively search out these specialty goods.

The relationship of the merchandise to other goods affects the location of a department. By grouping related merchandise together, such as bathing suits, summer clothes, and sports clothes, the consumer search could be limited to a single area and combination purchases made easier for customers. Many multilevel department stores devote entire floors to particular lines of goods such as women's wear, men's wear, and home furnishings.

QUESTIONS

1. Explain how a channel of distribution can help satisfy a consumer's need.
2. What are the benefits of a manufacturer using more than one channel to get its products to the consumer?
3. Design a channel of distribution for the following services and show how multiple channels could be used for the same service.
   a. education   b. banking   c. religion   d. medical
4. Because every member of a channel must add its desired profit to the cost of a product, how can it be said that channels reduce the cost of merchandise?
5. Identify and define the degrees of market coverage. Give examples of products and services for each degree.
6. Select a discount store and a specialty store in your town and discuss the product line in terms of width, variety, and depth.
7. Are specialty stores generally more expensive? Justify your answer.
8. Give an example of a store that you know practices scrambled merchandising. What are the advantages and disadvantages of the practice?
9. Discuss how a franchise can aid consumers during their search for a product or service.
10. Identify a service or product sold through mail orders and vending machines. What do you perceive to be the future of mail order selling and vending machine selling?
11. Identify several products you or someone you know have purchased through mail orders. Discuss why this method was selected over the others.
12. How would you classify the shopping area in which you do the majority of your shopping: unplanned shopping center or planned shopping center? Why?
13. Discuss the advantages and disadvantages a planned shopping center presents to consumers during their search for information.
14. The atmosphere of a store is created through the use of the senses. Go into a grocery store and identify the techniques the store uses to influence your senses.
15. Draw a layout of a specialty store in your town and discuss why you feel the store uses this design.

NOTES

1. Bert Rosenbloom, "Better Product Strategy Through Alert Channel Management," *Journal of Consumer Marketing*, Vol. 1 (1984), pp. 71–80.
2. William C. Black, "Choice-set Definition in Patronage Modeling," *Journal of Retailing*, Vol. 60 (Summer 1984), pp. 63–85.

3. John A. Carlson and Robert J. Gieseke, "Price Search in a Product Market," *Journal of Consumer Research*, Vol. 9 (March 1983), pp. 357–65.

4. Robert A. Westbrook, "Sources of Consumer Satisfaction with Retail Outlets," *Journal of Retailing,* Vol. 57 (Fall 1981), pp. 68–85.

5. Jack G. Kaikati, "Don't Discount Off-Price Retailers," *Harvard Business Review,* Vol. 63 (May–June 1985), pp. 85–92.

6. Richard T. Hise, et al., "Factors Affecting the Performance of Individual Chain Store Units," *Journal of Retailing*, Vol. 59 (Summer 1983), pp. 22–39.

7. Pradeep K. Korgaonkar, "Consumer Shopping Orientations, Non-Store Retailers, and Consumers' Patronage Intentions: a Multivariate Investigation," *Journal of the Academy of Marketing Research,* Vol. 12 (Winter 1984), pp. 11–22.

8. Jon M. Hawes and James R. Lumpkin, "Understanding the Outshopper," *Journal of the Academy of Marketing Science*, Vol. 12 (Fall 1984), pp. 200–18.

9. Subhash Sharma, William O. Bearden and Jesse E. Teel, "Differential Effects of In-Home Shopping Methods," *Journal of Retailing*, Vol. 49 (Winter 1983), pp. 29–51.

10. John A. Quelch and Hirotaka Takeuchi, "Nonstore Marketing: Fast Track or Slow?" *Harvard Business Review,* Vol. 59 (July–August 1981), pp. 75–84.

11. Dale Achabal, Wilpen L. Gorr, and Vijay Mahajan, "Multiloc: A Multiple Store Location Decision Model," *Journal of Retailing*, Vol. 58 (Summer 1982), pp. 5–25.

12. Charles A. Engene, "Productivity and Functional Shifting in Spatial Retailing: Private and Social Perspectives," *Journal of Retailing,* Vol. 60 (Fall 1984), pp. 15–33.

13. Thomas J. Maronick and Ronald M. Stiff, "The Impact of a Specialty Retail Center on Downtown Shopping Behavior," *Journal of the Academy of Marketing Science,* Vol. 13 (Summer 1985), pp. 292–306.

14. Phillip E. Downs and Joel B. Haynes, "Examining Retail Image Before and After a Repositioning Strategy," *Journal of the Academy of Marketing Science*, Vol. 12 (Fall 1984), pp. 1–24.

15. Philip Kotler, "Atmospherics as a Marketing Tool," *Journal of Retailing*, Vol. 49 (Winter 1973–74), p. 50.

16. Joseph A. Bellizze, Ayn E. Crowley, and Ronald W. Hasty, "The Effects of Color in Store Design," *Journal of Retailing*, Vol. 59 (Spring 1983), pp. 21–45.

17. Raymond A. Marquardt, James C. Makens, and Robert G. Roe, *Retail Management: Satisfaction of Consumer Needs,* 3d ed. (Hinsdale, Ill.: The Dryden Press, 1983), p. 220.

18. Robert Sommer and Susan Aitkens, "Mental Mapping of Two Super-Markets," *Journal of Consumer Research*, Vol. 9 (September 1982), pp. 211–25.

19. A. Edward Spitz and Alan B. Flaschner, *Retailing* (Cambridge: Winthrop Publishers, Inc., 1980), p. 159.

Promotion Influences

Consumer Search

CHAPTER OUTLINE

I. PROMOTION: DEFINITION AND OVERVIEW
   A. Promotional Tools Used to Influence Consumers
   B. Importance of Promotion to Consumers
   C. What Promotion Can Accomplish for Management
   D. Manner of Promotional Influence

II. PROMOTION AFFECTS INTERNAL SEARCH
   A. Promotion Directed at the Real Self
   B. Promotion Directed at the Ideal Self
   C. Promotion Directed at the Self Image
   D. Promotion Directed at the Reference Group Self

III. PROMOTION AFFECTS EXTERNAL SEARCH

IV. PROMOTION GAINS CONSUMER ATTENTION

V. PROMOTION EDUCATES CONSUMERS
   A. Message Presents Information
   B. Organization Provides Logic
   C. Other Information
   D. Related Principles of Learning

VI. PROMOTION MOTIVATES CONSUMERS
   A. Include Specific Appeals
   B. Use of Color to Motivate
   C. Typography Can Stimulate
   D. White Space as a Motivator
   E. Propaganda as a Motivator
   F. Related Principles of Influence

VII. PROMOTION MOVES CONSUMERS TO ACTION

CHAPTER OBJECTIVES

After completing your study of Chapter 13, you should be able to:

1. Define and give an overview of promotion.
2. Explain how promotion affects internal search.
3. Explain how promotion affects external search.
4. Discuss how promotion gains consumer attention.
5. Discuss how promotion educates consumers.
6. Discuss how promotion motivates consumers.
7. Explain how promotion moves consumers to action.

Perhaps no aspect of business strategy is more important for influencing consumers than promotion. Promotion is the part of strategy that reaches out beyond the firm to affect people in their homes, cars, and businesses. It also catches consumers at unsuspecting times when they may be vulnerable. Promotion can greatly affect the pattern of consumer search and the ultimate decision on whether to purchase or not. This chapter deals with the manner in which business uses promotion to accomplish its goals.

PROMOTION: DEFINITION AND OVERVIEW

One of the important questions asked by both profit and not-for-profit organizations is: "How can I best communicate with prospective customers and persuade them to buy my products?" The two key words in this question are communicate and persuade. Promotion involves any technique, under the control of a seller, that can communicate favorable, persuasive information about that seller's product to potential buyers, either directly or through others who can influence purchase decisions.[1]

Specifically, *promotion* is:

any form of informing, persuading, or reminding potential customers about the firm or its products and services.

Thus, promotion encompasses a wide range of activities.

Promotional Tools Used to Influence Consumers

Business managers possess four major promotional tools for influencing consumer decision making. They are advertising, personal selling, sales promotion, and publicity.

Advertising is any nonpersonal presentation of a good, service, or idea, paid for by a sponsor, for the purpose of making sales or influencing persons in some manner. Advertising is one-way communication because the recipient cannot respond immediately. It is presented over a variety of media, including radio, television, magazines, and newspapers. Of the promotional tools, advertising, on the whole, allows the greatest amount of creativity. Of course, there is less flexibility in altering the message since it must be printed or recorded before presentation.

Advertising is the most economical means of introducing generic new products and appealing to large markets, especially if they are scattered. Most businesses use some form of advertising to persuade consumers to use their products or services.

Personal selling is any face-to-face presentation of a good, service, or idea, paid for by a sponsor for the purpose of making sales or influencing persons in some manner. Personal selling involves two-way communication because the prospective buyer can reply to questions asked or points made by the salesperson. Hence the salesperson can adjust his or her appeal immediately. Unlike advertising, personal selling can reach only a limited number of persons in a given time. This makes it quite expensive unless the sales per call ratio is very high. Most businesses use some form of personal selling—door-to-door salespersons, clerks, or creative salespersons. As a part of business strategy, it often happens that advertising paves the way for the personal salesperson to close the sale.

Sales promotion can be defined as any presentation of a good, service, or idea, paid for by a sponsor, that supplements either personal selling or advertising. Sales promotion may have some of the characteristics of either personal selling or advertising. Some types of sales promotion include samples, contests, coupons, sweepstakes, trading stamp displays, point-of-purchase materials, cash rebates, and premiums.[2] Sales promotion establishes the notion that the buyer is getting something for nothing. It often paves the way for salespersons by stimulating positive attitudes toward the product or service. Furthermore, sales promotions, because of their variety, are extremely flexible, and they can be used at any stage in the consumer's decision-making process.

Publicity is any nonpersonal presentation of a good, service, or idea not paid for by a sponsor that results in making sales or influencing persons in some manner. Although publicity is not paid for, it is not free. Public relations personnel are paid to develop newsworthy releases and other material which the media can use. Some of the more common types of publicity are news releases, feature articles, press conferences, tapes and films, and editorials. For example, new models of automobiles typically are sufficiently newsworthy to make the papers when they are introduced each year. When a company executive becomes head of some charitable organization, it often makes the media. Because it can create goodwill, publicity can often be more effective than either advertising or sales promotion.

Importance of Promotion to Consumers

In our economy of abundance, businesses must constantly attempt to stimulate demand for products and services. They cannot trust to chance that consumers will become aware of their products through the passive agents of the market. Most businesses know that, if a better mousetrap is produced, consumers do not necessarily learn about it by themselves. It is the job of promotion to provide persuasive information to the consumer during the decision-making process.

Markets are flooded with thousands of products and brands. Consumers have a wide selection of products within most product categories. Faced with the decision each time a purchase must be made, consumers tend to favor the products that, within their limited experience, have yielded the greatest amount of

Photo 13-1
Personal selling is an effective method of promoting products.

satisfaction in the past. Manufacturers of new products must communicate persuasive information about their offerings in order to compete with established products. By using the promotional tools of advertising, personal selling, sales promotion, and publicity, businesses communicate to consumers product information in a persuasive manner that is designed to overcome consumer inertia.

The task of informing consumers does not cease with the market acceptance of a new product or product variation. Consumers must be continually reminded of the merits of an existing product because new products constantly arise to challenge the old. Businesses must also disseminate information because the market for a product undergoes constant change as births, deaths, changing family incomes, and other events take place.

What Promotion Can Accomplish for Management

Promotion is the basic competitive weapon possessed by any business. The product, no matter how good, cannot sell itself effectively; the product stays on the shelf and must be seen by the consumer to have any effect. Promotion, on the other hand, reaches out beyond the shelf or even the store to confront consumers in their homes, places of work, and automobiles. It can appeal to consumers when they least expect it. Even price must depend on promotion to get the consumer's attention. Thus, promotion is a powerful tool of business that is very necessary if management is to have anything more than a chance effect on consumers.

Promotion is designed to guide consumers along a path from a state of unawareness to some action desired by the firm. The action desired may be the acceptance of some idea or the development of a favorable attitude, but promotion is typically designed to induce consumers to purchase the firm's product. Table 13-1 relates the consumer's decision process, introduced and explained earlier, to management's stages of persuasion. The types of promotion are associated with these steps of persuasion.

Promotion during the awareness and interest stages is highly persuasive. Publicity, too, is much more important at these two stages. These are stages where management must aggressively sell the idea of the product because it is not

Table 13–1

Promotion and the Consumer Decision Process

Consumer Decision-Making Process	Stages of Persuasion	Type of Promotion
1. Problem Recognition	Awareness	*Advertising:* Announcements, descriptive copy, classified ads, slogans, signals, skywriters, teaser campaigns *Publicity:* News releases, press conferences, articles
2. Search for Information	Interest	*Advertising:* Competitive ads, argumentative copy, image ads, status and glamour appeals *Personal Selling:* Presenting facts, product comparisons, quality and performance *Publicity:* Articles, editorials, news releases
3. Evaluation	Evaluation and Trial	*Advertising:* Retail store ads, ads with emotional appeal, testimonials, price appeals *Personal Selling:* Product comparisons, fear appeals, last-chance appeals *Sales Promotion:* Point-of-purchase, contests, rebates, deals
4. Decision	Adoption	*Advertising:* Reminder ads, standard appeals *Personal Selling:* Clerks, answer final questions, close sale, write order *Sales Promotion:* Point-of-sales, feature displays *Publicity:* Model or price changes goodwill
5. Postpurchase Assessment	Confirmation	*Advertising:* Reminder ad, reinforcement appeals *Personal Selling:* Follow-up calls *Sales Promotion:* Feature display

generally known to consumers. At the evaluation and trial stages the emphasis changes from more factual information to more emotional appeals.[3] The use of publicity diminishes. It may be that the firm begins to use some comparison advertisements at this stage. The consumer has already been sold during the adoption and confirmation stages. The task of the promotion is simply to maintain the situation. Thus reminder advertisements, courtesy calls by salespersons, and sales promotion in the store become much more important.

In a business with multiple products, the promotions department may simultaneously have campaigns in which each of the five stages of persuasion are being emphasized. A new product campaign may be emphasizing highly persuasive advertising and personal selling, while another campaign may be conducted in a low-key fashion, using reminder advertising and courtesy sales calls. It must depend on which stage of the decision process a majority of the firm's customers are perceived to be in at the particular time. Even so, one would find considerable variety among different businesses concerning how they approached promotion at each of the stages of persuasion.

Manner of Promotional Influence

Promotion of all types affects the wants, motives, perceptions, and attitudes of consumers.[4] Furthermore, individuals who have been affected by advertising in turn influence other individuals through reference groups.

First, although promotion does not create consumer needs, it does make consumers aware of their latent wants and modifies or reinforces present wants.[5] Advertising and personal selling continually present to customers new or modified products and services that emphasize the person's present deficiencies. Of course, it may also happen that the result of a comparison of products reinforces the consumer's preference for present products or stores.

Second, advertising and personal selling continually cause each consumer to reevaluate feelings and attitudes. For example, an individual may consider a store high priced because of a previous experience. If this store continually emphasizes its low prices and sales, the consumer may decide to give the business another chance. Examples of cases where promotion changed consumer resistance can be found in automobiles, vacuum cleaners, TV dinners, and cigarettes. Promotion may also reassure the consumer of the soundness of previous decisions.

Third, promotion affects consumer wants and attitudes by conditioning perception. Advertising and personal selling affect individuals' perceptions of themselves, products, stores, other people, and the past and future. Of course, promotion has no magic power to cause people to perceive or act against their nature or wishes. For example, most people see topless attire as immodest but find nothing wrong with miniskirts. Long hair on men was once perceived as "sissified," but many people now view it as acceptable. Advertisers have shown reluctance to use black models in newspaper ads because of a fear of adverse white perceptions, but the evidence is that black models create greater visibility in the black community without alienating white consumers.

Fourth, promotion motivates consumers to action. A motivated state is a culmination of influences on wants, attitudes, and perception that convince the consumer of possible satisfaction. By making the consumer aware of the consequences of not acting, a negative type of motivation can also result.

PROMOTION AFFECTS INTERNAL SEARCH

We know that internal search involves relating a person's attitudes, or predispositions, to the consumer problem needing solution. Attitudes lie at the heart of a person's existence; who the individual is will, for the most part, determine how that person decides as a consumer. If managers are to be successful in affecting consumer search through the use of promotion, it is necessary to understand the self-concept.[6] *Self-concept* refers to the individual's perception of his or her attitudes and attributes. It is the function of promotion to create favorable attitudes within the individual toward the firm or the firm's product or services.[7] Many times promotion must change the person's existing attitudes toward the products and services of competing firms in order to accomplish its objective.

The self-concepts of (1) the real self, (2) the ideal self, (3) the self image, and (4) the reference group self were introduced earlier. Each of these self-concepts is important to promotion.

Promotion Directed at the Real Self

One can never completely understand or observe one's real self. How many of us are aware of the points of pettiness, greed, ambition, loneliness, and affection that reside deep inside our conscious or unconscious minds? How many of you know persons who have physical or mental quirks that they are not aware of? It is the same with consumers. We subconsciously prefer a certain color, a particular store clerk, or a particular price.[8] When purchasing products, a consumer follows personal patterns of conservatism or liberalism that may not register on the conscious mind. We get into ruts of travel or trade based on unconscious aspects of our nature.

The real self is extremely important to business. Contained in the real self are a person's basic physical and emotional requirements and characteristics. It is difficult for consumers to stray too far from their basic nature, even though they may not be completely aware of the motivation. Thus it is the real self that business would most like to research and know. In a practical sense, it is probably impossible for business to penetrate too far into this realm.[9] What consumers hide from themselves, they cannot report to business. Sometimes psychological techniques can bring out some parts of a person's nature, but it is difficult and costly.

It is very difficult for management to direct promotion at the real self because it is so difficult to identify. Such promotion typically is related to some observable physical aspect of a person. Ads promoting clothing for the portly or a retail store that identifies itself as "Tall Fashions" are examples of promotion directed at the real self.

Promotion Directed at the Ideal Self

The ideal self concerns a person's aspirations, his or her striving and desire to do and be better. Consumer attempts to achieve the ideal self can be seen in the purchasing of prestige products, such as mink coats, diamonds, and yachts. Attempts by consumers to buy products related to social climbing, snobbery, and leisure are also concerned with the ideal self.

The business executive is vitally interested in promotion directed at the consumer's ideal self. Furthermore, appeals directed at the ideal self are more likely to succeed, since this part of a person is more apparent. A person tends to be aware of aspirations and is frequently willing to discuss them, and much can be learned about the consumer's aspirations by observation. Aspirations can be studied by means of observed purchase behavior, style of living, and by surveys. Much of what we refer to as trading up, fashion buying, and "keeping up with the Joneses" relates to the ideal self. The business manager is also interested because of its effect on discretionary income.

For more than twenty-five years, Pepsi has promoted the "Pepsi generation," directed at the consumer's ideal of remaining youthful. Although the words have changed over the years, the general theme of idealized youth has remained. Some of the slogans follow.

1958–1961	"So young at heart"
1961–1962	"Now it's 2 for those who think young"
1963–1968	"Come alive. You're in the Pepsi generation"
1969–1973	"You've got a lot to live. Pepsi's got a lot to give"
1974–1976	"Join the Pepsi people, feeling free"
1977–1979	"Have a Pepsi day"
1980–1983	"Catch that Pepsi spirit! Drink it in"
1983–1984	"Pepsi Now"
1984–	"Pepsi: The choice of a new generation."[10]

Pepsi has made significant inroads into the Coca-Cola market using this promotion. It was a long-term investment that paid off.

Promotion Directed at the Self-Image

The self-image is how we see and understand ourselves and our aspirations. The self-image guides much of consumer decision making. In many respects, it is more important in purchase behavior than the real self. A consumer buys products that either support or improve the self-image.[11] It is difficult to get the consumer to go against his or her self-image in purchasing.

Knowledge of the self-image is perhaps the most important of all images to promotion. The self-image controls all normal expenditures that concern the consumer's present life-style. In a very real sense, a consumer is what that consumer buys. Information about the self-image can be obtained in the same manner as described above.[12] In some respects, it is even more easily gathered, and business utilizes it constantly. Salespersons can observe the self-image when they talk to a client. Advertisers deal with the self-image when they set the tone and appeals of their advertisements.[13] The clerk in a department store obtains clues to this image by the departments the consumer visits, the merchandise he or she handles, and the questions he or she asks. There is evidence that consumers who have a good image of themselves are more easily dealt with than consumers who have a poor image of themselves.

Promotion Directed at the Reference Group Self

The reference group image refers to how the consumer thinks others with whom he or she associates or identifies see them. It is not the image others necessarily have, but the reference group image that is an important motivator. We tend to behave as we think others want us to.

Consumer purchases related to group identification, group acceptance, pride and power are associated with the reference-group image. The individual is related directly to the environment by the reference group image and the image that others have. The reference group image is an emotional cognition; it is based on emotional or mental responses to facts that cannot be fully understood. Most concepts of self-image develop out of a social situation. Even our aspirations take on meaning in relation to other people.

Obviously, the reference group self is important to business. However, it is a very complex image. Next to the real self, it is perhaps the most difficult for business to pin down. Most of the time the consumer is not completely aware of the reference group self. Some indications can be obtained by complex psycho-analysis and depth interviewing; most businesses, of course, cannot afford to obtain such information. Yet it is an important motivator, and business needs more knowledge about the reference group self.

PROMOTION AFFECTS EXTERNAL SEARCH

Promotion by business management affects external consumer search in two ways. First, the firm's promotion is directed at providing individuals with new or different information not existing in their internal self-concept. The purpose of the promotion is to inform people about a store, a product, or a service they did not already know about, or to provide new information that brings into question the person's preference for a competing product. This effect is a one-step sequence because the promotion is directed at the consumer who reacts. The promotion attempts to induce the consumer directly to seek out and purchase the firm's product or service over competitor's product or service.

Second, promotion affects external search indirectly. This effect is a two-step sequence (like the two-step flow of communication) in which some individuals, who have been influenced by the firm's promotion, persuade other individuals about the merits of the product or service. An ad may be observed by hundreds of persons. Some of these persons, either because they purchased the product and like it, or because they were impressed by the ad, will discuss it with others. No doubt someone will try the product, at least in part, because of the recommendation given by the intermediary. It is easy to see that promotion has a powerful influence on the search and purchase patterns of consumers. Now let us turn our attention to the manner in which promotion influences.

PROMOTION GAINS CONSUMER ATTENTION

Promotion can accomplish four goals for management which are related to the stages of persuasion explained earlier. Promotion can gain consumer attention at the awareness stage. Promotion can educate consumers at the interest stage. Promotion can motivate consumers at the evaluation and trial stage, and promotion can move consumers to action at the adoption stage. This and the following sections explain each of these accomplishments of promotion. We begin by discussing how promotion gains attention. Promotion, whether it is personalized or employs media, gains awareness by the use of opening statements and logos and slogans.

Salespersons use several types of opening statements to gain attention. Some use jokes, while others make a provocative statement about the product or the prospect. For example, a salesperson may open with the statement, "I can save you $100 per month if you will give me just fifteen minutes of your time." The opening may be as simple as an introduction and handshake. Most retail stores teach their sales clerks to approach customers with some variation of, "May I help you?" They may also refer to the product, as with, "Isn't that a lovely dress? It would look great on you." Advertisements use the same type of openings as salespersons but they must be carefully expressed by means of logos and slogans, headlines, and illustrations.[14]

PROMOTION EDUCATES CONSUMERS

A primary function of any type of promotion is to inform people about the company and its products. Since most persuasion is founded on some type of information, nothing is more fundamental to the shaping of consumer decisions than information. We know that brands purchased most frequently are nearly always those with heavy promotion, because these are the brands most familiar to the consumer. Information increases consumer knowledge, and even though the consumer is left to his or her own devices concerning what to do with the data, its mere possession is influential. We cannot completely ignore information once we have it. Facts also influence by pointing out logical relationships. A sign, "Joe's Diner," relates hunger, diner, and satisfaction. There are several ways management has to get information across to consumers.

Message Presents Information

The basic tool of informing is the message. This is true whether the presentation is personal or through media. The salesperson presents the message by describing the product, its features, and its benefits. The salesperson may also compare the product to that of competitors or to earlier models. The salesperson has the advantage of being able to observe the customer's reaction and adjust the message.

The consumer is much more likely to act in a manner favorable to the firm if the message is understood.[15] Not only must consumers understand the facts, but they must interpret them in the manner intended by the business. A message understood is more difficult to ignore than one that is not understood. Besides, there is greater likelihood that the consumer will agree with the firm's position when that position is made clear.

Organization Provides Logic

    The organization of the total presentation provides logic which is essential to understanding. In a personal presentation, organization refers to the order and relationship of the points made. The salesperson should proceed with a logical sequencing of points that build to an inescapable conclusion by the consumer. Reputation can be, and should be used, as a part of the organization in order to add emphasis to the presentation.

    The layout is the primary organization used in the media.[16] Notice the positioning of the headline, copy, and photograph in Figure 13-1. Does it appeal to you?

Figure 13-1
Note the layout in this ad.

ONE LOOK
TELLS YOU
IT'S TURA

Nothing flatters like Tura eyewear, your most sensational accessory.
   Ask to see the Tura frame collection in all your wardrobe colors.

MAKE SURE IT'S A TURA.
LOOK FOR THE NAME.

© 1983 TURA, INC.

YOUR NAME AND ADDRESS

Tura, Inc.

Other Information

There are other types of information presented both by salespersons and through the media that educate consumers. Some of this information includes the name of the firm, brand, price, location where the product can be purchased, and what the consumer is expected to do. An ad may provide a considerable amount of other information, such as the brand name of the product, the specific item shown, the address of the company, and the company name. Salespersons, of course, provide other information verbally. They can provide specific other information requested by the customer.

Related Principles of Learning

There are several specific principles of learning that have been related to the effectiveness of educating consumers.[17]

1. *Appeals that are understood are remembered better than appeals learned by rote.*
2. *Unpleasant appeals can be learned as readily as pleasant appeals.* Appeals based on fear or risk, such as the appeal of insurance, can be effective. Reminder advertising that so often grates on the nerves can also be effective.
3. *Appeals have more effect when made over a period of time.* The policy of repeat calls by salespeople and repeat advertising is sound. On a given budget, it is better to promote periodically than to depend on one big splash. There is a direct correlation between initial interest and the ability to recall material over time.
4. *Appeals to several senses are more effective than appeals made to one sense.* On this basis, television rates higher than radio in its effect on consumers.
5. *Different or unique messages are better remembered.* The message stands out in a person's mind.
6. *It is easier to recognize an appeal than to recall it.* This makes brand such an important supplement to advertising. The advertising may get a message across that is recognized when the brand is observed in the store.
7. *Forgetting is rapid immediately after learning.* This is one reason why repeat promotion is so important.
8. *Knowledge of results increases learning of a message.* It is human nature to be interested in the payoff.
9. *Messages are easier to learn when they do not interfere with earlier habits.* People resist changing their patterns of behavior. A sufficiently strong appeal can change the consumer, but it takes more effort.
10. *Learning a new pattern of behavior can interfere with remembering something else.* Thus, promotion may serve as a partial block on competitors once the consumer has been convinced of the soundness of your argument.

PROMOTION MOTIVATES CONSUMERS

Promotion motivates consumers. At the preference stage of persuasion, promotion can provide strong emotional and factual reasons to believe the presentation. Some of the techniques used are specific appeal, color, typography, white space, and propaganda.

Include Specific Appeals

Specific appeals can be included in the promotion that motivate the consumer. One important appeal, *humor,* can relieve any tension that may be aroused when confronted with new information or a new perspective. Of course, humor can be used effectively by both the personal salesperson and in advertisements. Salespersons use jokes to evoke humor. A classic example of effective use of humor in the media is the Miller Lite campaign. In this campaign, celebrities discuss Miller Lite in humorous settings. One ad shows Bubba Smith on the golf course; Smith "shoots a birdie" and feathers fall. Another ad refers to the easy-opening can as Smith rips the can's entire top off.

Although the evidence is that humor can be effective, it should be used with caution. Several points can be made:

1. Humor attracts attention.
2. Humor can increase source credibility.
3. Humor may create a positive mood.
4. Humor may aid in recall of the message.
5. Humor may increase retention of the message.
6. Humor may offend a portion of the market.

One fact is clear: humor should not make fun of the company, its products, or services, and it should not dominate the message.

Audience *participation* in the promotion enhances its effectiveness. It is easy for the salesperson to gain participation by simply asking questions. It is more difficult with advertisements. However, it can be done. For example, describing the hazards of drinking would be less effective than having people participate in a quiz on the subject.

The use of *fear* appeals in promotional messages has had mixed results. Although consumers respond to moderate fear appeals, some research findings indicate that strong fear appeals may yield favorable responses. For example, Prudential Life Insurance Co. recently switched to a relatively strong fear appeal in its television ads for life insurance. In these ads, individuals are shown being revived from near-death situations (such as drowning or being caught in a fire), followed by the remark "At Prudential we know that most of us don't get a second chance." Preliminary tests of audience reactions to these ads have been quite positive.[18] Toothpaste and deodorants are just a few examples of products that have successfully used moderate fear appeals in their promotional messages, based on social factors, rather than physical ones.

Some promotional messages which use fear generate concern without pro-

Photo 13-2
Humor can be used effectively in selling.

viding clear and actionable recommendations. It is especially important to state clearly recommended action to alleviate the fear that has been generated. Promotional messages containing fear require especially strong recommendations that are clear and easily implemented. If it is not possible to provide this sort of information, some other type of appeal should probably be used.

Messages presented by personal salespersons and those in advertisements can be either *one-sided* or *two-sided*. In a one-sided message, only the firm's position is presented. A two-sided message presents both the firm's position and any opposing positions. An example of a two-sided promotion would be a comparative ad contrasting the firm's offering with that of competitors.[19] Comparison ads now account for 35 percent of all television commercials.

Use of Color to Motivate

Color has always been associated with emotional responses in individuals, and *color* is an important technique for motivating consumers. Because individuals have established color association, a consistent relationship exists between the colors used in a promotional message and the meanings that may be attached to it. Individuals cannot help but establish several color identifications early in their lifetimes. Not everyone reacts the same way to colors, but some typical symbolic meanings for certain colors are as follows:

Red: Danger, warning, warmth, blood, fire, heat, passion, anger; psychologically, red is also the most visible color.

White: Cleanliness, purity, health and medicine, virginity.

Blue: Peace, calmness, serenity, truth, formality. In Western culture, masculinity.

Orange: Harvest, fall, middle life, abundance.

Green: Nature, fertility, youth, spring, envy.

Purple: Royalty, richness, dignity.

Black: Death, mourning, evil, formality, mystery.

Gold: Wealth, high value, formal occasions.

In addition, several color combinations have become symbolic stimuli: red, white, and blue; red and green; orange and black; and gold, green and purple, representing patriotism, Christmas, Halloween, and Mardi Gras.

The exact emotion created by a color depends on the culture, the person, the product, and the situation. Because green is normally associated with freshness, nature, and fertility, menthol cigarettes, such as Salems, are promoted with basic green "nature shots" to imply that the products are natural and healthful.

Typography Can Stimulate

Type can be an important symbolic stimulus. It can create interest, draw attention to important aspects of the ad, and convey emotional meaning. Generally, block type is thought to be more formal, masculine, and modern. Script is considered feminine and modern. Roman type conveys tradition, formality, prestige, and permanence. Ornamental type may convey a variety of moods and backgrounds, historical and cultural.

In terms of the package, typography has to create a mood and portray the desired symbolic stimuli. For example, the laundry detergent Bold uses heavy, bold letters in the printing of the brand name on the package. The typography suggests a powerful detergent and exemplifies the product's name. The same type of lettering would be incongruous with a perfume product.

White Space as a Motivator

White space can be a stimulus. Try this test.[20] Get three ads, one from your local discount store, one from a specialty clothing shop, and one from an exclusive jeweler. Frequently, the discount store fills all the space in the ad with copy or illustrations. The ads for the clothing store and jeweler will often use white space rather extensively. With it they attempt to communicate a sense of elegance, refinement, and perhaps a feeling that they do not have to crowd their costly space. In the same way, they do not have to crowd their store itself. A sense of crowding, on the other hand, may be quite a welcome symbol for the cost-conscious shopper who associates low prices with massed merchandise and crowded stores. The decision about the use of white space should not depend on what is left over after all other verbal and nonverbal elements are included. White space is a symbolic stimulus as well. Compare the use of white space in the ads presented in this chapter. Which are most appealing to you?

Propaganda as a Motivator

There is some element of propaganda in nearly all advertising. Propaganda goes one step further than simple persuasion. Persuasive promotion attempts to influence by reasoning and the force and soundness of the argument. However, propaganda attempts to *condition* the consumer's thinking process by whatever means are available. Persuasive promotion deals with the truth, but "Propaganda, by definition, is biased, partial, and one-sided. It has an ax to grind, therefore it is always controversial. It is deliberately planned to make its readers and listeners take sides."[21]

Propaganda can be found in personal selling and advertising. Some of the techniques used by the propagandist are as follows:

1. *Name calling*: Getting consumers to reject the product or idea without a fair trial by associating it with a bad label.
2. *Testimonial*: Getting someone who is respected or hated to say the product or idea is good or bad.
3. *Card stacking*: Using facts, illustrations, logical and illogical statements presented in the best or worst possible way.
4. *Bandwagon*: All of us are doing it, so you should follow the crowd.[22]

Propaganda as such is neither good nor bad; it can be used honestly or dishonestly. We can clarify this point by considering the methods of the propagandist. They are:

1. Presenting one-sided arguments.
2. Showing data in the best light.
3. Selecting data to present.
4. Using innuendo and implication.
5. Modifying results.
6. Presenting false and/or untruthful information.

Most people agree that there is nothing much wrong with items (1) and (2). These two methods are considered by many to be a part of any persuasion. The selection of data and use of innuendo cause marketers more trouble. Is an advertiser justified in reporting that 80 percent of the people tested use his product, when mainly users were tested? Bayer aspirin has been criticized for advertising that it is "the best aspirin, " when there is only one kind. Shell oil has been under fire for suggesting that platformate gives better mileage than competing gasolines. Not everyone is in agreement as to the extent to which these types of propaganda are justified. Most marketers do agree that modifying results and false advertising are an improper use of propaganda.

Principles that relate to how the consumer is influenced by promotion may be described as follows:

1. *People selectively perceive communications that are favorable or congenial to their predispositions.*

2. *General or undifferentiated appeals have less influence on the audience than appeals directed at some particular interest.* The lesson is to know your audience and appeal to it directly.

3. *Persons of high intelligence tend to be influenced more by logical arguments.* This is true because the higher intelligence allows the person to follow the argument and draw valid conclusions.

4. *Persons of low intelligence tend to be influenced more by emotion, generalizations, or false, illogical, or irrelevant arguments.*

5. *The more aggressive, hostile, or unsociable a person is, the less likely he or she is to be persuaded by the majority opinion.* Often these people must be appealed to individually or left to make up their own minds without influence.

6. *Present a one-sided argument when the audience is friendly or when yours is the only position being presented, and present both sides when the opposite is true.*[23]

7. *Strong appeals to fear are less effective than mild appeals to fear.* Strong fear appeals develop tensions in the consumer that can actually cause the person to discount the entire argument. It may have happened in the case of the Surgeon General's appeal to people to stop smoking.

8. *It is better to state the conclusion rather than allow the audience to draw its own conclusions.* The argument may be, "Why take chances?" Actually, people given identical information come to different conclusions because of selective perception and because all information is interpreted in the light of the individual's motives and desires.

9. *The more trustworthy or creditable communicators appear to be, the greater the tendency to accept their conclusions.*

10. *Communicators can affect greater change in an audience if they express some views in common with the group.*[24] This promotes a community of interest. Besides, anyone we can agree with can't be all wrong.

PROMOTION MOVES CONSUMERS TO ACTION

"The proof of the pudding," as they say in any promotion, is whether the consumer takes the action desired by the firm. Promotion can move a consumer to act, and this is a separate stage from motivation. Just because a consumer has been convinced that the product is worthwhile does not mean that the consumer will immediately purchase it. It has been said that more sales are lost because the customer was never asked to buy than for any other reason. It is at the action stage that the customer is asked to buy.

Personal salespersons may evoke action by simply saying, "Do you wish me to wrap this for you?" or "You may sign here on this line." In an advertisement, it is equally important to ask the reader to take the desired action.

There is evidence of a *sleeper effect* with promotion where the persuasiveness of a message increases with time.[25] The consumer may take time just to get used to the idea—or to understand the idea fully. In any case, consumers may accept the point of view presented by the promotion, or they may purchase later even without additional reinforcement. This fact makes it difficult to appreciate fully the total effect of a promotion at the time of its occurrence.

QUESTIONS

1. Discuss the statement: "Perhaps no aspect of business strategy is more important for influencing consumers than promotion."
2. Identify and define the promotional tools for influencing consumer decision making.
3. Bring to class several examples of favorable publicity and unfavorable publicity and discuss their impact on the subject matter.
4. There are five stages of persuasion. Identify them and provide examples of advertisements for each stage.
5. Discuss the statement: "Promotion makes people buy things they don't want."
6. Promotion motivates consumers to action. Bring examples of advertisements that encourage individuals to take action.
7. Bring in examples of promotion that stress the ideal self-image. Discuss the implications.
8. Identify the individuals who fall within your reference group and discuss their influence on the different products or services you purchase.
9. You have just been given the job of a salesperson, develop an opening statement to gain attention for the following products.
   a. car   b. food   c. clothing
10. Identify the factors you should take into consideration when developing a message for your marketing target.
11. Bring to class several advertisements with different layouts and discuss the advantages and disadvantages of each example.
12. Appeals to several senses are more effective than appeals made to one sense. Bring to class several advertisements that appeal to more than one sense.
13. Make a list of products that are promoted with humor and those promoted with fear. Which assignment is easier? Why?
14. Identify and discuss the ways you can determine if your promotion is effective.
15. Which do you perceive to be a more reliable source: publicity or advertising? Why?

NOTES

1. William P. Dommermuth, *Promotion: Analysis, Creativity, and Strategy* (Boston: Kent Publishing Company, 1984), p. 4.

2. Gary F. McKinnon, J. Patrick Kelly, and E. Doyle Robison, "Sales Effects of Point-of-Purchase In-Store Signing," *Journal of Retailing,* Vol. 57 (Summer 1981), pp. 49–63.

3. Bent Stidsen, "Some Thoughts on the Advertising Process," *Journal of Marketing,* Vol. 34 (January 1970), pp. 47–54.

4. Robert Jacobson and Franco M. Nicosia, "Advertising and Public Policy: The Macroeconomic Effects of Advertising," *Journal of Marketing Research*, Vol. XVIII (February 1981), pp. 29–38.

5. Andrew S. C. Ehrenberg, "Repetitive Advertising and the Consumer," *Journal of Advertising Research*, Vol. 14 (April 1974), pp. 25–33.

6. Albert J. Della Bitta, Kent B. Monroe, and John M. McGinnis, "Consumer Perceptions of Comparative Price Advertisements," *Journal of Marketing Research,* Vol. XVIII (November 1981), pp. 416–27; George E. Belch, "An Examination of Comparative and Noncomparative Television Commercials: The Effects of Claim Variation and Repetition on Cognitive Response and Message Acceptance," *Journal of Marketing Research,* Vol. XVIII (August 1981), pp. 33–49.

7. M. Joseph Sirgy, "Self-Concept in Consumer Behavior: A Critical Review," *Journal of Consumer Research,* Vol. 9 (December 1982), pp. 287–300.

8. Kent B. Monroe, "Buyers' Subjective Perceptions of Price," *Journal of Marketing Research,* Vol. 10 (February 1973), pp. 70–80.

9. Ruth Ziff, "Closing the Consumer-Advertising Gap Through Psychographics," in Boris W. Becker and Helmut Becker, eds., *Marketing Educations and the World and Dynamic Marketing in a Changing World* (Chicago: American Marketing Assn., 1973), pp. 457–61.

10. Nancy Giges, "Time and Theme Is Now for Pepsi," *Advertising Age* (March 7, 1983), pp. 2, 62.

11. Edward L. Grubb and Bruce L. Stern, "Self-Concept and Significant Others," *Journal of Marketing Research,* Vol. 8 (August 1971), pp. 382–85.

12. J. Barry Mason and Morris L. Mayer, "The Problem of the Self-Concept in Store Image Studies," *Journal of Marketing*, Vol. 34 (April 1970), pp. 67–69.

13. Warren S. Martin and Joseph Bellizze, "An Analysis of Congruous Relationships Between Self-Images and Product Images," *Journal of the Academy of Marketing Science,* Vol. 10 (Fall 1982), pp. 473–489.

14. Julie A. Edell and Richard Staelin, "The Information Processing of Pictures in Print Advertisements," *Journal of Consumer Research,* Vol. 10 (June 1983), pp. 45–61.

15. Jolita Kisielius and Brian Sternthal, "Detecting and Explaining Vividness Effects in Attitudinal Judgments," *Journal of Marketing Research*, Vol. XXI (February 1984), pp. 54–64.

16. Esther Thorson, "A Microanalysis of the Advertising Communication Process," in Nancy Stephens, ed., *Proceedings of the 1985 Conference of the American Academy of Advertising* (Arizona State University and American Academy of Advertising, 1985), pp. 432–36.

17. Steuart Henderson Britt, "How Advertising Can Use Psychology's Rules of

Learning," *Printers' Ink*, Vol. 252 (September 1955), pp. 38–39.

18. Bill Abrams, "New Prudential Ads Portray Death as No Laughing Matter," *Wall Street Journal* (November 10, 1983), p. 31.

19. John Koten, "More Firms File Challenges to Rivals' Comparative Ads," *Wall Street Journal* (January 12, 1984), p. 27.

20. C. H. Sandage, Vernon Fryburger, and Kim Rotzoll, *Advertising Theory and Practice*, 10th ed. (Homewood, Ill.: Richard D. Irwin, Inc., 1979), p. 333.

21. Edmund D. McGarry, "The Propaganda Function in Marketing," *Journal of Marketing,* Vol. 23 (October 1958), pp. 131–29.

22. Alfred M. Lee and Elizabeth B. Lee, *The Fine Art of Propaganda*, (New York: Harcourt, Brace, & Co., 1939), pp. 22–24.

23. Michael Etgar and Stephen A. Goodwin, "One-Sided Versus Two-Sided Comparative Message Appeals for New Brand Introductions," *Journal of Consumer Research*, Vol. 8 (March 1982), pp. 460–64.

24. Anthony G. Greenwald and Clark Leavitt, "Audience Involvement in Advertising: Four Levels," *Journal of Consumer Research*, Vol. 11 (June 1984), pp. 581–92.

25. Darlene B. Hannah and Brian Sternthal, "Detecting and Explaining the Sleeper Effect," *Journal of Consumer Research*, Vol. 11 (September 1984), pp. 632–42.

CONSUMER EVALUATION
AND DECISION

SECTION A
ELEMENTS OF
THE CONSUMER DECISION

14. Introduction To Consumer Decision
15. Consumer Evaluation of Alternatives
16. Consumer Purchase Decision
17. Consumer Decisions Consistent with Personality

CHAPTER 14

Introduction To
Consumer Decision

CHAPTER OUTLINE

I. THE CONSUMER DECISION
   A. Consumer Dilemma When Deciding
   B. Consumer Decision Planning Is a Way Out
   C. Differences in Consumer Decision Planning

II. TYPES OF CONSUMER DECISION THEORIES
   A. Partial Explanation Theories
   B. Basic Explanation Theories

III. PERCEPTION UNDERLIES ALL CONSUMER DECISIONS
   A. Perception Defined
   B. Role of Perception in Decision Making

IV. MANNER OF PERCEPTION'S EFFECT ON DECISIONS
   A. Perceptual Process and Decision Making
   B. Perceptual Thresholds and Decisions

V. PERCEPTUAL CHARACTERISTICS AFFECTING DECISIONS
   A. Perception Is Selective of Data
   B. Perception Is Subjective of Relevance
   C. Perception Is Temporal for Retention
   D. Perception Is Summative of Data

VI. PERCEPTUAL FACTORS AFFECTING DECISIONS
   A. Technical Factors
   B. Perceptual Fixation
   C. Perceptual Habit
   D. Attention Is Necessary to Perceive
   E. Mental Set
   F. Mood of the Perceiver

VII. CONSUMER PERCEPTIONS CHANGE

CHAPTER OBJECTIVES

After completing your study of Chapter 14, you should be able to:

1. Discuss the consumer decision.
2. Discuss the types of consumer decision theories.
3. Explain why perception underlies all consumer decisions.
4. Discuss the manner of perception's effect on decisions.
5. Discuss the perceptual characteristics affecting decisions.
6. Discuss the perceptual factors affecting decisions.
7. Explain how consumer perceptions change.

Consumer purchase decisions are vital to consumer satisfaction because each decision is a specific commitment to a particular brand or store. The making of effective consumer purchase decisions is the central issue of consumer behavior. That is why we identify it as the goal of all consumers. The next several chapters of this text discuss how consumers make decisions. It follows logically after problem recognition and search for information in the consumer's decision process.

THE CONSUMER DECISION

The purchase decision appears to be the simplest step in the consumer's decision process. After all, the consumer simply selects the product, store, or method of purchase that is preferred. In fact, the purchase decision is never that simple or automatic. Consumer decision making is the step where all the information gathered in the search process is tested and compared in the mind. The consumer decision concerns a whole group of alternatives associated with choosing specific stores and products.[1]

To make a decision is to reduce uncertainty to the point where one can specify a course of action. *Consumer decision* is:

the selection, from among alternatives or preferences, of that market-related action which is indicated by available information.

On a given shopping trip, the consumer, even when knowing the type of product desired, may be simultaneously deciding on the brand, price, store, method of travel, services desired, personal treatment, product line expected, time of purchase, and more. Each of these types of decisions may involve multiple alternatives. Thus the consumer must establish a whole hierarchy of decisions.

Consumer Dilemma When Deciding

Consumers face a serious dilemma in the market; they cannot avoid making serious product and store decisions, but they do not have the means to make these decisions effectively. There are a number of reasons why consumers have difficulty making efficient decisions: too many desires, lack of capital, inadequate information, insufficient time, and poor training.

Photo 14-1
Consumers have difficulty making efficient decisions for many reasons.

First, consumers never run out of wants. Consumers want more and better products and services. They want greater variety and a wider range of styles in the products demanded. Fortunately, our society has been able to provide consumers with more and more goods and services, but the sheer number of product and service decisions reduces efficiency in making them.

Second, it takes money to function effectively in any market, and the consumer market is no exception. Insufficient funds not only limit the total amount of products and services that the consumer can have, but also force the consumer to make compromises on quality. Parents may be forced to purchase a cheap pair of shoes for their children, knowing full well that they will have to enter the market again in a month or six weeks.

Third, consumer information may be inadequate in several ways. The consumer may have too much information, too little information, or incorrect information. Some people argue that mass communication simply confuses people with conflicting information about products. Consumers have so many choices and so much conflicting data on each choice that they may tend to discount all such information.[2] Sellers may withhold pertinent product information that can help the consumer decide on a course of action. The consumer can fail to receive the entire message or may misunderstand the information received. The seller can add to the confusion by deliberately or accidentally distorting data.

Fourth, consumer market efficiency is reduced by a lack of time to compare and decide. The average consumer has too much to do each day and must often rely on habit, recommendation, or superficial examination or comparison when selecting merchandise.

Fifth, most consumers are not adequately trained to make sound choices in the market. The American society generally is preoccupied with production rather than consumption. Our entire educational system, and to some extent training in the home, centers around teaching skills in a profession or trade. Practically no effort is given to teaching our youth how to be a consumers—that is, how to obtain greatest satisfaction from the fruits of production.

The average consumer cannot tell which size bottle of detergent is really the cheapest, and most cannot rapidly figure the price per item for an item marked "3 for 89 cents." The situation is made worse because most consumers do not appear particularly interested in learning these things.

Consumer Decision Planning Is a Way Out

The consumer's dilemma in the market is real. The difficulties are too serious to be ignored, and they are too complex to be handled in any casual or ill-considered manner. There are no ideal solutions to consumer problems, but certainly these problems cannot be adequately solved by chance and guesswork. The consumer must find some sound basis for coping with this dilemma.[3]

It may appear to the reader that the complexity of market problems makes any useful market analysis impossible. Fortunately for the consumer, this is not the case. Consumer decisions can be meaningfully planned.

Planning may be defined as decision making in anticipation of needs or problems.[4] *Consumer decision planning* is:

the selection from among alternatives of a specific course of action in anticipation of particular needs or problems.

Consumer decision making does not need to be formal or highly complex; it is essentially nothing more than recognizing a problem and choosing how to handle it.

The consumer is generally aware of the products he or she owns, their deficiencies, and the means or preferred ways that these deficiencies can be corrected. Purchase planning improves the consumer's chances of successful buying in three ways. First, it forces the consumer to establish product goals and to consider specific means for achieving those goals. Thus, planning tends to encourage logical thought processes. Second, purchase planning forces the consumer to consider each problem as it arises. In much the same manner as management by exception, the consumer focuses attention on those products, or means of purchase, that are giving trouble at the time. Other decisions can be reduced to routine. The result is that the consumer reduces the number of decisions that must be handled at a given time to manageable proportions while focusing attention for more logical problem solving. Third, overall planning gives consumers a means to organize the many decisions they face. Separate decisions can be assigned priorities by importance or urgency; some decisions can be deferred until the consumer obtains more information.

Differences in Consumer Decision Planning

The fact that consumers employ decision planning does not mean that all the problems previously mentioned can be overcome. There is no way that the consumer can escape making decisions.[5] Every act of purchase requires one or more decisions: to part with the money or not, to take one product or brand over another, to follow previous purchase patterns or to change, or to approach one salesperson or another. The difference between consumers is not whether they make decisions, but how well they plan and execute these decisions. Consumer planning varies all the way from practically no planning at all to rather formalized, integrated planning.[6] Some consumers are so careful that their plans almost form a strategy. However, it is safe to say that this degree of decision planning is not characteristic of most consumers. Consumers often employ too little planning, improperly placed planning, and incorrect planning. These are the consumers that we refer to as poor marketers. Consumers are perhaps most often guilty of not giving sufficient consideration to the many problems they face. The important point is that consumers do make some effort to plan, and most consumers do employ some type of purchase planning most of the time. This decision planning is at least sufficient to keep them functioning.

TYPES OF CONSUMER DECISION THEORIES

We are now ready to take a look at the different types of decision theories. For the purpose of discussion, these theories have been divided into partial explanation theories and basic explanation theories. *Partial explanation theories* attempt to explain particular types of consumer decisions rather than all consumer decisions. *Basic explanation theories* attempt to develop a broad explanation of all consumer decisions, although exceptions may be recognized. Each of these groups of theories is discussed in turn.

Partial Explanation Theories

There are several types of partial explanation theories. Theories that view consumer decisions as based on (1) chance, (2) habit, (3) impulse, (4) social orientation, and (5) heredity, are partial explanation theories. *Chance* assumes that a consumer purchases without any planning simply because an opportunity presents itself. Essentially no thought is given to the purchase, and decisions are made, figuratively speaking, on the flip of a coin. *Habit* assumes that the consumer thinks out an original decision satisfactorily and makes each successive purchase the same way with little re-evaluation. Many consumer decisions are based on habit. *Impulse* is a decision made very quickly because a solution to a recognized problem presents itself, and there is relatively little thought given the purchase. Impulse is also frequently used. *Social orientation* is the proverbial "keeping up with the Joneses." It is buying on the basis of what the consumer feels others will think. Purchases based on *heredity* are made because of the inborn nature of the consumer.

The partial explanation theories have two ideas in common. Each theory views consumer deciding as almost entirely based on reaction or emotions, and each emphasizes the lack of factual information upon which consumer decisions are based. None of these theories offer a general explanation of consumer decisions, but none should be discounted. At one time or another consumers have made purchase decisions based almost entirely on one or the other of these concepts. Furthermore, almost every consumer purchase decision involves some aspects of the partial explanation theories. For example, we cannot underestimate the importance of chance or impulse on the individual when shopping or browsing, even when the general product desired is known in advance. Social orientation also is likely to be involved in most decisions to some degree, because all consumers are aware of their relationship with others. Thus, the fact that these concepts are called partial explanation theories indicates nothing of their importance. The name is given because each theory emphasizes a type of decision behavior rather than decision behavior in general.

Basic Explanation Theories

Basic explanation consumer decision theories consider the consumer as either (1) a risk reducer or (2) a problem solver. These basic explanation theories require some knowledge about the problem on the part of the consumer, but they do not require the perfect knowledge necessary for the concept of economic man. Each of the basic explanation theories is discussed below.

The *risk reduction* concept is based on the assumption that consumers enter into decision making in the market as a means of reducing risk.[7] The risk reduction theory requires the least amount of information for decision making, and this concept has been popular with many marketers in recent years. The basic idea is quite simple. Every consumer decision involves two elements—risk and consequence. No matter which course of action the consumer takes, there is the risk that the consequence will be unpleasant. The consumer, faced with a market decision, acts to get just enough information to reduce the risk to an acceptable level before acting.[8]

The consumer is faced with the risk of which branded item to buy, especially new product brands, which stores or trade areas to patronize, and which is the best alternative method of allocating funds among all wants.[9] The consumer depends on known risk-reducing strategies such as shopping familiar stores, purchasing only nationally advertised brands, trading with large stores, etc. The risk of information collecting is reduced by accepting more readily favorable information.[10]

Five major types of perceived risk have been identified. They are performance, financial, social, psychological and physical risk. The consumer always considers the consequence of any action, and the greater the consequence, the less risk the consumer is willing to assume. Thus expensive products, new products, durables, and new stores call for more information seeking. Risk reduction is a normal way for the consumer to handle purchasing because he or she is coping with a difficult situation in a reasonable manner.

Another theory of consumer decision making views the consumer as a *problem solver*.[11] Essentially, the view is that every consumer desire creates a problem within the individual. The consumer acts to solve the problem by deciding on a course of action consistent with his or her subjective desires. When the problem is fully solved, the purchase has taken place. The consumer solves the problem by acquiring information about the situation, determining alternative courses of action, and selecting one course from the alternatives.

The two primary differences between the risk and problem solver concepts are the definition of rationality and the amount of information needed to make decisions. Each concept requires a reasonable decision process, and each concept allows for emotions. The consumer as problem solver has a more rigidly defined analysis and requires more information as a basis for decision making. The consumer as risk reducer uses a great deal of emotion and very few facts. Each theory can serve as an adequate basis for consumer decision making.

PERCEPTION UNDERLIES ALL CONSUMER DECISIONS

At the heart of all consumer decision making is perception.[12] We define the term and then relate the role of perception to the consumer's decision-making process.

Perception Defined

In the simplest of terms, *perception* can be described as the process of interpreting directly through any of the senses.[13] More broadly, it includes information received through the senses. Perception is:

the entire process by which an individual becomes aware of the environment and interprets it so that it will fit into his or her own frame of reference.[14]

Young illustrates perceiving by the use of the following paradigm.[15]

$$\text{To perceive} = \begin{cases} \text{To see} \\ \text{To hear} \\ \text{To touch} \\ \text{To taste} \\ \text{To smell} \\ \text{To sense internally} \end{cases} \quad \text{Some} \quad \begin{cases} \text{Thing} \\ \text{Event} \\ \text{Relation} \end{cases}$$

Every perception involves a person who interprets through the senses, some thing, event, or relation, which may be designated as the percept. Nearly everything people know of the world around them comes through the senses. When a consumer reports that a particular department store has good bargains, the person is reporting something perceived through sensory experience. The way consumers think and behave is constantly being affected by their perception of changes in the environment. Perception is how consumers handle such new information psychologically by organizing and interpreting the stimuli impinging on their senses.

The senses of vision, touch, hearing, taste, and smell all produce effects that go beyond immediate sensation. The first time a youngster burns a finger on a match, the sensation of pain is related to the match, and the child perceives that the match caused the pain. Thus, sensation coupled with the mental association of two facts produces perception. Because perception involves learning, it carries over time. The youngster will associate the sensation of pain with matches at any future time a burning match is perceived. Sensory experiences are but one component of perception. The child's past experience, his or her background, the result of the encounter, and the activity engaged in at the time all contribute to the way in which matches are perceived. Hadley Cantril summed the concept of perception very well with the following story about three umpires who were discussing how they call the game.

> The first umpire said, "Some's balls and some's strikes and I calls 'em as they is." The second umpire said, "Some's balls and some's strikes and I calls 'em as I sees 'em." While the third umpire said, "Some's balls and some's strikes but they ain't nothing' till I calls 'em."[16]

If several customers observe a round, white object several inches in diameter in a retail store, each would most likely react differently to the object based on individual perception. Each person's needs, cultural background, past experiences, and motives will cause perception of the object to differ from that of the other individuals, even though the sensation is the same for all.[17] A round, white object may be perceived as a baseball by a ten-year-old. The child wants to purchase it. The parents may perceive the ball as a hazard or an expense and may not want to purchase it.

Since the identical sensation can be interpreted in differing ways, perceptions differ, and the resulting consumer behavior likewise differs. The sign proclaiming a National Football League exhibition game can be perceived as entertainment by the avid football fan, as traffic congestion by the motorcycle police officer, and as a revenue opportunity by the concessionaire. Each person's background and experience have altered individual interpretation of identical sensory data.

Role of Perception in Decision Making

It is the role of perception to provide a particular emphasis or flavor to the consumer's understanding of all considerations related to the decision process. None of the decision theories deal with fact. They all deal with the consumer's perception of fact. The risk reduction concept views the perception of risk and consequence as fundamental to how the decision is made. In the problem solver concept, the consumer's perception of problems begins the process, and the perception of alternatives, selection criteria, and what is reasonable determines how this perceived problem is decided. Decisions applying chance, habit, impulse, social orientation and heredity also have perception at their heart.

In other words, perception flavors the entire consumer decision-making process. The perception of problems starts the consumer's decision process. Perception governs which facts we accept and which facts we reject when searching for information. The perception of the importance of alternatives is critical in consumer choice. The perception of the success of the decision activates post-purchase assessment.

Illustration 14-1
Consumer perceptual process

MANNER OF PERCEPTION'S EFFECT ON DECISIONS

Perception affects consumer decision making in some rather specific ways. It is important that we understand what these ways are and the manner of the overall effect involved.

Perceptual Process and Decision Making

There are three elements to the perceptual process, and they are all involved in consumer decision making. First, *conveyance* is the act of getting sensations to the brain. The sensory organs previously introduced convey to the mind stimuli from the external world. In Illustration 14-1, the boy first observes the fancy sports car primarily through the senses of hearing and seeing. These external stimuli are conveyed to the brain via the central nervous system. At this point the observation means very little to a person as a consumer. Second, the stimulus is *elaborated* as a part of the mental process involving classifying the sensations according to knowledge and experience. In this way, the person finds out what the sensations are, whether there has been some past experience with them, and so on. In the illustration, the boy understands that he perceives a girl in a car, that he understands what has been conveyed to his mind, and that he has had previous experience with both girls and cars. Third, *comprehension* occurs when the stimulus has meaning for the consumer. In the illustration, the boy comprehends that he does not have a car like the one observed. He may feel he would be more successful socially if he did. This perception may motivate him to purchase a sports car, strive harder to be able to own a sports car, or engage in some alternative consumption as an alternative to owning a sports car. The point is that in every consumer decision there is conveyance, elaboration, and comprehension. Together they constitute consumer perception.

Perceptual Thresholds and Decisions

Each bit of perceptual information must be assigned some priority if our actions are to achieve continuity and direction. The factors that assign these priorities to the incoming data are not primarily the stimulus factors but factors such as interests, needs, and attitudes that can be measured by observing how a person reacts to various standard stimuli. Of particular importance to advertising, merchandising, and marketing research is the fact that the attention-getting value of the market stimulus depends not so much on the stimulus itself as on the individual the stimulus affects. We have pointed out that consumer behavior is very rarely controlled by a single stimulus affecting a single sense. Rather, consumer behavior is affected by a pattern of stimulation. The value and meaning of the market stimulus depend upon the context in which it is perceived. All of our senses have some limit to responsiveness to stimulation. In the literature these limits are referred to as thresholds.

There are three thresholds that correspond to each sense. They are as follows:

1. *Lower threshold*: Point beyond which the market stimulus is not sufficiently strong to be noticed by the consumer.
2. *Upper threshold*: Point beyond which increased stimulation produces no increased response.
3. *Difference threshold*: The smallest increment of stimulation that can be noticed by a consumer.[18]

These upper and lower thresholds do not correspond to the physical limits of market stimuli. Physical stimuli can be lower or higher than the threshold limits. Furthermore, these threshold limits apply to individual consumers and not to groups. Each consumer has a unique upper and lower threshold.

The consumer may be influenced by considerations he or she may not be able to identify, by responding to cues that are below the threshold of recognition. The product package is often spoken of as the "silent salesperson." A good package design has the ability to attract the customer's attention. The size of the package, its color, and its design may be influential, even though consumers may think they are interested only in price, brand name, or contents. The package may be so well designed that it breaks through the consumer's lower threshold. In advertising, marketers often observe that it is some simple, inexpensive bit of data that determines the way the entire advertisement is perceived. It is extremely important for marketers to gauge those factors people respond to, while at the same time acknowledging that this is not always possible.

PERCEPTUAL CHARACTERISTICS AFFECTING DECISIONS

Certain characteristics of perception are universal. Perception may differ among consumers, but perception displays four specific characteristics where found: It can be said to be (1) subjective, (2) selective, (3) temporal, or (4) summative. An awareness of these characteristics can greatly aid our understanding of how perception influences consumer behavior.

Perception Is Selective of Data

Perception is *selective* because individual minds fail to comprehend and interpret all the sensations that bombard the senses at any given time. When a person views a department store window, it is doubtful that one "sees" one-third of all the items present. Ask yourself what your initial perception is of the AIDS ad in Figure 14-1. Some persons shut out unpleasant stimuli as they are perceived. Three mechanisms existing in the perception of everyone determine which stimuli will "get through" to the mind and which will not. These mechanisms are perceptual overloading, selective sensitization, and perceptual defense.

Figure 14-1
Perception is selective.

AIDS: Our Deadly Enemy

How can you protect yourself?

AIDS stands for "acquired immune deficiency syndrome," a fearsome plague caused by a newly discovered virus that destroys the body's natural ability to defend itself against disease. Victims die because they can't fight common diseases like pneumonia or cancer. Around the world, medical researchers are mobilizing against the deadly AIDS virus. Here at home officially over 35,000 Americans have AIDS and, of these, more than 20,000 have died. Another 1,500,000 are carriers; their fate is uncertain. And AIDS is spreading every day. Think these things over—and act accordingly.

This advertisement presented as a public service by Reader's Digest.

1. Sexual intercourse of any kind with a person infected with the AIDS virus may transmit the virus to you. There's no way you can tell if the person is infected. Even he or she may not know.

2. Short of sexual abstinence, the surest way to avoid AIDS is the use of condoms. If you really want to be sure you're not infected, get a blood test for AIDS.

3. What if you're married? Experts say if you've both been faithful at least five years, you shouldn't worry.

4. Another common way to get AIDS is from a hypodermic needle soiled with contaminated blood. Victims are almost always intravenous drug addicts. Chances of contracting AIDS from a blood transfusion are extremely rare. From donating blood, no chance at all.

5. The AIDS virus is not spread by what you eat or drink, by utensils or glasses, by shaking hands, by toilet seats, coughs, sneezes, social kissing, hugging, sitting or working next to a person with AIDS.

6. Now that you know these basic facts, take due care. Change your habits or lifestyle, if need be. But don't make AIDS worse. Don't let it panic you.

Public Service Advertisement—August 1987 Reader's Digest

Photo 14-2
People are bombarded with 1500–1800 advertising messages of all types per day—even on clothing.

© 1981, Mark Wick

Perceptual overloading occurs because at any given time consumers can only take in and bring up to a conscious level relatively few of the stimuli confronting them.[19] The individual finds it impossible to respond to everything at once. Through perception a consumer is able to select from among the product or store stimuli. In this manner, an individual makes purchases manageable. The selective nature of perception may be regarded as the result of the subjective nature of people and of the limited capacity of a person's sensory equipment. *Selective sensitization* occurs when individuals perceive stimuli more accurately and rapidly because these stimuli are congruous with their value orientation. *Perceptual defense* occurs when a person's value orientation not only contributes to the selection of stimuli but acts to erect a barrier to those stimuli seen as threats. Thus, people are more than normally perceptive to some sensations and less than normally perceptive to other sensations. The result is a type of natural perceptual bias that exists in all purchase situations.[20]

The selectiveness of perception brought about by the physiological inability to take in more than a few stimuli at one time has importance to those in advertising. There are limits to the human capacity to absorb advertising messages accurately. The number of advertisements to which the average American consumer is daily exposed has been estimated to be from 1,500 to 1,800. A marketer's advertisement is thus competing with many others, yet only a small percentage of these are seen and brought to a conscious level by the consumer. Selective perception dictates not only carefully planned media selection but also the number of elements presented in the advertisement and they are presented. The selective nature of perception also plays a role in merchandising. Merchandising displays and assortments can be an important demand-creating force. However, if displays and merchandising techniques are utilized to the point that too many stimuli are present, they can actually cause a business to lose patronage.

Perception Is Subjective of Relevance

Perception is *subjective* because it exists in the mind of the individual and only in the mind. As consumers, we often block out things we do not want to emphasize, such as the price of the item or some possible defect in it.[21] We see what we want to see and hear what we want to hear. Thus, the consumer who wants to purchase perceives the good points of the product as more significant than the bad points. People are predisposed toward accepting certain information and rejecting other information. Consumers accept some data because it is more compatible with their background, feelings, or beliefs than other data.[22] Consumers tend to take in information that is agreeable, so as to protect their self-images and their egos. A person is the embodiment of certain beliefs, attitudes, and prejudices, and consumers buy in such a manner as to leave these factors intact and unchallenged. Illustration 14-2 illustrates one form of perceptual bias. Look closely and note what you see. Chances are you first saw the obvious, and the not-so-obvious only became apparent on further inspection.

Illustration 14-2
Perceptual bias

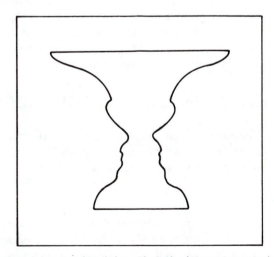

Illustration, "Perceptual Bias," from *Social Psychology: The Study of Human Interaction* by Theodore M. Newcomb, et al., copyright © 1965 by Holt, Rinehart and Winston, Inc., reprinted by permission of the publisher.

Perception Is Temporal for Retention

Most of our perceptions are *temporal,* that is, of short duration. Thus, products and services have difficulty holding the consumer's attention. This makes selective perception even more important and helps explain how a consumer can filter out an offensive advertising jingle. Temporal perception also partially explains why a well-known product can fail if advertising is cut off. Another partial explanation is that the market is changing.

A stimulus of constant intensity needs repetition if it is to be brought to the consciousness. A repeated, small ad may be more effective than a single, large ad. The temporal character of perception is the reason that reminder advertising is often successful. Individuals are constantly bombarded by market sensations, and practically none of the initial contacts are lasting. The slogan "Coke Is It" probably did not register in a lasting form the first time it was heard. It was only after numerous repetitions in a jingle that the idea was brought to a conscious level and remembered.

Perception Is Summative of Data

Perception tends to be *summative.* This means that consumers take many sensations that reach awareness almost simultaneously and sum these sensations into a complete and unified whole. Consider how you combine the information shown in Figure 14-2 with other known facts about "Post-It" to form a complete picture of the product. Consumers take the separate sensations of observing a building, hearing people move about, and observing various signs and colors, and put them together as a retail store. Consumers do the same thing when they observe an advertisement, a store sign, or a product design. Most sales messages are more effective when both audio and visual techniques are utilized rather than when either one or the other is used singly. The reason is that each sense message reinforces the others and aids in forming a consistent, unified impression. Consumers will add up a brand name, color, package features, approximate price, quality, past experience in using the product, and so on, to arrive at a purchasing decision. It is difficult to conceive how consumers could ever make up their minds to buy, if perception were not summative.

PERCEPTUAL FACTORS AFFECTING DECISIONS

The nature of the percept and the act of perceiving are affected by physical factors and subjective factors. It is impossible to discuss every factor, but some of the more important ones are explained below.

Technical Factors

When we refer to technical factors, we mean the actual things that are perceived by consumers. We do not mean the person's interpretation of the thing but rather the thing as it actually exists. There is evidence that technical (physical) considerations affect price-quality judgments of products more than nonphysical factors such as price or store image.[23]

Figure 14-2
Perception tends to be summative.

Courtesy of 3M Company

Whatever the consumer perceives is based on the actual thing, no matter how much the perception may become distorted in the beholder's mind. A pencil is a technical fact, but it can be perceived as an instrument with which to write a letter home, a means to curl hair, or a ruler. These perceptions are responses to a need. Technical factors refer to the things perceived, but these objects may be non-physical. Consumers perceive competition, efficiency, sales, and cost. These concepts are technical, but the differences consumers observe in them are perceptual.

Larger objects generally attract more attention than small objects, although there is no direct incremental relationship. Larger cans, larger ads, and larger stores attract more consumers. To some, size may also connote quality. Many people consider a large store to be automatically better than a small store. *Color* attracts more attention and makes a greater impression than black and white. An object in color is perceived quicker and is more likely to be remembered. Color can also emphasize various parts of an object, thus aiding learning. Used on labels, signs, and store fronts, color influences consumer perception. Color ads are 50 percent more effective than black and white, and newspapers using color have higher readership. *Loud, bright important*, and *significant* are words that convey intensity of an object. Greater intensity attracts and focuses attention. Intensity also affects memory and learning. Bright colors, important consumer decisions, and significant past experiences affect present consumer behavior.

Movement is a particularly good attention getter. Movement is an important element in TV commercials, point-of-sale aids, and in demonstrating products. Store signs that employ movement attract more customers. Where a thing is *located* affects perception. Consumers buy more products located shoulder-high on store shelves. The right-hand side and the upper half of a page get more of a person's attention. The placement of components in an advertisement help create interest and affect memory. Placement of products in a store can achieve the same effect. *Contrast* gains attention and creates interest much as color does. Contrast

Photo 14-3
Loud, bright elements gain attention from consumers.

Signs of the Times

is used effectively in ads, for interior and exterior store designs, for product placement, and on product labels. Contrast is achieved by varying the thought, color, size, pattern, or intensity. *Isolation* can also gain attention and influence perception. Even a small object, such as a knife, uniquely displayed attracts more attention than a window full of products. In addition, isolation of the headliner draws attention to the principal message.

It must be remembered that these attributes interact. High contrast may offset greater size. An object has its greatest impact on perception when several of the attributes function together.

Perceptual Fixation

The tendency of consumers to stabilize their perceptions of the environment is known as "perceptual fixation." Consumers tend to anticipate certain market stimuli in the environment and thus to stabilize their effects over time. You can say that individuals generalize some of their perceptions and retain them even after the basis for them has changed. For example, a consumer may perceive a quality image for a retail store even after evidence accumulates that the store has gone downhill. In the same way, consumers resist changing their image of a particular brand. They will continue to use inferior products long after better ones are available.

Perceptual Habit

We form habits in our perceptions as much as in our behavior. Individuals only break down old perceptions when they are forced to. A customer's performance in any situation may be partially determined by his or her habitual reaction. For example, those in the habit of shopping in small specialty stores giving a great deal of service may be slow to accept the discount house.

Attention Is Necessary to Perceive

Before perception can take place, the consumer's attention must be secured. If consumers are not attentive to a stimulus, there is no awareness. Attention consists essentially of focusing an awareness upon certain sensory processes aroused by the percept. Consumer awareness is usually characterized by the persistence and duration of the actual sensory processes or of the imagery set up by them.

Two factors affecting the attention process are the span of attention and fluctuation in attention. A consumer's *span of attention* is simply the number of discrete objects related to products or other market factors that a person is able to apprehend simultaneously. This can be tested experimentally by asking subjects to report the objects they can remember from a large number shown them for a brief period. It has been found that the average number reported correctly under such conditions is around eight. For maximum attention, therefore, consumer messages must be kept simple and pointed so as not to exceed the individual's span of attention. Familiar phrases, simple layouts, and fewer propositions all contribute to the success of staying within the limits of the consumer's span of attention.

Fluctuations in attention occur because consumers are unable to concentrate on one object for too long a period. Every four or five seconds, attention shifts. Radio advertisers using announcements repeated at intervals do so in recognition of fluctuations in attention. Although the listener's attention shifts, in this way it is shifted to the same message. Television commercials often rely on attention-getting visuals, but these risk shifting the viewer's attention to the visual rather than the message intended.

Package design, merchandising displays, point-of-purchase materials, radio and television commercials, and printed advertisements must all take into account both the span of attention and fluctuations in attention as factors in the perceptual process.

Mental Set

Closely related to the attention factor is the concept of mental set. Psychologists refer to mental set as a person's tendency, or readiness, to react to a given stimulus. This condition may be illustrated by the preparatory commands given by a drill sergeant or a pro football quarterback. When the quarterback gives such signals at the line as "down-hup-32-64-28," he knows that this team has been "preset" to react to the number "28" by charging forward.

In the same manner, consumers are set to perceive objects and events. Consumers perceive the way they are set to perceive by their cultural, social, and personal makeup.[24] Mental set involves the direction that our attention takes; it is not just a readiness to react but a tendency to react in a certain way. Sales trainers constantly use the concept of mental set. Sales personnel, for example, are told to be constantly alert to the overt responses of prospective customers. Thus, the salesperson is set to observe and adjust the sales presentation according to reactions that previously might have been ignored. The training is aimed at placing in the trainee's mental set as many such helpful elements as possible.

Mood of the Perceiver

Mood refers to our feelings, present attitude, or state of mind. It is of great importance to consumer perception. A person in the mood induced by illness does not perceive the world in the same way as does the person who feels well. An optimist will view a situation favorably that a pessimist sees as bad. Someone in a good mood is inclined to buy more and better things. Of course, some products may be more quickly bought when the consumer is in a bad mood. A person depressed by the future may more readily purchase insurance.

Because one derives enjoyment out of the buying situation, a person in a buoyant mood may take longer to purchase. Mood can be reflected in how the product, brand, store, and advertisement are presented. A product depicted as exciting has a greater appeal than one that appears dull. We have all had the experience of looking at a label and getting the impression that the product represents something old, traditional, and out of date. Another product label using a different combination of language, design, color, and typography may give us a feeling that the product is fashionable and will give prestige.

CONSUMER PERCEPTIONS CHANGE

Consumer needs and motives continually change in response to the environment, and this causes perceptions to change both during and between purchase situations.[25] This accounts for the consumer's willingness to try a new product, react to a new advertising campaign, or seek out a different retail store. Individuals trade with a certain retailer not because of what the store represents, but what that consumer perceives it to represent. Both the consumer and the perceptions the consumer holds about the market change. These changes in turn affect the individual's needs. An advertising campaign may cause a consumer to purchase a previously undesired product. Even though both the market and the consumer are in a state of flux, it must be pointed out that certain aspects of the situation are stable—we do live in a world that is organized and orderly. The things consumers observe and the relations they have with others change, but the changes are usually predictable in the short run. Each individual can rely on the relative accuracy of personal observation. There are always new stores and products, but the bulk of the stores and products available to consumers are reasonably stable.

It is important to remember that there is a relationship between needs and perceptions. Because individuals have different needs they may have different perceptions of the marketing manager's intentions. Perception is dependent on the individual's awareness whether or not a product, brand, or store message may help him or her to solve a problem, fulfill a need, or provide satisfaction.

A major determinant of people's perception is their motivation at the time with respect to the object or experience to be perceived. A person who believes that his or her family is deprived because they lack a new car or color television will take an active interest in a game or contest offered by a company where he or she could win a big cash prize. He or she may fantasize translating the cash prize that is big enough to purchase a new car and/or color television. However, another person who is not currently interested in acquiring new possessions or who has a low need for a new car or color television may barely notice the game or contest.

Persons participating in experiments in which they are deprived of certain items tend to distort their perceptions. Consider the classic experiment of Bruner and Goodman. Working with a group of "well-to-do" and "poor" children, they found that the poor children saw the coins as physically larger than did the well-to-do children. Presumably the greater value of the coins to the poor children influenced their perceptions and they amplified the sizes.[26]

Changing perceptions frequently cause consumers to re-evaluate their previous decisions. A solution to a problem that was satisfactory in the past may be modified as perceptions of the alternatives, information, criteria, and consequences change. However, consumer perception will play as important a part in the new situation as in the previous situation.

QUESTIONS

1. Discuss the statement: "The purchase decision is simple and automatic."
2. Identify and discuss the reasons why consumers have difficulty making efficient decisions.
3. "The largest size is always cheaper." Go to a grocery store and make price comparisons on the same product but different sizes and discuss if the preceding statement is true or false.
4. Discuss how purchase planning improves the consumer's chances of successful buying.
5. Discuss the statement: "There is no way that the consumer can escape making decisions."
6. Give several examples of how two individuals can see exactly the same thing but perceive it differently.
7. Discuss with examples the elements of the perceptual process.
8. Discuss why the product's package is often spoken of as the "silent salesperson." Give examples.
9. Give examples of how the consumer's perceptions can be changed.
10. Discuss why a repeated, small advertisement may be more effective than a single, large advertisement. Give an example where this is demonstrated.
11. Generally color attracts more attention and makes a greater impression than black and white. Can you give examples of products or product categories where this may not be true? Explain your answer.
12. Define and give examples of perceptual fixation.
13. Identify ways marketing managers attempt to overcome fluctuations in attention.
14. There are theories that view consumer decisions as being based on: (a) chance, (b) habit, (c) impulse, (d) social orientation, and (e) heredity. Give examples of products or services where these theories may hold true.
15. Basic explanation consumer decision theories consider the consumer as either a risk reducer or a problem solver. Identify the types of perceived risk and discuss how marketing managers can overcome these risks.

NOTES

1. James F. Bettman and C. W. Park, "Effects of Prior Knowledge and Experience and Phase of Choice Process on Consumer Decision Process: A Protocol Analysis," *Journal of Consumer Research,* Vol. 7 (August 1980), pp. 234–38.
2. For an interesting article on the role of ignorance, see Wilbert E. Moore and Melvin M. Tumin, "Some Social Functions of Ignorance," *American Sociological Review* (December 1949), pp. 787–95.
3. Michael Ursic, "Consumer Decision Making—Fact or Fiction? Comment," *Journal of Consumer Research,* Vol. 7 (December 1980), pp. 331–33; Richard W. Olshavshy and Donald H. Granbois, "Rejoinder," *Journal of Consumer Research,* Vol. 7 (December 1980), pp. 333–34.

4. G. David Hughes, *Demand Analysis for Marketing Decisions* (Homewood, Ill.: Richard D. Irwin, Inc., 1973), p. 16.

5. Robert C. Blattberg, Peter Peacock, and Subrata K. Sen, "Purchasing Strategies Across Product Categories," *Journal of Consumer Research*, Vol. 3 (December 1976), pp. 143–54.

6. J. Paul Peter and Lawrence X. Tarpey, Sr., "A Comparative Analysis of Three Consumer Decision Strategies," *Journal of Consumer Research*, Vol. 2 (June 1975), pp. 29–37.

7. Raymond A. Bauer, "Consumer Behavior as Risk Taking," in Robert S. Hancock, ed., *Proceedings of the 43rd National Conference of the American Marketing Association* (Chicago: American Marketing Assn., 1960), pp. 389–98.

8. James W. Taylor, "The Role of Risk in Consumer Behavior," *Journal of Marketing*, Vol. 38 (April 1974), pp. 54–60.

9. Joseph F. Dash, Leon G. Schiffman, and Conrad Berenson, "Risk- and Personality-Related Dimensions of Store Choice," *Journal of Marketing*, Vol. 40 (January 1976), pp. 32–39; Charles M. Schaninger, "Perceived Risk and Personality," *Journal of Consumer Research*, Vol. 3 (September 1976), pp. 95–100.

10. William K. Cunningham, "An Experiment in the Relative Effect of Favorable and Unfavorable Messages on Choice Motivation," in Fred C. Allvin, ed., *Relevance in Marketing: Problems, Research, Action* (Ann Arbor: American Marketing Assn., 1971), pp. 450–53.

11. John A. Howard, *Marketing Management: Analysis and Planning*, rev. ed. (Homewood, Ill.: Richard D. Irwin, Inc., 1973), Chap. 3.

12. David J. Reibstein, Christopher H. Lovelock, and Richard De P. Dobson, "The Direction of Causality Between Perception, Affect, and Behavior: An Application to Travel Behavior," *Journal of Consumer Research*, Vol. 6 (March 1980), pp. 370–76.

13. Good discussions of perception can be found in Perry Bliss, *Marketing Management and The Behavioral Environment* (Englewood Cliffs: Prentice-Hall, Inc., 1970), Chap. 6; Thomas S. Robertson, *Consumer Behavior* (Glenview: Scott, Foresman & Co., 1970), Chap. 2.

14. Adapted from Paul Thomas Young, *Motivation and Emotion: A Survey of the Determinants of Human and Animal Activity* (New York: John Wiley & Sons, Inc., 1961), pp. 289–99.

15. Ibid., p. 298.

16. Hadley Cantril, "Perception and Interpersonal Relations," *American Journal of Psychiatry*, Vol. 114 (1957), pp. 119–26.

17. J.R. Brent Ritchie, "An Exploratory Analysis of the Nature and Extent of Individual Differences in Perception," *Journal of Marketing Research,* Vol. 11 (February 1974), pp. 41–49.

18. James H. Meyers and William H. Reynolds, *Consumer Behavior and Marketing Management* (Boston: Houghton Mifflin Co., 1967), p. 3.

19. Lawrence A. Crosby and James R. Taylor, "Effects of Consumer Information and Education on Cognition and Choice," *Journal of Consumer Research*, Vol. 8 (June 1981), pp. 43–56.

20. Homer E. Spence and James F. Engel, "The Impact of Brand Preference on the Perception of Brand Names: A Laboratory Analysis," in P. R. McDonald, ed., *Marketing Involvement in Society and the Economy* (Chicago: American Marketing Assn., 1970), pp. 267–71; D. P. Spence, "Subliminal Perception and Perceptual Defense: Two Sides of a Single Problem," *Behavior Science*, Vol. 12 (1967), pp. 183–93.

21. Gerald J. Gorn and Charles B. Weinberg, "The Impact of Comparative Advertising on Perception and Attitude: Some Positive Findings," *Journal of Consumer Research,* Vol. 11 (September 1984), pp. 719–27.

22. Richard F. Yalch and Rebecca Elmore Yalch, "The Effect of Numbers on the Route to Persuasion," *Journal of Consumer Research,* Vol. 11 (June 1984), pp. 522–27.

23. See: I. R. Andrews and E. R. Valenzi, "Combining Price, Brand Name, and Store Cues to Form an Impression of Product Quality," *Proceedings of the 79th Annual Convention of the American Psychological Association, 1971,* Vol. 6 (1971), pp. 649–50; J. Jacoby, J. C. Olson, and R. Haddock, "Price, Brand Name, and Product Composition Characteristics as Determinants of Perceived Quality," *Journal of Applied Psychology,* Vol. 55 (1971), pp. 570–79; J. C. Olson and J. Jacoby, "Cue Utilization in the Quality Perception Process," *Proceedings of the 2nd Annual Convention of the Association for Consumer Research,* Vol. 2 (1972), pp. 167–79.

24. Alice M. Tybout and Richard F. Yalch, "The Effect of Experience: A Matter of Salience?" *Journal of Consumer Research*, Vol. 6 (March 1980), pp. 406–13.

25. Ronald J. Dornoff, Clint B. Tankersley and Gregory P. White, "Consumers' Perceptions of Imports," *Akron Business and Economic Review*, Vol. 5 (Summer 1974), pp. 26–29; William O. Adcock, Jr., Ugur Yavas, and Anthony J. Alessandra, "Consumer Reactions to a New Money Machine," *Atlanta Economic Review*, Vol. 26 (September–October 1976), pp. 52–54.

26. J. S. Bruner and C. C. Goodman, "Value and Need as Organizing Factors in Perception," *Journal of Abnormal and Social Psychology,* Vol. 42 (January 1947), pp. 33–44.

CHAPTER 15

Consumer Evaluation

of Alternatives

CHAPTER OUTLINE

I. **ALTERNATIVE EVALUATION AND PREFERENCE RANKING**

II. **IDENTIFY AVAILABLE CONSUMER ALTERNATIVES**
    A. Product Alternatives
    B. Store Alternatives
    C. Method of Purchase Alternatives

III. **ORGANIZE INFORMATION FOR EVALUATION**
    A. Informal Organization of Consumer Information
    B. Formal Organization of Consumer Information

IV. **SELECT CRITERIA FOR ALTERNATIVE PREFERENCE EVALUATION**
    A. Sources of Criteria
    B. Types of Criteria Used
    C. Problems with Criteria Selection

V. **COMPARISON OF CONSUMER PREFERENCE ALTERNATIVES**
    A. Types of Consumer Comparison
    B. Product Alternatives Compared to Criteria
    C. Store Alternatives Compared to Criteria
    D. Method of Purchase Alternatives Compared to Criteria

VI. **RULES FOR PREFERENCE EVALUATION**
    A. Conjunctive Rule of Evaluation
    B. Disjunctive Evaluation Rule
    C. Elimination by Aspect Rule of Evaluation
    D. Lexicographic Rule of Evaluation
    E. Compensatory Evaluation Rule
    F. Use of Evaluation Rules

VII. **CONSUMER DECISION READY STATE**
    A. Individual and Family Preferences May Differ
    B. Rank of Preferences Tentative

CHAPTER OBJECTIVES

After completing your study of Chapter 15, you should be able to:

1. Discuss alternative evaluation and preference ranking.
2. Discuss identifying available consumer alternatives.
3. Explain the importance of organizing information for evaluation.
4. Discuss selecting criteria for alternative preference evaluation.
5. Make comparisons of consumer preference alternatives.
6. Discuss the rules for preference evaluation.
7. Discuss the consumer decision ready state.

At some point in making a decision the consumer must compare perceived actions that are capable of satisfying her or his market-related problems. The success of consumer decision making is directly related to how these comparisons are handled.[1] If the consumer does not correctly identify relevant alternatives, does not understand the relevance of each alternative, or has a faulty basis for comparison, then the resulting decision is likely to be unsatisfactory. In this chapter we deal with the consumer's comparison of alternative actions in the marketplace.

ALTERNATIVE EVALUATION AND PREFERENCE RANKING

When we speak of *alternative evaluation* we have in mind:

the identification of each course of action, and its comparison with others, which may offer a solution to some recognized problem of the consumer.

Alternative evaluation is the prelude to consumer choice because it provides for the ranking of preferences necessary for choice. The ranking of preference is a natural outcome of evaluation. It involves taking information gained from the search process and relating it in some meaningful way to the consumer's recognized need, want, or desire.[2] Thus, the two previous steps of the purchase process, namely problem recognition and search, are necessary preconditions to alternative evaluation. Photo 15-1 depicts the nature of alternative evaluation by consumer.

Consumer alternative evaluation is complicated by a general lack of information.[3] Even if search has been extensive, there are typically gaps in what the consumer knows. Judgment is the only ingredient available to fill these gaps. There is also the difficulty of assigning proper weights to information that the consumer has. Which criteria are more important for ranking? How can two essentially similar alternatives be compared for ranking? How can one bring together for a ranking a variety of points to a cohesive pattern? All these factors, and others, complicate the evaluation and ranking process.[4]

The consumer's emotions have to be considered in every decision. All the facts may point toward the conclusion that the purchase of a $90,000 home is illogical, but the consumer may purchase anyway. Logic may indicate to a working couple that too much of the family income goes for clothing, but they still feel the desire to look nice at work.

The particulars of the situation also always affect consumer evaluation.[5] These include the purpose of the purchase, who else is involved, alternative products, and state of need. Some evidence suggests that the situational variables dominate the evaluation of alternatives. It would be premature to suggest that they dominate every consumer evaluation.

Consumer evaluation involves rather specific activities. The definition of alternative evaluation suggests four possible activities. They are:

1. Identify available consumer alternatives.
2. Organize information for evaluation.
3. Select criteria for alternative evaluation.
4. Compare consumer alternatives.

Each of these activities is discussed below.

IDENTIFY AVAILABLE CONSUMER ALTERNATIVES

The first activity associated with alternative evaluation is to identify and rank those alternatives that offer a reasonable chance to solve the consumer problem.

It can be useful at this time to review some of the more important product, store, and methods of purchase alternatives that are available to consumers at any given time.

Photo 15-1
Consumers are constantly deciding between alternatives.

Table 15–1

Purchase Priorities for Home Appliances

Consumer durable	Guttman scale	Average years of ownership	Percent ownership	Percent of appliances purchased used	Percent of appliances purchased with dwelling	Percent of appliances gifts from outside household
Refrigerator	1	15.4	97.0	14.4	10.8	5.0
Clothes washer	2	12.5	91.0	10.5	4.3	4.2
Color TV	3	6.0	84.7	8.8	0.3	8.3
Sewing machine	4	12.0	83.2	17.5	0.4	16.1
Kitchen range oven	5	11.3	83.1	23.1	35.1	3.0
Clothes dryer	6	8.4	80.9	11.9	4.7	5.5
Stereo AM-FM radio	7	5.2	70.1	6.5	0.5	10.8
Separate freezer	8	5.5	55.2	18.6	1.9	8.4
Dishwasher	9	3.4	48.7	16.8	30.7	5.7
Room air-conditioner	10	3.0	40.5	25.3	9.5	8.9
Microwave	11	0.3	16.9	5.7	4.7	10.0
Video recorder	12	0.1	5.0	6.5	0.0	5.9

Source: Peter R. Dickson, Robert F. Lusch, and William L. Wilkie, "Consumer Acquisition Priorities for Home Appliances: A Replication and Re-evaluation," *Journal of Consumer Research,* Vol. 9, (March, 1983), pp. 432–435.

Product Alternatives

Consumers can find alternatives among products, brands, prices, deals, and impulse purchases. It is important to recognize some of the more important of these alternatives related to different types of products.

The alternatives for types of products is almost infinite. Most consumers even have a very wide range of alternatives among products of the same type because of differences in materials, quality, size, shape, and color. Because all consumers have limited income, preferences must be established among these products. Even dissimilar products compete for the consumers' income.

Some scholars feel that there is an underlying common order to the acquisition of many products—particularly durables. Although this position cannot be proved for many types of products such as convenience goods, there is supporting evidence for durables. Several studies made over time indicate a rather consistent order of purchase. Table 15-1 has purchase priorities for home appliances. These appliances represent alternatives that consumers have, and which ones the consumers tend to select.

The two most popular appliances are the refrigerator and the clothes washer. It is interesting that clothes dryers are further down the priority list. It is also interesting that air-conditioning was only tenth on the list. Relatively few of these appliances were obtained as gifts outside the home or purchased with the home. The most popular gift items were sewing machines, stereos, and microwave ovens.

The most popular built-in appliance was the kitchen range/oven. The most popular appliances were also the most durable, as indicated by the average years of ownership.

Brand alternatives are as varied as are consumers, but most consumers have tended to prefer manufacturer's brands and have distrusted private brands. Nevertheless, a significant number of consumers prefer private brands, and the number is increasing as the larger chains, discount houses, and department stores promote confidence in their own brands. Generally, homemakers, consumers with higher education, and members of large families accept private brands as an alternative more readily than do others. A desire for lower prices and confidence in the retailer can help explain why the private brand alternative is becoming more viable.

The number of price alternatives available to consumers is also varied. Consumers are affected differently by price, which helps explain these alternatives. Attitude toward price levels varies by product and appears to be more important for staple or convenience goods. Some consumers display a proneness towards deals as an alternative to price or quality in products. Deal proneness is more frequent in younger homemakers and persons who are less loyal to brands. Deal proneness is also less when the consumer buys fewer brands or less units of a product.

Impulse purchasing is an alternative to a carefully thought out evaluation of product alternatives. The tendency to exercise impulse evaluations is greater for convenience goods than for shopping goods. It is no accident that grocery stores place such products as candy, gum, cigarettes, magazines, and batteries at the checkout counter where consumers may exercise the impulse alternative.

Store Alternatives

The types of store alternatives that may be considered by consumers in a given purchase situation include the type of store, display, shelf location, and store layout.

Factors that affect the consumer's selection of store alternatives include location, price lines, assortment, service, personnel, and atmosphere. The effect of these factors is so varied among customers that it is impossible to generalize on their importance to the alternatives.[6]

The number and type of displays and such considerations as shelf height, space allocated by product, and features do condition the store alternatives. However, there is evidence that these factors influence the store alternatives less than might be expected. Displays at the end of an aisle increase sales, but the increase varies by product. Sales also vary directly with the amount of shelf space allocated to a product, but again the increase is not great. There is clear evidence that the preferred alternative for products on the shelf is waist height to eye level. Consumers resist reaching and stooping.

The different types of store layouts offer alternatives that affect consumer decision making. Grocery stores usually place fresh produce on the right as the customer enters, meat in the back, canned and dry groceries on the aisles in the middle, and impulse items in display racks up front. The produce, meat, and checkout areas have the greatest traffic flow. Department stores and discount

Photo 15-2

Store layout is important. Customers prefer products placed between waist height and eye level.

houses have long recognized the importance of locating products by customer interest. Products with similar appeal are located together. Impulse and fashion merchandise tend to have front locations in these stores. Of course, there is considerable variation among all types of stores.

Method of Purchase Alternatives

The final broad group of consumer alternatives relates to the method by which the customer goes about purchasing. We consider the use of telephones, attitude toward distance traveled, and multiple-shopping alternatives.

Telephone shopping, as an alternative to visiting the store, has been on the increase. However, it still accounts for only a small part of total retail purchases. Consumers are particularly likely to consider this alternative when purchasing services, such as landscaping, repair service, and insurance. The telephone is frequently used to fill prescriptions, but it is also being used more by department and discount houses to solicit sales. The principal reason consumers exercise this option is convenience.

The choice between traveling and not traveling is an important one. Consumers show a clear reluctance to travel much over a half mile to purchase convenience goods or a mile to purchase shopping goods. In most shopping, consumers balance the convenience of closeness against a better choice and/or lower prices. One reason for the rapid development of shopping centers is found in the consumer's attitude toward time and distance as alternatives when purchasing. Increasingly, retailers have had to go where the customers are.

Consumers, in recent years, have demonstrated a clear tendency toward multipurpose shopping. They particularly tend to combine the purchase of: (1) food, hardware, drugs, and houseware items; (2) clothing, services, food, and personal items; (3) drugs, snacks, books, and hardware; and (4) furniture, records, and clothing.

ORGANIZE INFORMATION FOR EVALUATION

The second activity associated with consumer's preference evaluation of alternatives is to organize information that has been gained from the search process. Before one can evaluate alternatives, the data must be presented in a form suitable for consideration.[7]

This step can be highly complex when dealing with business problems. It can involve the use of statistics to compile graphs and charts and to provide figures on the relative homogeneity of the data. Consumers typically organize purchase information much more casually, but they do organize it. Consider consumers who select and compare automobile brochures, tear ads for food specials from the newspaper, and mentally record information given by a neighbor concerning the better of two retail stores. Consumers may organize data about a market problem either formally or informally.

Informal Organization of Consumer Information

An informal ordering of information is mostly mental. It does not require the use of tables or charts, and there is no need to alphabetize or arrange data numerically. An informal organization may be nothing more complex than recognizing that alternative A has certain characteristics and alternative B has certain others. For example, the consumer may simply recognize that the Chevrolet has better gas mileage, is less expensive, and has a high trade-in value, while the Pontiac offers prestige, better looks, and a better ride. Most consumers probably organize facts informally. There is nothing wrong with this. Many purchase decisions are not so important as to require any other type of organization. How much consideration would a person want to give to purchasing a loaf of bread, a pair of work pants, or a hamburger? The search for information is limited for many types of convenience products, and information organization is also limited.

Formal Organization of Consumer Information

A formal organization of information requires grouping facts together by categories. It frequently entails writing the facts down, because a formal organization typically occurs when the purchase is important or when a great many individual pieces of information are involved. A formal organization may be the only way to deal with these facts. Obviously, a formal organization may vary all the way from a simple list, as in the case of a grocery list, to a highly complex statement with specifications and prices, such as a list of materials to be used in making an addition to the house. A consumer may list the advantages and disadvantages of purchasing one house over another, selecting a landscape architect, or choosing a water bed. Consumers use formal organization more often than we may think.

SELECT CRITERIA FOR ALTERNATIVE PREFERENCE EVALUATION

The third activity associated with evaluation is to select proper criteria. These criteria become the basis for comparing preference alternatives discussed in the previous sections.[8] Information, even when organized, is of little value to the consumer unless there is a method of assessing its meaning to the decision. A *criterion* is any standard of value or evaluation used as a basis for judgment. Of course, in a given situation, different consumers apply different criteria. Nevertheless, the success of the decision is related to the criteria used.

Photo 15-3
Consumers use many criteria to make decisions. Price is important to many.

Table 15–2

Types of Evaluation Criteria

Cost	Performance	Suitability	Convenience
Price	Durability	Brand	Store location
Repairs	Efficiency	Style	Store layout
Installation	Economy	Store image	Store atmosphere
Operating cost	Materials	Product image	Store services
Cost of extras	Dependability	Time factor	Product extras
Opportunity cost		Appearance	

Data are illustrative rather than inclusive.

Sources of Criteria

The three major sources of consumer criteria are personal, reference groups, and business. *Personal criteria* are among the most important consumer standards, and they involve individual perception, needs, motives, and attitudes. Conservative consumers may have gray or blue as part of their standard in purchasing a new suit, but they may also seek high quality and therefore include high price as a part of the standard. The importance of *reference group criteria* cannot be underestimated for establishing consumer criteria. A person may insist that the new car be a Ford product because that is what the family has always purchased. The attitude of friends toward the type of house, car, furniture, and clothing helps determine the criteria for the products. *Business criteria* also furnish consumers with standards because much of what is in consumers' minds about pro-products and services was put there by promotion. Business has a particular influence on the individual's confidence in product quality, brand, and service.

Types of Criteria Used

Individual consumers do not always apply the same criteria, and consumers often disagree on the importance of given criteria.[9] Nevertheless, some standard is always necessary for decision.[10] Consumers use many types of criteria, including price, repairs, efficiency, durability, brand, store image, location, and credit. Fortunately, these criteria may be grouped under four major types, as shown in Table 15-2. Cost-related criteria have to do with getting and maintaining the product. Performance and suitability are criteria concerning the use of the product or desirability of a particular store. Convenience criteria involve time, pleasure, and extras that surround the purchase.

A couple of important points can be made concerning the criteria shown in Table 15-2. First, consumers typically use more than one criterion when evaluating choices. Second, the actual number of criteria used in a given situation is typically small, although it varies by consumers. Third, it is often assumed that product cost is the most important and consistently used consumer criterion.[11] Evidence does not support this position; rather it indicates that greater importance is placed on the less tangible criteria. Finally, it is often true that one particular criterion becomes the focal point of the decision. For example, a consumer may have complete trust in a brand; thus, the consumer selects this brand over similar lower-priced brands.

Problems with Criteria Selection

Criteria selection, like search, may be mental or physical and it may take a short or long time. One does not take as long deciding on the criteria in the selection of a new coat as between methods of redecorating the home. In fact, criteria selection is one of the weakest links in consumer decision making.

The success of the selection depends, in part, on the type and amount of information received from the search process. All too often the consumer has too much or too little information for effective criteria selection. Even when information is available, the consumer either does not take the time to consider it or is not capable of analyzing the information. How many consumers know anything about components of their car, television, furniture, etc.? The authors admit that, except in superficial matters, they could not tell the construction of a quality piece of furniture from junk. As a result, criteria selection is often poorly done. This failure is one of the principal reasons that so many consumer decisions are ineffective.

COMPARISON OF CONSUMER PREFERENCE ALTERNATIVES

The fourth activity associated with consumer evaluation is the specific comparison of the various alternatives. This is the point where the criteria selected are related to the information gathered about each alternative during the search process. It is a very important part of consumer evaluation.

Types of Consumer Comparison

There are two types of comparisons that the consumer can make; these are shown in Illustration 15-2. First, two or more alternatives can be compared directly, and they can be ranked by results.[12] This type of comparison is illustrated under A of Illustration 15-1. In this case, two alternative products, Brand X and Brand Y, are compared. Each is compared in terms of how well it meets the criteria that have been established. It is assumed that the consumer

Illustration 15-1
Types of comparisons

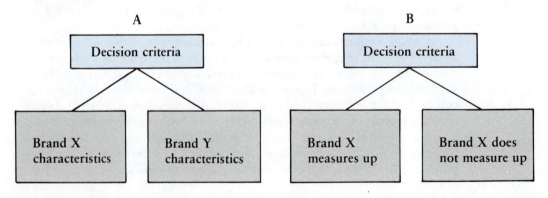

Part 4 – Consumer Evaluation and Decision

ranks the product highest that most nearly meets his or her criteria. For example, the consumer may be considering a Radio Shack recorder or a RCA recorder. The comparison may be in terms of price, features, quality, and which one is on sale.

Second, a single alternative can be directly compared to the criteria to determine if it measures up or not. This is the case with Example B in Illustration 15-1. The rank in this case is satisfactory or unsatisfactory. The consumer is considering Brand X, and no other product is involved. Brand X may be a paperback book. The consumer may consider the three criteria of reading as enjoyment, time, and price. If the consumer says, "That looks like a good book, I have the time to read, and I can afford a paperback," then the product measures up. It is ranked satisfactory, and the individual is likely to purchase.

Product Alternatives Compared to Criteria

We can now demonstrate how evaluation criteria are compared to the consumer's product, store, and method of purchase alternatives. We begin with product alternatives, as shown in Illustration 15-2.

The two major types of product alternatives are the type of product and the product brand. We observe that all the criteria do not necessarily apply to every product alternative. Consider the limited use of suitability and convenience criteria in Illustration 15-2. It is possible, although less likely, that a consumer could not use an entire category of criteria when evaluating given alternatives. It is clear that the most important criteria for product evaluation are cost and per-

Illustration 15-2
Product comparison

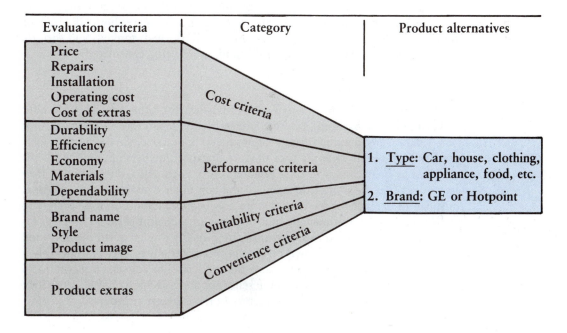

Evaluation criteria	Category	Product alternatives
Price Repairs Installation Operating cost Cost of extras	Cost criteria	
Durability Efficiency Economy Materials Dependability	Performance criteria	1. Type: Car, house, clothing, appliance, food, etc. 2. Brand: GE or Hotpoint
Brand name Style Product image	Suitability criteria	
Product extras	Convenience criteria	

Illustration 15-3
Store comparison

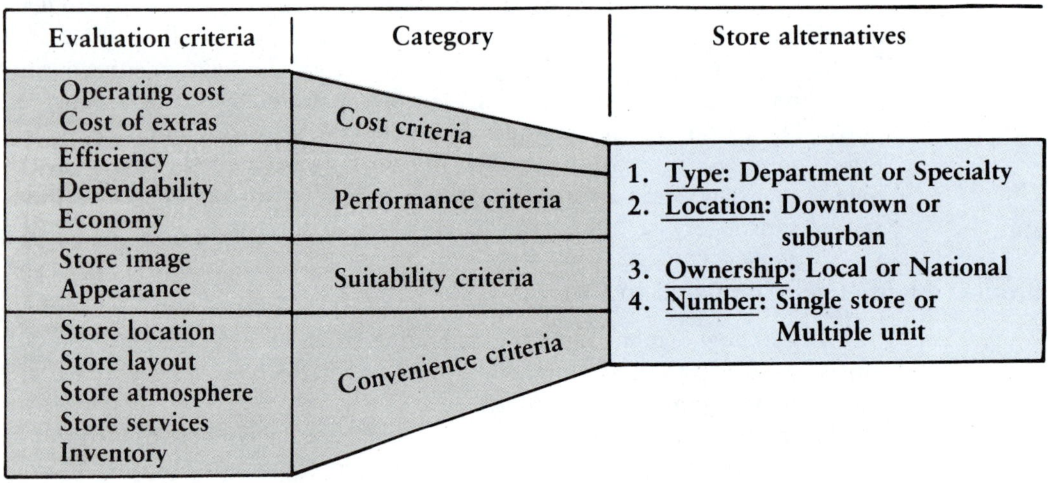

Evaluation criteria	Category	Store alternatives
Operating cost Cost of extras	Cost criteria	
Efficiency Dependability Economy	Performance criteria	1. **Type:** Department or Specialty 2. **Location:** Downtown or suburban
Store image Appearance	Suitability criteria	3. **Ownership:** Local or National 4. **Number:** Single store or Multiple unit
Store location Store layout Store atmosphere Store services Inventory	Convenience criteria	

formance criteria. Even so, the number of criteria used for selecting a product is not the same as the importance of a given criterion. For example, the consumer's decision may be made on the basis of product image even though consideration was given to the other factors listed. There is an increasing body of research which suggests that the comparison is not a simple adding of product criteria, but rather an averaging of the criteria.

If the consumer is considering buying a stove, and several brands are available, including GE and Hotpoint, the consumer compares both GE and Hotpoint to the criteria to see if each measures up. First one is ranked, and then the other. It would be the same if several brands were being considered.

Store Alternatives Compared to Criteria

Illustration 15-3 shows a typical comparison for some typical store alternatives used as a basis for ranking preferences.[13] There are more store alternatives than were found in the case of products. In practice, the consumer may be simultaneously evaluating the type of store, location, ownership, and number of units. It may be necessary to rank preferences for each. Also, one or two of these alternatives may be more important to the consumer evaluation. For example, consumer preference for the type of store may be more important than preference for whether to seek out a single-unit operator or a chain operator.

All four major categories of criteria are possibly important to the consumer when evaluating stores.[14] However, the specific criteria used vary considerably in many cases from those used to evaluate the product. The convenience criteria are very important in the ranking of preference for a store. For example, store location and layout are often deciding factors in the evaluation process.

Illustration 15-4
Method of purchase comparison

Evaluation criteria	Category	Method of purchase alternatives
Opportunity cost	Cost criteria	
Economy Dependability	Performance criteria	1. Travel: Car or Bus
		2. Type: Visit, mail order, or telephone
Time factor	Suitability criteria	3. Price: Single price or negotiated
Store atmosphere Store location Store services Inventory	Convenience criteria	4. Purchase: Single item or multiple 5. Payment: Cash or charge

Method of Purchase Alternatives Compared to Criteria

The method of purchase alternatives are as diverse as any alternatives faced by the consumer. They are also often given the least amount of attention when evaluating preferences. Illustration 15-4 shows some of the more important methods of purchase alternatives. They include method travel, type of contract, prices, manner of purchase, and preference for payment. For example, the consumer may have to balance economy and dependability when evaluating his or her preference for whether to use the automobile or bus to shop. The consumer may also have to establish preference for which day of the week and which hour of the day to grocery shop. The width of the inventory may be important to a consumer who wants to purchase several different types of items in one shopping trip.

The comparison of product, store, and method of purchase alternatives demonstrates that some of the criteria are used for every preference evaluation. Economy and dependability are criteria that may be important for the evaluation of products, stores, or method of purchase. The important consideration is that the consumer select the proper criteria and that those selected are given proper attention or the resulting preference may not be effective as a basis for making a purchase decision.

RULES FOR PREFERENCE EVALUATION

There are certain rules that can be used when evaluating consumer alternatives. These rules are concerned how the consumer deals with the criteria. There are five such rules. They are conjunctive, disjunctive, elimination by aspects, lexicographic, and compensatory.

Photo 15-4
Consumers can use many rules to help in decision making. The rules are usually consistent.

Conjunctive Rule of Evaluation

The *conjunctive rule* establishes minimum performance standards for each evaluation criterion and ranks any or all product, store, or method of purchase alternatives that surpass these standards. This rule is simple in concept and easy for the consumer to apply. In practice, the consumer accepts the first alternative that is satisfactory on the important criteria. Assume the information on rank of brands of paint as shown in Table 15-3.

Now suppose, for a consumer, the cut-off point for the four criteria is 9. In other words, the consumer will not consider a product with a total above 9. We can see that both Glidden and Olympic paints would meet the criteria. They are tentatively ranked equal, but the consumer would probably rank Olympic Paint first because of its better overall performance.

Table 15–3

Conjunctive Rule

Criteria	Brands of Paint			
	Weatherbeater	Glidden	Dutch Boy	Olympic
Price	1<	3	3	1<
Durability	2	2	3	2
Color	4	1<	2	2
Application	2	2	2	2
Total	10	(8)	10	(7)

Consumers may use the conjuctive rule because they have limited ability to process information. The consumer can focus on those alternatives which meet the criteria and eliminate others easily in the evaluation. It is also useful in low-involvement situations because the consumer can select the first alternative, thus reducing the time and effort spent shopping. It is perhaps true that the conjunctive rule underlies all other evaluation rules, and it is often used in combination with the others.

Disjunctive Evaluation Rule

The *disjunctive rule* uses cut-off points like the conjunctive rule, but they are used differently. When using the disjunctive rule, the consumer establishes cut-off points on each criterion, but any alternative is acceptable that is above cut-off on any single criteria. For example, in Table 15-3, if the cut-off point on any given criteria is 2, then Weatherbeater qualifies on price, Glidden qualifies on color, and Olympic qualifies on price. These cut-off points are indicated by a <, and these three alternatives are ranked equal. The consumer may choose any one of these brands. It could be that the consumer will select Weatherbeater, Glidden, and Olympic each one-third of the time. The consumer may also re-evaluate the three acceptable brands based on the use of a second evaluation rule to break the tie. For example, the consumer may still rank the Olympic brand highest because of its overall performance.

Elimination by Aspect Rule of Evaluation

The *elimination by aspect rule* of evaluation requires that the consumer rank each criterion by importance along with its cut-off point.[15] The consumer ranks first the product that is highest on the most important criteria. If more than one brand passes this cut-off point, the consumer considers the second most important criteria and so on until the preference ordering is made. Consider the information in Table 15-4.

The consumer begins the evaluation with price, which is the most important criterion. RCA, Zenith, GE, and Sharp are all below the $370 criterion for price. The consumer moves to the next criterion, style. RCA, Zenith, and GE are satisfactory at this point because each rates very good in style. Only Zenith is left after the evaluation of dependability since it receives an A+ on this criterion. Thus,

Table 15-4
Elimination-by-Aspect Rule

| Criteria | Television Sets | | | | |
	RCA	Zenith	GE	Sharp	Sony
1. Price	[$369]**	[$359]	$439	[$349]	$389
2. Style	[VG]	[VG]	[VG]	G	P
3. Dependability	A–	A+	A	A–	A
4. Repair Cost	M	M	L	H	H

*Evaluation criteria used: Price = $370; Style = VG, G, P; Dependability = A+, A, A–; Repair cost = L (Low), M (Medium), H (High).
**[ ] indicates the cut-off points.

the consumer ranks Zenith first because it rates best overall on the first three criteria. RCA and GE tie for second and Sharp ranks third. There is no need to consider the fourth criterion.

Lexicographic Rule of Evaluation

The *lexicographic evaluation rule* has the consumer rank the criteria by importance and ranks first the alternative that performs best on the most important criteria.[16] If there is a tie the consumer considers, in succession, each lower criterion until there is a clear choice. In Table 15-4, if repair cost rather than price were the most important criterion, then the consumer would immediately select the GE television because it performs best (L) where repairs are concerned. The price, style, and dependability factors would never come into play. However, Zenith is the clear choice if dependability is the most important criteria. There is no need for the consumer to consider criteria beyond the most important one unless two projects tie on the most important criterion.[17] This evaluation rule differs from the elimination by aspect in that there is no need to establish cut-off points for each criteria. It is overall performance on the criteria that decides.

Compensatory Evaluation Rule

We refer to the above evaluation rules as noncompensatory because good performance on one criterion cannot compensate for poor performance on another. There are occasions when the consumer may want to average out good features against poor features. In other words, the product may not excel on any feature, but be preferred because of overall high performance. Consider the example presented in Table 15-5. The consumer is attempting to evaluate the alternative of shopping downtown or in three different shopping centers. In the example, we observe that shopping center number 2 is ranked most preferred even though it did not rank first on a single feature in desirability. It even ranked above downtown, which was the most desirable shopping location based on two features. The reason for this preference was that shopping center number 2 was consistently high on all the desirable features.

Table 15–5

Use of Compensatory Rule

| Criteria | Shopping Locations | | | |
	Downtown	Shopping Center 1	Shopping Center 2	Shopping Center 3
Accessibility	3	3	2	1
Nearness	5	1	2	3
Size	1	4	2	2
Product Lines	1	3	2	4
Totals	10	11	8	10

Note: 1 = highest possible rating, 5 = lowest possible rating

Use of Evaluation Rules

It is understood that different consumers use the evaluation rules in a variety of ways, including a combination. There is currently no definitive evidence to indicate which of the rules are most used. One limited study is presented in Table 15-6. It deals only with the evaluation of an automobile, and it would be difficult to generalize from this data. However, the table does demonstrate an interesting pattern of use for the evaluation rules.

The lexicographic rule was by far the most important with individuals in this sample. The next most important was the compensatory rule. It is interesting that the third most important evaluation rule among these respondents was a combination of conjunctive and compensatory. The conjunctive rule was used very little by itself. In this study the use of a given rule did not change when the evaluation was made more difficult by the introduction of more types of automobiles.

Consumers tend to be fairly consistent in their use of evaluation rules. That is to say they tend to use the same type of evaluation rule in similar situations involving the same general type alternatives. Consumers tend to use the simple conjunctive, disjunctive, elimination by aspects, or lexicographic rules in low-involvement evaluations. They do this to reduce the mental cost of making a decision. High-involvement evaluations tend to use the more complex evaluation rules such as compensatory and the combination rules. It is also possible that in complex situations, different evaluation rules are used at different stages in the deliberation.

CONSUMER DECISION READY STATE

We know that consumer decision making on products, stores, and methods of purchase is the natural outcome of an evaluation that establishes preferences. Thus, when the consumer has a list of preferences, she or he is in a ready state to make the final decision. There are a couple of points that we must mention before moving on to the consumer's final decision.

Table 15–6

Use of Evaluation Rules in the Selection of Brand of Automobile

Brand Choice Rule	Verbal Description	Percentage Using this Choice Rule
Disjunctive	I chose the car that had a really good rating on at least one characteristic.	0%
Conjunctive	I chose the car that didn't have any bad ratings.	0.6%
Lexicographic	I looked at the characteristic that was most important to me and chose the car that was best in that characteristic. If two or more of the cars were equal on that characteristic, I then looked at my second most important characteristic to break the tie.	60.7%
Compensatory	I chose the car that had a really good rating when you balanced the good ratings with the bad ratings.	32.1%
Disjunctive-conjunctive	I first eliminated any car that didn't have at least one really good score and then chose from the rest the product that didn't have a really bad score on any characteristic.	0%
Conjunctive-disjunctive	I first eliminated the cars with a bad rating on any characteristic and then chose from the rest the one with a high score on any characteristic.	0%
Disjunctive-compensatory	I first eliminated any car that didn't have at least one really good rating and then chose from the rest of the cars that seemed the best when you balanced the good ratings with the ones that were bad.	1.1%
Conjunctive-compensatory	I first eliminated the cars with a really bad rating on any characteristic and then chose from the rest the one that seemed the best overall when you balanced the good ratings with the bad ratings.	5.4%

Source: Derived from M. Renly and R. Holman, "Does Task Complexity or One Intercorrection Affect Choice of an Information Processing Strategy: An Empirical Investigation, in W.D. Perrault, Jr., ed., *Advances in Consumer Research IV* (Chicago: Association for Consumer Research, 1977), p. 189.

Individual and Family Preferences May Differ

How individual consumers decide their preferences is reasonably clear when considering only a single person's involvement, as we have done in our discussion thus far. Our use of a single set of alternatives also simplifies the matter. The reason is that there are no complications caused by the interaction of persons within the family. If the individual or family always considered only its needs, one would be able to predict consumer decisions by relating them directly to needs. The problem is that individuals and families scale their preferences on the basis of many factors, including relationships within the family and with persons external to the family. This causes all types of unpredictable differences among consumers. We cannot predict with exactness a consumer's desire for goods and services until we explain the interactions and pressures that occur within these groups. One point is clear: individual and family preferences do differ. No two consumers or families are likely to weigh all the criteria relating to specific alternatives exactly the same way. The result is that each consumer and family is individualistic, desiring products to fit its particular requirements.

The effect of influences on preferences also varies between single-member and multimember families. In a single-member family that has no contact with any relations, the only considerations involved are personal preferences and reference group influences. In a multimember family, all the factors are at work but even here the effect varies. For example, a consumer living with relatives is not affected in the same way as one living with a spouse or with parents. A child is affected differently than a parent. Even the number of parents or children that make up a family can cause variations in the scales of preference held by the family.

Rank of Preferences Tentative

The total environment in which the individual functions is dynamic, not static. Thus, the ranking of personal preferences is always tentative until the actual sale takes place. A given circumstance may cause one consumer to act impulsively and immediately to change established preferences. For example, a father may start out to purchase new jeans for his son and end up with a new jacket for himself. The jacket was there to be seen, and it was just what the father had wanted for some time, although he had never consciously considered it a part of his assortment.

New information comes to the consumer right up to the moment of purchase. New information may cause consumers to re-evaluate their preference scale at any time. A family may have decided to buy living room furniture before a second car, but a particularly good offer on a new car may cause a quick reshuffling of preferences. The point is that consumers do scale preferences tentatively, and the scales influence their market behavior. Because references are tentative, the only positive way to determine a consumer's product preference is to observe the actual order of purchase. We can now turn our attention to how the negotiation takes place within families whose members have different established preferences for products and services.

QUESTIONS

1. Identify and discuss the activities involved in evaluation of alternatives.
2. Go to a grocery store in your town and identify all the brands of breakfast cereal in the store. Are they all product alternatives for you? Discuss your answer.
3. Do you consider price an important factor in selecting alternatives? Is this true for all products? Discuss your answer.
4. If you were a store manager with a limited amount of eye-level shelf space, what products would you put at eye level? Private brands or national brands? Explain your answer.

5. Are the criteria you use to evaluate alternatives the same for all products? Discuss your answer with examples.
6. Identify the three major sources of consumer criteria. Which has the most influence on you. Why?
7. Discuss why criteria selection is one of the weakest links in consumer decision making.
8. Discuss with examples the two types of comparison that the consumer can make when evaluating alternatives.
9. Define and discuss the conjunctive and disjunctive rule of evaluation.
10. Why is it important for marketing managers to know the evaluation rules of consumers?
11. Identify the several grocery stores in your town. Now rank them in your order of preference. Discuss the criteria you used.
12. Identify the methods of purchase available to you to purchase a pair of shoes. Rank the methods in order of preference. Discuss why you ranked them this way.
13. Why is it important for a marketing manager to know the evaluative criteria of a consumer?
14. Talk to three individuals and have them identify the factors that are most important to them when evaluating alternatives of automobiles. Why do you think there is or is not a difference in the factors?
15. Is your set of evaluative criteria the same as your parents? Discuss why or why not.

NOTES

1. Naresh K. Malhotra, "Multi-Stage Information Processing Behavior: An Experimental Investigation," *Journal of the Academy of Marketing Science,* Vol. 10 (Winter 1982), pp. 54–71.
2. Wilfried R. Vanhonacker, "Testing the Exact Order of an Individual's Choice Process in an Information-Theoretic Framework," *Journal of Marketing Research,* Vol. XXII (November 1985), pp. 377–87.
3. Noel Capon and Marion Burke, "Individual, Product Class, and Task Related Factors in Consumer Information Processing," *Journal of Consumer Research,* Vol. 7 (June 1980), pp. 314–26.
4. C. Whan Park and Richard J. Lutz, "Decision Plans and Consumer Choice Dynamics," *Journal of Marketing Research,* Vol. XIX (February 1982), pp. 108–15.
5. Russell W. Belk, "An Exploratory Assessment of Situational Effects in Buyer Behavior," *Journal of Marketing Research,* Vol. 11 (May 1974), pp. 156–63.
6. Jordan L. Louviere, "Using Discrete Choice Experiments and Multinominal Logic Choice Models to Forecast Trial in a Competitive Retail Environment: A Fast Food Restaurant Illustration," *Journal of Retailing,* Vol. 60 (Winter 1984), pp. 81–107.

7. Noel Capon and Roger Davis, "Basic Cognitive Ability Measures as Predictors of Consumer Information Processing Strategies," *Journal of Consumer Research,* Vol. 11 (June 1984), pp. 551–63.

8. Cathy J. Cobb, "The Use of Simplifying Choice Tactics in the Purchase of a Consumer Nondurable Product," in Donald R. Glover, ed., *Proceedings of the 1984 Convention of the American Academy of Advertising* (American Academy of Advertising, 1984), pp. 115–21.

9. Rashi Glazer, "Multiattribute Perceptual Bias and Revealing of Preference Structure," *Journal of Consumer Research*, Vol. 11 (June 1984), pp. 510–21.

10. James R. Bettman, "A Threshold Model of Attitude: Sales Factor Decisions," *Journal of Consumer Research*, Vol. 1 (September 1974), pp. 30–35.

11. Hazel F. Ezell and William H. Motes, "Differentiating Between the Sexes: A Focus on Male-Female Grocery Shopping Attitudes and Behavior," *Journal of Consumer Marketing,* Vol. 2 (Spring 1985), pp. 29–40.

12. Eric J. Johnson and Robert J. Meyer, "Compensatory Choice Models of Noncompensatory Processes: The Effect of Varying Context," *Journal of Consumer Research*, Vol. 11 (June 1984), pp. 528–41.

13. Hazel F. Ezell and Giselle D. Russell, "Single and Multiple Person Household Shoppers: A Focus on Grocery Store Selection Criteria and Grocery Shopping Attitudes and Behavior," *Journal of the Academy of Marketing Science*, Vol. 13 (Winter 1985), pp. 171–87.

14. Terry E. Powell, Daniel C. Bello, and Gregory A. Parker, "The Impact of Product Orientations on Retail Store Choice," in John H. Summey, Blaise J. Bergiel, and Carol H. Anderson, eds., *A Spectrum of Contemporary Marketing Ideas, 1982* (Southern Illinois University at Carbondale and Southern Marketing Assn., 1982), pp. 94–97.

15. Joel Huber and John McCann, "The Impact of Inferential Beliefs on Product Evaluations," *Journal of Marketing Research*, Vol. XIX (August 1982), pp. 324–33.

16. Eric J. Johnson and Robert J. Meyer, op. cit., pp. 528–41.

17. Michael D. Reilly and Rebecca H. Holman, "Marketing Strategy Based On Consumer Decision Style: The Lexicographic Critical Attribute," in Robert H. Ross, Frederic B. Kraft, and Charles H. Davis, eds., *1981 Proceedings Southwestern Marketing Association Conference* (Wichita State University and Southwestern Marketing Assn., 1981), pp. 134–37.

CHAPTER 16

Consumer Purchase
Decision

CHAPTER OUTLINE

I. CONSUMER DECISION

II. DECISION MAKING BY INDIVIDUAL CONSUMERS
  A. Choices Determined by Marginal Utility
  B. Modification in Utility Concept of Choice

III. FACTORS AFFECTING INDIVIDUAL'S DECISION
  A. Personal Needs
  B. Intended Use
  C. Degree of Motivation
  D. Experience with Product
  E. Price
  F. Logic of External Information
  G. Individual Consumer Decision

IV. DECISION MAKING WITHIN FAMILIES
  A. Personal Readiness to Negotiate
  B. Family Member Involvement
  C. Type of Negotiation

V. FACTORS AFFECTING FAMILY DECISION
  A. Ability to Persuade
  B. Power Within the Family
  C. Family Relationships
  D. Expected Outcome of Negotiation
  E. Family Income
  F. The Family Purchase Decision

VI. MISCONCEPTIONS ABOUT CONSUMER DECISIONS
  A. Normal Decisions and Correct Decisions
  B. Individual Versus Social View of Normality
  C. Habitual and Impulse Behavior
  D. Rationalization Is Normal

CHAPTER OBJECTIVES

After completing your study of Chapter 16, you should be able to:

1. Discuss consumer purchase decisions.
2. Discuss decision making by individual consumers.
3. Explain the factors affecting individual's decisions.
4. Discuss decision making within families.
5. Discuss the factors affecting family decisions.
6. Explain the misconceptions about consumer decisions.

The consumer's purchase decision is a natural follow-up to the selection of alternatives. The consumer cannot escape the hard conclusion, at some point in time, that certain products are preferred over others. No matter whether the choice is based on insufficient facts and inadequately thought out, the point remains that there can be no purchase without recognizing that one alternative is preferred over all others. In this chapter we deal with the purchase decision which establishes the preference for alternatives.

CONSUMER DECISION

Individual consumers have a variety of wants but limited means to satisfy them. Consumers therefore choose to satisfy some wants and to put off some, and to leave some unsatisfied. The *consumer decision* refers to:

the mental process of choosing the most desirable alternative from among those available.[1]

The consumer decision implies that consumers can order their preferences from among product, store, and method of purchase alternatives.[2] A consumer may have preferences for some products required immediately and preferences for products long before entering the market. Consumers may even have preferences for products that they never intend to purchase. The consumer's preferences may change several times before he or she actually enters the market.[3] The Armstrong ad shown in Figure 16-1 emphasizes the consumer consequence of making the correct decision.

If this ability to specify what is desired did not exist, then no consumer would ever purchase. It is difficult to imagine a person entering into a purchase agreement when wants are not known, when the mind cannot be made up between desired products, or when there is indifference to the alternative products offered for sale. The very act of sale is prima facie evidence that the consumer, at that moment, would rather spend money on the designated product than on any other thing. This is what scaling of preferences means.

A consumer may be in any of four possible decision states where a particular problem is concerned. They are: (1) rejected, (2) undecided, (3) partially decided, and (4) decided. A solution is rejected when the consumer consciously decides not to pursue that course of action. This state, more than any other, may cause the individual to seek a different solution. A person is undecided when he or she has no preference for a solution among the alternatives offered. In this state, the consumer cannot make up his or her mind. A person may have decided to buy an iron but be undecided as to which brand to purchase. A consumer in this state will not act. Indecision is a signal to obtain more information about the problem.

A partially decided state covers a wide range of possibilities, from practically undecided to practically decided. A person is partially decided when there is a tendency to accept one solution. The consumer may be "sold" on the product but feel that the price is just a little high. Just a little more negotiation can cause the person to act. When the consumer has decided some action, the action may be to

Figure 16-1
Advertisement emphasizing decision making

Go on, cut. You'll be brilliant. Armstrong guarantees it.

Install your new Armstrong sheet vinyl floor with a Trim and Fit kit, and if you goof while cutting or fitting, your Armstrong retailer will replace both the flooring and the kit.

Free. That's the Fail-Safe™ Guarantee. Just see your local home center or building supply retailer for details.

FREE. For a free Floor Project Planning Pack, call the Armstrong Consumer Line at 1 800 233 3823 and ask for Dept. 69GWD. Or, send this coupon: Armstrong, Dept. 69GWD, P.O. Box 3001, Lancaster, PA 17604

Name _____
(please print)
Street _____
City _____
State _____ Zip _____

Armstrong
so nice to come home to™

Courtesy of Armstrong World Industries, Inc.

buy, not to buy, or to defer the purchase until later. Business attempts to achieve a favorable decided state in consumers.

The consumer's decision would be much simpler to determine if only the individual's interest were involved. Often this is the case, but there are also situations in which others participate in the decision. Actually, the consumer decision can be divided into two separate types of situations. One situation involves the individual consumer buying personal requirements. The other situation occurs when the individual participates in establishing priorities for products that affect the family as a whole.[4] Most consumers must contend with both these situations, and in both cases the person is affected by external factors. In the first situation the consumer decides individual wishes in the light of external information. In the latter case, there is the extra consideration of negotiating over differences in each family member's individual priorities. The remainder of this chapter is based on these two types of consumer decisions.

DECISION MAKING BY INDIVIDUAL CONSUMERS

Traditional economics have made a significant contribution to consumer behavior in the area of choice.[5] The concept of marginal utility analysis necessarily deals with product choices. At this point we want to demonstrate its application to preference scaling and discuss some modifications necessary to apply the concept to the real world.

Choices Determined by Marginal Utility

In its essence, marginal analysis specifies that products with more utility to the individual are higher in order of purchases. *Utility* is:

the ability to satisfy a human want.

Marginal utility is:

the extra satisfaction derived from having one more incremental unit of the product.

Table 16-1 shows how marginal analysis can be used to rank consumer purchases for three products.

The individual apportions expenditures so that the marginal utility (MU) of each product considered is proportional to price (P).[6] In other words, MU/P must equal 1/1 for each product. When this condition exists, price measures a product's worth to the consumer and its rank compared to other products. Thus in Illustration A, where the consumer has $285 in income, he or she spends $180 on an apartment, uses up $90 in gasoline, and spends $15 on ham hocks. This allocation shows rent is twelve times and gasoline six times as important as ham hocks on the individual's preference scale.

Suppose our consumer is laid off from work (example B) and must resort to welfare. If the consumer's scale of preference is unchanged but income declines by $247, then expenditures must be reallocated. The person moves to a lower-priced

Table 16–1

Consumer Decision Making Using Marginal Analysis

Item	Distribution of income per month		
	A	B	C
A. $\dfrac{MU}{P}$ of rent	$180 (12:1)	$156 (12:1)	$165 (11:1)
B. $\dfrac{MU}{P}$ of gasoline	90 (6:1)	78 (6:1)	180 (12:1)
C. $\dfrac{MU}{P}$ of ham hocks	15 (1:1)	13 (1:1)	15 (1:1)
Totals	$285	$247	$360

( )means ratio of satisfaction and importance relative to ham hock.
*Two basic assumptions:
  a. Total money expenditure is fixed in each case.
  b. There is no diminishing marginal utility.

apartment and purchases less gasoline and ham hocks. Obviously, total consumer satisfaction has decreased even though shelter is still relatively the most important item.

Another change in circumstance, such as that in Illustration C, can cause a re-evaluation of the consumer's scale of preferences. Perhaps the person finds a better job than previously held, but it requires considerable driving. Thus gasoline becomes a number one on the product preference scale. It is followed by rent and ham hocks.

Modification in Utility Concept of Choice

The economic concept of marginal utility is a fair approximation of how consumers order preferences. However, several modifications must be explained in order to relate the concept to the real world.[7]

First, under marginal utility analysis, the individual always attempts to maximize dollar satisfaction between products using cold logic. In practice, consumer emotions get in the way of logic. The consumer may order preferences based on such nonmonetary factors as beauty, comfort, or uniqueness. A lack of sufficient information may often make it impossible to maximize. The consumer may be able to do no better than to optimize preference ranks. Furthermore, the ranking is much less factual than found in economics.[8] The consumer simply says, "We are going to buy a new floor polisher this month, and next month we can see about new clothes for the kids."

Second, most products are not made in infinitely small increments. The consumer must always choose between whole products which are often expensive. That is to say, consumers deal in discrete rather than incremental values. If a car, refrigerator, shoes, or other items could be purchased in one-cent increments, these items could rank high on many individuals' preferences who cannot even consider the outlay of hundreds of dollars for the items as actually sold. The only choice in reality is to go without.

Third, marginal analysis is based on an explicit comparison of products. Often in the real world, the individual doesn't even think in terms of comparisons. The only consideration absolutely necessary to make a decision is that the consumer be able to say, "I want that." Such a statement ranks the desired product first and all other products collectively second. For example, as an individual drives home after a difficult day, the thought emerges, "I'm sure tired. I believe I'll stop by the drugstore and pick up a book to relax with this evening." In this case, there is no direct comparison of products, but the consumer is aware that $3.95 will give more pleasure spent this way than any other way. If someone pins the consumer down at the time of the purchase, the individual is able to explain the reasons for the action taken.

Fourth, marginal analysis does not consider the reasons that lie behind the decision. Both individual and environmental factors do influence the decision. These factors are considered more completely below.

FACTORS AFFECTING INDIVIDUAL'S DECISION

Each individual consumer is responsible for ranking personal preferences, but there are always external influences that affect the decision.[9] Illustration 16-2 demonstrates the point. The internal factors affecting decision making are the physiological and psychological considerations that, taken together, summarize what the person is.[10] External influences may be derived directly from search, as discussed in the previous chapter, or may be the result of normal human interaction. Even though individuals make up a family, each person's external influences differ in some respects. We discuss in the following paragraphs some of the more important internal and external factors of individual decision making.

Personal Needs

Need is an important consideration to the consumer in decision making. Every individual has some needs different from others. As Figure 16-2 shows, the hair-care needs of individuals vary.

If it is spring and we do not have a lawn mower, we may plan to postpone including golf clubs in our current assortment. The lawn, because it does not stop growing, takes a higher priority. A certain proportion of our income must always go to fulfill our physical needs for such items as nutritious food and basic clothing. However, we must remember that our emotional needs can be just as strong. Therefore, our choices include provision for "pretty" clothes and "desirable" food along with the warmth and nutrition provided by these products.

Intended Use

Scales of personal preference cannot be separated from the consumer's attitude toward the intended use of the product. As individuals we get more pleasure out of some activities than others, and we select those products or brands in our assortment for which the use is compatible with our desires. A set of golf clubs ranks higher than a new rototiller on the scale of preferences of a

Illustration 16-1
Influences on individual preferences

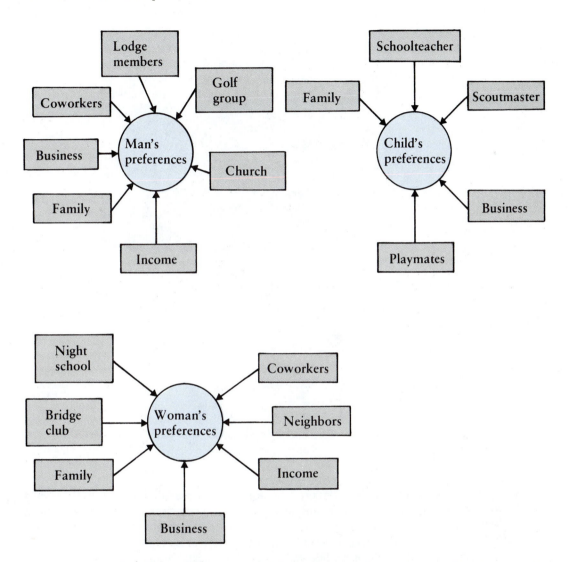

golfer. The rototiller may rank higher for a garden enthusiast. The difference between the two consumers is the attitude toward the activity to which the product is applied. One person's fun is another person's drudgery.

Degree of Motivation

The relative intensity of the consumer's motives plays an important part in decision making. No product or brand is included in our assortment scale until the motivation for it reaches a sufficient intensity level. What the individual is motivated toward is also important to the ranking. The level and direction vary

Figure 16-2
Hair-care needs of women

WHATEVER YOUR COLOR, HÄLSA HIGHLIGHTS YOU.

Every color of hair has its own special glow. Uncover yours with Hälsa.

WALNUT LEAVES
Deepens the
natural shine of
brown, dark brown
or black hair.

MARIGOLD
Brings out gold-
en highlights in
natural blonde
or lightened hair.

GINGER ROOT
Lights the fire of
red, reddish brown
or auburn hair.

CHAMOMILE
Warms the glow
of ash blonde, light
brown or light
chestnut hair.

HÄLSA SWEDISH BOTANICAL SHAMPOOS AND CONDITIONERS

© 1986, S.C. Johnson & Son, Inc.

S.C. Johnson & Son, Inc.

among people and between products for the same person. In effect, each product offers interference to the ranking of all other products. The longer a desire is postponed, the higher the product is placed on our preference scale. Also, a product toward which we have a more positive motivation tends to be ranked higher. For example, if the golf clubs have been put off from year to year, the consumer may plan to purchase them instead of the needed lawn mower in spite of the urgency of cutting the grass. The consumer may choose to borrow a lawn mower from a neighbor in order to obtain the clubs, even though this move is personally distasteful. In either case, brand is typically more important in selecting the clubs than the lawn mower.

Experience with Product

Past product experience is important for consumer decision making. Past experience with products or brands may involve known satisfaction or it may involve known dissatisfaction.[11] Both types of experience affect current decisions. We may have a preference for a particular brand of golf club, such as Wilson, because of our experience using these clubs borrowed from a friend. It should also be noted that our experience with lawn mowers may largely account for our preferring golf clubs to lawn mowers.[12] If we cannot find Wilson golf clubs, we may decide to choose the next best brand in our assortment; but the second choice may rank lower on our preference scale than the original choice. As a result, we may put off the purchase. An individual's desire for fresh, garden-ripe tomatoes may have to wait for spring. In the meantime, the person may, or may not, decide to take the half-rotten cold-storage tomatoes offered in the grocery store. If the consumer does not like cold-storage tomatoes, then tomatoes are placed further down the list of product preferences.

Price

Price is also a factor that influences consumer decisions. The importance of price rests on its effect on consumer income. Consumers may wish to rank many types of products or brands high on their preference list, but price makes this prohibitive. Evidence shows that consumers consider price important in their choice of brands and package size.[13] The evidence is that perceptions have considerable influence on the consumer's conception of price. Price is more important in determining rank for immediate wants than for future wants. When individual preferences are related to expectations, the consumer discounts price with the attitude that, "I will worry about that when the time comes." Of course, the consumer cannot put off considering price for purchases that are contemplated in the near future. Thus, a consumer may rank a very much desired but expensive product lower on the preference scale because the same money can buy several other needed products. Extra income can push some products, which could not be afforded before, up on the consumer's preferences.

There is evidence to support the fact that consumers can hedge the cost of new products by purchasing smaller quantities. A study of 1,480 individual new brand purchasers discovered this.[14] Consumers adjusted by purchasing a smaller package size rather than purchasing fewer units of the product. As one might expect, the respondents purchased a larger quantity on the second trial. Presumably, those who did not like the product did not have a second trial.

Logic of External Information

Consumers can be persuaded to select certain products by the logic of external information when it is received. Consumers may not always recognize sound and logical information when it is received, but they do react to perceived logic. If the logic is sound it can cause a re-evaluation of consumer internal needs and motivation.[15] The consumer may seek information from a business, but, if it does not make sense, the consumer will discount or discard it. Even information from a trusted friend is discounted if the consumer does not perceive it as "sound." Figure 16-3 has a strong appeal to logic based on a single point.

Logical external information may be discarded by a consumer when choosing products if it is not compatible with the consumer's own logic. On a given product choice, the consumer may receive a great deal of information, some sought and some unsought. The facts are filtered through the individual's thought processes, and that which is incompatible is either not used or not given the weight of other data. Of course, sufficient sound external information may cause the consumer to reassess his or her own position.

Individual Consumer Decision

An individual living alone and acting independently makes consumer decisions differently than does a member of a family. The independent consumer does not have to answer to anyone. When the individual reduces uncertainty that a given alternative is best to the point where she or he is willing to act, then the

Figure 16-3
Advertisement that emphasizes an appeal to logic

Quaker Oats

decision is made. Nothing stands between the consumer and the action chosen. Family members face another level of interaction, as we shall see in the next section.

DECISION MAKING WITHIN FAMILIES

Over any period of time, the average family buys some products for individual use and some products for use by the group. There are probably as many, if not more, instances of group need as there are of individual need. A different kind of product decision is necessary in these instances because the desires of others must be taken into account.

There are three important preconditions for family decision making: personal readiness to negotiate, family member involvement, and type of negotiation. We call these preconditions because they affect whether the individual is willing to negotiate as well as the nature of that negotiation.

Personal Readiness to Negotiate

Family members enter into product negotiations with their scales of preferences set, or they must very quickly place them in order. Photo 16-1 shows a family engaged in negotiation about a new car. Three situations may develop at

Photo 16-1
Family members enter into product negotiations with their scales of preference set, or they must quickly place them in order. Family members discuss purchases at home, while doing routine activities.

this point. First, if there is general agreement on the order of preferences, the negotiation stops there, and the family's assortment needs are determined. Second, if any family member refuses to compromise on preferences, the other members must either give in, overrule the holdout, or defer discussion to a later date. If a family member is given his or her way or if a decision is deferred, then the assortment, at least for now, is determined, and there is no further need for decision. Third, the family can compromise over differences in product ranking through discussion.[16] It is primarily in this third case that there must be a willingness on the part of family members to negotiate their differences. Without a willingness to negotiate, there can be no further progress toward a workable scale of preferences.[17]

Family Member Involvement

It is not necessary that each member of the family enter into negotiation over every product. Preference negotiation normally takes place between only those family members directly involved in the decision.[18] Parents don't usually consult the children in the negotiation over the inclusion of a new car, furniture, or appliances in the assortment. Mother and daughter may leave father out of the consideration of a new dress. In some cases, when product replacement is routine, no one need be consulted. One parent knows how new shoes for the kids, or a loaf of bread, rank for the family. The reader must be aware that the family assortment is a loose collection of products. At any given time, this assortment exists for the individual family member, for small groups within the family, and for the family as a whole. There is probably never complete understanding as to a final list of preferences except when an actual choice must be made at the moment of purchase.

If the individual is satisfied to remain an observer during the discussion, then no ordering of preferences may be necessary. The consumer may not see the discussion as relevant to the problem, or just may not care about the outcome. For example, an individual may remain passive as two friends discuss the merits of going fishing or doing yard work. In the case of family decisions, the passive individual has no say about the rank of the product under discussion in the family assortment.

If the individual wishes to enter into the discussion, he or she must either have formed prior opinions about the product(s) under consideration or must be capable of forming on-the-spot opinions about the product or its placement in the assortment. This fact is just as true between individuals and friends as it is between individuals and the family group. Unless one has opinions about the product's importance, one cannot discuss the problem intelligently. A quick decision is possible because the ordering of an individual's preferences is as much a mental activity as anything else. It does not require significant factual information to back up the opinions expressed. Needed facts can even be obtained during the discussion. When forced to decide, the individual states the feelings of the moment.

Type of Negotiation

Once the individual becomes involved in negotiating product preferences, the question becomes, "What type of negotiation is to be undertaken?" Four situations are possible. First, the individual consumer may enter into *direct interaction* with external social group members without any family consultation. This is most likely to happen with the single-member family, or when a family member is making a personal product decision that does not involve the family. The consumer may seek advice from these outside parties, or it may be offered without being sought. Second, the individual may enter into a *general discussion* with the entire family without any prior consultations among individual family members. The family members, as a group, may discuss such topics as whether to spend money on a vacation which may require curtailing expenditures for the children's clothing and family entertainment. Each member expresses his or her preferences between these expenditures freely, without any prior consultation with other family members or with outsiders.

Third, the individual may enter into *private negotiations* with individual family members prior to the general discussion. No external group advice is sought. It often happens that family members influence each other before any general discussion takes place. When this prediscussion occurs, there is likely to be joint action in the general discussion. Family members form coalitions or cliques in order to get their way. Children often gang up on parents in order to get a new toy or to gain permission to see a certain movie. Sometimes one parent prefers a different restaurant to the one selected by the other.

Fourth, the individual consumer may enter into *prior discussion* with family members, and one or more family members may also be obtaining information and advice from sources outside the family. The latter is the most complicated type of family negotiation. Any type of group agreement prior to general family discussion tends to give strength to one side when scaling preferences. Even when the influence is not intentional, it has the effect of increasing the chance of success of the group.

FACTORS AFFECTING FAMILY DECISION

Once there is negotiation over family decisions, no matter which type of negotiation is involved, certain factors come into play. These factors are:

1. ability to persuade
2. power within the family
3. family relationships
4. expected outcome of negotiation
5. family income

Ability to Persuade

Often the decisions that result from negotiation depend on the persuasive ability of each individual family member.[19] Most of us have observed the ability of children to get their way by a well-timed display of tears. Adults have also used the same device effectively. Family members use all the arts of communication to persuade other family members to give a preferred product higher priority. The use of fact, emotion, and outside support are all brought to bear in the negotiation. Also, the ability to use language and present a logical argument affects the outcome.

The status of the individual's own preferences plays an important part in the negotiation. A person resists giving in longer where the product ranks high on his or her preferences. It must be noted that a person may have a strong desire for or against a product. In either case, there is a tendency to hold out. The family member is inclined to give in when he or she doesn't care one way or the other about the product. A typical response to the question, "Which hat do you prefer?" is, "Take the one you like." If a family member were given a choice between buying a hat for another and not buying one, the reaction might be different.

Power Within the Family

Each member of a family has some power over the other members.[20] This power may be based on size, strength, recognized position in the group, or degree of control over money income.[21] Power can also be founded on apparent weakness. Spouses can prevail by appealing to the protective instinct of their mates. Where there is power, there is a degree of control over other family members. This control basically centers in the ability to reward or punish. However, the fact that a family member has power may work for or against that member in successfully persuading the group. The person may use his or her power to force personal product desires to a higher position in the assortment, or power can be used to trade off one favor for another. Who can resist the spouse who says, "You let me get the golf clubs and you can have a new camera." A member secure in his or her power may choose not to use it, thus giving in to another member's desires.

The contribution a member makes to the family may be an important source of power.[22] One member's contribution may be in keeping the home and taking care of the children. The other may help with these activities, but her or his primary contribution may be economic. How the members view their functions affects their power in the family. One may argue a lack of money for the washer, but the other counters by pointing out that the job cannot be done without the washer. The strength of each member's conviction affects the placement of the washer in the target assortment.

Family Relationships

Family relationships refer to how the family is organized to handle routine economic problems.[23] Decisions on who handles the money in certain situations, how routine purchases are made, which product brands are routinely preferred, and who makes the purchase come under family relationships.[24] These factors enter into the ordering of product preferences to the extent that one member is attempting to encroach on established routines or change the routines. For example, one of the children may want a brand of bread different from the brand routinely bought. Spouses may renegotiate meat purchases for the family. Instead of buying weekly quantities, it may be decided to buy all the meat, a side at a time. This decision may entail further negotiation over the purchase of a freezer that had been low on the family's scale of preferences. In more compatible families, the members have more characteristics in common, and there is a willingness to listen and cooperate. In such families cooperation predominates, and assortment preferences are easier to achieve. In families that are less compatible, the opposite tends to be true. There is argument over products, family members are more likely to act independently of the group, and there is less willingness to compromise. The products held in such families are more likely to reflect individual desires.

The individual's ego needs are a factor of family relationships. An individual may need love, satisfaction, power, recognition, approval, and so on. If a product meets any of these needs, singly or in combination, the individual will hold out longer for its high placement in the assortment. It may be that to give in affects the member's ego even though the product is not personally important. The product becomes secondary, and the important thing becomes the satisfaction of an ego need, such as maintaining one's power. A lot of what one considers obstinate behavior on the part of a mate is probably a desire for power or recognition, as when one spouse insists on replacing the station wagon before considering new furniture. An ego-oriented spouse is not likely to give in unless some way is found to salvage his or her ego.

A family member whose ego needs are secure finds it easier to give in. For example, love or respect for the other family members can cause one to give in more quickly in order to satisfy perceived ego needs of the other family members. A spouse may think, "I don't agree, but I love X, and if it makes X happy, we can get the new car before replacing the refrigerator." Love can also cause a member to hold out longer if the decision becomes a test of that love.

Expected Outcome of Negotiation

The expected outcome of negotiation influences a person's willingness to give in on the placement of a product in the target assortment. If one spouse feels that the other does not care as much about the argument, or that the other's knowledge of the product, the situation, or the circumstances is weak, he or she will hold out longer. Under these circumstances, the spouse will also put more effort into the argument, which affects the outcome. If, on the other hand, one spouse feels that the other is unyielding, the spouse may decide that the argument is not worth the trouble.

Family Income

Income is an important factor that can never be ignored when making product decisions. Income is both an opportunity and a restraint on the group. It is an opportunity because it represents the total amount available to spend. Several factors about income must be considered. First, the number of persons in the group earn income is important. The more earners, the greater the potential of products to include in the assortment. Second, it is important who earns the money. The spouse who earns income may have a greater say in how it is spent. Third, the willingness of family members to share income is important. Generally, parents have little choice in the matter of sharing, although there are families where each member keeps and spends his or her own earnings. Children are another matter. In low-income families, the tendency is for children to contribute more to the family group. In higher-income families, the children tend to keep their own earnings. Fourth, it is important how many persons must share the income. A single-member household has fewer required expenditures than a multi-member household. Fifth, it is important how much money is available; the more that is available, the more products other than necessities can be bought.

The Family Purchase Decision

The determination of product, store, and method of purchase decisions is similar to that described for individuals. Illustration 16-2 shows the similarity

Illustration 16-2
Family purchase decision

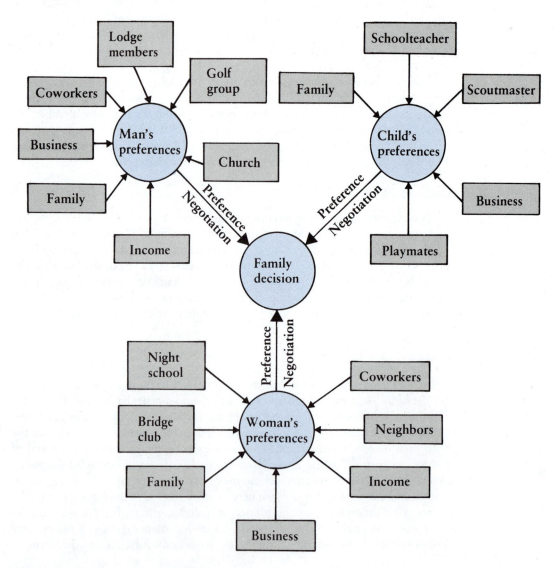

Part 4 – Consumer Evaluation and Decision

and differences. The external influences are exactly the same as those described for individual choices. The difference is that when several products are important to the entire family, individual preferences may be negotiated in order to arrive at a common decision.[25] The word "negotiation" sounds very businesslike, but family negotiation does not necessarily resemble that which takes place, say, between management and labor. In the family, the lines of battle are not so clearly drawn and the tools used are not so formal. Family negotiations may be more subtle and informal in their application. While the tools may not be formal, they are no less sharply honed or effective. Family members do utilize most of the tools that are found in business negotiations—including suggestion, persuasion, withholding favors, reprisals, coalitions, and arbitration. Anyone doubting the effectiveness of family tools of negotiation has only to ask a parent whose child has negotiated for a new garment. That parent knows the effects of the relentless pressure to compromise as a result of tears, the social outcast appeal, or the threat of the child's unhappiness.

Family purchase decisions involve the individual, reference groups, and family factors already discussed. These decisions are narrowing processes in which series of compromises are made concerning the factors important to the decision.[26] For example, one spouse may have a strong personal preference to purchase a boat before a dining room suite—based on personal needs, intended use, and compatibility of ideas presented by friends and coworkers. However, the individual's ability to push for her or his desires may be tempered by affection for the spouse, knowledge that the boat may not be as important to household operation, and the strong preference of the spouse. In the course of discussion, one single factor may become predominant. For example, the individual may give up the boat because of affection for the spouse even though the individual guesses that she or he could win the argument. It may even occur that both sides give way. For example, if one spouse wanted a boat and motor, the spouses may compromise on a boat and a less expensive dining room suite. Another type of compromise may call for giving up both in favor of a third product or saving the money temporarily.

Every family assortment decision involves some compromise. This fact is as true for the single-member family as for the multi-member family. Only one compromise may be necessary, or it may take several. The decision may be made quickly or involve considerable time. The decision may be accomplished by formal discussion or by hints and clues dropped here and there by the parties. The decision can be heated or quite calm, but the decision must be made or the family cannot function as an effective unit.

MISCONCEPTIONS ABOUT CONSUMER DECISIONS

We believe that consumer decisions are normal and reasonable. They may be correct or incorrect, but they were arrived at reasonably using available information.[27] This position has not always been accepted. As Illustration 16-3 demonstrates, under the traditional economic concept of decision making, only the maximization of economic motives was considered rational. The contemporary view perceives all decisions as rational because economic decisions are based on

Illustration 16-3
Perspectives of consumer decision making

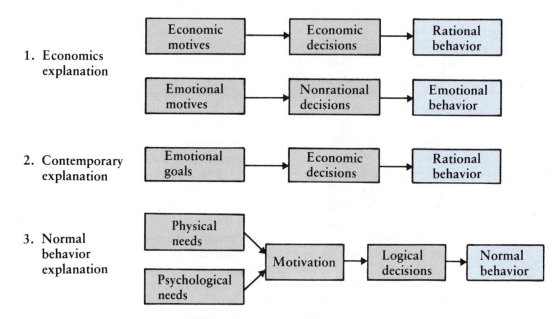

1. Economics explanation

| Economic motives | → | Economic decisions | → | Rational behavior |

| Emotional motives | → | Nonrational decisions | → | Emotional behavior |

2. Contemporary explanation

| Emotional goals | → | Economic decisions | → | Rational behavior |

3. Normal behavior explanation

| Physical needs | → | Motivation | → | Logical decisions | → | Normal behavior |
| Psychological needs |

emotional motives. The concept of normal decision making recognizes that consumers have both physical and psychological needs. These needs cause a motivated state in which there is logical deciding on the basis of known facts. Such a decision process is normal.

The traditional explanation, based on economic man, is deficient for two reasons. First, it fails to recognize the difference between the reason for a decision or action and the decision or action itself. It is just as normal or reasonable to retreat from the threat of an overpowering emotional fear as it is to attempt to purchase a vacuum cleaner at the lowest price based on a rational reasoning process. As a matter of fact, one can argue that it would be abnormal not to run from an overpowering fear.

Second, the economic man concept toward rationality implies that physical and emotional motives are two different things. In fact, we have shown that the two cannot be separated practically in people. Human beings are behaving in a normal manner when, by making a decision, they find a preferred solution to a problem. It does not matter whether the problem is emotionally based, physically based, or, as is more nearly the truth, based on a combination of physical and emotional motives.

The contemporary explanation is equally unsatisfactory. It contains a separation of efficiency factors and emotional factors. The difference is that they are supposed to occur in sequence. The actual fact is that emotions and physical considerations operate on the consumer's goals and decision processes. Even motivation is not free of emotions. While consumers do decide, in fact *must* decide, all market-oriented questions, they do not necessarily have to decide logically or efficiently. Furthermore, the concept of rational and nonrational behavior of consumers borders on the ridiculous. We have defined a decision as the ability to select from among alternatives, and nothing more is required from it.

The normal behavior explanation is a decision making concept, but it emphasizes the meshing of physical and emotional needs. Since the inputs to motivation involve emotions, it follows that motivation, as well as the decision making that follows, has some emotions involved. Just because physical and emotional aspects are involved in every consumer decision does not mean that each is involved proportionally. A given decision may involve more emotional considerations, or

Photo 16-2
Non-monetary factors can be important. This woman is more interested in beauty and uniqueness than price.

more physical considerations, or the two may be balanced. The combination depends on the individual and the circumstance. For example, one consumer may purchase a sport coat primarily for its style (an emotional consideration), while another consumer may purchase a coat because of its low price (an economic consideration).

Normal Decisions and Correct Decisions

The implication of the traditional explanation of rationality is that if a decision is incorrect it must have been nonrational. The contemporary explanation cannot recognize an incorrect decision. If the consumer was logically deciding on the basis of known facts, it had to be a rational decision *at the time of the purchase*. It is argued that the consumer may change his or her mind later as new facts are introduced, but at the time of the decision, the consumer's action was rational.

The fact is that consumer choices may be either correct or incorrect and still constitute normal decision behavior. A reasonable decision is determined by how it is made, not by whether it is correct or not. The consumer who is deciding is acting normally. In practice, consumers often make incorrect decisions. Four conditions may lead the consumer to make incorrect choices. First, the decision may be based on incorrect assumptions. A person who assumes all hair is green and is told that John has hair will conclude that John has green hair. The decision process is logical. The conclusion is wrong because the assumption was incorrect. A consumer who assumes that a discounted price is a low price can end up paying more for merchandise because the assumption is incorrect. Second, the facts upon which the consumer decides may be insufficient. Consumers often make incorrect decisions on product quality because they depend on price or brand as the determinants of value. Third, the facts may be incorrect. The seller may give the consumer misleading or incorrect information. Fourth, the consumer's judgment may not be sound. The facts may be present but either the consumer perceives these facts incorrectly or uses them ineffectively to make the decision. Nevertheless, the requirements for rationality are met when the consumer decides logically based on known facts.

Individual Versus Social View of Normality

Whether decision behavior is socially acceptable or not may depend on the point of view. Certainly, any individual who decides a problem in personal self-interest is acting normally according to our definition. Furthermore, the individual believes that the actions taken are reasonable. Society as a whole may view the individual's actions differently. What is normal and reasonable for the individual may be viewed by society as nonrational. For example, the individual consumer may not wear seat belts because they restrict movements. To the consumer, this is a normal and reasonable attitude, although society deems the behavior nonrational because it is life-endangering. A consumer may continue to smoke because the habit is too strong to give up, while society condemns the practice.

The position taken here is that both society and the individual consumer may be correct. The individual may consider his or her behavior perfectly normal, and still not conform to acceptable patterns of behavior prescribed for the group.

Social judgment may be that the town drunk, who purchases liquor instead of feeding the family, is nonrational. However, the town drunk may be a weak person and a poor provider, who, in spite of failure, does not like to see the family suffer. He or she may think that liquor consumed is necessary to stay sane. Given this person's assumption, this person is not irrational. The drunk's behavior is normal for the drunk; it is simply not normal for the majority of people. From a social point of view the drunk is nonrational, but from the drunk's own point of view he or she is rational. Society may prefer to see the drunk act differently, but that does not mean that those actions lack reason or thought. It simply makes the drunk's behavior different from what the group condones. Notice that society is not necessarily wrong in judging the nonuser of seat belts, the smoker, or the drunk as practicing unacceptable behavior. We may all agree that the total interest would be better served if they acted differently. Society is only wrong in judging their behavior nonrational. There is a real moral and ethical question as to how far society should go in forcing its will on individual consumers.

Habitual and Impulse Behavior

Habitual and impulse behavior are sometimes presented as examples of nonrational behavior. *Habitual behavior* occurs when, having made a decision once and found it satisfactory, the consumer automatically makes the same decision each time a similar problem arises. Suppose that a person purchases an Arrow shirt after carefully considering the merits of competitive products. This purchase is said to be based on a rational choice. However, when the shirt wears out, if the consumer buys another Arrow shirt without reconsidering the alternatives, the consumer is said to be nonrational because he or she has acted on habit rather than on reason.

Consumers would be nonrational if they didn't purchase to some extent by habit. Once you have found a satisfactory solution to a problem, it is not reasonable to waste time solving the same problem over and over. Habitual behavior is analogous to the management principle of management by exception. You apply your energy to those problems that are giving you trouble. If the consumer did not reduce many decisions to routine, he or she would not have sufficient time for deciding important problems. Besides, a sufficiently strong reason, such as a convincing advertisement of a superior product, can cause the consumer to reconsider habitual behavior. Thus habitual behavior is normal.

Impulse purchases are made on sight with little or no serious comparison of alternatives. Impulse buying is normal because the product receives as much attention as it deserves. Three factors account for impulse purchases:

1. Some individuals think faster than others.
2. The decision may not deserve a lot of thought or comparison.
3. The consequences of being wrong are small.

It would seem less than reasonable to devote a lot of time and thought to the purchase of a pack of gum when the consequence of choosing wrong is small. Competing gums are very similar, and if you don't make the best decision you are

Photo 16-3
This was an impulse purchase, but who can resist a balloon for a child in an amusement park?

Six Flags Over Georgia

only out a small amount of money. A normal person allocates more time to the purchase of a house than to the purchase of a car, and the car gets more attention than a new suit.

Rationalization Is Normal

There is nothing nonrational about rationalizing a purchase. *Rationalization* is:

justifying the need, internally or to others, after choosing a solution to a problem.

So long as consumers are using their mind to decide, they are acting normally. There isn't even anything really illogical about this type of decision making. Insofar as normal decision behavior is concerned, it does not matter whether the product is selected before or after the reasons are found. Normal behavior results from the way emotional and physical needs and motives are combined into a decision process. Although consumers are sometimes casual in their approach, they are not nonrational. Consumers do plan their moves in the market.

QUESTIONS

1. Identify and discuss the four possible decision states.
2. Discuss the statement: "The consumer's decision would be much simpler to determine if only the individual's interests were involved."
3. Identify and discuss the modifications needed to the marginal utility concept in order to relate the concept to the real world.
4. Each individual consumer is responsible for ranking personal preferences, but there are always external influences that affect the decision. Identify and discuss some of the external influences that affect your decisions.
5. Identify some product decisions that your family would negotiate over and product decisions they would not. Discuss your answer.
6. Discuss and give examples of the preconditions that affect family decision making.
7. Identify the factors you use in negotiation to influence family decisions. Are they some factors your parents use? Discuss your answer.
8. Discuss the relationship between income and ability to influence decision making.
9. Identify with examples the factors that are involved in the family purchase decision.
10. New information comes to the consumer right up to the moment of purchase. Identify and discuss the types of information that would influence your preference scales just prior to the purchase. Discuss why.
11. Discuss with examples why the traditional explanation, based on economic man, is deficient for explaining the decision making process?
12. Discuss the statement: "If a decision is incorrect it must have been nonrational."
13. Give examples where you consider your behavior perfectly normal, and you still do not conform to acceptable patterns of behavior prescribed for the group. Discuss your answer.
14. Define and give examples of habitual and impulse behavior.
15. Discuss and give examples to illustrate the difference between rational behavior and rationalization.

NOTES

1. Girish N. Punj and David W. Stewart, "An Interaction Framework of Consumer Decision Making," *Journal of Consumer Research,*, Vol. 10 (September 1983), pp. 181–96.
2. Robert B. Zajonc and Hazel Markus, "Affective and Cognitive Factors in Preferences," *Journal of Consumer Research,* Vol. 9 (September 1982), pp. 123–31.
3. Leigh McAlister, "A Dynamic Attribute Satiation Model of Variety-Seeking Behavior," *Journal of Consumer Research,* Vol. 9 (September 1982), pp. 141–150.
4. Robert F. Kelly and Michael B. Egan, "Husband and Wife Interaction in a Consumer Decision Process," in Phillip R. McDonald, ed., *Marketing*

Involvement in Society and the Economy (Chicago: American Marketing Assn., 1969), pp. 250–58.

5. Werner W. Pommerehne, Friedrich Schneider, and Peter Zweifel, "Economic Theory of Choice and the Preference Reversal Phenomenon: A Reexamination," *American Economic Review,* Vol. 72 (June 1982), pp. 569–74.

6. Dennis H. Gensch and Thomas F. Golob, "Testing the Consistency of Attribute Meaning in Empirical Concept Testing," *Journal for Marketing Research,* Vol. 12 (August 1975), pp. 348–54.

7. Jordan J. Louviere and George Woodworth, "Design and Analysis of Simulated Consumer Choice of Allocation Experiments: An Approach Based on Aggregate Data," *Journal of Marketing Research*, Vol. XX (November 1983), pp. 35–67.

8. Paul E. Green and Michael T. Devita, "A Complementarity Model of Consumer Utility for Item Collections," *Journal of Consumer Research,* Vol. 1 (December 1974), pp. 56–67.

9. Richard R. Batsell and Leonard M. Lodish, "A Model and Measurement Methodology for Predicting Individual Consumer Choice," *Journal of Marketing Research,* Vol. XVIII (February 1981), pp. 1–12.

10. Richard B. Westin and Peter L. Watson, "Reported and Revealed Preferences and Determinants of Mode Choice Behavior," *Journal of Marketing Research,* Vol. 12 (August 1975), pp. 282–89.

11. Kent B. Monroe, "The Influence of Price Differences and Brand Familiarity on Brand Preferences," *Journal of Consumer Research,* Vol. 3 (June 1976), pp. 42–49.

12. See: John H. Howard, *Marketing Management: Operating, Strategic, and Administrative,* 3d ed. (Homewood, Ill.: Richard D. Irwin, Inc., 1973), pp. 61–77.

13. Kent B. Monroe, "Buyers' Subjective Perceptions of Price," *Journal of Marketing Research,* Vol. 10 (February 1973), pp. 70–80; Zarrell V. Lambert, "Price and Choice Behavior," *Journal of Marketing Research,* Vol. 9 (February 1972), pp. 35–40.

14. Robert W. Shoemaker and F. Robert Shoaf, "Behavioral Changes in the Trial of New Products," *Journal of Consumer Research,* Vol. 2 (September 1975), pp. 104–9.

15. Earnestine Hargrove, Hiram Barksdale, Jr., and Terry Powell, "An Empirical Investigation of the Differences for Goods and Services," in John Summey, R. Viswanathan, Ronald D. Taylor, and Karen Glynn, eds., *Marketing: Theories and Concepts for an Era of Change, 1983* (Southern Illinois University at Carbondale and Southern Marketing Assn., 1983), pp. 99–101.

16. Alvin C. Burns and Donald H. Granbois, "Factors Moderating the Resolution of Preference Conflict in Family Automobile Purchasing," *Journal of Marketing Research,* Vol. 14 (February 1977), pp. 77–86.

17. C. Whan Park, "Joint Decisions in Home Purchasing: A Muddling-Through Process," *Journal of Consumer Research,* Vol. 9 (September 1982), pp. 151–62.

18. Harry L. Davis, "Decision Making Within the Household," *Journal of*

Consumer Research, Vol. 2 (March 1976), pp. 241–60.

19. Rosann L. Spiro, "Persuasion in Family Decision-Making," *Journal of Consumer Research,* Vol. 9 (March 1983), pp. 393–402.

20. Richard Hansen, Gary M. Munsinger, and Jean Draper, "A Dyadic Analysis of Power Roles in the Housing Decision Process," in Fred C. Allvin, ed., *Relevance in Marketing: Problems, Research, Action* (Chicago: American Marketing Assn., 1971), pp. 397–401; Kelly and Egan, "Husband and Wife Interaction in a Consumer Decision Process," pp. 250–258.

21. F. Robert Dwyer, "Are Two Better Than One? Bargaining Behavior and Outcomes in an Asymmetrical Power Relationship," *Journal of Consumer Research,* Vol. 11 (September 1984), pp. 680–93.

22. Robert M. Cosenza and Duane L. Davis, "The Effect of the Wife's Working Status on Familial Dominance Structure," *Journal of the Academy of Marketing Science,* Vol. 8 (Winter–Spring 1980), pp. 73–82.

23. Eli P. Cox, III, "Family Purchase Decision Making and the Process of Adjustment," *Journal of Marketing Research*, Vol. 12 (May 1975), pp. 189–95.

24. Robert M. Cosenza, "Family Decision Making Decision Dominance Structure Analysis—An Extension," *Journal of the Academy of Marketing Science*, Vol. 13 (Winter 1985), pp. 91–103.

25. Lakshman Krishnamurthi, "The Salience of Relevant Others and Its Effect on Individual and Joint Preferences: An Experimental Investigation," *Journal of Consumer Research,* Vol. 10 (June 1983), pp. 62–72.

26. Harry L. Davis, "Measurement of Husband-Wife Influence in Consumer Purchase Decisions," *Journal of Marketing Research,* Vol. 8 (August 1971), pp. 305–12.

27. C. Dennis Anderson and John D. Claxton, "Barriers to Consumer Choice of Energy Efficient Products," *Journal of Consumer Research,* Vol. 9 (September 1982), pp. 163–170.

CHAPTER 17

Consumer Decisions

Consistent with Personality

CHAPTER OUTLINE

I. CONCEPT OF PERSONALITY
   A. What Personality Is and Is Not
   B. Personality Defined
   C. Basis for Personality

II. CONSUMER DECISIONS CONTROLLED BY PERSONALITY
   A. Personality Affects Consumer Problem Recognition
   B. Personality Controls Type of Search
   C. Personality Underlies Thought Processes

III. PSYCHOANALYTIC CONTRIBUTION TO CONSUMER DECISIONS
   A. Consumers Motivated by Instincts
   B. Instincts Operate Through the Psyche
   C. Defense Mechanisms Affect Decisions
   D. Influence of Psychoanalytic Theory

IV. TRAIT CONTRIBUTION TO CONSUMER DECISIONS
   A. Consumer Attitudes and Traits
   B. Common Traits That Affect Consumer Decisions
   C. Individual Consumer Traits Also Affect Decisions

V. TYPE CONTRIBUTION TO CONSUMER DECISIONS
   A. Consumer Types and Stereotypes
   B. Basic Types Affect Decisions
   C. Social Types Affect Decisions

VI. GESTALT CONTRIBUTION TO CONSUMER DECISIONS

VII. PERSONALITY AND CONSUMER DECISIONS: AN EVALUATION
   A. Personality Is Basic to Consumer Decision Making
   B. Problems in Using Personality Theory

CHAPTER OBJECTIVES

After completing your study of Chapter 17, you should be able to:

1. Explain the concept of personality.
2. Discuss how consumer decisions are controlled by personality.
3. Discuss the psychoanalytical contribution to consumer decisions.
4. Discuss the trait contribution to consumer decisions.
5. Discuss the type contribution to consumer decisions.
6. Discuss Gestalt contribution to consumer decisions.
7. Make an evaluation of personality and consumer decisions.

Many scholars believe that the key to understanding consumer decision making lies with personality. The argument is that needs, motives, attitudes, learning, and perception, taken separately, constitute only bits and pieces of the totality that is a person. It is personality that ties all these pieces together. It is for this reason that we have left the discussion of personality until all the other parts of the individual have been explained. It is now time to examine how personality affects consumer decision making.

CONCEPT OF PERSONALITY

Human personality is a complex subject. Although all persons differ in personality structure, it is still possible to examine basic dimensions of human personality in order to develop a better understanding of how consumers think and behave.

What Personality Is and Is Not

The term "personality" is encountered in popular usage in phrases such as "personality kid" and "he or she has personality." There was even a song entitled "Personality." The term has come to mean whatever one person sees in another. In this casual usage, "personality" has a good connotation—to have personality is not a bad thing.

We want to make clear what personality is not. Personality does not refer to an ability to get along with others, nor is it the same thing as being popular within a group. Personality is not the ability to get votes. Personality is sometimes used to refer to an oddball or loner, but this is not personality. Personality constitutes a much broader concept than indicated by any of the above statements. Yet, because a person is uniquely what he or she is, that person may be popular, respected, or considered different. Although the term is used to describe such superficial things as popularity and friendliness, personality itself goes to the very core of the individual's being.

Personality Defined

Personality has broader and deeper connotations than its popular usage would indicate. One view perceives personality as those human characteristics which make one individual different from another. The focus of this definition is on differences in people. Another definition considers personality the total inner organization of the person. This definition focuses on the integration of internal psychological values. Our definition attempts to incorporate the best qualities of both of these. *Personality* is:

> *the inner organization of those characteristics, or qualities, that distinguish people and determine how they relate to the environment.*

First, personality refers to characteristics, traits, or qualities. Some consider only psychological qualities and others include physical characteristics. We include both because one's reaction to the environment is based as much on how one feels about one's physical self as on how one feels about one's psychological self. Second, personality does not vary from minute to minute. Rather, once established, it tends to hold for long periods, perhaps even the life of the person. Third, personality relates to individual behavior. How the person decides and the resulting behavior is based on that person's personality. What personality characteristics do you feel are being appealed to in Figures 17-1, 17-2, and 17-3?

Figure 17-1
Appeal to personality characteristics

Reprinted with permission of State Farm Insurance Companies

Figure 17-2
Appeal to personality characteristics

"You're so light and delicious, but are you really cholesterol-free?"

"Would an angel lie?"

Betty Crocker. Angel Food Cake

Light, tempting dessert you deserve, with no cholesterol. Indulge!

You Sweetalker, Betty Crocker

© General Mills, Inc. 1988

Used with permission of General Mills, Inc.

Basis for Personality

Traditionally, it was assumed that personality resulted from innate internal considerations, that a person's personality was fixed at birth and could never be changed. In short, personality was determined by the genetic makeup of the individual. This view is comforting because it relieves everyone of any responsibility for changing or modifying personality.

It is increasingly recognized that personality is a social product. The way a person feels and thinks, acts and talks, or even dreams or wishes, results from that person's experiences with other persons, events, and objects throughout a lifetime. Every time a consumer meets another person he or she reacts, in part, in terms of the interpretation of the other person's behavior—an interpretation which comes from past experience. If the consumer's actions, judged by responses received, proves inappropriate, the individual takes this into account before taking further action. A consumer may attempt to haggle over the price of a product, only to meet criticism from the clerk and stares from other customers. A consumer whose personality tends toward independence may pay no attention and

Figure 17-3
Appeal to personality characteristics

continue to haggle, but a consumer whose personality tends toward meekness will probably back down from the situation and seek to find a way out of the dilemma.

CONSUMER DECISIONS CONTROLLED BY PERSONALITY

A consumer's personality controls the entire decision process. Since personality is the totality of the individual, it affects everything that person thinks and does. We now summarize some of the important ways personality affects the consumer's decision making.

Personality Affects Consumer Problem Recognition

The consumer's personality has a direct bearing on how problems are perceived. A person who is outgoing and venturesome sees more and different kinds of problems than a person who is reserved and inclined to accept the status quo. The latter may not understand that the roof needs repairing until it begins to leak. Anxiety-prone people perceive more problems simply because they expect them. They worry about the proper kind of education and whether they have sufficient insurance. Sociable personalities come into contact with more problems concerning human relations, such as whether their clothing is correct or if a touch of hair color would make them look younger.

A serious-minded person is more likely to want to do something about problems perceived. They understand the importance of taking corrective action on the car brakes or saving money for the future. An adaptable person is more likely to take problems as they come without becoming overly apprehensive. An independent person is more likely to handle problems his or her own way, while a sociable person will seek advice. Thus, two persons can be faced with identical purchase problems but deal with them entirely differently because of the separate personalities involved.

Personality Controls Type of Search

The type of search that consumers engage in is directly affected by personality.[1] An outgoing person seeks more information than a reserved person. The former is more likely to shop and compare than the latter, or to seek the advice of friends. A person whose personality is achievement-oriented is more likely to seek information supporting a prestige car that supports his or her impression of accomplishments. An active personality is more likely to seek more information than a passive personality. A personality with a strong need to dominate will seek purchase information that favors his or her position in family negotiations.

Personality Underlies Thought Processes

Personality is certainly an important factor affecting the manner in which consumers decide on solutions to their problems.[2] Conservative persons seek conservative solutions. A person conservative by nature is more likely to buy a popular automobile, design a landscape similar to the neighbors, and wear conservative clothing.

Seldom, if ever, do persons go against their basic personalities when buying.[3] They think according to their personality, and their actions follow their thoughts. For example, a serious-minded young man is more likely to wear conservative clothing than an outgoing person. A serious person is likely to consider more alternatives more carefully when making a decision. Persons who have great emotional control are prone to put off purchase until the need is clear or urgent. Aggressive personalities tend to think aggressively and seek aggressive solutions to their problems. There can be no question concerning the importance of personality to the consumer's decision making. What a person buys is what that person is.

PSYCHOANALYTIC CONTRIBUTION TO CONSUMER DECISIONS

The psychoanalytic theory of personality is derived from the work of Sigmund Freud.[4] Freud based much of his life's work on the study of dreams in which he found clues to the unconscious. He laid the foundations for psychoanalysis in the methods he developed for the treatment of hysteria.

Consumers Motivated by Instincts

It was Freud's belief that a few basic instincts motivated people to decide problems in specific ways. The *life instincts* serve to protect the survival of the individual or the species.[5] Life instincts include hunger, thirst, and sexual drives. The *death instincts* involve our aggression toward others and our wish to self-destruct. The consumer's desire to have a better car, the drive to excel over others in work, and the depression that follows failure all relate to the death instincts.

Freud believed that these two basic types of instincts are inherited. They are fixed and cannot be changed over a person's life. Thus, according to Freud, the underlying manner in which a consumer approaches any problem is fixed. Thus, the primary influence on any given decision is the particular situation in which the consumer finds his or her self. Freud felt that sex was the strongest of the instincts. To him, the way a person decides on clothing, home, automobile, food, and recreation are related directly or indirectly to the sex drive.

Photo 17-1
Personality is a factor in purchase decisions. What can you tell about this consumer?

© *Richard Younker 1988*

Instincts Operate Through the Psyche

Freud pointed out that the personality is controlled by the *psyche* (mind), which exists on three levels, called the id, ego, and superego. The *id* is: the unconscious part of the psyche from which instinctual impulses and demands for the satisfaction of primitive needs arise. The demands of the id are unlimited. A newborn child is practically all id, since it has not yet learned conscious behavior. The *ego* derives from the id through contact with reality. It is: the largely conscious part of the mind, ruled by reason and mediating the unlimited demands of the id and bringing them in accord with everyday reality, in the interests of self-preservation. The *superego* is mostly unconscious, though partly conscious. It develops out of the ego through processes of internalization and introjection of influences and disciplinary actions of parents especially, but also other authority figures. Thus, the superego is a person's "moral law" that directly guides behavior and keeps the person in line with the rules of society. It is built up, more or less at random, out of childhood experience with parental and others' warnings, threats, punishments, advice, and example. The child looks upon these parental and authority figures as being omnipotent and omniscient.

Freud saw wishes as originating in the id to be met by the reason of the ego and the morality of the superego. If the wish is contrary to the standards set by the ego and supergo, it is suppressed into the unconscious mind. If the wish is deemed acceptable, it is permitted to affect behavior.

Defense Mechanisms Affect Decisions

Freud felt that the pleasure-seeking id, the moralistic superego, and the realistic ego were constantly in conflict. As a result, the individual consumer experiences frustration and conflict in all decisions and actions. The ego protects itself by several types of defense mechanisms. *Identification* is one powerful mechanism whereby the consumer attempts to relate to others in dress, mannerism, and buyer behavior. This mechanism helps explain the success of opinion and fashion leaders.

The defense mechanism known as *projection* occurs when the consumer sees decisions and behavior in others that are considered to be undesirable. Typically, the consumer wants to avoid engaging in the same type of behavior. Advertisers are taking advantage of this defense mechanism when they show persons with undesirable attributes that are associated with not using the sponsor's product.

Displacement is a defense mechanism whereby energy is transferred from one object (product) to another. A person may purchase a fancy car as a substitute for sex, or a family may buy a dog rather than take on the responsibility of having a child.

The mechanism of *rationalization* provides the consumer with acceptable reasons to act as they wanted to act in the first place. Most advertising and personal selling emphasizes a rational reason for buying. When deciding on any problem, consumers typically stress the factors in favor of doing what their emotions dictate that they want to do.

Influence of Psychoanalytic Theory

The great influence of Freud on scholars and practitioners cannot be underestimated. The great names in psychiatry and psychology tend to be either disciples or critics of Freud. As a result of criticism and modification, much of Freudian theory has been discarded by scholars, but it constitutes the original breakthrough in understanding personality. Alfred Adler believed that striving for superiority rather than sex was the basic factor of personality. Karen Horney saw personality as the result of anxieties a child learns to cope with that stem from the parent-child relationship. Erich Fromm considered man alone in society, and personality to him was the result of striving for love, brotherhood, and security. In short, the biological basis for personality advocated by Freud has been greatly broadened by the recognition that many factors influence human personality development.

The advertising industry seems inclined to stay with Freudian personality concepts. Freudian influence is observed throughout branding, advertising, and personal selling. The practice of making products sex symbols, as with "Mr. Clean" and the "Man from Glad," is strictly Freudian. The Hathaway shirt ads using a man with an eye patch, indicate the continuing power of Freud. Every salesperson who gains attention with a sensuous story is utilizing Freud. It is safe to say that Freudian appeals to sensuality, sex, and related subjects are the personality concepts most used by advertisers.

TRAIT CONTRIBUTION TO CONSUMER DECISIONS

We know that decision making by consumers is complex and so is personality. One way of dealing with this complexity is to break personality down to simpler constructs and relate these to consumer decision making. This is what the persons who advocate a *trait theory* of personality attempt to do. Of course, it is hoped that the totality of the person is not lost in the process.

Trait theory goes back to before the 19th century. In its simplest form, trait theory is based on the idea that people have powers or qualities that are located in the mind, and these powers determine behavior.[6] A more complex development of trait theory was offered by Allport.[7] Allport reasoned that traits were attributes that identify a person and make the person both whole and functional. Traits acted as regulators, and people with similar traits were believed to consume in a similar fashion. These persons were thought to have similar goals, and therefore it was concluded that the striving to achieve the goals would be similar also.

Each of us has a unique way of responding to environmental stimuli, and our responses are described by others as personality traits. A *personality trait* is any human characteristic, distinctive from other characteristics and consistent in effect, that distinguishes the behavior of one individual from another.[8] If we know that a person laughs, walks, or dresses, we know nothing to distinguish that person from others. However, if we know a person has a cackling laugh, walks with a limp, or dresses in the latest fashion, then we have an identifiable personality.

This is the reason that characteristics of personality must be distinctive. Personality traits must also be consistent—we cannot identify and classify people unless their distinguishing characteristics are reasonably stable.[9] Abilities are special types of traits that determine what people can do with body and mind.

Consumer Attitudes and Traits

Consumer attitudes, as we have seen, are formulated in reference to some particular object, such as a product or store. This is not the case with traits. Traits are not directed at anything in particular. An attitude is a predisposition to decide or act *toward* something; a trait is a characteristic manner of deciding everything.[10] Thus, a consumer may hold certain attitudes toward retailers, downtown congestion, and high prices; yet, when speaking of any of these topics, the individual may speak slowly and use certain mannerisms that distinguish personality.

Consumer attitudes result in our taking preferential action with respect to the market situation, whereas traits are more generalized tendencies to decide or act in a certain manner given the situation. Traits, because of their nature, may be appropriate or inappropriate to a specific situation. Attitudes are favorable, unfavorable, or neutral toward the situation, but traits do not refer to acceptance or rejection. Thus, the consumer's favorable attitude toward buying an electric can opener when combined with the trait to be cautious leads the consumer to deliberate before buying. The general trait of a consumer to be selfish or extravagant differs from the attitudes he or she may hold toward a retail store. A person may like the store but because of a frugal trait not want to purchase clothes there. A consumer may count pennies just as carefully when buying a suit he or she likes as when buying fly spray that he or she does not particularly care for.

Common Traits That Affect Consumer Decisions

One may well imagine that as the study of personality proceeds, the number of recognized traits tends to increase. One source lists 17,953,301 different words distinguishing one's human behavior.[11] Furthermore, the complexity of the human personality has not lent itself to any easy agreement on a single, unified list of personality traits. Several lists have been advanced, and there is some overlapping among them.

Listed below are eleven traits that appear common to most people. Each trait has its distinguishing characteristic, and each definitely affects consumer behavior.

1. *Activity*. Even babies have different activity levels. Activity shows up in consumers in their willingness to shop and spend time searching in the market.
2. *Masculinity*. Gestures, speech, habits, and attitudes found in one sex but not in the other. This trait is manifested in the type of products and stores favored by consumers. It is the basis for manufacturers giving their products sex attributes. All consumer behavior reflects this trait.

3. *Independence*. All people differ in their reliance on other people. A consumer's independence when deciding is reflected in dress, eating habits, preference for entertainment, and manner of shopping, just to name a few.

4. *Achievement*. Some people are characterized as achievers and others are not. Achievement is not dependent entirely on intelligence. Consumers with high achievement motivation are conscious of what others think of their behavior, manners, dress, and so on. These consumers may or may not conform to group norms.

5. *Anxiety*. Individuals display different degrees of sureness of themselves. Consumer anxiety shows up in the manner in which an individual handles the purchase situation. Salespeople do not usually intimidate a consumer who has self-assurance.

6. *Sociability*. The desire for interaction with others varies among people. Sociability affects decisions because shopping is social behavior, and some consumers are more willing to participate than others.

7. *Dominance*. Dominance is the desire to cause others to submit, and this important trait varies among people. Shopping for products gives individuals an outlet to display their need to dominate others. This trait makes a consumer aggressive and difficult to deal with in the buying process.

8. *Adaptability*. Some people can adapt to conditions of reality to a greater degree than others. If a desired product is not available, such consumers take a substitute.

9. *Aggressiveness*. Consumer aggressiveness shows up in many ways, including willingness to try new products, attitude toward price and service negotiation, and the seeking out of products and stores.

10. *Seriousness*. Some people take life seriously and others are carefree. A serious consumer gives more attention and consideration to a purchase decision.

11. *Emotional control*. People vary considerably in their ability to control their emotions. A certain amount of emotional control is necessary by consumers in all decision making, but it is perhaps more important in situations where service is slow or inadequate, when prices are exorbitant, when dishonesty is present, and when promises are not kept.

All these traits, of course, interact. The points made above apply only when considering each trait separately in connection with an individual consumer. For example, a consumer who is active, sociable, adaptable, and emotionally stable will consume differently from one who is active, sociable, aggressive, and serious. What a consumer actually does may be based on an internal compromise of traits, such as sociability and independence.

Individual Consumer Traits Also Affect Decisions

In addition to the common traits found in most people, there are traits, called individual traits, that are found in only one or a few persons. There are so many of these traits, and they vary so greatly, that it is impossible to provide a list. However, as an example, individual traits include: a person's particular guilt feelings, ego-defensive mechanism, and concept of self, taste, concept of beauty, and so on. These traits are crucial to consumer deciding because they play an important part in making each consumer's market reaction unique.[12] Furthermore, there is interaction within the consumer between common and individual traits that affects market decision making.

Personality traits are extremely important for understanding consumer decision making, but traits are also important for identifying consumer groups. One point of particular interest to marketers is the continuing attempt to identify systems of traits in consumers. That is to say, a market segment is really a group of consumers displaying some common personality traits. The marketer wants to put together a system of common traits from those in the list provided previously. Given these common traits, the marketer can discover the basic appeals to make to this group of consumers. This approach recognizes that groups of traits can in fact be a motivating force influencing consumer behavior.[13] For example, a marketer can appeal to groups of consumers who display anxiety or independence or aggressiveness. A marketer can also appeal to groups of consumers who display several of the traits.

TYPE CONTRIBUTION TO CONSUMER DECISIONS

Theories of personality based on human types are similar to trait theories. *Type theory* categorizes people into groups (types) based on either physical or psychological attributes. Personality types can be based on such physical attributes as color of hair and skin, sex, and so on. Psychological attributes include intelligence, emotions and emotional stability, and mental traits. The physical theory sees all human behavior as dependent on the physical structure of the person. This concept of personality goes all the way back to the Hippocratic school of medicine and the bodily humors of medieval physiology. The psychological concept of personality type considers consumer decision making and behavior to be controlled by the mind and not the body. The perceptual process and attitude formation play an important part in these theories.[14] Jung built his concept of personality around the manner in which a person perceived and developed attitudes toward his environment. Both the physical and psychological concepts of personality are self-restrictive. These concepts do not deal with the whole person, although they do provide for human change. The concepts are at best oversimplifications of human personality.

There are similarities and differences between type theory and trait theory. A human trait is the smallest single component of personality. A trait concerns specific individual mental or physical characteristics. *A personality type* is defined to mean:

a compatible group of human characteristics that, taken together, control behavior and distinguish between individuals.

The characteristics upon which types are classified can be either physical or mental. A personality type is a larger unit than a trait because several traits or other characteristics are necessary to constitute a personality type. The essential point of personality types is that people are classified according to a few key traits or characteristics.

Consumer Types and Stereotypes

Stereotypes are sometimes used synonymously with personality types, but there is a difference. *Stereotype* refers to:

> *a fixed notion held about a group of people and based on one, or a few, human characteristics.*

We are using stereotypes when we ascribe fiery tempers to redheads and scheming minds to people with narrow eyes. When we discuss French people as wine-drinking, fun-loving lovers, we are stereotyping French people. When we say that middle-income American consumers are conservative, home-oriented consumers, we are speaking in stereotypes. Both the French and middle-income Americans are more complex than the stereotypes indicate. Furthermore, no individual in a group will conform to the stereotype because stereotypes indicate average behavior. Can you identify a stereotype in Figure 17-4, either good or bad?

Figure 17-4
Stereotyping in advertising

Merrell Dow Pharmaceuticals Inc.

There exists no more agreement on personality types than on personality traits. Furthermore, personality types are not an infallible guide to consumer behavior.[15] Two individuals may be classified as the same type but decide and purchase differently. The reason is, of course, that the stereotyping of people is an oversimplification of the true complexity of these people.[16] Still, personality types do give us insights into the nature of people that are important for understanding their behavior.

Basic Types Affect Decisions

Another method of typing consumers places the emphasis on values that people hold.[17] This method identifies six classes of people, and it refers to both males and females:

1. *Theoretical Man.* The theoretical person is a seeker after truth and fundamental values. The scientist fits this group. A consumer fitting this group would be fact oriented, interested in change, and broad-minded when making product or market decisions.
2. *Economic Man.* This person is concerned with utility and maximizing. Many consumers fit this category to a degree. Such consumers are price conscious or interested in the good buy.
3. *Aesthetic Man.* This is the artistic person concerned with beauty in the world. All consumers fit this group to some degree.
4. *Social Man.* This person is motivated by love of others. He or she is motivated by group norms, and purchases reflect this.
5. *Political Man.* This consumer is concerned with power. He or she buys products that feed this power requirement.
6. *Religious Man.* This type is a mystic and is not completely bound to this earth. This consumer is more detached. He or she is not market- or product-oriented, and purchases out of necessity almost as an afterthought.

This classification is more nearly in line with personality as understood by marketers. It deals with values that can be appealed to as motivating forces within the individual.

Social Types Affect Decisions

An even more useful list for marketers focuses on the social values of consumers. It divides people into the:

1. *Tradition directed.* These persons are oriented toward the past and resist change. Tradition-oriented consumers are not fashion leaders except where traditional fashions are concerned, and they tend to decide purchases by habit more often.
2. *Inner directed.* These persons have their own internal value systems and keep command of their own activities, including their consumer behavior. They are independent nonconformists who are not easily influenced by others when making market decisions.

3. *Other directed*. The characters of these people are formed mainly by external influences. These people respond to and need others. Such consumers buy group-oriented products, and they tend to be fashion followers.

Personality types can be related to decision making in much the same manner as personality traits. They provide a simplified picture of consumer personality that can be used as a basis for discovering consumer appeals, meeting objectives, and increasing or creating motivation by means of either personal selling or advertising. Since type theory focuses on one or a few prominent traits or values, it is simpler to work with, and data can more easily be gathered. However, personality types are not as fundamental as traits, and many factors of human behavior can be hidden by a blind reliance on type.

GESTALT CONTRIBUTION TO CONSUMER DECISIONS

The term "Gestalt" was coined by the German psychologist Christian von Ehrenfels. Gestalt is derived from configuration, and it generally refers to the totality of a situation. Thus the term *Gestalt* came to describe:

a unity of perception in which the parts derive their meaning from the whole and cannot be separated from the total pattern or organization without losing their identity.

Some outstanding contributors to the development of Gestalt psychology were Kurt Lewin, Kurt Kiffka, Wolfgang Kohler, and Max Wertheimer.

Gestalt is intimately tied up with personality. The basic idea is that the whole of a person is greater than the summation of his or her parts, and personality cannot be determined by a consideration of separate characteristics. Personality is as much a product of the environment as it is of the individual's mind. Experiments prove that individuals respond to stimuli in relation to their experiences.[18] In Gestalt theory, personality is viewed as the result of the interaction between the person and the total environment—the two must be considered together as a patterned event. It is consistent with Gestalt theory that attitudes, perception, aspirations, self-concepts, satisfaction, frustration, motivation, etc., are all necessary to explain and understand human personality.

Consumers attempt to stabilize their psychological field by providing meaning to the surrounding world. Consumers, in making market decisions, strive to reduce tension and conflict between themselves and their environmental perceptions. For example, the use of average-looking people in television commercials is consistent with Gestalt theory. Such commercials assume that consumers can better identify with people like themselves. Businesses take advantage of the concept when they sell tension-reducing products such as deodorants, cosmetics, and life insurance. Personal selling and advertising that stress social acceptance or show people having fun, such as the beer commercials, are following Gestalt principles.

PERSONALITY AND CONSUMER DECISIONS: AN EVALUATION

So far our time has been spent discussing the major concepts of personality and relating these concepts to specific types of consumer behavior. It is now time to turn our attention to the evaluation of personality as a factor of consumer behavior.

Personality Is Basic to Consumer Decision Making

There is little question among scholars that personality is a major factor of consumer behavior. After all, we have shown that personality is related to the basic attributes of a person's nature, and a person seldom acts in opposition to his or her nature. We have also demonstrated that personality is affected by the environment. It is this knowledge that accounts for so much experimental work on personality. There is great promise that consumer action can be predicted by extrapolating from the basic attributes of individuals to specific consumer behavior.

A clear relationship between personality and general behavior has been recognized in the literature for some time.[19] Furthermore, it requires no more than personal intuition to recognize the logic of the relationship. Most of us can recognize specific personality traits or types of acquaintances. We are aware of how specific people tend to relate to their environment. The introvert or aggressive types tend to behave in expected ways. Persons who have the trait of hypertension show it in their decisions.

Problems in Using Personality Theory

There is a clear discrepancy between the promise of personality theory and the findings of researchers. The basic problem lies in assuming a simple relationship between personality traits and purchase patterns. This assumption leads to several fallacies.

First, there is the fallacy of the dominant attribute. It is assumed that one, or a few, attributes control consumer decisions. Actually, the total number of personality characteristics has never been determined. On any problem faced by the consumer, more than one of these attributes is at work. Furthermore, the attributes vary in intensity. Thus, a person may be shy but have a strong urge to excel; or a person may be aggressive and dislike conflict, but be highly sociable. The question is which trait, or traits, will control any given purchase situation. For any consumer, the answer depends on the number and strength of traits brought into play on a given purchase.

Second, there is the fallacy of attribute consistency. The notion is that if a person is dominant in one situation he or she is dominant in all situations, or that if a person is emotionally stable at one time, he or she is emotionally stable at all times. The effect of a personality trait on decision making depends largely on the situation and the object being considered. Someone may be personable and easygoing in social situations, but conflict-oriented at the office. By the same token, what is true about personality in one purchase situation may not be true in the next.

Third, there is the fallacy of time consistency. This is the notion that a person's personality does not change over time. In fact, a person can modify his or her personality as he or she develops. Introverts can learn to be more outgoing, and aggressive persons can develop restraint. Personality changes show up in purchases. For example, a person who is shy and intimidated by clerks may become more aggressive as the person's income increases.

Fourth, there is the fallacy that personality is the total person. This notion runs through all the research that has been cited. The fact is that personality attributes, whether traits or types, are just one of the variables of human nature. The environment, needs, motives, perceptions, and attitudes also enter into any purchase decision, as has been shown. A shy person may turn aggressive when his or her children are hungry and he or she is out of work. A sociable person may become belligerent if a sales clerk is discourteous.

Fifth, there is the fallacy that people with similar attributes purchase alike. Most personality traits have more than one possible product outlet. A social person can as easily display this trait by purchasing a garment as by purchasing a meal with a friend. A man's masculinity can be demonstrated just as well in the shaving lotion purchased, style of clothes, or manner of wearing his hair. Thus, consumers with similar personalities may purchase in entirely different ways.

The reader should not be discouraged about the future of personality as a predictor of consumer decision making. A clear relationship has been demonstrated. The studies that have been made are beginning to develop understanding of both how personality affects the purchase process and how complex the subject actually is. That constitutes more than a beginning. From this point on, both the research methods and the results are very likely to get better.

QUESTIONS

1. Describe your personality. Is it the same as your parents? Discuss your answer.
2. Discuss the implications of the statement: "A person's personality is fixed at birth and can never be changed."
3. What effect does your personality have on the products you buy? Give examples.
4. Seldom do persons go against their basic personality when buying. Give examples when this may not be true.
5. Do you believe that what a person buys is what that person is? Discuss your answer.
6. Define and discuss the different levels of the psyche.
7. The ego protects itself by several types of defense mechanisms. Identify and discuss these mechanisms.
8. Identify two people you feel are good shoppers, and identify the traits you feel they have. Discuss why they have or do not have the same traits.
9. Are personality traits a good basis for segmenting markets? Discuss your answer.
10. Identify and discuss examples of advertisements where the trait independence is reflected.
11. Identify and discuss examples of advertisements where stereotypes are present.

12. Identify and discuss examples of advertisements that are directed at the economic man, political man, and social man.
13. What effect does a person's environment have on his or her personality?
14. Identify and discuss the problems in using personality theories in marketing.
15. Give some reasons why two individuals with similar personalities may buy entirely different products.

NOTES

1. Werner Kroeber-Riel, "Activation Research: Psychobiological Approaches in Consumer Research," *Journal of Consumer Research*, Vol. 5 (March 1979), pp. 240–50.
2. Morris B. Holbrook, Robert W. Chestnut, Terence A. Oliva, and Eric A. Greenleaf, "Play as a Consumption Experience: The Roles of Emotions, Performance, and Personality in the Enjoyment of Games," *Journal of Consumer Research*, Vol. 11 (September 1984), pp. 728–39.
3. M. Joseph Sirgy, "Self-Concept in Consumer Behavior: A Critical Review," *Journal of Consumer Research*, Vol. 9 (December 1982), pp. 287–300.
4. See: Sigmund Freud, *Collected Papers* (London: International Psychoanalytic Press, 1922).
5. Mona A. Clee and Robert A. Wicklund, "Consumer Behavior and Psychological Reactance," *Journal of Consumer Research*, Vol. 6 (March 1980), pp. 389–405.
6. See: J. McCosh, *Psychology: The Cognitive Powers* (New York: Charles Scribner's Sons, 1888).
7. G. W. Allport, *Personality: A Psychological Interpretation* (New York: Henry Hols & Co., 1937).
8. Robert M. Liebert and Michael D. Spiegler, *Personality*, rev. ed. (Homewood, Ill.: The Dorsey Press, 1974), pp. 148–54; Harold H. Kassarjian, "Personality and Consumer Behavior: A Review," *Journal of Marketing Research*, Vol. 8 (November 1971), pp. 409–18.
9. Kathryn E. A. Villani and Yoram Wind, "On the Usage of 'Modified' Personality Trait Measures in Consumer Research," *Journal of Consumer Research*, Vol. 2 (December 1975), pp. 223–28.
10. Arnon Perry, "Heredity, Personality Traits, Product Attitude, and Product Consumption—An Exploratory Study," *Journal of Marketing Research*, Vol. 10 (November 1973), pp. 376–79.
11. G. W. Allport and H. S. Odbert, "Trait Names: A Psycholoexial Study," *Psychological Monograph*, Vol. 47 (1936).
12. P. S. Raju, "Optimum Stimulation Level: Its Relationship to Personality, Demographics, and Exploratory Behavior," *Journal of Consumer Research*, Vol. 7 (December 1980), pp. 272–82.
13. Charles M. Schaninger and Donald Sciglimpaglia, "The Influence of Cognitive Personality Traits and Demographics on Consumer Information

Acquisition," *Journal of Consumer Research,* Vol. 8 (September 1981), pp. 208–16.

14. C. G. Jung, *Psychological Types* (New York: Harcourt, Brace, & Co., Inc., 1946).

15. It has been pointed out on several occasions that many factors affect consumer behavior and that personality is only one of these factors.

16. Russell W. Belk, Kenneth D. Bahn, and Robert N. Mayers, "Developmental Recognition of Consumption Symbolism," *Journal of Consumer Research,* Vol. 9 (June 1982), pp. 4–17.

17. Kent L. Granzin and Kenneth D. Bahn, "Do Values Have General Application to Retail Market Segmentation?" in Robert H. Ross, Frederic B. Kraft, and Charles H. Davis, eds., *1981 Proceedings Southwestern Marketing Association Conference* (Wichita State University and Southwestern Marketing Assn., 1981), pp. 146–49.

18. Kurt Lewin, *Principles of Topological Psychology* (New York: McGraw-Hill Book Co., 1936).

19. Michel Laroche, K. Lee McGown, and Lise Herox, "Personality, Distraction and Time Pressure Effects on Product Label Information Processing," in David M. Klein and Allen E. Smith, eds., *Marketing Comes of Age, 1984* (Boca Raton, Fla.: Southern Marketing Assn., 1984), pp. 36–39.

SECTION B
BUSINESS POLICIES
INFLUENCE CONSUMER CHOICES

18. Price and Service Affect Consumer
    Decisions
19. Response To International Consumer
    Decisions

CHAPTER 18

Price and Service

Affect Consumer Decisions

CHAPTER OUTLINE

I. PRICE AND SERVICE ADJUST PHYSICAL PRODUCT

II. CONSUMER PRICES
   A. Function of Price
   B. Price Is Intended to Influence

III. PRICE POLICIES THAT INFLUENCE CONSUMERS
   A. Price Flexibility Policies
   B. Psychological Price Policies
   C. Price Lining
   D. Competitive Pricing
   E. Unit Pricing
   F. Special Event Pricing
   G. Professional Pricing
   H. Importance of Ethics in Pricing

IV. SERVICE TO CONSUMERS
   A. Public Attitude Toward Service Is Low
   B. Need for Service Responsibility

V. SERVICES THAT INFLUENCE CONSUMERS
   A. Credit Influences
   B. Warranty Influences
   C. Delivery Influences
   D. Installation Influences
   E. Repairs Influence
   F. Alterations Influence
   G. Other Services That Influence
   H. Service Standard Policies
   I. Service Cost

VI. SERVICE AFTER THE SALE

CHAPTER OBJECTIVES

After completing your study of Chapter 18, you should be able to:

1. Explain how price and service adjust physical product.
2. Discuss the function of price.
3. Discuss the price policies that influence consumers.
4. Explain the importance of service to consumers.
5. Discuss the services that influence consumers.
6. Discuss the services after the sale.

Business management cannot afford to leave store and product decisions entirely up to consumers. Just as managers implement specific policies designed to influence consumer search, so managers develop policies to affect the specific manner in which consumers decide on which products to purchase. This chapter deals with the price and service policies that affect the final consumer decision.

PRICE AND SERVICE ADJUST PHYSICAL PRODUCT

We noted earlier that consumer problems are founded in their needs, and management develops products to satisfy these needs. Products contain essential benefits which appeal to individual consumers. We also noted that business managers develop distribution and promotion policies to guide consumers in their search for information necessary for making wise store and brand choices. We arrive at the stage where the consumer makes a choice. Management can do a great deal to affect that choice. An important tool is price and service policies.

Business managers use price and service to adjust the final product more nearly to the consumer's specific needs. If a product costs too much, it may be necessary to use different raw materials or make other changes to make the product more affordable. Price relates the product to competitors. Competitors' products of about the same quality may cost more, or less, about the same, and consumers learn this when making decisions. Price also eliminates some products from consideration when deciding.[1] These products are simply too expensive for some consumers. A needed product with a surprisingly low price may allow the consumer to purchase another needed item that he or she had not thought was affordable.

Services add something to the physical product, sometimes at a higher price. Without the service, the product would not be usable, or it would not be as effective. Repair service and installation make products usable. Credit may be essential to owning the product, while wrapping makes handling the product more convenient. Consumers value these and similar services, and they are willing to pay for them. In making a decision, the consumer takes into account not only the service but also the addition to the price. The price and service package can be the deciding factors in the consumer's product decision. Thus, the price and service policies of management are a vital part of overall business strategy.

Photo 18-1
Service is an important factor in purchase decisions.

CONSUMER PRICES

Suppose a customer wants to haggle over a price. Does the manager stick to the established figure or lower it? Is the manager expected to follow suit when a competitor lowers price or hold the line? Assume a piece of costume jewelry costs $5.10, with a traditional markup of 40 percent. Should the manager set the price at $7.14, which carries the traditional markup but may look high to the consumer, or should the manager set the price at $6.99, which looks better but only carries a 37.1 percent markup? These and similar price decisions are handled every day as a part of management's price policy.

The term *price* refers to the perceived value of goods and services measured in some medium of exchange. The price of a product typically includes the cost of production and sale plus a markup which is the sellers profit. There are several types of prices. A *list, asking,* or *suggested* price is what the seller seeks to obtain. The *selling price* is the amount the seller actually obtains. A *discount* is any reduction from list or selling price. For example, a sale price is based on a discount. Management's *price policy* is:

> *the general guides that specify expected responses to price related issues under identified situations or circumstances.*

In other words, price policy prescribes how the manager should deal with the type of price related questions as those asked above.

Figure 18-1
Price used to influence

Function of Price

Price serves three functions for consumers: it indicates product quality, it determines affordability, and it identifies the good buy.

First, price indicates product quality. In fact, price and brand are the two most important ways used by consumers to estimate product quality. They are not always the most reliable indicators, but they are the most often used.[2] Consumers tend to select higher-priced products, such as waxes, razor blades, moth flakes, and cooking sherry, over lower-priced items when these products are perceived to have higher quality. Studies show that consumers express more doubts about the quality of low-priced products than they do about higher-priced products. High prices for products may even attract some consumers.

Second, price determines the affordability of products. No matter how well a product satisfies, there is no sale if it costs more than the consumer can pay. Therefore, price is a major factor in appealing to different market segments. It explains why managers sometimes refer to the low-, medium-, and high-price markets. They build quality into products in specific ways so that the product can be priced to appeal to one of these market segments.

Third, price identifies the good buy. Price is the factor that equalizes money and satisfaction in the consumer's mind. Any product is a good buy if the consumer feels he or she would rather have the satisfaction contained in the item than the money. This type of attitude is always necessary in trade because a consumer will not willingly give up more than is received. The purchase takes on an economy appeal when the consumer purchases primarily because of the lowness of price and not because of quality or other considerations.

Price Is Intended to Influence

Price policies are designed to influence consumers so that the firm can achieve its objectives. Figure 18-1 shows how price is used to influence. The price is very prominent in the ad and different prices are emphasized. Price information supplied by business persuades consumers at two levels: factual and psychological. Price facts persuade to the extent that they reflect product quality. Buyers rely on price to guide purchases, but facts also convey the social worth of products to people. Management designs price facts to have an influence on the consumer's decision. Price exerts psychological influence on consumers because it appeals to the emotions.[3] For example, a slightly lower price than a competitor's may be perceived by consumers as indicating a great quality difference in the two products. This response could be the deciding factor in the purchase. Low prices may be influential in causing poor persons to purchase or those who are socially conscious. The emotional response to affordability may cause one to overlook quality considerations related to the purchase. No matter which reason applies, management develops its price policy with specific influences on the consumer in mind.

PRICE POLICIES THAT INFLUENCE CONSUMERS

Policies used by management to affect consumer decisions are numerous. It is convenient for discussion to group these policies in some meaningful manner. We have grouped them into price flexibility policies, psychological price policies, price lining, competitive pricing policies, unit price policies, special event pricing, and professional pricing. In this section, we also address the issue of ethics in pricing.

Price Flexibility Policies

Every manager who engages in pricing, regardless of the type of institution in which he or she is employed, must decide on the degree of flexibility to allow. The overall choice is between a one-price or a negotiated price policy.

Managers who adopt a *one-price policy* offer the same price to all customers who purchase like quantities of the same product under similar circumstances. Typically, the price is marked on the merchandise or the shelf. The customer's choice is to accept or reject the product based on the indicated price. Lower offers are not normally accepted. The United States is characterized as adhering to a one-price policy because most sellers have adopted it. Businesses that generally "one-price" include department stores, discount houses, mass merchandisers, most specialty stores, and most wholesalers and producers. The same is true for such Westernized nations as West Germany, France, Norway, Greece, and Japan. The advertisement in Figure 18-2 is based on a one-price policy. If the price were negotiable it could not be displayed in an ad.

The one-price policy is popular with buyers for several reasons. It is easy to administer by the seller—it reduces record keeping and cuts the cost of training and supervising employees. These savings can be passed on to the consumers, which is persuasive. A one-price policy reduces the need for salespersons because less time is spent on each sale when there is no haggling. In addition, both buyer

Figure 18-2
Example of one-price policy

PINE SERVING TRAYS

If you paint or stencil, these unfinished trays are just what you're looking for. They can also be stained to match any decor. The best part of all is the price!

P-52 Large Tray 12x19x1¹/₂″ **$16.99** ppd.
P-5 Petite Tray 7x12x1⁵/₈″ **$8.99** ppd.

Catalog of over 100 unfinished wooden items $1.00

The Strawberry Tree, Inc.
One Merrimac St., Newburyport, MA 01950

WOMEN'S "SIZE" SPECIALIST

PETAL by Naturalizer
Perfect for tailor or dress wear. Open-toe pump, u-cut throat, covered heel, and soft leather upper topped with a delightful petal design. 13/8″ heel. **Navy, Black or Taupe.**

SS	S	N	M	W	WW
7-11	6½-11	6-11	4-11	5-10	5½-10

$45

Over size 10 Add $3
WW width Add $3 + $2 postage
MO residents Add 6¼% tax
SATISFACTION GUARANTEED

CHARGE ORDERS CALL:
(314) 946-0804
We accept Mastercard & Visa

WRITE FOR **FREE** CATALOG!

Send orders to:
Gene's
Dept. 2
126 N. Main St.
St. Charles, MO 63301

WE SPECIALIZE IN SIZES
3 to 12!

The Strawberry Tree, Inc., Newburyport, M.A. *Courtesy of Gene's Shoes, St. Charles, MO*

and seller know where they stand during the purchase. This saves the customer time and reduces confusion in the purchasing process. Furthermore, knowing the price makes possible self-service buying—without the use of clerks. Many customers do not like to deal with salespersons; they find them intimidating.

However, strict adherence to a one-price policy is seldom feasible or desirable. Even the most dedicated managements make exceptions. Exceptions may be necessary during special sales, or when disposing of old, out-of-fashion, or damaged merchandise. Competitors can undercut the price, thus making some bargaining desirable. The point is that a one-price policy is desirable for many businesses when applied with intelligence and judgment.

Managements that adopt a *negotiated price policy* sell the same product to different persons at different prices. There is no standard price, although a suggested price is sometimes marked on the merchandise. The actual price paid is determined by haggling in which each party makes offers and counteroffers until a price agreeable to both is decided on. There are still many nations where negotiated prices characterize economic activity. Egypt and other Middle Eastern nations are examples. Negotiated prices are also characteristic of many Third World nations in Africa and South America. It is an eye-opening experience to stand at the Cairo Bazaar and bargain at the top of your lungs for a cigarette box or a pendant worth no more than a dollar or two American.

Although haggling over everyday purchases is foreign to most Americans, price negotiation is not. We sometimes forget the extent to which it is possible to bargain over products in this nation. Anyone who has ever purchased appliances, automobiles, furniture, or a home is aware of the opportunity. There is nearly always haggling if a trade-in is involved with the purchase. The fact is that, given the right circumstances, Americans may find an opportunity to bargain over almost any purchase. We know of a person who recently purchased a pair of shoes and talked the salesperson into including the shoe polish. This purchase involved negotiation.

Many customers like negotiated prices and are greatly influenced by them. The negotiation itself represents a challenge to some buyers. It is a part of the psychological satisfaction we discussed earlier. The feeling of accomplishment that comes from bargaining the price down is quite real. Many customers feel that they obtain lower prices when they bargain, and they sometimes do. Negotiated prices also benefit the buyers because they allow the seller to adjust to changing supply and demand conditions.

A major problem with negotiated prices is the discrimination arising from selling the same item to different customers at different prices. This could cause legal problems, and the knowledge of negotiated prices can alienate customers. In addition, some customers do not like to bargain. Bargaining time on the part of both the buyer and the seller is costly. Furthermore, managers become concerned if salespersons lower price regularly as an easy way to make the sale. It can have a serious impact on the firm's profits.

Psychological Price Policies

The term *psychological pricing* refers to policies that influence consumers to purchase by means of emotional rather than rational responses. The three important types of psychological prices are odd-even pricing, loss leader pricing, and bait pricing.

When prices are set at odd amounts in order to convey to customers the idea of a bargain we have *odd pricing*. Odd pricing is based on the six "natural" breaks in any one, one hundred, or one thousand dollar(s). These breaks are 5, 10, 25, 50, 75, and 1. Many sellers feel that persons can be more easily influenced to purchase just below these breaks because buyers assume the price was lowered. In fact, the price may or may not have been lowered. It can as easily be raised. For example, would you assume that a tube of toothpaste marked 69 cents was marked up from 50 cents or marked down from 75 cents?

It is the attractiveness of the numbers themselves that gives rise to *even pricing* where only round numbers are used. It has been suggested that people are attracted emotionally to roundness and symmetry of words and numbers. Words and letters that display this symmetry get more attention and more favorable responses. Thus 66 cents is more attractive as a figure than 43 cents. It is suggested that a customer prefers $10.00 to $9.75 because of an emotional attachment to the numbers. Many managers attempt to combine the odd-even concepts when pricing. They assume that a price of $10.99 is both attractive and conveys the suggestion of a bargain to the consumer.

Many retailers practice *loss leader* or *leader* pricing where prices are greatly reduced on a few popular items in order to attract customers. Products that are popular, well-advertised, and purchased frequently are the ones that typically make good leaders. Some products that make good leaders include soft drinks, floor coverings, calculators, and used cars. It is thought that customers will come in to purchase the advertised leader but stay to buy other items at the regular markup. Management expects the increase in total volume to offset the lower price of the leader. Leaders are also used to trade up. In other words, the leader draws the customer into the store, salespeople attempt to get the customer to purchase a higher-priced product by using the quality comparison to the leader.

Loss leaders have been associated with sales below cost, and of course, it is the impression of a tremendous bargain that influences the consumer to buy. In fact, any unusually low price just above cost, at cost, or below cost can qualify as a leader. The idea is to create in the mind of the consumer the impression of low prices overall in the store, or to suggest an unusually good bargain on the leader item. Leader pricing is popular in supermarkets, department stores, and discount houses.

The practice of *bait pricing* exists in a situation where the seller attempts to attract business with a low price but does not intend to sell the merchandise. In all other respects, bait pricing is like leader pricing. This technique is common in the furniture industry and in door-to-door selling. There is a famous case of the "rebuilt like new" vacuum cleaner sold door-to-door in the 1940s and 1950s. Each salesperson was given one cleaner. If it was sold, it was not replaced. The rebuilt cleaner was used to get the customer's attention, then the salesperson pointed out all its bad features to keep the customer from buying it. In bait pricing, salespeople attempt to trade the customer up to a more expensive item or over to a similar item with a normal markup. Some furniture dealers have offered a dining room set for $1.00 to the first customer on a certain day. Of course, no matter when you arrive, someone just purchased the set. Such practices are not only unethical and illegal, but they are also poor business. Consumers should not be influenced by sellers using this practice.

Price Lining

Few business managers follow a policy of blind adherence to a single markup percentage. What would be the results if a hardware retailer bought bolts for 5 cents, 6 cents, 7 cents, 8 cents, 9 cents . . . and $1.00 per thousand, and marked each batch up 40 percent? We know that the results would be utter confusion over the large number of prices only 1 cent apart. Neither the customer's nor the seller's interests would be served. The concept of price lining was developed to reduce this type of price confusion.[4]

The term *price lining* refers to the seller establishing a small number of price points on similar merchandise, then taking varying markups. For example, a retailer may have a line of hats priced at $2.99, $5.99, $10.99, and $14.99. Any hat that costs up to $2.50 is priced $2.99, hats costing $2.51 to $4.50 are priced $5.99, etc. Although the markup on each hat varies, the retailer is expecting some target markup, say 30 percent over the entire line.[5]

Price lining influences consumers by its simplicity and cost saving. It allows the seller to keep cost low and better serve the buyer's interest at the same time.

Price lining offers many opportunities for the merchant to increase efficiency and lower price. It reduces the time clerks spend with customers explaining small price differences. It simplifies the pricing of merchandise, marking of items, and display. Stock planning is improved because customer demand is concentrated at the price points. Thus more items can be carried at these points, but fewer items are carried overall. The resulting simplification of the line saves time in purchasing, reduces storage space requirements, and makes physical movement easier.

Price lining reduces confusion for the customer in making decisions. There is less worry over small differences in quality. Buyers can concentrate on the one or two price ranges that particularly interest them. Furthermore, price lining provides the customer with greater merchandise choice at the price point.

Competitive Pricing

Competitive pricing concerns policies that relate the firm's prices to those of competitors. As a general statement, managers can price at the level of competitors, above competitors, or below competitors.

The term *prestige pricing* refers to a policy of consistently setting prices above those of competitors. Prestige pricing is used when the product is highly differentiated. The idea is to influence consumers, and place competitors at a disadvantage, by presenting your product as greatly improved, superior in quality, or possessing unique features. For example, Curtis Mathes proudly proclaims, "the highest priced television in the industry — and darn well worth it." Product quality and warranty are emphasized in Curtis Mathes advertising. Toyota, Lady Clairol, and Levi Strauss also tend to price above the market. You probably know of a retail jewelry or clothing store in your town that emphasizes prestige prices.

A special case of prestige pricing occurs when the product is so highly thought of that sales increase as the price increases and decline when the price is lowered. The influence here on consumers is based on a snob appeal. Rolls Royce, Cartier, Hummel Figurines, and Waterford Crystal are products with high prices based on a snob appeal. Their customers do not want to pay less. One of their pleasures is to report to others how much the products cost. Businesses with such products can price over a wide range and still effectively influence customers to purchase.

By *customary pricing* we mean setting price at the same level as competitors. Managers tend to use customary pricing under three circumstances. The first situation is when the product is nondifferentiated and the industry highly competitive. There is little influence on customers to buy one product over another, so price becomes very important. Perhaps the best examples are found in the markets for staple items such as bread, work clothing, and beer.

The second situation leading to customary pricing is when there is "traditional pricing" in the industry. Soft drinks, paperback books, ice cream, restaurant coffee, and candy are examples. This situation is like the first, except there is a strong tendency not to modify the price. Customers come to expect the traditional price and develop little resistance to buying at that price. The price influences because it is comfortable and expected.

The third situation that leads to customary pricing occurs when the number of sellers is small so that immediate adjustments to price changes are possible. In the first two cases, price tends to be the same because of competition, but in this latter case it is the lack of competition that accounts for price comparability. Customary prices are found in the automobile and mobile home industries where there are highly differentiated products. These prices are also found in the motel business where products are highly standardized. In each case the number of competitors is few and price adjustments can occur quickly.

When a marketing manager sets price below that of competitors it is known as *fighting brand pricing*. Honda and Sylvania are companies that price some of their product lines below the market. Consumers are influenced by the low prices that imply a bargain. The business attempts to establish in the consumer's mind the idea that it has quality products at low prices. The company takes the attitude that it will not be undersold on its fighting brands. For example, Anheuser-Busch Bavarian is a fighting brand. Fighting brand pricing denotes an aggressive posture. Promotion may be aggressive also and the firm attempts to take the market away from competitors.

Some businesses use a modifed form of price lining, *full line pricing,* in conjunction with competitive pricing. The firm uses three broad categories of products to price above, at, and below competitors at the same time, attempting to convey the notion that the firm has higher-quality products than competitors at lower prices. In one sense, the attempt is made to convey a confused price-quality image to customers. One of the better examples of full line pricing is found in the furniture industry. Within any product category, such as bedroom furniture, living room furniture or dining room furniture, the seller has a prestige line, a customary line, and a fighting brand line. On the fighting brands, the seller appeals to customers with small margins, low quality, and a price emphasis. The customary price line has normal markups, quality comparable to competitors, and prices that are competitive. Customers are influenced by differentiation, service, and promotion. The prestige line has high quality, high margins, and low sales. It makes the snob appeal to customers and provides an impression of class that pervades the entire operation.

Unit Pricing

The use of unit pricing is a relatively new way of influencing consumers. *Unit pricing* is the use of a shelf label that reports product price and the price per ounce, pound, pint, or some other standard measure. Unit price responds to the consumer's need to compare prices more easily. The proliferation of package sizes and "two for . . . " pricing makes price comparison almost impossible under the traditional manner of reporting in grocery stores, discount houses, and other wide line sellers.

Which carrots are the bargain in Illustration 18-1? It is difficult to tell without the unit price indicated on the shelf. Imagine how difficult it is to make price comparisons in a grocery store with perhaps 15,000 different items. Although several studies have been made of consumer use of unit pricing, the results do not show a clear pattern of use. The expectation by managers is that consumers will use this price technique more as they become used to it, and it will begin to have more effect on the way they make decisions.[6] It is in the seller's interest to promote unit pricing because it is in the consumer's interest.

Illustration 18-1
Unit pricing

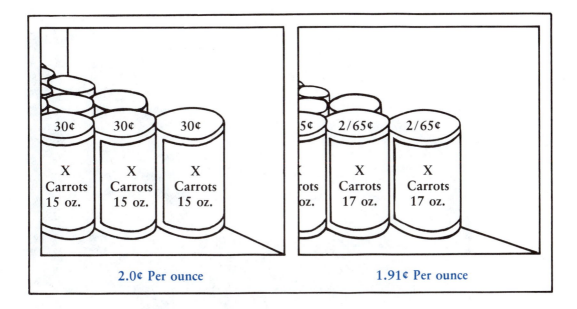

| 30¢ | 30¢ | 30¢ | 5¢ | 2/65¢ | 2/65¢ |
| X Carrots 15 oz. | X Carrots 15 oz. | X Carrots 15 oz. | X rots oz. | X Carrots 17 oz. | X Carrots 17 oz. |

2.0¢ Per ounce   1.91¢ Per ounce

Special Event Pricing

Pricing cannot be separated from other efforts to influence consumers. Pricing is often coordinated with promotion, or *special events,* in order to have greater impact on consumer decision making. Management frequently lowers the price on seasonal merchandise and promotes it heavily. We often find preseason and end-of-season sales in the clothing, automobile, and furniture industries. The price alone has an impact on consumers, but it is even more effective when combined with the persuasive power of promotion. The pre-Easter sales of many department stores are well-known special events, and so are the end-of-season sales on automobiles.

Special events do not have to be tied to seasons. Some other important special events include business openings, business bankruptcies, special anniversaries, and the introduction of new product lines. The expectation is that the lower price and increased advertising can create goodwill for the business and a favorable image in the minds of buyers.

Professional Pricing

Professional pricing involves the pricing of personal services sometimes based on great skill or education. Doctors, lawyers, and consultants sometimes use this pricing technique. The dentist charges $20 for a checkup and cleaning, $60 for a filling, etc. The lawyer charges $25 for a title search, $250 to draw up a will, and $500 for a divorce. These professionals feel the customer is paying as much for the education as for the service. Such prices inspire confidence in consumers, who

Photo 18-2

Professional pricing involves the pricing of personal services performed by highly educated and skilled professionals.

tend to associate the price with the level of skill of the professional. Even so, professionals do not want the price to appear out of line or to give the impression of gouging. In fact, many professionals do tend to underprice compared to what buyers are willing to pay for their service.

Importance of Ethics in Pricing

The importance of ethics in pricing cannot be overestimated. Consumers are becoming much more aware of ethical considerations related to business in general and to prices specifically. Many businesses are beginning to respond to this situation.

Many businesses today attempt to keep prices as low as possible in order to serve the interests of the largest possible segment of the public. Consumers are influenced by this attitude when they are aware of it. Although many firms practice ethics in pricing, it is often difficult to distinguish the results from fighting brand pricing or leader pricing. The difference lies in the reason for keeping the price low. If the reason is basically a commitment to public service rather than to greed or competition, then it is ethical pricing.

Johnson and Johnson Company practiced ethical pricing when it introduced Rhogan to protect pregnant mothers against incompatible RH blood factors in their unborn children. The Salk polio vaccine was introduced and made available to everyone at practically no profit to the manufacturers. There is some evidence that many drug companies practice ethics in their pricing. Even though the price of insulin, sulfa drugs, and penicillin may appear high, their manufacturers could probably charge much more. Demand is inelastic, and the user would pay almost anything in a life-threatening situation. Most of the prices charged by firms are ethical in the sense that they are designed to reflect the legitimate interests of the management in its customers and its need for profit.

SERVICE TO CONSUMERS

Service is as important to consumers as are physical things, and service adds to the cost of physical things. In fact, there is no product that does not involve both a physical thing and some service. For example, a movie theater sells entertainment, but it also involves a building, film, and popcorn. A doctor, lawyer, or consultant sells primarily a service, but none of these specialists could function without their tools, which are physical things. On the other hand, furniture stores or specialty dress shops sell primarily physical things, but they could not operate without the services of delivery, storage, credit, and personal attention by the sales personnel. The same is true for any other product.

With so much diversity possible, let us carefully consider what is meant by the term service. A *service* is:

any activity with intangible benefits or satisfactions which is offered for sale or is provided in connection with the sale of physical products.

We observe from this definition that services are activities or operations of a personalized nature that one performs for another. There are benefits for consumers associated with services in just the same way as with any other physical thing. These benefits as we shall see have the ability to influence the consumer when making store and product choices in the market. In fact, the services that surround the sale can be, and often are, the deciding factor in the decision. For example, a consumer would not purchase a washer that he or she could not transport home, and a consumer who is short of cash cannot buy without the extension of credit.

Public Attitude Toward Service Is Low

In general, the American consumer has a poor attitude toward the performance of service. Perhaps no sector of business has received more criticism in recent years. Although there are many outstanding examples of service performance, many customers feel that they are continually ripped off by too high service prices, performance of unnecessary work, poor-quality work, charges for work not done, and the use of inferior support products at quality prices. Some of the criticism is justified and some is not, but it all contributes to the poor service image existing today. The major complaints fall into four categories.

First, there is the overall problem of dishonesty. There is as much dishonesty in the sale of services as there is in the sale of products. It is easy for a business to be dishonest in service sales because customers typically lack the knowledge to judge work properly. However, services must stand the test of repeat business if the firm is to survive, and this curbs dishonesty. Customers tend to avoid businesses about which they have real or perceived complaints. Furthermore, other firms exploit the dishonest firm's weaknesses. Finally, law enforcement agencies are constantly on alert for dishonest sellers of service.

Second, there is the problem of performance. Inconsistent and incompetent work is often taken for dishonesty by consumers. Sometimes it is, but often it is simply poor execution. Quality varies considerably in the performance of service.[7] Consumers become suspicious when they must take the car to the shop several times with the same symptoms. It is even worse if the customer is charged for different repairs each time. Nevertheless, the problem is often not dishonesty but an attempt to cover up poor skill or to recoup the cost of an original honest mistake.

Third, the failure of replacement parts is often attributed to dishonesty. It is puzzling to buyers why a replaced TV tube, sparkplug, or shaver head fails after only a few weeks of operation. Many consumers feel service firms deliberately use inferior parts. No doubt this happens, but most service firms are just as upset with the failure, which reflects on the firm's good name. It is a fact that the performance of many parts cannot be predicted.

Fourth, many consumers do not understand the price structure for service. Consumers do not feel that a service charge of $12 to $15 enforced by appliance repairpersons, plumbers, and electricians is fair when the actual problem may be minor and fixed in minutes. These consumers do not consider the cost of equipment and training. Consumers wonder why doctors will not make a house call at any price, and whether carpenters, bricklayers, and painters are really worth between $15 and $30 per hour. Of course, most of these complaints are explained by the conditions of supply and demand, the existence of strong unions, and local market conditions.

In practice, it does not matter whether consumer criticism is justified or not. Management must respond effectively to retain repeat sales and continue to make a profit. If enough buyers become concerned, they will shift their trade, or they will operate through government officials and consumer groups to obtain redress. It is in the interest of service businesses to do everything in their power to obtain and maintain a favorable public image.

Need for Service Responsibility

No amount of reassurance by business can completely offset the current poor opinion of business services. Abuses do exist, and they are likely to continue. Whether the abuses are more serious in the sale of services than in the sale of physical goods is open to question. However, unless a responsible attitude is taken by management the result is likely to be more government control of business. Responsibility for improvement rests on both the business and the consumer. Business managers can help change the current poor service image by recognizing their responsibility to customers. The firm's need for repeat business demands such an enlightened attitude. It is suggested that each firm:

1. Work for buyer satisfaction.
2. Utilize human resources effectively.
3. Meet or counter competition.
4. Perform within the law.
5. Make adjustments for poor work.

Consumers also have a responsibility to protect themselves in the service market. The rules listed below can greatly reduce the chance of poor or dishonest service:

1. Trade with reputable firms.
2. Ask for an explanation for all repairs.
3. Get cost estimates before allowing work.
4. Ask for the return of replaced parts.
5. Complain to the Better Business Bureau or Chamber of Commerce when necessary.

Such actions will not eliminate dishonesty, but they will reduce individual cases and cause the honest service dealer to think twice about a dishonest act.

SERVICES THAT INFLUENCE CONSUMERS

Few physical goods, as they come off the assembly line, match the variety of needs individuals have. Some type of service accompanies every good to make it a complete product. The system demands that management consider the needs of consumers when developing service policies just as with physical goods. What is required is a service philosophy.

A *service philosophy* is the business's attitude toward the rendering of service. Some firms provide such services as credit, delivery, installation, and parking but play down the service and discourage its use by customers. This is a *nonaggressive service philosophy*. The firm considers service primarily a restraint or cost to the firm. The idea is to keep service cost low by limiting customer use of the service or by poor performance. For example, a firm may provide delivery but seldom inform customers of the service, employ poor delivery equipment, infrequent delivery schedules, and ineffective package control. Such a firm is always seeking ways to reduce customer use of the delivery service.

Some managements consider service an opportunity and use it to generate sales.[8] This is an *aggressive service philosophy*. The management attitude is that if a service is worth performing at all, it should be used to its fullest extent. The firm doesn't just make service available. Rather, the firm promotes its service as a competitive weapon that provides real benefit to consumers. Labor and equipment costs must be incurred once it is decided to render a service, and these are the most important costs. Thus it makes sense to get as much revenue as possible when incurring these costs, and this entails promoting the service to customers. They should be used to influence the consumer's decision.

Credit Influences

Credit is a convenience to buyers which allows products to be acquired today and paid for later.[9] Managers know that credit can be a powerful influence on consumer decision making. The most important effect is to lower the impact of product price on the consumer's decision. Products can be bought even when the person does not have the ready cash. Customers expect credit from some types of stores such as department and furniture stores, and they will not consider firms that do not grant the service. Some products, such as major appliances, autos, and homes, cost too much to be purchased without credit. Credit can be a competitive weapon used to influence customers away from other firms. For example, one firm may gain an advantage over others by offering credit when other firms do not, or by offering it in a different way.

Other reasons business uses credit to influence customers include the fact that credit increases sales, evens out sales over the month, and encourages quality buying. Credit that allows customers to purchase in anticipation of earnings is convenient because it reduces the daily need to carry cash and makes it easy to take advantage of sale prices when they occur.

The major disadvantage to credit for customers is that it is not always free; there is an interest charge. Consumers most frequently encounter the *30 day charge account* which allows unsecured charges to be made during the month with no interest if paid off at the end of the month. Interest, say 1.5 percent, is charged on any unpaid balance remaining at the end of the month. Many firms today use credit cards to identify their credit customers. *Installment credit* means that the customer makes a promise (contract) to pay a fixed amount, at regular intervals, over a specified period until the principal plus all interest is paid off. Installment credit is usually granted on durable, expensive items. It is secured by a *chattel mortgage*, which means that the item purchased is pledged against payment and can be repossessed upon default.

Warranty Influences

Warranty is a performance guarantee made by the seller to all types of consumers. Sellers must warrant their products, although there is an important element of customer satisfaction in the type of warranty provided.[10] The influence on consumers from warranties comes from the security provided.[11] If the product does not live up to expectations the seller is to provide relief. This security is so important that consumers consider it the deciding factor in the purchase of many products.

There are two types of warranties. First, an *implied warranty* affects all sellers, and it means that the merchandise conforms to the seller's statement of condition and is suitable for ordinary use. The seller can make a disclaimer of implied warranty, but it is up to the courts to decide if the disclaimer is valid. An *express warranty* is a definitive statement of specific operating conditions that are subject to adjustment by the seller if the product fails to perform. The expressed

Photo 18-3

Delivery can be a crucial factor with some items. Would the customer have this sign repaired if pickup and delivery weren't included in the repair service?

© *Copyright Photo 1988 by Larry Kolvoord*

warranty goes beyond an implied warranty to specify performance facts and type of adjustment. Express warranties may include guarantees on materials, workmanship, and defective parts for some stated period of time. Typically, the seller has the right to decide whether to repair or replace defective products. Any warranty may be written or oral, but oral guarantees are difficult to prove.

Delivery Influences

Delivery is transporting merchandise to the customer's home. Delivery is one of the most important services that influence consumers. Delivery influences in several ways that are important to the firm's management. First, it provides shopper convenience. Often customers simply do not want to be bothered with the merchandise. Perhaps they have other errands and the product would be in the way. Delivery is essential when the customer is purchasing by telephone or using mail order. Thus, while it is a convenience, it may be an essential convenience. Second, some items, such as furniture, pianos, and major appliances, cannot be physically carried by the consumer. The consumer must take into account any delivery charges when determining the total cost of the product. Third, layaway items require later delivery. Many seasonal items are purchased in advance for later delivery. Fourth, some consumers obtain psychic satisfaction from having the store deliver. It may provide a feeling of power, or it may be important to consumers to have neighbors observe the store's truck at their home.

Although some businesses charge for delivery, most provide free delivery within a specified area, say fifty miles from the store. Even when the firm charges, it is typically a nominal fee which does not cover the total cost of the service. The firm's management must consider the effect of delivery charges on the customer's decision when instituting this practice.

Installation Influences

Installation goes beyond delivery and includes mounting, hook-up, testing, and in some cases operational training for consumers. Major appliances, heating and cooling systems, and carpeting are examples of products that typically require installation. The cost of installation is typically included in the price of the product, but some businesses make a separate charge. Most managements have no choice about providing installation. If the product requires the service, it must be offered. There are important competitive advantages to be had from the efficiency with which the service is performed. Quite often the efficient use of the product is directly related to installation.

Installation is one of those services that many customers take for granted. They are not aware of its influence until the service is not available or until they are charged for it. Therefore, its influence is strategic, but it often goes unnoticed in the total decision process. The essential fact is that many products could not be obtained by consumers were it not for installation.

Repairs Influence

Repairs are corrective actions taken on products after the consumer has begun using them. Repairs are made both to honor warranties and to make a profit on the service itself. Any type of mechanical device breaks down in time. Thus, there is a large market for the repair of these items. Consumers are influenced by repairs in much the same way they are influenced by products; repairs make the items usable, thus rendering specific functional satisfaction. The repair service may or may not be important to the consumer when making the initial decision to purchase. Often consumers making purchase decisions do not think about the likelihood of breakdowns, although they should. Repairs over time can add significantly to the cost of the product, and they can have an important impact on the consumer's satisfaction with the product purchased.

There are two types of repairs: (1) routine maintenance of items under warranty and (2) repairs made on unwarranted products. Most firms that sell equipment and other mechanical devices offer repair service. The firm must honor warranties anyway, and it makes sense to attempt to make a profit off the service by extending its use. Some managements that provide repair service to their customers have an independent agent perform the service. The agent may obtain a commission on each item handled for the seller. Of course, this arrangement means that the manager must exert effective control over the agent to be sure that customers receive proper satisfaction.

Alterations Influence

Alteration is a service designed to give a product an exact fit. Alterations relate more to clothing than to any other type of products. The importance of alterations to the consumer is that they have the capacity to negate completely any otherwise desirable product. Like repairs, alterations usually go unnoticed until they are not available or are poorly executed. Then the consumer becomes very concerned about alterations. Alterations also involve the inconvenience of a delay in obtaining the product. Many consumers prefer to purchase ready-made items so that they do not have to have them altered. Of course, the fit may not be good.

It is not necessary for retailers to alter the clothing they sell, but most do because: (1) it is expected, (2) it creates goodwill, (3) competitors make it necessary, and (4) it generates store traffic. Minor adjustments in length and waist measurements are typically performed without charge. The cost of such alterations are included in the price of the product. However, more and more retailers are beginning to charge for even these alterations. Major alterations, affecting the overall fit of the clothing, may carry an extra charge. Even so, the price of alterations seldom completely covers the cost of performing the service.

Other Services That Influence

There are several other types of retail services that influence the consumer's decision to purchase. These include provision for parking, product wrapping, gift wrapping, providing customer information, baby-sitting, leasing, handling of complaints, and provision for returns. Most of these services are a convenience to customers and influence for this reason. Services affect the final decision on the product only marginally. However, in particular instances that can be the deciding factor. For example, if consumers do not obtain proper directions on the location of a product from a store's information desk, they may become discouraged and leave without buying.

Leasing is becoming more important to retailers. Today, such less expensive items as typewriters, storage bins, office furniture and carpet cleaners, as well as automobiles and movies, are leased by customers. The reasons given for leasing include:

1. It is cheaper than owning in some instances.
2. It does not require "up front" money as in owning.
3. It allows one always to have the latest model.
4. It may be that one can lease a more expensive model than one can own.
5. There is less headache with service and maintenance.

Many retailers are expanding their leasing service because consumers want it and because it offers excellent opportunities to make a profit.

Service Standard Policies

Standards are essential in order to control a service program; the essential word is "control." The cost of satisfying everyone is usually prohibitive, so the seller of a service must maintain performance within reasonable limits that are fair to the customer and to the business. There are many things that management can do to aid in the control of service. A first step is to see to it that service personnel understand what is expected of them.[12] Service procedures and rules should be carefully explained. For example, it does not cost much for personnel to be pleasant and attentive when dealing with the public. The desired behavior is more likely when personnel understand what is expected.

It is essential to maintaining service standards that personnel be adequately trained. In some businesses, where home service is an integral part of the sale of the product, management conducts regular training. Even factory training of retail personnel is not uncommon in some industries such as the automotive, appliance, and equipment industries. Factory training tends to assume that competent instructors conduct the training, and it tends to provide more uniform performance among different firms. In the automobile industry, retail mechanics return to the factory on a regular basis to review service practices and learn about new models.

The organization can establish specific service standards. For example, management may set the average time for providing a service, set a minimum number of calls a person is to make in a day, place limits on the number of dissatisfied customers in a period, determine the cost per customer contact, etc. For example, a TV repairperson may be expected to average a certain number of calls per day. A hairdresser may be expected to create a certain hairstyle in thirty minutes.

Where standards are established, it is important to monitor the work. When the work is performed at the business, monitoring may be done by personal observation of the manager. Monitoring can also be done by use of reports where the activity is performed outside the business. Reports can show which employee did the work, the date, where it was done, how long it took, what action was taken, and the charge. Most managers attempt to use a combination of personal observation and reports to control service. When standards are established and effectively monitored, they not only facilitate the control of service activities, but they help assure customers of consistent quality.

Service Cost

At some point in the process of establishing service policy, the firm must develop a policy toward service cost. With rising prices and increasing consumer demand for service, this decision is becoming more important.

Service costs can be absorbed by the seller. This practice results in a lower gross margin unless the increased cost is offset in some way by higher sales volume. The manager may absorb service cost if the increased service increases product sales or if the increased cost is due to more or better service which increases demand for the service. Service cost may be passed on to the buyer. If the price is competitive or if performance is superior at a higher price, then this can be an effective policy. If there are sufficient buyers who want the service, even at higher prices, then a differential appeal to the market is possible. For example, traditional department stores that specialize in service at a price, and discount houses that offer little service, but lower prices, can both be successful. Some firms use a combination policy whereby the firm and the customer share the cost of service. Such a policy is designed to recoup part of the expense of service while affecting demand only minimally. The policy can be effective, but it is used less than the previous two mentioned.

SERVICE AFTER THE SALE

The seller has not completed his or her responsibility when the sale is made. The final responsibility is to make sure that the consumer continues to be happy with the decision to purchase the product; this requires service after the sale. After-sale service involves several activities. It may be as simple as calling the customer to check on the product's performance. Some firms use this as a chance to make new sales. For example, a store may call and note that you purchased children's clothing three months ago. They may inquire about performance and remind you that it is time to restock. Other activities may be involved in service after the sale. Some minor adjustments may be necessary in the product. This situation is fairly typical in the purchase of automobiles and some appliances. Customers may be reminded of routine maintenance requirements. A note can be sent thanking the customer for the business.

Service after the sale is extremely important. The major reason is that dissatisfied customers do not typically make repeat purchases, and these lost sales affect profits. Perhaps even more damaging to the firm's long-run market and profit position is the fact that dissatisfied customers often express their displeasure to others. The result can be a poor image, and no firm can afford for such an image to be held by large numbers of customers. On the other hand, satisfied customers not only come again, but they bring others. Therefore, after-sale service should be considered part of the total sales process.

QUESTIONS

1. Give examples of how managers use price and service to adjust the final product more nearly to the consumer's specific needs.
2. Name the three basic functions served by price for the consumer and give examples of each.
3. Price information supplied by business persuades consumers at two levels. Identify and discuss these levels with examples.
4. List money-saving reasons for management to adhere to a one-price policy in the pricing of merchandise.
5. Identify and discuss the different types of psychological prices.
6. The term "price lining" refers to a range of markup prices on similar items. Discuss and give examples where this technique might be used.

7. Are there products you would not buy because the price was too low? Discuss your answer.
8. Which brands generally have higher prices, private brands or national brands? Discuss your answer with examples.
9. What is the importance of unit pricing to the consumer? Do you use the unit price during shopping? Discuss why or why not.
10. Is it more difficult to price professional services or products? Discuss your answer with examples.
11. Discuss the statement: "The services that surround the sale can be, and often are, the deciding factor in the purchase decision."
12. Do you perceive the attitude of the public toward services as low? Discuss why or why not.
13. Discuss the implications of the statement: "We are in business to satisify all consumers."
14. Discuss the statement: "If an individual has to use credit it is an indication they are poor managers of their money."
15. Discuss why some individuals are willing to pay high prices for a product at a specialty store when they could get the same product at a lower price at a discount store. Give examples.

NOTES

1. Verkatakrishva V. Bellue, "Consumer's Awareness and Attitude Towards Repricing," *Journal of the Academy of Marketing Science,* Vol. 10 (Spring 1982), pp. 125–39.
2. Eitan Gerstner, "Do Higher Prices Signal Higher Quality?" *Journal of Marketing Research,* Vol. XXII (May 1985), pp. 209–15; Chr. Hjorth-Anersen, "The Concept of Quality and the Efficiency of Markets for Consumer Products," *Journal of Consumer Marketing,* Vol. 1 (1984), pp. 35–41.
3. G. Ray Funkhouser, "Using Consumer Expectations as an Input to Pricing Decisions," *Journal of Consumer Marketing,* Vol. 1 (1984), pp. 35–41.
4. David J. Reibstein and Hubert Gatignon, "Optimal Product Line Pricing: The Influence of Elasticities and Cross-Elasticities," *Journal of Marketing Research,* Vol. XXI (August 1984), pp. 259–67.
5. Shmuel Oren, Stephen Smith, and Robert Wilson, "Pricing a Product Line," *Journal of Business,* Vol. 57 (January 1984), pp. 873–99.
6. David A. Asker and Gary T. Ford, "Unit Pricing Ten Years Later: A Replication," *Journal of Marketing,* Vol. 47 (Winter 1983), pp. 118–22.
7. Jack J. Kasulis and Marie Adele Hughes, "Husband-Wife Influence in Selecting a Family Professional," *Journal of the Academy of Marketing Science,* Vol. 12 (Spring 1984), pp. 115–27.
8. Michael R. Solomon, Carol Surprenant, John A. Azepiel, and Evelyn G. Gutman, "A Role Theory Perspective on Dyadic Interactions: The Service Encounter," *Journal of Marketing,* Vol. 49 (Winter 1985), pp. 99–111.

9. A. Parasuraman, Valerie A. Zeithaml, and Leonard L. Berry, "A Conceptual Model of Service Quality and Its Implications for Future Research," *Journal of Marketing,* Vol. 49 (Fall 1985), pp. 41–50.

10. Ellen Day and Richard J. Fox, "Extended Warranties, Service Contracts, and Maintenance Agreements a Marketing Opportunity?" *Journal of Consumer Marketing,* Vol. 2 (Fall 1985), pp. 77–86.

11. Elizabeth C. Hirschman, "Consumer Payment Systems: The Relationship of Attribute Structure to Preference and Usage," *Journal of Business,* Vol. 55 (October 1982), pp. 531–45.

12. Ronald E. Michaels and Ralph L. Day, "Measuring Customer Orientation of Salespeople: A Replication with Industrial Buyers," *Journal of Marketing Research,* Vol. XXII (November 1985), pp. 443–46.

Response To International
Consumer Decisions

CHAPTER OUTLINE

I. **MULTINATIONAL CONSUMERS**
   A. Importance of Multinational Markets
   B. Is Consumer Decision Making Different Worldwide?

II. **MANAGEMENT MUST BE AVAILABLE IN THE MARKET**
   A. Organization for International Trade
   B. Methods of Reaching International Markets

III. **MANAGEMENT MUST BE CULTURE-CONSCIOUS**
   A. Language Is Necessary to Interact
   B. Education Defines the Interaction
   C. Class Structure Decides Type of Interaction
   D. Religion Underlies Social and Moral Behavior
   E. Different Personal Tastes and Different Responses

IV. **INCOME LIMITS PURCHASING POWER**

V. **MANAGEMENT MUST RESPOND TO ATTITUDES**
   A. Attitudes Toward Materialism
   B. Don't Force Change
   C. Be Aware of Marketing Practice
   D. Overcome Suspicion of Foreign Products
   E. Take Advantage of Shopping Preferences

VI. **TIPS FOR INTERNATIONAL MANAGERS**

CHAPTER OBJECTIVES

After completing your study of Chapter 19, you should be able to:

1. Discuss multinational consumers.
2. Discuss the importance of multinational markets.
3. Explain why management must be available in the market.
4. Explain the importance of management being culture wise.
5. Discuss why income limits purchasing power.
6. Discuss the importance of management responding to attitudes.
7. Discuss the tips for international managers.

We have pointed out how various segments of American consumers differ in their decision-making process. Even more diversity exists among the members of the world community. Marketing managers must understand these inherent differences so they can better appeal to the international consumer by means of more effective marketing strategies. In this chapter we discuss some of the more important considerations that affect marketing in multinational markets.

MULTINATIONAL CONSUMERS

No doctor would dare operate on a patient without understanding something about his or her psychological as well as physical condition. It is the same in international marketing. No manager would dare enter the world market without understanding about the nature of consumers as well as their numbers. In this book, a *multinational consumer* is anyone from a country other than the seller's who determines personal wants, buys products, and uses those products. As with any other consumer, more than one person may be involved in this purchase process. The manager gains information about multinational consumers by means of analysis.[1] *Multinational consumer analysis* is the study of persons from nations other than the seller's to discover their wants, behavior, and purchase tendencies. It is expected that much of this analysis centers on the differences between consumers in the seller nation and consumers external to the seller nation.[2] Multinational consumer analysis uses economic, social, cultural, and psychological characteristics of the people as a basis for designing effective marketing strategies. Because of national differences, it is typically necessary to conduct multinational consumer analysis in each country in which the seller markets.

Importance of Multinational Markets

The importance of multinational markets to business cannot be underestimated.[3] Foreign products sold in the United States affect nearly every business in the nation. Much of our steel comes from Europe, our clothing from Hong Kong, our knickknacks from Taiwan, and our raw materials from Africa and Central America. American companies ship grain, high-tech equipment, arms, and other finished products all over the world. Every American firm has the potential to become involved in international trade. Some American firms such as

Photo 19-1

Many products we use every day are manufactured by foreign-owned companies.

Coca-Cola, IBM, and TWA do over half their business overseas. Such foreign firms as Unilever, Shell, and Nestlé have substantial operations in the United States.

There are five major reasons why American firms enter foreign markets. First, there is potential profit. There are almost infinite possibilities for firms to serve and make money on a multinational basis. Second, entry into foreign trade may be based on surplus production at home. Foreign markets may be an attractive alternative to laying off workers and closing plants. Third, diversification may be the company stimulus that causes entry into foreign markets. There are many ways of diversifying, including adding products, entering new industries, entering new geographic regions, consolidating with other companies, and developing foreign markets. Entry into foreign markets can provide a hedge against sales declines at home. Fourth, a business may enter a foreign market because of political pressure. This pressure may come in many forms such as political pressure to conserve resources, military pressure, or the need for an economic lever. Fifth, a business may seek foreign markets for humanitarian reasons. The opportunity to serve and to aid the people of emerging nations can be a strong motivator in some companies. In most cases, a business enters foreign markets for a combination of these reasons.

Is Consumer Decision Making Different Worldwide?

The answer to the question, "Is consumer decision making different worldwide?" is "yes and no."[4] As indicated by Table 19-1, the basic consumer decision process is the same the world over. However, the manner in which con-

Table 19–1

Multi-national Consumer Decision Process

Stage of Decision Process	Comments
Problem recognition	Problems differ
Search for information	What to buy, where to buy, when to buy, and how to buy differ
Purchase decision	Consider different factors
Post-purchase assessment	Attitudes toward redress differ

sumer decisions are handled varies widely among nations.[5] A few examples will serve to make the point.

In many Westernized nations, problems relate to which product brands to purchase, how much, and when. In many developing nations, problems revolve around simply finding sufficient food, clothing, and shelter to survive. The entire recognition step is affected by particular needs faced by the consumer.

Culture, as well as existing facilities, affects search patterns among consumers. For example, in some Mediterranean, African, and South American nations it is common to shop each day for food. A person may spend the entire morning buying the day's meals. Many nations do not have automobiles or other rapid transit systems; this greatly limits the manner of search. Even many European nations do not have the number and variety of stores found in the United States. For example, Europe is just now experimenting with supermarkets. The specialty store is still the most important type in most nations.

The purchase decision reflects the various degrees of importance of specific factors to people in the nation. For example, the restricted merchandise offerings in Russia, Central America, India, China, and other nations affects the purchase decision. Low income in many nations plays a major role in the products to be decided on and may require long-range commitments to own items such as automobiles, homes, and furniture. In Egypt the waiting period for a Fiat is about ten years.

Consumer attitudes toward postpurchase redress differ among nations. If the consumer has no hope of redress for poor, ineffective or faulty products, there is little need to get upset about it. Some of these consumers take a fatalistic attitude about products that they have purchased. In nations such as the United States where consumer rights are protected by business and the law, it is different. Consumers are more likely to take action if products are not satisfactory. It is obvious that while the consumer decision process is the same worldwide, there are considerable differences in how consumers in the various nations go about making the decision.

MANAGEMENT MUST BE AVAILABLE IN THE MARKET

If business management is to take advantage of the opportunities offered by international markets, the firm must be physically available in the target nation.

Illustration 19-1
Domestically organized company

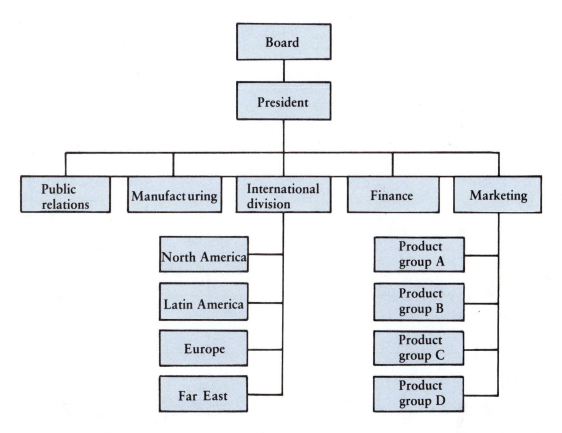

Two important points must be explained relative to this issue. They are how the firm is organized to operate in the international market and the methods for reaching those markets.

Organization for International Trade

There are two basic way‿ that business can organize to operate in international trade. A *domestically organized company* treats the home market as primary and the foreign market as secondary. Illustration 19-1 demonstrates a domestically organized company. The central offices with top management are located in the home nation; only operating managers, if any, are located in the foreign nations. The marketing manager distributes to the entire home market, and one international division is responsible for the remainder of the world. Manufacturing, promotion, sales, financing, and public relations are geared for the home market and are only adapted for international trade. Managers think of the home market first in everything. This type of organization often has problems that make it difficult to succeed in international markets. There are communications problems between home and overseas representatives. Functional areas,

Illustration 19-2
Internationally organized company

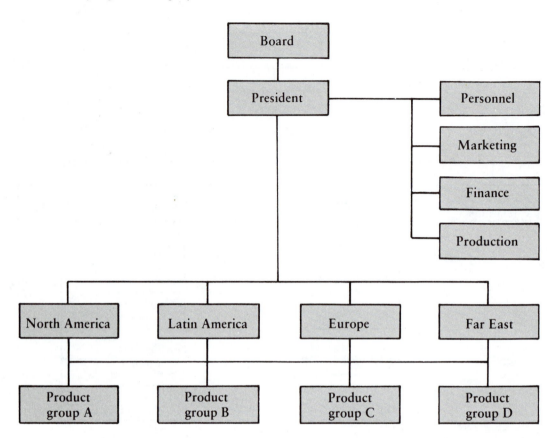

such as promotion and finance, geared for home markets, are often not suited for overseas operations. There is often no real understanding of the local situation in the overseas market. Lack of interest by home management leads to a poor international effort.

An *internationally organized company* treats all markets, domestic and foreign, as primary markets.[6] Illustration 19-2 shows an internationally organized company. In this company, top managers are located in regional foreign offices with their staffs. Middle managers are operating out of the nation they serve, with local staffs typically provided from the country. All markets are considered equal, and the products, along with all promotion, finance, etc., are tailored for the particular nation. The company does not consider itself an American, British, or French company. Rather, it considers itself a multinational company. More and more companies are taking on some variation of this type of organization.

Methods of Reaching International Markets

It is not enough to have an effective organization to operate in the international arena. The company must also provide for the physical movement of pro-

Illustration 19-3
Alternative international channels

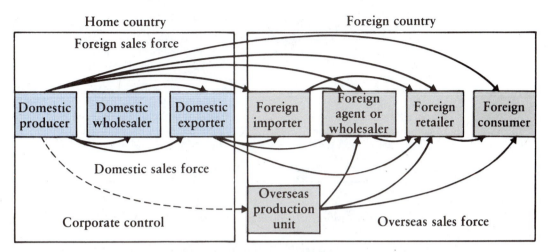

Source: C. Glenn Walters and Blaise Bergiel, *Marketing Channels* (Glenview, Illinois: Scott, Foresman and Company, 1982) p. 516.

ducts between nations.[7] Illustration 19-3 demonstrates most of the possibilities. Notice the long supply lines existing with the use of a domestic sales force. Compare this distribution system to the overseas sales force. The overseas production unit could just as easily be a regional sales office. Management has much greater control over financing, product, sales force, promotion, publicity, and personnel when the channel is short. These functions can be adapted to the local situation; when local personnel are used the problem of communication and appeals is greatly reduced.[8] Of course, it is more costly to operate overseas offices. Sometimes overseas managers lose identification with the home office, which can be a problem.

MANAGEMENT MUST BE CULTURE-CONSCIOUS

We know that culture refers to learned behavior, passed down from one generation to the next, and in this chapter we use the term broadly to mean a country's "national characteristic." There are varying definitions of the elements of culture, including one that counts seventy-three "cultural universals." For the purpose of this discussion, we divide culture into: (1) language, (2) education, (3) social structure, (4) religion, and (5) personal tastes.

Language Is Necessary to Interact

Language is the primary means of communication between people. It is the single most important cultural element. When managers in one nation seek to trade with managers in another nation, the first hurdle they must overcome is the language. Before managers can interact they must be able to communicate through the spoken word, gestures, expressions, or body movements. Clumsy use of language, at best, can lead to inaccurate information; at worse, it can offend.

Table 19–2
Problems with Translation

American English	Translation
"Body by Fisher"	"Corpse by Fisher" (Flemish)
"Come Alive with Pepsi"	"Come out of the grave with Pepsi" (German)
Braniff's 747 Rendezvous Lounge	Braniff's 747 Meet-your-Mistress" Lounges (Portugese)
Exxon's Engros fertilizer	Exxon's "in bulk" Fertilizer (French)
"Accessories for your closet"	"Accessories for the toilet" (British)
"Let Hertz put you in the driver's seat"	"Let Hertz make you a chauffeur" (Spanish)
"Sticks Like Crazy"	"Sticks Foolishly" (Japan)

Business managers cannot afford such problems when their whole purpose is to inform or persuade.

Management has two methods of dealing with foreign languages. First, interpreters are used—only at the point of contact with customers. In all other activities the seller's native language is used. The problem is that the more times thoughts are transferred, the greater the chance for misunderstanding. Interpreters seldom understand all languages with equal competence, and misunderstanding can result.

Second, managers can learn the language of the nation with which they wish to do business. This is more difficult, but it pays dividends in the long run. Unfortunately, it is not enough to be able to parrot words in another language. To really function effectively, the manager must understand what lies behind the words. This means learning about the culture along with subtle differences in meaning of words. Note the differences in meaning of phrases in Table 19-2. Can you imagine the problems any one of the companies would have if they attempted to use these perfectly acceptable American phrases in their overseas promotion? In fact, several of these businesses did make that mistake.

Language has a subtle role in our lives. It directs our thinking and constrains us. Linguists emphasize the predominance of action verbs in American English. Far Eastern languages are comparatively rich in terms to describe abstract concepts and philosophies. Spanish has a rich vocabulary of terms to present ideas without revealing the speaker's true feelings. In order to function effectively in foreign markets, management must understand these differences. For example, what did the Englishman mean when he announced, "He put some petrol in his lorry, drove to his girlfriend's flat, took the lift to her floor, knocked her up, and then they threw up a cake"? He said, "He put some gas in his truck, drove to his girlfriend's apartment, took the elevator to her floor, rang the doorbell, and then they made a cake." It does matter how you say it.

Only by having individuals immersed in the culture of the nation can all language barriers be eliminated. This achievement is very difficult. English is rapidly becoming the universal language of business around the world; French also serves this function to some extent. This has led many nations to become bi-

Photo 19-2
American companies that expand into foreign countries need employees who understand the language and culture.

Marathon Oil Company

lingual, and it has relieved some responsibility for Americans to learn other languages. It does not solve the problem, however. American managers, like managers of other nations, must strive to pick up on language variations even in English. Sometimes the words differ even when speaking a common language. "Table the report" in the United States means to postpone it, but in Great Britain it means "bring the matter to the forefront."

Education Defines the Interaction

Language is the communicator of culture, but education defines the manner of interaction. Two persons cannot communicate what is neither known nor understood. Education refers to one's collection of facts and ideas. We tend to think of education in association with school, but it is much broader than that. Every experience we have adds to our education. In Westernized nations, formal education tends to be associated with school, but this is not true in all nations. In some

Table 19–3

Public Expenditure for Education and Illiteracy, Selected by Country

| Country | Year | Public Expenditure for Education | | Percent of adult population illiterate, 1985 |
		Percent of total public expenditure	Percent of gross national product	
United States	1981	(NA)	6.8	(NA)
Afghanistan	1982	6.4	(NA)	76.3
Algeria	1982	(NA)	4.7	50.4
Argentina	1982	14.5	2.5	4.5
Australia	1981	14.5	5.8	(NA)
Bangladesh	1983	8.6	1.9	66.9
Brazil	1983	17.0	3.2	22.3
Burma	1977	12.2	1.6	(NA)
Canada	1983	(NA)	8.0	(NA)
Chile	1982	(NA)	5.8	5.6
China: Mainland	1982	10.0	2.3	30.7
Colombia	1983	21.5	3.0	11.9
Czechoslovakia	1983	(NA)	5.1	(NA)
Egypt	1983	8.9	4.1	55.5
Ethiopia	1982	11.3	4.1	44.8
France	1980	(NA)	5.1	(NA)
German Dem. Rep.	1982	(NA)	5.5	(NA)
Germany, Fed. Rep. of	1982	(NA)	4.6	(NA)
Ghana	1981	(NA)	2.0	46.8
Hungary	1983	6.6	5.8	(NA)
India	1982	(NA)	3.2	56.5
Indonesia	1981	9.3	2.2	25.9
Iran	1982	15.6	(NA)	49.2
Iraq	1982	8.5	(NA)	10.7
Italy	1979	11.1	5.0	3.0
Japan	1982	19.1	5.7	(NA)
Kenya	1983	15.3	4.8	40.8
Korea, Republic of	1983	(NA)	3.4	(NA)

African countries, schools are more often limited to the role of preparing individuals for lives in the modern world. Elders and oral historians transmit traditions and values to young people in these countries.

It is very difficult for persons with widely differing educational levels to communicate, even if both are aware of the problem. There is just too much variation in the total understanding and experience of the two parties. Table 19-3 shows the wide range of education across the world. Managers must make a special effort to understand this problem and adjust their policies to deal with it. The problem is that you cannot afford to talk up to or down to consumers.

Pepsodent was unsuccessful in Southeast Asia because it promised white teeth (expected by highly educated persons) to a market where black or yellow teeth are symbols of prestige. In Quebec, a canned fish manufacturer tried to promote a product by showing a woman dressed in shorts, golfing with her husband, and

Table 19–3 (Continued)

| Country | Year | Public Expenditure for education | | Percent of adult population illiterate, 1985 |
		Percent of total public expenditure	Percent of gross national product	
Malaysia	1982	(NA)	7.5	26.6
Mexico	1983	6.4	2.7	9.7
Morocco	1983	22.0	7.5	66.9
Mozambique	(x)	(NA)	(NA)	62.0
Nepal	1982	(NA)	2.5	74.4
Netherlands	1982	(NA)	7.7	(NA)
Nigeria	1983	(NA)	2.1	57.6
Pakistan	1983	(NA)	2.0	70.4
Peru	1983	14.7	3.3	15.2
Philippines	1982	(NA)	2.0	14.3
Poland	1982	8.9	4.1	(NA)
Portugal	1981	(NA)	4.7	16.0
Romania	1983	7.5	2.3	(NA)
Saudi Arabia	1983	10.5	4.7	(NA)
South Africa	1976	15.0	4.3	20.7
Soviet Union	1983	10.2	6.6	(NA)
Spain	1979	16.4	2.6	5.6
Sri Lanka	1983	7.0	3.0	12.9
Sudan	1980	9.1	4.7	(NA)
Syria	1983	12.1	5.9	40.0
Tanzania	1983	15.3	5.8	(NA)
Thailand	1983	(NA)	3.9	9.0
Turkey	1983	(NA)	3.4	25.8
Uganda	1983	(NA)	1.8	42.7
United Kingdom	1982	11.9	5.5	(NA)
Venezuela	1982	21.2	6.5	11.4
Yugoslavia	1982	(NA)	4.3	8.8
Zaire	1980	32.3	5.8	38.8
Zimbabwe	1982	15.9	7.8	26.0

Source: *Statistical Abstract of the United States* (Washington D.C., U.S. Dept. of Commerce, 1987), p. 823.

planning to serve canned fish for dinner. This promotion was inconsistent with the local image of women. Maxwell House advertised itself as the "great American Coffee" in Germany but discovered that the Germans have little respect for American coffee. African men were upset by a commercial for men's deodorant that showed a happy male being chased by women. They have been taught that they should be strong and not be ruled by women. In Japan, photograph frames aimed at the office market flopped. It is engrained in the Japanese from childhood that the workplace is not for pictures. The Japanese put photos into albums and show them only to friends.

It may be necessary sometimes for a firm to hire special consultants to deal with educational differences. Many Americans have had some college. Check the literacy rate in Table 19-3 for most other nations. It is possible to study all promotional material and sales talks to determine if each is suited to the consumer that they are directed toward.

Low literacy rates also cause problems with product labels and instructions about a product's use. Advertisers must rely heavily on radio and television commercials and billboards and print ads that use pictures rather than words. However, even the use of these media can present a problem if you do not understand the host consumer. Illustration 19-4 depicts a possible laundry soap advertisement that could be used on a billboard—or could it? The advertisement shows that if you take a dirty shirt and use the soap, the result will be a bright clean shirt. This would be an acceptable advertisement if the consumer reads from left to right. However, what are the implications if the consumers are Chinese and read from right to left? Brand names and trademarks are especially important because people recognize and remember products by the pictures or symbols on the labels.

The multinational marketer is further concerned about the educational situation in foreign markets because it is a key determinant of the nature of the consumer market. Some implications are:

1. Well-educated consumers tend to want more sophisticated information about products and tend to use more sources of information when making purchase decisions.
2. If girls and women are largely excluded from formal education, marketing programs will differ greatly from those aimed at American females.
3. Conducting marketing research can be difficult, both in communicating with consumers and in getting qualified researchers.
4. Products that are complex or need written instructions may need to be modified to meet the educational and skill levels of the market.

Literacy appears to have its strongest association and causal impact on openness to change and on potential for change. Becoming literate appears to unlock creative abilities that enable consumers to picture themselves using the product being sold. The higher the literacy skills of consumers and the more accustomed they are to reading, the greater their flexibility in thinking. Greater flexibility in thinking increases the readiness to accept new products and new ideas. The greater the consumers' reading abilities and the more materials they read, the more likely it is that they will possess the knowledge or skills necessary to accept and use new products to satisfy their problems.

Class Structure Decides Type of Interaction

Although education defines the manner of cultural interaction, class structure, more than any other factor, determines with whom you associate. Every culture has a class structure which determines social status. Class structure has a direct bearing on consumption. Preferences for food, alcoholic beverages, clothing, entertainment, housing, and home furnishings are all related to one's social class.

Illustration 19-4
A billboard advertisement without language

One notable characteristic of class structure is social mobility. In the United States, persons born in the working class are able to move into the middle class via education and occupational achievements. In India, class structure is less fluid; a person's inherited class restricts his or her educational and occupational opportunities. Consumer behavior is much more likely to be different across social classes in India than in the United States.

Not only is social mobility an important dimension of class structure and consumer behavior, but the relative size and number of distinct classes within a society is also significant. Illustration 19-5 shows the relative sizes of different social classes in six different societies.

Consumers in the upper classes in almost all countries seem to be more similar to each other than they are to the rest of the consumers of their own society. Consumers in the lower classes tend to be more culture-bound; that is, they are less aware of other cultures or of these cultures' solutions to the problems of life. They are, therefore, more distinct from each other in the ways they dress, the food they eat, and how they spend leisure time and discretionary income. Consumers in the middle classes are more apt to do cultural "borrowing" from other classes when there is some social mobility from lower to middle class and within the middle classes. Therefore, the larger the upper and middle classes, the more likely the consumers are to buy products and services that are not culture-bound— food, clothing, household items, and personal care products.[9]

The social class system of a society affects consumer behavior, first, through value systems induced by social class, and second, through the desires of con-

Illustration 19-5

Class structure in different societies: The top rectangle shows the size of the upper class relative to middle and lower classes for each society in the figure.

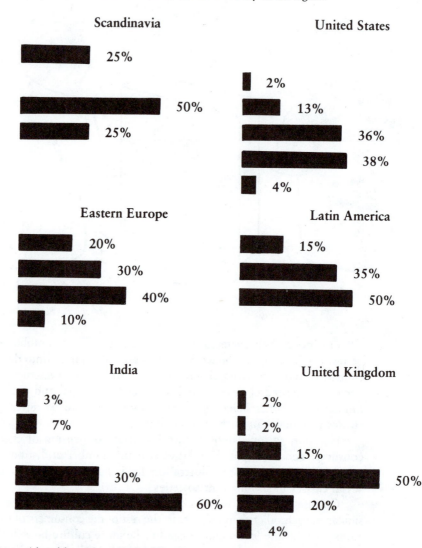

Source: Adapted from Edward W. Cundiff and Mary T. Hilger, *Marketing in the International Environment,* (Englewood Cliffs: Prentice-Hall, Inc., 1984), p. 117; *Statistical Abstracts of the United States,* 1984, Section 33.

sumers to gain prestige from socially approved class symbols. In general, status symbols have logical, utilitarian origins, whether they be cattle in African tribes or a VCR in the United States. But a distortion of economically logical purchasing priorities develops when desires to own certain products become widespread because of social pressures; for example, when a middle-class Mexican family buys a refrigerator (often prominently displayed in the living room because it is a symbol of affluence) rather than putting the money into more education for their children or some other investment. By the same token, the Western fashion industry creates social pressure to conform to frequent changes in dress styles, skirt lengths, and the like, that go well beyond practical needs for clothing or even aesthetic satisfactions of variety in appearance.

In any social class system, each class has somewhat distinct problems, consumption patterns, and behavior in satisfying these problems.

Religion Underlies Social and Moral Behavior

Religion underlies all of any society's social and moral beliefs. There is no society that does not depend heavily on religion to provide the moral and ethical rewards and sanctions common to its people. However, moral positions vary among nations. European religious positions are more tolerant than their American counterparts toward sex and nudity.

Nearly all nations that follow Christianity subscribe to the Protestant ethic. According to this ethic, God rewards hard work with success and the accumulation of material things. These material acquisitions are seen as good. People are expected to dominate the physical environment and the animals. On the other hand, Islam and Hinduism consider emphasis on material wealth ignoble. Hinduism also prescribes vegetarianism and lays special stress on abstinence from beef. Moslems are prohibited from drinking alcoholic beverages or eating pork. Jews are prohibited from eating pork or shellfish. All these religions take a stand on how one can behave and which products are acceptable to consume.

Other activities affected by particular religions include social behavior, manner of dress, ways of doing business, and relations between people. Religion also influences male-female roles and societal institutions and customs such as marriage and funeral rites. Islam restricts the role of the female to the household. She is also confined to an inferior role in society. In addition, a Moslem man may have more than one wife, but a woman must practice monogamy. Traditional Hinduism also restricts women, following the occasional belief that to be born a woman is a sign of sin in a former life. In Hinduism, marriages are arranged by relatives; although a man may remarry if widowed, a woman may not.

In India several firms have shown an awareness of religion and capitalized on a return to "traditional thinking." One of them, Ciba-Geigy, introduced an herb-flavored version of its Binaca toothpaste, based on the herbs and medications discussed in the *Yajur Veda*, a 4000-year-old text on the science of life. Helene Curtis introduced an acne cure, Pimponyle, containing camphor and herbs, which was also based on the *Yajur Veda*.

Religion tends to establish rules of moral and ethical behavior. The Ten Commandments of the Christian and Jewish Bibles and the rules of the Koran are examples of religious effects on morality and ethics. Thus how consumers feel about shoplifting, stealing in general, abiding by contracts, dealing honestly, and telling the truth in all buying situations has basic roots in religion.[10] For example, there is very little stealing in Moslem countries because it is forbidden by religion and the punishment is very severe.

A question that any management operating in a foreign nation must answer is, "Under whose morals and ethics do we operate?" Do we conform to what is legal and ethical in our own nation or do we conform to the manner of conduct in our host nation? These are not simple questions. For example, American firms are expected to abide by the ethical and legal rules of the American society. This places American firms at a decided disadvantage in countries where government and other officials expect to be bribed. Such conduct is often condoned culturally, and the bribes pay the officials' primary income. Most firms tend to conform to the standards of conduct in the host nations. This can get them into legal trouble at home. If the market is worth it, the firm simply pays the fine and considers it a cost of doing business in that nation.

Different Personal Tastes and Different Responses

There are differences in tastes, or aesthetics, perceived by persons in different nations.[11] We are referring to the consumer's understanding of fine art, music, drama, and dancing. These aesthetic values are manifest in product design, styles, colors, expressions, and symbols.

Cultural aesthetics have significant implications for consumer behavior. For example, in the design of product or package, the firm should be sensitive to the local consumers' aesthetic preferences. A washing machine manufacturer serving the British, French, and German markets found that the generally accepted ideas about what constitutes good design were different in each market. The German consumer preferred a design that was larger and more sturdy in appearance, that gave a feeling of sound engineering and durability. The French consumer preferred a smaller, lighter-appearing machine that did not overly dominate a small kitchen.

Refrigerator manufacturers from the Western nations initially encountered great difficulty in selling their products in Japan. The refrigerator motors were simply too noisy for the typical Japanese home. Sears is cited as one of the companies most successful in the sale of Western refrigerators in Japan. It achieved this status by designing a refrigerator specifically for use in the local conditions.

In Britain, products like Jell-O are preferred in solid-wafer or cake form, Germans usually buy salad dressing in tubes, and most of the industrialized countries outside the United States employ the metric system for measurements. American firms have made design modifications in response to all of these cultural aesthetics.

Color is a large, though often subliminal, part of a marketing effort to better aid the consumer during his or her decision-making process. Color in advertisements, on packages, and on the product itself may communicate different impressions to international consumers.

The significance of different colors on consumer behavior can vary from culture to culture. In America, for instance, we use colors to identify emotional reactions; for example, we "see red," we are "green with envy," or we "feel blue." Certain colors have particular meanings because of religious, patriotic, or aesthetic reasons. The marketer needs to know the influence of color on consumer behavior in planning products, packages, and promotion. For any market, the right choice of colors, illustrations, and appeals is related to the aesthetic sense of the *buyer's* culture rather than that of the *marketer's* culture.

For example, blue is considered a warm color in Holland and a cold color in

Table 19–4
Positive and Negative Colors of Selected Cultures

Japan	India	Europe	Latin America	Mexico	Middle East
Positive colors are in muted shades. Combinations of black, dark gray, and white have negative overtones.	Positive colors are bold colors such as green, red, yellow, or orange. Negative colors are black and white if they appear in relation in weddings.	Generally white and blue are considered positive. Black often has negative overtones.	Popular colors are generally bright or bold yellow, red, or green. Purple connotes death.	Yellow flowers connote death. Red flowers are thought by the superstitious to cast spells and white flowers to lift them.	Positive colors are brown, black, dark blues, and reds. Pink, violets, and yellows are not favored.

Sweden. Green is a restful color to consumers in the United States, but is repugnant to those in Asian countries, where it connotes the illness and death of the jungle. In China and Korea, white is for funerals and red is popular. Red, however, is not popular in Africa. Purple is associated with death in Brazil and in many Spanish-speaking countries. Yellow flowers are a sign of infidelity in France, but one of death in Mexico, and they can be a sign of disrespect to a woman in the Soviet Union. These and the other examples in Table 19-4 illustrate that marketers must be careful to check if colors have any special meanings before using them in their marketing programs.

To most of the world, blue is thought to be a masculine color, but it is not as manly as red in the United Kingdom or France. Although pink is believed to be the foremost feminine color by Americans, most of the rest of the world considers yellow to be the most feminine color. Color, as it applies to the concept of culture, offers many general and specific insights into the behavior of consumers. This is a starting point for marketers who wish to understand consumers. It is imperative for the marketer to appreciate cultural nuances governing the relevant marketplace whether it be in the United States or abroad.

INCOME LIMITS PURCHASING POWER

Income, like culture, is a basic factor in consumer decision making worldwide. Income limits the amount and type of products that people can buy, and this fact is directly related to what business can sell. Table 19-5 illustrates the wide range in gross national product (GNP) between nations. In current dollars the Soviet Union only has 56 percent of the purchasing power of the United States. The next closest nations are Japan (35 percent), the German Federated Republic (21 percent), and France (17 percent).

The standard of living in most nations of the world does not approach that of the United States. This does not mean that products cannot be exported and sold in these nations, but it does mean that the seller must fit the types of products to the purchasing power of the consumers in the nation. Products that Americans

Table 19–5

Gross National Product in Current and Constant (1982) Dollars and Per Capita: 1975 to 1983

Country	Current Dollars					
	1975	1979	1980	1981	1982	1983
United States	1,556.1	2,421.0	2,632.8	2,942.9	3,056.9	3,297.8
Afghanistan	1.8	2.7	3.0	3.0	3.2	4.0
Algeria	17.8	31.0	35.1	39.3	43.6	49.9
Argentina	35.7	50.7	55.4	55.1	54.6	56.5
Austria	32.8	49.9	56.1	61.4	66.1	69.9
Bangladesh	4.7	7.9	9.0	10.5	11.3	12.4
Belgium	45.0	65.9	73.2	78.4	84.2	87.8
Brazil	121.8	204.5	237.6	253.4	269.5	272.0
Bulgaria	28.2	39.6	42.0	47.3	51.6	52.7
Burma	2.3	3.8	4.5	5.2	5.9	6.4
Canada	149.0	223.2	243.0	273.9	278.9	299.4
Chile	10.8	18.8	22.0	25.2	22.1	22.6
China: Mainland	145.0	239.0	274.0	309.0	353.0	401.0
Taiwan	15.8	31.7	36.8	42.2	46.7	52.2
Colombia	17.1	28.1	32.0	35.4	37.7	39.6
Czechoslovakia	61.8	87.4	97.6	106.4	115.0	121.0
Egypt	9.2	18.3	22.0	25.2	28.5	32.2
Ethiopia	2.2	3.2	3.7	4.1	4.4	4.8
France	272.2	413.5	456.4	499.7	538.7	564.3
German Dem. Rep.	77.3	110.3	123.0	137.6	145.2	153.2
Germany, Fed. Rep	339.8	518.6	575.2	629.0	662.3	699.0
Ghana	21.1	28.1	31.3	32.3	32.2	32.1
Greece	19.4	30.8	34.1	37.0	39.2	40.9
Hungary	37.5	53.4	58.9	65.0	71.4	73.3
India	80.2	116.4	135.2	156.3	170.8	189.6
Indonesia	32.7	56.0	66.8	79.8	87.2	93.5
Iran	65.7	96.8	92.2	94.6	104.0	110.1
Iraq	14.1	34.5	39.7	24.5	25.2	25.5
Italy	172.6	262.0	296.9	321.8	341.6	350.7
Japan	465.9	743.9	849.2	963.9	1,059.8	1,137.8
Kenya	2.6	4.2	4.9	5.6	6.0	6.6
Korea, Dem. Peo. Rep.	9.0	14.4	15.5	18.6	20.5	21.6
Korea, Rep. of	26.8	52.5	54.2	62.9	70.8	80.7
Madagascar	1.8	2.4	2.7	2.6	2.8	2.9
Malaysia	9.0	16.2	19.2	22.5	25.2	27.3
Mexico	66.7	110.0	129.2	150.7	158.2	157.6
Morocco	6.9	11.0	12.4	13.3	15.0	16.1
Mozambique	2.8	3.6	4.0	4.5	4.9	4.9
Nepal	1.2	1.9	2.0	2.3	2.5	2.6
Netherlands	74.2	109.4	120.2	129.8	136.3	143.8
Nigeria	40.2	61.8	67.5	70.1	70.4	69.5
Pakistan	13.1	21.3	25.3	29.6	32.7	36.6
Peru	11.4	14.9	17.3	19.6	30.9	19.1
Phillipines	16.5	27.9	31.7	36.0	39.4	41.6
Poland	122.4	168.9	179.9	186.5	196.0	212.9
Portugal	10.5	16.6	18.8	20.4	22.1	23.0

Part 4 – Consumer Evaluation and Decision

Table 19–5 (Continued)

Country	Constant U.S. Dollars			Per capita (dol.)		
	1975	1980	1983	1975	1980	1983
United States	2,573.8	3,066.2	3,163.9	12,027	13,465	13,492
Afghanistan	3.0	3.5	3.8	225	225	269
Algeria	29.5	40.9	47.0	1,845	2,176	2,269
Argentina	59.1	64.5	54.2	2,318	2,330	1,824
Austria	54.2	65.3	66.8	7,226	8,713	8,908
Bangladesh	7.8	10.5	11.9	99	118	124
Belgium	75.5	85.2	84.2	7,603	8,605	8,505
Brazil	201.5	276.8	261.0	1,857	2,268	1,987
Bulgaria	46.6	48.9	50.6	5,352	5,492	5,684
Burma	3.9	5.2	6.2	126	152	173
Canada	246.5	283.0	287.2	10,859	11,792	11,535
Chile	17.8	25.7	21.7	1,744	2,331	1,886
China: Mainland	239.8	319.1	384.7	254	314	376
Taiwan	26.2	42.8	50.1	1,626	2,405	2,663
Colombia	28.3	37.2	38.0	1,175	1,500	1,342
Czechoslovakia	102.3	113.7	115.7	6,910	7,430	7,511
Egypt	15.2	25.7	30.9	412	608	674
Ethiopia	3.6	4.3	4.6	126	143	147
France	450.2	531.5	541.4	8,543	9,898	9,896
German Dem. Rep.	127.8	143.2	147.0	7,562	8,576	8,800
Germany, Fed. Rep	562.0	670.0	670.6	9,093	10,875	10,903
Ghana	34.9	36.5	30.8	3,384	3,014	2,300
Greece	32.0	39.7	39.2	3,560	4,137	3,963
Hungary	62.0	68.5	70.3	5,909	6,405	6,570
India	132.7	157.5	181.9	215	227	248
Indonesia	54.1	77.8	89.7	394	514	541
Iran	108.6	107.4	105.6	3,261	2,766	2,485
Iraq	23.4	46.3	24.2	2,086	3,533	1,667
Italy	285.5	345.8	336.5	5,116	6,067	5,924
Japan	770.6	989.0	1,091.6	6,904	8,467	9,149
Kenya	4.3	5.7	6.3	315	344	339
Korea, Dem. Peo. Rep.	14.9	18.1	20.7	936	1,008	1,079
Korea, Rep. of	44.3	63.1	77.4	1,207	1,586	1,870
Madagascar	2.9	3.1	2.8	381	360	295
Malaysia	14.9	22.3	26.2	1,200	1,594	1,746
Mexico	110.3	150.4	151.2	1,878	2,215	1,997
Morocco	11.4	14.5	15.4	625	690	673
Mozambique	4.7	4.7	4.7	515	389	360
Nepal	2.0	2.3	2.5	153	154	153
Netherlands	122.8	140.0	138.0	8,962	9,926	9,581
Nigeria	66.5	78.6	66.7	1,012	1,019	782
Pakistan	21.6	29.4	35.1	287	337	373
Peru	18.9	20.1	18.3	1,220	1,142	984
Phillipines	27.3	36.9	39.9	634	752	734
Poland	202.5	209.5	204.3	5,954	5,884	5,580
Portugal	17.4	21.8	22.1	1,851	2,205	2,206

Table 19–5 (Continued)

Gross National Product in Current and Constant (1982) Dollars Per Capita: 1975 to 1983

Country	Current Dollars					
	1975	1979	1980	1981	1982	1983
Romania	50.7	81.2	87.2	96.0	104.4	108.7
South Africa	35.1	49.8	58.7	67.2	71.3	72.1
Soviet Union	892.3	1,418.2	1,579.0	1,715.0	1,843.4	
Spain	97.3	137.8	152.1	165.9	178.8	190.1
Sri Lanka	2.0	3.2	3.7	4.2	4.7	5.1
Sudan	4.1	7.2	4.9	9.3	10.4	10.7
Sweden	56.2	76.4	84.3	91.0	96.7	102.5
Switzerland	55.3	75.6	85.9	96.4	101.1	105.4
Syria	6.0	9.3	11.3	13.3	15.0	16.4
Tanzania	2.6	4.1	4.5	4.9	5.1	5.0
Thailand	14.2	24.5	28.2	32.3	35.6	39.5
Turkey	26.2	39.3	42.3	48.2	53.7	57.7
Uganda	3.6	3.8	4.0	4.6	5.3	5.9
United Kingdom	263.1	378.9	405.5	435.0	475.0	507.5
Venezuela	35.4	55.2	59.5	65.6	68.2	69.7
Yugoslavia	27.3	46.4	51.9	56.6	60.2	61.6
Zaire	3.3	4.1	4.5	4.9	5.2	5.5

take for granted are far beyond the reach of consumers in Nepal, Kenya, Ethiopia, Burma, and Zaire. These consumers are concerned with providing basic food, clothing, and shelter. These nations are markets for basic farm commodities, simple work clothing, and building materials.

Even nations such as Egypt, Bulgaria, Chile, Korea, and Peru have limited purchasing power. Many items that Americans consider essential for everyday life—such as automobiles, refrigerators, stoves, typewriters, fashion clothing, restaurant dining, watches, and television—are beyond the reach of the majority of consumers. They cannot afford American prices. Where these products are made available in these nations, they are provided by internal suppliers at much lower prices. Of course, any nation is a market for any product on an extremely small scale. For example, although most people of such oil-producing nations as Saudia Arabia, Iran, and Iraq cannot fulfill their basic wants, the privileged classes can afford anything and are willing to pay whatever is necessary to indulge themselves. The seller cannot be too careful when analyzing foreign markets for product fit.

MANAGEMENT MUST RESPOND TO ATTITUDES

Every culture has a set of attitudes and values which influences nearly all aspects of consumer behavior and the decision-making process. The more marketers can learn about certain key attitudes, the better prepared they will be to under-

Table 19–5 (Continued)

Country	Constant U.S. Dollars			Per capita (dol.)		
	1975	1980	1983	1975	1980	1983
Romania	83.9	101.6	104.3	3,956	4,576	4,613
South Africa	58.0	68.4	69.2	2,273	2,769	2,240
Soviet Union	475.9	1,651.6	1,768.6	5,799	6,220	6,490
Spain	161.0	177.1	182.4	4,547	4,736	4,774
Sri Lanka	3.4	4.3	4.9	245	290	315
Sudan	6.8	5.7	10.3	425	306	510
Sweden	92.9	98.2	98.4	11,334	11,833	11,850
Switzerland	91.4	100.1	101.1	14,281	15,635	15,552
Syria	9.9	13.1	15.8	1,331	1,490	1,609
Tanzania	4.2	5.3	4.8	274	284	236
Thailand	23.4	32.8	37.9	552	688	746
Turkey	43.4	49.3	55.4	1,071	1,071	1,125
Uganda	6.0	4.6	5.7	519	362	407
United Kingdom	435.2	472.3	486.9	7,771	8,433	8,690
Venezuela	58.5	69.3	66.8	4,609	4,007	3,977
Yugoslavia	45.2	60.5	59.1	2,113	2,699	2,584
Zaire	5.5	5.3	5.3	220	184	198

Source: *Statistical Abstract of the United States* (Washington, D.C., U.S. Department of Commerce, 1987), p. 824.

stand why consumers behave as they do, especially when their reactions are different from what the marketer has learned to expect in dealing with their consumers.

Attitudes Toward Materialism

How the people of a nation feel about acquiring material wealth is an important factor of foreign trade. The United States has been called the "affluent society" and "the achieving society." The reason is that Americans subscribe to the Protestant ethic, and they strive to acquire more and better products to improve their standard of living. We are oriented toward owning things, and wealth is considered a sign of social status. Most Westernized nations, especially those of Western Europe, have more or less the same attitude toward owning products. It is much easier for consumers in such nations to justify buying. Appeals can be made to social acceptance and status. It is possible to explain how the product will make living easier for the owner. Products can be freely displayed without concern for public reaction.

There are many nations in the world that take the opposite attitude toward wealth and product ownership. In Buddhist, Hindu, or Moslem societies, such as Burma, India, Bangladesh, and Afghanistan, which have a large part of the world's population, "wantlessness" is an ideal. People are not so strongly motivated to consume. They are less interested in the appeals mentioned in the previous paragraph, and they do not try new products or brands early. Appeals to function, harmony with nature, and the serene life are more likely to succeed with these consumers.

Photo 19-3
Many foreign countries are consumers of American farm commodities.

Port of Tacoma

Don't Force Change

When a firm enters a foreign market, it invariably brings change by introducing new ways of doing things and new products to satisfy consumers. Americans in general accept change. The word "new" usually has a favorable connotation in America and even facilitates change when used to describe techniques and products. Many societies are more tradition-oriented, revering their ancestors and their traditional ways of producing and consuming.

The international marketer as an agent of change has a different task in such traditional societies. Rather than emphasizing what is new and different about the product, it might be better to relate it to traditional values, perhaps noting that it is similar but better.[12] In seeking to gain acceptance of its new product, the firm might try to get at least a negative clearance—that is, no objection—from local religious leaders or other elite opinion leaders. While any product must meet consumers' needs, it must also fit in with the overall value system if it is to be accepted. The more consistent a new product is with society's attitudes and values, the more quickly it will be adopted.

Be Aware of Marketing Practice

There is considerable difference in marketing practices among nations. What is accepted as sound marketing in one nation is frowned on in another. The manager in international trade must be aware of these differences, take advantage of the opportunities, and avoid the pitfalls where possible. This accomplishment takes careful analysis.

In a free enterprise market, consumers are as important as the other groups in the firm's environment. Managers devote considerable effort to satisfying these consumer wants. Prices, services, and appeals are controlled mostly by the market, with relatively little government intervention. Marketing as a business activity thrives in this type of setting. Products are made available according to consumer wants and not according to government wants. Any reasonable appeal that is ethical and legal can be made to consumers, and all the various media are employed to get the job done. The marketing function is very important to the business and receives considerable attention as a part of operations. Highly trained personnel engage in personal selling, advertising, publicity, and sales promotion. Much time and effort are spent developing product brands, labels, and logos.

In a totalitarian or socialist society where government is more important than consumers, things are different. The government, not the market, determines what is produced and consumed. Consumers receive according to their needs and not their contribution, so both the standard of living and productivity tend to be low. In such nations, marketing is not popular. Only goods have value; the services of marketing are not thought to add value to the product. Society frowns upon most forms of promotion; only basic information is considered appropriate. Brands are not important. Management must subscribe to these conditions when distributing in government-controlled societies. It makes distribution difficult, but it can be done.

There is considerable variation in the importance of marketing even within capitalistic nations. These differences arise out of cultural, social, and legal considerations historical to the country. A magistrate in Italy banned the sale of bottled Coca-Cola because he felt that the ingredient information should be provided on the bottle rather than on the bottle cap. Coca-Cola can adjust, but the change is costly. Canada requires that labels be in both French and English. Firms operating in Canada can comply, but it increases the cost of selling in that nation. France requires that only the French language can be displayed on products. This requires that all label and promotional material be translated.

In Great Britain the pharmaceutical industry was required to reduce its advertising-to-sales ratio from 14 percent to 10 percent within two years. Foreign sellers must conform to this standard. Many countries either prohibit or severely restrict the context of television advertising. In France, as in some other European nations, there is no advertising on TV during or between programs. All commercials are presented together at a specific time. In Costa Rica, products connected with health must be submitted for government approval before sale. In France, children may not be used in promotion. International sellers can conform to these requirements, but they must first understand what they are and adjust prices for the extra cost involved.

The widely accepted practice of using premiums to influence consumers during their decision-making process can cause problems to multinational firms. In Austria, premium offers to consumers come under the discount law, which prohibits any cash reductions that give preferential treatment to different groups of customers. Since it is considered that most premium offers would result in discriminatory treatment of buyers, they normally are not allowed. Premium offers in Finland are allowed with considerable scope as long as the word "free" is not used and consumers are not coerced into buying products. France makes premium offers, for all practical purposes, illegal, since it is illegal to sell below cost or to offer a customer a gift or premium conditional on the purchase of another product. Furthermore, a manufacturer or retailer cannot offer products different from the kind regularly offered—for example, a detergent manufacturer cannot offer dish towels; the cereal box offers common in the United States would be completely illegal under this law.

Overcome Suspicion of Foreign Products

Many persons view anything foreign as potentially threatening. Workers fear these products will take away jobs or reduce salaries. Business fears the competition. Governments worry about the balance of trade and the influx of foreign capital.[13] Consumers also worry that foreign products are inferior or unsafe. Many Americans still remember the attitude immediately after World War II that Japanese products were cheap and inferior. It has taken years for the Japanese automobile industry to overcome this image. When a foreign seller's product has a poor image there are two courses of action available. The seller can do as Nissan did, engaging in an active, long-term campaign to change the attitude. This alternative is more likely with a company that has a strong brand in other international markets and operates primarily from the seller's country. The other alternative is to downplay the fact that the product is foreign. Few Americans are even aware that Shell Oil Products, Norelco razors, and Nescafé products are not made by American firms. This policy is more likely when the seller has some production and management staff in the foreign nation to which it is selling.

Not all views toward foreigners and foreign products are negative. Foreign products of high quality may be perceived as exotic rather than threatening. Belgian lace, French wine, Japanese cameras, and German microscopes are all viewed as distinctive and of extra-high quality in world markets. In these instances, the foreign identification actually provides an advantage in the marketplace. Success in a foreign market may depend on the firm's ability to blend in with the local scene and develop a domestic identity or the ability to convince local consumers that "foreign" means better.

Take Advantage of Shopping Preferences

The manager should study carefully the shopping preferences of a nation and conform to these where possible.[14] Of course, there are advantages in attempting to change shopping behavior, as with the introduction of a new type of retail operation.

Shopping behavior is partly a result of options. For example, housewives in the United States tend to shop more often in large supermarkets, which are common in the United States, while French housewives tend to patronize small traditional stores, which are more common in France.

Photo 19-4
In many foreign countries, families shop every day for staple foods.

© *Charles Marden Fitch/Taurus Photos*

A few examples illustrate how buying habits are influenced by cultural elements. One-stop shopping is unknown in most parts of the world. In many foreign markets people buy in small units, sometimes literally on a meal-to-meal basis. Also, they buy in small specialty stores. To buy food for a weekend, a consumer in West Germany may visit the chocolate store, the dairy store, the meat market, the fish market, and possibly some other specialty food stores. While this may seem to be an inefficient use of time, we must recognize that a shopping trip is more than just a chore to be done as fast as possible. It is a major part of the consumers' social life. They visit with friends and neighbors in these shops. It is only in recent years that large supermarkets have appeared in some Western European countries.

U.S. consumers also tend to use more convenience products than their French counterparts. This is especially true in relation to take-out dinners, packaged cold cuts, and paper plates and cups, all of which are widely available in the United States and not in France. On the other hand, more common convenience products such as instant desserts and canned main dishes, which are found in most stores in both France and the United States, appear to be used with similar frequency in both countries.

It is possible to argue either that differences in the retail environment affect consumer shopping habits or that differences in consumer preferences affect the retail environment. Attitudes toward shopping may differ in different cultures; many Americans see shopping as a chore, and most Europeans do not.

In many cultures, the old order is changing with regard to shopping habits. This is particularly true in parts of European countries, Japan and Hong Kong, where there is a growing tendency to adopt American-style goods and shopping habits.

Hong Kong, like many other Asian cities, has witnessed a revolution in food-buying habits during the past ten years. Whereas the Chinese traditionally preferred fresh food, the trend now is toward buying imported, frozen, prepared, or canned items. To this extent, the time-honored daily visit of the Hong Kong consumer to street markets for fresh meat, fish, fruit and vegetables is becoming less of an institution; supermarkets are growing in popularity.

Supermarkets are not the only retailing institution gaining in popularity. Fast-food franchises are also gaining acceptance in some countries. One of the lessons American food executives have learned, however, is that it is often possible to introduce a new concept abroad, but more difficult to take an item domestic consumers have traditionally eaten and offer it in a new form. McDonald's hamburgers gained quick acceptance in Hong Kong, where hamburgers were a totally new concept.

TIPS FOR INTERNATIONAL MANAGERS

The reader is no doubt aware by now that there are both opportunities and problems involved with international marketing that do not apply to domestic marketing. While we cannot cover most of these considerations, we can offer some important tips for international managers.

First, before venturing into international markets make sure that your internal markets are reasonably secure.[15] International marketing is hazardous, and it is essential that management have a base of operations to fall back on in case of need. Second, management should develop a positive attitude designed to find opportunities to serve the international customer. The attitude should be that international customers will be treated with the same importance as the internal customer. Third, the company should obtain the best people possible and train them extensively—both in management techniques and in the new culture. Where possible, local managers and employees should be utilized. Bilingual managers should be either hired or trained.

Fourth, managers should become involved in the country in which they are operating. This means, whenever possible, living in the nation, working there, and interacting on a daily basis with the people of the nation. Fifth, foreign markets should be carefully analyzed for potential. Sixth, management must make sure that its products are not only of high quality, but that they are designed and promoted in accordance with the requirements of the nation to which they are sold.[16]

Seventh, management must keep prices competitive. It may be necessary to design a price strategy specifically for foreign trade, perhaps on a nation-by-nation basis. Finally, the best marketing tools available should be used. These tools must conform to the legal and ethical conditions in the foreign nation. Application of these tools should be carefully thought out, appropriate to the market, and efficient.

QUESTIONS

1. Why is the study of international consumer behavior important?
2. Identify and discuss the reasons why American firms enter foreign markets.
3. Identify several foreign firms that have operations in the United States.
4. Discuss the problems with the statement: "Consumers are the same worldwide."
5. Why may a firm have to reorganize for international marketing?
6. Would researching international markets be more difficult than researching home markets? Explain your answer.
7. Identify some terms that are unique to your area. Demonstrate how they might be used in promoting a product.
8. What methods would you use to promote a product in a country with a low literacy rate? Give examples.
9. Discuss, with examples, how different religions can affect marketing a product in a foreign market.
10. What guidance on ethics would you give an individual going into international marketing?
11. Identify some business practices that are acceptable in the United States but not in other countries.
12. Many persons view anything foreign as potentially threatening. Discuss why.
13. Identify ways in which marketing managers can induce change in international consumers.
14. Discuss with examples when it would be to a company's advantage to stress nationalism, i.e., "Made in America," "Made in France."
15. Identify and discuss some of the important tips for firms going international.

NOTES

1. Robert T. Green and Arthur W. Allaway, "Identification of Export Opportunities: A Shift-share Approach," *Journal of Marketing,* Vol. 49 (Winter 1985), pp. 83–88.
2. Nikhilesh Dholakia and Ruby Roy Dholakia, "Colloquium: Comparative Marketing in the Emerging World Order," *Journal of Macromarketing,* Vol. 2 (Spring 1982), pp. 47–56; Hiram C. Barksdale and L. McTier Anderson, "Comparative Marketing: A Review of the Literature," *Journal of Macromarketing,* Vol. 2 (Spring 1982), pp. 57–62.
3. Theodore Levitt, "The Globalization of Markets," *Harvard Business Review,* Vol. 61 (May–June 1983), pp. 92–102.
4. Robert T. Green, Jean-Paul Leonardi, Jean-Louis Chandon, Isabella C. M. Cunningham, Bronis Verhage, and Alain Strazzieri, "Societal Development and Family Purchasing Roles: A Cross-National Study," *Journal of Consumer Research,* Vol. 9 (March 1983), pp. 436–42.
5. Stephen J. Arnold, Tae H. Oum, and Douglas J. Tigert, "Determinant Attributes in Retail Patronage: Seasonal, Temporal, Regional, and Interna-

tional Comparisons," *Journal of Marketing Research,* Vol. XX (May 1983), pp. 149–57.

6. William H. Davidson and Philippe Haspeslagh, "Shaping a Global Product Organization," *Harvard Business Review,* Vol. 60 (July–August 1982), pp. 125–32.

7. John J. Brasch, "Using Export Specialists to Develop Overseas Sales," *Harvard Business Review,* Vol. 59 (May–June 1981), pp. 6–8; Olga Quintana, "Co-Production: A Viable Consideration for Developing Nations," *Journal of the Academy of Marketing Science,* Vol. 12 (Winter 1984), pp. 38–48.

8. J. Peter Killing, "How to Make a Global Joint Venture Work," *Harvard Business Review,"* Vol. 60 (May–June 1982), pp. 120–27.

9. Edward W. Cundiff and Marye Tharp Hilger, *Marketing in the International Environment,* Englewood Cliffs: Prentice-Hall, Inc., 1984), pp. 116–17.

10. Jyoti N. Prasad and C. P. Pao, "Foreign Payoffs and International Business Ethics: Revisited," in David M. Klein and Allen E. Smith, eds., *Marketing Comes of Age, 1984* (Boca Raton, Fla.: Southern Marketing Assn., 1984), pp. 260–64.

11. Lisa Uusitalo, "Environmental Impact of Changes in Consumption Styles," *Journal of Macromarketing,* Vol. 2 (Fall 1982), pp. 16–30.

12. Gary M. Erickson, Johnny K. Johansson, and Paul Chao, "Image Variables in Multi-Attribute Product Evaluations: Country-of-origin Effects," *Journal of Consumer Research,* Vol. 11 (September 1984), pp. 694–99.

13. John J. Nevin, "Doorstop for Free Trade," *Harvard Business Review,"* Vol. 61 (March–April 1983), pp. 88–93.

14. Phillip Niffengegger, Gill M. Howison, Lochie B. Overbey, "A Cross-National Comparison of Consumer Product Use," in Daniel R. Comigan, Frederic B. Kraft, and Robert H. Ross, eds., *1982 Proceedings Southwestern Marketing Association Conference* (Wichita State University and Southwestern Marketing Assn., 1982), pp. 141–47.

15. Craig M. Watson, "Counter-Competition Abroad to Protect Home Markets," *Harvard Business Review,* Vol. 60 (January–February 1982), pp. 40–42.

16. Solvieg Wikstrom, "Another Look at Consumer Dissatisfaction as a Measure of Market Performance," *Journal of Consumer Policy,* Vol. 6 (1983), pp. 19–35.

CONSUMER ASSESSMENT
OF PURCHASE

SECTION A
CONSUMER'S CHECK
ON PURCHASE RESULTS

20. Introduction To Postpurchase Assessment
21. Favorable Assessment Results In
    Consumer Loyalty
22. Consumer Actions When Dissatisfied

CHAPTER 20

Introduction To

Postpurchase Assessment

CHAPTER OUTLINE

I. CONSUMER ASSESSMENT DEFINED

II. NATURE OF CONSUMER ASSESSMENT
   A. Why Assessment Is Important
   B. Types of Consumer Assessment
   C. Assessment Responsibility
   D. Formal or Informal Assessment
   E. Time Element of Assessment

III. CONSUMER EQUILIBRIUM: THE DESIRED STATE

IV. ASSESSMENT RESULTS FROM DISSONANCE
   A. Dissonance Is Normal
   B. Physical- and Emotional-Based Dissonance
   C. Dissonance Requires New Information
   D. Factors That Cause Dissonance
   E. Management Creates Dissonance

V. CONSUMER RE-ESTABLISHES EQUILIBRIUM
   A. Review the Facts
   B. Mental Resolution
   C. Seek Reassurance
   D. Sell Your Misery to Others
   E. Consumer Always Changes
   F. Management Helps Maintain Equilibrium

VI. RESULTS OF PREPURCHASE ASSESSMENT

VII. RESULTS OF POSTPURCHASE ASSESSMENT
   A. Consumer Behavior When Satisfied
   B. Consumer Behavior When Resigned
   C. Consumer Behavior When Dissatisfied
   D. Management Awareness of Assessment Results

CHAPTER OBJECTIVES

After completing your study of Chapter 20, you should be able to:

1. Define consumer assessment.
2. Discuss the nature of consumer assessment.
3. Discuss consumer equilibrium, the desired state.
4. Explain how assessment results from dissonance.
5. Discuss how the consumer re-established equilibrium.
6. Discuss the results of prepurchase assessment.
7. Discuss the results of postpurchase assessment.

Historically, managers have spent much time, effort, and money in order to understand how consumers evaluate product alternatives and decide on the particular item to purchase. This "evaluation and decision" is perceived by the manager as the most important consideration in the firm achieving its goals. Very little attention has been given by managers to the other steps in the decision process — problem recognition, search for information, and assessment. This attitude is beginning to change as more managers realize the need to understand the entire purchase process as a basis for achieving their goals.

Assessment in particular has been neglected by managers. The reason seems to be an attitude by managers that consumer decision making ends with the purchase and that businesses have no responsibility for the purchase beyond this point. We know that this is incorrect, that assessment is a vital step in the purchase process because it has important implications for the next decision. Certainly, we take the position that consumer assessment is as important as any other step in the consumer purchase process. In this chapter, we consider consumer assessment, including what it is, how it is carried out, and its results.

CONSUMER ASSESSMENT DEFINED

An assessment is the review of some action to establish the success of the outcome. The definition of consumer assessment, however, does not follow logically. The problem stems from the understanding of what is assessed. It is generally agreed that consumer assessment is limited to review of the consumer's purchase decision. That is to say, it is a postpurchase activity that is restricted to only consideration of whether the product bought provides satisfaction or not. This is a very narrow interpretation of consumer assessment, since it leaves out any review of the thought processes and actions taken by the consumer prior to the purchase of the product. These prepurchase considerations are far too important to be excluded.

A broader definition of consumer assessment is used in this text. *Consumer assessment* is defined as:

> *the review of the results of engaging in problem recognition, search for information, evaluation of alternatives and the product decision to determine the relative success of the undertaking.*

This definition involves the entire consumer decision process. Each step can be evaluated separately, or the entire decision may be re-evaluated by the consumer. The results of this evaluation affect the consumer's next decision. The significance of this definition becomes clearer as we proceed.

NATURE OF CONSUMER ASSESSMENT

There are several considerations related to the nature of assessment that must be explained. They expand the definition of the concept and lay a foundation for the discussion to follow.

Why Assessment Is Important

Assessment is important to consumers for four reasons. First, it adds to the consumer's experience. It is through assessment that the results of shopping and buying are internalized as part of the consumer's frame of reference. Thus it identifies successful and unsuccessful market activities and broadens the consumer's personal needs, ambitions, drives, perceptions, and attitudes.

Second, assessment provides the consumer with a check on market-related decisions; it provides an indicator of success. Consumer satisfaction is related to the person's expectations before purchases, as illustrated in Table 20-1. Satisfaction with a purchase is a function of the initial performance expectations and perceived performance relative to those expectations.[1] As a general rule, consumers are dissatisfied only if the product performance is below their expectation level.

Third, assessment forms the basis for the consumer's store and brand loyalty. Consumers tend to be loyal to products and stores where their doubts have been resolved favorably. They tend to ignore products and stores where their doubts have ended in frustration. This fact is one of the reasons why it is so important for managers to understand the effects of assessment on their sales and revenue.

Table 20–1
Relationship Between Expectations, Performance, and Satisfaction

Perceived Performance Relative to Expectations	Consumers Expectation Level	
	Expectation from Purchase below Minimum Desired Performance Level	Expectation from Purchase at Minimum Desired Performance Level
Better performance than expected	Satisfaction	Satisfaction
Same performance as expected	Nonsatisfaction	Satisfaction
Worse performance than expected	Dissatisfaction	Dissatisfaction

Source: Derived from R.L. Oliver, "Measurement and Evaluation of Satisfaction Process in Retail Settings," *Journal of Retailing,* Fall 1981, pp. 25–48.

Fourth, the results of consumer assessment are frequently transmitted back to business. This transmittal too frequently takes the form of complaints and returns, but it is valuable information for the organization nevertheless. Management can take the initiative and monitor consumer assessments to discover their favorable attitudes as well as those that are unfavorable. Such information is plugged into policy formulation that affects future customer satisfaction.

Types of Consumer Assessment

There are two broad types of assessment that consumers make, and each is shown in Illustration 20-1. First, there is prepurchase assessment. *Prepurchase assessment* is defined as a review that involves problem recognition, search for information and evaluation of alternatives.[2] Prepurchase assessment is nearly always overlooked in the literature, but it is as important as any other type.[3]

Illustration 20-1
Assessment in the decision process

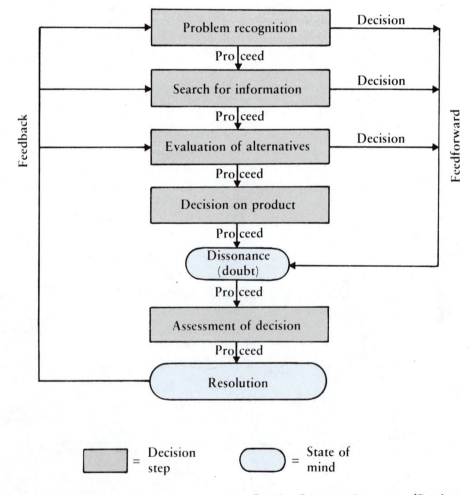

Photo 20-1

Pre-purchase assessment takes place prior to a buying decision.

Any time a consumer makes a decision, there exists the possibility of questioning the outcome of that decision—or assessment. Prepurchase assessment takes place before the final product decision is made. Any decision related to problem recognition, search, or evaluation causes dissonance or doubt, which results in assessment and a resolution which is expressed as feedback. Only when the consumer is satisfied with a decision at a particular stage in the purchase process will he or she proceed to the next stage in the process. This transaction from one stage to another is all lines marked "proceed."

Second, there is postpurchase assessment. *Postpurchase assessment* is defined as a review of the product's performance after purchase to determine if it meets expectations or not. At this point the die is cast, and there is probably no turning back from the decision. Either the product provides satisfaction as expected, or the person must take some positive steps to come to grips with the dissatisfaction. Thus the sequence in Illustration 20-1 is product decision, dissonance, assessment, resolution, and feedback.

The consumer has to resolve any doubts or remain in a state of frustration. If the consumer is resolving some doubt during problem recognition, then the feedback is related only to problem recognition as a part of prepurchase assessment. If the consumer has purchased the product, then the information is feedback to problem recognition, search for information and evaluation.

Assessment Responsibility

Who is responsible for assessment? The answer is not so simple. In Chapter 1, we defined a consumer as one or more persons who determine wants, buy products, and use products. The responsibility for assessment does not exactly parallel these activities of consumption. The parallel would be exact if the same person acts as the demander, the shopper, and the user. That person would engage in prepurchase assessment and postpurchase assessment. The variation occurs if different persons perform the activities of consumption. For example, a husband (demander) asks his wife (shopper) to pick up a Wok he needs to prepare a Chinese dinner for the entire family (users). Only the husband has problem recognition dissonance because he is the only one with a problem. The wife, as shopper, can have dissonance related to search for information and evaluation. The entire family may express dissonance with the output of the product purchased. Any one of the family may also individually express dissatisfaction with the product. Thus, when responsibility for consumption is specialized, the assessment process may also be specialized.

Formal or Informal Assessment

Consumer assessment can be either formal or informal. A *formal assessment* is a carefully thought out, written evaluation of (1) the problems with a decision or (2) the specific element related to the performance of a product. It is very unlikely many consumers use formal means when engaging in prepurchase assessment. An example is the person who has decided to purchase a new home, and makes out a list of the advantage of staying where he or she is or going on with the search for a new place. A formal assessment is more likely with postpurchase assessment. For example, a formal assessment would be involved when a person who has repeated trouble with a new Pontiac J2000 lists out and considers each problem that has occurred and his or her reaction to it.

An *informal assessment* occurs strictly in the mind; it is quickly made and quickly acted on. The informal technique is used with both prepurchase and postpurchase assessment, but it is especially important with prepurchase assessment. One reason is that decisions are made too frequently to give them formal attention. Another reason is that the consumer is not likely to consider any one decision in a series that important. For example, a consumer sets out on a shopping trip. There may be a fleeting thought about the prudence of visiting one store over another, but there is no time or inclination to go into it formally. A few minutes later the consumer may wish he or she had remembered a wallet, but the frustration must be resolved immediately, so there is little formal analysis. Informal postpurchase assessment occurs all the time. An example would be the consumer who is dissatisfied with the bow on a new dress. The consumer thinks a minute or two, then cuts it off, and the dissonance is solved.

Time Element of Assessment

Most dissonance occurs immediately after the decision; therefore, assessment tends to be immediate. The reason is that the decision is still fresh in the consumer's mind. A consumer evaluates three alternative products and marginally decides that one is preferred over the others. Then the question arises, "Is it really?" Now, the consumer must deal with this doubt immediately or the purchase process comes to a stop. The consumer is not going to buy a marginal product if there is doubt about its performance.

There are many times when dissonance is delayed, and so is assessment. Delayed dissonance is more likely after the purchase than before. It is frequently associated with performance. For example, high-cost durable items such as automobiles, appliances, and fashion clothing may have to be used for awhile before the doubt sets in.

There can be instances when dissonance recurs. This is also most likely to occur when the purchase is some durable product. You buy a new couch. It looks great in the store, but when you get it home you begin to wonder if the color is just right or if it goes with the other pieces of furniture. You think this out and decide that it is fine. Later you change the carpeting, and the dissonance concerning the couch returns. Dissonance may recur as the couch begins to wear out or when the style begins to lose its popularity. You can clearly understand that dissonance is frequently associated with beginning the purchase process. The consumer is dissatisfied with something that he or she has and wants to replace it. This dissatisfaction is a type of dissonance.

CONSUMER EQUILIBRIUM: THE DESIRED STATE

We know from our discussion of motives that consumers seek to establish and maintain equilibrium in their body states—what is sometimes called *cognitive consistency*. Equilibrium describes a state where the consumer is at peace. Scien-

Photo 20-2
Consumers are frequently in a state of consumer equilibrium with respect to their market behavior.

tists use the term *homeostasis* to refer to the tendency of persons toward achieving a relatively stable internal environment. Homeostasis is very closely associated with motivation, as discussed in Chapter 4. When the consumer is in equilibrium, there is no perception of a serious want, no motivation to seek out new or different products, no understood dissatisfaction with the things owned, and no important decisions to be made relative to buying. At first thought, you may consider that such a state is beyond attainment; it is no more than a concept. However, in the practical sense this is not the case.

Consumers are frequently in a state of equilibrium with respect to their market behavior. They may, or may not, be in equilibrium with respect to their human behavior, but that is not our concern. We refer to a condition where the body may be functioning to carry out its normal thought and activity, and, indeed, there may be problems in association with these activities, but nothing the person is doing has any direct relationship to consumer decision making. The person is mentally at rest in the sense that he or she is not being challenged to make market-related decisions.[4] This equilibrium may describe a person preparing dinner, watching a football playoff game or reading a good book before bedtime. We could go on describing situations when the consumer is in equilibrium. As a matter of fact, there is nothing unusual about this situation.

Consumer equilibrium does not mean that consumers have no wants or that all their wants are temporarily satisfied. We know wants are insatiable. We also know that a condition where the consumer was completely satisfied would be unlikely. Rather, our equilibrium simply describes a situation where the consumer, for whatever reason, is not concerned with the problems associated with purchasing.

ASSESSMENT RESULTS FROM DISSONANCE

We noted earlier in this chapter that dissonance is doubt or inconsistency between the consumer's perception of the state he or she wants to exist and the state that actually exists. We purchase a new hair dryer and we expect it to work over a reasonable period of time. If it does not, then we have doubts about our purchase. Dissonance disrupts the consumer's equilibrium with this doubt causing the person to seek relief. This relief is assessment, and it is the direct result of dissonance.

Dissonance Is Normal

Dissonance is a mental state because the doubt exists in the mind. Some scholars also argue that it is a reactive, or "knee-jerk," response to deciding. It is argued that the simple fact that consumers make decisions causes dissonance as the reaction. These scholars perceive dissonance to be present after every product decision. This position relates to postpurchase dissonance only because they do not recognize prepurchase dissonance. Even so there is no proof that every product decision results in dissonance. There is evidence to the contrary because some consumers have reported in studies experiencing no dissonance after purchases.

Photo 20-3

Not all purchases cause dissonance. This woman will in all likelihood not think about this purchase after consuming it.

The notion that there could be prepurchase dissonance after every decision in the purchase process seems even more far fetched. Can you imagine a person questioning the decision to purchase a loaf of bread when the problem is recognized just before lunch? It may happen, but it does not have to.

There is no question that dissonance occurs in a great many, if not all, buying situations.[5] We consider dissonance to be normal after a decision or product selection—but not inevitable. It may occur for no other reason than that the consumer wants to check the results of the decision to be sure. Furthermore, as we shall see there are a lot of external forces at work to assure the consumer has dissonance. It is certainly important enough in consumer decision making for us to give it our most careful attention.

Physical- and Emotional-Based Dissonance

Although dissonance is a mental state, the doubt can be either physically or emotionally based.[6] *Physical-based dissonance* results when there is inconsistency between a consumer's perception of an expected physical need fulfillment and the actual fulfillment. Physical-based dissonance results from the basic need for food, water, warmth, and sleep. Assume a person purchases a new sport coat, but discovers when it is worn it binds the shoulders. The mind immediately picks up on this physical problem and expresses doubt about the purchase of the coat. A college student buys a water bed. It felt fine at the store, but it feels cold. The mind picks up a doubt about the decision to purchase. Most physical-based dissonance occurs after the purchase.

Emotional-based dissonance results when there is a difference between the perceived and actual psychological condition of the consumer. Postpurchase dissonance based on emotional considerations is very common. When purchasing a new car, the consumer may check prices on several different manufacturers' makes and models. Each of these has certain advantages and disadvantages—prestige versus economy, style versus comfort, and combinations of accessories. Once the individual selects a car, dissonance can develop because economy may have been sacrificed for additional prestige, or the wrong combination of accessories was included. Of course, dissonance is inevitable if the consumer wants economy and prestige in equal amounts. The cigarette smoker develops dissonance because the pleasure of smoking is inconsistent with the medical reports linking cigarettes to cancer.

Prepurchase dissonance based on emotional considerations is more easily identified. A consumer who decides to shop downtown rather than in the closer mall may experience dissonance related to the emotional strain of traffic, parking, and automobile fumes. In the example of purchasing an automobile, there may be emotional-based dissonance because obtaining a lower price may entail leaving off some accessories or considering an alternative with less power.

Physical and emotional dissonance have been treated here as if they were entirely different things. In practice, this is not the case. Most often physical and psychological inconsistencies occur together. In the case of the sport coat mentioned earlier there is psychological doubt about how the coat looks along with the physical doubt related to discomfort. The smoker can develop real physical problems that create doubt along with the psychological doubt associated with smoking.

Dissonance Requires New Information

Both prepurchase and postpurchase dissonance require new information. To understand this, we must understand what happens when exchange takes place. For there to be exchange, both the buyer and the seller must feel, at the time of the purchase, that they are getting more than they are giving up. Exchange occurs when a consumer is willing to swap something of value (money), which he or she holds, for something of value ("things" or services) held by sellers. It is inconceivable to imagine a consumer saying, "The money is more important to me than the 'thing,' but I will buy it anyway." Such would be irrational behavior. If the money is more important, then the consumer will keep it. It follows that, at the moment of exchange, the consumer is satisfied with the transaction.

A consumer who is satisfied will experience dissonance only if some new information causes him or her to question whether the "thing" is actually more important than the money.[7] That is why we say dissonance is always based on new information. An example can serve to make the point. A consumer wants to buy a portable telephone. This consumer shops carefully and makes comparisons. The preferred brand is found at an acceptable price and purchased. This consumer has no doubts because the product is worth more to him or her than the price. Now, the very next day this consumer observes a television ad featuring the same brand of portable telephone for substantially less money. Now, the consumer has information not available at the time of the purchase which changes the whole perception of the exchange—causing dissonance.

The new information that we speak of can be anything.[8] It may be knowledge of a lower price. It may be knowledge of a product promoted as superior to the one purchased. It may be that the product does not perform as expected. In the case of the telephone, the consumer may be unhappy with the constant static characteristic of many portable telephones. The purchase experience itself can constitute new information. Thoughts and conversations that occurred during this purchase experience, and repressed at the time, may be recalled later to cause dissonance. "Did the salesperson mean it was as good as the competitor's or not?" "Why did the salesperson keep changing the conversation when I asked for comparisons?" Once these facts are recalled, they can modify how the consumer feels about the decision.

Factors That Cause Dissonance

There are several factors that make dissonance highly likely both before and after the purchase. First, there is price. As a rule, the higher the price, the greater the possibility of dissonance. The price level may itself evoke a reaction on the part of the consumer. The consumer may say, "Why am I shopping for an item costing that much?," "This product costs too much for me to give it that much importance on my preference list," or "Why did I spend that much money?" Second, there is psychological importance. As a rule, the more psychological satisfaction derived from the decision or the product, the less the dissonance. If the consumer very badly wants something, it will take a great deal of inconsistent information to cause that consumer to doubt either the product or the decisions associated with its purchase.

Third, there is product performance. This factor applies primarily to dissonance after the sale. Table 20-2 gives some of the reasons why a sample of consumers was dissatisfied with repairs and general services. Dissonance increases as product performance fails to live up to consumer expectations. Failure to perform or to perform up to expectations is the most important reason for postpurchase dissonance.

Fourth, there is the number of rejected alternatives. The more alternatives available to the consumer, the greater the likelihood that dissonance will occur; the consumer is more likely to wonder if one of these rejected alternatives could have been better. This is especially likely if the selected alternative does not meet expectations. For example, you pass up several stores in order to shop at a particular store you know has the brand you want—and they no longer carry it. Or you purchase a specific brand when you perceive others to be almost as good—only to find that performance has declined in the brand you bought.

Fifth, and closely associated with the number of alternatives, is the perceived performance of alternatives rejected. If the consumer perceives performance of rejected alternatives to be close to the one selected, dissonance is more likely to occur. This tendency also increases if the selected alternative does not prove satisfactory. The consumer may wish he or she had gone to the other store or purchased the other product.

Sixth, the credibility of the source of new information affects the amount of dissonance it causes. If you make a decision, and a salesperson in another store tells you it is a poor decision, you are less likely to be concerned than if a friend or relative tells you the same thing. If you believe the source of inconsistent information, you are more likely to show dissonance.

It should be clear why we indicated earlier that dissonance is normal. There are simply too many opportunities for the buyer to question some aspect of prepurchase or postpurchase decisions. This possibility increases when you consider that all the above factors occur in some combination. It is a poor manager who does not have some knowledge of this dissonance and policies to combat it. More will be said on this subject shortly.

Table 20–2

Reasons for Dissatisfactions: Repairs and General Services

Reasons for Being Dissatisfied	Total	Number	Named	Most
The service was provided in a careless, unprofessional manner	31	64.6%	10	43.5%
Services were rendered in an incompetent manner, with very harmful results	18	37.5	2	8.7
Performance of the item was worse after the repairs than before	17	35.4	2	8.7
The quality of parts or materials was inferior	15	31.3	1	4.3
The service was not completed in the agreed time	13	27.1	1	4.3
Results fell short of those claimed by ads	9	18.8	1	4.3
I was charged for work that was not done	8	16.7	4	17.4
The fee was much higher than the amount agreed in advance	6	12.5	0	0.0
I was charged for parts that were not furnished	4	8.3	0	0.0
Unauthorized repairs were made and charged to me	2	4.2	2	7.0
I was tricked by a salesman into buying services I did not want	2	4.2	0	0.0
I was harassed by bill collectors	1	2.1	0	0.0
The warranty did not cover everything that went wrong	1	2.1	0	0.0
Credit terms were misrepresented to me	0	0.0	0	0.0
	127		23	

Source: Ralph L. Day and Muzaffer, "Consumer Response to Dissatisfaction with Services and Intangilies," in *Advances in Consumer Research*. Vol. 5, Proceedings of the Eighth Annual Conference on Consumer Behavior, 1978, pp. 267 and 269.

Part 5 – Consumer Asessment of Purchase

Photo 20-4
Consumers make decisions about the worth and importance of each alternative at the evaluation stage.

Management Creates Dissonance

The fact that dissonance is likely in consumers is one of the more useful types of information managers have. It is the basis for most business efforts to lure consumers away from competitors.[9] As long as a competitor's customers are satisfied, there is little chance of inducing them to change stores or brands. However, if one firm can create dissonance in the minds of another firm's customers, there is a chance to induce those customers away.

Much of the effort of personal salespersons and advertising is designed to create this dissonance. It is done deliberately, but there is nothing wrong with the effort. It is fundamental to a free enterprise system.

Salespersons use the same technique to create dissonance. They may make comparisons showing competitors' products unfavorably, or they may simply point out the superior features of their product compared to competitors. In either case, managers know the first step in luring competitors' customers is to cause them to doubt their loyalty to the competitors' product.

CONSUMER RE-ESTABLISHES EQUILIBRIUM

Once dissonance occurs in the mind of the consumer, something must be done. No consumer can remain in a constant state of doubt or dissatisfaction. This is the point at which homeostasis, as previously explained, comes into play.

The body, out of equilibrium, will seek by whatever means possible to return to equilibrium. In fact, it can be argued that dissonance, because it is inconsistency or doubt, causes motivated behavior to correct the situation. There are several courses of action available to the consumer for re-establishing equilibrium.

Review the Facts

The consumer can review the facts in the original decision. There must have been some compelling reasons why the consumer chose the original course of action. A review of the facts may reinforce the original decision as correct, thus eliminating the dissonance. A review of the facts probably occurs automatically anytime there is dissonance. That is to say, this activity probably does not stand alone as a means of re-establishing equilibrium, but it is a part of every other means of re-establishing equilibrium.

A consumer reviews the facts to determine how any new information, which caused the doubt, fits the situation. For example, a friend tells you that the typewriter you bought was $15 cheaper in a nearby larger city. You may review the situation and determine that it would not have been worth $15 to travel to the city to make the purchase and be forced to travel farther for repairs and adjustments. Thus you may decide that the new information would not have affected the original decision.

Mental Resolution

Mental resolution means that the consumer simply finds excuses to discount the new information that has created dissonance. In effect, consumers talk themselves out of the dissonance. The consumer may think, "The difference in price isn't important," or "We'll chalk it up to experience." Mental resolution of dissonance is perhaps the most common means of re-establishing equilibrium. For example, a homeowner hired a contractor to build and install rigid plastic panels around the screened porch. The consumer wanted to create a Florida room to extend the living room in winter when entertaining and to protect plants from freezing weather. The job was poorly done, and the customer had the contractor take the panels back, but the customer lost the cost of the materials. The consumer argued, "It was still a very good idea that was just not executed correctly." The cost of the materials was chalked up to experience, and the consumer vowed to have the job redone. The consumer was mentally satisfied.

Seek Reassurance

Some consumers handle dissonance by seeking reassurance from others. It is always comforting to know that others are in the same boat. That is why a person who buys a lemon of a car constantly asks friends or colleagues who have the same type of car about performance. When they explain how satisfied they are in spite of small problems, the consumer can think, "I'm just being picky. The car is O.K. I'm having the same type of problems as others." Actually, the consumer's problems may be much more serious than those of friends. Deep down the consumer may know this but continues to seek the reassurance. A consumer may seek reassurance on any aspect of a decision. A man buys a new suit, but someone comments that it looks a little old for him. This man may ask friends what they think of shopping in the store where the suit was purchased. He is seeking reassurance that others have been successful shopping in that store. A consumer may seek reassurance on a decision. For example, an individual considering shopping in a particular store may ask a friend what he or she thinks of this particular store.

Sell Your Misery to Others

Some consumers use the technique of selling their own misery to others as a means of reducing dissonance.[10] The person who buys the car that is a lemon may talk up the virtues of the car to friends. He or she may even attempt to get the friend to purchase the same type of car. This activity is based on the old adage that misery likes company. The consumer just feels better about his or her own problem if an acquaintance is in the same boat.

Consumer Always Changes

The consumer is always changed as a result of assessment. Although the individual achieves equilibrium, it is a new equilibrium, not a return to the equilibrium that existed before the dissonance. The reason is experience. The experience gained as a result of recognizing and coming to grips with dissonance leads to new experiences which the consumer internalizes as feedback.[11] It may be a new understanding of oneself, a better appreciation of product performance, a knowledge of how others feel about the decision, a better feel for alternatives, and a perception of possible new products to purchase.

This experience becomes a part of the consumer's knowledge that is used in the next purchase situation. It relates to internal search, as we explained in a previous chapter. This knowledge can help the individual avoid some of the pitfalls of decision making the next time a similar product must be purchased. As a result, the entire purchase process can be made more efficient.

Management Helps Maintain Equilibrium

Business management helps consumers maintain equilibrium with respect to their purchase decisions. It is common knowledge that nearly all businesses depend on repeat sales to survive and make a profit. Thus it is necessary to encourage loyalty to the store and its products. It follows that management seeks ways to maintain consumer equilibrium where the firm's products are concerned. The manager seeks to reaffirm that the decision to buy from the store previously was a good one that should be followed in the future. In this sense, management is attempting to offset attempts by competitors and others to create dissonance in the mind of their customers. Management uses all available means to accomplish its ends, including personal selling, sales promotion, advertising and publicity.

RESULTS OF PREPURCHASE ASSESSMENT

No matter how the consumer deals with dissonance, certain results can be anticipated when equilibrium is achieved. In the case of prepurchase assessment, the result is a continuation of the purchase process. For example, a consumer is in the problem recognition stage when he or she perceives a lack of proper clothing for a new job. The consumer begins to question this judgment as soon as the problem is recognized. "Can I get by for a couple of months with the clothes I have? My old clothes are really not so bad." Only after the consumer has dealt with this dissonance and is satisfied with the decision to purchase will he or she proceed to the search stage.

At the search stage the consumer makes decisions about the method of search, and these immediately create dissonance. "Is the day right for shopping?" "Did I select the most appropriate stores?" "Can I trust my friends' advice?" The consumer must resolve these doubts satisfactorily to proceed to the evaluation stage. Of course, the consumer may withdraw from the decision process anytime a doubt cannot be resolved.

Our consumer again makes decisions concerning the worth or importance of each alternative at the evaluation stage. A new group of doubts arises at this point. "Do I really prefer the red suit over the blue?" "Perhaps I'm making a mistake to buy three shirts at this time." All these and similar doubts must be resolved before the consumer purchases the product. The consumer must be satisfied at every stage of the purchase process to proceed; the result of prepurchase assessment must be either satisfaction or termination of the prospect of buying.

RESULTS OF POSTPURCHASE ASSESSMENT

A consumer may take a much greater variety of actions during postpurchase assessment than during prepurchase assessment. No matter which one of the methods used by the consumer to re-establish equilibrium, the result is going to be satisfaction, dissatisfaction, or a state of resigned product use.[12] We introduce these results here, and we will expand upon them in the next chapter.

Consumer Behavior When Satisfied

Consumer satisfaction is an expected result of buying. Illustration 20-2 shows how the consumer behaves when satisfied with the purchase.[13] If the product was bought to satisfy a one-time need, such as braces to correct the teeth, then the product is discontinued with no future action required. There are two conditions where a product is repeatedly used, but its purchase is re-evaluated each time. If there is a good deal of style change or innovation, the consumer wants to make sure the product is still superior with each successive purchase. If the product does not change much and the purchases are habitual, there is no re-evaluation because satisfaction is carried over. The consumer is fairly sure the previous product will still satisfy. However, even with these types of products, there may be some periodic reassessment of the decision after a long period of use.

Illustration 20-2

Consumer behavior when satisfied

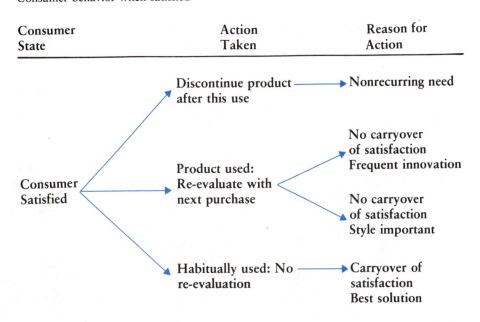

Consumer State	Action Taken	Reason for Action

Consumer Satisfied

Discontinue product after this use → Nonrecurring need

Product used: Re-evaluate with next purchase

No carryover of satisfaction Frequent innovation

No carryover of satisfaction Style important

Habitually used: No re-evaluation → Carryover of satisfaction Best solution

Consumer Behavior When Resigned

Consumer behavior is quite different when the consumer is only resigned to the use of the product. The consumer is neither very satisfied or very dissatisfied, so there are three major courses of action available. We observe these courses of action in Illustration 20-3. The consumer will discontinue to use the product when there is a one-time need. A consumer may routinely use the product if it is the best available and the consumer lacks the motivation to seek a better solution. Perhaps the individual could not afford a better product, the product in use did not have certain features that were desired, or the consumer wanted a favorite brand that was not available. The consumer simply makes the best of the situation because it is the best available. Lack of motivation usually means that the consumer is not being displeased enough to do anything.

The consumer may decide to continue using the product but reconsider with the next purchase; the consumer's resignation to the use of the product this time does not carry over to future purchases.

Consumer Behavior When Dissatisfied

There are two major types of consumer behavior when the person is dissatisfied with the purchase. These are shown in Illustration 20-4. The consumer may eliminate the product after this use if the need is nonrecurring or if for some reason the consumer decides to remain unsatisfied. This latter situation may occur if the product is too expensive or not immediately available or if the purchase is very time-consuming. If the dissatisfaction is not too strong, as in the case of an inexpensive item, the consumer may just live with the dissatisfaction until

Illustration 20-3

Consumer behavior when resigned

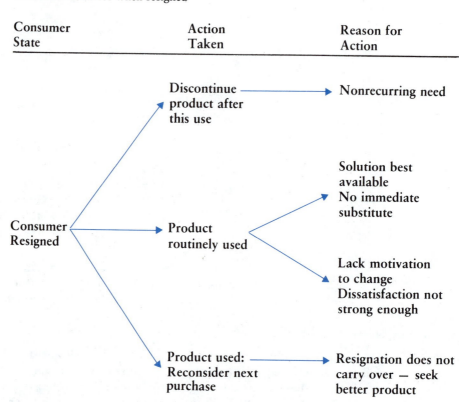

Consumer State	Action Taken	Reason for Action
	Discontinue product after this use	Nonrecurring need
Consumer Resigned	Product routinely used	Solution best available No immediate substitute Lack motivation to change Dissatisfaction not strong enough
	Product used: Reconsider next purchase	Resignation does not carry over — seek better product

the next purchase. This case is very similar to the resigned stage explained earlier.

There are three types of immediate action that the consumer can take when discontinuing an unsatisfactory product. The consumer can redefine the problem and seek a better product in the market. In our example of the consumer who was dissatisfied with a contractor's installation of plastic panels around a screened porch, the consumer may redefine the problem from making the porch a Florida room to making it a room. The consumer could then wall up the porch and install windows. The consumer could seek redress from the seller. The consumer could also redefine the solution and seek a better product. For example, the consumer may decide that even though the original contractor did poor work, another contractor can be found to do better. The result could be a better type of panel to be installed on the porch. We will return to these results in the next two chapters.

Management Awareness of Assessment Results

Managers need to be more aware of the results of assessment. If managers realize the types of consumer behavior that are likely to result from satisfaction, resignation, and dissatisfaction, they can develop policies to deal with each situation. Knowledge of the results of a previous purchase can help managers do a better job of establishing policy.

Illustration 20-4
Consumer behavior when dissatisfied

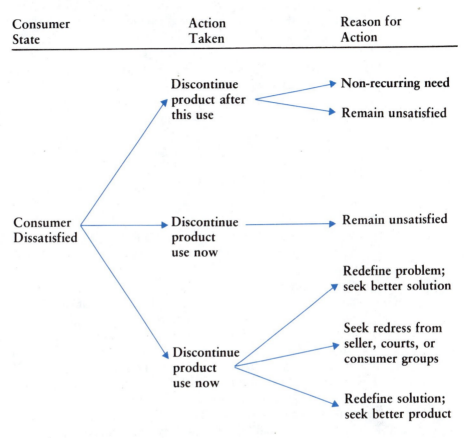

Consumer State	Action Taken	Reason for Action
Consumer Dissatisfied	Discontinue product after this use	Non-recurring need Remain unsatisfied
	Discontinue product use now	Remain unsatisfied
	Discontinue product use now	Redefine problem; seek better solution Seek redress from seller, courts, or consumer groups Redefine solution; seek better product

QUESTIONS

1. Discuss why consumer assessment is as important as any other step in the consumer purchase process.
2. What generally holds the greatest importance to you—prepurchase assessment or postpurchase assessment? Discuss your answer.
3. What are the reasons to conduct an informal assessment?
4. What are the reasons to conduct a formal assessment?
5. How does a marketing manager influence you during an informal assessment? During formal assessment?
6. Discuss what is meant by the statement: "Consumer equilibrium does not mean that consumers have no wants."
7. Does dissonance occur after every purchase? Discuss your answer.
8. Give examples of products in which you experienced emotional dissonance. Discuss the reasons why.

9. What sources of information do you turn to when you experience dissonance? Why these sources?
10. Why would management create dissonance? Give examples.
11. What are the ways you reduce dissonance? Give examples.
12. How can a marketing manager reduce dissonance in a consumer? Give examples.
13. Give examples of products with which you were satisfied but did not repurchase. Discuss why not.
14. Discuss why it is important for a marketing manager to know who the firm's satisfied and dissatisfied customers are.
15. Identify some ways a marketing manager can become more aware of satisfied and dissatisfied customers.

NOTES

1. R. A. Westbrook, "Intrapersonal Affective Influences on Consumer Satisfaction with Products," *Journal of Consumer Research,* Vol. 7, No. 1 (June 1980), pp. 49–50.
2. For the sake of convenience throughout this text we have treated evaluation and decision together as one step. The nature of this discussion makes it necessary to separate them for the sake of clarification.
3. Robert B. Woodruff, Ernest R. Cadotte, and Roger L. Jenkins, "Modeling Consumer Satisfaction Processes Using Experience-Based Norms," *Journal of Marketing Research,* Vol. XX (August 1983), pp. 296–304.
4. Michael J. Etzel and Bernard I. Silverman, "A Managerial Perspective on Directions for Retail Customer Dissatisfaction Research," *Journal of Retailing,* Vol. 57 (Fall 1981), pp. 124–36.
5. John E. Swan and I. Frederick Trawick, "Disconfirmation of Expectations and Satisfaction with a Retail Service," *Journal of Retailing,* Vol. 57 (Fall 1981), pp. 49–67; Robert A. Westbrook, "Sources of Consumer Satisfaction with Retail Outlets," *Journal of Retailing,* Vol. 57 (Fall 1981), pp. 69–85.
6. Lynn Langmeyer, "A Comment on Dissonance Theory and Self-Perception," in David M. Klein and Allen E. Smith, eds., *Marketing Comes of Age, 1984* (Boca Raton, Fla.: Southern Marketing Assn., 1984), pp. 32–35.
7. Raj Arora, "Is 'Cognitive Dissonance' Simple 'State Anxiety'?" in Carol H. Anderson, Rajinder Arora, Blaise J. Bergiel, Sion Raveed, and Ronald L. Vaughn, eds., *Midwest Marketing Association 1981 Conference Proceedings* (Southern Illinois University at Carbondale and Midwest Marketing Assn., 1981), pp. 94–99.
8. Jerome B. Kernan, "Some Thoughts on Unfavorable Information: When Does Sheep's Clothing Hide the Wolf?" in David M. Klein and Allen E. Smith, eds., *Marketing Comes of Age, 1984* (Boca Raton, Fla.: Southern Marketing Assn., 1984), pp. 269–72.

9. Gregory M. Pickett, "Stimulating Consumer Dissatisfaction: A Management Approach Via Equity Theory," *1983 Proceedings Southwestern Marketing Association Conference* (North Texas State University and Southwestern Marketing Assn., 1983), pp. 10–13.

10. Marsha L. Richins, "Negative Word-of-Mouth by Dissatisfied Consumers: A Pilot Study," *Journal of Marketing,* Vol. 47 (Winter 1983), pp. 68–78.

11. Ralph L. Day, Klaus Grabicke, Thomas Schaetzle, and Fritz Staufach, "The Hidden Agenda of Consumer Complaining," *Journal of Retailing,* Vol. 57 (Fall 1981), pp. 86–106; Kenneth L. Bernhardt, "Consumer Problems and Complaint Actions of Older Americans: A National View," *Journal of Retailing,* Vol. 57 (Fall 1981), pp. 107–23.

12. R. Neil Maddox, "Two-factor Theory and Consumer Satisfaction: Replication and Extension," *Journal of Consumer Research,* Vol. 8 (June 1981), pp. 97–102.

13. William O. Bearden and Jesse E. Teel, "Selected Determinants of Consumer Satisfaction and Complaint Reports," *Journal of Marketing Research,* Vol. XX (February 1983), pp. 21–28.

CHAPTER 21

Favorable Assessment

Results In Consumer Loyalty

CHAPTER OUTLINE

I. CONSUMER BEHAVIOR WHEN SATISFIED OR RESIGNED
  A. Discontinue Product Use
  B. Re-evaluate after Each Use
  C. Habitual Use

II. SATISFIED CONSUMERS ARE LOYAL
  A. Consumer Loyalty Defined
  B. Degrees of Loyalty
  C. Types of Consumer Loyalty
  D. Loyal Markets
  E. Loyalty Is Learned
  F. Loyalty Is Related to Attitudes
  G. Loyalty Conditions Consumer Motivation

III. ADVANTAGES OF LOYAL CUSTOMERS TO SELLERS

IV. REASONS WHY CONSUMERS ARE LOYAL
  A. Achievement of Satisfaction
  B. Image of Superiority
  C. Consumer Inertia
  D. Tendency to Conform
  E. Avoidance of Risk
  F. Simplify Consumer Decisions
  G. Market Conditions

V. FACTORS THAT CAUSE CONSUMER SWITCHING
  A. Curiosity Causes Switching
  B. Reassurance and Switching
  C. Chance Switching
  D. Switching from Dissonance
  E. External Pressure

VI. CREATE A CLIMATE FOR LOYALTY

CHAPTER OBJECTIVES

After completing your study of Chapter 21, you should be able to:

1. Discuss consumer behavior when satisfied or resigned.
2. Explain why satisfied consumers are loyal.
3. Discuss the advantages of loyal customers to sellers.
4. Discuss the reasons why consumers are loyal.
5. Discuss the factors that cause consumer switching.
6. Discuss how to create a climate for loyalty.

We know that the consumer purchase decision is not complete until assessment has taken place. We know that the result of assessment is that the consumer is either satisfied, resigned, or dissatisfied. Furthermore, we know that the consumer will engage in rather specific types of future behavior depending on whether he or she is satisfied, resigned, or dissatisfied. In this chapter we consider in detail the behavior of consumers who are either satisfied or resigned to use the product. Consumer loyalty is the result of consumer satisfaction, and it is the result that most business managers seek when attempting to influence consumer behavior.

CONSUMER BEHAVIOR WHEN SATISFIED OR RESIGNED

The results of consumer decision making tend to be similar when the person is satisfied or resigned. For this reason we discuss these two results together. The three results involved with satisfied or resigned consumers are to discontinue product use, re-evaluate after each use, or engage in habitual use.[1]

Discontinue Product Use

A consumer can be completely satisfied with a product or service and still discontinue its use. A satisfactory product is discontinued when it has been purchased in response to a nonrecurring need. The product is used, but no repeat purchase is necessary. Once the doctor has taken out a patient's appendix, there is no need for further service. The same can be said for the use of crutches, orthopedic shoes, retirement homes and many other types of products or services.

Sellers of one-use products must continually seek different customers to use their products.[2] These sellers typically know that a certain portion of the population requires the product at a given time. Effective promotion must keep potential customers advised of the product or service. The seller is interested in having satisfied customers because they become testimonials to others who may need the product or service.

Re-evaluate after Each Use

Many products are used by consumers, and they are satisfied, but they do not automatically purchase the same product the next time the need arises. Rather, the consumer engages in the entire purchase process again—including problem recognition, search, evaluation, selection, and assessment. This situation develops when there is no carryover satisfaction from one purchase to the next. For example, a person buys a Ford LTD, likes the car, uses it regularly, and even recommends it to his or her friends. However, when time comes to purchase a new car, the consumer seeks out information on several different makes and models. Products that are subject to frequent modification and innovation—such as computers, typewriters, watches, automobiles, and those with a significant element of fashion such as dress clothing, shoes, and furniture—are most likely to be re-evaluated before each purchase.

Sellers of these products must be in the market continually influencing consumers to purchase their products. Product modification and personal selling, creative advertising, publicity, and the other means of promotion are regularly used for this purpose. Such methods are necessary because the consumer demonstrates no consistent loyalty to the firm or its products. Such customers are the most difficult to retain and the easiest to induce away from competitors. The consumer tends to be influenced by perceptions of which products lead the others in new ideas or style. Emotion plays a considerable part in the decision to buy, but the emotion must be backed up with realistic facts.

A resigned consumer may also use a product fully but seek a different solution the next time the need arises. This happens when the individual is neither highly dissatisfied nor highly satisfied with the product. There is not enough of a problem to change the product already bought, but the customer will seek a different product next time. An individual not completely comfortable with a new coat may wear it for a season until she or he can justify purchasing a different style. Continuing to use a type of shaving lotion although not completely satisfied is another example of making the best of a product until next time. Of course, marketing managers do not want their product in this category. The marketing manager must try to persuade the resigned consumer to become a satisfied consumer.

Habitual Use

We know that habitual use occurs when a consumer purchases a product repeatedly without giving any real thought to alternative products or brands. This is the type of buying that most business managers seek. Figure 21-1 shows a product bought habitually by many consumers. Habitual buying can occur in two different situations. First, the consumer may be completely satisfied, and the satisfaction carries over from one need situation to another. For example, a person uses Dial soap, likes it, and sees no reason to consider any other soap. Many types of branded products, convenience products, and staple products are purchased habitually. Such branded products as Campbells's soup, Revlon cosmetics, and Coors beer are habitually purchased by large segments of the population. Of course, there is *no* product or brand that is purchased habitually by everyone.

The second type of situation occurs when a consumer is resigned to the product's use, but nonetheless purchases routinely. This can happen when the customer is not completely satisfied, but the consumer perceives the product as

Figure 21-1
Product type bought habitually by many consumers

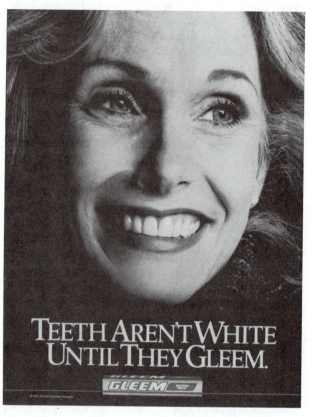

Courtesy of Proctor & Gamble Co.

the best one available. A person buys a Trim fingernail clipper but is not completely satisfied because the file is not effective. The individual continues to use the Trim repeatedly because he or she perceives that none of the other files included with fingernail clippers are any more effective. The consumer may not be sufficiently concerned to seek an alternative solution. Almost any type of product can fall into this type of repeat purchase. It is primarily a matter of how the consumer considers that product and the alternatives.

This chapter focuses mostly on habitual consumer behavior, the behavior most desired by marketing managers.

SATISFIED CONSUMERS ARE LOYAL

Consumer satisfaction and consumer loyalty go hand in hand.[3] Consumer loyalty generates repeat sales for the firm and provides stability to markets. In a very real sense, it is the creation of satisfied consumers who are loyal that is the

Illustration 21-1
Loyalty and satisfaction between business and consumers

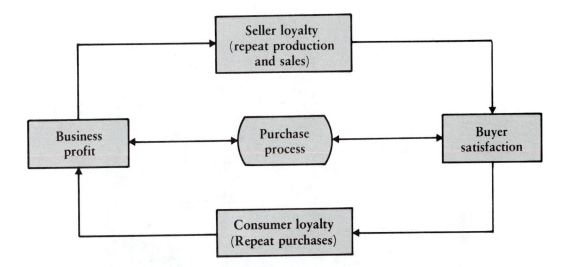

payoff of all consumer behavior.[4] When consumer decision making is successful, as shown in Illustration 21-1, the consumer becomes loyal to either the product, the brand, and/or the store, and marketing management obtains its goal of profit. In Illustration 21-1, business representatives and consumers interact during the purchase process. Consumers receive satisfaction from this process because of the products acquired. This satisfaction builds consumer loyalty and repeat sales. The business achieves profit from the repeat sales, which makes it possible to buy or produce more products for sale.

Consumer Loyalty Defined

Consumers may be loyal to the product, the brand, the store, or any combination. Consumer loyalty refers to a degree of unwillingness on the part of the consumer to switch products, brands, or stores. Consumer loyalty has been introduced, but it is now necessary to clarify our understanding of the term. For the purpose of this text, *consumer loyalty* is defined as:

> *the propensity of a customer to purchase the same product (brand) or frequent the same store each time the same need requires a solution.*

Consumer loyalty expresses a tendency rather than an absolute.

Degrees of Loyalty

The degree of loyalty exhibited by consumers differs among products, brands, and stores. Such differences are inevitable because of personal differences in self-concept and perception of the environment. Let us provide some illustrations of what is meant by loyalty.[5] An individual who buys Polo shirts 80 percent

Photo 21-1
Satisfaction is the result of many factors.

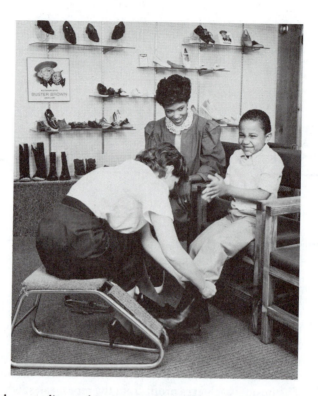

of the time when needing a shirt is more loyal than a person who purchases Polo shirts 60 percent of the time. A person who buys from Sears 35 percent of the time when seeking clothing is more loyal than a person who buys clothing from Sears 20 percent of the time. In these examples, both the purchasers of Polo shirts were more loyal to that product than either of the customers of Sears.[6] We can see there are degrees of loyalty, and we can say that both Polo and Sears have loyal customers. However, a more definitive identification of loyalty is desirable because it aids us in recognizing variations that exist among consumers. We will discuss two methods of identifying degrees of loyalty, one based on purchase sequence and the second on familiarity.

Suppose the consumers in your town distribute their grocery purchases among six stores in the following manner:

A&P	20 percent
Winn-Dixie #1	15
Winn-Dixie #2	10
Kroger	18
I.G.A.	16
Ma & Pa	21
	100

In other words, each consumer bought 20 percent of the time from A&P, 15 percent of the time from Winn-Dixie #1, etc. Now we can say that more customers are loyal to the Ma & Pa store than to any other single store or location in town. However, we can see that loyalty was fairly evenly divided among the businesses.

Brown reported in a classic article the degrees of loyalty among one hundred housewives.[7] He assigned the letters A, B, C, D, E, and F to specific product brands, and identified four degrees of loyalty:

1. *Undivided loyalty*—purchases were in the sequence AAAAAA
2. *No loyalty*—a purchase sequence of ABCDEF
3. *Divided loyalty*—a purchase sequence of ABABAB
4. *Unstable loyalty* a purchase sequence such as AAABBB

In the final analysis, we recognize that consumer loyalty is a much more complex subject than is suspected.

Types of Consumer Loyalty

Over the years, we have come to recognize three major types of consumer loyalty. They are product, brand, or store recognition; product, brand, or store preference; and product, brand, or store insistence.

Product, brand, or *store recognition* is simply the ability to identify store, products, or brands with no detailed knowledge about them. Recognition is the least loyal classification of customers. While these consumers at least remember having heard of or observed a store, product, or brand, they feel no particular identification; they do not know enough about it to have preferences. The consumer may purchase the brand or frequent the store if alternatives in the area are even less recognized. The likelihood of purchase is low, and marketing managers want to get their offerings out of this category if they possibly can. Much creative personal selling, sales promotion, advertising, and publicity is designed to get products, brands, and stores out of this category.

Product, brand, or *store preference* is a definite bias toward the store, product, or brand; but consumers in this category will accept a substitute before going without. A purchaser of soft drinks is an example. An individual may prefer Pepsi but will accept another brand before not drinking. Consumers can often express preferences for automobiles, appliances, canned foods, and doctors. Product, brand, or store preference is the state of loyalty when many consumers purchase from habit and experience. For example, a consumer who generally prefers Maxwell House coffee might buy another brand on special sale or if Maxwell House is out of stock. Sellers have a loyal customer as long as they maintain a competitive advantage and the product is generally available.

Product, brand, or store insistence is when the consumer will not willingly accept a substitute. The consumer will go without the product before accepting a substitute or the consumer will not shop in any other store. Insistent consumers will go to considerable trouble to purchase the desired product or brand, or purchase from the desired store. This is an objective of most marketing managers.

Here, the store, product, or brand may enjoy a very inelastic demand curve. A case of complete insistence is seldom found. There is usually some periodic switching between alternatives, even by the most loyal customers.

Loyal Markets

A highly loyal market is said to be one that contains a large number of undivided and insistent loyal consumers. The individuals who spent time, money and effort to inform the Coca-Cola company that they wanted the "old Coke" back were considered a loyal market. It appears the company did not identify the loyal market until New Coke was introduced.

Loyalty Is Learned

What we know about consumer loyalty is closely related to learning. Implicit in consumer loyalty is the assumption that consumers learn from past experience and that future behavior is influenced by what was learned. However, just as the accepted models of learning differ, so do the opinions on how consumer loyalty is established. The learning concepts discussed in Chapter 8 emphasize past behavior as the cornerstone to learning. However, consumer loyalty is not based only on past behavior. The concept of consumer loyalty must also incorporate the commitment to the decision over time. Learning influences future behavior, but it will not always lead to consumer loyalty.

The learning curve presented in Chapter 8 shows a relationship between the number of trials and the probability of response. As the number of trials increases, the probability of response increases. Illustration 21-2 shows that we can identify a corridor along the plotted line of the curve that represents degrees of commitment to a particular product. There are a number of product alternatives during the early trial stages, as shown by the dotted lines above the learning curve. Few of the alternatives have been rejected at this stage. Most alternatives are perceived as acceptable. As the consumer gathers more and more information about the alternatives, the rejections begin to increase.[8] These rejections are shown below the learning curve. As you can see from the illustration, the rejections increase and the number of acceptable alternatives decreases until only the final acceptable alternative is left. As the consumer gains more learning experience, the likelihood of repeatedly making the same choice is increased.

Loyalty Is Related to Attitudes

Consumer loyalty is directly related to consumer attitudes. The attitude acquired toward each alternative (product, brand, or store) plays a large part in that alternative's acceptability. Positive attitudes lead to a favorable assessment, while negative attitudes cause an alternative to be dropped. The intensity of the attitude, whether positive or negative, is a factor in determining the quickness and the finality of the consumer's decision. It follows that consumers tend to be more loyal to those alternatives toward which they have a strong positive attitude. Once this attitude is learned it takes some strong dissonant information to break the established pattern of response.

Illustration 21-2
Loyalty and learning

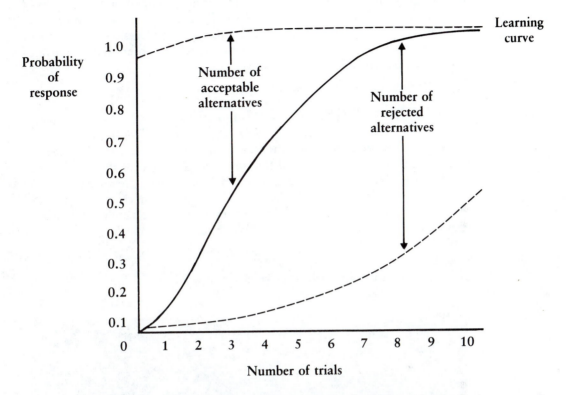

Probability of response

The transferable nature of attitudes is also a factor in developing consumer loyalty. Favorable attitudes previously developed toward one product in a line may carry over to others, and so does the related loyalty. This is the reason that some sellers (Campbell's soups, Betty Crocker, Heinz, Alpo, and Ortho, for example) identify and promote families of products. These carryover attitudes of consumers make it possible for the seller to develop instant loyalty for a product even though the person has no previous experience with it. Their favorable attitude toward other products in the family can carry over to the new offering. If the new product performs adequately, then it further strengthens loyalty toward the entire family. In order to change the consumer's attitude and loyalty, there must be some change in the consumer's information or perception of the product, brand, or store.

Loyalty Conditions Consumer Motivation

Loyalty tends to condition motivation because a loyal consumer does not perceive dissonance to the extent that others might.[9] A loyal consumer is a satisfied consumer; satisfaction tends to reduce motivation. Without motivation to change, the consumer will stay loyal.

On the other hand, a consumer who does not display loyalty for the firm's product, brand, or store offers a challenge. The marketing manager must motivate this consumer to try the product, brand, or store, to learn about its advantages, and to be convinced of its worth. The manager uses all appropriate variables of the marketing mix to accomplish this end. The manager wants to convince the consumer that the product, brand, or store offers satisfaction which can be developed over time into loyalty. Thus, how and why the consumer is motivated has a direct bearing on consumer loyalty.

ADVANTAGES OF LOYAL CUSTOMERS TO SELLERS

There are several rather specific reasons why sellers prefer loyal customers. First, there is *ease in selling*. Loyal consumers are already convinced of the basic worth or usefulness of the product, brand, or store. They have repeatedly made the conscious decision to use this product or brand or frequent this store. Thus they do not have to be sold—only reminded. Marketers must simply keep reinforcing the consumer's original decision. This reinforcement is much easier than per-

Photo 21-2
One way to gain customer loyalty is by keeping your word.

Part 5 – Consumer Assessment of Purchase

Figure 21-2
Example of reminder advertisement

Best Western International

suading them to purchase the first time. Repeat calls by salespersons and reminder advertising such as the one in Figure 21-2 are the primary tools of reinforcement selling. They are much less expensive, both to develop and to display, than their persuasive counterparts.

Loyal customers also provide *market stability.* The firm's share of the market can be predicted with more accuracy; it does not display the wide swings in sales associated with less loyal customers. A stable market allows management to plan more accurately and use its resources more effectively, which reduces cost.

Third, loyal customers allow *control over pricing.* Loyal customers are not quite so concerned about small swings in price, since they perceive overall satisfaction to be the important thing. Businesses such as Neiman Marcus and Federated Stores enjoy a price advantage because of their relatively loyal customers. Products such as Bayer aspirin, Corning cookware, Polo shirts, and Tide detergent have the same advantage. The managements of firms with loyal customers have more discretion in setting price levels and margins.

Fourth, loyal customers *encourage impulse buying*. Loyal customers of a store tend to frequent that store more; while there, they see and purchase products that they did not intend to buy. The carryover effect of loyalty from one product to another also encourages impulse purchases. The loyalty developed from prior satisfaction will be extended to the new offerings of a firm. Part of the attraction of Anacin-3 is its connection with the original Anacin, a product with a long record of public acceptance and loyal customers.

Fifth, loyal customers aid the *seller in distribution*. When customers are loyal to a particular product or brand they place pressure on wholesalers and manufacturers to supply that product or brand in sufficient quantity to meet everyone's demand. This fact makes it easier for the retailer to obtain supplies and to develop regular purchase patterns; this strengthens supplier relations and lowers cost.

REASONS WHY CONSUMERS ARE LOYAL

There are several reasons why consumers are loyal to specific products, brands, or stores.[10]

Achievement of Satisfaction

The basic ingredient in all consumer loyalty is perceived satisfaction with the firm's store, product, or brand. No consumer is likely to consider seriously repeating purchases when there is no real benefit. At least this is true when the consumer has meaningful alternatives; that is to say, they are not faced with a monopoly such as a public utility.

Satisfaction can be based on certain aspects of the firm's store, brand, or product.[11] The customer may have a strong feeling for the salespeople or the store's atmosphere. Satisfaction may relate to the brands carried, the line of products, or the prices. It may be the availability of such services as credit, returns, delivery, or warranty. Obviously, satisfaction does not have to apply to every aspect of the business for customers to be loyal. The brand image may be so satisfying that the customer overlooks poor salesperson performance, or low prices may create sufficient satisfaction to offset a narrow product line. The point is that loyalty depends on an overall favorable assessment of the business.

Image of Superiority

Perhaps the underlying reason for all consumer loyalty is an image of superiority the customer associates with a brand, product, or store. This image is more than simple satisfaction. There may be several products, brands, or stores that can provide essential satisfaction, but the consumer perceives one product, brand, or store to be superior to any others. This image can be so strong that it precludes, at least in the short run, even the desire to test the market periodically for a possibly better solution. Of course, sooner or later nearly every consumer re-evaluates the original decision to purchase. But in the short run, an image of superiority is the most powerful single factor causing the consumer to remain loyal to a particular product, brand, or store.

Consumer Inertia

Consumer inertia is not the most important foundation for loyalty, but it can be critical in conjunction with other factors. Consumer inertia means that there is no compelling reason to seek out an alternative product or store. It is simply easier for the consumer to continue purchasing the same product or brand or visiting the same store than it is to change.[12] Inertia has to be overcome in nearly every decision. If inertia is coupled with an image of superiority, the consumer is very unlikely to make any new decision. Inertia can often be overcome if the consumer finds out about some new product, brand, or store without having to make any effort. For example, one sees a startling new product advertised while watching television, or a friend informs one of an outstanding new store that has just opened.

Tendency to Conform

Consumer conformity is closely associated with inertia. Conformity means that if the image of the product, brand, or store is compatible with what the consumer's friends and associates deem to be satisfactory, the consumer may develop loyalty in order to be like these people. The individual may not want to question the judgment of associates. Then too, it may mean something to a circle of friends to be observed using the product in question or visiting the proper store. A consumer may develop loyalty to a product or brand that is not personally considered the best because of the necessity to conform. There are executives, for example, who own a London Fog coat or a Rolex watch because of the image it conveys to their associates.

Avoidance of Risk

Loyalty can aid the consumer in reducing or avoiding risk. When consumers remain loyal to a product, brand, or store they avoid the possibility of being wrong.[13] In other words, one way to avoid the risk of dissatisfaction from a new product, brand, or store is to remain with a familiar product, brand, or store. The essential considerations for the consumer where risk is concerned are (1) how strong is the perception that there is a risk, and (2) how important is it to avoid the risk of being wrong.[14] Of course, these two considerations vary greatly among individuals. There is evidence that customer loyalty is greater among persons who perceive considerable risk in brand, product, or store selection but who have already found a satisfactory solution to their problem.

Simplify Consumer Decisions

At any given time, the average consumer is faced with a vast array of product, brand, and store decisions. The number of alternatives available to satisfy even the simplest of problems can be tremendous. For example, a medium-sized grocery store can carry 15,000 to 25,000 separate items. It is said that General Motors could make cars around the clock for a year and never have two exactly alike. Consider the number of drugstores or furniture stores in your own town. Now add to that the other stores in your community that handle drug items and furniture. The possible combinations can be staggering. How can the consumer make reasonable decisions under these circumstances? Even if the person could come to a logical conclusions, who has time to give proper consideration to the issue?

Loyalty can help the consumer in these and similar decision situations; it simplifies future decisions. Loyalty reduces the number of decisions that the consumer has to make. Loyalty assumes that it is not efficient to solve the same problem repeatedly. If the consumer knows she or he can rely on the taste of Pepsi or the quality of Wal-Mart products, then the decisions related to buying soft drinks and clothing have been greatly simplified. There is evidence that consumers try to avoid extended problem solving. One study shows that in the United States about 60 percent of consumers consider themselves likely to "try to stick to their purchase decisions."[15]

Market Conditions

Consumer loyalty can result from conditions in the market. For example, if there are no alternatives in the market, the consumer must either be loyal or go without. Municipal services, such as garbage collection, electricity, and street repairs, are handled as monopolies, and consumers have no choice in their purchase. The consumer may even have to pay whether the service is desired or not.

Contractual arrangements can lead to loyalty. If the consumer purchases a service agreement on a new refrigerator, that person is forced to continue repairs from the company that sold the agreement. This contract greatly reduces the consumer's ability to shop around for repair service.

The trade-in can also aid in creating customer loyalty. Some tire dealers will reduce the cost of new tires based on the usable tread left on tires being traded in. The dealer does this only on the firm's own brands. Thus the consumer must make repeat purchases from the same dealer to obtain the discount.

Market isolation can aid in creating loyal customers. No store ever had more loyal customers than the general store. It was typically located in a rural area with no near competitors. Many customers had no choice but to frequent the general store. Even today in many small towns there may not be more than one store of a type; consumers are considerably restricted in their choice. It can be difficult and time-consuming to travel to nearby cities to seek out alternatives. Many consumers find it simpler to trade with the local merchant.

FACTORS THAT CAUSE CONSUMER SWITCHING

Loyalty is a tendency, not an absolute condition. Satisfaction is seldom absolute, and there is probably no such thing as a completely loyal consumer. We have indicated that even the most loyal of consumers buy different or competing products or brands sometimes. Customer loyalty will develop and be strengthened as long as there is positive reinforcement of beliefs, all other things being equal.[16] However, every consumer will, on occasion, seek novelty and deliberately go against established beliefs and attitudes. We must remember that product, brand, or store switching are as normal among consumers as loyalty. In the cereal market, individuals switch brands as often as ten times a year, and a new brand has only six months to establish itself before losing out to a more popular competitor.[17] It is estimated by Chrysler Corporation management that automobile switching takes place more often among individuals who purchase small domestic cars than those who purchase imports.[18] Consumer switching appears to have accelerated during the past decade. If this is true, consumer loyalty has declined.

There are some compelling reasons why consumers switch products, brands, and stores. Some of the more important ones are explained here.

Curiosity Causes Switching

Curiosity is an important reason for switching. We live in a world characterized by change, and people want to know about these changes. When people discover interesting new ideas, they want to apply them to their life-style. They naturally want to determine if the idea or product will solve their current problems. This tendency to apply new ideas or products exists even if the problem is currently being satisfied by another product. In this way, curiosity leads to switching. Good examples of consumer switching are found in the sale of laundry detergents and patent medicines. Consumers regularly switch among Bold, Tide, Cheer, All, etc., even though some of these brands are sold by the same business.

Switching is more likely to take place due to curiosity when there is not a lot of money involved and when the switch does not imply permanence. If the money involved is small, the consumer feels little risk. If the switch is not permanent, the consumer feels it will be easy to return to the former product. Once the curiosity of the consumer is satisfied, he or she may or may not return to the original product. It may turn out that the new product is a better solution to the person's problem.

Reassurance and Switching

It may sound unlikely, but many consumers switch products, brand, or stores in order to remain the same. The idea behind this type of switching is to be sure that the preferred product, brand, or store is still the best choice. In most cases consumers switch to recognized brands or directly competitive stores, so that the comparison is a legitimate one. However, in some cases consumers deliberately purchase products that are inferior in order to reassure themselves about their previous choice. Obviously, in most of these cases the consumer goes back to the familiar brand after a short trial of the new brand, product, or store.

It is also possible that customers switch in order to reassure themselves of a particular quality or price of product. At one time Izod products had a quality image, and they were purchased by specific customers who sought the product for its prestige. Later, the prestige of Izod changed and the price was lowered. A majority of customers who wanted to maintain the prestige image switched to Polo and similar brands that had the image formerly associated with Izod.

There is one other type of reassurance switching. This occurs when consumers change over time and switch to products, brands, or stores more in keeping with their new life-style. Consumers seek the reassurance that they are maintaining the desired image. We already know that people grow and develop over the "family life cycle." Over this life cycle consumers may change products, brands, or stores in order to reassure themselves that what they purchase is keeping pace with their manner of living.

Chance Switching

Consumers may switch their product, brand, and store loyalty because of chance. The consumer tries a new brand of drink mix at a friend's house, likes it, and decides to purchase it. A person may receive a sample brand in the mail and try it. Perhaps the individual liked a brand of coffee served in a restaurant and asked the management about it. There are any number of ways that consumers come into contact with new products, brands, or stores that they had not previously given any indication of purchasing. Sometimes these chance encounters lead to a modified purchase pattern.

In a study made by the A.C. Nielsen Company, it was found that 58 percent of the loyal customers who could not find their favorite brand were willing to switch to a competing brand.[19] It was chance because it was the available alternatives that determined which product the consumer chose. Whether the chance switch is permanent or temporary depends in part on the strength of the former habit and the performance of the new product, brand, or store.

Switching from Dissonance

One of the most important reasons for switching is the dissonance that results from disappointment with the product, brand, or store.[20] It often happens that a person buys a product habitually because of specific features, but the product changes over time. The quality of the features declines, and the consumer becomes disappointed. It may be that the seller attempts to improve the product, but in the process creates a combination of features that no longer appeals to some consumers. In these cases, the dissonance can cause the consumer to seek a new product. One only has to remember the disappointment created by Coca-Cola when they tried to improve the taste of Coke. The seller could also gradually allow quality standards to slip, thus alienating some consumers. It is the same with stores. A store that was once desired may over time modify its product assortment, its prices, or its service package. The new combination just may not appeal to the customer, and switching is the result.

Illustration 21-3 helps to explain how loyalty and dissonance are related as the business changes its offerings over time. The "Wheel of Retailing" is based on the notion that new firms tend to enter the market as low-status firms (low prices, low services, low margin, low quality), and, if successful, they evolve into high-status firms (high prices, high service, high margin, high quality). As the firms evolve, a void in low-status firms results. This causes new, innovative low-status firms to develop, forcing high-status firms to lower prices, services, and margins to meet the competition. As the low-status firm moves toward a higher status, price-conscious consumers become dissatisfied. They begin to have dissonance toward the firm's product, and they begin switching to the newer low-status firms as they develop. The same happens with quality-conscious consumers. As pro-

Illustration 21-3
Wheel of retailing and switching

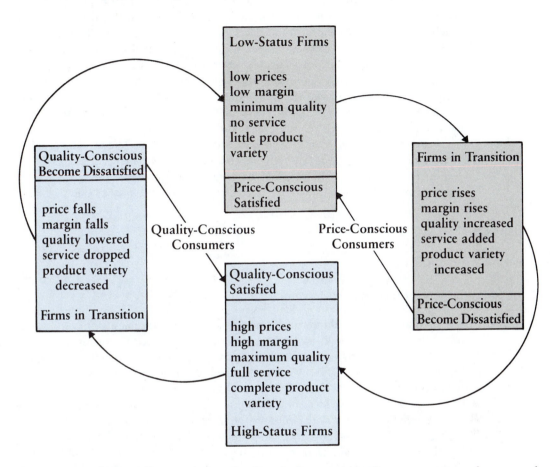

duct quality, service, and prices decline, ensuing dissonance causes them to seek out the emerging high-status firms. This cycle is repeated over and over.

External Pressure

Consumers sometimes switch because of external pressure. This external pressure comes from two sources. First, family, friends, and associates cannot help giving advice and offering suggestions to help the consumer make decisions. Some of this advice is sought out and some is not. Second, there is the external pressure exerted by business. We know that a principal purpose of promotion is to influence consumers. Of particular importance to switching are sales promotion techniques such as "cents-off coupons," rebates, and two-for-one price deals. Evidence demonstrates that such techniques do induce many consumers to switch. However, after the specials have run their course, the consumers may switch back to their original selection. There is little evidence that these sales promotion techniques have any long-run effect on consumer loyalty.

CREATE A CLIMATE FOR LOYALTY

We have already said that the key to success lies in repeat purchases. Of course, some managements are more successful than others. Loyalty tends to be much higher for supermarkets than for fashion specialty stores. One study shows that at least 75 percent of supermarket shoppers were exclusive one-brand users of such products as salt, vinegar, dinner rolls, popcorn, waxed paper, oven cleaner, yogurt, and doughnuts.[21] Managers must create a climate in which customer loyalty can thrive. This is not an easy task, but it is a goal worthy of the manager's most careful attention. There are several factors that contribute to this climate for loyalty which require explanation.

First, management must provide a satisfactory product. The product must be satisfactory, not only to consumers, but to all groups in the environment that affect the firm. As we have observed throughout this text, these "other groups" also affect consumers. In Chapter 1 we described a *perfect product* as one that is:

1. Profitable to the firm
2. Wanted by consumers
3. Legal
4. Competitive
5. Socially acceptable
6. Efficient in resource use

Such a product could not fail, since it meets the requirements of every group in the firm's environment, and it also meets the firm's need for profit. Although we recognize that providing this perfect product is very difficult, if not impossible, it is a worthy goal. The closer to the ideal management we come, the greater the likelihood of success. The firm should have these six objectives in mind every time it innovates a new idea, produces a product, and promotes a product.

Second, let people know about the product, brand, or store. There is an old saying, "Build a better mousetrap and the world will beat a path to your door," but there is not a grain of truth in it. If you do not get out there and beat the bushes, the mousetrap will sit on your shelf. Managers must let consumers know that they have a good product, and this can only be done by effective promotion. People need to know that there are products worthy of their loyalty. They must be induced to try these products, and the initial trial must be reinforced until buying becomes automatic. To change consumer loyalty, management must make sure the alternative is known and understood.

It is the same with stores. Consumers must be informed about the special advantages of the store, and how these advantages relate to the individual. It is just as important that the business be emphasized in sales effort and advertising as it is for the product.

Third, make your product accessible. Only in the case of brand insistence or store insistence will consumers go without rather than purchase a substitute. If your product, brand, or store is not accessible, then buyers turn to those alternatives that are. Having stores located near consumers is a very important form of accessibility; convenience grocery stores have significantly eroded chain store sales by locating near customers. But accessibility can take several other

Part 5 – Consumer Assessment of Purchase

forms—including selling by mailorder, by telephone, and door-to-door. It is important to find the type of accessibility that is most effective for the operation and to use it effectively.

Fourth, keep your word as an enterprise. Whatever the business says through its clerks, outside salespersons, managers, or promotions should conform to consumers' and society's concepts of what is honest, ethical, and just. Managers should not state in their warranty that defective tires will be replaced if they only mean that they will replace the tires to the extent that tread wear indicates. Managers could not state that they have the friendliest salespeople in the business if they do not do everything in their power to train and maintain salespeople who can meet this standard. Nothing turns a consumer off faster than feeling managers are promoting standards that cannot be met in practice. The consumer has been cheated. If it is possible, consumers will get back at stores that treat them unfairly. Their revenge may take the form of withholding purchases, talking friends or relatives out of buying from the firm, or otherwise undermining the organization's profit position. It pays to keep your word to customers, because satisfied customers are much more likely to become loyal customers.

Fifth, make buying easy. The easier it is for the consumer to locate and finalize the purchase, the more likely that consumer is to make the same decision next time. Most persons tend to take the path of least resistance. If their mental condition is product recognition or product preference, they will accept substitute merchandise. Very often the difference between a loyal and a disloyal customer is the ease with which that person can locate the item in the store and make payment. Thus management should remove all possible barriers between the customer and the merchandise to the extent that this is feasible. We must recognize that customer safety cannot be overlooked, and neither can the possibility of theft. Some merchandise, such as jewelry and watches, must be kept locked in showcases. Even such items as expensive clothing must be sometimes locked to the rack. Nevertheless, the goal should be to make buying easy. That is the basic notion behind the self-service store. Let the customer wait on him- or herself and expedite checkout. Making the purchase easy may also entail the use of salespeople. Some products, such as fashion clothing, appliances, and automobiles, cannot be fully understood by the customers without help. It is the store's responsibility to provide this help when necessary.

Sixth, treat customers with respect. No one has to purchase from a given store. Often the difference between a loyal customer and one that shops around is the manner of treatment in the store. It costs very little for clerks and salespersons to be courteous and responsive. Many people feel that this is the area in which most firms fail to meet customer expectations. One cannot help but wonder why so many store employees cannot deal effectively with the public. The reason is all too often that the management of the firm does not understand the importance of customer relations. Too little time and training goes into how clerks and salespeople deal with customers. Managers assume, often incorrectly, that employees already know the importance of being courteous, polite, responsive to needs, and pleasant. There is no aspect of store operations where a little effort can gain more customer loyalty than customer relations. Almost every retail organization could profit from greater effort in this direction.

QUESTIONS

1. Identify products that you have purchased and are satisfied with. Would you buy these products again without a search? Explain your answer.
2. Define habitual use. Are there any products for which you are a habitual user? Explain why or why not.
3. Discuss the relationship between habitual use and loyalty.
4. Give examples of products in which you have: undivided loyalty, no loyalty, divided loyalty, and unstable loyalty. Why the difference?
5. Why is it important for a marketing manager to know that loyalty is learned?
6. Discuss the advantages to a marketing manager to have loyal customers.
7. Discuss reasons why individuals become loyal consumers.
8. Identify some product where you have switched brands. What were your reasons for switching?
9. Who switches brands most often, you or your parents? Discuss your answer.
10. Identify a store in your town which you feel has evolved through the wheel of retailing. Discuss the changes it went through.
11. Consumers sometimes switch their loyalty because of external pressure. Identify some of the sources that influence or could influence you. Why?
12. To create a climate for loyalty, first, management must provide a satisfactory product. Is this an easy task? Explain your answer.
13. Discuss how the marketing mix relates to creating a climate for loyalty.
14. One cannot help but wonder why so many store employees cannot deal effectively with the public. Discuss how management can rectify this problem.
15. Relate the major types of consumer loyalty to the classification of consumer products.

NOTES

1. Richard L. Oliver, "Measurement and Evaluation of Satisfaction Processes in Retail Settings," *Journal of Retailing,* Vol. 57 (Fall 1981), pp. 25–48; John E. Swan and I. Frederick Trawick, "Disconfirmation of Expectations and Satisfaction with a Retail Service," *Journal of Retailing,* Vol. 57 (Fall 1981), pp. 49–67.
2. Claes Fornell and William T. Robinson, "Industrial Organization and Consumer Satisfaction/Dissatisfaction," *Journal of Consumer Research,* Vol. 9 (March 1983), pp. 403–12.
3. Klaus Peter Kaas, "Consumer Habit Forming, Information Acquisition, and Buying Behavior," *Journal of Business Research,* Vol. 10 (March 1982), pp. 3–16.
4. F. Stewart DeBruicker and Gregory L. Summe, "Make Sure Your Customers Keep Coming Back," *Harvard Business Review,* Vol. 63 (January–February 1985), pp. 92–98.
5. S. P. Raj, "Striking a Balance Between Brand 'Popularity' and Brand Loyalty," *Journal of Marketing,* Vol. 49 (Winter 1985), pp. 53–59.

6. Richard A. Werbel, "An Evaluative Review of Measures of Brand Loyalty," in John C. Crawford and Barbara C. Garland, eds., *1985 Proceedings Southwestern Marketing Association Conference* (North Texas State University and Southwestern Marketing Assn., 1985), pp. 66–70.

7. George Brown, "Brand Loyalty—Fact or Fiction?" *Advertising Age,* Vol. 23 (9 issues between June 19, 1952 and January 26, 1953).

8. Geoffrey P. Lantos, "The Influences of Inherent Risk and Information Acquisition on Consumer Risk Reduction Strategies," *Journal of the Academy of Marketing Science,* Vol. 11 (Fall 1983), pp. 358–81.

9. S. P. Raj, "The Effects of Advertising on High and Low Loyalty Consumer Segments," *Journal of Consumer Research,* Vol. 9 (June 1982), pp. 77–89.

10. Gilbert Churchill, Jr. and Carol Surprenant, "An Investigation into the Determinants of Customer Satisfaction," *Journal of Marketing Research,* Vol. XIX (November 1982), pp. 491–504.

11. M. Joseph Sirgy and A. Coskun Samli, "A Path Analytic Model of Store Loyalty Involving Self-Concept, Store Image, Geographic Loyalty, and Socioeconomic Status," *Journal of the Academy of Marketing Science,* Vol. 14 (Summer 1985), pp. 265–91.

12. Susan E. Holland, "An Exploratory Study of Products Used for Enjoyment and Enhancement Purposes I. Reasons for Choice Among Brands," *Journal of the Academy of Marketing Science,* Vol. 12 (Spring 1984), pp. 205–17.

13. Gilles Laurent and Jean-Noel Kapferer, "Measuring Consumer Involvement Profiles," *Journal of Marketing Research,* Vol. XXII (February 1985), pp. 41–53.

14. Peter H. Bloch and Marsha L. Richins, "A Theoretical Model for the Study of Product Importance Perceptions," *Journal of Marketing,* Vol. 47 (Summer 1983), pp. 69–81.

15. Bill Abrams, "Brand Loyalty Rises Slightly, But Increase Could Be Fluke," *Wall Street Journal* (January 7, 1982), p. 23.

16. Gregory S. Carpenter and Donald R. Lehmann, "A Model of Marketing Mix, Brand Switching, and Competition," *Journal of Marketing Research,* Vol. XXII (August 1985), pp. 318–29.

17. "Food in the A.M.," *Time* (March 31, 1980), p. 53.

18. *Wall Street Journal* (October 9, 1980), p. 1.

19. J. O. Peckham, Sr., "The Wheel of Marketing," *The Nielsen Researcher* (1973), pp. 9–11.

20. Priscilla A. LaBarber and David Mazursky, "A Longitudinal Assessment of Consumer Satisfaction/Dissatisfaction: The Dynamic Aspect of the Cognitive Process," *Journal of Marketing Research,* Vol. XX (November 1983), pp. 393–404.

21. "Progressive Grocer's Guide to Usage of Supermarket Product," *Progressive Grocer* (July 1983), pp. 39–41.

CHAPTER 22

Consumer Actions

When Dissatisfied

CHAPTER OUTLINE

I. INDIVIDUAL RESPONSES TO DISSATISFACTION
  A. Take No Action
  B. Trade Elsewhere
  C. Work with Company Representatives
  D. Take Legal Action

II. GROUP APPROACH TO DISSATISFACTION: CONSUMERISM

III. DEVELOPMENT OF CONSUMER COOPERATION TO SOLVE PROBLEMS
  A. Period of Innocence
  B. Period of Public Awareness
  C. Period of Consumer Achievement

IV. CONSUMERISM TODAY
  A. Types of Consumer Organizations
  B. Objectives of Consumerism
  C. Tools of the Consumer Movement

V. CURRENT SOURCES OF CONSUMER DISSATISFACTION
  A. Economic Issues
  B. Social Issues
  C. Issues of Business Ethics

VI. WHAT CONSUMERISM HAS ACCOMPLISHED
  A. Consumer Bill of Rights
    1. Right to Safety
    2. Right to Be Informed
    3. Right to Choose
    4. Right to Be Heard
  B. More Effective Legislation
  C. Increased Consumer Awareness in Business
  D. Marketing Opportunities

VII. FUTURE OF CONSUMERISM

CHAPTER OBJECTIVES

After completing your study of Chapter 22, you should be able to:

1. Discuss individual responses to dissatisfaction.
2. Discuss the group approach to dissatisfaction.
3. Explain the development of consumer cooperation to solve problems.
4. Discuss consumerism today.
5. Discuss current sources of consumer dissatisfaction.
6. Discuss what consumerism has accomplished.
7. Discuss the future of consumerism.

For the most part, when one thinks of consumer dissatisfaction, a picture comes to mind of the solitary shopper attempting to oppose large, well-financed corporations. It is an image of the individual against the business system trying to overcome high prices, confusing product claims, sales inefficiency, and sometimes dishonesty. This picture is beginning to change. Consumers are increasingly aware that they have a variety of options, and they often take action to alleviate their dissatisfaction.[1] This chapter examines the actions consumers take when dissatisfied.

INDIVIDUAL RESPONSES TO DISSATISFACTION

The individual consumer is not helpless when dealing with frustrations toward businesses. Although most businesses have managers who want to perform up to their customers' expectations because it is good business, sometimes they do not. Typically, the problem is an honest misunderstanding concerning what the company or its products can do. The firm may not have explained its product or service fully, or the consumer may have misunderstood the information. The product, although performing up to its design specifications, simply may not have performed up to the consumer's expectations. The product could have been defective. No matter what the cause, the consumer does have means of dealing with such situations.

You will recall from a previous chapter that the consumer can engage in two types of behavior when dissatisfied. The consumer can discontinue the product after this use if the purchase was one-time or if he or she is willing to remain dissatisfied. The consumer can discontinue the product immediately if he or she is willing to remain unsatisfied. The consumer can discontinue the product now and take direct action to obtain redress from the seller. These actions can be summarized as:

1. Take no action.
2. Trade elsewhere.
3. Work with company representatives.
4. Take legal action.
5. Cooperate with consumer groups.[2]

Take No Action

A dissatisfied consumer may choose to take no action against the offending firm, simply deciding that confronting the business would not be worthwhile. This is likely if the dissatisfaction is not serious, if the product cannot easily be obtained elsewhere, or if the consumer is convinced that he or she cannot win against the firm. For example, the consumer is not likely to do anything if the product costs less than $5.00. Some consumers will take considerable abuse from the phone company or other utilities rather than taking the chance of having their service discontinued.

Trade Elsewhere

One of the most effective instruments of redress possessed by consumers is withdrawal of trade, as depicted in Photo 22-1. Most firms depend on repeat sales for success, and if a sufficient number of customers are dissatisfied and take their business elsewhere then the firm must either take some corrective action or go out of business. A problem with this course of action is that it seldom works for individuals. Few businesses miss one or two customers. Even so, consumers

Photo 22-1
Dissatisfied customers shop elsewhere.

may obtain considerable satisfaction from withdrawing their trade. Perhaps most consumers have taken this course of action toward a business at some time, even if they begin trading with the firm again later. The business may never know that a customer was offended, and the business may never have the opportunity to take corrective action unless the customer takes the time to explain why he or she is withdrawing trade.[3]

Work with Company Representatives

The most popular single method of handling consumer problems is working through the company. The person goes to a company representative and explains the situation in order to find a solution. Company representatives include salespersons, department managers, complaint departments, product return departments, customer relations departments, and, in some cases, top managers.

Typically, customers take their complaints either to the salesperson or department manager where the dissatisfaction occurred. If the problem is a faulty price, a defective product, discourteous salespeople, or something similar, this is a good place to begin. It is safe to say that most customer problems are solved there. If the problem cannot be handled in the department, the customer may be referred to the complaint, returns, or customer relations departments, whichever is appropriate. For example, a customer wants a product refund but has no sales slip. If the firm's policy is not to grant refunds without this slip, there is a difficulty. If a customer purchases a product with certain expectations of performance which is different from performance as expected by the firm, there is a difficulty.[4] Only if the company is willing to give in to the customer can the individual achieve his or her satisfaction. Otherwise, the firm may be correct in its response and still have a dissatisfied customer.

Take Legal Action

If all else fails, the customer has the right to take legal action against the business. This course should never be taken unless the problem is serious or involves a large sum of money. Even then, the individual should consult carefully with an attorney prior to taking action to determine if the case is strong enough to proceed.

Legal action is seldom used by individual consumers because of the time and cost involved. The chance of individuals winning in court against a large, well-financed business is small. The business has available the best legal minds. Most individuals cannot match the business attorneys. Even if the individual goes to court and wins, the company can drag out proceedings with delays and appeals that cause a real financial strain on the consumer. People often give up even when their case is very strong.

GROUP APPROACH TO DISSATISFACTION: CONSUMERISM

Consumer dissatisfaction over the years has resulted in attempts to improve the situation through group action. Consumer groups have ranged all the way from a small number of housewives picketing a local meat market to state and national consumer leagues—including the federal Consumer Protection Agency. Some of the organizations are more successful than others, but individuals have learned that there is strength in numbers. This movement has become known as the consumerism movement, or just consumerism. The remainder of this chapter is devoted to the consumer movement because of its importance in educating and protecting the individual consumer.

The consumer movement is quite old, but consumerism is a term of recent origin. Its inclusion in the language attests to the growing emphasis our society is placing on the consumer. Consumerism is a rejection of the doctrine of *caveat emptor* (Latin for "let the buyer beware"), in which the buyers were viewed as having both the will and the means to protect themselves in the market.[5] Like most new doctrines, consumerism has been advanced from more than one perspective. Consumerism has been shown to be organized consumers, a social force, and the activities of various agencies. Buskirk and Rothe indicate: "Accordingly, consumerism is defined as the organized efforts of consumers seeking redress, restitution, and remedy for dissatisfaction they have accumulated in the acquisition of their standard of living."[6] Aaker and Day define consumerism as: "The widening range of activities of government, business and independent organizations that are designed to protect individuals from practices that infringe upon their rights as consumers."[7]

Both definitions are somewhat restricted—the first, because it ignores agencies other than consumers, and the second, because it de-emphasizes individuals. Furthermore, consumerism, as it has evolved, includes much more than consumer protection or redress of wrongs. For the purpose of this book, *consumerism* is defined as:

> an organized effort by consumers within the environment designed to aid and protect consumer rights by efforts directed at, and through, government, business and private organizations.

DEVELOPMENT OF CONSUMER COOPERATION TO SOLVE PROBLEMS

The beginning of the consumer movement is, of course, lost in time.[8] However, it is safe to say that the first disgruntled consumer probably occurred simultaneously with the first marketing institution. After all, there is some basis for natural antagonism between buyers who seek the lowest price for goods and sellers who seek the highest price. Most consumers feel that everything they purchase costs too much, since, if each item cost less, the consumer could spread his or her income further.

There is no general agreement on the specific causes for the rise of modern, organized consumerism. When business, consumer, and government representatives were given twenty-eight reasons popular in the literature to explain the rise of consumerism, there was little agreement. A consensus existed on only the seven items listed below.

1. The political appeal of consumer protection legislation.
2. The mechanical and impersonal nature of the marketplace.
3. The language of advertising.
4. A bandwagon effect.
5. Greater public concern for social problem.
6. A feeling that business should assume greater "social responsibilities."
7. A change in national attitude.[9]

A complete history of consumerism is not necessary or desirable at this time, but a summary of the high points of progress can place consumerism in proper perspective.[10] The consumer movement can be divided into three periods: (1) the period of innocence, (2) the period of public awareness, and (3) the period of consumer achievement. This definition is sufficiently flexible to encompass most institutions involved in consumerism, and it points to the need for consumer aid as well as protection.

Period of Innocence

The period of innocence is so named because the mass of people naively believed that they had no power to affect business or had faith in the system to provide for their requirements. This period lasted from the dawn of history until approximately 1900. The early part of the period was characterized by suppression of the masses. The barons of England had achieved a measure of freedom from King John with the signing of the Magna Charta in 1215, but the benefits had not been passed on to the average person. A very strict class system existed in all nations. The gentry ruled and enjoyed the good life, which was supported on the backs of the commoners who had little or nothing. Even so, there were isolated, and usually spontaneous, instances of resistance to the low standard of living. Occasionally, the serfs would rise up against the baron, or commoners would wreck the local trade center. The legendary tales of Robin Hood, although fictional, depict true situations in which the poor attempted to gain better economic conditions.

The American revolution in 1775 began with the consumer-related problems of tariffs, sales taxes, and product shortages. Only later did it become a fight for freedom. The Boston Tea Party was an early consumer uprising and product boycott. The French Revolution in 1789 was largely due to a desire of the common people to share more in the good life. These two struggles changed the course of history and gave the ordinary person a large measure of freedom.

The 19th century continued the advance in human freedom in America, but saw no real upswing in consumer action from the sporadic types that had previously occurred. The writings of Alfred Marshall and Adam Smith had popularized a concept of economic balance that precluded any opportunity to change the inevitable. Despite evidence to the contrary, most people believed in pure competition which automatically allocated resources perfectly. The "unseen hand" controlled the system, and the individual consumer was caught in its power. Furthermore, the average person's recently won freedom worked against any concerted consumer movement in an organized sense. Individualism, pride in self-achievement, and self-sufficiency were the order of the day. Americans did not want to depend on group action, the government, or private agencies to achieve their goals. This dependence was viewed as a restriction of freedom. The American dream envisioned advancement based on personal merit and hard work. There was not much chance for organized consumer action.

Period of Public Awareness

Consumerism had its beginning around 1900, although the first consumer protection law was passed in 1872. The period of awareness occurred between 1900 and 1960, and it is so named because a real change in the American attitude toward consumer problems occurred during this period.[11]

Events in the late 1800s and early 1900s caused people to become increasingly aware of the existence of market inequities. The builders of the transcontinental railroad, completed in 1869, had, with government cooperation, made tremendous profits from land grabs, exploitation of labor, and the abuse of Indians and settlers alike. The Grangers were instrumental in bringing these abuses to light, and this knowledge began to open some eyes. The growth of large business after 1880, with some instances of conspiracy, interlocking directors, price fixing, and dividing up territories between companies, added impetus to the awakening.

Like most causes, the consumer movement needed leadership and a catalyst to get it moving. The leadership was beginning to appear by 1891 when the first

Photo 22-2
The Boston Tea Party was an early consumer revolt.

THE BOSTON TEA PARTY—DESTRUCTION OF THE TEA IN BOSTON HARBOR, DECEMBER 16, 1773.

The Bettmann Archives

Consumer League was formed, and by 1898 this organization had become a national federation. The catalyst came in the form of two books published between 1900 and 1930. Upton Sinclair's *The Jungle* was a graphic exposé of working conditions in Chicago's meat packing industry.[12] This book told of rats, dirt, and even human parts finding their way into the packaged meat. The book became popular and was instrumental in the passage of the landmark Food and Drug Act of 1906. *Your Money's Worth* was one of the first attacks on advertising and high-pressure selling.[13] Thus by 1930, the consumer movement was established, but it still had not gained cohesion as a movement.

Consumerism grew slowly but steadily during the 1930s. Writers continued to focus attention on consumer problems. *100,000,000 Guinea Pigs* dealt with the manner in which business experimented on the American public with new products, and *American Chamber of Horrors* focused on unsafe cosmetics and quack medical cures.[14] When the Food and Drug Administration pushed for new protective legislation in the early 1930s, only the American Economic Association and the National Congress of Parents and Teachers were interested. Due largely to these two books, the scope of the problem was brought home to the public, and sixteen national women's organizations joined the fight. As a result, new legislation was passed in the food and drug area.

Period of Consumer Achievement

The period of consumer achievement began in the 1960s and continues to the present. In this period, consumerism began to reach its potential.[15] The period is characterized by consumer action on several fronts. In the 1960s, much legislation was passed dealing with labeling of products, food and drug standards, lending, product safety, and promotion truth and honesty. Furthermore, the general public was finally made aware to the point of identification with the consumer movement. It is for these reasons the period is identified with achievement.

Consumerism has become a popular cause with government officials, better-business bureaus, academicians, movie stars and even business leaders.[16] The movement began to show some efforts toward organization, and by 1969 there were over twenty-nine states with consumer leagues or similar organizations. The most active consumer groups were in Louisiana and Arizona. Even so, the movement was still characteristically identified with specific personalities. Ralph Nader is probably the name most identified with the modern consumer movement. However, Betty Furness, Vance Packard, David Caplovitz, and Jessica Mitford are also important symbols of consumerism. In the next sections of this chapter, we can more clearly identify the present status and accomplishments of consumerism today.

CONSUMERISM TODAY

Consumerism has evolved over time into a viable movement that has had an impact on how users and sellers behave in the market. What consumerism is today can be summarized in the types of organizations involved, their objectives, and the tools they use to accomplish their goals.

Types of Consumer Organizations

The consumer movement has attracted a wide variety of groups with diverse interests, and it is difficult to keep these groups working together. Today, temporary coalitions are formed as the interests of specific groups coincide, but they seldom include a majority of available organizations, nor are they of long duration when organized. Herrmann says:

> . . . the constituent groups in these coalitions include labor organizations, consumer cooperatives, credit unions, consumer educators, the product-testing and consumer education organization (Consumer Union), state and local consumer organizations, plus other organizations with related interests such as senior citizens groups and professional organizations.[17]

To this list should be added such federal agencies as the Federal Trade Commission, the Food and Drug Administration, the Federal Communications Commission, and the Department of Agriculture. Furthermore, there is clear evidence that the consumer movement depends heavily on the favor of the White House for any legislative improvement. Presidential support was particularly important in the Kennedy and Nixon terms. Perhaps the most consistent consumer participants are Consumers Union and the state and local consumer organizations.

Objectives of Consumerism

There are, of course, as many different consumer objectives as there are consumer organizations. Labor unions may be primarily concerned with wages, cooperatives may want favorable legislation to extend their sphere of influence, credit unions may want to become involved in legislation relating to lending and interest rates, and educators may be primarily concerned with student understanding of the consumer movement. However, there are three logical objectives of consumerism that underlie all the above organizations, whether recognized or not. They are:

1. Consumer education.
2. Consumer self-protection.
3. Business acceptance of responsibility.

First, consumers must be informed. Information provided may include tips on when and where to shop, how to determine merchandise quality, when to compare and when not to, tips on good buys, how to compare prices, and how to take advantage of sales.[18] Other types of information include lists of ethical and cooperative dealers and lists of businesses caught, or suspected, of actions detrimental to consumers. There is evidence that a lack of information concerning rights is one of the more serious problems of consumerism.[19] Second, consumer self-protection takes two forms. Consumers, under the guidance of some agency, may attempt redress by refusing to buy from certain stores or by refusing to purchase certain types of merchandise. The meat boycott of 1973 is an example of this type of action. Consumer organizations also seek self-protection of consumers through the support of, or opposition to, specific legislation that affects consumers. Third, consumer organizations, by direct action and education, seek to get business voluntarily to accept its responsibility to consumers and society.

Tools of the Consumer Movement

Publicity is, and has been throughout the history of consumerism, the single most important tool of the movement. We have already cited the effect of books used to expose specific conditions in business. Other publicity tools include news releases, published lists of offending firms, and newsletters. Consumer organizations work hard at uncovering genuine news items the news media can pick up. Newsletters are sent primarily to the membership of the various consumer organizations and are one of the prime methods of consumer education.

Political action is the second most important tool of consumerism. It ranks behind publicity because political action is dependent on publicity. Consumerism uses three types of political action. First, organization members study the platforms of political candidates, give support to those in line with consumer goals, and educate consumers on candidates to support. Second, there exists both an organized and unorganized lobby in favor of consumerism in Washington. The lobbyists are mostly unpaid, but often quite effective, especially when supported by spontaneous write-ins from constituents. Third, write-in campaigns are sometimes organized at the local level to support candidates or legislation favorable to the consumer movement. These campaigns can be quite effective.

Direct action is the least important of the consumerism tools. The prime means of direct action is the consumer boycott or threat of boycott. The effectiveness of a boycott is limited because it is difficult to organize group action and sustain it over any length of time. Thus the boycott is used only as a last resort, or when it is the result of spontaneous action. The meat boycott of 1973 was organizationally successful, but it had mixed effect on meat prices—mostly because there were sound economic reasons for meat prices to be high.

CURRENT SOURCES OF CONSUMER DISSATISFACTION

It is apparent from the previous discussion that consumerism has come a long way since 1900. Even so, the movement remains largely fragmented and lacking in overall direction. Just getting the attention of a group as large and diverse as American consumers is a monumental task, and obtaining cooperative action from them staggers the imagination. The immensity of the group is perhaps consumerism's chief enemy. Group size probably accounts for the fact that the peaks and valleys of interest in consumerism follow closely publicity of emotionally charged national issues associated with purchasing power or health problems. Only such issues are capable of obtaining broad consumer support over periods of time. A discussion of the issues, objectives, organizations, and tools of consumerism can greatly aid in clarifying these points.

Consumerism finds its reason for being in a great many issues that create common dissatisfactions. These issues range from inflation and business ethics to

Figure 22-1

Consumerism involves issues such as protection or minorities.

These are the words of a very
spirited man who has pushed and
pushed hard to obtain his goals.
Born deaf, his greatest joy while
growing up was watching the famous
Hollywood musicals choreographed
by Busby Berkeley on TV. As a child,
he recognized his overwhelming
response to music and dance.
"I didn't have to hear the music
because the music was inside my
body. I feel proud and beautiful
when I dance."
His interest in dance,
theatre and story-
telling began during
his early school
years and continued
through college to the
present time.
As for most schools
for the deaf, Sam Edwards
states emphatically, "Hearing Authorities refuse
to listen to deaf people's
opinions. They are deaf and
blind. They want deaf people
to talk, to wear hearing aids and
to be like hearing people. Many
deaf people including myself are left
with bad scars because of our experiences at school."
One of the points that Sam
Edwards stresses is that there is
already too much violence in the
world and he doesn't believe in being
violent or militant on his behalf or for
deaf people as a group.
So Sam Edwards' militancy
takes the form of encouraging other
deaf people to pursue all art forms as
a means to express their creativity
and to gain exposure anywhere and
everywhere possible. In fact, he
wants deaf people to become the
visible as opposed to the invisible
minority.
President's Committee on
Employment of the Handicapped
Washington, D.C. 20210
Produced by The School of Visual Arts Public Advertising System

President's Committee on Employment of the Handicapped

pollution and protection of minorities, as shown in Figure 22-1. Fortunately, these dissatisfactions can be meaningfully grouped around three broad topics: (1) economic issues, (2) social issues, and (3) issues of business ethics.

Economic Issues

The general operation of our business system gives rise to economic issues. Of these issues, inflation causes the greatest concern among consumers, although the abuse of technology, depletion of resources, and productivity are important. Inflation, which reflects the general price level of goods, affects every consumer's pocketbook. Americans have learned to live with a little inflation, since it is preferred to any deflation. However, any sharp rise in prices, such as occurred in the late 1960s and 1970s, erodes real income and leads to discontent.

The abuse of technology is a broad area of consumer concern that involves business stewardship over tools, methods, and techniques of production.

Americans believe in technology, because it leads to productivity and a higher standard of living. We have even come to recognize that some unemployment is tolerable because it occurs while unskilled workers are being moved to more skilled and higher-paying jobs. However, there is a growing feeling, whether right or wrong, that excess technology is not sound because of its effect on people and the environment. Business is criticized for moving too quickly into technology, as seen by criticism of the expenditures on space, opposition to atomic energy plants, and the scrapping of the SST. Business is also criticized for too slow a rate of technology, as seen by the current attacks on the internal combustion engine, failure to install pollution abatement devices in industry, and the federal interstate highway system, railroads, and rapid transit.

Consumers are becoming increasingly concerned about the failure of productivity to keep in step with rising prices. The American public has become astute enough to recognize the connection of productivity with the balance of U.S. payments abroad and foreign imports.

The depletion of resources has suddenly been introduced to consumer issues in recent months. The most striking example was the gasoline shortage of several years ago, but many of our natural mineral, wildlife, and scenic resources are rapidly being depleted. Of course, it can easily be seen that these economic problems are often directly related to social and ethical goals.

Social Issues

The major social issues directly related to consumerism are environmental protection, protection of minorities, and protection of health and safety. The environment is a real social problem. However, consumers appear about as confused over how to handle it as does business. Consumers insist on a lessening of pollution, but refuse to give up their oversized, dirty automobiles or the products of polluting factories. Consumers actively seek improvement in the safety of products, such as flammable materials, dangerous toys and poisons, but refuse to use their seat belts, object to the cost of safety devices, and do not remove medicine from children's reach or safely dispose of old refrigerators. The attitude often appears to be that it is up to business to find a way to protect the environment and the consumer without the individual giving up anything.[20] Given sufficient time, business will probably do just that.

Issues of Business Ethics

Business has always been under attack by some group. The criticism is sometimes justified and sometimes not. It is the author's experience that business people are about as honest and ethical as the average of the population. It should be understood that the above statement leaves plenty of room for improvement. The fact is that business is an easy target for disgruntled members of society. Some business people are often stupid, inefficient, and dishonest, and the first two may be more serious than the latter. Thus, any attack is likely to contain some elements of truth. Consumers feel that business is so impersonal that no one is really hurt by such attacks and that the industry is really too vast to fight back on a personal basis.

The overriding issue of business ethics is fair, honest, and equitable treatment for consumers.[21] Of course, this issue can be broken down into several problem areas, including truth in promotion, unit pricing, high-pressure selling, restraint of trade, and service standards. The problem is that the great variety of stores, the number of generic products, and the specific brands available make it impossible for the consumer to be fully informed when buying. Therefore, the consumer is an easy target for various types of deceptions by dishonest, misinformed, or incompetent business firms. Some of the more common types of deceptions include: promoting a No. 303 can as larger than a No. 2 can; selling factory seconds or damaged merchandise without identification as such; using large packages not completely full to give the appearance of more; use of bait pricing; making false and misleading statements about the store or its merchandise; selling essentially the same merchandise for different prices; charging exorbitant interest on credit purchases; overcharging merchandise; and misidentifying merchandise for pricing purposes.

It does not matter that the majority of business people are honest, and may take strong ethical stands, as shown in Figure 22-2. The consumer measures the worth of the entire group by the bad encounters. Besides, where abuses take

Figure 22-2
Businesses do take ethical stands.

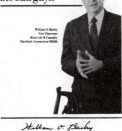

#8 in a Series on Civil Justice Reform

Responsibility Repealed

In order for someone to haul you into court today, the product you make doesn't have to be defective or shoddily made. It just has to have some kind of inherent risk.

The classic example is the vaccine manufacturer who makes a product essential for millions, but harmful to a few. The constant threat of liability and the astronomical costs associated with litigation have stopped many manufacturers from producing life-saving vaccines.

And in today's legal environment, you can even be held retroactively liable for *conduct* that was considered careful, responsible and acceptable at the time it occurred.

Consider the Federal Superfund law. Should a company be liable for clean-up costs when it had followed accepted procedure at the time it disposed of waste? And should one company have to pick up the whole tab even if it was only marginally responsible?

I've been dealing with the civil justice system for more than 30 years. In years past, I saw this system play a very valuable role in deterring careless and irresponsible behavior. The system once protected the careful and responsible from legal harassment, but not anymore. Our civil justice system has lost the ability to distinguish between the good guys and the bad guys.

We *can* have a liability system that recognizes responsible behavior. Let's restore the notion of fault to the system. Let's crack down on frivolous suits. And

let's not impose liability and added costs on those who exercise due care in making a product.

The American people are ready for reforms like these and America is desperately in need of them. I hope you will join me in working for meaningful reform of our civil justice system.

I welcome your thoughts and ideas on how we can work together to restore balance to this system. And I would be pleased to send you information on efforts that already are under way.

"Our civil justice system has lost the ability to distinguish between the good guys and the bad guys."

William O. Bailey
Vice Chairman
Aetna Life & Casualty
Hartford, Connecticut 06156

William O. Bailey

Courtesy of Aetna Life & Casualty

place, the consumer has a right to have these abuses corrected. The problem is that no amount of consumer vigilance or government action can completely eliminate dishonest or unethical business practices. However, such action can act as a deterrent and improve the overall performance of business.

WHAT CONSUMERISM HAS ACCOMPLISHED

There is no question but that the accomplishments of the American consumer movement have been significant.

Consumer Bill of Rights

Perhaps the most important single accomplishment of modern consumerism is the recognition that consumers have certain rights. In 1962, the late President John F. Kennedy, in a *Special Message on Protecting the Consumer Interest*, outlined consumer rights as: (1) the right to safety, (2) the right to be informed, (3) the right to choose, and (4) the right to be heard. Although specific acts of legislation have probably had a more immediate impact on consumers, the clear statement of consumer rights means more in the long run. Its publication by the president carried great symbolic weight and attracted more publicity than specific laws. In addition, the enumeration of consumer rights provides a standard for evaluating business service to the community. Third, the bill of rights will provide a basis for future legislation of far-reaching impact. The existence of a consumer bill of rights overshadows all other accomplishments of consumerism. Let us take a closer look at these rights.

Right to Safety. This is the right of the consumer to be protected against the sale of products hazardous to health or life.[22] The right is not absolute and must be applied with reason, since any product can be potentially dangerous. Gasoline used in automobiles can explode, screwdrivers can put out eyes, some people are allergic to specific chemicals, and appliances can short-circuit. However, no one seriously wants these products removed from the market. The right to safety is directed at unusually hazardous products such as narcotics, unclean food, fire hazards, defective products, or products with hazards the consumer cannot detect. No amount of government action can eliminate all health and safety hazards, and the consumer is expected to use intelligence and reasonable caution when using any product.[23]

The federal government has been active in the area of consumer safety by (1) limiting the sale of diseased meat, narcotics, and dangerous patent medicines; (2) regulating the use of drugs and chemicals by consumers themselves; (3) initiating programs of highway, waterway, and air safety; and (4) establishing standards that eliminate or control conditions of manufacture and sale of goods. The Consumers Product Safety Commission puts out an index of hazardous products. According to the index, the most hazardous products are:

1. Stairs, ramps, landings (indoor, outdoor)
2. Bicycles and bicycle equipment
3. Baseball-related equipment and apparel

4. Football-related equipment and apparel
5. Basketball-related equipment and apparel
6. Nails, carpet tacks, screws, thumb tacks
7. Tables (nonglass)
8. Architectural glass
9. Chairs, sofas, and sofa beds
10. Swings, slides, seesaws, and playground climbing apparatus
11. Beds (including springs and frames)
12. Skating-related equipment and apparel
13. Glass bottles and jars
14. Cutlery and knives
15. Desks, cabinets, shelves, bookcases, footlockers
16. Ladders and stools
17. Lumber
18. Drinking glasses
19. Swimming-related equipment
20. Cans and other containers[24]

Of course, all these products bring consumer benefits, and it is difficult to balance safety against consumer wants. It is not an easy decision to make.

Right to Be Informed. This consumer right concerns protection against fraud, deception, and grossly misleading information, promotion, labeling, and other practices. It also establishes the consumer's right to have the facts needed for intelligent product choice. The right to information does not relieve the consumer of responsibility of market awareness. Each seller has the right to present his or her product most favorably, and there is nothing that requires such full disclosure as: whether better or cheaper competitive products exist; exact performance; or features that are unsuited or unnecessary to the specific consumer. It is still the consumer's responsibility to shop, compare, and use relevant market information efficiently.

The right to be informed raises some sticky moral and ethical questions. The most difficult question is where to draw the line between truth and untruth or fact and deception. For example, is the use of cartoons untruthful because cartoons are not real? How about the use of actors to depict average persons in commercials? Is it deceitful of an aspirin manufacturer to advertise that its product is the best, when, in fact, none is best—although several are just as good? Is it ethical to promote toys on the morning TV cartoon shows for viewing by the susceptible young? Are appeals to sex, beauty, and happiness factual in promoting drugs and cosmetics? Ask your acquaintances about these and similar questions of information presentation, and you may be surprised at the variety of answers you receive. Marketers are equally in doubt. They must wait for clarification by the legislatures and courts. The federal government has already passed significant legislation in this area. Furthermore, the government supports efforts of the Bureau of Home Economics, the Department of Agriculture, and the Food and Drug Administration to provide consumers with product standards and market information.

Right to Choose. This right assures consumers, when possible, of a variety of products and services at competitive prices.[25] It is understood that in such industries as public utilities, government regulation substitutes for the competitive mechanism to provide these goods and services. Government action in the arena of consumer choice has focused primarily on the passage of legislation affecting competition. The most active watchdogs of American competition within the government are the Department of Justice, the Federal Communications Commission, the Federal Trade Commission, and the U.S. Patent Office.

Several important issues of consumer choice have not been effectively clarified. How much choice is enough? Is the consumer sovereign? Which products do consumers want? How should product warranty be regulated? These are not easy questions for either business or the consumer to answer. It may take years, and many court decisions, to settle these questions.

Right to Be Heard. This is the right of consumers to be assured that their interests will receive full consideration in the establishment of government policy and quick and fair treatment in administrative agencies. Agencies are urged to begin to develop a dialogue with consumer groups and individual consumers.

In July 1962, the Consumer Advisory Council was established to study this particular right of consumers. After lengthy investigation, the council reported ten critical areas needing attention. They are:

1. *Consumer standards, grades, and labels*—To study governmental consumer standards of identity, quality, quantity, safety, and product performance, including assessment from the consumer point of view of system of grades, labels, and quality designation.

2. *Two-way flow of information and opinion between government and the consumer*—To prepare recommendations for improving the two-way flow of information and opinion between government and the consumer public.

3. *Effective consumer representation in government*—To examine and advise on different structures and procedures for achieving effective representation of, and participation by, the consumer in government.

4. *Consumer credit*—To examine consumer credit (including mortgage credit) in order to assess its effect on the family and the nation, to evaluate contract terms as they facilitate or inhibit efficient and intelligent use of credit by consumers, and to appraise procedures used in cases where consumers have made excessive use of credit.

5. *Interrelation among federal agencies and between federal and state agencies in areas of consumer protection*—To examine and advise on such relationships with a view to improving the effective administration, enforcement, and scope of their programs.

6. *Acceleration of economic growth*—To examine and advise on the process of economic growth with the objective of submitting the consumer's point of view on basic economic policies designed to promote a higher level of national product, income, and employment— with special attention to the factors determining consumer decisions to save or consume and the improvement of economic opportunities.

7. *Improvement of levels of consumption of low-income groups.*
8. *Antitrust action and prevention of price fixing.*
9. *Provision of adequate housing for the nation's families.*
10. *Medical care.*[26]

As a result of the council's report, the government has begun to move on a broad front of consumer rights. It will probably be some time before the action of the council and the government agencies can be evaluated.

More Effective Legislation

The immediate accomplishments of consumerism are most apparent in the legal sphere. We have deliberately skirted the question of legal action so that the pertinent laws can be presented together and in sequence. This is done in Table 22-1.

It is difficult to evaluate the impact of these consumer protection laws individually. They cover such a wide range of violations. Generally speaking, consumers are not as aware of their rights as they might be. One study of 234 consumers found mixed results concerning awareness of the Truth in Lending Law.[27] While over 58 percent of the respondents stated that they were aware of the law, only about 27 percent could answer questions about it. Of course, knowledge is necessary if the application of the law is to be effective. It was also found that knowledge varied by demographic factors.

The reader will observe a clear trend of wider and more comprehensive coverage over time. Basic drug protection in 1906 had been extended to include such areas as child protection, credit, environmental quality, smoking, product safety, and packaging. There can be no doubt of the progress made over the period. On an individual basis certainly, the Food and Drug Act of 1906 was a milestone that opened the door for consumer protection. The "Truth-in-Packaging" Act of 1965, the "Truth-in-Lending Act of 1968," and the Consumer Product Safety Act of 1972 were also extremely important in establishing legal trends. The impact of consumerism can almost be measured by the snowballing of legislation between 1900 and 1972. The total impact of the legislation has been to change the thinking of the nation on the subject of consumer protection. The American economic system has gone from "let the buyer beware" to one approaching "let the seller beware."

Increased Consumer Awareness in Business

Another area of accomplishment for consumerism lies in business awareness.[28] There are two sides to business awareness. One side is the recognition of public responsibility, and the other side is to see opportunity in public service, as shown in Figure 22-3.

Business leaders are generally aware of the consumer movement—its social goals, organization, and leadership. Of course, awareness is not acceptance, but it is a necessary first step in that direction. Table 22-2 provides an indication of how chief executives and controllers in some three hundred major firms view their business responsibility. These results indicate that the business managers polled are basically inward looking where responsibility is concerned. However,

Table 22–1
Significant Consumer Legislation

Year	Legislation
1906	*Food and Drugs Act of 1906.* It regulated misbranded and adulterated foods, drinks, and drugs in interstate commerce.
1914	*Federal Trade Commission Act.* It established the Federal Trade Commission; has among the responsibilities "unfair methods of competition" including deceptive advertising.
1936	*Federal Food, Drug, and Cosmetic Act of 1936.* It added cosmetics and devices to the Food and Drug Act of 1906; required clearance prior to distribution of new drugs; and established standards of identity, quality, and fill for food in containers.
1938	*Wheeler-Lea Amendment.* It gave the Federal Trade Commission power to prosecute for deceptive advertising or sales practices.
1939	*Wool Products Labeling Act.* It requires labeling wool products for the kind and amount of wool contained.
1951	*Fur Products Labeling Act.* It prohibits misbranding, false advertising, and false invoicing of fur products.
1953	*Flammable Fabrics Act.* It prohibits transporting easily ignited wearing apparel or material in interstate commerce.
1958	*Automobile Information Disclosure Act.* It requires posting of the suggested retail price on all new automobiles.
1959	*Textile Fiber Products Identification Act.* Added most textile products not covered by the Wool or Fur Products labeling Acts.
1960	*Federal Hazardous Substances Labeling Act.* It required the labeling of hazardous household chemicals.
1960	*Color Additives Amendment.* It gave the Food and Drug Administration, under the Food and Drug Act, the right to regulate conditions of safe use for color additives to foods, drugs, and cosmetics.
1962	*Kefauver-Harris Drug Amendments.* It amended the Food and Drug Act, requiring manufacturers to lise new drugs with the FDA; to provide generic labeling and to provide pretesting.
1965	*Drug Abuse Control Amendments.* It gave several powers to the Food and Drug Administration, including: requiring drug handlers to keep records of suppliers and sales; power to seize illegal supplies; power to serve warrants and to arrest violators.
1965	*Fair Packaging and Labeling Act (Truth-in-Packaging).* It regulates the packaging and labeling of consumer goods.
1966	*Child Safety Act.* It amended the Hazardous Substances Labeling Act of 1960 to prevent marketing potentially harmful toys, and it allowed the Food and Drug Administration to remove harmful products from the market.
1966	*Cigarette Labeling Act.* It required manufacturers to place, "Caution: cigarette smoking may be hazardous to your health," on all cigarette packages.
1967	*Wholesome Meat Act.* It required high standards for meat inspection and cleanup of unsanitary meat plants.
1967	*National Commission on Product Safety Act.* It set up a commission to review hazardous household products and to filed recommendations for legislation.
1968	*Consumer Credit Protecting Act (Truth-in-lending).* It established full disclosure of annual interest rates and financial charges on consumer loans and credit.
1968	*Wholesome Poultry Product Act.* It required states to have inspection systems for poultry and poultry products.

Table 22–1 (Continued)

Year	Legislation
1968	*Hazardous Radiation Act.* It established performance standards to limit or prevent radiation emissions from electronic products.
1969	*Child Protection and Toy Safety Act of 1969.* It amended the Federal Hazardous Substances Act to include electrical, mechanical, or thermal hazards.
1970	*Fair Credit Reporting Act.* It regulated the reporting and use of credit information by business.
1972	*Consumer Product Safety Act.* It protected against the unreasonable risk of injury from unsafe products.
1974	*Fair Credit Billing Act.* It required that a creditor must take steps if a debtor complains of an error within sixty days of the receipt of a bill.
1974	*Real Estate Settlement Law.* It required the disclosure of all real estate costs to buyers prior to the transaction.
1975	*Magnuson-Moss Warranty, Federal Trade Commission Improvement Act.* It required that warranties disclose the terms of the warranty in simple readable language.
1975	*Consumer Goods Pricing Act.* Repealed the Miller-Tydings Act which permitted retail price maintenance.
1975	*FTC Improvement Act.* Extended power to Federal Trade Commission promulgation of rules specifying acts on practices prohibited as unfair or deceptive.
1976	*Toxic Substance Control Act.* Regulated commerce and protects human health and the environment by requiring testing and necessary use restriction on certain chemical substances.
1976	*Medical Devices Amendment.* Provided for safety and effectiveness of medical devices intended for human use.
1976	*Preservation of Consumers' Claims and Defenses, Unfair or Deceptive Acts or Practices.* It required credit contracts to contain provisions warning the consumer as to what would happen if there is non-payment.
1977	*Foreign Corrupt Practices Act.* Established written ethical guidelines pertaining to bribes, kickbacks and extortion payments.
1978	*Airline Deregulation Act.* Deregulated airline industries, making them more competitive.
1980	*2nd FTC Improvement Act.* Specifically, this stated that the agency must defer publication of any trade rule concerning unfairness in commercial advertising for a three-year period.
1980	*Fair Debt Collection Act.* To eliminate the harassment of debtors and ban false statements to collect debts.
1980	*Motor Carrier Act.* Deregulation act to make the motor carrier industries more competitive.
1981	*Depository Institutions Act.* Designed to make the industry more competitive.

the results are encouraging. Chief executives, who have the greatest long-run influence on business policy, rank customers third in importance even though chief executives were not included on the questionnaire. No significant percentage of either chief executives or controllers recognized responsibility to satisfy society as a whole. Thus the problem now is to turn business awareness into acceptance of responsibility.

Figure 22-3
A business demonstrating public responsibility

"I never understood when Mom made me eat my vegetables because 'there were places where kids were starving.' Now...in two weeks I walk into a Dow laboratory and begin work on new ways to help grow more and better grain for those kids who so desperately need it. I can't wait!"

Dow lets you do great things.

Photo Courtesy of The Dow Chemical Company

Marketing Opportunities

A positive attitude toward consumerism by business can lead to new opportunities. After all, the route of least resistance in acquiring profits is to produce and market what society wants. The trick is now, as it has always been, finding out what consumers want. When Ford attempted to promote a safe car in the 1950s, consumers rejected the move. This situation has changed today as a result of the consumer movement, and the car would be accepted today. As a result, the marketer can find significant opportunities for successful marketing in social needs.

There are four major categories of product opportunities. *Desirable products* have high immediate satisfaction and long-run benefit to consumers (new "miracle drugs," automobile engines, and fabrics). These products should receive

Table 22–2

How Chief Executives and Controllers Rank Responsibility to Selected Groups

	Percent of chief executives giving rank of 1	Percent of control less giving rank of 1	Average rank
Stockholders	81.9	86.2	1
Employees	12.1	10.5	2
Customers	26.1	0.0	3
Creditors	11.8	11.0	4
Society	5.5	0.0	5

Source: Arthur W. Lorig, "Where Do Corporate Responsibilities Really Lie?," *Business Horizons* (Spring 1967), pp. 51–54.

the marketer's greatest effort. Their very nature makes them easy to sell and highly profitable. *Pleasing products* have high immediate satisfaction, but are harmful to consumers over time (cigarettes, narcotics, and alcohol). There are great marketing opportunities here, but they lie in developing alternatives to the harmful products. The development of alternative products include: low-lead gasoline, products that aid in stopping smoking, antipollution devices for cars and factories, rapid transit systems, and safe sugar substitutes. Of course, there is a risk associated with such products because consumers are not always willing to change. Some are successful and some are not. *Salutary products* have low appeal to consumers but are highly beneficial over time. Since the lack of basic consumer appeal is inherent in such products, the challenge for marketers is to make the product pleasing or to promote an effective change in attitude toward it. These actions are more difficult than the opportunities previously cited, but the rewards can be great when successful. *Deficient products* have no immediate appeal and no lasting benefit. The marketer should simply avoid these products since there is no basis for successful marketing. However, it is clear that consumerism has created marketing opportunities, and the payoffs are great for farsighted business leaders.[29]

FUTURE OF CONSUMERISM

The future of consumerism is bright. In fact, the movement is likely to pick up momentum in the next few years. In summary:

1. Consumerism was inevitable.
2. Consumerism will be enduring.
3. Consumerism will be beneficial.
4. Consumerism is promarketing.
5. Consumerism can be profitable.

These points have been the focus of attention of this entire chapter. The movement needs to move away from dependence on personalities and toward a closer, cleaner organization. Effort must also be directed toward clarifying objectives and getting these objectives across to the several agencies participating in the movement and to the average person. These are difficult chores, but they are inevitable.

QUESTIONS

1. Identify several products and/or services that you have been dissatisfied with. Discuss what you did about them. Was it the same action for all products? Why or why not?
2. When would you take legal action because you were dissatisfied? Discuss your answer.
3. Identify groups which influenced your dissatisfaction of a product. Discuss your examples.
4. Identify and discuss the three periods which make up the consumer movement.
5. Consumerism has become a popular cause with government officials; discuss some of these causes and why you think they have become so prominent.
6. What are the three logical objectives of consumerism which underlie all types of consumer organizations (i.e., labor, education)? Discuss some common problems or goals for all of these groups.
7. There are three major tools in the consumer movement: publicity, political action, and direct action. Discuss these three tools as they have been used in any movement with which you are familiar.
8. Consumerism finds its reason for being in (1) economic issues, (2) social issues, (3) issues of business ethics. List examples of each.
9. The late President John F. Kennedy gave the first outline of consumer rights in 1962 in a *Special Message on Protecting the Consumer Interest*. List these rights and discuss their relevance in various situations.
10. Discuss at least three of the acts listed under consumer legislation and give examples of how they have made changes in our society.
11. The American economic system has gone from "let the buyer beware" to one approaching "let the seller beware." Discuss this statement.
12. Discuss a major U.S. manufacturer who is using business or product awareness to increase self-regulation.
13. In your own words, what areas do you believe will become important in the consumer movement in the next five years?
14. Discuss how consumerism can be profitable for businesses.
15. What factors would motivate you to become involved in a consumer movement? Give an example.

NOTES

1. Solveig Wikstrom, "Another Look at Consumer Dissatisfaction as a Measure of Market Performance," *Journal of Consumer Policy,* Vol. 6 (1983), pp. 19–35.

2. Ralph L. Day, Klaus Grabicke, Thomas Schaetzle, and Fritz Staubach, "The Hidden Agenda of Consumer Complaining," *Journal of Retailing,* Vol. 57 (Fall 1981), pp. 86–106.

3. Claes Fornell and William T. Robinson, "Industrial Organization and Consumer Satisfaction/Dissatisfaction," *Journal of Consumer Research,* Vol. 9 (1983), pp. 403–12.

4. Alan J. Resnik and Robert R. Harmon, "Consumer Complaints and Managerial Response: A Holistic Approach," *Journal of Marketing,* Vol. 47 (Winter 1983), pp. 86–97; Claes Fornell and Robert A. Westbrook, "The Vicious Circle of Consumer Complaints," *Journal of Marketing,* Vol. 48 (Summer 1984), pp. 68–78.

5. Warren C. Magnuson, "Consumerism and the Emerging Goals of a New Society," in Ralph M. Goedeke and Warren W. Etchenson, eds., *Consumerism* (San Francisco: Canfield Press, 1972), pp. 3–7.

6. Richard H. Buskirk and James T. Rothe, "Consumerism—An Interpretation," *Journal of Marketing,* Vol. 34 (October 1970), pp. 61–65.

7. David A. Aaker and George S. Day, "A Guide to Consumerism," *Journal of Marketing,* Vol. 17 (July 1970), pp. 12–19.

8. The modern consumer movement is of much more recent origin. Most scholars date it from about 1900. See Robert O. Herrmann, "Consumerism: Its Goals, Organizations, and Future," *Journal of Marketing,* Vol. 34 (October 1970), pp. 55–60; Ralph M. Gaedeke, "The Movement for Consumer Protection: A Century of Mixed Accomplishments," *University of Washington Business Review,* Vol. 29 (Spring 1970), pp. 31–40.

9. Ralph M. Gaedeke, "What Business, Government and Consumer Spokesmen Think about Consumerism," *The Journal of Consumer Affairs,* Vol. 4 (Summer 1970), pp. 7–18.

10. William J. Wilson, "Consumer Reality and Corporate Image," *California Management Review,* Vol. 16 (Winter 1973), pp. 85–90.

11. Herrmann divides the modern consumer movement into three eras: (1) early 1900, (2) 1930s, and (3) 1960s. See Robert O. Herrmann, *The Consumer Movement in Historical Perspective* (University Park: Department of Agricultural Economics and Rural Sociology, 1970), pp. 2–31. The first two eras coincide with our period of public awareness, and the third period coincides with the period of consumer achievement.

12. Upton Sinclair, *The Jungle* (New York: Doubleday, Page and Co., 1906).

13. Stuart Chase and F. J. Schink, *Your Money's Worth* (New York: The MacMillan Co., 1927).

14. Arthur Kallet and F. J. Schlink, *100,000,000 Guinea Pigs* (New York: Grosset and Dunlap, 1933); Ruth De Forest Lamb, *American Chamber of Horrors—The Truth About Food and Drugs* (New York: Farrar and Rinehart, 1936).

15. Paul N. Bloom and Stephen A. Greyser, "The Maturing of Consumerism," *Harvard Business Review,* Vol. 59 (November–December 1981), pp. 130–39.

16. Paul N. Bloom, "How Marketers Can Help Consumer Educators," *The*

Journal of Consumer Affairs, Vol. 10 (Summer 1976), pp. 91–95.

17. Robert O. Herrmann, "Consumerism: Its Goals, Organizations, and Future," *Journal of Marketing* (October 1970), pp. 55–60.

18. Paul N. Bloom and Gary T. Ford, "Evaluation of Consumer Education Programs," *Journal of Consumer Research,* Vol. 6 (December 1979), pp. 276–279.

19. William H. Cunningham and Isabella C. M. Cunningham, "Consumer Protection: More Information or More Regulation?" *Journal of Marketing,* Vol. 40 (April 1976), pp. 63–68.

20. W. Kip Viscusi, "Market Incentives for Safety," *Harvard Business Review,* Vol. 63 (July–August, 1985), pp. 133–38.

21. Larry J. Rosenberg, "Retailers' Responses to Consumerism," *Business Horizons* (October 1975), pp. 37–44; Stephen A. Greyser and Steven L. Diamond, "Business Is Adapting to Consumerism," *Harvard Business Review* (September–October 1974), pp. 38–58.

22. Paul Busch, "A Review and Critical Evaluation of the Consumer Product Safety Commission: Marketing Management Implications," *Journal of Marketing,* Vol. 40 (October 1976), pp. 41–49.

23. Robert H. Malott, "Let's Restore Balance to Product Liability Laws," *Harvard Business Review,* Vol. 61 (May–June 1983), pp. 67–74.

24. Consumer Product Safety Commission, *1980 Annual Report: Fiscal Year 1979* (Washington, D.C.: U.S. Government Printing Office, 1979), pp. A2–Ar.

25. Robert Wuthnow, "The Moral Crisis in American Capitalism," *Harvard Business Review,* Vol. 60 (March–April 1982), pp. 76–83.

26. *Consumer Advisory Council, First Report,* Executive Office of the President (Washington, D.C.: U.S. Government Printing Office, 1963), pp. 5–8, 18–31.

27. William H. Bolen, "Consumer Awareness of Truth in Lending," *College of Business Ideas and Facts,* Vol. 7 (Fall 1976), pp. 37–41.

28. Kenneth E. Goodpaster and John B. Matthews, Jr., "Can a Corporation Have a Conscience?" *Harvard Business Review,* Vol. 60 (January–February 1982), pp. 132–41.

29. Mary C. Gilly and Richard W. Hansen, "Consumer Complaint Handling as a Strategic Marketing Tool," *Journal of Consumer Marketing,* Vol. 2 (Fall 1985), pp. 5–16.

SECTION B
BUSINESS ADJUSTS
TO CONSUMER CHANGE

23. Business Use of Consumer Research
24. Management Adjusts To Market Changes

CHAPTER 23

Business Use of
Consumer Research

CHAPTER OUTLINE

I. NATURE OF CONSUMER RESEARCH
   A. Business Purpose and Use of Consumer Research
   B. Broad Approaches to Consumer Research
   C. Steps in Consumer Research
   D. Two Major Types of Consumer Research

II. SOURCES OF CONSUMER DATA
   A. Primary Sources
   B. Secondary Sources
   C. Assessment of Sources

III. DEMOGRAPHIC CONSUMER RESEARCH
   A. Nose Counting
   B. Consumer Audit

IV. COGNITIVE UNSTRUCTURED-UNDISGUISED RESEARCH
   A. Depth Interview
   B. Focused Group Interview
   C. Behavior Sampling

V. COGNITIVE UNSTRUCTURED-DISGUISED RESEARCH
   A. Word Association
   B. Sentence Completion
   C. Pictorial Projectives
   D. Verbal Projectives

VI. COGNITIVE STRUCTURED-DISGUISED RESEARCH

VII. COGNITIVE STRUCTURED-UNDISGUISED RESEARCH
   A. Self-Rating Scales
   B. Likert Scales
   C. Thurstone Scales
   D. Semantic Differentials

VIII. CONSUMER RESEARCH ETHICS

CHAPTER OBJECTIVES

After completing your study of Chapter 23, you should be able to:

1. Discuss the nature of consumer research.
2. Identify the sources of consumer data.
3. Explain demographic consumer research.
4. Explain cognitive unstructured-undisguised research.
5. Explain cognitive unstructured-disguised research.
6. Explain cognitive structured-disguised research.
7. Explain cognitive structured-undisguised research.
8. Discuss consumer research ethics.

We have discussed in depth how business uses various means to influence consumer decision making. We know that business managers are most successful in influencing consumers when they have the knowledge to relate the firm's assets to the consumer's needs. It is very difficult to affect people when you know nothing about them. It is consumer research that measures the nature and tendency of consumers in the marketplace. Armed with this information, managers can design marketing policies to be both effective and efficient.

Almost every business uses some consumer research, either gathered themselves or borrowed from someone else. It is essential to business success. This chapter discusses consumer research and how it is used to provide managers with the data needed to meet their own objectives while satisfying consumers.

NATURE OF CONSUMER RESEARCH

In its broadest sense, research is the search for truth. Marketing research is the search for truth about marketing. We can define *marketing research* as:

the systematic and objective process of gathering, recording, and analyzing data for marketing decision making.[1]

Consumer research is logically a part of marketing research, and it takes its definition from the broader field. *Consumer research* is defined as:

the systematic and objective process of gathering, recording, and analyzing data relating to final household consumers.

Although we emphasize business benefits in this discussion, nearly every sector of our society can benefit from a knowledge of consumers. Consumer research can be used by governments as a basis for devising better laws to protect consumer rights and to aid the consumer-oriented candidate who seeks political office. Consumer protection groups need consumer research to understand the consumer decision-making process better in order to help individuals buy more efficiently. Not-for-profit organizations need consumer information to serve their markets better in much the same way as businesses.

Business Purpose and Use of Consumer Research

The purpose of consumer research is to serve the interest of business management in achieving the firm's objectives. In order to serve this purpose, consumer research attempts to discover the essential nature of consumers, individually and in groups—their numbers, location, characteristics, needs, problems, motives, attitudes, and actions. Management seeks to learn enough about its market to be able to identify tendencies upon which it can base its marketing strategy.[2] Of course, management would like to be able to predict consumer decision making, but such a goal is not likely to be achieved in the near future. In fact, such control over the actions of consumers appears to be beyond any reasonable expectations.

Consumer research has many uses. The most important one is to determine the drives that cause people to buy. However, this is not the only application.[3] Some of the more important uses are classified in Table 23-1. The actual number of uses for consumer research are as varied as the firms that apply the information.

Table 23–1
Uses for Consumer Research

Nature of markets	Motivation	Attitudes	Preference	Intentions
Customer location	Analyze motives for purchase	Establish attitude toward store	Determine store preferences	Estimate purchase intentions
Customer characteristics	Evaluate factors influencing motives	Establish attitude toward product brand	Determine product preferences	Analyze relationships between aspirations and purchase intent
Customer change	Establish motives behind product and store preferences	Determine problems of consumer dissatisfaction	Estimate store loyalty	Determine degree of intent realization
Market comparisons	Analyze motives for shopping and comparing products	Analyze relative strength of attitudes	Estimate product loyalty	
Determine market potentials		Determine store image	Establish trade area preferences	
Estimate sales		Determine product image	Determine purchase frequency	
		Analyze attitude toward distance traveled to shop		
		Evaluate attitude toward purchase planning		

Broad Approaches to Consumer Research

There are four broad approaches to the conduct of consumer research. They are: (1) synthesis, (2) survey, (3) observation, and (4) experiment.

Synthesis involves taking information that is already known, organizing it in some new or meaningful way, and drawing new inferences or conclusions. For example, one may synthesize information from several published government sources and come to a conclusion on economic conditions for the coming year. The research lies in how the data are organized and analyzed rather than in breaking new ground in the design and collection of the data. Synthesis is one of the more popular forms of consumer research.

The *survey* involves selecting a sample from the total population, designing a questionnaire with the questions you want answered, administering the questionnaire to the sample, then analyzing the results. A survey, unlike a synthesis, collects new data. It is one of the more complex and difficult means of obtaining data on consumers.[4] Yet it is the most used when performing original research. Surveys can be conducted by means of personal interviews, telephone interviews, and by use of mailouts.

In *observation,* the researcher perceives (through the sense of sight) the person, object, or actions of interest. There is no personal contact and no communication, therefore, it is the simplest approach to research. For example, a researcher may simply stand in a retail grocery store and observe how customers proceed down the various aisles. These observations can have importance for the layout of the store.

In an *experiment,* the researcher introduces selected factors into a situation where all other factors are controlled (held constant). The new factor may be manipulated, and its effect on the situation is measured and evaluated. This is the most difficult approach to consumer research, but since it is the closest approximation of the scientific method, some feel that it is the most valuable. For example, a firm may continue its present promotional campaign in all but one area of the nation. In this test market, a new promotion is introduced and the difference in sales is measured between the new promotion and the rest of the nation. In this way, the effect of the new promotion can be estimated.

Steps in Consumer Research

No matter which of the above approaches to consumer research is used, there are certain necessary steps in the conduct of consumer research:[5]

1. *Problem Recognition*—Identification of some aspect of consumer behavior that is a concern to management. For example, a firm would know it had a problem if it did not know how many consumers were in its market, or if it was unaware of product preferences. Do not be fooled. Problem recognition is one of the most difficult steps in research. It is not easy to recognize what management is not tuned to.

2. *Research Design*—A procedural guide is developed, using the identified problem as a guide. Each activity is specified that must be undertaken to solve the problem. This guide typically contains types and location of data and the means to obtain and analyze it. The research design

must be carefully detailed or the results will be defective.

3. *Data Collection*—The activity of physically acquiring the information needed. The sample size is determined, personnel are hired and trained as needed, and the procedure is undertaken with proper supervision.

4. *Analysis of Data*—The data collected are arrayed into some meaningful classification involving editing, coding, and tabulation, then the essentially mental process of determining what the data mean is undertaken. This stage must be completed accurately or the results are meaningless.

5. *Report Preparation*—A document is prepared and submitted to the appropriate person(s) summarizing the entire research procedure and all results. Conclusions and recommendations are included as a part of the report.

It is not necessary to engage in all these steps, but they are common to most research. For example, once the problem is recognized the solution may be obvious, so one goes directly to the report. The conduct of consumer research can vary from relatively simple to highly complex, but in either case it is essential that the researcher proceed with care and deliberation. Remember, the manager's decision is no better than the information upon which it is based.

Two Major Types of Consumer Research

Consumer research is a much broader area of study than is often realized. There is a tendency to equate consumer research with motivation research, but whereas motivation research concerns why consumers do certain things or act in some specified manner, consumer research concerns all the vital aspects of understanding consumers. Consumer research can be classified into broad methods according to the nature of the research: (1) demographic research and (2) cognitive or motivation research.

Demographic research deals with vital statistics about consumers—their numbers, location, sex, occupation, income, age, ethnic group, and marital status.[6] It attempts to chronicle what consumers are in terms of observable attributes. Primarily concerned with nose counting, this type of research is easily quantifiable. The importance of demographic studies cannot be overestimated. Some of our most important work on consumer behavior has developed from such studies.

Cognitive research, or what was historically termed motivation research, deals with a consumer's mental process and his or her relationship to his environment.[7] Cognitive research deals with the consumer's mental processes—attitudes, perception, motivation, personality, learning, communications, beliefs, and convictions. It also relates the consumer's mental processes to the environment by means of investigation of social class, group influence, culture, and family operation. Cognitive research also deals with the consumer decision processes. Boyd and Westfall said, "Research on motivation is not limited to any specific type of behavior, but includes the entire area of human behavior that may be related to marketing."[8]

Cognitive studies attempt to get below the surface of observable attributes and discover why consumers behave in specific ways. Cognitive research concerns the recognition, classification, and evaluation of the fundamental motivating forces manifest in consumer behavior. Consumer motives, perceptions, beliefs, etc., are difficult to quantify, and research in this area depends heavily on judgment.

SOURCES OF CONSUMER DATA

There are a great many sources of data available for consumer research. These sources can be grouped under the two headings of primary sources and secondary sources. Illustration 23-1 makes the distinction between these two types. When we discuss *primary sources,* we mean data that is garnered by the researcher for the purpose of the investigation at hand. Said another way, a source is primary if it furnishes unpublished data gathered directly from the original holder by the user—whether that user is an individual, a company, a government, or some other agency. In the figure we note that primary sources can be internal or external to the business.

Secondary data are always supplied by some third party to the researcher. *Secondary sources* supply data that is already published, or available in some other form, to be used in some different research. The data may have been original with the supplier, but it is secondary to the researcher who acquires it for a new purpose. Illustration 23-1 notes that secondary sources are always external to the acquiring unit, whether it is a person, a company, a government, or some other agency.

Primary Sources

The two most important sources of primary data for business are company records and the consumers themselves.

Illustration 23-1
Primary and secondary data sources

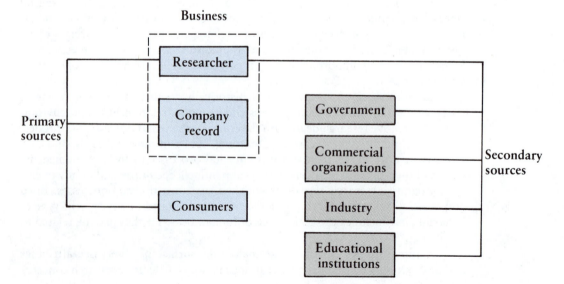

Part 5 – Consumer Assessment of Purchase

Most business firms have a wealth of information about consumers available in their own *company records*. Very often this information is either overlooked or not put to full use. The first place to begin searching for answers to any problem is in company records. Company sources include (1) credit records, (2) inventory records, (3) sales slips and tapes, (4) credit application records, and (5) accounting records.

Credit and sales records are excellent sources of customer information and should not be overlooked. Typically, the credit application records of a company contain information on the customer—name, residence, occupation, income, marital status, sex, age, and payment record. The sales slips usually have information on type of merchandise sold, price, quantity sold, date sold, selling department, and/or name of salesperson. This information is exactly the type included later in this chapter on the customer profile. It is, therefore, possible for the store to construct profile data using these two prime information sources.

No source of consumer information is more important than *consumer sources*. This source requires original research directed at some sample of consumers.[9] Most consumer analysis that deals with motivation and attitudes must be obtained directly from consumers. A considerable proportion of this chapter is devoted to explaining methods of obtaining data directly from consumers.

Secondary Sources

There are four principal secondary sources of consumer information for the business. They are: (1) governments, (2) commercial, (3) industry, and (4) educational.

Government sources are a most fertile ground for secondary consumer information. All governments, local, state, and federal, supply data. Local and state governments have population and economic data related to their boundaries. The federal government supplies more and more general types of information.

The Bureau of the Census, which operates under the Department of Commerce, is an important supplier of information useful to business. A description of the eight major census studies is presented below.

1. *Census of Population*: Provides detailed information on the population makeup (age, sex, race, citizenship, education, family composition, occupation, and income) of states, counties, cities, and town.
2. *Census of Housing*: Covers type of housing unit, value of property, size of mortgage, type of heating and number of bathrooms in the units. For cities of 50,000 and over, these data are available by individual blocks.
3. *Census of Agriculture*: Topics such as farm ownership, number of acres, crops harvested, number and type of livestock, equipment, and facilities.
4. *Census of Business*: This report covers three segments of business establishments—retail trade, wholesale trade, and selected services. The statistics pertain to nature of the business, location, dollar sales, payroll information, legal form of organization, etc.
5. *Census of Manufacturers*: Includes information about all manufacturing establishments with one or more paid employees. Covers value and

quantity of individual products shipped, employment and payroll dollar volume, and expenditures for plant and equipment.

6. *Census of Mineral Industries*: Covers a variety of minerals, including fuels, metallic ores, sand and gravel, and stone. It covers capital expenditures, person-hours, value added in mining, and quantity and value of individual products.

7. *Census of Transportation*: The newest of the census studies, it covers passenger transportation, truck inventory and usage, in-depth statistics on the movement of people and products throughout the United States.

8. *Census of Governments*: The information collected includes such topics as the number and type of government, value of property owned, revenues, expenditures, and size and payroll of their work forces.

Marketing managers should not overlook state and local government "registration data." This is data collected as part of legal requirements—records on births, deaths, marriages, sales tax payments, auto registrations, new home starts, property improvements, etc. The County Recorder's Office, the Motor Vehicle Office, and the County Planning Office are the main sources of the registration data useful to business. For example, the Motor Vehicle Division has information on the number and make of new cars sold every week within the city as well as the transfer of ownership of secondhand cars.

Certain state and city commissions, as well as Chambers of Commerce, also publish information sheets wherein they proclaim their virtues and give reasons why people of industries should choose a particular locale. While such information is quite biased, these reports also contain a great deal of useful statistics on schools, population, average temperatures, etc., and thus can be of use to consumer researchers.

Another important secondary source of consumer information is *commercial organizations*. The demand for consumer data has given rise to a number of vendors of marketing information. In 1984 there were over 1,600 such firms operating throughout the United States. Such firms typically fall into one of two categories. Some of the firms restrict their research to specific problems faced by their clients. This can be considered the collection of primary data; consequently, consideration of these companies and their work is not relevant here. Consider the following information types.

1. *Nielsen Retail Index*—Based on national samples of 1,600 supermarkets, 750 drugstores, and 150 mass merchandisers, taken every two months. The following information is provided: sales to consumers, purchases by retailers, retail inventories, dealer support, prices, number of days' supply, major media advertising, etc.

2. *Nielsen Television Index*—An audimeter (electronic device) is installed in TV sets in approximately 1,200 households. It records when the TV set is turned on, what channel it is tuned to, and when it is turned off. It is tied into a central computer, and twice a day the information is transferred to the computer, where it is analyzed.

3. *Market Research Corporation of America*—Uses a consumer panel

consisting of 7,500 families to obtain information on what, when, and where families buy. Every week the families submit detailed diaries of their purchases of such product lines as food, drugs, clothing, and household supplies.

4. *Selling Areas—Marketing, Inc.*—Provides information to manufacturers who sell through retail food stores. The data show manufacturers the sales of their brands and the competing brands in each of the markets.

5. *Starch Advertisement Readership Service*: Measures the reading of advertisements in magazines and newspapers. Some 75,000 advertisements in 1,000 issues of consumer magazines, business publications, and newspapers are assessed each year using over 100,000 personal interviews.

6. *National Menus Census (by Market Research Corporation of America)*—Collects information on each menu served at each meal, snack item, and carryout food items; other items served at the same meal; how the item was prepared; temperature on that day; who was present at the meal; what was done with the leftovers, and so on.

Other well-known research firms are Market Facts, Inc.; National Family Opinion; and the R. L. Polk Company. The number of such firms will continue to increase since the trend among firms is to seek more defined target markets. Whereas in the past, firms sought data about the "average American," today, for example, they want to know about single parents living in New York with incomes between $30,000 and $35,000 and with all children aged five to ten.

The group of *industry sources* includes information from organizations that exist to serve primarily their own industry. Each major industry or profession has one or more magazines specifically aimed at its members. For example, a tremendous amount of information about the grocery industry can be found in such trade publications as *Chain Store Age, Progressive Grocer,* and *Food Topics.* A consumer researcher should be aware of the various trade publications and indexes such as *Business Publication Rates and Data* and *Ayer Directory of Publications.*

Another source is trade associations. The coordinating offices of such operations generally compile and publish useful data for their members. The *Encyclopedia of Associations* lists associations' names, addresses, staff, number of members, and most important, their publications.

Educational sources include reports coming out of institutes, individual research undertakings in the academic world, and the output of various research centers. An important educational source is the *American Doctoral Dissertation Index,* and another is the *Index of University Publications of Business and Economic Research.* Some of the more important professional publications with an academic influence are the *Journal of Consumer Marketing* and the *Journal of Consumer Research.* The *Journal of Marketing, Journal of Retailing,* and *Journal of Marketing Research* frequently have articles dealing with consumers.

Assessment of Sources

The primary advantages of primary data are that it is timely, it can be tailored to need, and the researcher can control collection and analysis. It is timely because it is collected only when the researcher requires it. It is tailored to need because the researcher can design the research to do that which is specifically required for the study. The method of tabulation and analysis can also be customized so that there is no wasted effort in determining results. The major disadvantages of primary research is that it is very costly and difficult to obtain. Primary research is useless if it is not undertaken by someone knowledgeable in the subject and expert in research design and execution.[10]

The primary advantage of secondary research lies in its cost savings. It is less costly because it is already available. Most government publications and the various information existing in libraries are easily and quickly obtainable. Individual investigators usually cannot match the quality that governments and large organizations can put into their research. Some of the information available in secondary research is not available by any other means. For example, no private agency could duplicate the government's various census reports. Furthermore, secondary data collected by an independent agency is often less subject to the biases that might occur in the research of individual researchers or company employees.

There are several drawbacks to the use of secondary research. Secondary data were developed for purposes other than the researcher's specific project. Problems can arise because of (1) differences in definitions, (2) differences in units of measurement, (3) timeliness, and (4) accuracy of the data. Definitions used by the Bureau of the Census and the American Marketing Association are to some extent arbitrary and have not been uniformly accepted. Problems with measurement are common.[11] Consumer income, for example, may be measured by individual, family, household, or tax return. Each gives a different total. Timeliness is always a problem with government data. For example, government census data are comprehensive but are collected only about every five years. It may not be available when the researcher needs the information, or some interpolation, which affects accuracy, may be necessary. Accuracy must always be checked very carefully when using someone else's information.

DEMOGRAPHIC CONSUMER RESEARCH

The remainder of the chapter deals with the two broad types of consumer research, demographic and cognitive. Demographic research deals with the vital statistics of consumers. It is the easiest research to conduct because it mostly involves secondary data. It is also the most used type of consumer research, and it can be applied to a wide variety of consumer problems.

There are two types of demographic research, nose counting and consumer audit.

Nose Counting

Nose counting is quite simple in concept, but sometimes more difficult in execution. Nose counting involves determining some characteristic of the population you want to know about, then adding up the number of times this characteristic appears. For example, a person considering starting a maternity store in Scotts Bluff, Nebraska may want to know the number of births in Scotts Bluff county. This information is available at the courthouse, and it can be obtained by a nose count. Table 23-2 shows nose counting of the labor force by sex and race. The Bureau of Labor Statistics has simply counted the number of persons in each occupation class by sex and race. Many businesses may be able to use this information as it stands. Others may want to do some further compiling. For example, a seller of health supplies may want to combine the following from the table: physicians, dentists, registered nurses, and therapists. The principle of nose counting is the same in either case.

Consumer Audit

Audit is an accounting term meaning a formal periodic checking of something. A consumer audit is a formal periodic checking of some aspect of consumer behavior. For example, the products the consumers in a sample hold in inventory may be checked periodically to determine what they purchase, the brands, the amounts, and how purchases change over time. The frequency of consumer shopping may be audited to determine the location of stores visited, manner of travel, distance, and type of store visited. This type of information is easily assembled, it can be quite accurate, and it is timely. Many business managers can use consumer audit information in their planning process.[12]

COGNITIVE UNSTRUCTURED-UNDISGUISED RESEARCH

Cognitive research studies consumer mental states. We begin our discussion with cognitive unstructured-undisguised research. The terms disguise and structure refer to whether the respondent knows the purpose of the interview and whether there is a formal procedure for the questioning. Thus, unstructured-undisguised means that there is no formal process to the questioning and the respondent knows the purpose of the interview. The three most important types of unstructured-undisguised research are the depth interview, focused group interview, and behavior sampling.

Depth Interview

The depth interview as used in consumer research is an adaptation of the method employed by clinical psychologists. It is simple to describe, difficult to practice. Depth interviewing is not usually undertaken without the services of highly trained interviewers.

Table 23–2

Employed Persons by Sex, Race, and Occupation: 1985

Occupation	Total employed (1,000)	Percent of Total		
		Female	Black	Hispanic origin
Total	107,150	44.1	9.8	6.2
Managerial and professional specialty	25,851	42.7	5.9	3.3
Executive, administrative, and managerial	12,221	35.6	5.3	3.5
Officials and administrators, public	462	40.7	8.7	3.3
Financial managers	394	35.7	3.1	3.1
Personnel and labor relations managers	394	35.7	3.1	3.1
Purchasing managers	99	24.4	4.0	2.7
Managers, marketing, advertising and public relations	419	23.8	3.9	2.5
Administrators, education and related fields	419	23.8	3.9	2.5
Managers, medicine and health	106	59.2	8.1	4.6
Managers, properties and real estate	342	41.0	5.1	5.9
Management-related occupations	3,318	45.7	6.5	4.0
Accountants and auditors	1,263	44.1	5.9	4.2
Professional specialty	13,630	49.1	6.3	3.0
Architects	130	11.3	3.1	4.6
Engineers	1,683	6.7	2.6	2.6
Electrical and electronic	544	8.3	3.4	2.0
Mechanical	272	3.7	2.2	2.1
Mathematical and computer scientists	571	31.1	5.6	2.8
Computer systems analysts, scientists	359	28.0	5.5	3.1
Natural scientists	376	20.8	2.9	2.4
Health diagnosing occupations	728	14.8	3.2	3.1
Physicians	492	17.2	3.7	3.9
Dentists	131	6.5	2.6	2.1
Health assessment and treating occupations	2,006	85.6	7.0	2.4
Registered nurses	1,447	95.1	6.8	2.1
Therapists	257	76.2	7.2	4.2
Teachers, college and university	643	35.2	3.9	3.0
Teachers, except college and university	3,523	53.0	9.2	3.1
Prekindergarten and kindergarten	329	98.8	11.9	5.4
Elementary school	1,360	84.0	11.1	2.7
Secondary school	1,175	54.0	7.6	3.2
Counselors, educational and vocational	177	55.9	11.7	5.8
Librarians, archivists, and curators	215	84.7	6.1	2.6
Librarians	201	87.0	6.6	2.8
Social scientists and urban planners	286	42.6	5.2	3.1
Psychologists	150	50.4	6.6	3.4
Social, recreation, and religious workers	873	45.6	12.6	4.7
Social workers	438	66.7	17.6	5.6
Lawyers and judges	671	18.2	3.3	2.3
Writers, artists, entertainers, and athletes	1,725	44.5	4.7	3.3
Technical, sales, and administrative support	33,231	64.7	8.4	5.0
Technicians and related support	3,255	47.2	8.9	4.0
Health technologists and technicians	1,115	83.4	13.6	4.1
Licensed practical nurses	402	96.9	19.6	4.5

Table 23–2 (Continued)

Occupation	Total employed (1,000)	Percent of Total		
		Female	Black	Hispanic origin
Engineering and related technologists and technicians	904	18.1	6.4	4.9
Electrical and electronic technicians	304	13.1	9.1	5.0
Science technicians	211	33.3	8.1	3.8
Technicians, except health, engineering, and science	1,026	36.4	6.2	3.2
Computer programmers	534	34.3	6.4	2.5
Sales occupations	12,667	48.1	5.5	4.4
Supervisors and proprietors	3,316	31.2	3.8	4.0
Sales representatives, finance and business services	2,099	41.0	3.4	2.7
Insurance sales	541	27.7	4.7	2.7
Real estate sales	659	51.6	2.3	2.7
Securities and financial services sales	266	24.6	2.2	1.2
Sales representatives, commodities, except retail	1,509	17.5	2.2	1.2
Sales workers, retail and personal services	5,682	68.5	8.2	5.6
Cashiers	2,174	83.1	12.1	6.4
Sales-related occupations	63	63.7	2.1	3.1
Administrative support, including clerical	17,309	80.2	10.4	5.6
Supervisors	712	53.4	12.3	4.5
Computer equipment operators	779	66.4	13.5	5.9
Computer operators	774	66.5	13.5	5.9
Secretaries, stenographers, and typists	5,002	97.7	8.2	4.5
Secretaries	4,059	98.4	6.5	4.3
Typists	880	95.6	16.0	5.8
Information clerks	1,257	90.1	8.4	6.4
Receptionists	679	97.6	6.7	6.2
Records processing occupations, except financial	842	81.1	14.1	7.0
File clerks	290	81.0	17.4	8.5
Financial records processing	2,503	90.3	5.5	4.2
Bookkeepers, accounting, and auditing clerks	2,037	91.5	4.7	4.1

Source: Adapted from U.S. Dept. of Commerce, *Statistical Abstract of the United States,* (Washington, D.C., Bureau of the Census, 1987), p. 385.

The interviewer makes the respondent as comfortable and relaxed as possible. He or she then asks many questions about the subject, product, or problem under investigation. The order of questioning is determined as the interview progresses and fruitful avenues for investigation arise. The questions are usually indirect but designed to evoke responses, and the respondent is prompted to give as much detail as possible. The interviewer either types the interview or makes notes. These records become the basis for the analysis of findings. The researcher may spend hours or days analyzing the results before reaching final conclusions.

Depth interviewing is designed to obtain a large amount of information about a limited subject.[13] Its greatest market use is for determining underlying reasons or motives that help explain buyer behavior. The major problems with depth interviewing are: Few quantifiable results are obtained; it lacks structure; and qualified researchers are hard to find.

Focused Group Interview

The focused group interview is similar to the depth interview, but it differs on two counts.[14] First, several people are involved. Second, the focused group interview depends largely on the interaction of ideas between members of the group. The basic concept of depth interviewing is followed in the group interview. A group of typical consumers is brought together and prompted, by questioning, to provide detailed information on their feelings or attitudes or beliefs about some product or problem.[15] Group depth interviews have been used to explore corporate image, political issues, container design, advertising themes, and new product research. The results are recorded and analyzed in much the same manner as with depth interviewing. Focused group interviews have proven productive for evaluation of proposed advertising themes, stimulating ideas for new creative concepts, stimulating new ideas about older products, and securing impressions on new products.

Behavior Sampling

In behavior sampling, the respondent is asked to relive certain specified buyer situations. The respondent is placed in a relaxed atmosphere and asked to recall every detail involved with the buyer situation under study.[16] Even seemingly irrelevant information, such as the time of day or the color of the sky, is sought. It may be that some seemingly unimportant factors were actually crucial in the purchase decision.

Behavior sampling is useful for analyzing the buyer's decision processes and for determining the factor of buyer influence and the sequence of activities involved in purchasing.

COGNITIVE UNSTRUCTURED-DISGUISED RESEARCH

Many individuals are unwilling or unable to provide researchers with insight into their conscious or unconscious motives and attitudes. Disguised methods, usually referred to as projective techniques, have been developed to overcome this problem. These techniques are most often open-ended, so they are referred to as unstructured.

Projective tests operate on the simple principle that a person will answer more freely and more truthfully if relieved of direct responsibility for what is expressed. Projective tests are designed to break through the subject's bias and natural desire for secrecy to get to his or her essential emotions. Unconscious attitudes which a respondent cannot verbalize, or conscious attitudes which a respondent cannot report because they are socially unacceptable, may be explored in this manner. The most important types of unstructured-disguised research are word association, sentence completion, pictorial projectives, and verbal projectives.

Word Association

Association tests are among the oldest tests of motivation, and they are simple to administer. All association tests are based on the idea that a proper stimulus leads to an immediate response. The respondent is asked to respond to a series of key words or ideas with the first thought that comes to mind. These words are those associated with the product or service about which information is desired. In addition, a number of unrelated words are included to provide concealment and make responses easier. By carefully structuring the sequence of words or phrases, a rhythm is established so that the responses become automatic. In this way, the inner motives of the respondent can be brought out. The most important types of association tests are the free word association, successive word association, and sentence completion tests.

Association tests can be very useful for a variety of marketing problems. They can be used to determine consumer attitudes toward products, stores, advertising appeals, product features, store services, and store personnel. In short, the technique can be used in any instance where attempts are made to determine consumer attitudes.

Free word association involves presenting the respondent with a series of words, one at a time.[17] The subject responds freely to each word presented with the first word that comes to mind. The group of words presented to the respondent usually contains some *neutral* and some *stimulus* words. The stimulus words pertain to the study, the neutral words do not. For example, in a study of margarine or cooking oil purchasing, key words included might be *health, cholesterol, convenient, butter, cost,* and so on. As each word is read, the time it takes the respondent to answer is recorded. Thus, the researcher can determine which responses are automatic and which are reasoned. Of course, the researcher is looking for automatic or free responses. The respondent is not allowed to write replies, because this gives time to think. The researcher may write the answers or check them off from a prepared list of typical replies.

Although the collection of data is simple using the free word association technique, the interpretation of results is not. The typical method of tabulating results is to divide responses by frequency of occurrence into typical responses, thought-out responses, and nonresponses. Thought-out responses and nonresponses are useful only to the extent that they denote resistance to answer or indecision or weak attitudes toward the subject. Typical responses are usually further categorized by type to indicate respondent attitudes.

Successive word association is the same as free word association except that instead of asking for a single-word response, a series of single-word responses are sought for each word asked. The respondent may be asked to give the first three or four words that come to mind. These words are ranked in order by the researcher. It is felt that this technique can obtain information on several layers of responses. The data are analyzed in the same manner as for free word association.

Controlled word association is a variation used to measure the impact of advertising. The idea behind this approach is to use the terms generated in a work-association task as the stimulus words in a second round of associations. For example, the term *soap* generates relatively few associations. Among these are *clean* and *fresh.* Clean and fresh, however, generate additional responses such as *free, relaxed, unhindered, nature, country,* and *sensual.*[18] The value of information of this type for advertising is apparent.

Photo 23-1

Many methods, such as surveys, exist to help marketers find out about customer needs and wants.

Sentence Completion

The sentence completion test is similar to the free word association test. The main difference is that the respondent is given a series of incomplete statements designed to evoke responses about a particular subject rather than single words. Also, since the answers can be written, the respondent has some time to think about the reply.

The respondent is asked to complete the sentences with the first "idea" that comes to mind. In comparing margarine and butter, one might state, "A housewife using margarine instead of butter is . . . ," or "The healthfulness of margarine is . . . . " The sentence completion test may give more information about the respondent's inner feelings, since he or she has a chance to qualify statements, but it does give the respondent an opportunity to consider the answer. In order to adjust to this factor, the subject is timed. Responses that take too long are classified as thought-out.

Pictorial Projectives

Several pictorial methods are used in the projective method. The three most popular are the Rorschach inkblot test, the thematic apperception test, and cartoons.

The *Rorschach test* is a device used primarily in clinical psychology. A series of nonstructured "pictures" composed of inkblots are shown to the respondent. The subject is asked to explain what he or she sees in the picture. Evidence demonstrates that persons will project their own personalities into explaining the blots.[19] The organization that the subject imposes upon an unstructured form is revealing of underlying personality structure.

The *thematic apperception test* (TAT) asks the subject to explain a series of ambiguous pictures. The respondent may be asked such things as what conditions gave rise to the situation, what is happening, and what the outcome will be. The assumption is that in explaining the picture, subjects will tell something about themselves. This occurs because subjects are asked to tell a story about a picture where few clues are available. This means that they must resort to their own experience and imagination. The theory behind such a technique rests on the assumption that when persons are called upon to structure an unstructured or ambiguous situation, it is necessary for them to rely on their own personality attributes. The TAT test is useful for obtaining customer reaction to products or product features and for gaining insight into the personality or personality traits of individuals in social situations.[20]

A variation of the TAT method is found in the use of cartoons (Illustration 23-2). The principle is the same, but cartoons are simpler and easier to administer and interpret. The respondent is shown an ambiguous cartoon—for example, the

Illustration 23-2
Example of pictoral projective

What do you think of Samuel's department store?

Response:

_____
_____
_____
_____
_____
_____

one shown in Illustration 23-2. One consumer asks, "What do you think of Samuel's Department Store?" The respondent is asked to give the reply of the other consumer. Like the TAT, the cartoon projective uses an indirect approach to get at basic human traits, feelings, and attitudes.

Other similar projective techniques include attitude batteries, psychodrama, puppetry, and finger painting. Most of these methods vary only in the manner in which the information is gathered.

Verbal Projectives

Verbal projectives use words instead of pictures to describe a social situation. The basic technique is to describe a product, situation, or problem and ask the respondent what others would do under the described circumstances. In a classic case, an auto manufacturer asked people what they wanted in a car. The answer came back that these people wanted a safe, functional, conservative car. When this same manufacturer asked respondents what *their neighbors* wanted in a car, they obtained a different answer. People said their neighbors wanted a flashy car with lots of chrome, horsepower, and style. Very few respondents, in this case, mentioned safety.

COGNITIVE STRUCTURED-DISGUISED RESEARCH

When the purpose of the study can be disguised there is less problem with having persons express their inner emotions. If the study can also be structured it adds confidence to the results because there is less need for judgments. The idea underlying structured-disguised research is that individuals will reveal their attitudes by the extent to which their answers to objective questions vary from the correct answers.

Individuals are given questions which they are not likely to be able to answer correctly. Therefore, they are forced to guess at the answers. The direction and extent of these guessing errors is assumed to reveal their attitudes on the subject. For example, individuals tend to gather information which supports their attitudes and, therefore, the extent and kind of information individuals possess on a given subject indicates something of their attitude. Conversely, individuals tend to see differently and forget situations and items that are inconsistent with their preconceived attitudes.

This idea would suggest that one way of avoiding the socially acceptable response in securing an individual's attitude toward drinking and the need for antidrinking legislation would be to ask the person what he or she knows rather than how he or she feels. Thus the questions could be structured as follows: "What is the status of the antidrinking legislation listed below?" A number of bills would be listed, some actual and some hypothetical, and the respondent would be asked to check the box that best describes the current status of the legislation. Some of the descriptions might be: "In Committee," "Passed by the House but not the Senate," "Vetoed by the President," and so on. Respondents' attitudes toward the need for more legislation would then be assessed by the accuracy of their responses.[21]

COGNITIVE STRUCTURED-UNDISGUISED RESEARCH

Structured-undisguised research offers the opportunity to present formal questions with the respondent aware of what is being asked and the purpose of the study. This research technique has become closely associated with scaling. *Scaling* consists of rules for assigning numbers to objects in such a way as to represent quantities of attributes.[22] For example, we assign numbers to the various levels of heat and cold and call it a thermometer.

The basic idea behind all rating scales is that respondents can rate their attitude to some object along a continuum. Scales can be conveniently divided into four major types. They are self-rating scales, Likert scales, Thurstone scales, and semantic differentials.

Self-Rating Scales

The simplest of all scales is the *self-rating scale*. In this type of scale, the respondents are asked to rate themselves with respect to two bipolar factors. For example, a respondent may be asked, "Do you feel the majority of TV advertising is honest or dishonest?" The respondents, in answering the question, are classified into two categories—those who believe TV advertising is honest and those who believe TV advertising is dishonest.

The unstructured scale is very flexible. Almost any type of question can be asked, and, should the researcher desire more detail about a given attitude, a sequence of questions bearing on the point can be asked. Another variation is to ask open-ended questions. For example, we could ask, "What do you feel about the honesty of TV advertising?" We would receive a variety of answers that could be ranked into several categories by the intensity of the attitude expressed.

Likert Scales

Likert scales, or summed scales, involve three considerations.[23] First, a group of statements about some subject is constructed, such as the following statements about candy:

1. Candy provides energy.
2. Candy is fattening.
3. Candy causes tooth decay.
4. Candy tastes good.
5. Candy is messy.

Second, a group of agreement-disagreement responses is provided:

1. Strong agreement.
2. Agreement.
3. Undecided.
4. Disagreement.
5. Strong disagreement

The responses are given numerical values as indicated. Third, a respondent is asked to match the statement to the number of the response that most nearly expresses his or her attitude.

The responses are summed based on the numbers 1 to 5. The sum total of all responses is the score for each respondent. In the example described, low scores indicate agreement with the statements and high scores indicate disagreement. Cohen uses a Likert scale in his study of the relationship between consumer market behavior and complaint, aggression, and detached interpersonal orientations.

Thurstone Scales

The *Thurstone (equal-appearing interval) scale* recognizes the difficulty in assigning quantitative values to highly qualitative attitudes. Thurstone based his method of equal-appearing intervals on the concept that, even though people could not assign quantitative measurements to their own attitudes, they could tell the difference between the attitude represented by two different statements and could identify items that were approximately halfway between the two. The procedure is as follows:

1. Collect at least one hundred statements related to the overall attitude.
2. Have a set of judges rate the statements in terms of their favorability from one to eleven.
3. Select the ten to twenty statements which get the most consistent ratings and assign the median value from the one to eleven scale given them by the judges.
4. Have subjects indicate which of the statements they agree with.
5. The sum of the scale values in (3) for the statements that the subjects checked is their attitude score.

A five-position list of statements about attitudes toward children's commercials might be:

1. All children's commercials should be prohibited by law.
2. Most children's commercials are pretty bad.
3. I have no feeling one way or the other about most children's commercials.
4. Most children's commercials are pretty interesting.
5. I think there should be more children's commercials.

Most respondents will agree with only one statement or with a few statements that are from immediately adjacent scale positions. For example, a respondent might agree with statements whose scale values were 4 and 5. Such an agreement in the above list on children's commercials would be interpreted as representing a favorable attitude toward children's commercials. Respondents' scores are computed as the median of the item numbers with which they agree. If respondents agreed with statements 2 and 5, it would be interpreted to indicate they did not have organized attitudes on the topic. If the scale has been properly prepared, few respondents should show such a varied group of attitudes.

Semantic Differentials

A *semantic differential* obtains responses to a stimulus in terms of semantic categories, and it is based on bipolar scales. Illustration 23-3 illustrates a semantic differential for a retail store. When using a semantic differential, three, five or seven positions can be designated. The middle position is neutral relative to any bipolar scale, since it divides the scale equally. Respondents are asked to place a check by the position that most nearly describes their attitude toward the product, store, or subject under investigation. The semantic differential makes it possible for the researcher to develop an image profile by summing the positions checked as shown in Illustration 23-3. Can you profile the three stores shown in the illustration? It is possible to compare the images of more than one unit in this matter.

CONSUMER RESEARCH ETHICS

Ethical issues involve complex questions that cannot adequately be addressed here. In fact, addressing ethical issues frequently raises more questions than answers. In considering ethical issues, remember that they are in fact philosophical in nature. There is no general agreement, even among philosophers, about answers to questions of ethics.[24]

The American Marketing Association adopted a Marketing Research Code of Ethics in 1962, which since then has been revised. As is the case with most codes of ethics, this one merely represents minimum standards and does not prescribe an all-encompassing list of "dos and don'ts." The AMA code covers two areas involving research participants:

Illustration 23-3
Semantic differential for hypothetical stores

What do you think of the store?

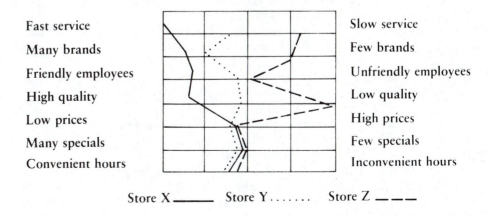

Store X ——— Store Y .... Store Z — — —

The activity must be research and not have as its real purpose the sale of merchandise to the respondent. If so informed, the participants' anonymity must be protected.

These two areas just scratch the surface of possible ethical issues pertaining to consumer behavior research. Other areas in research that can give rise to ethical concerns are:

1. Involving individuals in research without their knowledge or consent.
2. Coercing individuals to participate.
3. Exposing the research participant to physical or mental stress.
4. Invading the privacy of the individuals.

The researcher should carefully weigh the need for the research against the potential for adverse effects.[25] A source of guidance is the statements of ethical practice issued by such professional organizations as the American Marketing Association and the American Psychological Association. When in doubt, it is probably best to consider if you would want it done to you or your family. If not, do not do it to anyone else.

QUESTIONS

1. What is the biggest difference between marketing research and consumer research? Give an example.
2. Discuss how you would use consumer research to determine store preference.
3. Distinguish between the four approaches to the conducting of consumer research.
4. Discuss the statement: "Problem recognition is one of the most difficult steps in research."
5. Identify the types of data you would collect with demographic research and cognitive research. Give examples of each.
6. Can a research project be completed without primary data? Explain your answer.
7. Identify a public agency in your town that provides secondary data and discuss the types of data they provide.
8. Discuss the advantages and disadvantages of secondary data.
9. Discuss when information may be more accurate from sampling than from gathering information from the total population.
10. Give an example of a word association test that you would use to determine an individual toward a product.
11. What are the advantages and disadvantages of unstructured research?
12. What are the advantages and disadvantages of structured research?
13. Develop four questions using the Likert scale to determine the attitude of an individual toward a product.
14. Using Illustration 23-3, develop four categories that you could add to the study to aid the marketing manager.
15. Discuss some of the ethical problems that could be encountered when using individuals in consumer research.

NOTES

1. American Marketing Association, Committee on Definitions, *Marketing Definitions: A Glossary of Marketing Terms* (Chicago: American Marketing Association, 1960), p. 17.

2. Leonard M. Lodish and David J. Reibstein, "New Gold Mines and Minefields in Marketing Research," *Harvard Business Review,* Vol. 64 (January–February 1986), pp. 168–170.

3. Yoram Wind and Thomas S. Robertson, "Marketing Strategy: New Directions for Theory and Research," *Journal of Marketing,* Vol. 47 (Spring 1983), pp. 12–25.

4. Roahit Deshpande and Gerald Zaltman, "Factors Affecting the Use of Marketing Research Information: A Path Analysis," *Journal of Marketing,* Vol. XIX (February 1982), pp. 14–31.

5. Terry C. Wilson, "Creativity and Scientific Method in Marketing Research," in David M. Klein and Allen E. Smith, eds., *Marketing: The Next Decade, 1985* (Boca Raton, Fla.: Southern Marketing Assn., 1985), pp. 316–19.

6. Donald S. Tull and Del I. Hawkins, *Marketing Research: Meaning, Measurement, and Method* (New York: Macmillan Publishing Co., Inc., 1976), Chap. 15.

7. See: Robert J. Holloway, Robert A. Mittelstaedt, and M. Venkatesan, eds., *Consumer Behavior: Contemporary Research in Action* (Boston: Houghton Mifflin Co., 1971); Stuart Henderson Britt, ed., *Psychological Experiments in Consumer Behavior* (New York: John Wiley & Sons, Inc., 1970).

8. Harper W. Boyd, Jr., and Ralph Westfall, *Marketing Research: Text and Cases,* 3d ed. (Homewood, Ill.: Richard D. Irwin, Inc., 1972), p. 617.

9. Peter Hodgson, "Sampling Racial Minority Groups," *Journal of Marketing Research Society,* Vol. 17 (April 1975), pp. 104–6.

10. Eleanor Singer, "Public Reactions to Some Ethical Issues of Social Research: Attitudes and Behavior," *Journal of Consumer Research,* Vol. 11 (June 1984), pp. 501–9.

11. Roland T. Rust, "RECAT: A Program to Recategorize Secondary Data," in Robert H. Ross, Frederic B. Kraft, and Charles H. Davis, eds., *1981 Proceedings Southwestern Marketing Association Conference* (Wichita State University and Southwestern Marketing Assn., 1981), pp. 247–48.

12. Danny R. Arnold, Louis M. Cappella, and Garry D. Smith, "Competitive Audits for Retailers," in Daniel R. Comigan, Frederic B. Kraft, and Robert H. Ross, eds., *1982 Proceedings Southwestern Marketing Association Conference* (Wichita State University and Southwestern Marketing Assn., 1982), pp. 167–71.

13. Laurence Siegel and Irving M. Lane, *Psychology in Industrial Organizations* (Homewood: Richard D. Unwin, Inc., 1974), pp. 442–45.

14. Keith K. Cox, James B. Higginbotham, and John Burton, "Applications of Focus Group Interviews in Marketing," *Journal of Marketing,* Vol. 40 (January 1976), pp. 77–80.

15. Edward F. Fern, "The Use of Focus Groups for Idea Generation: The Effects of Group Size, Acquaintanceship, and Moderator on Response Quantity

and Quality," *Journal of Marketing Research,* Vol. XIX (February 1982), pp. 1–13.

16. Terry L. Childers and Michael J. Houston, "Conditions for a Picture-Superiority Effect on Consumer Memory, *Journal of Consumer Research,* Vol. 11 (September 1984), pp. 643–54.

17. Paul E. Green, Yoram Wind, and Arun K. Jain, "Analyzing Free-Response Data in Marketing Research," *Journal of Marketing Research,* Vol. 10 (February 1973), pp. 45–52.

18. J. Langer, "Story Time Is Alternate Research Technique," *Marketing News,* September 13, 1985, p. 24.

19. Morris B. Holbrook and William L. Moore, "Feature Interactions in Consumer Judgements of Verbal Versus Pictorial Presentations," *Journal of Consumer Research,* Vol. 8 (June 1981), pp. 103–13.

20. Kenneth D. Bailey, *Methods of Social Research,* 2d ed. (New York: The Free Press, 1982), p. 206.

21. Adapted from: Gilbert A. Churchill, Jr., *Marketing Research: Methodological Foundations,* 3d ed. (Chicago: The Dryden Press, 1983), p. 189.

22. Ibid., p. 242.

23. For the basic work in the field, see Rensis Likert, "A Technique for the Measurement of Attitudes," *Archives of Psychology,* Vol. 22 (June 1932), p. 55. Further material is presented in G. Murphy and Rensis Likert, *Public Opinion and the Individual* (New York: Harper & Bros., 1938), p. 316.

24. M. M. Pressley, D. J. Lincoln, and T. Little, "Ethical Beliefs and Personal Values of Top Level Executives," *Journal of Business Research* (December 1982).

25. Shelby D. Hunt, Lawrence B. Chonko, and James B. Wilcox, "Ethical Problems of Marketing Researcher," *Journal of Marketing Research,* Vol. XXI (August 1984), pp. 309–24; Stephen W. McDaniel, Perry Verille, and Charles S. Madden, "The Threats to Marketing Research: An Empirical Reappraisal," *Journal of Marketing Research,* Vol. XXII (February 1985), pp. 74–80.

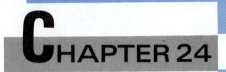

CHAPTER 24

Management Adjusts
To Market Changes

CHAPTER OUTLINE

I. MANAGEMENT MUST RESPOND TO MARKET DYNAMICS

II. TOTAL U.S. MARKET INCREASES—BUT SLOWLY

III. MARKETS BASED ON HOUSEHOLD CHARACTERISTICS
    A. Traditional Household Markets
    B. Markets Based on Age of Household Head
    C. Markets Based on Household Size
    D. Working Women Market Segment

IV. INCOME CONDITIONS HOUSEHOLD MARKETS
    A. Household Buying Depends on Income
    B. Occupation Conditions How Income Is Spent
    C. Education Affects the Level of Income
    D. Income Varies with Race

V. EXPENDITURE PATTERNS OF CONSUMERS
    A. Patterns of Buying
    B. Household Spending Power Declines
    C. Product Prices Affect Expenditures

VI. GEOGRAPHIC MARKET CHANGES
    A. Regional Markets
    B. Urban-Rural Markets
    C. Metropolitan Markets: Definition
    D. Metropolitan Markets: Population
    E. Metropolitan Markets: Income
    F. Metropolitan Markets: Significance
    G. Interurban Markets
    H. Small City Markets Important

CHAPTER OBJECTIVES

After completing your study of Chapter 24, you should be able to:

1. Discuss why management must respond to market dynamics.
2. Discuss the increase in the total U.S. market.
3. Discuss the markets based on household markets.
4. Explain how income conditions household markets.
5. Discuss the expenditure patterns of consumers.
6. Discuss the changes in geographic markets.

Throughout this book, we have pointed out that consumer decision making is dynamic. Therefore, it is very difficult for business managers to predict consumer behavior with respect to the purchase of particular products and brands. We have discussed throughout the book how business management can use consumer data for making decisions. We have shown that consumer knowledge is vital to the success of the business. In this chapter, we demonstrate how the changes that occur in consumer decision making require that businesses remain flexible. To succeed, businesses must adjust to consumer changes.[1]

MANAGEMENT MUST RESPOND TO MARKET DYNAMICS

The adjustment of business to consumer changes is very difficult—and very critical to the firm's success.[2] Since the market is always dynamic, so business management must be dynamic to meet the challenge.[3] In fact, business management has no alternative but to respond to market changes. It is very difficult to predict changes in individual consumers' mental attitude. However, it is possible to follow broad changes in the market structure. Changes in the number of persons and their location, income, expenditure patterns, and family size provide clues that the manager can use when planning responses to the market. In the final analysis, it is these quantifiable factors of consumer behavior upon which most business managers depend.[4]

TOTAL U.S. MARKET INCREASES—BUT SLOWLY

Figures on total U.S. population show the size and direction of change in the American market. Total population underscores all other changes in the economy. The population of the United States has been increasing since the beginning of our nation, and, as Table 24-1 shows, this increase has been consistent, although there are variations in the numbers. The figures show a slower increase in population caused by the depression between 1930 and 1940. The significant increase in population after each world war is also evident, but the big growth in population occurred after 1940. The 1950s witnessed a larger increase than ever before, but in the 1960s the steep climb dropped drastically. The Bureau of the Census estimates that the nation's population will continue to increase through 2000. The underlying explanations for these figures are a progressively larger base of population, a high birth rate, and a lower death rate.

Part 5 – Consumer Assessment of Purchase

Table 24-1
Total U.S. Population, 1900 to 1986 (000)

Year	Total Population	Population Change
1900	76,094	
1910	92,407	16,313
1920	106,461	14,054
1930	123,077	16,616
1940	132,457	9,380
1950	152,271	19,814
1960	180,671	23,400
1970	205,052	24,381
1975	227,757	22,705
1980	239,283	11,526
1986	241,489	2,206

Source: Adapted from U.S. Bureau of the Census, *Statistical Abstract of the United States: 1987* (107th edition), Washington, D.C. 1987, p. 8.

Total population figures dramatically illustrate that the total market in the United States is increasing—at varying rates over time, but always increasing. We will observe that there are many segments within this total market and that opportunities abound for business. Still, the market's increasing explains why so many businesses are able to increase the number of their stores and the volume of their sales.

MARKETS BASED ON HOUSEHOLD CHARACTERISTICS

The basic component of all markets is the family or the household. All products in our society are purchased either for individuals who make up the household or for the household as a unit. Thus we refer to the household as *the basic spending unit*. Let us consider some of the more important types of market segments based on households.

Traditional Household Markets

The traditional—married couple—family household is the largest market segment in the United States. This market, as illustrated in Table 24-2, accounts for about 58 percent of all households, in 1985.

Male households (no spouse present) account for almost 3 percent of the total, whereas female households (no spouse present) account for almost 12 percent of the total. A look at the persons per household indicates that most of these households have children present. The average household size—three to four people—conditions how so many products are made. Most houses have three bedrooms, cars accommodate four, most canned foods serve three to four, and meat is packaged for this same number. The best-selling products are those priced to fit the income of young married couples with one or two children whose earnings have not yet peaked. It follows that the traditional household market is the largest and safest market, generally speaking, for a business to seek to satisfy.

Table 24–2
Traditional Household Markets: 1980 and 1985

| Type of Household | Households | | | | | | Persons in Households, 1985 | | Persons per household, 1985 |
| | 1980 | | 1985 | | Change 1980–1985 | | | | |
	Number (1,000)	Percent distribution	Number (1,000)	Percent distribution	Number (1,000)	Percent distribution	Number ( )	Percent distribution	
Total households	80,776	100.0	86,789	100.0	6,013	7.4	233.5	100.0	2.69
Family households	59,550	73.7	62,706	72.3	3,156	5.3	204.5	87.6	3.26
With own children under 18	31,022	38.4	31,112	35.8	90	.3	123.0	52.7	3.95
Without own children under 18	28,529	35.3	31,594	36.4	3,065	10.7	51.4	34.9	2.58
Married couple family	49,112	60.8	50,350	58.0	1,238	2.5	166.0	71.1	3.30
With own children under 18	24,961	30.9	24,210	27.9	-751	-3.0	101.2	43.3	4.18
Without own children under 18	24,151	29.9	26,140	30.1	1,989	8.2	64.8	27.8	2.48
Male householder, no spouse present	1,733	2.1	2,228	2.6	495	28.6	6.7	2.8	2.99
With own children under 18	616	.8	896	1.0	280	45.5	2.7	1.1	2.96
Without own children under 18	1,117	1.4	1,331	1.5	214	19.2	4.0	1.7	3.00
Female householder, no spouse present	8,705	10.8	10,129	11.7	1,424	16.4	31.8	13.6	3.14
With own children under 18	5,445	6.7	6,006	6.9	561	10.3	19.1	8.2	3.19
Without own children under 18	3,261	4.0	4,123	4.8	662	26.4	12.7	5.4	3.07
Nonfamily households	21,226	26.3	24,082	27.7	2,856	13.5	29.1	12.5	1.21
Living alone	18,296	22.7	20,602	23.7	2,306	12.6	20.6	8.8	1.00
Male householder	8,807	10.9	10,114	11.7	1,307	14.8	13.4	5.7	1.32
Living alone	6,966	8.6	7,922	9.1	956	13.7	7.9	3.4	1.00
Female householder	12,419	15.4	13,968	16.1	1,549	12.5	15.7	6.7	1.12
Living alone	11,330	14.0	12,680	14.6	1,350	11.9	11.9	12.7	1.00

Source: U.S. Bureau of the Census, *Statistical Abstract of the United States: 1987* (107th edition.) Washington, DC. 1987, p. 45.

Part 5 – Consumer Assessment of Purchase

Markets Based on Age of Household Head

Table 24-3 illustrates that the number of households has increased dramatically since 1970. The percentage with female and black heads of household has also increased, while male heads of household have declined. The important trend based on age is the number of households with both young and older heads. Let's consider the impact of these trends on business.

Households with heads ages fourteen to thirty-four increased from 25.3 percent in 1970 to 29.4 percent in 1985. These households with younger heads are more recently formed. They tend to require more of all types of products, including transportation, food, clothing, household items, and housing. However, managers must be aware of the change if they are to appeal to this group. Households headed by young heads tend to be more liberal in their approach to life. They are more modern when it comes to selecting style in clothing, transportation, and home furnishings. If their income will allow, they are more inclined to purchase a sporty car than a family car. They may buy a smaller but more modern home or choose a stylish apartment. Their taste in music, entertainment, and clothing tends to be more like the singles group they just left than established married couples. Managements that understand their increased numbers may be able to tailor their operations to appeal specifically to these young household heads.

Households with heads over sixty-five have increased from 19.5 percent in 1970 to 20.9 percent in 1985. These older households now constitute 20 percent of all American families. That represents a significant market for business to tap. The business must adopt a different management philosophy to attract these family members. They tend to be conservative in their outlook. They are careful with their money and they do not get around as well as their young counterparts. Thus it may be important for businesses to specialize in their offerings to the older market in much the same way as they would for the young household. It may be necessary for these specialized firms to locate closer to the areas where older households live. Certainly the style of stores must be toned down to present a comfortable atmosphere for these customers. The number and attitude of salespersons is also important. Older customers tend to need more help in the store, and they may be especially sensitive to the manners of salespersons.

It is sometimes difficult to cater to families with young household heads and families with older household heads at the same time. The young sometimes resent the presence of older customers. They suspect the merchandise handled by a store that has older customers shopping there. This fact has caused some merchants deliberately to discourage older shoppers. Fortunately, this practice is not widespread, but it does indicate the need for separate facilities for older and younger family shoppers.

Markets Based on Household Size

The size of American families tends to vary, as indicated in Table 24-4. It can be clearly observed that the size of the American family was decreasing over time. In 1960, 40.9 percent of all households had one or two persons, but by 1985 this figure had increased to 55.3 percent. That is a significant increase. Equally important is the decrease in the number of households with three or more children.

Table 24-3
Households by Age of Head: 1968 to 1982

Characteristic	1970	1974	1975	1976	1977	1978	1979	1980	1981	1982	1983	1984	1985
Total (million)	63.4	69.9	71.1	72.9	74.1	76.0	77.3	80.8	82.4	83.5	83.9	85.4	86.8
Percent Distribution													
Male	78.9	77.1	76.4	75.8	75.4	74.6	74.2	71.8	71.2	70.6	70.6	69.5	69.2
Female	21.1	22.9	23.6	24.2	24.6	25.4	25.8	28.2	28.8	29.4	29.4	30.5	30.8
White	89.5	88.7	88.5	88.4	88.1	88.0	88.0	87.6	87.3	87.2	87.2	87.1	86.8
Black	9.8	10.1	10.2	10.3	10.5	10.5	10.4	10.6	10.7	10.7	10.6	10.8	10.9
Age of householder:													
15–24 years old	6.8	8.4	8.2	8.1	8.1	8.2	8.2	8.1	7.8	7.3	6.8	6.5	6.5
25–34 years old	18.5	20.5	21.0	21.3	21.8	22.1	22.0	22.9	23.2	23.1	22.8	23.2	23.1
35–44 years old	18.6	16.8	16.7	16.8	16.8	17.1	17.2	17.3	17.6	18.3	19.1	19.4	20.1
45–54 years old	19.5	18.5	18.2	17.6	17.4	16.6	16.3	15.7	15.4	15.0	14.7	14.6	14.6
55–64 years old	17.1	16.0	15.9	16.0	15.9	16.0	15.9	15.5	15.4	15.5	15.6	15.4	15.1
65 years old and over	19.5	19.9	20.1	20.3	20.0	20.0	20.4	20.5	20.5	20.7	21.1	21.0	20.9

Source: U.S. Bureau of the Census, *Statistical Abstract of the United States: 1987* (107th edition.) Washington, D.C., 1987, p. 48.

Table 24-4
Household Size: 1960 to 1985

Size of Household	1960	1970	1975	1977	1978	1979	1980	1981	1982	1983	1984	1985
Total	52.6	63.4	71.1	74.1	76.0	77.3	80.8	82.4	83.5	83.9	85.4	86.8
1 person	6.9	10.9	13.9	15.5	16.7	17.2	18.3	18.9	19.4	19.3	20.0	20.6
1 person	6.9	10.9	13.9	15.5	16.7	17.2	18.3	18.9	19.4	19.3	20.0	20.6
Male	2.3	3.5	4.9	5.6	6.4	6.5	7.0	7.3	7.5	7.5	7.5	7.9
Female	4.6	7.3	9.0	9.9	10.4	10.7	11.3	11.7	11.9	11.8	12.4	12.7
2 persons	14.6	18.3	21.8	22.8	23.3	23.9	25.3	25.8	26.5	26.4	26.9	27.4
3 persons	9.9	10.9	12.4	12.8	13.0	13.4	14.1	14.6	14.6	14.8	15.1	15.5
4 persons	9.3	10.0	11.1	11.6	12.0	12.3	12.7	12.8	12.9	13.3	13.6	13.6
5 persons	6.1	6.5	6.4	6.3	6.4	6.2	6.1	6.1	6.1	6.1	6.1	6.1
6 persons	3.0	3.5	3.1	2.9	2.7	2.6	2.5	2.5	2.5	2.5	2.4	2.3
7 persons or more	2.9	3.2	2.5	2.3	1.9	1.8	1.8	1.6	1.6	1.6	1.4	1.3
Percent of total:												
1 person	13.1	17.1	19.6	20.9	22.0	22.2	22.7	23.0	23.2	22.9	23.4	23.7
2 persons	27.8	28.9	30.6	30.7	30.7	30.9	31.4	31.3	31.7	31.5	31.5	31.6
3 persons	18.9	17.3	17.4	17.3	17.2	17.3	17.5	17.7	17.5	17.6	17.7	17.8
4 persons	17.6	15.8	15.6	15.7	15.7	15.9	15.7	15.5	15.4	15.9	15.9	15.7
5 persons	11.5	10.3	9.0	8.5	8.4	8.0	7.5	7.4	7.3	7.3	7.1	7.0
6 persons	5.7	5.6	4.3	3.9	3.6	3.3	3.1	3.1	3.0	2.9	2.8	2.6
7 persons or more	5.4	5.0	3.5	3.1	2.5	2.3	2.2	2.0	1.9	1.9	1.6	1.5

Source: U.S. Bureau of the Census, *Statistical Abstract of the United States: 1987* (107th edition), Washington, D.C., 1987, p. 45.

The smaller households mean that managers must modify their entire approach to marketing. The size of packages must be modified to reflect a need for less quantity, and room must be made on the shelves for these new types of packages. The increased space can come from the deletion or reduction in the number and types of products carried for children. Fewer children means that there is an increased opportunity for businesses specializing in vacations, vacation homes, eating out, and entertainment. Note the rapid increase lately in fast food establishments, home video shops, and recreational boat firms. On the other hand, families are spending less on education and medical care, although the cost per person has increased. That there are fewer children on which these expenditures must be made accounts for the difference.

Working Women Market Segment

The working woman has become a significant part of the American family.[5] Observe the figures in Table 24-5. The trend of women working was already well established in 1970, when 37.7 percent of the work force was female. By 1985,

Table 24–5
Employed Persons by Selected Characteristics: 1970 to 1985

Age, Sex, and Marital Status	1970	1975	1979	1980
Total employed	78,678	85,846	98,824	99,303
16–19 years	6,144	7,104	8,083	7,710
20–24 years	9,731	11,885	14,327	14,087
25–34 years	16,318	21,087	26,492	27,204
35–44 years	15,922	15,953	18,981	19,523
45–54 years	16,473	16,190	16,357	16,234
55–64 years	10,974	10,827	11,585	11,586
65 years old and over	3,118	2,801	2,999	2,960
Male	48,990	51,857	57,607	57,186
16–19 years	3,409	3,839	4,300	4,065
20–24 years	5,237	6,484	7,791	7,532
25–34 years	10,936	13,205	15,688	15,832
35–44 years	10,216	9,891	11,202	11,355
45–54 years	10,170	9,902	9,735	9,548
55–64 years	6,928	6,722	7,015	6,999
65 years and over	2,094	1,811	1,876	1,835
Married, spouse present	37,982	38,249	39,740	39,004
Single (never married)	8,426	10,313	13,424	13,515
Widowed, divorced, separated	2,582	3,294	4,443	4,668
Female	29,688	33,989	41,217	42,117
16–19 years	2,735	3,263	3,783	3,625
20–24 years	4,494	5,401	6,538	6,555
25–34 years	5,382	7,882	10,802	11,370
35–44 years	5,706	6,061	7,779	8,168
45–54 years	6,303	6,288	6,622	6,686
55–64 years	1,023	989	1,124	1,125
Married, spouse present	17,572	19,788	23,126	23,532
Single (never married)	6,613	7,943	10,386	10,567
Widowed, divorced, separated	5,505	6,258	7,706	8,018

this figure had increased to 44.1 percent. In fact, today women are approaching parity with males in the work force.[6] Women in the work force had increased by 59 percent between 1970 and 1985, while males increased only 22 percent.

Women work for a number of reasons, but the most important reason is that they must. We have observed the number of single, widowed, divorced, and separated women in our society. Many of these women have children. They are household heads and must work to provide products required by the home. Some women work to help their husbands make ends meet, and some women work because they enjoy their careers. In many families where both husband and wife work, it is because the income of both is necessary to support the family. There are also some instances where women work in order to provide "extras" for the household.

Working women—and men—make many purchases that are different from women or men who spend most of their time in the home.[7] Working people require more and better clothing and transportation to and from their place of employment. Executives may be required to entertain more and to travel out of

Table 24–5 (Continued)

Age, Sex, and Marital Status	1970	1975	1979	1980
Total employed	99,526	100,834	105,005	107,150
16–19 years	6,549	6,342	6,444	6,434
20–24 years	13,690	13,722	14,207	13,980
25–34 years	28,149	28,756	30,348	31,206
35–44 years	20,879	21,960	23,598	24,732
45–54 years	15,923	15,812	16,178	16,509
55–64 years	11,414	11,315	11,395	11,474
65 years old and over	2,923	2,927	2,835	2,513
Male	56,271	56,787	59,091	59,891
16–19 years	3,379	3,300	3,322	3,326
20–24 years	7,197	7,232	7,571	7,339
25–34 years	16,002	16,216	17,166	17,584
35–44 years	11,902	12,450	13,309	13,800
45–54 years	9,234	9,133	9,326	9,411
55–64 years	6,781	6,686	6,694	6,753
65 years and over	1,776	1,770	1,703	1,695
Married, spouse present	38,074	37,967	39,056	39,248
Single (never married)	13,304	13,783	14,699	15,022
Widowed, divorced, separated	4,892	5,036	5,335	5,621
Female	43,256	44,047	45,915	47,258
16–19 years	3,170	3,043	3,122	3,105
20–24 years	6,492	6,490	6,636	6,640
25–34 years	12,147	12,540	13,182	13,644
35–44 years	8,977	9,510	10,289	10,933
45–54 years	6,689	6,678	6,852	7,097
55–64 years	4,634	4,629	4,700	4,721
65 years and over	1,147	1,157	1,133	1,118
Married, spouse present	24,053	24,603	25,636	26,336
Single (never married)	10,785	10,996	11,444	11,758
Widowed, divorced, separated	8,438	8,447	8,835	9,165

Source: U.S. Bureau of the Census, *Statistical Abstract of the United States: 1987* (107th edition.) Washington, D.C., 1987, p. 378.

town. They must spend more on products associated with good grooming. Often working couples do not have time for preparing meals, so the family eats more frozen dinners, easy-to-prepare meals, and fast foods. If there are children, the family may use day-care or baby-sitters. It is no accident that businesses that cater to working women and working couples have been increasing in numbers.

INCOME CONDITIONS HOUSEHOLD MARKETS

As we have noted, markets are more than people in households. Those people must have the means to purchase. It is income that provides that ability, and so now we turn our attention to the income of households.

Household Buying Depends on Income

Table 24-6 has data on household income. The median was $26,433 in 1984. The median income of female household heads was only about 55 percent that of male heads. However, the highest median income for all households occurred where both the husband and wife were employed. The largest number of families earned between $25,000 and $34,000 in income. Even so, the number of families earning under $15,000 is significant. Of course, the more earnings in a family the more products that can be purchased. At some point in every family, income becomes sufficient to provide for necessities and that which is left over can be used to purchase the "extras" that make life worth living. Income left after providing for necessities and paying taxes is called *discretionary income* because the consumer has more options on how to spend it.

Greater income in families means that these persons can purchase more and better products. This accounts for the recent trend to upgrade the quality of merchandise in so many retail stores. A good example is Sears, which has changed

Table 24–6
Household Income, 1984

	Number of families	Income Level			
Type of family		Under $5,000	$5,000 – $9,999	$10,000 – $14,999	$15,000 – $19,999
All families	62,706	3,144	5,894	6,780	6,790
Married-couple families	50,350	1,149	3,374	4,882	5,235
Wife in paid labor force	26,938	826	858	1,339	2,038
Wife employed	25,401	247	681	1,339	2,038
Wife unemployed	1,537	79	178	186	192
Wife not in paid labor force	23,412	824	2,514	3,357	3,005
Male householder, no wife present	2,228	144	273	270	227
Female householder, no husband present	10,129	1,851	2,248	1,626	1,328

from essentially a low-priced, staple-product store in the 1930s to a quality merchandiser of a large variety of products today. This trend is likely to continue into the future. However, there are still many poor persons in our society, and there will always be a place for the low-priced, low-end merchandiser.

Occupation Conditions How Income Is Spent

Income is not the same for all occupations. Furthermore, the source of the income has some effect on how consumers spend their money.

In Table 24-7, employment increased significantly between 1970 and 1984, but the increase was not uniform. Some industries decreased employment over the period. The professional, technical, and construction groups increased employment the most between 1970 and 1984. We continue our trend toward more skilled workers, as these figures show.

Persons in the skilled occupations tend to earn more income, so they can purchase more. There are also differences in how skilled and unskilled workers spend their income. Skilled and/or white-collar workers put more income into their home, home furnishings, savings, and investments. They also spend more on medical care, education, and travel. Unskilled and blue-collar workers tend to spend more on personal consumption items such as television, automobiles, clothing, alcoholic beverages, and fast foods. The two groups do not even read the same type of books or seek the same type of recreation. Skilled workers tend to read *Time, Playboy, Ladies' Home Journal,* and *National Geographic.* Unskilled workers tend more toward sports magazines, sensational magazines, and special-interest magazines such as boxing, boating, fishing, etc.

Education Affects the Level of Income

The amount of income a household has to spend is directly affected by the education of the wage earners in that household. Table 24-8 sheds light on this

Table 24–6 (Continued)

	Income Level				
	$20,000 – $24,000	$25,000 – $25,000	$35,000 – $35,000	$50,000 and over	Median income (dol.)
All families	6,730	11,931	11,550	9,889	26,433
Married-couple families	5,486	10,328	10,544	9,341	29,612
Wife in paid labor force	2,746	5,968	6,986	6,297	34,668
Wife employed	2,533	5,670	6,741	6,152	35,352
Wife unemployed	214	298	244	146	23,114
Wife not in paid labor force	2,740	4,361	3,567	3,044	23,582
Male householder, no wife present	287	433	325	258	23,325
Female householder, no husband present	957	1,159	671	289	12,803

Source: U.S. Bureau of the Census, *Statistical Abstract of the United States: 1987* (107th edition), Washington, D.C., 1987, p. 439.

Table 24-7
Employment by Industry: 1970 to 1995

Industry	Employment					Annual Average Rate of Change			
	1970	1980	1984	1990	1995	1970–1980	1980–1984	1984–1990	1990–1995
Total	82,519	102,703	106,841	116,865	122,760	2.2	1.9	1.5	1.0
Agriculture	3,300	2,860	3,293	3,164	3,059	–1.4	3.6	–.7	–.7
Dairy and poultry products	765	436	374	324	305	–5.5	–3.9	–2.4	–1.9
Meat animals and livestock	742	533	472	448	404	–3.3	–3.1	–.9	–2.1
Food and feed grains	589	612	604	555	506	.4	–.3	–1.4	–1.9
Agricultural products, n.e.c.	984	1,182	1,155	1,155	1,157	1.9	–.6	'	.1
Agricultural services	321	495	564	574	576	4.4	3.3	.3	.1
Mining	514	723	651	659	631	3.5	–2.7	.2	–.9
Coal mining	147	247	198	199	185	5.3	–5.7	.1	–1.5
Crude petroleum, natural gas (excl. drilling)	156	246	285	291	289	4.7	3.8	.3	–.2
Construction	4,387	5,865	5,920	6,189	6,636	2.9	.2	.7	1.4
New construction (including oil well drilling)	3,555	4,327	4,674	4,857	5,232	2.0	2.9	.6	1.5
Maintenance construction	897	1,463	1,246	1,332	1,404	5.0	–4.1	1.1	1.1
Manufacturing	19,665	20,673	19,779	20,913	21,124	.5	–1.1	.9	.2
Durable goods	11,399	12,423	11,744	12,872	13,216	.9	–1.4	1.5	.5
Household furniture	300	301	295	317	321	'	–.5	1.2	.3
Millwork, plywood products	301	363	360	380	381	1.9	–.2	.9	.1
Blast furnaces, basic steel	627	512	335	311	261	–2.0	–11.0	–1.3	–3.6
Fabricated structural metal	435	522	448	496	525	1.8	–3.9	1.7	1.1
Fabricated metal products, n.e.c.	300	359	344	387	402	1.8	–1.1	2.0	.7
Metalworking machinery	324	381	313	360	377	1.6	–5.1	2.4	.9
General industry machinery	285	324	273	309	325	1.3	–4.4	2.0	1.0
Nonelectrical machinery, n.e.c.	234	321	301	338	356	3.2	–1.6	2.0	1.1
Computers, peripheral equipment	236	376	479	640	713	4.8	6.2	4.9	2.2
Radio, communication equipment	362	378	472	556	607	.4	5.7	2.7	1.8
Electronic components	367	554	673	797	846	4.2	5.0	2.9	1.2

Table 24–7 (Continued)

Industry	Employment					Annual Average Rate of Change			
	1970	1980	1984	1990	1995	1970–1980	1980–1984	1984–1990	1990–1995
Total	82,519	102,703	106,841	116,865	122,760	2.2	1.9	1.5	1.0
Motor vehicles	801	791	863	852	828	–.1	2.2	–.2	–.6
Aircraft	670	676	634	692	714	.1	–1.6	1.5	.6
Scientific, controlling instruments	181	221	222	268	304	2.0	.1	3.2	2.5
Nondurable goods	8,266	8,250	8,035	8,041	7,906	–	.7	.1	–.3
Meat products	348	363	361	345	331	.4	–.2	–.8	–.9
Canned and frozen foods	288	312	286	287	275	.8	–2.2	.1	–.9
Fabric, yarn, and thread mills	600	510	440	406	361	–1.6	3.8	–1.4	–2.4
Apparel	1,213	1,101	1,023	924	818	–1.0	1.9	–1.7	–2.5
Paper products	483	488	486	486	480	.1	.1	·	–.3
Newspaper printing and publishing	382	441	463	512	548	–1.4	1.2	1.7	1.4
Periodical and book printing and publishing	209	238	274	298	313	1.3	3.6	1.4	1.0
Other printing and publishing	549	656	725	826	890	1.8	2.5	2.2	1.5
Industrial chemicals	297	330	300	302	306	1.1	2.4	.1	.2
Plastic products, n.e.c.	314	467	544	659	712	4.0	3.9	3.3	1.6
Transportation	2,887	3,250	3,240	3,507	3,692	1.2	.1	1.3	1.0
Railroad	636	534	378	323	283	–1.7	9.0	–2.7	–2.7
Local transit and intercity buses	321	312	317	325	330	–.3	.4	.4	.3
Truck	1,225	1,497	1,560	1,750	1,868	2.0	1.0	2.0	1.3
Water	217	216	206	218	230	–	1.2	.9	1.1
Air	356	461	498	538	579	2.6	2.0	1.3	1.5
Transportation services	114	209	262	333	382	6.2	5.8	4.1	2.8
Communications	1,132	1,362	1,353	1,485	1,585	1.9	.2	1.6	1.3
Radio and television broadcasting	139	203	237	263	290	3.9	4.0	1.7	2.0
All other (telephone and other)	993	1,159	1,116	1,222	1,295	1.5	1.0	1.5	1.1
Public Utilities	713	839	907	965	1,027	1.6	2.0	1.0	1.3
Electric, excluding public	397	513	569	617	677	2.6	2.6	1.4	1.9
Gas, excluding public	221	221	223	227	226	–	.2	.3	–.1

Table 24–7 (Continued)
Employment by Industry: 1970 to 1995

Industry	Employment					Annual Average Rate of Change			
	1970	1980	1984	1990	1995	1970–1980	1980–1984	1984–1990	1990–1995
Total	82,519	102,703	106,841	116,865	122,760	2.2	1.9	1.5	1.0
Trade	17,060	22,493	24,290	27,106	28,272	2.8	1.9	1.8	.8
Wholesale	4,250	5,597	5,897	6,710	6,985	2.8	1.3	2.2	.8
Retail, except eating and drinking places	9,872	11,948	12,660	13,926	14,351	1.9	1.4	1.7	.6
Eating and drinking places	2,938	4,948	5,733	6,470	6,936	5.4	3.7	2.0	1.4
Finance, insurance, real estate	3,977	5,702	6,296	6,991	7,397	3.7	2.5	1.8	1.1
Banking	1,049	1,572	1,678	1,780	1,865	4.1	1.6	1.0	.9
Credit agencies and financial brokers	636	952	1,239	1,467	1,621	4.1	6.8	2.9	2.0
Insurance	1,411	1,794	1,904	2,150	2,237	2.4	1.5	2.0	.8
Real estate	881	1,384	1,475	1,594	1,675	4.6	1.6	1.3	1.0
Services	14,050	21,097	23,886	28,142	31,170	4.1	3.2	2.7	2.1
Hotels and lodging places	1,079	1,571	1,914	2,146	2,299	1.4	5.0	2.0	1.4
Personal and repair	1,193	1,244	1,388	1,535	1,664	.4	2.8	1.7	1.6
Beauty and barber shops	616	622	663	570	675	.1	1.6	.2	.1
Miscellaneous business	1,756	3,404	4,612	6,200	7,245	6.8	7.9	5.0	3.1
Miscellaneous professional	1,101	1,930	2,295	2,823	3,335	5.8	4.4	3.6	3.4
Automobile repair	576	845	1,022	1,079	1,194	3.9	4.9	.9	2.0
Motion pictures	244	290	328	358	390	1.8	3.2	1.5	1.7
Amusements and recreation	515	832	869	1,045	1,135	4.9	1.1	3.1	1.7
Doctors' and dentists' offices	815	1,408	1,650	1,949	2,190	5.6	4.1	2.8	2.4
Hospitals	1,871	2,754	3,001	3,242	3,256	3.9	2.2	1.3	.1
Medical, except hospitals	733	1,517	1,821	2,449	2,886	7.5	4.7	5.0	3.3
Educational (private)	1,240	1,772	1,928	2,057	2,147	3.6	2.1	1.1	.9
Nonprofit organizations	1,784	2,142	2,182	2,339	2,486	1.8	.4	1.2	1.2
Private households	2,280	1,598	1,242	1,148	1,023	– 3.5	– 7.0	– 1.3	– 2.3
Government	12,554	16,241	15,984	16,598	17,144	2.6	.4	.6	.7

Source: U.S. Bureau of the Census, *Statistical Abstract of the United States: 1987* (107th edition), Washington, D.C., 1987, p. 389.

point. The fact is that income varies directly with an increase in education. The median income of college graduates is $39,506, compared to $10,124 for persons with less than eight years of education. The number of families with income above $25,000 increases as education increases. Also, the United States is a highly educated nation; over 35 percent of the householders have a high school degree and over 38 percent have some college education.

This increase in education makes it possible for consumers to have more of almost all kinds of products. It augments the finding for occupation in that it tends to make customers more discriminating. They can afford better merchandise, better treatment in stores, and better store atmosphere when shopping. The smart managers are the ones that have noted these trends and modified their operations accordingly.

Income Varies with Race

Income varies greatly by race in the United States, as Table 24-9 demonstrates. Black household median income in 1985 was only 59 percent that of white households. The same relative percentage prevailed in 1970.

Thus, blacks had far less to spend and they were not making any progress over the period in improving their ability to purchase goods and services. The relationship clearly shows classes by income. Black households were much more concentrated below $15,000. This limitation in income affects every single thing that black families purchase, including their home, transportation, foods, clothing, recreation, education, and health. They cannot purchase as much or as high quality as their white counterparts.

Spanish-speaking households were in much better shape than blacks. Their median income was 72 percent that of whites in 1975 and 70 percent in 1985. Spanish-speaking households lost purchasing power significantly compared to whites over the period. This decline was probably due to a change in the nature of the population. Fewer middle-class Hispanic persons were coming into the country, and more peasants were entering from Mexico to perform low-paying menial and farm tasks. Even so, as a group, Hispanic income was higher than black income.

EXPENDITURE PATTERNS OF CONSUMERS

The proof of the pudding for any market depends on how consumers actually spend their income. It is the inclination to buy specific items that determines how well businesses do in the market. Although it is difficult to predict how any specific consumer will purchase, there are patterns of expenditure when we consider consumers as a group. These patterns indicate something about the willingness to consume.

Patterns of Buying

A look at Table 24-10 makes it very clear how American households spent their income between 1970 and 1985. There were significant changes in the way households spent their income over the years. Total dollar expenditures increased

Table 24–8

Money Income of Households—Percent Distribution by Money Income Level by Selected Characteristics: 1985

Characteristic	Total households (1,000)	Percent Distribution of Households by income level (in dollars)			
		Under 5,000	5,000 – 9,999	10,000 – 14,999	15,000 – 19,999
Education attainment of householder:					
Elementary school	12,335	17.8	27.0	17.4	11.5
Less than 8 years	6,618	20.5	29.0	17.9	11.1
8 years	5,717	14.7	24.7	16.9	11.9
High school	42,338	8.5	13.5	13.2	12.5
1–3 years	11,067	13.9	19.3	16.3	13.2
4 years	31,271	6.6	11.5	12.2	12.2
College	33,785	2.9	5.7	7.1	8.8
1–3 years	15,300	4.3	8.7	9.4	10.6
4 years or more	18,485	1.7	3.3	5.2	7.3
Tenure:					
Owner occupied	56,408	4.6	9.2	9.5	9.6
Renter occupied	30,516	12.8	18.0	14.9	13.3
Occupier paid no cash rent	1,534	18.1	22.5	16.9	12.3

drastically between 1970 and 1985; the increase was over 300 percent. Overall, nondurable goods had a decrease in expenditures, from 42 percent in 1970 to 35 percent in 1985. There was a slight increase for durable goods, from 13 percent to 14 percent. These changes are partially due to gasoline prices and to high interest rates, which had a tremendous impact on housing. The increase in the expenditure for service was the most dramatic of all the changes. It is clear that there is a major shift taking place in consumer expenditures from goods to services.

There is a lesson here for all business managers to remember. Just because a market is important today does not mean that it will be equally important in the future. Markets sometimes get better and sometimes they decline. If markets become more favorable, then management must be ready to expand to meet the increased demand. If there is a decline in the market, management must be flexible enough to transfer money from that market into another, more promising one. It never pays to ignore market dynamics.

Household Spending Power Declines

There are two major economic factors that affect the ability of consumers to purchase. They are the changes in consumer income and the inflation rate which affects the price of products bought by consumers. We consider changes in income first.

Table 24-11 demonstrates what has happened to median income of households between 1967 and 1985. Although median income has increased for all American households, purchasing power has declined. We can see from the

Part 5 – Consumer Assessment of Purchase

Table 24–8 (Continued)

Characteristic	Percent Distribution of Households by Income Level (in dollars) 20,000– 24,999	25,000– 34,999	35,000– 49,999	50,000– and over	Median income (dollars)
Education attainment of householder:					
Elementary school	7.9	9.8	6.0	2.6	11,309
Less than 8 years	7.0	8.2	4.5	1.9	10,124
8 years	8.9	11.7	7.7	3.5	12,970
High school	10.9	17.8	14.8	8.7	20,934
1–3 years	9.7	12.9	9.7	5.0	15,171
4 years	11.3	19.6	16.7	10.0	23,134
College	9.7	18.5	20.5	26.8	33,250
1–3 years	11.4	20.4	19.5	15.8	27,337
4 years or more	8.2	16.9	21.3	35.9	39,506
Tenure:					
Owner occupied	9.6	18.4	19.2	20.1	29,001
Renter occupied	11.0	14.5	9.9	5.6	16,518
Occupier paid no cash rent	8.7	12.5	6.3	2.7	12,615

Source: U.S. Bureau of the Census, *Statistical Abstract of the United States: 1987* (107th edition), Washington, D.C., 1987, p.432.

table that the median income in current dollars increased from $7,143 in 1967 to $23,618 in 1985. Median income increased for whites, blacks and Hispanics. Blacks had the greatest increase in median income over the period; however, they still have the lowest income. The facts are quite different when we take inflation out of the figures. In constant dollars, household income actually increased from $23,015 in 1967 to $20,618 in 1985. Hispanic households experienced declines in income from $19,741 in 1972 to $17,465 in 1985. Black median income increased by $584 and white median income increased by $907, but Spanish median income declined by $2,276.

It is obvious that while incomes were increasing over the period, consumers did not greatly increase their standard of living. The increase was being taken away by inflation and taxes. Over the period, personal income tax increased by 406.3 percent.[8] This figure represents a rather important increase in taxes which reduces the amount that consumers have to spend. The total impact was obviously great.

These changes in income explain why many shoppers have become more cautious in the marketplace. The increasing importance of the discount house and the trend of some grocery stores back to a strict price appeal can be traced, in part, to these changes. It also helps to explain the continued success of retail store sales and the popularity of off-season merchandise. This erosion of individual income helps explain why so many families have moved in the direction of multiple members in the work force. It has been the only way to buck the trend in spending power.

Table 24–9

Money Income of Families: 1970 to 1985

Race and Spanish Origin of Householder and Year	Number of households (1,000)	Percent Distribution, by Income Level			
		Under $5,000	$5,000 – $9,999	$10,000 – $14,999	$15,000 – $19,999
All households					
1970	64,778	8.4	11.2	10.6	10.7
1975	72,867	6.9	13.3	11.6	11.2
1978	77,330	6.6	12.5	11.3	10.9
1979	80,776	7.0	12.1	11.5	10.8
1980	82,368	7.5	13.1	11.1	11.5
1981	83,527	7.8	13.2	12.6	11.2
1982	83,918	8.1	13.3	12.4	11.1
1983	85,290	8.0	12.9	12.2	11.5
1984	86,789	7.5	12.9	11.8	11.3
1985	88,458	7.7	12.4	11.5	10.9
White					
1970	57,575	7.6	10.4	10.0	10.5
1975	64,392	6.0	12.2	11.3	11.1
1978	68,028	5.7	11.6	10.9	10.8
1979	70,766	5.9	11.4	11.0	10.7
1980	71,872	6.3	12.2	11.4	11.5
1981	72,845	6.6	12.2	12.2	11.3
1982	73,182	6.8	12.4	12.0	11.2
1983	74,170	6.7	11.9	11.9	11.5
1984	75,328	6.2	11.9	11.4	11.2
1985	76,576	6.4	11.7	11.2	10.8
Black					
1970	6,180	16.2	18.4	15.3	13.0
1975	7,489	15.0	22.0	14.0	12.3
1978	8,066	14.7	20.4	14.1	11.7
1979	8,586	15.7	19.7	15.1	11.9
1980	8,847	17.7	20.4	14.7	11.7
1981	8,961	18.5	21.2	15.5	10.9
1982	8,916	19.0	19.9	16.1	10.6
1983	9,243	18.8	21.0	14.2	12.1
1984	9,480	17.9	20.2	15.1	11.9
1985	9,797	17.6	18.8	14.0	12.4
Spanish Origin					
1975	2,948	9.3	16.6	16.8	13.9
1978	3,291	7.8	15.5	14.4	14.6
1979	3,684	8.2	15.3	14.6	13.6
1980	3,906	10.1	16.5	16.0	13.5
1981	3,980	9.4	16.9	15.4	12.8
1982	4,085	10.8	19.3	15.1	12.8
1983	4,666	11.3	18.6	14.5	13.9
1984	4,883	12.0	17.0	14.0	11.9
1985	5,213	10.8	17.9	14.7	12.2

Table 24–9 (Continued)

Race and Spanish Origin of Housekeeper and Year	Percent Distribution, by income level				Median income (dollars)
	$20,000 – $24,999	$25,000 – $34,999	$35,000 – $49,999	$50,000 and over	
All households					
1970	11.4	20.0	16.5	11.1	24,197
1975	10.6	18.4	16.6	11.5	23,585
1978	9.6	18.0	17.3	13.8	24,839
1979	9.8	18.0	17.2	13.5	24,396
1980	10.1	18.1	16.0	12.1	23,121
1981	10.5	17.2	15.6	11.7	22,561
1982	10.9	17.3	14.9	12.1	22,480
1983	10.3	17.1	15.3	12.8	22,694
1984	10.1	16.8	15.8	13.8	23,215
1985	10.0	17.0	15.8	14.8	23,618
White					
1970	11.5	20.7	17.4	11.9	25,203
1975	10.6	19.0	17.5	12.3	24,665
1978	9.7	18.5	18.2	14.7	25,822
1979	10.0	18.6	18.0	14.5	25,579
1980	10.2	18.7	16.8	13.0	24,392
1981	10.7	17.8	16.5	12.7	23,837
1982	11.1	17.9	15.6	13.0	23,535
1983	10.6	17.7	16.1	13.7	23,792
1984	10.4	17.4	16.6	14.8	24,491
1985	10.1	17.5	16.5	15.8	24,906
Black					
1970	10.5	13.8	9.0	3.9	15,340
1975	10.3	13.5	9.0	4.0	14,807
1978	9.3	14.2	9.9	5.7	15,518
1979	8.8	13.4	10.3	5.0	15,018
1980	9.3	13.0	9.0	4.3	14,053
1981	9.2	12.4	8.5	3.8	13,377
1982	9.7	12.9	8.4	3.5	13,388
1983	8.5	12.1	8.8	4.6	13,468
1984	8.6	12.0	9.1	5.2	13,952
1985	8.5	12.9	9.9	5.8	14,819
Spanish Origin					
1975	11.4	17.5	9.9	4.5	17,719
1978	10.8	17.3	13.1	6.4	19,462
1979	11.4	17.2	12.1	7.6	19,329
1980	11.0	15.4	11.6	6.1	17,822
1981	12.3	15.6	11.5	6.0	18,097
1982	11.3	14.6	10.5	5.7	16,916
1983	10.6	14.5	10.6	6.0	17,054
1984	11.2	15.5	11.6	6.7	17,598
1985	10.8	15.2	11.0	7.3	17,465

Table 24–10

Income, Expenditures, and Wealth

Personal Consumption Expenditures in Current and Constant (1982) Dollars—By Type of Expenditure: 1970 to 1985 (in billions of dollars)

Type of Expenditure	1970	1975	1979	1980	1981	1982	1983	1984	1985
Total, current dollars	640.0	1,012.8	1,566.8	1,732.6	1,915.1	2,050.7	2,234.5	2,428.2	2,600.5
Food and tobacco[1]	152.9	233.7	336.6	369.9	399.2	423.5	450.1	479.8	501.2
Food purchased for off-premise consumption	104.4	158.5	220.8	242.3	262.6	278.4	290.4	307.0	318.6
Meals and beverages, purchased[1]	34.9	55.8	90.5	100.2	106.7	112.9	123.5	134.4	141.9
Tobacco products	10.8	15.1	19.3	20.8	22.7	24.7	28.2	29.9	31.8
Clothing, accessories, and jewelry[2]	57.6	85.6	125.0	135.0	148.2	142.2	167.2	182.4	192.2
Clothing and accessories	39.8	60.4	86.5	91.9	100.9	105.4	114.7	125.4	132.2
Women's and children's	25.6	38.8	56.3	60.0	66.1	69.5	76.3	83.7	88.8
Men's and boys	14.3	21.6	30.2	32.0	34.8	35.9	38.4	41.6	43.5
Shoes	7.8	10.3	15.7	16.9	18.8	18.9	20.2	21.9	22.9
Jewelry and watches	4.1	8.1	13.3	15.4	16.7	16.7	18.0	20.0	21.3
Personal care	11.8	16.7	25.3	27.2	29.3	30.6	34.1	36.5	38.6
Toilet articles and preparations	6.6	10.3	15.2	16.4	17.9	18.8	20.3	21.9	23.0
Barbershops, beauty parlors, baths, health clubs	5.2	6.5	10.1	10.8	11.4	11.7	13.8	14.5	15.6
Housing[2]	94.0	148.4	231.1	261.5	295.6	321.1	344.1	372.2	403.9
Owner-occupied nonfarm dwellings-space rent	61.3	98.8	156.8	178.3	200.7	218.1	233.9	253.3	276.3
Tenant-occupied nonfarm dwellings-rent	16.0	39.0	55.7	61.9	71.1	77.9	84.7	92.3	101.7
Rental value of farm dwellings	3.3	5.4	9.3	11.0	12.6	12.9	12.1	12.2	10.6
Household operation	84.7	135.2	211.2	233.1	255.2	272.4	294.1	317.1	329.3
Household utilities	22.7	42.3	70.9	83.7	93.4	103.2	110.8	117.2	121.2
Electricity	9.6	19.4	30.8	37.2	42.5	47.1	51.0	55.4	60.2
Gas	5.6	9.1	16.1	19.1	21.0	25.7	29.0	29.4	29.7
Water and other sanitary services	3.1	5.3	8.3	9.3	10.5	11.8	13.3	14.5	15.6
Fuel oil and coal	4.4	8.4	15.8	18.0	19.4	28.6	17.5	17.9	15.7

Table 24–10 (Continued)

Type of Expenditure	1970	1975	1979	1980	1981	1982	1983	1984	1985
Telephone and telegraph	10.1	17.7	25.8	27.8	31.2	35.6	37.9	39.7	39.9
Furniture[4]	8.6	12.8	20.3	20.9	22.1	21.6	23.8	26.5	27.5
Cleaning and polishing preparations[5]	8.2	12.5	18.1	20.1	21.6	22.6	23.6	25.1	26.2
Kitchen and other household appliances	7.3	10.6	15.6	16.4	17.5	17.7	19.6	21.7	23.0
Medical care[2]	56.1	99.1	162.9	187.7	219.3	245.4	268.7	296.4	325.9
Privately controlled hospitals and sanitariums	19.7	40.1	70.0	82.2	96.8	110.3	119.6	129.9	138.4
Physicians	14.0	23.5	36.3	42.0	49.0	54.4	61.1	67.1	73.3
Professional services,[6] other	3.2	5.8	11.9	14.2	18.4	20.5	23.1	28.4	34.3
Drug preparations and sundries[7]	8.1	12.0	17.3	18.8	20.8	22.1	24.4	26.6	28.5
Dentists	4.9	8.2	12.3	13.7	16.1	17.4	18.5	19.8	21.3
Health insurance	4.4	6.6	10.9	12.3	13.2	15.1	16.0	17.9	22.8
Personal business	32.1	52.2	85.3	96.7	103.5	116.3	136.7	148.1	171.5
Transportation	81.5	131.2	222.0	238.5	261.5	267.6	295.4	327.3	349.8
User-operated transportation[2]	74.5	119.9	203.5	216.8	238.0	243.7	270.5	299.4	320.3
New autos	21.9	29.3	49.3	46.4	50.7	53.3	66.2	77.8	87.2
Gasoline and oil	21.9	39.7	66.1	83.7	92.7	89.1	90.2	90.7	91.9
Repair greasing, washing, parking storage, and rental	12.3	19.8	31.1	32.2	34.8	35.4	38.4	42.8	47.8
Used autos, net purchases	5.2	8.5	14.8	14.9	17.8	19.6	21.6	27.9	28.1
Other motor vehicles	2.7	7.7	17.6	12.3	12.9	15.6	20.7	25.4	29.8
Tires, tubes, accessories, and other parts	6.1	10.3	15.3	16.7	19.1	20.2	21.9	23.4	24.1
Insurance premiums less claims paid	3.8	3.8	8.4	9.4	8.9	9.1	10.3	10.0	10.0

Table 24–10 (Continued)

Income, Expenditures, and Wealth
Personal Consumption Expenditures in Current and Constant (1982) Dollars—By Type of Expenditure: 1970 to 1985 (in billions of dollars)

Type of Expenditure	1970	1975	1979	1980	1981	1982	1983	1984	1985
Purchased intercity transportation	4.0	7.3	13.0	15.9	17.3	17.6	18.4	21.0	22.4
Purchased local transportation	3.0	4.0	5.6	5.8	6.2	6.4	6.5	6.9	7.2
Recreation[8]	42.7	70.2	106.2	115.0	128.6	138.2	152.1	165.3	176.3
Private education and research	10.1	16.3	24.0	27.2	30.6	32.6	35.8	38.9	41.9
Religious and welfare activities	12.0	19.6	32.4	36.8	41.0	44.4	47.8	52.4	56.1
Foreign travel and other, net	4.5	4.4	4.6	4.1	3.0	5.1	8.5	11.9	13.8
Total, constant (1982) dollars[2]	1,492.0	1,711.9	2,004.4	2,000.4	2,024.2	2,050.7	2,146.0	2,246.3	2,324.5
Housing[2]	216.1	265.7	304.1	312.5	318.9	321.1	325.4	333.8	342.7
Household operation[2]	102.2	117.5	138.3	142.6	142.0	143.4	146.2	148.6	151.4
Electricity	29.0	37.0	45.0	47.0	46.7	47.1	49.4	50.5	53.0
Gas	25.4	26.2	26.1	26.0	25.3	25.7	24.7	25.0	25.4
Water and other sanitary services	8.3	10.1	11.1	11.7	11.7	11.8	12.3	12.6	12.8
Fuel oil and coal	26.7	24.2	26.2	21.6	19.2	18.6	18.6	18.6	17.0
Personal business	80.3	91.4	107.7	111.2	110.7	116.3	124.4	127.6	138.2
Transportation	59.8	69.4	82.9	77.4	73.3	69.7	71.4	75.9	81.0
Private education and research	27.0	29.2	31.4	31.8	32.5	32.6	34.3	35.7	37.0
Religious and welfare activities	29.9	33.4	41.8	42.0	43.0	44.4	46.4	49.0	51.4

[1]Consists of purchases (including tips) of meals and beverages from retail, service and amusement establishments, hotels, dining and buffet cars, schools, school fraternities, institutions, clubs, and industrial lunch rooms. [2]Includes other expenditures not shown separately. [3]Includes luggage, excludes shoes. [4]Includes mattresses and bed springs. [5]Includes miscellaneous household supplies and paper products. [6]Consists of osteopathic physicians, chiropractors, private duty nurses, chiropodists, podiatrists, and others providing health and allied services. [7]Excludes drug preparations and related products dispensed by physicians, hospitals, and other medical services. [8]For additional detail, see table 365.

Source: U.S. Bureau of Economic Analysis, *The National Income and Product Accounts of the United States, 1929–82,* and *Survey of Current Business,* July issues.

Table 24–11
Median Income by Race: 1967 to 1985

	Median Income in Current Dollars			
Year	All households	White	Black	Spanish origin
1967	7,143	7,449	4,325	(NA)
1970	8,734	9,097	5,537	(NA)
1971	9,028	9,443	5,578	(NA)
1972	9,697	10,173	5,938	7,677
1973	10,512	11,017	6,485	8,144
1974	11,197	11,710	6,964	8,906
1975	11,800	12,340	7,408	8,865
1976	12,686	13,289	7,901	9,569
1977	13,572	14,272	8,422	10,647
1978	15,064	15,550	9,411	11,803
1979	16,461	17,259	10,133	13,042
1980	17,710	18,684	10,764	13,651
1981	19,074	20,153	11,309	15,300
1982	20,171	21,117	11,968	15,178
1983	21,018	22,035	12,473	15,794
1984	22,415	23,647	13,471	16,922
1985	23,618	24,908	14,819	17,465

	Median Income in Constant (1985) Dollars				Annual Percent Change of Median Income of All Households	
Year	All households	White	Black	Spanish origin	Current dollars	Constant dollars
1967	23,015	24,001	13,935	(NA)	(x)	(x)
1970	24,197	25,203	15,340	(NA)	6.9	1.7
1971	23,980	25,083	14,816	(NA)	3.4	– .9
1972	24,935	26,159	15,269	19,741	7.4	4.0
1973	25,447	26,669	14,698	19,714	8.4	2.1
1974	24,426	25,545	15,192	19,428	6.5	– 4.0
1975	23,585	24,665	14,807	17,719	5.4	– 3.4
1976	23,973	25,113	14,933	18,083	7.5	1.6
1977	24,093	25,446	14,951	18,901	7.0	.5
1978	24,839	25,822	15,518	19,462	11.0	3.1
1979	24,396	25,579	15,018	19,329	9.3	– 1.8
1980	23,121	24,392	14,053	17,822	7.6	– 5.2
1981	22,561	23,837	13,377	18,097	7.7	– 2.4
1982	22,480	23,535	13,338	16,916	5.8	– .4
1983	22,694	23,792	13,468	17,054	4.2	1.0
1984	23,215	24,491	13,952	17,598	6.6	2.3
1985	23,618	24,908	24,819	17,465	5.4	1.7

Source: U.S. Bureau of the Census, *Statistical Abstract of the United States:* 1987 (105th edition), Washington, D.C., 1987, p. 431.

Table 24–12

Consumer Price Index, 1950 to 1985

| Year | All items | Food | | Shelter | | Fuel oil and coal | Gas and electricity |
		Total	Away from home	Total	Rent, residential		
1950	72.1	74.5	(NA)	(NA)	70.4	72.7	81.2
1951	77.8	82.8	(NA)	(NA)	73.2	76.5	81.5
1952	79.5	84.3	(NA)	(NA)	76.2	78.0	82.6
1953	80.1	83.0	(NA)	76.5	80.3	81.5	84.2
1954	80.5	82.8	70.1	78.2	83.2	81.2	85.3
1955	80.2	81.6	70.8	79.1	84.3	82.3	87.5
1956	81.4	82.2	72.2	80.4	85.9	85.9	88.4
1957	84.3	84.9	74.9	83.4	84.5	90.3	89.3
1958	86.6	88.5	77.2	85.1	89.1	88.7	92.4
1959	87.3	87.1	79.3	86.0	90.4	89.8	94.7
1960	88.7	88.0	81.4	87.8	91.7	89.2	98.6
1961	89.6	89.1	83.2	88.5	92.9	91.0	99.4
1962	90.6	89l9	85.4	89.6	94.0	91.5	99.4
1963	91.7	91.2	87.3	90.7	95.0	93.2	99.4
1964	92.9	92.4	88.9	92.2	95.9	92.7	99.4
1965	94.5	94.4	90.9	93.8	96.9	94.6	99.4
1966	97.2	99.1	95.1	96.8	98.2	97.0	99.6
1967	100.0	100.0	100.0	100.0	100.0	100.0	100.0
1968	104.2	103.6	105.2	104.8	102.4	103.1	100.9
1969	109.8	108.9	111.6	113.3	105.7	105.6	102.8
1970	116.3	114.9	119.9	123.6	110.1	110.1	107.3
1971	121.3	118.4	126.1	128.8	115.2	117.5	114.7
1972	125.3	123.5	131.1	134.5	119.2	118.5	120.5
1973	133.1	141.4	141.4	140.7	124.3	136.0	126.4
1974	147.7	161.7	159.4	154.4	130.6	214.6	145.8
1975	161.2	175.4	174.3	169.7	137.3	235.3	169.6
1976	170.5	180.8	186.1	179.0	144.7	250.8	189.0
1977	181.5	192.2	200.3	191.1	153.5	283.4	213.4
1978	195.4	211.4	218.4	210.4	164.0	298.3	232.6
1979	217.4	234.5	242.9	239.7	176.0	403.1	257.8
1980	246.8	254.6	267.0	281.7	191.6	556.0	301.8
1981	272.4	274.6	291.0	314.7	208.2	675.9	345.9
1982	289.1	285.7	306.5	337.0	224.0	667.9	393.8
1983	298.4	291.7	319.9	334.8	236.9	628.0	428.7
1984	311.1	302.9	333.4	361.7	249.3	641.8	445.2
1985	322.2	309.8	346.6	382.0	264.6	619.5	452.7

Product Prices Affect Expenditures

The second factor that affects consumer expenditures is the price of products. Table 24-12 shows trends in consumer prices between 1950 and 1983. Note that 1967 represents 100. Since 1967, consumer prices have inflated over 200 percent. The greatest increases were in fuel and coal (620) and gas and electricity (453). The cost of public transportation and medical care also rose considerably. Overall, services experienced greater inflation than did commodities.

Table 24-12 (Continued)

Year	Apparel and upkeep	Transportation Private	Transportation Public	Medical care	All commodities	All services
1950	79.0	72.5	48.9	53.7	78.8	58.7
1951	86.1	75.8	54.0	56.3	85.9	61.8
1952	85.3	80.8	57.5	59.3	87.0	64.5
1953	84.6	82.4	61.3	61.4	86.7	67.3
1954	84.5	80.3	65.5	63.4	85.9	69.5
1955	84.1	78.9	67.4	64.8	85.1	70.9
1956	85.8	80.1	70.0	67.2	85.9	72.7
1957	87.3	84.7	72.7	69.9	88.6	75.5
1958	87.5	87.4	76.1	73.2	90.6	78.5
1959	88.2	91.1	78.3	76.4	90.7	80.8
1960	89.6	90.6	81.0	79.1	91.5	83.5
1961	90.4	91.3	84.6	81.4	92.0	88.6
1962	90.9	93.0	87.4	83.5	92.6	86.8
1963	91.9	93.4	88.5	86.6	93.6	88.6
1964	92.7	94.7	90.1	87.3	94.6	90.2
1965	93.7	96.3	91.9	89.5	95.7	92.2
1966	96.1	97.5	96.2	93.4	98.2	96.3
1967	100.0	100.0	100.0	100.0	100.0	100.0
1968	105.4	103.0	104.6	106.1	103.7	106.2
1969	111.5	106.5	112.7	113.4	108.4	112.5
1970	116.1	111.1	128.5	120.6	113.5	121.6
1971	119.8	116.6	137.7	128.4	117.4	128.4
1972	122.3	117.5	143.4	132.5	120.9	133.3
1973	126.8	121.5	144.8	137.7	129.9	139.1
1974	136.2	136.6	148.0	150.5	145.5	152.1
1975	142.3	149.8	158.6	168.6	158.4	156.5
1976	147.6	164.8	174.2	184.7	165.2	180.4
1977	154.2	176.6	182.4	202.4	174.7	194.3
1978	159.6	185.0	187.8	219.4	187.1	210.3
1979	166.6	212.3	200.3	239.7	208.4	234.2
1980	178.4	249.2	251.6	265.9	233.9	273.3
1981	186.9	277.5	312.0	294.5	253.6	305.7
1982	191.8	287.5	346.0	328.7	263.8	333.3
1983	196.5	293.9	362.6	357.3	271.5	344.9
1984	200.2	306.6	385.2	379.5	280.7	363.0
1985	206.0	314.2	402.8	403.1	286.7	381.5

Source: U.S. Bureau of the Census, *Statistical Abstract of the United States:* 1987 (107th edition), Washington, D.C., 1987, p. 463.

The higher prices of all products means that consumers must adjust by buying lower-quality products. It no doubt results in more careful shopping by many consumers. We know that consumers have reduced their cost of gasoline by traveling less or changing to other modes of transportation. This has spurred the market for small cars, bicycles, and pedicycles. High prices and high interest rates have kept the housing market depressed for several years. This fact has greatly affected such businesses as contractors, architects, plumbers, carpenters, and similar business persons. Another result has been a tremendous rise in the number of trailers sold. This particular market is booming. Every problem is an oppor-

Table 24–13
American Population Mobility: 1980 to 1985

Age and Region	Total (1,000)	Nonmovers (same house in 1980)	Movers (different house in U.S., 1980)					Movers from abroad
			Total	Same country	Different county			
					Total	Same State	Different State	
Total	216,108	58.3	39.9	22.1	17.8	9.1	8.7	1.8
5–9 years	16,566	47.9	50.0	29.8	20.2	9.6	10.6	2.1
10–14 years	17,226	57.8	40.5	23.9	16.6	8.2	8.4	1.7
15–19 years	18,325	64.4	33.4	19.2	14.2	7.4	6.8	2.2
20–24 years	20,466	39.1	58.0	30.8	27.2	14.7	12.5	2.9
25–29 years	21,106	26.5	70.4	37.7	32.7	16.7	16.0	3.2
30–34 years	19,752	40.9	56.5	31.8	24.7	12.7	12.0	2.6
35–44 years	31,299	58.8	39.4	21.7	17.7	8.6	9.1	1.8
45–54 years	22,398	72.9	26.2	14.1	12.1	6.2	5.8	.9
55–64 years	22,151	79.0	20.2	10.4	9.8	5.2	4.5	.9
65 years and over	26,818	83.5	16.2	9.2	6.9	3.6	3.3	.3
Northeast	46,058	66.9	31.3	18.8	12.5	7.3	5.2	1.8
Midwest	54,214	60.9	38.2	22.9	15.4	9.1	6.3	.8
South	73,167	56.0	42.4	21.5	20.8	9.8	11.0	1.6
West	42,669	49.6	47.2	25.9	21.3	9.8	11.5	3.3

Source: U.S. Bureau of the Census, *Statistical Abstract of the United States: 1987* (107th edition), Washington, D.C., 1987, p. 25.

tunity for some business. The secret is for management to be tuned to the changes occurring and to take advantage of them as they occur.

GEOGRAPHIC MARKET CHANGES

Just as the composition of the population of the United States does not remain constant so there are changes that take place geographically.[9] Americans have been characterized as a people on the move. Table 24-13 shows that 39.9 percent of our population moves every year. Thus, on the average, the total population moves every three years. Persons up to about thirty-four years of age tend to move more. Older people tend to settle down in one place. Only about 13.6 percent of the population over forty-five moved to a different state between 1980 and 1985. The largest number of moves were made within the same county. As for regions, the most moves were made in the West.

Regional Markets

There is considerable variation in the importance of markets across the United States, and they are changing at varying rates.[10] These and other points can be observed from Illustration 24-1. Population and markets were moving to the South and West between 1960 and 1982. The South and West increased in population over the entire period. The Northwest and North Central regions

Illustration 24-1
Regions and geographic divisions of the United States: population and income*

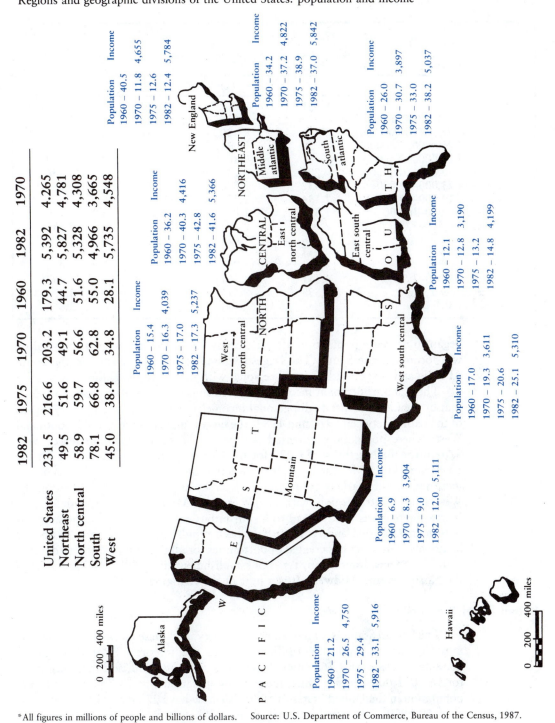

*All figures in millions of people and billions of dollars.   Source: U.S. Department of Commerce, Bureau of the Census, 1987.

Table 24–14

Urban-Rural Population: 1960 to 1980

| Class and Size | Places | | | Population (1,000) |
	1960	1970	1980	1960
United States	(x)	(x)	(x)	179,323
Urban	6,041	7,062	8,765	125,269
Places of 1,000,000 or more	5	6	6	17,484
Places of 500,000–1,000,000	16	20	16	11,111
Places of 250,000–500,000	30	30	34	10,766
Places of 100,000–250,000	81	100	117	11,652
Places of 50,000–100,000	201	240	290	13,836
Places of 25,000–50,000	432	520	675	14,951
Places of 10,000–25,000	1,134	1,385	1,765	17,568
Places of 5,000–10,000	1,394	1,839	2.181	9,780
Places of 2,500–5,000	2,152	2,295	2,665	7,580
Places under 2,500	596	627	1,016	690
Other urban	(x)	(x)	(x)	9,851
Rural	13,749	13,706	13,764	54,054
Places of 1,000–2,500	4,151	4,191	4,434	6,497
Places under 1,000	9,598	9,515	9,330	3,894
Other rural	(x)	(x)	(x)	43,664

began to decrease population after 1975. By 1982, the largest total population was located in the South. The largest regional gains were posted in the South Atlantic and West South Central regions, with the West just behind.

The trend in personal income measured in constant dollars tends to follow that of population. Although personal income shows an increase in every region of the nation between 1970 and 1982, the largest increases were in the South and West, where population increased the most. The actual dollar increases were $1,046 for the Northeast, $1,020 for the North Central region, $1,361 for the South, and $1,187 for the West. It follows that the South and West are becoming more important markets. The largest increases in personal income were in the West South Central region, with $1,699, and the Mountain region, with $1,207. Increasing markets always lead to a shift in business, so it is not surprising that both manufacturing and retailing have been rapidly moving into the South and Southwest. This fact has created opportunities for all types of business to develop there. In the meantime, many types of establishments have fallen on hard times in the Northeast and Midwest. It is a part of the changing times.

Urban-Rural Markets

The United States is largely an urban society, and these markets are by far the most important. Table 24-14 demonstrates the importance of these urban markets. There were 8,765 cities classified as urban in 1980, and they accounted for 167,051,000 people. Thus, the urban population was 73.7 percent of total population in the United States in 1980. We now have 22 cities with populations over 500,000. These urban markets mean that stores can be concentrated,

Table 24–14 (Continued)

Class and Size	Population (1,000)		Percent of Total Population		
	1970	1980	1960	1970	1980
United States	203,212	226,546	100.0	100.0	100.0
Urban	149,325	167,151	69.9	73.5	73.7
Places of 1,000,000 or more	18,769	17,530	9.8	9.2	7.7
Places of 500,000–1,000,000	12,967	10,834	6.2	6.4	4.8
Places of 250,000–500,000	10,442	12,158	6.0	5.1	5.4
Places of 100,000–250,000	14,286	17,015	6.5	7.0	7.5
Places of 50,000–100,000	16,724	19,786	7.7	8.2	8.7
Places of 25,000–50,000	17,848	23,328	8.3	8.8	10.3
Places of 10,000–25,000	21,415	27,645	9.8	10.5	12.2
Places of 5,000–10,000	12,924	15,356	5.5	6.4	6.8
Places of 2,500–5,000	8,038	9,368	4.2	4.0	4.1
Places under 2,500	727	1,260	.4	.4	.6
Other urban	15,186	12,663	5.5	7.5	5.6
Rural	53,887	59,495	30.1	26.5	26.3
Places of 1,000–2,500	6,656	7,038	3.6	3.3	3.1
Places under 1,000	3,852	3,563	2.2	1.9	1.7
Other rural	43,379	48,594	24.3	21.3	21.4

Source: U.S. Bureau of the Census, *Statistical Abstract of the United States:* 1987 (107th edition), Washington, D.C., 1987, p. 15.

salespersons need to travel less, and more customers can be served in a shorter period of time.

The rural population declined from 30.1 percent of the total in 1960 to just 26.3 percent in 1980, and rural population continues to decline as the market moves to the city. However, the rural population continues to make up a significant market that many firms cater to successfully. It is interesting that farm families now are just 1.8 percent of total United States families. Their income is lower than average; farm families have a median income of $17,205, while their nonfarm counterparts have a median income of $20,238. Thus, the rural market is small and highly specialized. The South continues to have the largest rural population (33.1 percent), followed by the North Central region (29.5 percent), Northeast (21.8 percent), and the West (16.1 percent).

Metropolitan Markets: Definition

The metropolitan markets are the largest ones in the United States. Before we can deal with these markets, we must come to some understanding about what they are. The United States Census defines a *Standard Metropolitan Statistical Area* (SMSA) as a city with 50,000 population, all of whose surrounding counties are at least 50 percent urbanized. Each SMSA has a *central city* (CC) defined by its political boundaries or city limits and *suburbs* (sub) defined as that area of the SMSA outside the central city. Illustration 24-2 shows the 323 SMSAs in the United States as defined by the 1981 census. The number has been growing over time. There were only 172 SMSAs in 1950. Each central city of SMSA has a *central business district* which is the major retail trade area of the city.

Illustration 24-2

Standard metropolitan statistical areas of the United States. Areas defined by U.S. Office of Management and Budget, June 1981

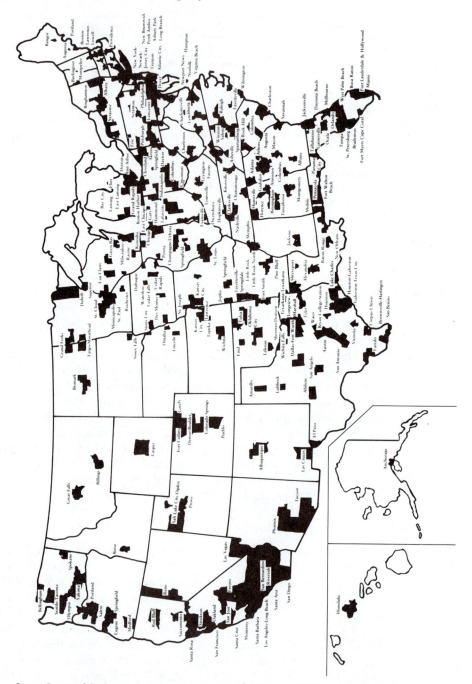

Source: Bureau of the Census, *Statistical Abstract of the United States,* (Washington, D.C., U.S. Government Printing Office, 1984), p. 49.

Part 5 – Consumer Assessment of Purchase

Illustration 24-3

Population by residence (total population each year = 100 percent)

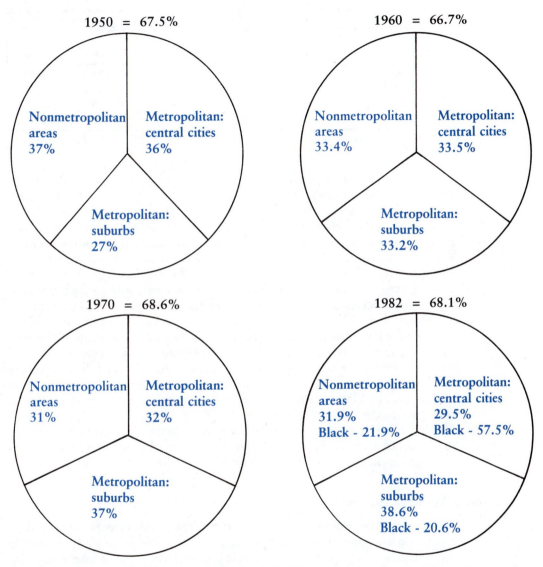

1950 = 67.5%

Nonmetropolitan areas 37%

Metropolitan: central cities 36%

Metropolitan: suburbs 27%

1960 = 66.7%

Nonmetropolitan areas 33.4%

Metropolitan: central cities 33.5%

Metropolitan: suburbs 33.2%

1970 = 68.6%

Nonmetropolitan areas 31%

Metropolitan: central cities 32%

Metropolitan: suburbs 37%

1982 = 68.1%

Nonmetropolitan areas 31.9% Black - 21.9%

Metropolitan: central cities 29.5% Black - 57.5%

Metropolitan: suburbs 38.6% Black - 20.6%

Source: *Statistical Abstracts of the United States,* (Washington, D.C., U.S. Government Printing Office, 1984), p. 49.

Metropolitan Markets: Population

The population figures in Illustration 24-3 point out the rapid growth of standard metropolitan statistical areas since 1950. These areas have increased from 62.5 percent of total population in 1950 to 68.1 percent of the total in 1982. However, this growth has not been uniform. The population of central cities has decreased rather dramatically over the period while the suburbs have shown tremendous increase.

Table 24–15

Income Distribution in Metropolitan Markets: 1983

Area	All Families		Blacks	
	Number (1,000)	Median Income	Number (1000)	Median Income
In Metropolitan Areas	35,465	27,948	5,123	15,304
In Central Cities	12,336	24,730	3,580	13,885
Outside Central Cities	23,131	29,893	1,544	18,900
Total	89,399	36,083	11,798	15,036

Source: U.S. Bureau of the Census, *Statistical Abstract of the United States:* 1987 (107th edition), Washington, D.C., 1987, p. 451.

In terms of market potential, the tendency is for poorer, less well-educated persons to move from the nonmetropolitan areas directly to the central cities. They perceive advantages in terms of improved employment opportunities, better education for themselves and their children, better services, and more diverse recreational and entertainment opportunities. The more affluent of them tend to move directly to the suburbs where there is more casual living and a better environment for raising children. Those central city dwellers who succeed in increasing their standard of living tend to make a second move to the suburbs. If central city dwellers do not make it, their children tend to move to the suburbs.

Notice that in 1982 there was a decrease in persons living in metropolitan areas. There is a clear shift back to the nonmetropolitan areas, primarily by persons living in central cities. Often these central city dwellers are disappointed with what they find in the city. Opportunities do not materialize, and the annoyances of the city affect the quality of their life. Many of these persons are opting to go back to the small towns rather than move to the suburbs. It will be interesting to see to what extent this trend continues.

Illustration 24-3 shows the distribution of blacks in metropolitan areas. Blacks concentrate in the central cities (57.5 percent) much more than whites (29.5 percent). There are far fewer blacks in the suburbs than whites.

Metropolitan Markets: Income

The importance of income to markets has already been demonstrated, and income is no less important to metropolitan markets. Table 24-15 shows how wide the variation in income is among the areas of the SMSAs. Some interesting relationships can be determined from this table that bear on markets.

Median income was lower in central cities for both whites and blacks. This fact indicates the tendency reported earlier for the less privileged to move into this area. Median income was lower for blacks in every area of the SMSAs, and the difference was quite large. Nevertheless, incomes for both whites and blacks within metropolitan areas was greater than was found for persons living outside these metropolitan areas. When you consider that most persons live in the suburbs and that incomes in the suburbs are higher, this area clearly represents

Part 5 – Consumer Assessment of Purchase

the larger markets. The market for blacks is concentrated in the central cities and their lack of purchasing power makes it quite a different type of market from that of whites.

Metropolitan Markets: Significance

The significance of metropolitan markets cannot be underestimated for business. As both population and income begin to concentrate in these areas, they offer the greatest opportunity for almost any type of business. In fact, retail stores have been growing the fastest in metropolitan markets over all other markets for the past forty years, although we do note some tendency for that situation to change.

The fact that metropolitan markets are so concentrated offers significant opportunities for management to cut costs. For example, it is possible for a door-to-door salesperson to reach tremendously more people within a metropolitan market in a given amount of time. The inside traffic for almost every type of business is greatly increased in metropolitan markets. Therefore, management can design much larger and more efficient stores to take advantage of the situation. Shoppers have much more opportunity to compare in these areas, hence retailers are more competitive in pricing and promotion. The diversity of population creates diversity of businesses. It would be difficult to imagine the same number of important department stores, discount houses, variety stores, and large drug-stores outside the metropolitan market. These stores are simply made for the high-density metropolitan markets.

Interurban Markets

Although the rate of growth is likely to slow in the future, the general tendency of people to move to the suburbs will continue. Already, in some sections, metropolitan areas are beginning to fuse, giving rise to a new type of supercity even larger than the standard metropolitan area. The name *interurbia*, or *megalopolis*, has been given to these supercities. Today a person can travel from Boston, Massachusetts, to Norfolk, Virginia, a distance of over 600 miles, without effectively going outside the "city." This area, known as the Atlantic seaboard megalopolis, contains over 20 percent of the U.S. population on 6 percent of the land area. Illustration 24-4 shows other examples of emerging interurbia.[11] The Lower Great Lakes megalopolis spreads from Pittsburgh, Pennsylvania, to Buffalo, New York, on the east, and to Chicago, Illinois, and Milwaukee, Wisconsin, on the west. The Great Lakes and Atlantic seaboard megalopoles are beginning to merge through Ohio and Pennsylvania. Two other developing interurban areas are the California megalopolis, running from San Francisco and Oakland through Los Angeles to the Mexican border, and the Florida megalopolis that curves from Orlando through Tampa and St. Petersburg to Miami. This latter region is the fastest growing of all the supercities. Not only will most consumers of the future be city dwellers, but the consumption of products associated with clean water, recreation, waste disposal, and environmental pollution will increase.

Table 24–16

Population by City Size, 1960 to 1980: Urban and Rural Population

Class and Size	Places 1960	Places 1970	Places 1980	Population (1,000) 1960
United States	(x)	(x)	(x)	179,323
Urban	6,041	7,062	8,765	125,269
Places of 1,000,000 or more	5	6	6	17,484
Places of 500,000–1,000,000	16	20	16	11,111
Places of 250,000–500,000	30	30	34	10,766
Places of 100,000–250,000	81	100	117	11,652
Places of 50,000–100,000	201	240	290	13,836
Places of 25,000–50,000	432	520	675	14,951
Places of 10,000–25,000	1,134	1,385	1,765	17,568
Places of 5,000–10,000	1,394	1,839	2.181	9,780
Places of 2,500–5,000	2,152	2,295	2,665	7,580
Places under 2,500	596	627	1,016	690
Other urban	(x)	(x)	(x)	9,851
Rural	13,749	13,706	13,764	54,054
Places of 1,000–2,500	4,151	4,191	4,434	6,497
Places under 1,000	9,598	9,515	9,330	3,894
Other rural	(x)	(x)	(x)	43,664

Small City Markets Important

In spite of the obvious importance of metropolitan areas, we cannot overlook the small city market. Table 24-16 indicates their continued importance. There were more cities below 25,000 added to the total than any other size of city. These smaller cities show the growth between 1970 and 1980 rather than the larger cities. This fact supports our earlier observation that population is tending to leave the SMSAs for smaller towns. The largest change in population was in the cities with between 5,000 and 50,000 population. It is clear that marketers cannot afford to ignore the smaller cities and towns when they seek out customers. It appears that these smaller cities will become even more important in the future.

QUESTIONS

1. Consumers modify their purchase decisions for several reasons. Identify the reasons why you have modified any of your purchase decisions.
2. Identify the different products that may be affected by the change in market size. What products would not be affected? Why?
3. Identify the different products that might be purchased by a household but not a family and a family but not a household. Why the difference?
4. The number of households with female heads is expected to increase. Will

Table 24–16 (Continued)

Class and Size	Population (1,000)		Percent of Total Population		
	1970	1980	1960	1970	1980
United States	203,212	226,546	100.0	100.0	100.0
Urban	149,325	167,151	69.9	73.5	73.7
Places of 1,000,000 or more	18,769	17,530	9.8	9.2	7.7
Places of 500,000–1,000,000	12,967	10,834	6.2	6.4	4.8
Places of 250,000–500,000	10,442	12,158	6.0	5.1	5.4
Places of 100,000–250,000	14,286	17,015	6.5	7.0	7.5
Places of 50,000–100,000	16,724	19,786	7.7	8.2	8.7
Places of 25,000–50,000	17,848	23,328	8.3	8.8	10.3
Places of 10,000–25,000	21,415	27,645	9.8	10.5	12.2
Places of 5,000–10,000	12,924	15,356	5.5	6.4	6.8
Places of 2,500–5,000	8,038	9,368	4.2	4.0	4.1
Places under 2,500	727	1,260	.4	..4	.6
Other urban	15,186	12,663	5.5	7.5	5.6
Rural	53,887	59,495	30.1	26.5	26.3
Places of 1,000–2,500	6,656	7,038	3.6	3.3	3.1
Places under 1,000	3,852	3,563	2.2	1.9	1.7
Other rural	43,379	48,594	24.3	21.3	21.4

Source: U.S. Bureau of the Census, *Statistical Abstract of the United States:* 1987 (107th edition), Washington, D.C., 1987, p. 15.

this lead to any changes in the products demanded? Discuss your answer.

5. What marketing strategies must marketing managers take as they see their black and Hispanic household markets are increasing?

6. Identify the products that would be affected by a decrease in household size. Explain your answer.

7. Discuss the statement: "Working people make many purchases that are different from people who spend most of their time in the home."

8. Discuss the statement: "Just because a market is important today does not mean that it will be equally important in the future."

9. Identify the products in which sales have suffered because of increasing prices and those in which sales have not suffered because of increasing prices. Why is there a difference?

10. Identify the regions of the United States that have had the biggest increase in growth. What products and services would be affected by this change? Why?

11. Identify the Standard Metropolitan Statistical Area in your area. Why is this information important to marketing managers?

12. Discuss the relationship between population shifts and occupations.

13. What regions of the United States do you think will offer the greatest potential income for you? Why will there be differences in income potential?

14. What do you think is the best marketing technique to reach the interubia and small town markets? Why?

15. What are the biggest changes you think marketing managers will face in the future?

NOTES

1. B. G. Yovovick, "Finding the Answers," *Advertising Age* (July 20, 1981), pp. 41–45; "A New Way to View Consumers," *Dun's Review* (August 1981), pp. 42–46.
2. John M. McCann and David J. Reibstein, "Forecasting the Impact of Socioeconomic and Demographic Change on Product Demand," *Journal of Marketing Research,* Vol. XXII (November 1985), pp. 415–23.
3. Peter E. Drucker, "The Discipline of Innovation," *Harvard Business Review,* Vol. 63 (May–June 1983), pp. 67–84.
4. Stephen A. Greyser and Steven L. Diamond, "U.S. Consumers View the Marketplace," *Journal of Consumer Policy,* Vol. 6 (1983), pp. 3–18.
5. Lore Harp, "The Entrepreneur Sees Herself as a Manager," *Harvard Business Review,* Vol. 60 (July–August 1982), pp. 140–150; Don Beliante and Ann C. Foster, "Working Wives and Expenditure on Service," *Journal of Consumer Research,* Vol. 11 (September 1984), pp. 700–707.
6. Joanne Miller and Howard H. Garrison, "Sex Roles: The Division of Labor at Home and in the Workplace," *Annual Review of Sociology* (1982), pp. 237–62.
7. Judith Langer, "Changing Demographics: Stimulus for New Product Ideas," *Journal of Consumer Marketing,* Vol. 1 (1984), pp. 35–43; Sharon Y. Nickols and Karen D. Fox, "Buying Time and Saving Time: Strategies for Managing Household Production," *Journal of Consumer Research,* Vol. 10 (September 1983), pp. 197–208.
8. U.S. Dept. of Commerce, Bureau of the Census, *Statistical Abstracts of the United States* (Washington, D.C. 25: U.S. Government Printing Office, 1984), p. 326.
9. Gerald Albaum and Del I. Hawkins, "Geographic Mobility and Demographic and Socioeconomic Market Segmentation," *Journal of the Academy of Marketing Science,* Vol. 11 (Spring 1983), pp. 97–113.
10. Gregory A. Jackson and George S. Masnick, "Take Another Look at Regional U.S. Growth," *Harvard Business Review,* Vol. 61 (January–February 1983), pp. 76–87.
11. Compare this map to the one showing metropolitan areas.

INDEX

A

Achievement, and social class, 242
Achievement (trait), 407
Activities, interests, and opinions (AIO) rating, 223
Activity (trait), 406
Adaptability (trait), 407
Adjustment function, 183
Adler, Alfred, 405
Adopters, 146–147
Adoption of a product, 145–146
Advantage, relative, 148
Advertising, 306–307. *See also* Promotion; and fantasy, 76; as information source, 169; psychoanalytic theory in, 405
Aesthetic man, 410
Aesthetic values, 67–69; in multinational markets, 456–457
Affectional needs, 69
Age: of customers, 569; subcultures based on, 267–274
Agents (brokers), 282
Aggressiveness (trait), 407
All-or-nothing solution, 96
Allport, Gordon, 405
Alternatives, consumer: comparison of, 358–361; evaluating, 23–24, 350–367; identifying, 351–355
American culture, 260–262, 520–521
American Marketing Association, 561–562
Anticipatory reference group, 234
Anxiety (trait), 407
Appliances, home, 352–353
Architecture of stores, 295
Assessment. *See* Consumer assessment
Atmospherics in stores, 296–298
Attention: customer's, getting it, 313–314; span of, 343–344

Attitudes, 12, 182–183; adjustment, value expressive, ego defensive, and knowledge functions of, 183–185; changes in, reasons for, 196–199; completeness property of, 194; conflicting, 196; and consumer behavior, 192–194; in internal search, 182–199; learned, 185–191; and loyalty, 500–501; personality trait and, 406; positive and negative, 192, 500–501; stability of, factors in, 194–196; strength of, 192–193, 198; transferring, 193–194
Audience participation, 317
Audit, consumer, 551
Automatic reference group, 233
Automobile, shopping by, 293
Awareness of product, 145–146

B

Bachelor stage, 218–219
Bait pricing, 424
Bandwagon appeal, 320
Bargaining, 421–423
Bayton, James A., 69
Behavior, 9; consumer. *See* Consumer behavior; determined by culture, 254–255; habitual and impulse, 391–392
Behavior sampling, 554
Belief, 182–183
Belonging needs, 63–65
Bias, 183
Blacks: demographics of, 263; income of, 579; integration of, 235–236; purchasing patterns of, 263–266; subculture of, 263–267
Boutiques, 302
Boycotts, consumer, 524
Branch operations, 289

Brand(s): alternatives in, 353; and consumer search, 283–284; loyalty toward, 499–500
Branding, 148–150
Brand name, 150
Bribes, in international trade, 456
Brokers. *See* Agents
Business: and consumerism, 531–533; criticism of, 525–528; influence on consumer, 12; information from, 169, 547; norms of behavior, 255–258
Business firms: abilities of, and marketing target, 103–105, 111–113; change in, 508–509; consumer research used by, 542–543; ethical standards of, 511, 526–528; in multinational markets, 444–447, 466; promotion as basic tool of, 308–311; withdrawal of trade from, 508–509, 517–518
Buyer. *See* Consumer(s)
Buyer power, discretionary, 71–72

C

Caplovitz, David, 522
Card stacking, 320
Career, and family orientation, 210–211
Cartoon test technique, 557–558
caveat emptor doctrine, 518
Census, Bureau of, 547–548
Central business districts, 293, 593
Central city, 593
Chain stores, 288–289
Chance: and consumer decision, 331–332; and switching, 508
Change, in traditional societies, 462
Channels of distribution, 280–283; in international trade, 446–447; length and cost of, 281–282

Charge account, 30-day, 432
Chattel mortgage, 432
Children: consumer behavior of, 267–270; and family orientation, 209–210; in full nest, 220–221; marketing to, 198–199
Choice. *See also* Alternatives; consumer, right to, 530
Cities: large, 592–593; small, 598
Cognitive consistency, 82, 477–478
Cognitive dissonance. *See* Dissonance
Cognitive research, 545, 551–561
Cognitive theories, 187
College students, 271
Color: and consumer decision making, 341; as motivator, 318–319; national differences in, 456–457
Commercialization, 138
Communication, 161–164; and consumer behavior, 13; in consumer search, 161–170; intent of (casual, informative, persuasive, or reminder), 163; noise in, 167–168; one-way or two-way, 164–165; personal vs. mass, 163; two-step flow concept of, 165–167; vertical vs. horizontal flow, 166; written, verbal, or physical, 163
Companies. *See* Business firms
Compatibility of a product, 148
Compensatory evaluation rule, 364
Competition: intensity of, 119–120; legislation re, 530; during product life cycle, 140–142; pure, 520–521
Competitive pricing, 425–426
Competitors: customers of, 483; as marketing target, 14–16, 114–115; needs and motives of, 114–115
Complaints, consumer, 152, 518
Complexity of a product, 148
Compliance, 238
Conditioning, 187
Conflict, resolution of, 93
Conformity, 238; in American culture, 262; and loyalty development, 505
Congruence, 196
Conjunctive rule, 362–363
Connectionist theories, 187
Consumer(s). *See also* Customers; behavior of. *See* Consumer behavior; defined (three roles of), 4–5; final, vs. industrial buyers, 8; getting their attention, 313–314; and government, 530–531; identifying them, 4–8; vs. influencer, 5; information on. *See* Consumer data; learning by,

Consumer(s) *(continued)*
185–191; loyal. *See* Loyalty, customer; as marketing target, 14–19, 102–113, 124; market segmentation of, 106–113; multinational, 442; poor consumer skills of, 328–331; potential vs. realized, 5–8; research on. *See* Consumer research; rights of (to safety, to be informed, to choose, to be heard), 528–531; satisfied. *See* Satisfaction; skills of, improving, 328–331
Consumer analysis, 442
Consumer assessment, 472–473. *See also* Postpurchase assessment; Prepurchase assessment; formal or informal, 476; immediate or delayed, 476–477; importance of, to consumers and management, 473–474; responsibility for, 476; types of (prepurchase, postpurchase), 474–475
Consumer assortment, 43–44; attributes of (width, variety, depth), 44–45; as consumer problem, 43–48; expanding or deleting, 50–51; individual differences in, 45–48; open and closed, 48
Consumer audit, 551
Consumer behavior, 9. *See also* Behavior; acceptable and forbidden, 256; age group and, 267–274; of children, 267–270; communication and, 13; culture as affecting, 255–274; knowledge of, affecting marketing strategy, 13–19; motivation and, 82–83, 95–97; overall view of, 8–13; reason for studying, 2–4; sex interest and, 205; of teenagers, 270–271; of young adults, 271
Consumer data. *See also* Consumer research; problems in accuracy of, 550; sources of, primary and secondary, 546–550
Consumer decisions, 328, 372–374. *See also* Consumer search; Purchase decisions; alternative evaluation and, 350–367; correctness of, 390; decision states, 372–374; by families, 381–392; by individuals, 374–381; motivation and, 80–81; in multinational markets, 443–444; as normal and reasonable, 387–392; partial and basic explanation theories of, 331–333; perception in,

Consumer decisions *(continued)*
333–345; personality and, 398–413, 406–408; planning, 330–331; problems of consumers in making, 328–331; process of, 19–27; promotion and, 309–311; rationalization of, 77; ready state, 365–367; simplified, due to loyalty, 505–506
Consumer inventory, 48–54; casual and formal, 52; complete and partial, 51–52; long- and short-run, 52–54
Consumerism, 519; accomplishments of, 528–535; business and, 531–533; consumer organizations, 523; future of, 535–536; history of, 518–522; legislation on behalf of, 531; marketing opportunities created by, 534–535; methods and tools of, 524; objectives of, 523–524; in recent times, 522–523
Consumer League, 522
Consumer motives/motivation. *See* Motives/motivation
Consumer needs. *See also* Needs; products that satisfy, 61–62
Consumer panel, 137
Consumer preference grouping, 302
Consumer problem(s). *See also* Problem(s); consumer assortment as, 43–48; consumer inventory identifying, 48–54; degree of specification of, 54–55; derived from needs, 60–62, 75–77; recognition of, 34–43, 401–402; sequence of, 37
Consumer Reports, 84
Consumer research, 542–543. *See also* Consumer data; Marketing research; ethics of, 561–562; steps in, 544–546; structured and disguised dimensions, 551–561; types of (demographic, cognitive), 545–546
Consumer search, 169–170; active and passive, 173–174; amount and length of, 170–172; casual or formal, 174–175; communication in, 161–170; in consumer decision, 21–23; continual or intermittent, 174; culture's effect on, 258–262; distribution methods and, 280–303; importance of studying, 161; information search in, 169–170; internal and external sources in, 23, 160–161, 168–170, 182–199, 311–313; local or extended, 175; nature of, 160–161; patterns of, 172–177;

Consumer search (continued)
personality and, 402; promotion and, 306–322
Consumers Product Safety Commission, 528–529
Consumers Union, 523
Consumption: and family orientation, 211–212; process of, 4–5
Contrast, visual, 342–343
Control, emotional, 407
Convenience cost, 283
Convenience goods, 283
Costs, types of (product, convenience), 283
Credibility, of sources of information, 170
Credit sales, 152–153, 432
Criteria, evaluation: sources of (personal, reference group, business), 357; types used (cost, performance, suitability, convenience), 357–358
Crowds, in stores, 298
Cultural norms. See Norms
Culture, 252–253; American, basic characteristics of, 260–262; attributes of (handed down, ideational, adaptive, integrative), 258–260; behavior determined by, 254–255; consumer behavior affected by, 255–274; function of, 254–255; identification with, 252–253; influence of, 12; institutional sources of, 253–254; national, contrasts in, 447–457, 460–466
Curiosity, and switching, 507
Customers. See also Consumer(s); age of, 569; flow of, in stores, 298–302; respect toward, 511
Customs, 256

D

Deal proneness, 353
Decision. See Consumer decisions; Purchase decisions
Decision states, 372–374
Decline stage of a product, 142
Decoding, 163
Defense, perceptual, 338
Defense mechanisms. See Ego defense
Deferred actions, 95–96
Deficiency: vs. equilibrium, 82; and needs, contrasted, 61
Deletion of a product, 144
Delivery service, 433–434
Demander, 4–5
Demographic research, 107–109, 545–546, 550–551
Departmentalized stores, 286–288
Department stores, 286–287

Depth interview, 551–553
Depth of assortment, 44–45
Desires, 59–60
Diffusion, of innovation, 146–148
Direct marketing, 291–292
Discontinuance of use, 494–495
Discount, 419
Discount houses, 287
Discretionary buyer power, 71–72
Discretionary income, 574
Disinvestment, 142
Disjunctive rule of evaluation, 363
Displacement (defense mechanism), 404
Dissatisfaction. See also Satisfaction; consumers' reasons for, 524–528; group responses to, 518–519; individual responses to, 516–518
Dissonance: causes of, 481–483; immediate or delayed, 476–477; new information and, 480–481; physical- and emotional-based, 480; and postpurchase assessment, 478–479; and switching, 508–509
Distribution: channels of. See Channels of distribution; intensity of (intensive, exclusive, selective), 283–284; methods, 280–303; policy, 14–15, 18
Distributors, 280–283
Dominance (trait), 407
Door-to-door selling, 292
Durable goods, 352–353

E

Easterners, 224
Economic man, 387–388, 410
Economic value, maximizing, 387–388
Economy, the: and consumer dissatisfaction, 525–526; influences on consumers, 12
Education: and income, 575–579; in multinational markets, 449–452; and social class, 242
Ego, 404
Ego defense, 69, 184–185, 404
Ego needs, 69
Elimination by aspect rule of evaluation, 363–365
Emotional control (trait), 407
Empty nest, 221
Encoding, 163
Energy mobilization, 80
Environmentalists, 236
Equal-appearing interval scale, 560
Equality, ideal of, 261
Equilibrium, 477–478; vs. deficiency, 82; re-establishment of, 483–485

Esteem, need for, 65
Ethics: of business firms, 511, 526–528; in consumer research, 561–562; in multinational markets, 455–456; in pricing, 428–429; in promotion, 529; in services, 429–431
Evaluation. See Alternatives, consumer, evaluating
Expectations, and purchase decisions, 93–95
Experience theory, 187
Experiments, consumer research, 544
Expressive role in family, 212–213
External pressure, and switching, 509
External search, 160–161, 311–313

F

Families, 204–205. See also Households; of birth vs. of marriage, 207–208; compatible-integrated dimensions of, 208–209, 384–385; consumer decision by, 381–392; consumer problem recognition by, 39–43; culture inculcated by, 254; external and internal roles in, 214–215; formation of, and product consumption, 205, 208; functions of (social, economic, procreative), 205–207; influences on behavior, 12; instrumental and expressive roles in, 212–213; negotiation in, 381–383; nuclear, extended and compound, 208; orientation of (family-, career-, consumption-centered), 209–212; power relationships in, 384; "purchasing agent" in, 39–43; roles in, and consumer decisions, 212–218, 382, 384–385; types, classified by composition, 207–208
Fantasy, needs resolved by, 76
Fear, in promotions, 317–318
Feedback, 164
Feelings, 183
Final consumer market, 8
Fixation, perceptual, 343
Food and Drug Act of 1906, 522
Foreign countries. See also Multinational market; gross national product of, 457–460; products from, suspicion of, 464; purchasing power of, 457–460; shopping habits in, 464–466
Forgetting, 76, 190–191
Formality, of reference group, 231–232
Franchising, 289

Free-flow layout of stores, 301–302
Freud, Sigmund, 402–405
Fromm, Erich, 405
Full nest, 220–221
Furness, Betty, 522

G

General stores, 287
Generation gap, 210
Generic grouping, 302
Geography. *See* Location; Regions
Gestalt psychology, 411
Goal, perceived, 80
Goods, convenience vs. shopping, 283–284
Government. *See also* Legislation; and business, 119–120; and consumer interests, 523; consumers' role in, as right, 530–531; information sources of, 547–548; as marketing target, 14–16, 113–114; minorities and, 236; needs and motives of, 113–114
Grid layout of stores, 299–300
Grocery stores, 287
Gross national product, 457–460
Group. *See* Social group
Group interview, 554
Growth stage of a product, 140–141
Guilt feelings, advertising and, 76

H

Habit: and consumer decision, 331–332; perceptual, 343; purchasing out of, 83, 391, 495–496
Heredity, and personality, 331–332
Heterogeneity, between social classes, 240
Hierarchy of social class, 240
Hispanics: income of, 579; subculture of, 262–263
Homeostasis, 478
Homogeneity, within social class, 240
Homosexuals, 236
Horney, Karen, 405
Households, 204–205. *See also* Families; head of, 567–569, 572–574; income of, 574–579; purchasing power of, 580–581; size of, 569–572; traditional, 567
Humanitarianism, 262
Humor, in promotions, 317
Husbands, role of, 212–218, 235

I

Id, 404
Idea generation. *See also* Innovation; internal and external sources, 135; in product develop-

Idea generation *(continued)*
ment, 134–135; screening phase of, 136
Ideal self, 311–312
Identification: with culture, 252–253; with norms, 238; with reference group, 230–231
Identification (defense mechanism), 404
Impulse buying, 83, 331–332, 353, 391–392, 504
Inclination, 183
Income: discretionary, 574; education and, 575–579; of households, 385–386, 574–579; of metropolitan markets, 596–597; and motivation, 91–92; and purchasing patterns, 574–581; race and, 579; social class and, 242
Independence (trait), 407
Individuals: consumer decision by, 374–381; personality of, 398–399, 407–408; vs. society, 390–391
Industrial buyer, 8
Inertia, consumer, 505
Inflation, 525, 581; as market opportunity, 588–590
Influence: of others, 12–13, 75; theoretical principles of, 321
Influencer, 5
Informal group, 232
Information: commercial vendors of, 548–549; confidence in (credibility), 170; on consumers. *See* Consumer data; in consumer search, 168–171; consumers' right to, 529; flow to, 529; flow of, variations by social class, 242; limited, and attitude change, 198–199; logic of, 379–380; new, and dissonance, 480–481; organizing, formal and informal, 355–356; search for. *See* Consumer search; seekers and receivers of, 165–166; sensory. *See* Perception; sources of, 168–171, 314–316
Inhibition, 76
Inner-directed man, 410
Innovation. *See also* Idea generation; Product, new; diffusion of, 146–148
Innovators: vs. opinion leaders, 166; in product adoption, 146
Installation service, 434
Installment credit, 432
Instinct, 82–83, 403
Instrumental role in family, 212–213
Interaction, in reference group, 232
Internalization, of norms, 238

Internal search, 160–161, 311–313; attitudes in, 182–199; promotion affecting, 311–313
International trade. *See also* Multinational markets; business organization for, 444–446; channels of distribution in, 446–447
Interurbia, 597
Interview: depth, 551–553; focused group, 554
Introduction of a product, 140, 145–148

J

Jung, C. G., 408

K

Kennedy, John F., 528
Knowledge, need for, 65–66
Knowledge function of attitudes, 185

L

Labeling, 152
Laggards, in product adoption, 147–148
Languages, foreign, 447–449
Laws, 257
Layout of stores, 298–302
Learned response, motivation and, 83
Learning, 11–12; of attitudes, 185–191; curve, 188–189; principles of, 316; theories of, 186–191
Leasing, 435
Legal action by customers, 518
Legislation. *See also* Government; on competition, 530; pro-consumer, 531; on safety, 528–529
Leisure time, 72
Lexicographic rule of evaluation, 365
Life cycle, 218; stages of, 218–222
Life style, 223; examples of, 224; and information sharing, 222–226; and market segmentation, 110–111; regional, 224–226
Likert scale, 559–560
Limited-line stores, 285–286
Literacy, 451–452
Location: and market segmentation, 107; perception of, and consumer decisions, 342–343
Logic: and consumer decision, 379–380; in promotional message, 315
Loss leader pricing, 423–424
Lower class, 245
Loyalty, customer, 497. *See also*

Loyalty, customer (continued)
Switching; advantages of, to marketers, 502–504; degree of, 497–499; forced, due to market conditions, 506; how to create, tips on, 510–511; learned, 500–501; and motivation, 501–502; reasons for, 504–506; satisfaction and, 496–502, 504; target of (product, brand, store), 499–500; types of (recognition, preference, insistence), 499–500
Luxuries, 59

M

Mail-order selling, 291–292
Majority, in product adoption, 147
Malls, 294–295
Management. See Business firms
Manufacturers, distribution methods of, 281–283
Marginal utility, 374–376
Marketing: objective of, 13–14; during product life cycle, 140–144; strategy, 13–19, 140–144; test. See Test marketing
Marketing audit, 103–105
Marketing mix, 14; in product development phase, 136–137
Marketing research, 542. See also Consumer research
Marketing target, 102; feasibility of success in attaining, 117–120; identifying, 14, 102–117; single, segmented, and multitarget approaches, 121–124; strategy planning for achieving, 120–124
Markets, 106; changes in, responding to, 566; by geographic area, 590–598; growth of, in U.S., 566–567; heterogenous and homogeneous, 106; household as basic unit, 567; interurban, 597; isolated, 506; loyal, 500, 502, 506; metropolitan, 593–597; multinational, 462–464; regional, 590–592; rural, 592–593; size of, 119–120; urban, 592–593
Market segment, 17; identifying, 106–113, 408
Market share, loss of, 144
Markup, 419, 424
Marriage: demographics of, 273; subcultures based on, 267–274
Married couples: with children (full nest), 220–221; empty nest, 221; newly married, 219–220
Masculinity (trait), 406
Maslow, Abraham, 62, 69
Materialism, Western attitudes

Materialism (continued)
toward, 461
Maturity stage, of a product, 141–142
Maximization, of economic value, 387–388
McGregor, Douglas, 69
Megalopolis, 597
Membership, group, types of (participation, automatic, anticipatory, negative), 232–234
Men, role of, 216–218
Mental set, 344
Merchandising, visual, 298
Merchants, 281–282
Message (communication), 163; one-sided or two-sided, 318
Metropolitan markets, 593–597
Middle class, 244–245
Middlemen. See Distributors
Midwesterners, 226
Minorities, in government, 236
Mitford, Jessica, 522
Mood, and perception, 344–345
Mores, 256
Motives/motivation, 11–12, 80; conflicting, 93; conscious and unconscious, 87; and consumer behavior, 82–83, 95–96; and consumer decisions, 80–81, 377–378; directional, 95; income and, 91–92; individual differences in, 89–92; and learned response, 83; loyalty and, 501–502; multiple motives and multiple effects, 93; origin of, 82; patronage and selective, 87–89; physiological and psychological, 85–86; positive and negative, 89; primary and secondary, 86–87; promotion and, 317–321; satisfaction as reducing, 84; types of, 85–89; variations over time, 92–93
Multinational markets, 442. See also Foreign countries; consumer decisions in, 443–444; cultural factors in, 447–457, 460–466; importance of, to American firms, 442–443; management in, 444–447, 466; marketing practices in, 462–464; success in, tips for managers, 466
Murray, Henry, 69
Music, background, in stores, 296–298

N

Nader, Ralph, 522
Name calling, 320
Natural resources, depletion of, 526

Necessities, 59
Needs, 11–12, 58–60. See also Consumer needs; awareness of, 61; basic, 59; categories of, 62–69; conflict of, 72–75; consumer problems derived from, 60–62; fantasy as resolving, 76; hierarchy of, 69–75; individual differences in, 90–92; innate, physiological and psychological, 60–61; nonrecurring, 494; personal, 376; repression of, 75–76; satisfaction of, 75–77, 84; theories of, 69–75
Negative reference group, 234
Negotiation: expected outcome of, 385; in families, 381–383; of prices, 421–423; types of (general discussion, private negotiations, etc.), 382–383
Nest, full and empty, 220–221
Newly married, 219–220
Noise (communication), 167–168
Nonbehavior, 82
Nonconsumer, 5–6
Normality, in decision making, 387–392
Norms, 238; rewards and sanctions of, 258; types of (customs, mores, laws), 256–257
Nose counting, 551

O

Observability of a product, 148
Observation technique in consumer research, 544
Obsolescence, types of (planned, technological, style, and built-in), 139
Occupation: and purchasing patterns, 575; and social class, 241
Old people. See Senior citizens
Opinion, 183
Opinion leaders: importance of, to marketers, 166–167; who they are, 167
Other-directed man, 411
"out" condition, routine, 49–50
Overloading, perceptual, 338

P

Packaging, 150–151
Packard, Vance, 522
Participation: audience, 317; in social group, 232–233
Party-plan selling, 292
Patronage, 88–89
Peers, culture inculcated by, 254
Perception, 11–12, 333–334; change in, 198, 345; characteristics of (selectivity, subjectivity, temporality, summativeness),

Perception (continued)
337–340; in consumer decisions, 333–345; steps in (conveyance, elaboration, comprehension), 335–336; thresholds of, 336
Personality, 11–12, 398–399; and consumer decision, 398–413; experience as shaping, 400–401
Personality theory: problems with, 412–413; types of (psychoanalytic, trait, type, Gestalt), 402–411
Personality trait, 405–408
Personality type, 408–411
Personal selling, 307
Persuasion, 383–384
Pictographs, as signs, 299–300
Pictorial projectives, 556–558
Political action, in consumerism, 524
Political institutions, culture inculcated by, 254
Political man, 410
Pollution, 526
Population: of metropolitan markets, 595–596; projected growth of, 268–269, 566–567
Postpurchase assessment. See also Satisfaction; in consumer decision, 24–27; dissonance and, 478–479; results of, 486–488
Preference ranking, 350; individual vs. family preferences, 366–367; rules for (conjunctive, disjunctive, elimination by aspect, lexicographic, compensatory), 361–365
Preference scaling, and marginal utility analysis, 372–376
Prepurchase assessment, 486
Price(s): consumer alternatives in, 353; and consumer decision, 379; control over, with loyal customers, 503; ethical, 428–429; flexibility of (one-price vs. negotiated pricing), 421–423; functions of, to consumers, 420; inflation of. See Inflation; influence of, on consumers, 421–429, 508–509; policies, 14–15, 18–19, 419–429; as product benefit, 418; types of (list/asking/suggested, selling/actual), 419
Price lining, 424–425
Pricing: competitive, prestige, customary, 425–426; fighting brand, full line, 426; loss leader, bait, 423–424; odd, even, 423; psychological, 423–424; special event, professional, 427–428; unit, 426
Primal repression, 75–76
Primary group, 232

Priorities, of problems, 96
Problem(s), 34. See also Consumer problem; all-or-nothing solution to, 96; deferred, 95–96; multiple, single and partial solutions to, 97; priorities of, 96
Problem recognition: during adoption and diffusion stages, 145–148; in consumer decision, 19–21; product attributes and, 148–153; during product development, 133–139; over product life cycle, 140–144
Problem-solving theory, 187; and consumer decision, 332–333
Product(s), 130–132; accessibility of, 510–511; adoption of, 145–146; alternatives in, 352–353, 359–360; assortment of. See Consumer assortment; attributes of, and problem recognition, 148–153; awareness of, 145–146; as benefit, 111, 130–132, 418, 534–535; categorized by usefulness (desirable, pleasing, salutary, deficient), 534–535; change in, 197–198, 508–509; consumer needs satisfied by, 61–62; consumers' past experience with, 378–379; costs of, 282–283; decline stage of, 142; deletion of, 144; developing. See Product development; discontinuing use of, 494–495, 516; failure rate of, 134–135; family formation, and demand for, 205; foreign, suspicion of, 464; growth stage of, 140–141; intended use of, 376–377; introduction of, 140, 145–148; location of, in stores, 302–303; loyalty toward, 499–500; maturity stage of, 141–142; new, 134–135, 138–139. See also Innovation; one-time-use, 494; opposition to, 138–139; "perfect" (competitive, wanted, profitable, legal, resource efficient, socially acceptable), 102, 510; policies, 14–15, 17–18; satisfaction with, 494–496; searching for. See Consumer search; service components of, 131–132, 418, 429; status of, 46–48; switching among. See Switching; unsafe, 528–529; value of, and length of consumer search, 171
Product development: commercialization stage, 138; prototyping phase, 136–137; stages of, 133–138; technological factors in, 139; test marketing phase,

Product development (continued)
137–138
Product group, 302
Product item, 132
Product life cycle (PLC), 139–148; competition during, 140–142; marketing strategies during, 140–144
Product line, 132; of stores, 284–288
Product mix, in stores, attributes of (width, variety, depth), 132
Professional fees, 427–428
Projection (defense mechanism), 404
Projective tests, 554–558
Promotion, 306. See also Advertising; and consumer decision, 309–311; and consumer search, 306–322; ethical, 529; importance of, to consumers and marketers, 307–308; influences of, on consumers, 310–322; informative value of, 314–316; and loyalty creation, 510; policy, 14–15, 18–19; specific appeals in, 317–318; types of (advertising, personal selling, sales promotion, publicity), 306–307
Propaganda, as motivator, 320
Protestant ethic, 261, 455
Prototyping, 136–137
Psyche, 404
Psychic satisfaction, 283
Psychoanalytic theory, 402–405; in advertising, 405
Publicity: by consumer movement, 524; by firms, 307
Purchase(s): closing the sale (asking customer to buy), 321–322; as equivalent exchange, 480–481; habitual, 83, 391, 495–496; impulse, 391–392; past, market segmentation by, 111; repeat, 510; timing of, 9
Purchase decisions. See also Consumer decision; autonomic vs. syncratic, 216; components of (whether, what, when, where, and how), 9–11; environmental influences on, 12–13; expectations and, 93–95; family members responsible for, 213–218; group influence on, 238–240; joint and individual, routine and nonroutine, 213–214; risk in, 83–84
Purchasers. See Customers
Purchasing: discontinuance or reevaluation of, 494–495, 516; ease of, 511; income and, 574–581; methods of, consumer

Purchasing (*continued*)
    alternatives in, 354–355, 361;
    occupation and, 575; patterns,
    574–581
Purchasing power: of foreign coun-
    tries, 457–460; of households,
    580–581

Q

Quality, consciousness of, and
    switching, 508–509

R

Race, and income, 579
Rationality, in decision making,
    387–392
Rationalization: of consumer deci-
    sions, 77, 392; defense mechan-
    ism, 404
Ready state, 365–367
Real self, 311
Reassurance, and switching,
    507–508
Receiver (communication), 163
Recovery, spontaneous, of informa-
    tion, 190
Reevaluation of produce use,
    494–495
Reference group. *See also* Social
    group; in consumer search,
    168–169; identification with,
    230–231; influence of, 238–240;
    as information source, 230–240;
    overlapping, 234; role in,
    234–235; and self-concept, 313;
    status in, 236–238; types, by
    function, formality, interaction,
    and membership type, 231–234
Reflex behavior, 82–83
Regions: life style of, 224–226; as
    markets, 590–592
Registered trademark, 148
Reinforcement, 187
Relative advantage, 148
Religion: belief in, 261; culture
    inculcated by, 254; in multi-
    national markets, 455–456; sub-
    cultures based on, 267
Religious man, 410
Repair service, 152, 434
Repression, primal, 75–76
Research and development (R&D),
    135
Resignation, consumer, 487; prod-
    uct use after, 494–496
Resources, natural, depletion of,
    526
Response, 187; learned, 83
Retailing, 282; non-store, types of,
    290–292; in stores, 284–289
Retail store, 169
Retired people, 221–222

Rewards, 188; formal and infor-
    mal, 258
Risk: avoidance, 505; perceived,
    83–84; reduction, 332–333
Role: ascribed or achieved, 235; in
    reference group, 234–235
Rorschach test, 557
Rural markets, 592–593

S

Safety: as consumer right,
    528–529; legislation on, 526;
    need for, 63
Sale, closing the, 321–322
Sales promotions, 307; effective-
    ness of, 509
Sanctions, formal and informal,
    258
Satisfaction, 486–488. *See also* Dis-
    satisfaction; Postpurchase assess-
    ment; and loyalty, 496–502,
    504; motivation reduced by, 84;
    product use after, 494–496;
    psychic, 283
Scaling, 559–561
School, culture inculcated by, 254
Scrambled merchandising,
    287–288
Screening, preliminary and final,
    136
Search. *See* Consumer search
Secondary group, 232
Selective motives, 87–88
Selective perception, 337–339
Self-actualization, need for, 65
Self-concept, 311–313
Self-fulfillment needs, 69
Self-image, 312
Self-rating scale, 559
Self-service stores, 511
Selling: to loyal customers,
    503; personal, 307
Semantic differential, 561
Sender (communication), 163
Senior citizens, 221–222, 271–272,
    569
Sensitization, selective, 338
Sensory perception. *See* Perception
Sentence completion, 556
Seriousness (trait), 407
Service, 429; consumer criticism of,
    429–431; cost of, to firm,
    436–437; customer service de-
    partments in stores, 152; influ-
    ence of, on consumers, 431–437;
    philosophy of (aggressive or not),
    431–432; post-sale, 437; and
    product, compared, 131–132,
    418; and sale of products, 429;
    standards of, policies, 436; types
    of (credit, warranty, etc.),
    432–435

Sex instinct, 205, 403
Shopping: by automobile, 293; day
    of week and time of day for,
    175–177; in foreign countries,
    464–466; multipurpose, 355;
    number of stores visited, 177
Shopping centers (planned), types
    of (neighborhood, community,
    regional/mall), 294–295
Shopping districts (unplanned),
    types of (central, secondary,
    neighborhood, string street),
    293–294
Shopping goods, 283–284
Sight, sense of, importance of, to
    sales, 298
Signs: exterior, 295–296; interior,
    298–299
Sinclair, Upton, 522
Single-line stores, 285–286
Single people, 272–274
Situation orientation, 14
Size, perception of, and consumer
    decisions, 341–342
Smell, of stores, as stimulus, 296
Smith, Adam, 520
Sociability (trait), 407
Social class, 240; indicators of,
    240–242; as information source,
    240–247; mobility within,
    245–247; in multinational mar-
    kets, 452–455; theories of,
    242–245; upper, middle, and
    lower, 243–245
Social group: norms. *See*
    Norms; primary and secondary,
    232
Social influence, 12; identification
    and, 230–231; importance of
    knowing about, 248
Social institutions, culture incul-
    cated by, 253–254
Social man, 410
Social mobility, 245–247
Social needs, 69
Social orientation, and consumer
    decision, 331–332
Social problems, and consumer dis-
    satisfaction, 526
Society, vs. individual, 390–391
Solitary survivor, 221–222
Southerners, 224
Special events, pricing for, 426
Special interest groups: attitude
    toward businesses, 119–120; as
    marketing target, 14–16,
    115–116; needs and motives of,
    115–116
Specialty stores, 285–286
Standard Metropolitan Statistical
    Area (SMSA), 593
Standard of living, 261; decline in,

Standard of living (*continued*) 580–581; foreign, 457–460
Status: of products, 46–48; in reference group, 236–238
Stereotypes, 409–410
Stimulus, 186–187
Stores. *See also* Retailing; consumer alternatives in, 353–354, 360; exterior design, 295–296; interior design, 296–302; layout of, 298–302; location of, 293–295, 355; loyalty toward, 499–500; merchandise grouping, 302–303; product line of, 284–288; product mix in, 132; single or chain, 288–289; types of (limited line, departmentalized, superstores), 284–288
Subcultures, 253; age and marriage as basis, 267–274; racial and ethnic, 262–267; religious, 267
Subjectivity, of perception, 339
Subliminal stimuli, 87
Suburbs, 593
Summativeness, of perception, 340
Summed scale, 559–560
Superego, 404
Superiority, perceived, of a product or store, 504
Superstores, 288
Suppliers: availability, quality, and cost of, 119–120; as marketing target, 14–16, 117; needs and motives of, 117
Supportive services, 152–153
Survey, consumer, 544
Switching. *See also* Loyalty, customer; reasons for, 506–509
Synthesis of information, 544

T

Target market grouping, 302
Taste. *See* Aesthetic values
Taxation, 581

Technical factors in perception, 340–343
Technology: belief in, 262; dissatisfaction with, 525–526; in product development, 139
Teenagers, as consumers, 270–271
Telephone, shopping by, 354–355
Temporality, of perception, 340
Testimonials, 320
Test marketing, 137–138
Thematic apperception test (TAT), 557
Theoretical man, 410
Thought processes, personality and, 402
Thresholds of perception, 336
Thurstone scale, 560
Time, discretionary, 72
Timing, of purchase, 9
Touching, importance of, to sales, 298
Trade, withdrawal of, 517–518
Trade-ins, 423, 506
Trademark, 148
Trade practice grouping, 302
Traditional societies, 462
Tradition-directed man, 410
Traits, change vs. consistency in, 412–413
Trait theory of personality, 405–408
Transmission (communication), 163
Traumatic experience, 197
Triability of a product, 148
Trial and learning, 189
Truth in Lending Law, 531
Type theory of personality, 408–411
Typography, as motivator, 319

U

United States: population and market size, 566–567; values of. *See*

United States (*continued*) American culture
Unit pricing, 426
Upper class, 243–244
Urban markets, 592–593
User, 4–5
Utility, marginal, 374–376

V

Value expressive function, 183–184
Values. *See also* Culture, national, contrasts in; American. *See* American culture; personality types as determined by, 410–411
Variety of assortment, 44
Variety stores, 287
Vending machines, 292
Verbal projectives, 558
Visual merchandising, 298

W

Wants, 59
Warranty, 153; implied and express, 432–433
Westerners, 226
Wheel of Retailing, 508–509
White space, as motivator, 319–320
Wholesalers, 282
Widows/widowers, 221–222
Width of assortment, 44
Wife: as purchaser, 39–40; role of, 212–218
Windows, store, 296
Withdrawal of trade, 517–518
Women: role of, 216–218, 235; working, 216–218, 572–574
Word association, 554–555

Y

Young adults/marrieds, 271